COLLECTION LATOMUS
VOLUME 183

THE WHEEL AS A CULT-SYMBOL
IN THE ROMANO-CELTIC WORLD

LATOMUS
REVUE D'ÉTUDES LATINES
18, av. Van Cutsem, B. 7500 Tournai

La revue **Latomus**, fondée en 1937 par M.-A. **Kugener**, L. **Herrmann** et M. **Renard** et dirigée actuellement par MM. Léon Herrmann et Marcel Renard, publie des articles, des variétés et discussions, des notes de lecture, des comptes rendus, des notices bibliographiques, des informations pédagogiques ayant trait à tous les domaines de la latinité : textes, littérature, histoire, institutions, archéologie, épigraphie, paléographie, humanisme, etc.

Les quelque **1000 pages** qu'elle comporte actuellement contiennent une riche documentation, souvent **inédite** et abondamment **illustrée**.

Montant de l'abonnement au tome XLIII (1984) :

Abonnement ordinaire :

Prix pour la Belgique : 1.855 FB, TVA comprise.
Prix pour l'étranger : 1.750 FB.

Port et expédition en sus.
Prix des tomes publiés avant l'année en cours :
— pour la Belgique : 2.120 FB, TVA comprise,
— pour l'étranger : 2.000 FB.
Les quatre fascicules d'un tome ne sont pas vendus séparément.

C.C.P. **000-0752646-23** de la **Société d'études latines de Bruxelles.**

Pour l'achat des tomes I à XXI, s'adresser à :
Johnson Reprint Corporation,
111, Fifth Avenue, New York 3, New York.

Correspondants :

ARGENTINE : M. le Prof. Fr. Nóvoa, Laprida, 1718, Buenos-Aires.
ÉTATS-UNIS ET CANADA : M. le Prof. J. R. Workman, Brown University, Providence 12, Rhode Island.
ESPAGNE : J.-M. Blázquez, Instituto de Arqueologia, 4, Duque de Medinaceli, Madrid.
FRANCE : M. J. Heurgon, Membre de l'Acad. des Inscr. et Belles-Lettres, Le Verger, Allée de la Pavillonne, 78170 – La-Celle-St-Cloud.

GRANDE-BRETAGNE : M. le Prof. Fergus Millar, Dept. of History, University College of London, Gower Street, London WC1E 6BT.
ITALIE : Mlle M. L. Paladini, 13, Via Bellotti, Milano.
PAYS-BAS : M. le Dr. K. H. E. Schutter, 6, Sloetstraat, Nimègue.
SUÈDE : M; le Prof. G. Saeflund, 52, 1 tr. Vasagatan, 11120, Stockholm.
SUISSE : M. A. Cattin, 14, Grand-Rue, Cormondrèche (Neuchâtel), Suisse.

Bronze Wheel-God ; Le Châtelet (C2). Height : 10.3 cm.

COLLECTION LATOMUS
Fondée par Marcel RENARD
VOLUME 183

Miranda Jane GREEN

The Wheel as a Cult-Symbol in the Romano-Celtic World

With Special Reference to Gaul and Britain

LATOMUS
REVUE D'ÉTUDES LATINES
BRUXELLES
1984

For my mother and father

ISBN 2-87031-123-0
D/1983/0415/100

Droits de traduction, de reproduction et d'adaptation réservés pour tous pays.
Toute reproduction d'un extrait quelconque, par quelque procédé que ce soit et notamment par photocopie ou microfilm, est strictement interdite.

TABLE OF CONTENTS

Preface	5
Acknowledgements	7
Introduction	9
Chapter I. Early Wheel-Symbolism in non-mediterranean Europe	15
Chapter II. Analysis of Romano-Celtic Miniature Wheels in Relation to other Models in North-West Europe and Britain	45
Chapter III. The Significance of Miniature Wheels and other Models in Romano-Celtic Europe	73
Chapter IV. Descriptive Analysis of Stone Monuments relating to Wheel-Symbolism in Roman Gaul, the Rhineland and Britain	103
Chapter V. Descriptive Analysis of Miscellaneous Material	135
Chapter VI. Significance of Monuments and Cult-Objects relating to Wheel-Symbolism	155
Chapter VII. Classical Jupiter and Celtic Sky-God in Britain	217
Chapter VIII. Taranis and the Celtic Jupiter	251
Chapter IX. Realism and Non-Realism in Cult-Wheel Representation	265
Conclusion	295
Catalogue A	305
Catalogue AB	323
Catalogue AX	326
Catalogue B	329
Catalogue C	348
Catalogue D	359
Catalogue E	360
Bibliography	371
Catalogue of Illustrations	403
Plates	411

PREFACE

The thesis was begun, part-time, in January 1978. From October 1978 to 1981 I held a full-time internal research studentship at the Open University, and I have been in receipt of an Open University Research Grant.

One bibliography, comprising references both to the text and the catalogues, will be found at the back. The Harvard system of bibliographical references is used throughout. Journals and book-titles are generally referred to in full ; minimal use has been made of abbreviations.

British sites are referred to by their new county ; where possible French sites are referred to by Département ; those in Germany by region.

Within each of the five catalogues (A - E) each entry has been given a number. Where catalogue-numbers are referred to in the text they are preceded by the relevant letter.

Access to published material has posed few problems. In the main I have utilized the library facilities of the Ashmolean Museum, Oxford ; the Society of Antiquaries of London ; the Society for the Promotion of Roman Studies ; the National Museum of Wales ; and University College, Cardiff. Inevitably, however, there will be continental reference works which are not readily available in Britain.

Physical access to archaeological material in Britain has been reasonably satisfactory, although in some cases, owing to the nature of museum storage, it has been impossible to obtain a photographic record. Access to items in continental museums has been variable. Belgium (apart from Namur), Switzerland, Germany and Austria posed no difficulties. Problems, however, have been encountered in some French museums, notably at the Musée des Antiquités Nationales, St. Germain-en-Laye, where free access to material was not granted ; and at Toulouse, Musée St. Raymond, where no access whatever was permitted.

There have sometimes been problems, both with regard to published and unpublished material, where it has not always been possible to set down all factual information about a given object. If an item has to be photographed through a display-case there can be no scale, neither can its size be exactly recorded. Sometimes, in published work, details as to date or size are not given (¹).

---

(1) Unless otherwise specified by date, reference to Espérandieu in text or catalogues is to his catalogue of stonework (ESPÉRANDIEU 1907-1966).

ACKNOWLEDGEMENTS

First, I should like to express my special gratitude to the British Academy and to the Open University for their financial sponsorship of this book. I would like to express my great gratitude to the Open University, both for the three years research grant, and for generous financial allowance towards travel and photographic expenditure. I am also deeply grateful to the Regional Office of the Open University in Wales, who provided office space and many facilities.

I wish to thank the staff of the following museums for their cooperation and for access to their collections:

Aix-en-Provence, Musée Granet ; Arles, Musée Lapidaire, Musée St.-Trophime ; Augst, Römermuseum ; Avignon, Musée Calvet, Musée Lapidaire ; Bern, Historisches Museum ; Béziers, Musée Lapidaire ; Bonn, Rheinisches Landesmuseum ; Brussels, Musées Royaux ; Hallein, Keltenmuseum ; Köln, Römisch-Germanisches Museum ; Liège, Musée Curtius ; Luxembourg, Musée des États ; Lyon, Musée de la Civilisation Gallo-Romaine ; Mainz, Mittelrheinisches Landesmuseum, Mainz Zentralmuseum ; Montpellier, Musée Lapidaire (Société Archéologique de Montpellier) ; Namur, Musée Archéologique ; Narbonne, Musée Archéologique, Musée Lapidaire ; Nîmes, Musée Archéologique ; Orange, Musée de ; Paris, Musée Carnavalet, Musée de Cluny, Musée des Antiquités Nationales, St.-Germain-en-Laye ; Saalburg, Roman Fort Museum ; Saint-Rémy-de-Provence, Musée des Alpilles (Pierre de Brun) ; Salzburg Museum ; Saverne, Musée Archéologique, Château de Rohan ; Steyr, Schloss Lamberg ; Strasbourg, Musée Archéologique, Château de Rohan ; Stuttgart, Württemburgisches Landesmuseum ; Tongeren, Provinciaal Gallo-Romeins Museum ; Trier, Landesmuseum ; Vaison-la-Romaine, Musée de ; Vienne, Musée des Beaux-Arts, Musée Lapidaire ; Vienna, Historisches Museum, Naturhistorisches Museum ; Zürich, Schweizerisches Landesmuseum.

Bath, Roman Bath Museum ; Birmingham, City Museum ; Bristol, City Museum ; Cambridge, University Museum of Archaeology and Anthropology ; Cardiff, National Museum of Wales ; Carlisle, Tullie House

Museum; Carmarthen County Museum; Chedworth, Roman Villa Museum; Chester, Grosvenor Museum; Chesterholm, Vindolanda Museum, Chesters Museum; Cirencester, Corinium Museum; Colchester and Essex Museum; Corbridge, Corstopitum Museum; Devizes Museum; Dorchester, Dorset County Museum; Edinburgh, National Museum of Antiquities of Scotland; Exeter, Royal Albert Museum; Gloucester, City Museum; Housesteads Museum; Ilkley, Manor House Museum; Keighley Museum; Keswick Museum; Kettering, Westfield Museum; Leicester, Jewry Wall Museum; Lincoln, City and County Museum; London, British Museum, Museum of London; Lydney Museum; Malton, Roman Malton Museum; Manchester Museum; Netherhall Museum; Newcastle, University Museum of Antiquities; Newport (Gwent) Museum; Northampton, Central Museum; Norwich, Castle Museum; Nottingham, Castle Museum, University Museum; Oxford, Ashmolean Museum; Peterborough, City Museum; Reading Museum; Rydale, Folk Museum; St. Albans, Verulamium Museum; St. Mary's, Isles of Scilly Museum; Scunthorpe Museum; Shrewsbury Museum; Taunton Museum; York, Yorkshire Museum.

I should like to thank, first and foremost, my external supervisor, Professor John Ferguson, for his generous support, help and advice throughout the period of study. Special thanks should go also to my internal supervisor, Dr. Chris Emlyn-Jones.

Of the many individuals who have contributed help and encouragement I should mention the following by name: E. B. & E. R. Aldhouse (who did many of the illustrations for this book); D. Baatz; F. E. Barth; T. Bees; G. C. Boon; P. D. C. Brown; G. Coulomb; T. Cross; B. W. Cunliffe; P. Filtzinger; A. Follman; P. Garmy; D. Greene; N. A. Griffiths; E. Halmos; J. J. Hatt; C. Hocking; S. Hopkin; C. Horton; M. G. Jarrett; C. E. King; E. Künzl; M. Lassalle; J. Liversidge; G. Lloyd-Morgan; W. H. Manning; M. Martin; S. Murgatroyd; D. Nash; P. Nölke; O. Pagett; P. Perrin; J. Cl. Richard; S. Rieckhoff-Pauli; G. Rogers; A. Sheratt; D. J. Smith; D. A. T. Thomas; J. M. C. Toynbee; D. Viner; J. J. Wilkes.

Finally, I must express the greatest gratitude to Stephen Green for his unwearying and generous help at all stages of the work.

INTRODUCTION

Background and Scope of the Research

This study commenced with a dissertation entitled *The Religions of Roman London*, submitted to University College, Cardiff in 1969 as part of the B. A. Honours, Archaeology degree-requirement. My M. Litt., submitted to the University of Oxford in 1974, was entitled *The Religions of Civilian Roman Britain*. This was published in 1976 as a British Archaeological Reports Monograph. In 1977, I held a British Academy Research Award to study small cult objects in the military areas of Roman Britain. The results of this project, entitled *A Corpus of Small-Cult-Objects from the Military areas of Roman Britain*, were published as a British Archaeological Reports Monograph in 1978. In 1977, I held a Society of Antiquaries Research Award to study representations of the Wheel-God in the Musée des Antiquités Nationales, St.-Germain-en-Laye. In 1978, I held a Leverhulme Research Fellowship in order to study the Roman Bronze Figurines in the Ashmolean Museum, Oxford.

Specific research on the Wheel as a cult-symbol began with a number of articles on individual British items (see Green, 1974-1979). The Society of Antiquaries award enabled me to publish a preliminary survey of British and some Gaulish material in the review *Latomus* (Green, 1979).

Material from sites mentioned in the text are indexed in a series of catalogues. Where site-names in these catalogues are not organized alphabetically a concordance-table is provided.

Content of Text and Catalogues

The text is divided into ten chapters, of which the first comprises a survey of early pre-Roman symbolism. With Romano-Celtic material, descriptive analyses and interpretative sections have been treated separately. Chapter IX includes a stylistic assessment of a sample of 274 cult-wheels.

The main areas of study comprise Britain, France, Belgium, Switzerland and West Germany (the Roman provinces of Britannia, Gallia,

Germania Superior, Germania Inferior, Raetia). However, other Celtic regions are also referred to where relevant. These include northern Italy, Yugoslavia and Austria.

The main evidence for the wheel as a cult-symbol is archaeological, i.e. iconographical. The few classical literary references have been taken into account. However, no study has been made of early Irish or Welsh literature. Any attempt to link archaeological data of the Roman period with post-Roman historical material is at best suspect. Epigraphic material has been analysed.

The archaeological evidence for Romano-Celtic wheel symbolism occurs on items of stone, metal, clay and bone. A sharp distinction may be made between monuments of stone and other, portable, items. A stone altar was probably not traded very far from its place of manufacture ; therefore local distribution of types may well be significant. By contrast, small votive or ceremonial objects, especially models, could be exported over wide areas. Still, even though this is the case, patterns of distribution will sometimes reflect regional preferences. Distinctions should also be made within the framework of technology. A cast or moulded object — such as a bronze or pipe-clay figurine, or a brooch — may indicate stereotyped models ; a stone-carving will be more likely to reflect individual preferences. No two altars are exactly alike, whilst wheel-models fall into a number of distinct groups.

Caution must be exercised with regard to decoration. The presence of ornament on a wheel portrayed on a stone representation or accompanying a figurine, is almost certainly of significance. The same is true of genuine models. Brooches and pendants, however, are jewellery and in themselves have a decorative function. Thus ornament on such items may pertain to this rather than a ritual purpose.

The time-span of the main study comprises the period of Roman influence on Celtic lands, in the case of Britain from the mid 1st Century A.D. until the beginning of the 5th, and commencing somewhat earlier in Gaul. In Chapter I, I survey wheel-symbolism in non-Mediterranean Europe in detail from the Middle Bronze Age to the later Iron Age. It is frequently difficult to assign a close date within the Roman period to ritual wheels. I have considered detailed chronology where evidence is available.

Within the limitations discussed above and below the aims and objectives of the present research are as follows :

a) the production of a catalogue and illustrative record of material which may serve as an index of reference for a specific Romano-Celtic cult. The catalogues are not intended to be a fully comprehensive corpus. However, in the case of stonework and figurines, it is hoped that the vast majority of extant depictions have been included. Comprehensiveness in the case of models is both less important, and virtually impossible to achieve.

b) the examination, analysis and interpretation of the archaeological evidence for a cult which integrates Roman and Celtic beliefs in a celestial power, and whose iconography has a wheel as a common element. Attempts have been made to interpret cult-items by means of intrinsic composition of objects, their distribution, context and association. Geographical, cultural, functional, economic and social questions have all been considered. Occurrence of the wheel-symbol and its derivative alone, without an associated divinity-representation, has also been examined to show whether or not it has a specific religious significance. It is thus hoped to contribute a detailed study of one divine manifestation, to serve as a complement to other works, such as that of Magnen & Thevenot (1953) on Epona ; Thevenot (1955) on the Celtic Mars ; Tudor (1976) on the Danubian Rider-God ; and Speidel (1978) on Jupiter Dolichenus. At the same time, however, it is recognized that whilst one deity may be represented by a pipe-clay figurine in the Allier district of Central France, and the same god by a stone monument in Germany, that is not to assume that all wheel-symbolism is part of the same religious phenomenon. A wheel-model worn around the neck, or a swastika scratched on a piece of tile may be nothing more than good-luck symbols.

The present study is, as far as I am aware, the first major examination of the Wheel as a Romano-Celtic cult-symbol. Gaidoz, in two articles (1884, 1885) looked at some of the Gaulish evidence. Wheel-monuments formed a substantial chapter in Lambrechts' important survey (1942). Such symbolism has also been discussed in general works on Romano-Celtic religion, such as that of Duval (1957); de Vries (1963); Ross (1967); and Thevenot (1968). Espérandieu (1907-1966) and Reinach (1894) are major contributors to 'catalogues raisonnés' of iconographical data, as is Déchelette (1914, 1910, 1913).

Preliminary Note

THE ORIGIN OF THE ROMANO-CELTIC PEOPLES

The title of this book is *The Wheel as a Cult-Symbol in the Romano-Celtic World*. The term 'Romano-Celtic' perhaps requires brief clarification. The period of Roman influence on the Celtic lands of western and central Europe involved interaction between two cultures; that of the Mediterranean peoples of the classical world and of the Celts. It is this latter ethnic group which needs some explanation.

Keltoi were defined as such by Greeks by about 500 B.C. (Powell, 1958, 15; Fischer, 1972, 109-124). Sixty years later a mention, locating Celts at the sources of the Danube (i.e. the hills of the Black Forest), is recorded (Herodotus, II, 35; Fischer, 1972, 109-124; Powell, 1958, 15). The origins of the people called 'Celts' by classical writers have long been the subject of speculation. Coles and Harding (1979, 367) are of the opinion that the process of celticization was fairly gradual and that no one culture or time should be sought as the immediate source of Celtic beginnings. Burgess (1980, 277-278) endorses this view. The Celts, whether in Europe or Britain, did not suddenly come from anywhere, but were people who had become Celtic by accretion in process of time. It is, he postulates (*ibid.*), senseless to enquire when the Celts first appeared, since the Celts who were known and recognized as such by classical writers were the lineal descendants of generations stretching right back to Neolithic farmers.

Megaw (1970, 13) sees Celtic material culture stemming, in origin, from about 1200 B.C., the beginning of the later Bronze Age in technological terms. He cites economic turmoil and folk movement, emanating partly from the Black Sea; the downfall of concretions of power, such as the Hittite and Mycenaean Empires and the lessening of external demands on local mineral resources; the development of skills, by Central and Eastern European metalsmiths, which were ultimately of eastern Mediterranean origin, for instance sheet-bronze vessels, decoration in the form of abstract, geometric designs but also of sun-signs and aquatic birds. Megaw would also see the 8th Century B.C. (when the

Dorian invasions were taking place in Greece) as heralding the use, for the first time in Central Europe, of horses for riding, as opposed to merely for traction, with all the cultural paraphernalia which would accompany such an event. Coles and Harding (1979, 367) admit to the possibility that the origins of Celtic material culture may be sought during the Bronze Age, but emphasize that there is little specifically Celtic in the cultural repertoire of Urnfield Europe. They also (*ibid.*) argue that there is no particular motive for assuming that the presence of Hallstatt warriors at the end of the Bronze Age means the introduction of Celts into Central Europe.

The traditional Bronze Age, at any rate in England and Wales, is over by 600 B.C. and iron commonplace in Britain and Ireland (Burgess, 1980, 277). On the mainland of Europe the pre-Roman Iron Age may be said to begin somewhat earlier. It is about a hundred years later that Celts are named in classical sources (Fischer, 1972) which so describe the barbarian peoples who occupied much of northwestern Europe. The term covered a multitude of tribes of different ethnic and varying customs. Nevertheless, it is a useful generalization. Archaeological research has indicated that by the 5th Century B.C. large parts of Europe, from Britain to Romania, and from North Italy to Belgium, shared some cultural elements. We cannot speak of a Celtic nation but processes of trade and exchange by folk-movement and convergent evolution caused the peoples of barbarian Europe to develop a degree of cultural similarity. It was that which impressed classical observers when they wrote of Celts (Cunliffe & Wiseman, 1980, 12). If one speaks entirely archaeologically, it is possible to say that Iron Age Celts originated in Central and West Central Europe (Piggott, 1968b, 36, Fig. 1).

Pre-Roman Iron Age Celtic art (through the medium of which we may sometimes observe, if not interpret, expressions of religious belief) was for the most part an aristocratic phenomenon. Thus, when assessing continuity and change of ideas and themes as expressed in art, one should be aware that, whilst peasant crafts may demonstrate great continuity, aristocratic art-ideas may easily be transmitted long distances from one point of Europe to another ; and one should not discount the possibility of sudden innovation (Piggott, 1976, 283-284). In a heroic society a chief's treasury may have contained a number of art-items collected over a period of time, and these, together with coins, could present a repertoire of art where craftsmen could examine different styles (*ibid.*). It behoves us to remember also that craftsmen themselves added to the fluidity of art in later prehistoric Europe, since they themselves would have been essentially peripatetic (*ibid.*, 286).

There is, as stated below (Chapters I, IV, VI), pre-Roman iconography attesting directly to religious beliefs and to the worship of formally recognizable god-forms (Megaw, 1970, *passim*). But it is scarce compared to the archaeological record in the Roman period. It is against the backdrop of later prehistoric Europe that we must view the Roman presence and the introduction of Romano-Celtic art and religion. Apart from a relatively few instances, it was with the advent of the Romans to the Rhineland, Gaul and Britain that deities were first presented iconographically as sculptured, cast or moulded images. The transformation of previously aniconic ideas of divinity to formalized images involved cross-pollination of ideas. Such a process appears to have been based on a Roman assurance that the barbarian deities worshipped by the Celts were disguised members of their own pantheon and on the willingness of the indigenous population to accept Roman physical god-types whose natures included at least one function which paralleled their own, previously formless, divinities (Linduff, 1979, 818). Nevertheless, there are specifically Celtic iconographical features to a number of these anthropomorphic and theriomorphic images (Ross, 1967, *passim* ; Green, 1976, *passim*). It is the physical manifestation of one such image of deity or divine element which is the subject of this study.

CHAPTER I

Early Wheel-Symbolism in non-mediterranean Europe

INTRODUCTION

In the millennia preceding the Roman era, it seems possible to trace a form of solar cult symbolism expressed in artifactual remains. In this chapter evidence from Britain, France, Germany, North Italy, Scandinavia, Yugoslavia and Eastern Europe will be considered. When dealing with prehistoric cult evidence of any description it is easy to be accused, and indeed guilty of, what Sprockhoff would call rushing 'through the space and time of prehistory in seven-league boots' (Sprockhoff, 1955, 278), and it is necessary to harness speculatory tendencies with regard both to space and time. Scepticism is natural if one attempts to link up, for example, the second millennium B.C. with the immediate pre-Roman Iron Age. Yet in prehistory it is possible to argue extreme conservatism in religious beliefs and practices. The factors of a relatively small population and of difficult and limited communication may often combine to produce at least a sluggish rate of progress and change. Space is a more serious problem. The whole question of connections in belief spanning thousands of miles is a vexed one. However, in prehistory, numerous associations and connections in types of artifact, in widely spread areas, have been established and their validity is not in question. Since communication and in some cases actual migration did occur, then, notwithstanding the previous plea for conservatism, one may also assume the transmission of ideas even if the precise mechanism involved may often be obscure.

In the discussion which follows, I have restricted detailed consideration of the prehistoric evidence to approximately the last 1500 years B.C.

BRONZE AGE CHRONOLOGY

The absolute dating of events in Bronze Age Europe has seen frequent changes of opinion over the years, and, moreover, it is necessary to make a distinction between radiocarbon and calendar years. It is now known that the natural rate of production of ^{14}C in the earth's atmosphere has not been constant through time (Burleigh, 1975). There is only a slight discrepancy in A.D. dates but radiocarbon dates B.C. become progressively too young so that a difference of around three centuries obtains at 1500 radiocarbon years B.C. I propose here to use calendar years, and in dating will generally follow Burgess' suggested divisions for the Bronze Age (Burgess, 1976, 74). The earliest date when it is possible to see evidence of a cult which might have some kind of continuity as far as the early Iron Age is around the middle of the second millennium B.C. If one is supposing (for a particular area) a continuity in beliefs or at any rate in cult-expression, 1500 years is not a very long time. A tangible example of ancient continuity and conservatism may be cited in Egypt where, from the earliest dynastic period, circa 3000 B.C., until the Roman era, cults and deities survived, albeit with certain innovations and changes (British Museum, 1969). It remains now to examine the evidence for a sky-cult in the Middle and Late Bronze and Iron Ages in non-Mediterranean Europe.

Model Objects

There is evidence for solid wheel-models as early as the 4th millennium B.C. in the Upper Euphrates and the Caucasus (Piggott, 1979, 5) (see also Chapter III). Wheels, axes and other models occur consistently right through the Bronze Age in Europe. One may cite, for example, Hungary during the 2nd millennium B.C. (Coles & Harding, 1979, 90, 141) where a ritual building in a fortified promontory site at Salacea in the Carpathian Basin contained a clay model altar, wheel-models, clay carts and a clay boat-model (Coles & Harding, 1979, 86-87).

Although we are essentially concerned with wheel and sun-symbolism, it is important, nevertheless, to survey the whole practice of depicting items in miniature during the earlier part of the Bronze Age. What we find is a steady flow of evidence from Europe both of models in general and of wheel-models in particular. Where it is necessary to be circumspect is in the interpretation of miniature wheels which appear in isolation (i.e. not certainly part of pins, pendants, wagons or chariots/carts). Were they sun-talismans carried in hope of protection against evil forces, or were they in fact part of model vehicles which may represent an entirely different kind of cult, or merely have been a toy ?

Spoked Wheels and their Symbolism

Spoked wheels first appear in the Near East around the beginning of the 2nd millennium B.C. (Piggott, 1979, 11). One of the earliest datable wheeled vehicles from mainland Europe is the four-spoked war-chariot carved on a grave-stele of a rich tomb, Shaft Grave IV at Mycenae in about 1500 B.C. (Childe, 1951, 188). Wagons and carts with spoked wheels spread to Italy, East and Central Europe and Scandinavia by the mid 2nd millennium B.C. (Anati, 1960a, 50 ; Piggott, 1979, 1ff). At this time, models of four-spoked wheels are recorded in the Central European Únětician Culture (Gimbutas, 1965, 316 ; Pittioni, 1954, 323) and elsewhere in Central and Eastern Europe (Tihelka, 1952, 373-434 ; Miske, 1908, pl. 56, 13 ; 15-16).

Middle and Later Bronze Age Solar Motifs

Butler (1963) refers to 'the golden sun-disc', symbol of a Bronze Age cult or religion common to the British Isles, Northern Europe and wider areas as well (Butler, 1963, 167-175) and lists six golden 'sun-discs' from southern Scandinavia and five from Britain (Jacob-Friesen, 1931, Abb. 25a, b ; 26a, b ; 27a ; British Museum, 1920, fig. 7, fig. 91). The most famous North European 'sun-disc' is that forming part of the Trundholm chariot-group probably to be dated around 1300 B.C. (Bing, 1934 ; Müller, 1903 ; Coles & Harding, 1979, 314, pl. 12a). This find, from north-west Zealand, Denmark, comprises a model bronze horse drawing a bronze disc plated on one side with gold sheeting (Glob, 1974, 99-103). The whole was set on a base carried on three pairs of bronze wheels. The disc itself, c. 15,5 cm diameter, has a parallel at Helsingborg also in Denmark, where model oxen and horses were discovered together with spearheads and parts of a model wagon and bronze disc (*ibid.*). In speaking of 'sun-discs' of this general type we may note that two of the Irish examples (Butler, 1963 ; Jacob-Friesen, 1931) bear cruciform patterns, which could indicate some kind of solar/wheel/sky symbolism.

It is possible that in the earlier Bronze Age, as early as the late third millennium B.C., sun-symbolism may be recognized on small sheet-gold objects, sometimes called 'sun-discs' but which may be button-caps (Clarke, 1970, 439). Numerous examples are known from the British Isles (Clarke, 1970, 298) and we may note here, as examples of the type, the finds from a Beaker burial at Mere in Wiltshire where a Wessex/Middle Rhine Beaker was associated with an archer's bracer, a tanged copper dagger and two thin sheet-gold discs ornamented with equal-armed crosses (Piggott, 1938, 78). Gimbutas (1965, 56) quotes gold discs bearing spiral decoration from Central Europe, which she dates to between 1800-1650 B.C. (for example her fig. 21), and would like to see a connection here with Mycenae, citing a gold plaque with spiral decoration from Shaft Grave III. Gimbutas attests other links between the Aegean and Central Europe at about this time (*ibid.*, 58).

There is a wealth of Middle Bronze Age Scandinavian symbolism. Gold bowls from this area of Northern Europe bear concentric circles similar to some of the later sun-discs mentioned above (Broholm, 1952). Glob (1974, 124) cites Danish gold repoussé vessels bearing a 'wheel-sign' on their bases and some also with handles in the shape of horse-heads, for example that from Borgbjerg (*ibid.*, pl. 37). Also to the Middle Bronze Age belong certain ritually ornamented bronze knives from Sweden and Denmark. They are decorated with swan-heads and wheels (Déchelette, 1910, 412ff). One example (*ibid.*, fig. 169 ; Déchelette, 1909, fig. 15a) has a model wheel-motif in the round attached to the end of the blade. Waterbirds associated with wheel-symbolism become ubiquitous in the later Bronze Age, as shall be discussed below. But in some of these Scandinavian knives appears a symbolic association which has already been seen, for instance at Trundholm, that is horse and sun/wheel symbolism on one and the same item (Déchelette, 1910, 412ff).

Moving to Central Europe, certain articles of metalwork may have links with a sun/sky cult in the middle part of the Bronze Age. Belonging to the Tumulus Culture (c. 1400-1200 B.C.) are certain Lusatian pins with large disc-heads (Gimbutas, 1965, 290), some of these decorated with motifs which Gimbutas would identify as solar symbols. Concentric circles, spirals, swastikas and stars are all included in the ornamental repertoire of the pin-makers (Gimbutas, 1965, fig. 196). Even earlier than this period, in the late Únětician phase in Central Europe (c. 1500-1400 B.C.) are found model four-spoked wheels (*ibid.*, 316) apparently not as part of pins, pendants or miniature vehicles. The Salacea (Hungary) model wheels (see above) are of similar date.

Apart from the gold (and bronze) sun-discs already mentioned from Ireland and Scandinavia, two other occurrences, in Britain and in France respectively, should be noted. The British item is the Caergwrle Bowl from Powys in Wales. It is a boat-model, made of shale (Green *et all.*, 1980, 26-30) and probably of later Bronze Age date. What is interesting about the item is its gold-leaf decoration which includes a gold band ornamented with concentric circles stamped-on below the rim. Analogies may be seen between these circles and the Hiberno-Nordic sun-discs of the Middle Bronze Age. The French goldwork comprises two gold sheets from Courtevant and Le Theil (Sandars, 1957, 114). Miss Sandars suggests that the technique of decoration, with possible solar symbolism, is similar to that on the discs from Ireland and Scandinavia.

A phenomenon which may well have links with the Tumulus Culture disc-headed pins already noted, is that of wheel-headed pins, which occur in France, Central and Northern Europe in the Middle Bronze Age (Torbrügge & Uenze, 1968, 212, 241). The homeland of wheel-pins (Sandars, 1957, 67) appears to be the Middle Rhine and Lower Main in West Germany. As their name suggests, they comprise a long shank with a vertically mounted circular head in the form of an openwork wheel with a varying number of spokes. In a find from Hesse in West Germany (Holste, 1939) two pins were found, obviously having been worn as a pair on the breast. Sandars suggests (1957, 67) that these were dress-pins worn as a normal component of female garb, in pairs. Certainly, in Alsace graves (Schaeffer, 1926) they frequently occur in pairs in female tombs. Wheel-headed pins seem to begin in the earlier part of the Bronze Age (for discussion of wheel-pin types and chronology see Lawson, 1979, 82ff ; Kersten, 1936 ; Bergman, 1970 ; Laux, 1971) and although their main *floruit* appears to be the Middle Bronze Age, they do continue into the later Bronze Age and even into the Iron Age (Sandars, 1957, 178). Finds of wheel-pins in Germany are numerous. One may cite, for instance, the Middle Bronze Age grave-find from Baierseich, South Germany (Behrens, 1916, pl. 18, n° 3). At Mühltal (*ibid.*, pl. 7, n° 13) only the four-spoked head of a wheel-pin survives and it may be that the shaft was deliberately broken off for burial and therefore for ritual, defunctionalizing purposes (for ritual breakage in prehistory see Grinsell, 1953, 36-37 ; Grinsell, 1961, 475-491 ; Castaldi, 1965). A similar occurrence may be noted in the area of the River Oder, where a pin has lost most of its shaft and has the appearance of a later Bronze Age wheel-pendant (Claus, 1978, 24, Abb. 4). There may be no ritual significance to be attached to these pins, in terms of solar symbolism, but broken examples may be interpreted as instances of the enhancement of the wheel-sign for burial. There is also a great similarity between these pins (especially the broken ones) and the wheel-pendants of Urnfield and Hallstatt Europe, which may well have ritual significance (see below).

The Evidence of Rock Carvings

In this section the vast topic of petroglyphs will be considered briefly. Some of the Scandinavian and northern Italian rock-art can be dated by their representation of Bronze Age weapons which may be dated typologically. I do not consider that the petroglyphs of Scandinavia have necessarily any direct relevance to Celtic wheel-symbolism of later periods. However, examination of this evidence is of relevance to the symbolism of other areas since there is evidence of great similarities between Scandinavia and Central Europe at any rate during the Urnfield phase of the Bronze Age; in addition, there are close links between the iconography of the rock-carvings of Scandinavia and northern Italy, which may have Celtic connections.

The wheel occurs, as a symbol, on rock-carvings in Danish burial-mounds, probably to be dated within the later Bronze Age (Glob, 1974, 1969). A number of interesting features should be noted. One is the association of horse, sun-wheel and ship (sometimes with bird-head terminals), for example at Kalleby (Glob, 1974, pl. 61) and at Herrestrup (*ibid.*, pl. 54; 1969, 14, figs. 8a, B). Another feature is the fact that concentric circles are used as alternatives to wheel-symbols (Glob, 1969, 38, fig. 22), a phenomenon which I believe occurs on Romano-Celtic monuments (see Chapter IV). A third is the specifically solar nature of the spoked wheels on Danish carvings, which total in excess of one hundred, verified by their position in relation to other iconography (Glob, 1969, 286-318, e.g. fig. 22d).

The majority of Swedish petroglyphs cannot be dated more closely than between 1500-400 B.C. (Gelling & Davidson, 1969), but some probably date to the Middle and Later Bronze Ages. A solar cult is well-represented in Sweden (Bronsted, 1938-1940, 148) where ships and wheel/suns are again depicted, together with human representations (Gelling & Davidson, 1969, 9-26). Again a number of features exist in parallel both with prehistoric and later Romano-Celtic solar evidence. The discs themselves take many different forms – wheels with four or eight spokes, some on stems or stands (*cf.* Bad Dürkheim, Chapter IV). The discs sometimes represent shields (*cf.* Romano-Celtic Jupiter-column depictions (Chapter IV, VI). Axes and wheel/suns are frequently associated (*ibid.*, 27-42) and appear to have a solar connection. The ship and 'solar' disc are also frequently associated, and on one occasion a boat is carried on a wheel with spokes set diagonally as if in motion (*ibid.*, fig. 21f), recalling the 'X' sign represented on some Romano-Celtic monuments (see Chapter VI). Davidson (Gelling & Davidson, 1969, 117-135) draws attention to similar themes in North European Urnfield metalwork from about 1000 B.C.

As in the case of the Danish petroglyphs one must pose the question as to whether isolated wheels are portrayals (*pars pro toto*) of chariots or of the sun itself. Gelling (Gelling & Davidson, 1969, 9-26) interprets spoked wheels as sun-symbols. In my opinion he is probably correct, but one should note that there is doubt among some scholars (e.g. Coles & Harding, 1979, 318) about the wisdom of assigning too much significance to wheels as suns here.

The motifs on North Italian rock-carvings, like those from Val Camonica, bear brief examination (Anati, 1960b). Camonica Valley is in the Italian Alps near the city of Brescia. Petroglyphs here appear to date from the Neolithic to the Iron Age (*ibid.*, 61). Anati believes (*ibid.*, 83) that the Celts were present in the Iron Age and that before that the Camunians had steady relationships with Central European Urnfield cultures. The major 'solar-cult' phase appears to be during the Bronze Age. Once again certain features of the petroglyphic iconography should be specifically noted. One is the very frequent representation of the sun as a ring-and-dot motif, seemingly replaced at a later period by four-spoked wheels and rayed circles. Another is the association between solar wheels, stags and bulls (Coles & Harding, 1979, 175 ; Bicknell, 1911). A further noteworthy phenomenon is the association of humanoid figures with wheels, warrior-equipment and, in one instance, a long shafted hammer (Glob, 1969, 152, figs. 179-180). It is suggested (Coles & Harding, 1979, 175) that in Anati's Phase III (Bronze Age) the association of house-depictions with sun-motifs, stags and humans, may indicate the representation of temples and worshippers (and/or gods).

Recent work outside our area in Asian Russia (Littauer, 1977) has discovered rock-carvings dating around the second to first millennium B.C. These carvings show a startling similarity with the Swedish depictions (Althin, 1945) with wheels alone associated with wheeled chariots (Hančar, 1943, 26f ; 1956, 154-155). What is of particular interest is that, whereas these chariots are generally seen as portrayals of sun-carriages hurtling across the sky and therefore part of a sky-cult (Kozhin, 1968), Littauer would postulate that the artist is depicting the vehicles and beasts as if he is looking down on the contents of a tomb. Thus it may be a funerary ritual rather than a straightforward sky-cult that is sometimes symbolized here.

The Urnfield Period in Central and Northern Europe

The chronology of the Late Bronze Age Urnfield is based on contacts between Central European cultures and those of Greece during the late Helladic period, and subsequently between the late Urnfield and Villanovan and pre-Villanovan cultures of northern Italy. The Urnfield culture is roughly coincident with the decline of Mycenaean power (Coles & Harding put the Late Bronze Age between 1300 and 700 B.C. (1979, 335)), when Central Europe adopted a new burial-rite − cremation in flat cemeteries. The widespread appearance of urnfields around the close of the 2nd millennium B.C. provides a sufficiently coherent phenomenon for some prehistorians to attempt an equation of Urnfield groups and proto-Celts. By the beginning of the 1st millennium B.C. the use of wheeled and spoked-wheeled vehicles was widespread over most of Central Europe (Piggott, 1979, 14).

Childe (1929, 299) and Torbrügge (1968) would see a definite connection between wheel-headed pins and later wheel-pendants which are endemic in the Urnfield phases of the later Bronze Age. Déchelette (1910, 289-298) and Torbrügge (1968, 212, 241) suggest that there is solar symbolism behind the manufacture of both types of object.

Wheel-pendants and wheel-models of the European Bronze Age are a feature in material culture from about the 12th Century B.C. I will look first at wheel-pendants (Pls. L, LI). It is possible that in some cases they were part of horse-harness ; there are good parallels to this function for wheel-shaped bronzes in the Iranian Late Bronze Age (Moorey, 1971, 109-111, pls. 110, 111). Others, however, should be interpreted as true pendants, worn around the neck or dangled from belts, as they frequently possess suspension-rings. Unlike wheel-pins, pendants would, for the most part, appear to have had no specific function, and may well have been primarily decorative in purpose but with possible talismanic, presumably solar, significance.

The Spindlersfeld hoard near Berlin, dating from the commencement of the Urnfield period in Central Europe, contained a series of pendants, one wheel-shaped, and one wheel-model, possibly itself a pendant or amulet (Sprockhoff, 1938, Taf. 82, nos. 34, 19). In a grave at Grünwald, Germany (Müller-Karpe, 1959, Taf. 183) a female burial was associated with seven five-spoked wheels and a four-spoked example with a ring threaded through it. A number of Central European examples come from graves (as is the case with wheel-pins). Other examples include those from

Grammeitlingen, Baden-Württemburg (Grave 529) (Schauer, 1971, 177, pl. 14b, nos. 26-28), and from an urnfield in the North Tyrol at Hötting (Grave 18) (Wagner, 1943, pl. 3, no. 10). In Czech hoards wheel-pendants are of early mid-Urnfield date (dated by pin-types) (Rihovsky, 1979, Taf. 79, B2). Wheel-pendants are ubiquitous in Hungarian contexts during this period (Patek, 1968 ; Hampel, 1886-1896 ; Parvan, 1928, pl. 3, no. 3). A number of Swiss wheel-pendants are known, both of naturalistic and stylized forms including examples from Zürich and Montlingerberg (Schweizerisches Landesmuseum, Zürich). One Swiss pendant, from Sierre (cast in Schweizerisches Landesmuseum) has a hand-amulet attached (see below for later hand-symbolism). A number of sandstone moulds for wheel-pendants (e.g. Pl. L, Fig. 2) are also recorded (Wyss, 1967, 11, Taf. 10). In France too the pendants occur in the early Urnfield period, for example an eight-spoked bronze from Courchapon (Girardot, 1883 ; Kossack, 1950 ; Sandars, 1957, 139). Hoards such as that from Réallons (Hautes-Alpes) (Pl. L, Fig. 1) (Reinach, 1921, 203) and Épine (Hautes-Alpes) (Courtois, 1957, fig. 10) date to about the 10th Century B.C. A late Urnfield tumulus at St. Bernard (Ain) (Sandars, 1957, 185, fig. 44, no. 6) has yielded a ring or wheel-pendant.

A number of Late Bronze Age wheel-pendants have interesting associations which perhaps give some clue as to their religious symbolism. It is at the beginning of the Urnfield period, according to Gimbutas (1965, 310), that bird-figures appear first as part of pendants, frequently associated with wheel-motifs. The Urnfield cemetery at Grünwald, mentioned above, has yielded wheel-pendants and others ending in water-bird heads (*ibid.*, 129-131). The same association occurs, for example, in the Yugoslav hoard found between Bingula and Divos (Holste, 1951 ; Gimbutas, 1965, 316). On a Hungarian bronze pendant stylized bird-bodies support wheels (Hampel, 1887 ; Gimbutas, 1965, fig. 231). The Charroux pendant from near Gannat (Allier) (de Longpérier, 1867, pl. 25, fig. 31) comprises a wheel-symbol on a boat with bird-heads at bow and stern. De Vallon (Ardèche) (*ibid.*, fig. 33) and Vaison (Vaucluse) (Reinach, 1890, 172) show similar motif-associations. Swiss lake-dwellings (Déchelette, 1910, 409ff ; Keller, 1866) have yielded similar pendants, probably dating to the very end of the Bronze Age. One pendant, from a North Italian settlement (Déchelette, 1910, fig. 185, 3 & 205, 3) bears the motifs of disc, swans and an axe-symbol (the last a symbol of especial significance for later imagery). Déchelette suggests that this kind of pendant was worn under the chin or on the stomach, and cites as parallels in idea the miniature bronze wheels slung on Celto-Italian brooches during the Iron Age (1910, 409ff).

True wheel-models (as opposed to objects which are overt pendants) are common also during the later Bronze Age in Europe. Bone and clay wheel-models are recorded from Italian Terramare sites, for example Castione (Anati, 1960a, 50-53 ; Peet, 1909, 353 ; Keller, 1866, pl. LXII). A number of bronze Italian wheel-models occur in graves, as at Gorzano in the Modena area (Woytowitsch, 1978, Taf. 50). The majority of Late Bronze Age wheel-models are probably amulets although some have no intrinsic evidence of having been worn. An Urnfield cremation grave (A3) at Gemeinlebarn, Lower Austria has produced a miniature four-spoked wheel very similar to Iron Age examples from, for instance, La Tène (see below) (Naturhistorisches Museum, Vienna). Swiss lake-settlements, like Eaux-Vives and Paquis (Deonna, 1915a, 47, fig. 24) have produced wheel-models, as has Uetliberg (Keller, 1866, 376, pl. XCII). Clay models with four spokes come from Wallishofen-Haumesser in Switzerland (Schweizerisches Landesmuseum, nos. 25059-25100 ; 14425). Model wheels and a cult wagon come from the village of Culciul Mare, belonging to a Romanian Urnfield cremating group (Coles & Harding, 1979, 404). French wheel-model finds include those from Beaujeu (Haute-Seine) associated with flat cremations (Sandars, 1957, 204 ; Piroutet, 1903, 685 & 1913, 584). A late Bronze Age hoard from Petit Villatte (Cher) includes a model wheel, star and spiral-shaped items (Reinach, 1921, 217). Central European finds include Ockstadt (Oberhessen) (Behrens, 1916, pl. 12, no. 21) and a bronze wheel from a grave (No. 15) at Hühlau (N. Tyrol) (Wagner, 1943, pl. 17, no. 8).

An association, on certain pendants, of the wheel and water-bird symbols has been noted above. If we look at some sheet-bronze vessels of the Late Bronze Age, it is apparent that this linking of themes is ubiquitous on this distinct class of bronze item. It is during the Urnfield period that sheet-bronze vessels bearing 'sun' and bird or bird-boat symbols are first introduced. Situlate vessels thus ornamented are found from Italy and Yugoslavia to Germany, Denmark and Eastern Europe (von Merhart, 1952). The vessels possess uniformity in decoration, generally executed in repoussé-work. Motifs consist essentially (Déchelette, 1910, 289ff) of more or less stylized water-birds flanking discs, sometimes a definite wheel, like that from the Hajduböszörmeny hoard of North East Hungary (Kovacs, 1977, pl. 7b ; Hampel, 1876, pl. 65, fig. 3), and Siem in Denmark (Déchelette, 1910, fig. 173, 1 ; Undset, 1891, 244, fig. 12). On others the pattern is more degenerate, with the wheel merely a circle and the birds represented as 'S' shapes.

Cult wagons should be briefly examined at this point. A particularly important piece of iconographical evidence is the composite clay item from Dupljaja, Banat, Yugoslavia, which may date as early as the 11th Century B.C. (Coles & Harding, 1979, 408, pl. 19a), though Grapinat (1970, 54-56, fig. 7) sees it as Iron Age. A male deity is depicted with sun-symbols (of ring-and-dot form) on his body; the statuette is mounted on a bird-drawn vehicle, the rear wheels of which also bear ring-and-dot motifs (Gimbutas, 1965, 342, pl. 67; Sandars, 1968, 174-175, pl. 168), and a four-spoked wheel is incised on the bottom of the wagon. Other, bronze, cult-wagons may have solar associations. Some bear vessels with the sun and bird motifs. Coles and Harding (1979, 369-370) allude to their interpretation as expressions of a possible solar cult but refer also to the suggestion that the cult could be connected with weather-deities, the vessels carried being symbolic containers to encourage and collect rain (*ibid.*, Bouzek, 1977, 200); or they could be funerary vessels (Coles & Harding, 1979, 36809), like the full-size funerary wagons or hearses of the Urnfield and Hallstatt periods (Childe, 1951). A number of the cult-wagons are drawn by birds, and resemble miniature carts. It may be that sun, water and death-images are being combined here.

A number of utilitarian items in the later Bronze Age demonstrate solar religious symbolism using a sun or wheel-motif. A razor-fragment from an Innsbruck cremation-grave has a four-spoked wheel as part of the handle (Naturhistorisches Museum, Vienna). An Urnfield greave, which dates to the 11th Century B.C. is decorated with ducks perched on top of a four-spoked wheel (Gimbutas, 1965, 341; von Merhart, 1957, 91-147). Déchelette (1910, 409) mentions the recurring image of the swan on North Italian armour at the end of the Bronze Age. Urnfield belt-plates frequently bear solar symbolism, as at Uioara de Sus in Transylvania (Gimbutas, 1965, 124-125). A similar type of plate (in silver) found at Syros in the Cyclades (*ibid.*, 117; Lambrechts, 1942, 64-80) depicts a solar symbol associated with possible horse and a winged human figure. The dotted line technique perhaps links this piece with Central European material (the Kameiros, Rhodian, wheel and duck symbolism (see Chapter III) may have similar associations). The Syros human figure has parallels in late Helladic Greece (c. 1200 B.C.) (Furumark, 1941, 115).

We shall see that, in Romano-Celtic contexts, wheels and axes appear frequently as models and that there may be a solar connection between the two (see Chapter III). Axes would appear also to play some part in the seemingly great solar cults of the European later Bronze Age. The association of axe-symbols, disc and water-birds in a lake dwelling in North Italy has already been mentioned above. Other evidence supports this association both in the case of functional axes and of models. Two Late Bronze Age axes, unprovenanced but from Italian contexts (Reinach, 1921, 65), bear swastika-motifs. At Bologna an axe with an incised wheel is recorded ; from north of the Po comes an axe-blade bearing a swastika ; axes decorated with bird-motifs are also known (Déchelette, 1910, 409ff). The Urnfield site of Magyasco in Hungary has produced an axe with a central wheel-pattern (Sprockhoff, 1955, fig. 4, 4).

The most common model items, apart from wheels, are axes. The bronze axe-model from Maure-de-Bretagne (Ille-et-Vilaine) was strung on a bronze thread passed through a hole (Reinach, 1921, 204). Urnfield double-axe pendants occur, for example, in the Lemaud-Bourget site, at Fort Harrouard (Eure-et-Loire) (Sandars, 1957, 275, fig. 17, 18) and at Bourget (Savoie) (Girardot, 1883, 273-303). It is difficult to see these double-axe symbols as unrelated to those of Minoan Crete (see Chapter III). Apart from metal models, clay axe-miniatures and tiny clay thrones were placed in Hungarian Urnfield graves (Childe, 1929, 286).

In addition to frequent association of water-birds with sun-symbolism, bull-imagery often appears (Gimbutas, 1965, fig. 109, 1 ; Jorns, 1960) The importance of this beast as a cult-animal can be shown (see below) to manifest itself through the Iron Age and the Roman period in Western Europe, and the bull may have some significance with sun/wheel cults in prehistoric Central Europe at least. A late Urnfield Danish spout-cover has a triple-horned bull's head (Kossack, 1954, 52, fig. 14, 3). The three-horned nature of the bull becomes of increasing significance when seen in relation to the familiar North-East Gaulish triple-horned beast of the Roman period. Sometimes waterbirds associated with cult-vessels or vehicles are themselves bull-horned (Gimbutas, 1965, 341). North German Late Bronze Age hoards, like those from Löcknitz and Neu-brandenburg, contain both bull and water-bird figurines (Sprockhoff, 1937, pl. 30). Swiss lake-dwellings and Central European sites have produced curious clay horns, sometimes with stylized wheel-signs between them (Schweizerisches Landesmuseum).

The rare occurrences of relevant Late Bronze Age stone sculptures should be mentioned here. Swiss stone blocks, probably Late Bronze Age in date, decorated with swastikas and wheels, are recorded, for instance above Zermatt and at Zmutt (Valais) (Reber, 1907, 63ff ; Sauter, 1976, 111). Rocks dating from the end of the Bronze Age and bearing crudely incised wheels occur in the Ariège area of France (Glory, 1954, fig. 1). At Substantion, Hérault, a stone slab is decorated with a concentric-ribbed, notched shield (of Late Bronze Age type (Coles, 1962)), three four-spoked wheels and a possible spear (Coles & Harding, 1979, fig. 158).

Pottery served sometimes for probable solar cult-expression in the later part of the Bronze Age. Italy, for instance, has produced urns and other clay vessels bearing swastikas. The lake-dwellers of Lac-du-Bourget used pottery bearing this sign (Bertrand, 1897, 143, fig. 6). The Pilin cemetery in Hungary has produced swastika-patterned pots (Hampel, 1886-96). Northern Urnfield bronze bowls, for instance at Sophienhof near Demmin (Sprockhoff, 1955, 264, fig. 5, 8) bear swastika-patterns which were perhaps copied by potters.

Gimbutas (1965, 341) has convincingly demonstrated that in the Late Bronze Age Urnfield period, bird-sun symbolism was common to the whole of Central Europe. According to Sauter (1976, 110), Late Bronze Age religion is discernible by personal ornaments, such as wheel-symbols, and attendant creatures, for example horses, swans and ducks. In concluding this section it is difficult to do better than to quote Gimbutas :

> 'The sun-disc, the concentric circle, the wheel, the cross, the water-birds, the bull-horns and the clattering pendants represent a gamut of 'celestial' symbolism'.
>
> (Gimbutas, 1965, 342).

THE HALLSTATT IRON AGE (C. 750/700-500 B.C.)

The cemetery at Hallstatt in Austria produced both cremations and inhumations ; it is the finds of wealthy bronzework associated with most of the cremation-graves which have given their name to particular types of object found all over Europe at the beginning of the Iron Age. It is worth here briefly restating the well-known ambiguity in the term 'Hallstatt' to define cultural material. Occupation of the type-site began during the later Urnfield period of the Central European Late Bronze Age. The Bronze Age phases are generally known as Hallstatt A & B. The Hallstatt early Iron Age, when iron was in everyday production and use in Central Europe, is accurately referred to as Hallstatt C & D and follows the end of the *floruit* of the Urnfield cultures. By 'Hallstatt' then in this context I refer to C and D — the traditional date for the commencement of C being between 750 and 700 B.C.

According to Duval (1977, 43-44), in the Hallstatt era Bronze Age traditions mingled with Greek, Etruscan and other foreign influences. This mixture of cultural components should ever be borne in mind. However, many themes and motifs in Central European bronzeworking carried over smoothly from the Urnfield period through to the beginning of the Iron Age in Central Europe. There appears to be little change in the use of symbols, and, if anything, the features noted for the Late Bronze Age become more pronounced in the later Hallstatt cultural record.

A number of graves from the Hallstatt cemetery itself have produced sheet bronze vessels bearing duck or swan and sun-symbols, which were prominent on earlier Urnfield *situlae*. Grave 507 has produced a cylindrical bronze container with alternating wheel/suns and aquatic birds (Kromer, 1959, 119, pl. 101, no. 3 ; pl. 225). Grave 697 has yielded a bucket-lid with knob-ended rayed sun-signs (Pittioni, 1954, 545, Abb. 380). The knobs recall later wheel-brooches and possibly also knobs on bull-horns in Late Iron Age or Roman contexts (see Chapters II, III, VII). There are many similar examples (e.g. British Museum, 1925, 30-31, fig. 25 ; Kromer, 1959, 44, pl. 1, no. 23 ; 80, pl. 42, no. 7 ; 134, pl. 119, no. 4 ;157-158, pl. 162, no. 4). Hallstatt itself and contemporary cemeteries, for example in the Forest of Hagenau (Rhineland), have produced numerous vessels bearing not only the sun-wheel and water-bird motif but also horses, human figures, concentric circles, radiate discs and four-spoked wheels (Déchelette, 1910, 409ff. ; fig. 175). At Kleinklein, Steiermark, Austria, a bucket-cover bears stylized human figures, crosses, four-spoked wheels and crested water-birds, and hanging triangular 'rattles' (Pittioni, 1954, 615, Abb. 435). As far away as Denmark, as in the earlier Urnfield phase, the same theme pervades sheet bronzework. The biconical beaten bronze 'amphora' or *situla* from Lavindsgaard Mose, Fyen, dated to c. 750 B.C. bears the familiar sun-boat and water-birds (Hawkes, 1948, pl. facing 206), the sun here taking on the definite character of an eight-spoked wheel. Finally here should be mentioned the 7th-6th Century B.C. bowl in chased pure gold (908 grams) depicting stylized beasts, crescent moons and either full moons or suns, from Zürich-Altstetten (Sauter, 1976, pl. 52).

Pottery vessels appearing in the Hallstatt Iron Age in the 7th-6th centuries B.C. bear relevant motifs. Geometric painted vases occur, for example, in Gaul at Arles, bearing circles, stars and swastikas (Déchelette,

1914, 1494ff; fig. 684). From Bavaria comes a painted Hallstatt vase bearing a swastika-sign (Grapinat, 1970, fig. 8). In the Rabensburg area of Austria pottery of 'graphitverzierte' type dating to c. 600-500 B.C., bears four-spoked wheel-symbols around the belly of the vessel (Pittioni, 1954, Abb. 419).

Wheels or swastikas appear as motifs on a number of non-vessel items of Hallstatt bronzework. A Hallstatt grave contained a ribbed bronze bucket and an iron dagger with sheath and with an elaborate gilt hilt in the form of two adjacent wheels (Harding, 1978, 95). Belts, once again, bear wheels, stars, crescents and swastikas, sometimes associated with water-birds, horses and stags (Déchelette, 1913a, 373-380).

Wheel-models and pendants continue to form a fundamental part of the archaeological record during the Hallstatt phases. Most na Soci (Czechoslovakia) has produced a bronze open-naved wheel-pendant (Pl. LI, Fig. 3) (Naturhistorisches Museum, Vienna). A double, knobbed wheel-model on a stand, decorated with ring-and-dot motifs, comes from Byčiskala Höhle, Adamov (Moravia, Czech.) (Naturhistorisches Museum, Vienna), and another wheel-model, a pendant in the same museum, bears ring-and-dot symbols on the solid nave. The Charroux (Allier) pendant mentioned above, in the form of wheel with stylized bird-boat beneath, may come from a Hallstatt Iron Age rather than a later Urnfield context (Ferrier, 1971, 64, fig. 70a). A pectoral pendant from the Forêt de Moidons (Jura) comprises an openwork rectangular band with suspension-rings from which hang joined rings ending in seven-spoked wheel-pendants; an outward-facing duck is at each end of the rectangle (Ferrier, 1971, 67, fig. 75). The finds from Eberdingen-Hochdorf, Landkreis Ludwigsberg, are of relevance to the question of pendants. A grave of 6th century date contained eight supports of the funeral couch in the form of female figurines riding single six-spoked wheels and wearing pectoral wheel-pendants (Biel, 1978/9, 3-10, Abb. 2 & 3). A brooch from a Hallstatt grave at Brezje-Pri Trebelnem, Yugoslavia, is of relevance to the Urnfield pendant from Sierre, Switzerland which has hand-amulets attached to a ribbed spoked wheel-symbol. The brooch has a chain from which hangs a triangular pendant with ring-and-dot decoration from which in turn hang three hands with ring-and-dot ornament (Naturhistorisches Museum, Vienna). The Frögg (Villach-Land, Carinthia, Austria) lead grave-finds comprising ducks, horsemen and multi-wheel amulets, of probable Hallstatt C or D date, could have been amulets but were more probably applied as decoration for bronze vessels or pots (suggestion from Dr. Barth, Naturhistorisches Museum, Vienna) (Aigner-Foresti, 1978/9, 43-47, Taf. 1, fig. 1).

Bronze wheel-models, used as attachments to items of clothing, presumably possess a talismanic function. Belts frequently bear such amulets (Déchelette, 1913a, figs. 375-6). Déchelette (*ibid.*) notes also the presence of wheel-models attached to brooches and collars and placed in graves on vital parts of the body, presumably with an apotropaic function. Wheel-models with chains and rattles attached, like that fom Grave 507 at Hallstatt (Kromer, 1959, pl. 98, no. 3), and that from Chilly (Jura) – with dangling wheel-pendants attached (Déchelette, 1913a, 373-380 ; Piroutet, 1900) – may have been ceremonial rattles carried in processions, like later Romano-Celtic pole-tips. Simple wheel-models may occur in bronze, like the naturalistic 14-spoked example from Hallstatt (Grave 827 ; Kromer, 1959, pl. 183, no. 12) or in clay, as at Deerndorf (Parsberg area) where a miniature clay wheel and water-bird were found in a grave (Torbrügge & Uenze, 1968, no. 239).

We have noted the association of horsemen, wheels and water-birds at Frögg (above). Indeed, as early as 1300 B.C. at Trundholm, sun and horse appear to be associated (see above). We have also postulated that, in the Late Bronze Age, the axe may have been a celestial symbol. This idea appears to continue. A miniature bronze axe-pendant from Grave 641 at Hallstatt bears the image of a horseman (Kromer, 1959, 138, pl. 137,222). Cremation Grave 504 contained a miniature bronze axe with ring-and-dot decoration, on which is perched a miniature bronze horse (Naturhistorisches Museum, Vienna). Grave 734 contained a bronze model axe with ring-and-dot ornament (repeated several times, as on the pendant cited above), with a horse on top with a ring-and-dot motif on his neck (Anon, 1980a, 8.45). Torbrügge has suggested (1964) that the miniature clay wheel with long shaft from Grave 75 at Altmühl, near Regensburg, could be part of an axe-model.

Finally in this section the full-size bronze-sheathed funerary wagon from Býciskala (Czech) should be mentioned. Covered in new bronze the vehicle would have gleamed in bright light. Of particular note are both the ribbed spokes which would especially catch and reflect light (paralleled both on Late Bronze Age wheel-pendants and on Romano-Celtic wheel-brooches [Chapters II, III]) and the repoussé swastikas on the sides of the wagon (Anon, 1980a, 11.2). Other Hallstatt tombs have yielded swastika-decorated bronze plaques (Bertrand, 1897, 144) and, although this form of ornament may be entirely secular and perhaps derived from classical themes, there may be some solar symbolism here, as in later, Romano-Celtic, swastika-motifs.

The Pre-Roman Celtic Iron Age

It is important, when assessing the Hallstatt and later pre-Roman Iron Age phases in Europe, to remember the extensive Greek and Italian influence in material culture (Reinach, 1917, 202ff.) and the consequential difficulty in divorcing classical from Celtic or proto-Celtic emblems and symbols. Jacobsthal states 'Celtic art has a triple root :Italy, the East and Hallstatt' (1944, 155).

Another major point to be borne in mind when looking at material evidence from the pre-Roman Iron Age – as in other prehistoric periods – is that use of iron began at different times in different places. There may have been more than a century between the commencement of the Iron Age in Italy and the first use of the metal in say Germany or France. Because of this ambiguity I will assess the evidence for a non-classical solar-cult in Villanovan (and related) Italy first before proceeding to the rest of Europe.

The Italian Evidence

The Italian Iron Age traditionally begins c. 900 B.C. (Barfield, 1971, 104). Thus in terms of absolute chronology, there is overlap between this era and the Late Bronze Age of North-West and Central Europe.

In the various pre-classical cultures of Italy it is possible to see certain symbols which are similar to and *may* have associations with material trends in other parts of Europe. There appears to have been consistent communication between, at any rate, the northern areas of Italy and Central Europe (Barfield, 1971, 105). One may, as one item of evidence, cite the horned bird-wagon from Tarquinia, Viterbo, dating to the 9th-8th Century B.C. (Woytowitsch, 1978, Taf. 28, no. 135).

I do not propose to consider the Italian material in detail, but certain features may be noted. The Este culture of Venetia began in the 9th Century B.C. and several tombs here have revealed bronze material with Urnfield or Hallstatt sun/wheel and bird motifs (Randall-MacIver, 1927, 18, fig. 6 ; 14-15, fig. 5). A *fibula*-pendant model axe also comes from here (*ibid.*, pl. 6, no. 7). Later, but similar, evidence, includes a probably 4th Century girdle decorated in repoussé with eight-spoked wheels, from the Cerinasca Cemetery (Barfield, 1971, 151 ; Randall-MacIver, 1927, pl. 22, no. 8). Other similar girdles are recorded (Déchelette, 1910, 409ff.).

Villanovan Iron Age cultures in the North Italian Plain were centred on Bologna between 900 and 525 B.C. (Barfield, 1971, 106). A great deal of wheel and swastika-symbolism may be traced in Villanovan and other northern Italian grave-goods. Brooches decorated with swastika-symbols (Bertrand, 1897, fig. 23 ; Randall-MacIver, 1927, pl. 32, no. 9) and swastika-brooches themselves (Bertrand, 1897, 167 ; Gozzadini, 1854, pl. VIII, fig. 3) are recorded, for instance at Terni. Villanovan brooches also sometimes incorporate water-bird motifs (Déchelette, 1910, 409ff.).

Pottery in the Iron Age cultures of North Italy also bears evidence of the constant recurrence of 'solar' themes (Barfield, 1971, 112 ; Randall-MacIver, 1924, pl. 9 ; Déchelette, 1910, fig. 174 ; Randall-MacIver, 1927, 19).

Weapons and armour of the North Italian Iron Age were adorned with sun-signs, presumably for symbolic (perhaps protective) purposes − a phenomenon seen already on Central European Urnfield and Hallstatt material. Wheels and water-birds occur on helmets (Reinach, 1921, 88, fig. 41 ; Déchelette, 1910, fig. 486, 476). A dagger-scabbard from near Verona bears wheel-decoration (Déchelette, 1914, fig. 572, no. 4 ; 1312 ; Naue, 1888, pl. 1). There is an interesting parallel to this possible protective use of solar signs on arms and armour, on Italo-Greek vase-painting in southern Italy where one particular figured scene shows a warrior with two swastikas on his body and a wheel-motif at his belt. On another vessel a warrior has a swastika at his genitals and there is a wheel marked on the flank of his horse (Bertrand, 1897, 171 ; Déchelette, 1910, fig. 178).

Wheel-models and axe-models occur also in Iron Age Italy. A La Tène cemetery at Guibiasco near Bellinzona has produced a fragment of chain-belt with a bronze wheel-ornament attached (Déchelette, 1914, 1299ff. ; fig. 564). Déchelette (*ibid.*) has cited Italian *fibulae* with wheel-pendants attached (see above). A Villanovan grave in Etruria (Randall-MacIver, 1924, 68, fig. 11) has produced an axe-model, and allusion has already been made to the *fibula*-pendant model axe from Este (Randall-MacIver, 1927, pl. 6).

The 'La Tène' Iron Age in North-West and Central Europe

Metalwork is by far the most common medium for symbolic expression in the Early Iron Age in North-West and Central Europe, as is the case with Italy. Arms and armour, jewellery and now, for the first time, coinage, all imply that the cult of sky or sun remained dominant. Now, and again for the first time, quantities of wheel-models occur together ; the swastika is still present, seemingly as a wheel-substitute, and there begins to emerge the pattern of material evidence which was to survive throughout later prehistory into the Romano-Celtic era in North-West Europe, especially in Gaul.

Wheel-models are perhaps the most important phenomenon ; a large number are from graves. It is worthwhile citing a number of these in order to illustrate their widespread use. The whole question of miniature wheels is problematical since they are commonly found without attachments and there can be no way of knowing their precise function. In a La Tène grave in Switzerland, provenanced 'du Valais', an anthropomorphic-hilted dagger (a characteristic La Tène weapon [Jope, 1961, 341]) was found with a belt-fragment suspended from which was a four-spoked wheel-pendant (Chantre, 1880, pl. xx). At Diarville (Meurthe-et-Moselle) a La Tène burial contained a skeleton wearing a torc around its neck with a wheel-shaped ornament behind the head (British Museum, 1925, 50). It is suggested in the publication that the position of the wheel argues for its possibly having been part of, or originally attached to, a leather helmet. This is quite feasible for we have seen, and will see, evidence for wheel-symbols on armour including helmets. However, in this instance, the wheel could just as well have been some kind of pendant hung around the neck and displaced as the body decomposed, or have been part of a brooch-attachment (of possible significance is the absence of evidence for weapons or other armour in the grave). A skeleton from Chaffois (Doubs) buried in a tumulus, bore at his belt a bronze 'barrette' carrying eight wheel-symbols (Lerat, 1968, 440, fig. 10).

Elsewhere in Gaul numerous instances of wheel-models alone or in groups have been recorded. At the site of La Tène itself a number of simple wheel-models are known in association with coinage (Castelin, 1980, nos. 981-986). At Basel about ten four-spoked wheel-models from a late La Tène (1st Century B.C.) cemetery are the only objects recorded as found with certain burials (Major, 1940). Two other late La Tène wheels from a Basel grave were found with jewellery (Berger, 1966-76, 60ff. ; Abb. 14, 72). Of interest are a number of Romano-Celtic wheel-models recorded from the Roman *colonia* at Augst three miles away from Basel (see Chapters II, III). From Fully ("Baudon"), also in Switzerland, comes a curious nine-spoked wheel-model, the spokes of which jut out beyond the felloe (Primas, 1966-76, 98, Abb. 10). Another Swiss wheel-let comes from Münsingen, Grave 27 (Pauli, 1975, Abb. 9).

Quantities of wheel-models are recorded from French Iron Age contexts. A number come from *oppida* like Bibracte (Reinach, 1921, 109), Nasium (Bertrand, 1897, 358ff.) and Alesia (Flemming, 1908-9, 391-2) where moulds for such wheels are also known (Jullian, 1920, 78). Other Gaulish examples include late Iron Age wheels in lead and bronze from Châlon-sur-Saône (information from Dr. Max Martin, Augst Römermuseum); Argonne in lead (Chenet, 1919, 243-251), and Lavoye (*ibid.*), where Late Iron Age and Roman models are recorded in lead and bronze. It is possible that the hundreds of miniature wheels found in the Loire near Orléans may be pre-Roman (Flemming, 1908, 391ff. ; Déchelette, 1910, 409ff.), but without a context it is impossible to say with any certainty whether these are Iron Age or Romano-Celtic.

Eastern and Central Europe have produced a number of wheel-models, some of potential interest and significance. Hradīstĕ near Stradoniče (Bohemia) has produced a bronze wheel-model from a Celtic *oppidum*. Another, from the same site, forms a brooch-attachment (Déchelette, 1914, 1296ff.). Finds from the second half of the 1st Century B.C. show wide trade-connections with Roman lands (Filip, 1960, pl. XXXV, bottom centre). Another Czech *oppidum* find is that fom Stáre Hradisko (Meduna, 1970, fig. 7, 53). In a hoard at Regöly, S. Hungary, miniature gold wheels of 1st Century B.C. date are associated with gold beads (Megaw, 1970, no. 208). This is of interest if one recalls the gold wheel-models from Romano-Celtic contexts (see Chapters II, III). A grave at Mannersdorf (Lower Austria) dating to the early La Tène period (350-300 B.C.) produced a realistic bronze wheel-model with a long, perforated nave, as if from a model vehicle, and with uneven spoke-distribution (Grave 13 ; Anon, 1980b, no. 50). The Dürrnberg has produced several wheel-models. Grave 96 yielded a five-spoked model with the nave projecting both sides (Pauli, 1975, Abb. 6, no. 27). Grave 55/2 contained jewellery belonging to a six to twelve year old child, and dating to about 450-400 B.C. It includes a four-spoked wheel-model with perforated nave, glass beads and bronze armlets (Pauli, 1975, Abb. 6, no. 21). Of extreme interest is Grave 71/2 (430-400 B.C.), the tomb of a young girl containing a bronze wheel-model and a miniature axe (Anon, 1980b, no. 98 ; Pauli, 1975, 18, Abb. 3, no. 27). Another grave of 5th Century B.C. date (Grave 77/3) contained an axe-model with a ring-and-dot mark at the junction of the haft and the blade, and the blade itself doubling as a horse-head (Pauli, 1975, 21, Abb. 5, no. 9). This evidence is indicative of possible solar symbolism in that a wheel and axe are associated in one grave and, in another, ring-and-dot and horse-symbolism occur on a model axe. Other axe-models of this date are recorded, for example from a south German grave at Moorsingen, with a large suspension-ring (Pauli, 1975, Abb. 14,2). Other Central European wheel-models include the four-spoked wheel from a grave at Mülheim, southern Germany (Pauli, 1975, Abb. 14, no. 15). The Libna bei Krsko (Yugoslavia) find is of particular note in establishing the presence of contact between Hallstatt and La Tène cult-ideas. A 5th Century B.C. ceremonial bronze 'rattle' from here has close affinities with the Hallstatt example from Grave 507 alluded to above. It comprises a five-spoked wheel-model attached by a long chain to a 'mace-top'. The wheel has knobs with rings for the suspension of a hand-amulet bearing ring-and-dot decoration (Anon, 1980b, no. 100). This hand and wheel-symbolism is a recurrent theme. A hand-talisman attached to a bunch of keys comes from Alesia (where a number of wheels are recorded) (Deonna, 1925, 108-113, fig. 1). The author (*ibid.*) cites Italian Iron Age hand-models with concentric circle ornament ; this occurs also in the Hallstatt brooch with hand-pendants at Brezje (Yugoslavia) already cited and the Late Bronze Age wheel-pendant with hands attached from Sierre. At the Musée de Sion, Valais, Switzerland, is a bronze wheel-pendant with six spokes, supporting five hand-like pendants (Deonna, 1925, 108-113). The significance of the association of wheel and hand is obscure. It is of note that Scandinavian rock-art depicts hand-symbols (Gelling & Davidson, 1969), and that, in Provence in the Roman era, hand and hammer-symbols frequently occur associated on small altars (Musée de St-Rémy-de-Provence).

There is little British evidence for pre-Roman wheel-models, but a possible Iron Age context should be ascribed to the example from Hounslow (AB6 ; Pl. LXIII, Fig. 25) (British Museum, 1925, 147-148, fig. 172). This wheel has a parallel in the Late Iron Age metalwork find at Stanwick, Yorkshire (Macgregor, 1962).

It is probable that all Iron Age wheel-models were amulets. Their quantity in some contexts, however, and their frequent association with coinage (Blanchet, 1912, 1905, 27) have led some scholars to argue for their use as currency. Plain rings (sometimes known as 'ring-money') and wheel-models have been found together. At Naix, for example (Déchelette, 1914, 1286, fig. 560, 9 ; de Mortillet, 1876) wheel-models and rings are recorded as being slung on metal strips. All I would venture to say is that if wheel-models were used as currency it was probably in part on account of the symbolism attached to them ; Gaulish coinage itself (see below) seems to have combined a definite religious symbolism (including that associated with the wheel) with a purely economic function (see below).

Wheel or solar symbolism occurs on three main kinds of jewellery – brooches, pins and torcs. Wheel-miniatures are found attached to torcs, especially in the Marne area of North-East France, during the La Tène period. One example, from Pogny (Marne), is decorated at the front with a wheel-symbol flanked or supported by aquatic birds (Déchelette, 1914, 1299 ; fig. 563, 1). A Catalauni (Marne) torc has ornament in the form of wheels and birds (Sprockhoff, 1955, 259) ; and another Marne torc, from Attacourt, bears a pair of duck-prowed boats (*ibid.*). Sprockhoff points out the close similarities between the motif on the Attacourt necklet and that on the Urnfield Late Bronze Age bronze basin from Rossin, Pomerania (*ibid.*, 1955, fig. 3, 3). Another Iron Age torc (British Museum, 1925, 60, fig. 60, 3) bears a wheel-motif at the front.

Brooches too bear 'solar' motifs. The Suippes (Marne) *fibula*, and that from Stradoniče (already alluded to above) bear wheel-models attached to them by chains or wires (Déchelette, 1914, 1296ff. ; de Mortillet, 1876, 15, fig. 12). An 'S'-shaped amulet attached to a chain from the Marne region (Déchelette, 1914, 1296ff.) may embody a degenerate water-bird motif, and could possibly reflect later Romano-Celtic spiral symbolism (see Chapter VI).

In the Yugoslav Iron Age, one finds the motif of the wheel-headed pin (Alexander, 1958 ; 1964, 175-6), similar in form to Middle Bronze Age examples (see above). One pin actually bears a model bronze wheel mounted horizontally on the shaft (*ibid.*, 1964, fig. 9, no. 5). In Britain, a find from Danes Graves (Yorkshire) comprises a Swan's Neck pin with its 'ring'-head in the form of a four-spoked and coral-inlaid wheel (Stead, 1979, 77, fig. 30, no. 3, p. 78).

Celtic La Tène armour has very obvious parallels with North Italian Iron Age and Hallstatt material, being frequently marked with what may be interpreted as solar symbolism. The motifs appear on helmets, shields, body-armour and weapons. On a coin from Marseilles, a helmeted head with a wheel-symbol is depicted (Déchelette, 1914, 1566; Blanchet, 1912, 20, figs. 15, 16). The Orange Arch probably dating to the second half of the 1st Century B.C. (Powell, 1958, 266-267) depicts La Tène weapons including helmets with wheel-symbols attached. One of these helmets has bull-horns (Pobé & Roubier, 1961, no. 101, 61, pl. 101; Reinach, 1917, 41-2). The combination of bull-horns and wheel-symbol is repeated on the Gundestrup Cauldron (Chapter V; C1; Chapter VI) where a man wearing a bull-horned helmet carries a large wheel (Olmsted, 1979). According to Duval (1977, 25), Celtic metal helmets were frequently ornamented with apotropaic symbols including horns and wheels. Sprockhoff's view of the occurrence of solar motifs on helmets is appealingly and eloquently put:

> '... the appearance on Celtic helmets of a wheel-motif which, isolated on a flat surface, almost seems like the emblem of a secret society'
> (Sprockhoff, 1955, 261).

Other arms may be marked with celestial signs. A La Tène inhumation grave from Hallstatt yielded a sword-sheath of iron and bronze bearing decoration including horsemen, wrestlers and two sets of two men holding a wheel which has a marked resemblance to a rayed sun (Anon., 1980a, 15.7). The art-style would appear to be composite in that, according to Jacobsthal (1944, Cat. no. 96), the horses have Celtic affinities ; the human figures seem closest to North-East Italian (Venetic) styles ; and the wheel-men's garb has oriental associations. We are reminded of Jacobsthal's comment on the composite allegiances of Celtic art (1944, 155) and of Duval's statement regarding foreign influences on Celtic metal-work (1977, 43-44). A Middle La Tène sword from München-Untermenzing (Torbrügge & Uenze, 1968, no. 226), bears sun and moon-symbols. The Mainz dagger encrusted with gold symbols of sun and moon is also possibly Iron Age (Reinach, 1917, 202). One is reminded of Caesar's remark about German religion :

> 'They count as gods ... Sun, Fire and Moon ...'
> (de Bello Gallico, VI, 21).

A form of evidence comparable to that of the helmets on the Orange arch is the sculpture from Pergamum in Asia Minor. Celtic trophies were carved on the balustrade of the temple of Athene Nikephoros in the reign of Eumenes III (197-159 B.C.), the son of Attalos I who overcame the Celtic outlying province of Galatia (Powell, 1958, 266). A cuirass on the carving is decorated with swastikas and 'S' signs (Déchelette, 1914, 1156; Reinach, 1917, 39, fig. 31). The Battersea Shield bears a swastika similar to that on a bronze (?) yoke-terminal from Llyn Cerrig Bach (Fox, 1958, 28, fig. 83, F44 ; Savory, 1976, 57-59, 83, figs. 13, 14). It is difficult to judge whether the swastika in these instances, is entirely decorative, as it frequently was in the Mediterranean world (Grapinat, 1970, 54-56), or whether it has an apotropaic symbolism similar to that argued for the wheel.

The final type of armour here considered is belts or girdles. The 'barette' at belt-height on a skeleton from Chaffois, with wheel-models attached, has already been noted above. A chain-belt, with wheel and swans, occurs at Nemejice in Czechoslovakia (Déchelette, 1913a, 373-380 ; fig. 377 ; Pič, 1905, 638).

Bronze vessels bearing solar motifs are not as dominant in the later Iron Age archaeological record as in Late Bronze Age and Hallstatt Europe. A possible survival from these earleir periods is the bronze-mounted Aylesford (Kent) bucket bearing a wheel-motif below the rim (British Museum, 1925, 125). Sprockhoff would go further, and actually suggests a sun and bird motif on the Kentish vessel (1955, 265, fig. 6, 5). Such a survival of symbolism is not unreasonable. It has been pointed out already that the bird/wheel motif is present on La Tène torcs. Another piece of metalwork for which an Urnfield sun-boat symbolism is alleged is a Late Iron Age bronze disc (Sprochhoff, 1955, fig. 2, 6 ; Jenny, 1935 ; Mahr, 1939, 11, fig. 9, 2 ; 11, 4).

Pottery vessels too bear what may be celestial signs. A few instances may be cited ; an amphora-neck from Martigues (Vieille-Couronne), of 6th Century B.C. date, bears a swastika-mark (Benoit, 1958, 426, fig. 21a). The fact that a single swastika-sign only is present may imply true symbolism. By contrast the line of stamped swastikas on a sherd from Trogouzel (Finistère) may be merely decorative (Clement, 1979, 53-63, fig. 1).

Other, miscellaneous, items should briefly be noted. These include the bronze key in the form of a swastika from the Belgic *oppidum* of Nasium (Meuse) (Bertrand, 1897, 155). Stone sculpture, like the swastika-marked pyramidal stele from Kermaria (Brittany) (Clement, 1979, fig. 2), and the Robernier stele, which may be Roman rather than La Tène, (see Chapters IV & VI) with swastika, concentric circle and associated equine depictions, may embody celestial symbolism. The 'spoke'-decorated stone spindle-whorls from North Wales (Savory, 1976, 104, fig. 34) may or may not be significant. Childe dismisses clay whorl-discs with radial patterns out of hand because these patterns appear also on conoid or biconical shapes, morphologically incapable of simulating wheels (Childe, 1951, 177-178). However, on the North Welsh discs the markings could not have been seen when in use and thus could have been symbolic, though decoration on a circular object must always be suspect since shape and ornamentation are here inextricably linked.

Coinage

The role of wheel-symbolism on Gaulish pre-Roman coinage (copied and adapted by the Celts from Greek and Roman prototypes as early as the later 3rd Century B.C. (Allen, 1980, 3) is worthy of consideration, especially in the light of the suggestion that model wheels may have themselves been money. In Central and Western Gaul staters of the 4th and 3rd Centuries B.C. bear swastika-motifs. One coin has a swastika with horse-head arms (*cf.* the Romano-Celtic swastika-brooch from Cologne (Pl. 27c)) the symbolism on this coin is enhanced by the concentric circle in the centre of the Swastika (*cf.* the Romano-Celtic swastika-brooches from Tongeren (Pl. 27a)) (Hucher, 1874, figs. 12, 13). On North Gaulish coins numerous motifs may have sun or sky symbolism (Bertrand, 1897, 230). Particularly noteworthy is the occurrence of sun/wheel and axe-motif on one and the same coin (Déchelette, 1914, 1566, fig. 726, 4). Duval (1977, 140-141) mentions the occurrence, between the Loire and the Seine of curious coins bearing the motif of a horse surmounted by a bird of prey (*ibid.*, pl. 141); he postulates elsewhere (*ibid.*, 162) that the eagle may well have been sacred to the Celts before Roman influence and ritual took hold in Gaul. If this is so then we may have a significant link betwen pre-Roman sky-cults and the later Romano-Celtic equation of a sky-deity with the classical Jupiter and his theriomorphic emblem the eagle.

A number of coins show distinct sun/wheel motifs associated sometimes with other features of significance. A coin of Togirix shows stag, ram-horned serpent and a solar symbol beneath the stag's body (Vauthey & Vauthey, 1965, 255-273). Coins of the Nervii (Dhenin & Dhenin, 1976, 1-4, pl. 2, nos. 15-21), and of the Catuvellauni and Atrebates in Britain (Allen, 1958, pl. 1, 1 ; pl. 2, 10, 11) show horse and sun/wheel associated. On some coins (British Museum, 1925, pl. XIII, nos. 5, 13, p. 167) a wheel is represented between the fore and hind limbs of the beast. In the latter publication it is suggested that the wheel in this position represents the sun rather than a stray chariot-wheel. This need not be so. Many Gaulish coins used as their prototypes the Macedonian staters of Philip of Macedon, with the head of Apollo on the obverse and with a charioteer on the reverse. The British Museum example no. 5 (*ibid.*) has a sun-wheel above the horse (a likely position for the sun). The lower wheel probably represents part of a degenerate chariot.

The presence of naturalistic sun/wheel-symbols on Gaulish coins, in an otherwise frequently abstract art-medium, appears to demonstrate the important role of the object as a symbol. Wheels, crescents, and swastikas are all common (Allen, 1976, 265-266). The horse is present in almost all Gaulish areas ; boars too are supraregional. A number of detailed points about the iconography of Celtic coinage are worth making. The heads on the obverse seem frequently to be those of deities (Allen, 1980, 38-39). Often, for instance in Armorican Gaul, a symbol, such as a wheel or boar, accompanies the head, presumably to give it a personality (Allen, 1980, 135). From the early 4th Century B.C. the Greek colony of Rhoda in south-western Gaul struck fine silver drachmae with a rose on the reverse (*ibid.*, 54-55). The Celtic copiers misunderstood this rose and converted it into a wheel, sun or cross-pattern. Later the *calices* of the rose were used to divide the reverse into quadrants filled with symbols, including 'S's, eyes and axes. Allen suggests (*ibid.*, 50) that certain areas adopted the classical horse and rider or charioteer not as a random theme but because such an image meant something to the choosers. He further postulates that the original Philip of Macedon stater was chosen because of a particular appreciation of the horse and chariot by the Gauls. It may be significant that the wheel frequently survives intact whilst the rest of the original motif disintegrates.

> 'The need to look behind the surface of Celtic coin-types has made a happy hunting-ground for the crankish interpreter in pursuit of devious religious symbolism'

Such is Allen's warning (1980, 148). Nevertheless, he himself believes in the presence of symbolism (*ibid.*, 149) as would Daphne Nash (personal communication, 1980). Allen postulates (*ibid.*) that rings, wheels and rosettes on coins were meant in general as solar symbols and that four, six and eight-spoked wheels were probably at one and the same time both representative of wheels themselves and solar depictions. The same thing appears to be true of Romano-Celtic wheel-symbols (see Chapter IX).

The association between wheel-signs and other iconography on coins is of potential significance with regard to later Romano-Celtic associations. For instance, on an Aeduan coin (Allen, 1980, no. 309) the wheel-sign beneath the horse is replaced by a concentric circle, as if wheel and the latter motif were interchangeable. We have seen this phenomenon on prehistoric rock-carvings (above), and I would postulate the same occurrence in Romano-Celtic iconography (Chapter VI). Other significant

Gaulish coin-associations (Nash, pers. comm., 1980) include boar and tree-symbolism (present on the Netherby Romano-Celtic sculpture [BB18]) and the ram-horned snake (present on the Lypiatt Park sculpture [BB13]). The most powerful association, however, must be that of horse and wheel. The presence of this beast as a recurrent companion of the Wheel-God in Romano-Celtic contexts could carry over from the symbolism of coinage.

The Gundestrup Cauldron

This cult-bowl is discussed below in Chapters V and VI. Although it is probably of immediate pre-Roman date (Olmsted, 1976; 1979), it belongs more with Romano-Celtic than with pre-Roman iconography. Worthy of note here is the association of ram-horned snake, wheel and bull-iconography on the same silver plate (C1). Both ram-horned snake and bull appear to have Romano-Celtic solar associations (see Chapters IV, V, VI, VII).

SUMMARY AND CONCLUSION

A great deal of material evidence, ranging over a millennium and a half has been surveyed in the course of this chapter, and a number of themes relating to a possibly dominant sky or sun-cult of some kind have been distinguished.

I must stress first that I am not endeavouring to prove specific continuity of divinity or ritual from the Bronze Age to the Roman period. The most that may be said is that the evidence from Roman Europe for some form of sky and/or sun worship takes the form of circles, wheels or swastikas, and that these signs, in various forms, have been recorded consistently right through later European prehistory. What I have tried to do is to put the occurrences relating to a Romano-Celtic sky-cult in pre-historical perspective. Thus, one need not imagine that the wheel takes its place for the first time as a sky-symbol when we find it linked with Jupiter's sky-cult in Roman Gaul and in Britain.

One or two phenomena of particular interest may be singled out. The first involves the use of model objects, and specifically model axes and wheels, from very early indeed in the European archaeological record. It is these two latter items which most frequently occur in miniature form both in the prehistoric and in Roman periods. We have seen that there is good evidence to support a connection between the symbolism of axe and wheel, and the culmination of this may be seen in the miniature axe, bearing an incised swastika-symbol, from the Romano-Celtic shrine of Woodeaton in Oxfordshire (AX20 ; see Chapters II, III). Models in general deserve examination and will be considered in detail below. All we need say here is that the practice of manufacturing miniature objects in imitation of full-size articles is one that goes back some millennia on the Continent and in the Near East (see Chapter III).

A second point to emerge from this survey lies in the general connection of sky and funerary ritual. Most finds relevant to our study, especially in earlier periods, do occur in sepulchral contexts (although one must always be wary of tomb-bias in archaeological survival). There seems also to be an association between Late Bronze Age and Hallstatt funerary vehicles and sky-symbolism epitomized in the Hallstatt 'hearse' from Býciskala (above).

The protective, talismanic properties of the wheel-sign are most evident in prehistory. Pins, amulets, pendants and necklets are all present in the form of the wheel. Above all we have the evidence of armour and the need of a soldier to be shielded from harm at his most vulnerable parts — the head, genitals and vital organs.

Two final points should be made. One is that occasionally in prehistory we catch glimpses of humanoid representations which could represent either worshippers or deities themselves associated with solar symbolism. We have the evidence of Bronze Age rock-art ; we have the Dupljaja clay figure ; the wheel-turners of the Hallstatt sword-scabbard could perhaps depict priests of a sky-cult. The heads with wheels on the obverse of Celtic coins could denote a sky-divinity. At the boundary between prehistory and Romano-Celticism we have the deity associated with a wheel on the Gundestrup Cauldron. Thus it may not have been too great a step for the historical Celts after the Roman occupation to see their own sky-god in terms of the classical equivalent.

Certain beasts, all of which recur in the Romano-Celtic archaeological record, appear to have had a specific association with a prehistoric European sky-cult. They include the horse, bull, swan or duck, ram-horned serpent, boar and stag. Of these the most important are the horse, water-bird and bull. The Romano-Celtic era in western Europe sees a consistent connection between a horse or horseman with that of a celestial divinity (see Chapter VI). In the Bronze Age especially, the horse's role in a sun/sky ritual is unequivocal ; and in the later periods the horseman begins to appear. The presence of the bull is likewise an early feature and persists throughout the Bronze and Iron Ages. The most enigmatic creature of all is the water-bird whose inextricable association with the sun-wheel apparently remains virtually unaltered for over a thousand years. The occurrence of composite theriomorphism — such as the bull-horned aquatic birds — is presumably intended to intensify the symbolism ; the same is perhaps true of the ram-horned snake (see below).

In assessing the evidence we have surveyed in this introductory chapter we must pose the question as to whether it is valid in prehistory to draw conclusions as regards continuity or idea-sharing within time and space. Sprockhoff (1955, 259) has asked if one can viably trace continuity of trends and ideas between the Central European Late Bronze Age and the Celtic Iron Age. All I feel able to say is that there are traces of a sky-cult, using the wheel as a symbol sometimes associated with other motifs which recur over several centuries and over wide distances. The importance of studying the prehistoric evidence in what is otherwise a work concerned with Romano-Celtic religious symbolism cannot, however, be underestimated. A number of the symbols and beasts which have a ritual function connected with a sky-cult in the Bronze and Iron Ages, appear once again in the Roman period. Whilst I would not postulate unilinear continuity of ideas within prehistoric Europe or between prehistoric and Romano-Celtic Europe, I do argue a common heritage or circumstance of origin.

CHAPTER II

Analysis of Romano-Celtic Miniature Wheels in Relation to other Models, in North-West Europe and Britain

MODELS IN ROMANO-CELTIC EUROPE [1]

No attempt is made here to provide a comprehensive corpus of model wheels and other miniature items from the Continent. It would be an impossible undertaking to visit every museum, archaeological centre and private collection in north-western Europe. Nevertheless, museum-collections in Belgium, Luxembourg, Alsace, West Germany, Switzerland, Austria and the South of France, have been studied in detail ; it has, in addition, been possible to gain a reasonable overall impression of other French material, from an examination of the collections of the Musée des Antiquités Nationales, St-Germain-en-Laye (although it was not always possible to remove objects from display-cases for purposes of study).

With the exception of certain grave-groups from the Cologne and Bonn areas of the Rhineland (to which I shall return later) the western European archaeological record has produced nothing like the variety or diversity of model items found in the British province. Apart from model wheels and wheel-brooches, which are far more numerous in Gaul and on the Rhine frontier than in Britain, isolated models of all types are comparatively rare in continental contexts. Axes are reasonably common, especially in Switzerland (Forrer, 1948), but other miniatures outside the German grave-finds are sparse. It is the striking cluster of sepulchral groups in the Rhineland, containing large numbers of models which are of particular interest outside Britain (Rottländer, 1973-74). They are almost exclusively of an agricultural nature, but two grave-groups are of direct relevance to

---

[1] See Catalogue A for detailed description and full references to Wheel-Models.

our study since they are accompanied by model wheels (A12, A12a) (Rottländer, 1973-74, 143-152, Abb. 9, 15).

Wheel-Models on the Continent

Context

As stated above, the Romano-Celtic finds of miniature wheels are extremely numerous in Gaul and the Rhineland. Very frequently context cannot give any aid in interpretative significance since, for the most part, continental wheel-models are either stray finds in or away from Roman sites, or the exact findspot has not been recorded by the collector or the museum concerned. However, a significant number of these miniatures has turned up on specifically Roman sites, and of these some are from graves or shrines. Others, like those from the Loire near Orléans (A84), come from the beds of rivers.

If we look at the distribution of wheel-shaped brooches on the Continent (Pls. XIX-XXII) it seems immediately apparent that they are far more thickly scattered than in Britain, where they are relatively scarce. They occur in varying quantities in almost all the museums visited and there are a large number recorded in publications from excavated sites (see Catalogue A).

A most prolific site for wheel-symbols is the cemetery at Wederath near Trier (A52), which has produced at least half-a-dozen miniature wheels from the Roman and Celtic site of Belginum, published by Haffner (1971, 1974, 1978) as 'Anhänger' or pendants. The models are all around 2 cm diameter (Haffner, 1971, grave 268, 59, pl. 64, no. 18 ; grave 368, 80, pl. 92, no. 4 ; 1974, grave 463, 6, pl. 144, no. 10 ; grave 492a, 12, pl. 150, nos. 5-7). All the wheels found in the cemetery were simple four-spoked examples – merely crosses within circles. It is of interest that a recent discovery at Augst in Switzerland (A126), from a specifically Roman context, comprised a mould for just such wheel-amulets – four-spoked and of precisely the dimensions of the Wederath-Belginum examples (Pl. LVII, Fig. 14). This mould, with pouring channel clearly visible, was incised on a scrap of broken tile. Whilst I do not suggest that this particular mould was used to cast the Belginum models, we may assume that this type of simple amulet was by no means confined to the Valley of the Moselle.

There is a substantial amount of evidence for wheels as grave-finds on the Continent, especially in the Rhineland, unlike the situation in Britain (see below). An elaborate four-spoked wheel-brooch decorated with knobs round the outside of the circumference, comes from the St. Kunibert area of Cologne (A2). Although there is no precise sepulchral context for the brooch, it is from a district where a number of Roman graves have been recorded. A six-spoked wheel-shaped brooch comes from a cemetery associated with the Roman town of Strasbourg (A41) (Forrer, 1927, pl. 39, 324). Trier has produced a wheel-brooch from a grave in the Maar area in the North of the city (A44 ; Pl. LIV, Fig. 10), and another example from Aachenstrasse in western Trier (A45) may also be from a cemetery, though no certain evidence survives. A third brooch comes from Paulin, definitely from a burial (A48). In Belgium, evidence of wheel-brooches in sepulchral contexts comes from a number of sites including Élouges (A56 ; Pl. LVI, Fig. 12) ; Juslenville (A58) and Tongeren (A60) where four brooches were probably from graves. A small enamelled brooch from Lavacheri (A57) also comes from a cemetery. Gaulish examples from France include models or brooches of wheel-shape from Lanslevillard (A100) ; Villeneuve (A179) ; Blanc-Pavé (A196) ; and Nîmes (A207). It is of interest in this connection that at Basel near Augst, a late Iron Age cemetery of 1st Century B.C. date produced nothing but simple wheel-models (information Dr. Max Martin, Augst Römermuseum). We shall see, below, that in the Roman period Augst itself has produced a substantial number of wheel-models.

Wheel-models or wheel-brooches as temple-finds are rarer than those discovered associated with burials, but they do exist, and were, in all probability, much more frequent than the evidence now available suggests. At Gusenburg (A50 ; Pl. LV, Fig. 11) two large and identical wheel-brooches, each with six ribbed spokes and beautifully-enamelled, were discovered in or near a temple-precinct. A temple at Dhronecken (A51) (Hettner, 1901, Taf. V, no. 54, 51) yielded a wheel-brooch. A wheel-model (not a brooch) comes from the Altbachtal temple-precinct in Trier (A109). The Champlieu model (A72) could be from the Romano-Celtic shrine known ; the Bolards (A173-5) and Bourbonne (A206) finds are from temples or their vicinities. Lardiers (A180-1) is a temple-site producing both wheel and swastika-shaped brooches. It is suggested that the Augst examples (A137-41 ; Pl. LVIII), found in Insula 17, are from a temple.

The only other type of site-context worthy of mention is that of rivers. In the collections of St-Germain-en-Laye, provenances are frequently extremely imprecise, but there is evidence for large numbers of miniature wheels having been deposited in rivers (Courcelle-Seneuil, 1910, 73 ; Reinach, 1894, 34ff.). The latter authority has recorded several hundred model wheels in the bed of the Loire near Orléans (A84). He omits to state whether there is evidence for their use as brooches or whether they were true models without any specific secular function. I myself have examined a number of miniature wheels in St-Germain-en-Laye (Pls. LII-LIII), but it was not possible to remove examples from display to look for this kind of information ; those in reserve collections did appear to be straightforward miniatures. Riverine finds, apart from the Loire, include examples from the Marne (A64) ; Oise (A67 ; Pl. LII, Fig. 6) ; the Seine (A68 ; Pl. LII, Fig. 6), and the Mayenne (A205).

Leaving aside the question of the presence of wheels in possible ritual contexts, these models are found alike in military and civilian sites. Civil examples (for instance A1-9 ; 44-48) have already been noted. Finds from Roman forts (which retained a military function throughout their existence include Saalburg (A20, 23) ; Straubing (A29) ; Stockstadt (A90) ; Zugmantel (A89) and Rückingen (A93).

Descriptive Analysis of Wheel-Models

The model wheels listed in Catalogue A may be divided into the following categories :

        a) true models
        b) brooches
        c) brooch-variants
        d) swastika-brooches
        e) pendants
        f) miscellaneous

There is an inevitable problem where, as sometimes happens, the evidence available does not lend itself to the distinction between true model and brooch. Where this is the case I will classify the item as a query model.

a) *True Models*

A8 ; A9 ; A12 ; A12a ; A23 ; A42 ; A52 ; A54 ; (?) A62 ; A63 ; A64 ; A65 ; A66-72 ; A76-83 ; (?) A84 ; A101 ; A106-109 ; A119 ; A123 ; A136 ; A137-145 ; A148 ; A154 ; A168 ; A169 ; A175 ; A180 ; A183 ; A184 ; A186-192 ; A200 ; A205 ; A206 ; A207-8 ; A210.

Most of the wheels cited above are plain models of cart-wheels ; they vary greatly in the number of spokes, and this factor would appear to have little or no significance; Attention should be drawn, however, to one or two points. One is the extremely small size of some models, for example A8, 52, 186, 187-9, 207 and 208 ; and the large size of others, like A123. Another point is that whilst the great majority of sites have produced models of bronze, occasionally other metals have been employed. Many of the Lavoye examples (A186-9) are of lead, as are A83, and some of the examples from Naix (A78). Other Naix wheels are of silver. A79 and A80 are gold. Some wheel-models have features which may be of interpretative significance and will be examined again below (Chapter III). The Champagne model (A210) bears concentric-circle decoration on the felloe at the spoke ends. The two models (A82) with denticulate ornament around the outside of the circumference should be noted. Some wheels, for example A69, A106, A123, may have been part of model carts or chariots, like that from the Rodenkirchen grave-group (Rottländer, 1973-74, 143-152) and thus cannot be treated as isolated miniature wheels. The Strasbourg item (A42) is of interest since it is of sheet bronze and, although there is no direct evidence for this, it may have formed some kind of decoration, applied, perhaps, to a wooden surface. It is unlikely to have been used by itself as an amulet. A most curious model is that from Grand-Jailly (A101) which comprises a wheel-shape decorated with three small 'S'-shaped plaques welded or soldered onto one surface. Only one of these applied ornaments survives but the position of the solder indicates the past existence of the other two 'S' symbols. In addition, on each surface the hub of the wheel is decorated with a rosette. The 'S' motifs may be particularly significant since the bronze figurine of the Wheel-God from Le Châtelet near St. Dizier (C2) bears 'S' or spiral-shaped items hanging from a ring on the deity's shoulder. We will return to the possible ritual implications below.

One Augst wheel-model (A140 ; Pl. LVIII, Fig. 16) is of particular interest since it actually bears the remains of a votive inscription. A bronze Lavoye model (A191) has a highly polished surface and pointillé decoration on the felloe ; a Bern wheel (A136 ; Pl. LIX) has an indented nave, as if for a cord-attachment.

The context or associations of these true wheel-models should now be considered in detail. Two of the Cologne grave-groups contain small wheel-models (A12 ; A12a). One group (A12) (Behrens, 1939, 56-59 ; Rottländer, 1973-74, Abb. 9) contained two adze-hammers, two ox-yokes, a ladder, two keys, two lizards, a pair of scales and a four-spoked wheel-model. The other (A12a) (Rottländer, 1973-74, Abb. 15) included a model bell, mattock, axe, key, yoke and a six-spoked wheel. The models from Grignon near Le Châtelet (A76) are interesting since a number were allegedly discovered in the same area as the Celtic Wheel-God statuette, and one could speculate on the possibility of there being a sacred place, dedicated to the god, where model wheels were offered by devotees of the Wheel-God cult. At Guignicourt (A77) more than forty wheel-models were found together in a gravel-pit. At Naix (A78) two vessels were discovered, one filled with silver and lead wheels, the other containing wheels and coins, both of Gaulish and Roman date (de Villefosse, 1881, 12). At Langres miniature wheels (A80) were found associated with mosaics, wall-paintings, Celtic and Roman coins, an altar and a carving of the Deae Matres (Drioux, 1934, 111). Near Orléans we have the large group of riverine wheel-deposits (A84), which could have been made over a long period of time but equally could have been the contents of a ritual hoard. The wheel-models from Langenheim (A119) and Böhming (A123) came from the vicinity of Roman forts but no further information as to ritual or other association is available. The Bourbonne (A206) and Bolards (A173, 5) wheels came from shrines — the Bolards examples possibly associated with a head of Jupiter. The Augst models (A137ff.) are very probably from shrines.

A review of the association-evidence of true wheel-models, therefore, gives little clue as to their religious significance. They are occasionally found in temples or graves. There is little hint at deity-association, but the possible link between wheels and the Mother-Goddesses at Langres is of great potential interest (see below). The Cologne grave-groups are anomalous. The presence in many of them of animals like lizards, crested serpents and batrachians, makes it most likely that an eastern mystery-cult is represented. There were a large number of oriental soldiers on the Rhine and the presence of votive bronze hands of the god Sabazius (e.g. Ristow, 1975, pl. 56) also bearing these symbols suggests some cult-association between this Thraco-Phrygian divinity and these burials.

b) *Wheel-Brooches*

A1-5 ; A16 ; A18-20 ; A26 ; A32-37 ; A39-41 ; A43 ; A44-48 ; A50-51 ; A53 ; A54-60 ; A85-87 ; A93 ; A96-97 ; A99-100 ; A104 ; A105 ; A111-112 ; A117 ; A118 ; A125 ; A127 ; A130 ; A132 ; A134 ; A145 ;

A146 ; A147 ; A155 ; A156 ; A157-158 ; A160 ; A161-166 ; A167 ; A170-171 ; A174 ; A176 ; A178 ; A179 ; A182 ; A185 ; A193 ; A194-197 ; A199 ; A209.

Once again I shall comment on any stylistic features which merit particular note, and then discuss context and association. One curious feature common to a number of wheel-shaped brooches is the ribbed decoration frequently present on the spokes and the circumference, for example that from Cologne (A1) ; from Strasbourg (A40) ; Gusenburg (A50 ; Pl. LV) ; Dhronecken (A51) ; Vienne (A165) ; Augst (A147) ; Blois (A195) and Nijmegen (A160). Another decorative feature appearing on several wheel-brooches, especially in the Rhineland, is the presence of knobs or lugs around the outside of the circumference; A four-spoked brooch from Cologne (A2) bears such excrescences, as does another (A3) from the same city. Again from the same site (A4) a much more elaborate example is ornamented with curlicues and very pronounced knobs. Yet another Cologne wheel-brooch bears lugs not only around the outside of the rim but also sprouting from the nave itself (A5). A Koblenz brooch (A19) bears decoration in the form of open-work knobs, thus differing from the closed lugs on the Cologne brooches. A Sarre-Union item (A39) has similar open-circle decoration. In the Pas-de-Calais region of North-West France was found a wheel-shaped brooch with a large and elaborate knob at the top and smaller lateral lugs (A36). Bavay, also in northern France (A59 ; Pl. LIII, Fig. 9), Reims (A85) and Alpentäler in Switzerland (A96) have all produced lugged brooches, as have Châlon (A164, 165) ; Bolards (A174) ; Néris (A176) ; Montot (A178) and Blois (A195). Nave-knobs occur at, for example, Trègnes (A155) ; Juslenville (A58) ; Châlon (A164) ; Villeneuve (A179) and Alesia (A185). A Vienne brooch (A165) bears curious trilobate ornaments in place of felloe-lugs.

Other curious ornamental features include dotted felloe-decoration at Trègnes (A155) ; the octagonal nave at Vesqueville (A167), and circular felloe-decoration at Néris (A176) and Villeneuve (A179).

Unlike true models, wheel-shaped brooches are frequently ornamented with red and/or blue enamelwork. This is not, of course, a feature unique to wheel-shaped brooches, but common especially to skeuomorphic, solid circular, and zoomorphic types. Red "enamel" appears to have been in use by early in the La Tène period. The decoration is, strictly speaking, not enamel but an opaque red glass heated until soft enough to be pressed into the inlay cavity (Hughes, 1972). The Namur enamellers' workshops in Belgium were prolific before the Roman period and one, at Anthée near

Namur, was worked until the mid 3rd Century, producing the Viet, Dinant wheel-brooch (A156), and also possibly that from Mainz (A158) (Henry, 1933, 66, 67, 123-4). There is evidence, too, for pre-Roman enamelling at Bibracte. Here model wheels were actually discovered in the workshops of enamellers and bronzesmiths (Reinach, 1921, 109). Particularly splendid examples of beautifully enamelled wheel-brooches include that from Haegen (A43); the pair from Gusenburg (A50; Pl. LV); and the brooch from Weisenthaum (A118).

One curious, and possibly significant, feature of some enamelled wheel-brooches is the presence of 'solar' or floreate decoration incised into panels of enamelling on the felloe. This occurs at Trègnes (A155); Bavay (A166); Nijmegen (A160) and in the British Museum example from a French or German context (A104).

A characteristic of some wheel-shaped brooches is the presence of a ring attached to the outside of the felloe. This feature has been noted, for example, at Weisenthaum (A118) and on the Gusenburg brooches (A50; Pl. LV). There are three possible purposes for such a ring. The first is that the wheel-symbol could be used either as a brooch or as a pendant – round the neck or attached to a belt. The second is that the brooch itself had something suspended from it, in which case the suspension-ring must obviously be positioned at the bottom of the wheel. The third possibility is that the brooches were worn in pairs and that a length of chain joined two together on a garment. There is some evidence for both latter ideas. A number of pendants, discussed below, do have items hanging from them. As for the third suggestion, there is evidence that bow-*fibulae* sometimes have suspension-rings (there are several such examples in the Ashmolean Museum); occasionally two such brooches have been found together attached by a wire or chain (Cunliffe, 1968, pl. XXXI, fig. 66, for example). With regard to suspension, the Iron Age wheel from Stradonitz in Central Europe should be noted. Here a four-spoked wheel was suspended from a brooch by a short length of chain (Pič, 1906, pl. X, 24).

A few further stylistic features should briefly be noted. A wheel-brooch from Mainz (A26) is curious in having four double spokes; the Weisenthaum enamelled brooch (A33) is interesting in that the spaces between the wheel-spokes are formed by oval holes in a solid circle, so that the spokes are implied rather than genuine, and the wheel itself takes on a floreate, roseate, appearance. One of the Alpentäler brooches is essentially similar (A97) in that the spokes are distinctively concave-sided. Sometimes, as at Lanslevillard (A100), Viet (A156), Mainz (A158) and the

British Museum brooch (A104) the spokes are conversely convex-sided. The Augst brooches (A146 ; Pl. LVIII, Fig. 17) are all distinctive in having four concave-edged spokes ; wedge-shaped spokes appear, for example at Châlon (A162). The central dolphin on the Bavay brooch (A59 ; Pl. LIII, Fig. 9) should also be noted.

Grave-contexts for wheel-brooches are attested from a number of sites (for instance A2, A41, A44, A48, A56, A57, A58, A100 ; A179 ; A196). Those from Gusenburg (A50), Dhronecken (A51), Argentomagus (A193) and Lardiers (A180) are from shrines or their immediate vicinity.

A word should be said about wheel-shaped brooches in general. For present purposes only those which are definite wheel-imitations with recognisable spokes within an openwork frame, are accepted. Thus I would discount the brooches made up of discs and knobs, belonging late in the Roman Empire, which at first glance look as if they could belong to the same group (Thomas, 1963, 344-350). Again, I would reject solid circular brooches, with or without lugs. This classification is supported by Feugère (1978), who groups solid circular enamelled brooches as his Type 34, as distinct from wheel-brooches, which he classifies together with other skeuomorphic brooches, as Type 40. My only exception to this 'true wheel' rule is the brooch from Carnuntum (A197) which is a normal wheel-brooch with an additional solid back-plate.

c) *Brooch-Variants*

A21 ; A22 ; A38 ; A88 ; A114 ; A152.

There are only a few examples of these. 'S'-shaped brooches (A21) and a triskele-shaped example (A22) from Saalburg, may be variants of the wheel/swastika-type. As stated above, the 'S' motif appears to have a connection with wheel-symbolism, on the evidence of the Grand-Jailly wheel (A101), and of the Le Châtelet statuette (C2). The triskele brooch appears to have more in common with the swastika than with the true wheel-symbol. It should be recalled that Saalburg has also produced a large number of swastika-brooches (A20). One very strange piece of jewellery is the composite *fibula* from Illkirsch (A38), which is composed of a double wheel — two separate wheels joined together by a number of interconnecting bronze strips. It is an awkward-looking object and the multiplication of the symbol may have other than a purely decorative significance. It is possible that a stylistic representation of a chariot-axle is intended ; alternatively the popular Celtic idea of enhancement of a symbol's potency by duplication may explain this curious item. Amiens

(A88) and Augst (A152) have produced a variant of the wheel-type in a *fibula* of conventional bow-type but with a wheel set horizontally as part of the bow. The wheel itself possesses ribbed spokes like some of the true wheel-brooches described above. A similar theme is expressed in the brooch from Eisenstadt (A114), the catchplate of which is ornamented with an openwork wheel-motif. It is of interest that authorities on Roman *fibulae* (information from D. Mackreth, Nene Valley Research Committee), working from iconographic evidence, suggest that brooches were fastened with the cross-spring facing downwards, so that the catchplate and any decoration on it might be easily visible. The convention in publication, until recently, has been to illustrate *fibulae* with the cross-spring uppermost, frequently obscuring the catchplate. A similarly decorated brooch-plate, with a wheel-motif with curving, almost 'S'-shaped spokes, comes from Intercisa (Hungary), one of a pair of massive silver brooches (Ashmolean Museum). One final brooch which should be noted, though not a true model of any kind, is the solid round brooch from Carnuntum (A98) which is decorated with an enamelled swastika-symbol.

d) *Swastika-Brooches*

A6 ; A7 ; A14 ; A17 ; A24 ; A25 ; A27 ; A29 ; A49 ; A61 ; A90 ; A91 ; A92 ; A94 ; A100 ; A116 ; A120 ; A121 ; A124 ; A129 ; A133 ; A150 ; A151 ; A159 ; A181.

Swastika-brooches do not, of course, represent true models. Nevertheless, it is apparent that wheels and swastikas probably form part of a common Romano-Celtic (and later prehistoric) solar symbolism. The connection between the two motifs may be borne out by the occurrence of swastika-in-circle brooches at, for example, Augst (A150) and Slavonin (A159), which appear to combine elements of both symbols ; and by the existence of small Pyrenean stone altars bearing wheels and swastikas (see Chapters IV, VI). As far as I am aware there are no small metal swastika-shaped objects apart from brooches in the Roman period. Plain swastika-brooches are recorded, for instance, from Bonn (A4, A17) ; Saalburg (A24) ; Zugmantel (A25) ; Mainz (A27) ; Stockstadt (A90) ; Miltenberg (A91) (unusual in that it is made of tin rather than bronze) ; Rückingen (A92) ; between Gunzenhausen and Kipfenberg (A94) ; Wetteraulinie (A95) ; Pfünz (A110), from the *uicus* rather than the fort itself ; Feldberg (A121) and Namur (A124).

The decoration on some swastika-brooches is of interest. A Cologne example (A7) has arms terminating in horse-heads. We shall see (below) that the horse appears to have a connection with solar symbolism. Other ornament, which may be of interpretative significance, may be divided into two types (i) ring-and-dot and (ii) St. Andrew's Cross. From my select index of continental data I have noted ring-and-dot motifs on the swastika-brooches from Tongeren in Belgium where, on two brooches, the symbol occurs at the arm-angles and at the central junction of all four arms (A61). The same motif occurs on the brooch from Baden-Württemburg (A116), and that from Buch (A120). Ring-and-dot ornamentation may or may not mean anything in ritual terms. It appears frequently on bracelets in late Roman contexts, for example at the Lydney Park temple-site in Gloucestershire in Britain (Wheeler, 1932, 82, fig. 17E) and at the late Roman cemeteries in southern Germany (Keller, 1971) and is not in these circumstances considered to bear any religious symbolism. However, the sign itself may possess intrinsic associations with sun-symbolism. It appears on the 'stèles-maisons' from the Vosges region, together with crescents, star-signs and wheel-symbols (Linckenheld, 1927). More significantly, it occurs on some model axes, for example on a pin from Richborough (Green, 1978, 70); Straubing (Walke, 1965, Pl. 98, 27); and Pfünz (*O.R.L.*, 1901, Taf. 12, no. 15). It is just possible that the Nassington wheel-brooch (Ashmolean Museum) also bearing this motif (around the rim) may be Roman, although Nassington is well-known as an early Saxon site. Certainly the motif occurs on both wheel-models and axes during the later Bronze Age and Iron Age in Central Europe.

The St. Andrew's Cross or diagonal cross-motif occurs, for example on the swastika-brooches from Cologne (A6 ; Pl. LX, Fig. 20), and Straubing (A29) – a silver-washed bronze *fibula*. It is difficult to decide what this cross represents. In both cases it appears at the junction of the four arms. In my opinion there are two possibilities as to its purpose (if such exists). The first is that it represents cord-binding marks, found, for example, on miniature axes from, for example, Hockwold in Norfolk (Green, 1975c, no. 17, fig. 2), and Woodeaton (*ibid.*, no. 30c, fig. 3). The other is that it was some kind of ritual sign, perhaps a stylized rimless wheel (see Chapter VI).

Only one contextual feature should be noted with regard to swastika-brooches ; that is the occurrence of both wheel and swastika brooches in the vicinity of the Lardiers shrine (A181).

e) *Pendants*

A28 ; A30 ; A31 ; A74 ; A75 ; A102 ; A103 ; A113 ; A115 ; A122 ; A131 ; A135 ; A149 ; A172 ; A177 ; A198 ; A201 ; A202 ; A203.

Whilst it is arguable that model wheels were probably frequently used as pendants, there is some specific evidence for such usage, on particular specimens. The Mainz item (A28) has a silver pin ornamented with a coiled cone-shaped terminal from which hang three wires with a pendant attached to each. Two of these pendants are mere knobs but the middle one is in the form of a wheel-model. This immediately recalls La Tène *fibulae* (see Chapter I) with wheel-pendants attached by wire or chain (like that from Stradonitz cited above). It also gives credence to the notion that pins themselves may carry a ritual as well as a purely functional significance. Even if one disregards the very early pre-Roman wheel-headed pins of the Central European Middle Bronze Age, and the Yugoslav Iron Age, there is evidence in the Roman period of model items in the form of pins (Green, 1975c).

A wheel-shaped amulet which is apparently of early Roman date comes from Dieburg in Hessen (A31) ; it is composed of a bronze wheel with ordinary spokes alternating with foliate lobes. The Rheingönheim (A113) pendant, is of filigree-work, but is complex in comprising a double-conoid wheel-shape. It comes from a Roman fort and is early in date (Ulbert, 1969, pl. 40, no. 5, 49 & pl. 55, nos. 20-21). The ornament has parallels with a pendant from the Celto-Roman cemetery at Belginum near Trier. Also early Roman, or even perhaps late pre-Roman, is the bronze wheel-shaped pendant, decorated with red enamel, from Vaison in southern Gaul (A115) from which, interestingly enough, there is a great deal of lithic material relating to wheel-symbolism (see Chapter IV). One other bronze item to be looked at is in fact not a pendant in itself. The object comes from Kapersburg (A122) and comprises an openwork three-spoked wheel with a pendant attached to its circumference. A final bronze pendant is that from Saalburg (A131), a twelve-spoked filigree example.

A distinctive group of wheel-pendants occurring both in continental and British contexts is that consisting of small gold wheels, sometimes associated with chains or bead-bracelets. Some of these take the form of true wheels, either with six or eight spokes, as at Lyon (A198). Others are extremely stylized, with voluted spoke-decoration, as at Obfelden (A135). Gold jewellery such as this is a phenomenon distinct from that of bronze wheel-brooches which are endemic to the Celtic world. It cannot be taken *ipso facto* as necessarily having any cult-purpose at all in terms of Romano-Celtic religion. According to Higgins (1961, 186) a popular type of Roman necklace incorporated a wheel either as pendant or finial. It occurs, for example at Pompeii and Boscoreale in Campania in the 1st Century A.D. and at Eleutheropolis (Palestine) in the 2nd Century (de Ridder, 1924). At Olbia on the Black Sea a gold four-spoked (?) pendant comes from a tomb (Marshall, 1911, no. 2976, 354). Galliou (1974) divides gold wheel-pendants into a series of types, both stylistic and functional. He also cites Boscoreale (Pfeiler, 1970, 13-14, pl. 19 ; de Villefosse, 1899, 270) and Pompeii (Siviero, 1954, no. 168, pl. 139). Galliou's Type I is almost entirely confined to Italy ; Type III to the North-West Empire, Gaul and Britain ; Type II is widely distributed from Palestine to Britain (Backworth [see below]).

My own opinion regarding whether this group should be included as examples of Romano-Celtic wheel-symbolism is that whilst in origin this reasonably homogeneous group of jewellery is simply decorative, in Romano-Celtic lands wheel-pendants may possibly have a secondary cult-purpose. It is difficult to believe that their presence in the unequivocally cult-hoard at Backworth (see below) is secular. Other, Gaulish, occurrences reinforce a ritual view. The Thérouanne example is of particular interest in that associated with this wheel is a model club-pendant. The gold wheel from Langres (A80) may well be part of another such pendant. The Balèsmes model wheel (A102) has a suspension-ring ; it has eight filigree spokes and is extremely close in style both to the Backworth and Dolaucothi examples (see below). Associated with the wheel-symbol from Balèsmes are the motifs of double-axe and crescent, which are soldered or welded onto the two central spokes making up the horizontal diameter of the wheel (Déchelette, 1913b, 260ff.).

f) *Miscellaneous*

A10 ; A11 ; A13 ; A15 ; A73 ; A126 (pl. 22a) ; A153 ; A204.

The following small group comprises anomalous data which are possibly of relevance to the present study, but which do not fall into any of the definite categories outlined above.

In Cologne Museum, and from sites in or near to the Roman city, are a number of white pipe-clay model wheels, each with eight or nine spokes (A10). Taken as isolated items, their interpretation as true clay wheel-models seems a natural one (clay miniatures representing wheels are recorded in prehistoric contexts ; see Chapter I). However, also from

Cologne (A11) are three pipe-clay four-wheeled carts, each drawn by a pony with a human rider. It is more than likely that the models mentioned come from other such vehicles. The carts themselves may be best interpreted as toys from the graves of children (pipe-clay figures including what must be playthings are recorded from a child's grave in Colchester [Toynbee, 1962, Cat. no. 143]). Nevertheless it could be argued that the survival intact of so many wheels without their carts may be significant, and that these models possessed a secondary, talismanic, property. Pipe-clay was a natural medium in Cologne since this city was one of two centres for the manufacture of Romano-Celtic clay figurines (the other being the Allier district of Central Gaul [Jenkins, 1957b ; 1958]). It should also be remembered that central Gaulish figurines of the Celtic Jupiter are frequently associated with pipe-clay wheels, some of which occur as isolated models, with merely a hand attached.

Another clay object which may or may not be ritually significant is a spindle-whorl in the form of a spoked wheel from the Bonn area (A15). This is very reminiscent of Iron Age stone whorls with radiate lines (Savory, 1976, 64-65, fig. 34A). Whilst Childe (1951), 177-195) would deny any wheel-symbolism, secular or otherwise, for such spindle-whorls, it is worthwhile keeping an open mind. On the one hand a small circular object may only have a limited range of decorative possibilities ; radiating lines are not necessarily the result of profound thought. On the other hand it could be argued that the act of scoring such lines on a purely utilitarian object, where the ornamentation could not even be seen when in use, means that a talismanic property may have been introduced.

Five final items remain to be examined. The first is the bronze star-shaped item from a Cologne multi-model grave-group (A13). One might interpret this as a wheel-symbol-derivative, in the same light as the swastika-sign, or one might assume that the item does in fact represent a star, in which case an image of the heavens by night instead of by day is presumably being portrayed. The second item comprises a curious lead ornament from Plessis-Barbuise (A73). It consists of a lead wheel-shape inside which is the figure of a standing divinity bearing a sceptre or lance in his right hand and a thunderbolt in his left. The presence of the latter makes it particularly likely that the deity represented is Jupiter. It is worth commenting upon the use of lead here. If a sky-god is portrayed, lead seems a curious choice; However, we have evidence of other lead model wheels (see above) and several models of other types, for example at Chester (Green, 1978, 54).

Two bronze bracelets may next be considered. They come from Augst (A155) and Starigrad (A204) respectively. Each bears a six or eight-spoked silver wheel set into the bezel. At Starigrad the outer rim is knobbed at each spoke-terminal. This site is of even greater interest since a Roman cemetery produced a similar bracelet but decorated with a crescent or *lunula* in place of the wheel (Abramic & Colnago, 1909, 103-104, fig. 73).

The final item in this heterogeneous category is the mould from Augst (A126 ; Pl. LVII, Fig. 14). The casting-shape is for a simple four-spoked wheel, without a suspension-ring or other details. Close comparison between this mould and the wheel-models from Belginum has already been noted above. Moulds such as the Augst example must have been common and it is interesting that few of Roman date appear to survive. Other wheel-model moulds do occur but usually in Iron Age contexts, as at Bibracte.

Distribution of Romano-Celtic Wheel-Models [2]

Wheel-models and brooches occur all over Gaul, West Germany and Switzerland, but there is a concentration of wheel and swastika-brooches on the German-Raetian frontier. Some areas of Gaul appear to have great gaps, but this may be due to lack of publication rather than reality. The different physical types are scattered, but it is possible that distinctive examples like those from Dinant (A156), Mainz (A158) and others with thick felloes and convex spokes, may come from the Namur workshops. The Augst wheel-brooches are all of a very similar type one to the other but this type also occurs far away from Switzerland, at Icklingham, Suffolk (see below). In very general terms wheel-models show a north-easterly Gaulish and German slant. Swastika-in-circle brooches tend to occur on Pannonian sites ; swastika-brooches occur very rarely in civilian Gaulish contexts. Finally we know of seven swastika-brooches at Dura Europos on the Euphrates. There is evidence here for imports of metalwork primarily from Gaul and the German *limes* (Frisch & Toll, 1949, 62). Of the swastika-brooches from here (*ibid.*, nos. 137-143, pl. 16, 64) one (no. 137) possesses 'binding-marks', both diagonal and vertical, at the arm-joints and terminals. It has already been noted that the gold wheel-pendants occur all over the Roman world, from North Britain to Palestine (Galliou, 1974).

[2] See Pls. XIX-XXII.

British Wheel-Models [3]

    a) True Models
    b) Brooches
    c) Pendants
    d) Mould
    e) Swastikas

a) *True Wheel-Models*

AB5 ; AB6 ; AB8 ; AB9 ; AB10 ; AB15 ; AB17 ; AB23.

All true wheel-models occurring in Britain are bronze, except for the Colchester wheel which is made from brass. By the Roman period zinc was being deliberately added to copper alloys to make brass (Tylecote, 1962, 53), the metal being manufactured by mixing the zinc-ore Calamine ($ZnCo_3$) with copper under reducing (non-oxidizing) conditions, using charcoal for the smelting process. The technological procedure involved was not easy (since zinc has a very low melting and boiling point) and it may be that brass was employed to make this particular Colchester wheel-model for a specific reason, either to make it more durable or to produce a brighter and more heliolatric effect. One thing which seems clear, and we also obtain this picture from continental data, is that the number of spokes on wheel-models would appear to be entirely at random, normally varying in Gaul from four to ten (Toutain, 1920, 192ff.) ; in Britain, where the evidence survives, wheel-models may have four spokes (AB6), six (AB8 ; AB10), eight (AB15) or even as many as twelve (AB5).

A few other features of British wheel-models may be noted. The Hounslow miniature has a particularly thick rim, a solid cylindrical nave and four extremely thin spokes (AB6 ; Pl. LXIII, Fig. 25). It has a close parallel in the silvered bronze wheel-brooch from Andernach (A86). The Icklingham wheel (AB8 ; Pl. LXI, Fig. 22) is fragmentary and in two parts ; four spokes survive but there were probably originally six ; the model has a protruding, naturalistic nave. The Verulamium model (AB15) is complete but is coarsely-cast compared with the delicacy of the Hounslow wheel, or that from London (AB10). The Verulamium wheel has a thick felloe and a hollow centre. The twelve-spoked Felmingham wheel (AB5 ; Pl. LXII, Fig. 24) is the most striking model ; it is large, with a dished nave, fine rim and narrow spokes. The Chester fragment (AB23)

(3) See Catalogue AB.

was probably once a true model rather than a brooch ; it is noteworthy in being extremely thin, only 1 mm thick. It probably had at least eight spokes.

b) *Wheel-Brooches*

AB3 ; AB7 ; AB11 ; AB13 ; AB14 ; AB16 ; AB18 ; AB19 ; AB21 ; AB24 ; AB25 ; AB27 ; AB28-30.

Once again there is variation in the number of spokes. Margam (AB11) and Icklingham (AB27 ; Pl. LX, Fig. 21) and Nor'nour (AB19) each possess four ; the brooches from Sewingshields (AB13), Hadrian's Wall Turret 18B (AB14) have six ; those from Corbridge (AB3 ; Pl. LXIII, Fig. 26) and Housesteads (AB7 ; Pl. LXI, Fig. 23) had eight. Like the many brooches from northern Gaul and the Rhineland, the Corbridge and Nor'nour examples have lugs or knobs round the exterior circumference ; in the former case (AB3 ; Pl. LXIII, Fig. 26) the lugs correspond with the outer terminals of the eight spokes. Several of the British and continental wheel-brooches are enamelled (unlike true wheel-models) and British examples fall into the same type-series as those of Romano-Celtic Europe, namely Feugère's Type 40 (Feugère, 1978). Particularly well-preserved is the enamelled decoration on the Corbridge brooch (Pl. LXIII, Fig. 26) and that from Hadrian's Wall (AB14) ; in both instances the enamelling is in the form of small rectangular panels set into the rim. The Corbridge brooch is an especially magnificent item ; more than 5 cm diameter, it has a large, solid, flat nave with eight small depressions corresponding to the inner ends of each spoke. The Housesteads fragment (AB7 ; Pl. LXI, Fig. 23) is also from a large brooch but it is of thin, flat-sectioned and undecorated bronze, with the feature, unique in Britain, apart from the new Lakenheath example (AB28) of extremely convex edged spokes, paralleled by some European examples already discussed. The Lakenheath brooch (AB28) is of interest since its elaborate enamelling, large size and convex spokes show marked similarities with continental examples, for instance those from Mainz (A158) and Viet, Dinant (A156). It may even have been manufactured in the Namur workshops. The site itself may have been a sanctuary. The Icklingham brooch (AB27 ; Pl. LX, Fig. 21) may have significance in that it is tinned or silvered. A particularly ornate brooch comes from Silchester (AB30). It is knobbed, and has six angled but convex spokes, and raised concentric circles around the felloe. The Icklingham brooch (AB27) and the Verulamium model (AB15) have in common the perforation of the central nave, almost as if a chariot or cart-wheel, linked to its fellow by an axle-bar, was being depicted. The Kettering brooch (AB18) is peculiar in Britain in that the spokes are ornamented with horizontal ribs, like brooches from continental sites such as Cologne (A1).

c) *Wheel-Pendants*

AB1 ; AB4 ; AB12.

This group of pendants in wheel-form is small in number but of extreme interest. They fall into the same category of Roman jewellery as the continental gold wheel-pendants looked at above. Five are of gold, one is silver, and all have been discovered in association with gold or silver chain-necklaces or bracelets. In addition the wheels themselves bear a remarkable similarity to each other as well as to continental examples. The Backworth gold wheel-models (AB1) (Marshall, 1911, nos. 2738 ; 2740) are made in filigree-work and one of the chains has a crescent attached, like those from Dolaucothi (AB4) and the silver example from Newstead (AB12) (Hawkins, 1851, 35-44). It has been suggested (Mann, 1975, 39) that the bracelet or necklet, which includes fifteen hollow gold beads, probably dates to the 1st Century A.D. Nevertheless, something as valuable as this may well have been guarded as a precious possession for a very long time. Mann (*ibid.*) states that it was definitely imported, probably from Italy. This may be so, and Galliou's study (1974) certainly seems to imply such an event. But if the find is an import then it could have equally well come from North-West Gaul (we have a substantial amount of evidence for gold wheel-pendants from this area). However, the Dolaucothi, Dyfed, wheels (AB4) (Marshall, 1911, nos. 2741, 2742) were found in a goldwork hoard in the vicinity of Roman goldmines, so they surely could have been made on site − in which case all the gold wheels from Britain could have been made locally. All the British pendants are fitted with eye-loop fastenings for attachment to their associated chains. On the surviving Dyfed wheel (AB4) the remains of a rod with looped ends soldered behind the wheel may be seen, probably the original attachment for the chain. The Newstead (AB12) item is different from the Backworth/Dolaucothi group in being made from silver rather than gold. It too is fitted with a solid bar across the back, ending on either side with a suspension loop. As in the Durham and Dyfed finds a small crescent-pendant is associated. It is of interest that the Newstead wheel is repeatedly published as having nine spokes (e.g. Clarke *et all.*, 1980, 40, no. 30) but in fact has eight.

d) *The Mould*

The Gateshead stone mould (AB22) is of interest principally because it is unique in a British context. It comprises a small oblong slab of stone, with the matrix of a wheel or wheel-shaped brooch, and next to it the trace of another wheel-rim (Green, 1978, pl. 49). Wheel-moulds are recorded in pre-Roman Gaulish contexts, such as Nasium, Bibracte and Alesia (see Chapter I), and in a Roman context at Augst (A126). So far, this is the only British example which has come to my notice, although one might have expected such a find, for instance, from the bronzesmithing establishment at Nor'nour. The rarity of British moulds could imply import of most of our wheel-models, but their scarcity also in Europe argues against such an assumption.

e) *Swastika-Brooches*

AB2 ; AB26.

The only two swastika-brooches at present recorded from Britain come from Benwell, a fort near the eastern end of Hadrian's Wall and from Denholme Hill Farm in southern Scotland. Bearing in mind the concentration of swastika-brooches at some Rhineland forts, it is abundantly clear that this form is essentially an east Gaulish and Rhine frontier type, certainly not made in Britain. Both brooches are of plain, undecorated form, and bear close resemblance, both in size (around 3 cm 'diameter') and style to those from, for instance, Saalburg and Zugmantel. It is worth noting that at least one inscription from Benwell (*R.I.B.* 1328) attests a Rhineland cohort at Benwell, the First Cohort of Vangiones.

Distribution of British Wheel-Models [4]

Wheel-models of all kinds are scattered sparsely all over the province. If one may speak of concentrations with such very small numbers wheel-models are most common in the east of the country and on the Northern British frontier. This (see below) reflects the distribution of British models of all kinds. The wheels are reasonably evenly distributed between north and south Britain, there being seventeen from civilian and twelve from military or northern contexts. The two swastikas are from the North. What is of interest is that almost all of the true (non-jewellery) models are from southern areas. The true model wheels from the south are

[4] See Pl. XXIII.

concentrated in the extreme east and south of the country ; East Anglia, Hertfordshire, Surrey and the London area. Brooches are wider spread, occurring in Northamptonshire, Wiltshire and even the extreme south-west. In the western frontier regions only Margam Beach (AB11), Wroxeter (AB16) and Chester (AB23) have produced wheel-symbols. Otherwise the motifs are spread out along the eastern part of Hadrian's Wall. The most northerly outliers are Newstead (AB12) and Denholme Hill Farm (AB26).

Context

No wheel-symbol from Britain definitely comes from a temple site. This may be entirely due to chance, but it could suggest their function as talismans or amulets rather than votive offerings as such. However, wheel-models occur in other contexts which imply some kind of ritual connection. In the first place they appear as grave-finds at Leatherhead (AB9) and probably at Colchester (AB17), the latter being found in an urn together with beads and a shale armlet. Second, there are a number of wheel-models in what one may term ritual deposits or hoards, i.e. found in association with other material of a votive nature. This is the case certainly at Backworth (AB1) and at Felmingham Hall (AB5 ; Pl. LXII, Fig. 24). Other possible ritual depositions occur at Dolaucothi (AB4) ; Hounslow (AB6 ; Pl. LXIII, Fig. 25) ; Icklingham (AB8, 27 ; Pl. LXI, Fig. 22, LX, Fig. 21) and Nor'nour (AB19).

Undoubtedly, as far as context is concerned, it is the Backworth and Felmingham Hall hoards which are of the greatest interest. The latter deposit comprises a group of about twenty-three items found in a pot (Gilbert, 1978). The most important votive objects consist of a bronze wheel-model ; a bronze male bearded head (with lentoid eyes) – probably representing Jupiter ; two bronze figurines of ravens ; a mask of a radiate god (perhaps Jupiter Helioserapis) ; a pole-tip or terminal of a ceremonial stave ; a bronze statuette of a dancing *Lar* and a coin of A.D. 260 – providing a *terminus postquem* for the deposition of the hoard. The most likely suggestion for the circumstances of deposition is that it was buried for safety by temple-priests or by temple-looters, neither of whom survived or were able to return to collect their treasure. It would be indulging in the wildest speculation to infer that the deposition of the hoard was the result of Christian persecution in the 4th Century, but if priests or devotees felt it necessary to hide valuable shrine-furniture, then there must have been a fairly pressing need. One interesting point about this hoard is the cosmopolitan nature of the inclusions. The radiate mask would appear to depict an oriental sun or sky-divinity ; classicism is represented by the presence of the *Lar* ; the model wheel would appear to be a Romano-Celtic sky-motif or symbol, and elements of the hollow 'Jupiter'-mask betray celticism in, for instance, the shape of the eyes. The 'pole-tip', a triangular spear-shaped item, has holes for the suspension of pendants, perhaps bells ; the object may have been the terminal for a wooden stave or sceptre, carried in processions and maybe shaken so that the hanging bells or metal strips would make a jangling sound (Green, 1975a ; Leuzinger, 1960, 25). These rattles or *sistra* are known in Romano-Celtic contexts in Britain, for example at Brigstock in Northamptonshire (Greenfield, 1963, 228ff. ; Green, 1976, pl. XXVa, b). In London, however, *sistra* may have been employed in oriental cult-practices (London Museum, 1930, 108, pl. 48). A final feature which should be alluded to briefly here (and will be discussed in more detail below) is the association between the wheel-symbol and the mask which may portray Jupiter in either Roman or Celtic guise (see Chapter VII).

The Backworth hoard (AB1) is similar to the Norfolk group in some respects, in that the ritual material was deposited in a vessel. In a saucepan-shaped *patera*, or sacrificial container, had been placed three gold chains with eight-spoked wheel-pendants, five gold finger-rings and a number of coins. The *patera*-handle and one of the rings bear dedications to the *Deae Matres*, the finger-ring having the added epithet *Coccae* (which may perhaps mean 'red' [Ross, 1967, 169]). Two of the coins are dated to the reign of Antoninus Pius, thus providing a *terminus postquem* for the hoard-deposition. The positive association here between Mother-Goddesses and the Wheel-God will be commented upon below.

Of the other possible ritual depositions alluded to the only one which, in itself, has no religious association is that from Dolaucothi (AB4). The gold chain necklace and two wheel-pendants come from a hoard of goldwork probably made at the mining-site, but nothing else in the group suggests a cult-purpose. However, the one filigree wheel which survives (the other being lost) and its chain are so similar to the Backworth items that it would seem folly to dissociate them in terms of ritual. The finds from Hounslow (AB6) ; Icklingham (AB8) ; Nor'nour (AB19) and Lakenheath (AB28) were discovered in close proximity to other cult-objects ; whilst in none of these cases is there a definite, sealed or archaeological association, it is possible to speculate the one-time existence of some kind of shrine (domestic or public), ritual hoard, or at least a *'locus consecratus'*.

The model wheel from Hounslow (AB6 ; Pl. LXIII, Fig. 25) is generally considered to belong to the late Iron Age, although there is no specific evidence to support this. The suggestion is based on the presence in the same field, of a number of bronze animal-figurines, including three bronze boars. The other beasts are indeterminate and fragmentary but the boars are of a distinctively Celtic and pre-Roman style. We have to be careful in assigning an Iron Age context to the bronze wheel-model since there may well have been a shrine here spanning a period both pre-Roman and Roman in date. Examples of these occur, for instance at Frilford, Oxon (Bradford & Goodchild, 1939, 1ff.) and Worth, Kent (Klein, 1928, 76ff.). If this is the case then the Hounslow finds may have been deposited over a hundred years or more. The Nor'nour wheel-shaped brooch (AB19) was discovered on a remote site, on a small island in the Scillies, occupied in the Bronze and Iron Ages and in the Roman period. There is evidence of bronze-workers and enamellers' workshops on the site, which probably produced the wheel-brooch and also a number of other *fibula*-types. What is of interest, however, is the presence of several fragments of pipe-clay 'Venus'-figurines and 'Deae Nutrices'. As in the case of the Backworth association, we have a possible connection on one and the same site between wheel-symbolism and Romano-Celtic Mother-Goddess representations.

The two final 'associations' to be examined are those from Icklingham (Suffolk) (AB8, 27) and Lakenheath (AB28). There may well have been a sanctuary at the latter site or its vicinity, evidenced by finds of face-urns and a bronze *Lar* with double *cornucopiae* in the area (Green, 1976, 213). At Icklingham, which produced a wheel-model, wheel-brooch and eagle's wing all in bronze, there is a probable villa and/or temple-site (carding-combs from the site attest an agricultural function [Liversidge, 1968, 167]). The site or its vicinity has produced a number of votive items including bronze snakes, phallic amulets, figurines of Mercury and Hercules (Heichelheim, 1935-1937, 52-68) and three items which may be connected with the Celtic and classical Sky-God respectively (Green, 1975b, 55-70).

Continental Axe-Models

1) *Axe-Models with Possible Intrinsic Solar or Sky-Symbolism*

It is important to recognize that wheel-models are only one specific group within a large class of miniature implements occurring in the

Romano-Celtic world and in prehistory (see Chapter I). Of these the large group of axe-models has a definite connection with wheel and solar symbolism (see Chapter III). Only those axes which appear to bear unequivocal and intrinsic sky-symbolism are catalogued (AX), but it should be borne in mind that all miniature axes may well have close ritual associations with celestial cults.

The Catalogue (AX) includes those axes bearing either diagonal crosses or ring-and-dot motifs, both of which, in the present connection, may have relevance (cf. marks on swastika-brooches). These models are AX2 ; AX3 ; AX4 ; AX5 ; AX6 ; AX12 ; AX22. It also includes models combining axe and double-axe motifs (AX7 ; AX10 ; AX9 ; AX13). The double-axe (see Chapters I, III) has a long association with sky-symbolism, and the association of axe and double-axe may well be important. One should remember the Balèsmes gold wheel-pendant found in association with a double-axe-model (A102) A clay double-axe from Trier is also included here (AX11), as are two axes from Switzerland dedicated to Jupiter (AX1 ; AX8), which indicate unequivocal associations between a Sky-God and axe-models.

The context and associations of these particular axe-models may be significant. The Engehalbinsel-Bern site (AX3) has produced a number of miniature axes with St. Andrew's Cross (AX2), and ring-and-dot decoration ; the Tiefenau sector has also produced a wheel-model (A136). The multi-model Cologne grave-groups have produced axes including one (AX5a) with an 'X' mark, and wheel-symbols (A12, A12a). Winterthur-Lindberg (AX12) has produced an axe-model with ring-and-dot decoration, associated with a statuette of Mercury, a dog and a horse. The aquatic deposits from Solothurn (AX8) and (?) and Allmendingen (AX1) may also be significant with regard to a water-association for wheel-motifs (see above and Chapter VI). The terra-cotta double-axe from Trier (AX11) comes from a temple-site ; it is crudely-fashioned, with a short, thick shaft and surmounted by a double-triangular blade.

Finally it should be noted that the ring-and-dot motif on axe-models has an Iron Age parallel at the Dürnnberg, Hallein in Austria (Keltenmuseum, Hallein), and a Hallstatt one from Hallstatt itself.

2) Other Continental Axe-Models

The context-association or intrinsic symbolism on other axes are noteworthy in establishing their essentially ritual nature. Five axe-models from Allmendingen, near Bern, bear inscriptions to Minerva, the Deae

Matres, the Matronae, Mercury and Neptune (Staehelin, 1931, 486, Abb. 131 ; Degen, 1966-1976, 123ff., Abb. 15, 132 ; Forrer, 1948). The Cologne and Bonn region grave-groups (Rottländer, 1973-1974, 143-152) contain axe-models and other predominantly agricultural models, believed to be cult-objects associated with the worship of Sabazius (who did have a connection with Jupiter [see Chapter III]) (Manning, 1966, 50-59).

As with wheels continental axe-models may occur as brooches, as at Straubing (Walke, 1965, pl. 95, 34) ; Jagsthausen (*O.R.L.*, 1909, 39, no. 12, Taf. III, fig. 8) ; as pins, as at Junkerath (Trier Museum, Acc. no. 12168) ; Cologne (Cologne Museum) ; Jagsthausen (*O.R.L.*, 1909, 39, n. 13, Taf. III, fig. 7) ; Pfünz (*O.R.L.*, 1901, Taf. XII, 14 & 15) ; or as true models, for example at Cannstatt (*O.R.L.*, 1907, Taf. VIII, no. 50) ; Cologne (Cologne Museum) and Trier (Trier Museum).

Regarding the question as to whether jewellery in the form of models has the same ritual function as true models it is of interest that at, for example, Straubing, a true axe-model and an axe-brooch were found together.

Other models with a possible connection with a Jupiter-cult include miniature thunderbolts found near a spring at St. Tau, Gissey-sur-Ouche (Drioux, 1934, 40). If these were dedicated to Jupiter then the aquatic association is of interest. A bronze model altar 4.3 cm. high from a French site (Babelon & Blanchet, 1895, no. 31, 14) is dedicated to Jupiter and is decorated with representations of thunderbolts between two snake-limbed creatures. Of particular interest with regard to Celtic sky-symbolism is a find from Isômes (Haute-Marne) composed of a small bronze ring from which hang nine miniature items including something published as a 'sun-symbol', a crescent and a votive hand (Drioux, 1943-1944, 289-290).

Other Continental Models

The occurrence of models in the continental archaeological record; apart from wheels and axes, should be noted in brief. We have mentioned already the predominance of agricultural models in the Rhineland grave-groups (Rottländer, 1973-1974, Abb. 2). The uniqueness of these particular deposits lies in the frequent presence of specific beasts – reptiles and batrachians. Chronological evidence from coins associated with these groups – coins minted in the reigns of Severus Alexander, Elagabalus,

Probus, Maximinus Thrax and Gallienus attest to the *floruit* of the cult in the mid 3rd Century A.D.

Bells are common model items, perhaps for attachment to ceremonial staves, as at London (London Museum, 1930, pl. 48). The Pfünz bell, however, is on a chain, presumably to be worn (*O.R.L.*, 1901, Taf. XIII, no. 8). Bronze and iron bell-models together with an iron knife-model come from a sanctuary associated with Augustan coinage at Pupillon (Lerat, 1970, 345-365). A bronze 'charm' bracelet from Daubeuf-la-Champagne (Eure) supports a ring, two discs and a bell-model (de Boüard, 1968, 347-372).

Miniature pots are reasonably well-represented. One may cite, for instance the clay amphora, 1.5 cm high found at Nantes (Parenteau, 1869, 82, no. 170).

British Axe-Models with Possible Intrinsic Sky-Symbolism

As with continental examples I will first consider axe-models with positive implications for sky-symbolism. The reasons for looking briefly at models other than wheels, already mentioned, include the light that other miniatures, especially axes, may shed on the role of wheel-models (it should always be recalled that wheels form part of a much larger group of miscellaneous model items) and the possibly close interpretative affinities between wheels and other models.

A number of British axe-models with overt sky-symbolism bear 'X's (AX14 ; AX15 ; AX16 ; AX17 ; AX20 ; AX21). If one is arguing the possible interpretation of the X-motif as a rimless wheel (see above and Chapter VI) then one Woodeaton example is of particular interest (AX20 ; Pl. LXIV, Fig. 27). This has an 'X' symbol but with horizontal ligatures above and beneath the mark, thus forming a link between the 'X' and a true four-spoked wheel-sign. Other Woodeaton axes are of note, in that one bears a swastika-sign (AX20) and another a ring-and-dot motif. The argument for 'X' marks on axes being skeuomorphic binding-marks cannot always be maintained. At Kirmington (AX15) the blade itself bears the mark, not the junction of blade and haft. At Richborough (AX16) one axe-model bears the 'X' at the haft and blade-junctions as if imitating binding, but another such mark appears on the blade. Binding-marks sometimes are definitely represented on other British axes, as at Corbridge (Forster & Knowles, 1901, fig. 33) and Hockwold Green, 1975c, no. 17).

At Woodeaton (Green, 1975c, fig. 3, no. 30c) one axe-model has definite 'X' marks as binding lines.

Apart from 'X' markings some British axes bear ring-and-dot motifs (AX18 ; AX20). A double-axe-model from Richborough (AX18) bears such a symbol. A brooch combining axe and double-axe motifs occurs at South Shields (AX19), almost certainly an import from the Rhineland (cf. AX7, AX9).

British Axe-Models : some General Observations

British axe-models have much more contextual evidence for a ritual function of some kind than either continental axes or British wheel-models. Those from Brigstock (Greenfield, 1963, 228ff.), Caistor (Norwich Castle Museum), Cold Kitchen (Devizes Museum), Harlow Wilson *et al.*, 1971, 273), Hockwold (Green, 1975c, no. 17), Nettleton (Bristol City Museum), Springhead (Penn, 1964, 172ff.), Woodeaton (Kirk, 1949, 32ff.) and Wycomb (Lewis, 1966, 47) come from in or the vicinity of shrines. Those from Howletts (Dewey, 1924, 276-277) and Poundbury (Farrar, 1952, 98ff.), Sussex (Manning, 1966, 50-59) and Winchester, Lankhills (information Ashmolean Museum) come from graves. They do occur also in secular contexts, as at the villa-sites of Bradwell, Bucks (Bradwell Abbey Field Centre), Hambledon (Cock, 1921, 141-198) and Rockbourne (Morley Hewitt, 1969, pl. XVa). Stray finds include London (London Museum, 1930, 112) and Kenchester (Green, 1975c, no. 19). The Silchester axes (*ibid.*) may or may not be from urban shrines.

There is certain evidence for pre-Roman antecedents for British axe-models, as at Arras, from a La Tène cemetery (Stead, 1965, 82 ; Manning & Saunders, 1972, 281), and at Meare (Bulleid & Grey, 1953, pl. XLIX, G74 ; Manning and Saunders, 1972, 282). An interesting and unpublished group of Wiltshire finds (information Devizes Museum) may be Roman or Iron Age, but are perfect miniature replicas of Bronze Age socketed axes.

The distribution of axes (and indeed other models) shows general similarities with that of wheel-models – the south-east of Britain and a few in the region of Hadrian's Wall.

It may not be of significance but there are a number of sites where both wheel-models and axes occur. Corbridge has produced both an axe-headed pin and a wheel-brooch ; Kettering has similar evidence (Westfield

Museum); London has both types of model, as has Silchester (Reading Museum) and Wroxeter (Shrewsbury Museum). This may well have no significance in terms of archaeological association but it is perhaps worth noting, if one remembers the Iron Age Dürnnberg grave which produced both model-types.

Miscellaneous British Models

Other models apart from axes are reasonably frequent British occurrences. Weapons include lead spears at Chester (Hartley & Kaine, 1954, 35-36, fig. 12, nos. 2-5), bronze spears at, for example, a Welwyn Roman cemetery (Westall, 1930, 37ff.) and several such, some bent double, at Woodeaton (Kirk, 1949, 32ff.). Iron Age shields occur at Worth (Klein, 1928, 76ff.) and shields and a sword at the pre-Roman shrine at Frilford (Bradford & Goodchild, 1939, 1ff.). The three latter sites are sanctuaries. Miscellaneous tools occur, for example, a sickle at Aylesbury (Green, 1979c); an anvil at Brough-on-Humber (Green, 1978, pl. 122, left) and one of lead at Chester (Newstead, 1928, 22, pl. XI; Green, 1978, 54, nos. 1, 2); a knife at Chester (Petch, 1975, 35, fig. 8, no. 2); a shovel at Cirencester (British Museum, 1951, 72) and one from Oxfordshire (Green, 1977a). Several different models come from a shrine at Lamyatt Beacon (Leach, 1980, 332). A cauldron model comes from a possible temple-site at Ancaster (Anon, 1957-1958, 99-101); anchor-models from Woodeaton and Barton Court Farm, Oxon (Green, 1979b); a bale-of-goods, in clay, comes from Skye (Robertson, 1970, 198ff.; Curle, 1931-1932, 277ff.; Mann, 1975, 31); a galley-prow from London (British Museum, 1922, 90); bells, for example from Langton, East Yorkshire (Corder & Kirk, 1952, 70, fig. 18), and Mildenhall, Wiltshire (Green, 1976, 192).

Miniature pots are also common, coming from such sites as Chalk, Kent (Allen, 1956, 252); Chester (Green, 1978, pl. 119); Exeter (Fox, 1968, 1ff.); Haslemere (Anon, 1905-1907, 221-228); Norton, North Yorkshire (Green, 1978, pl. 120); Stanton Harcourt, Oxon (Thomas, 1955, 21); Thatcham, Berks (Harris, 1935, 128), and Islands Thorn, Hants (British Museum).

The purpose of this resumé has been to emphasize the vast range of model implements from Romano-British sites, a substantial number being from ritual contexts, of which large group wheel-models are merely a part.

CHAPTER III

The Significance of Miniature Wheels and other Models in Romano-Celtic Europe

Introduction

Miniature wheels (Catalogue A), usually made of bronze, and generally from about 2-6 cm diameter, form a substantial part of the archaeological record, relating to a possible sky-cult in pre-Roman and Romano-Celtic contexts both in Britain and on the European Continent. However, model wheels have to be viewed in their context rather than in an isolated vacuum (as stated in Chapter II), since they are but one type of miniature replica of full-size objects which may occur in a very wide variety of forms (see Chapter II). The term 'model' or 'miniature' object may be taken to mean, in the main, minute copies of full-size Roman items. All true models in this present context should be recognizable as potentially usable items (apart from their extremely small dimensions). Judging by the foregoing criteria, one might, as one anomaly, point to swastika-shaped brooches. However, I believe it possible to demonstrate that the swastika is a derivation of (or shares ideas with) the motif of the wheel and thus it may be included in the same group (see Chapter VI). It may obviously be argued that a great many cult-objects are miniatures – figurines, for instance, are tiny replicas of personified deities or animals. The categories of miniatures assessed here, however, do cohere in their essentially utilitarian nature.

The Concept of Ritual Models in Antiquity

The rôle played in prehistory by models has been discussed in Chapter 1, which assesses some of the evidence for pre-Roman wheel-symbolism. Nevertheless it is necessary to look again at the original significance given to miniatures in a cult-context. In order to understand the use of model items in general as possible expressions of ritual, it is essential briefly to step outside the boundaries of Europe to glance first at Egypt and the Near East.

As seen in Chapter I models occur in ritual contexts in the Near East (Woolley, 1934, 64), and even those found in secular situations could have religious significance (Littauer & Crouwel, 1974, 20-36). Egypt, however, has far more concrete evidence for a very specific use of models. The practice, especially in the 3rd millennium B.C. and particularly in the 6th Dynasty (1st Intermediate Period c. 2180-2050 B.C.) (British Museum, 1971, 159-160) of placing miniature objects, mainly tools, in tombs, was prompted by a magical intention similar to that underlying the graphic representations of items on tomb-walls; models served in place of actual, usable articles. The original reason for the manufacture of items in miniature is presumed to have been an economic one, but later they were apparently chosen in preference to life-size objects because they could thus be made specifically for funerary purposes; they could be more elaborately fashioned, of better, longer-lasting materials. Models of hoes, baskets and other implements were interred for use by the deceased or his 'shabti' for carrying out work on the land in the afterlife. An example of such a tomb-find is at Heqreshu (British Museum Acc. no. 32693). In the British Museum is a group of model copper objects from the tomb of the 6th Dynasty priest whose name was Idy (British Museum, 1969, fig. 54). In graves of the late Old Kingdom and the Middle Kingdom wooden models of, for example, boats, items representing ploughing, and pottery models of houses are recorded. The Egyptian practice has a close parallel in modern times. Although it is fully recognized that present-day ethnographic comparisons are fraught with perils, nonetheless it is worthwhile examining one. In traditional Chinese society (which is still of relevance to life in the Hong Kong New Territories) paper models (though not in miniature), including cars and power-boats, were made and ritually burnt with the dead. By the act of incineration the models were believed to have been transformed into material possessions in the Underworld, to be utilized in the afterlife, in a world envisaged as being essentially similar to that of earth (Barker, 1978).

Central and Southern Europe too have early evidence for models, frequently with an apparently ritual purpose. Wheels themselves occur as models in clay from the 4th millennium B.C. (Bona, 1960, 83-111), but it is uncertain whether such items were isolated models or originally part of miniature vehicles (Piggott, 1968a, 266-318). Miniature bronze double-axes occur in Minoan Crete from around 2000 B.C. (Evans, 1902-1903, 59ff. ; 101, fig. 58 ; Higgins, 1974, 142, fig. 174 ; Hawkes, 1937, 145, 149, fig. 3 ; Cook, 1925, 543-559). The sign of the double-axe frequently occurs on representations of sacred cattle, situated between the horns, at Mycenae (Déchelette, 1910, fig. 204 ; Schliemann, 1878, 298) and at Knossos (Evans, 1902-1903, 114, fig. 70). There may well have been a connection between this axe-form and Zeus from very early indeed. Double-axe miniatures occur at the shrine of Zeus at Olympia (Déchelette, 1910, fig. 206), one of the Sky-God's main sanctuaries (Hardwick, 1979, 68). Single-axe models are recorded from the shrine of the Oracle of Zeus at Dodona (Carapanos, 1878, 100f.) and these may date from as early as the 13th or 12th Century B.C. There is no question but that these early Greek double-axe and single-axe models are votive objects. Some of the Minoan examples (Higgins, 1974, fig. 174) are of gold ; Dodona and Olympia are unequivocal sanctuaries.

Very probably of religious significance are the Kameiros finds of the Archaic period (8th-7th Century B.C) on Rhodes, which could conceivably be connected with Urnfield trade (Sprockhoff, 1954). Graves here have revealed bronze wheel-models in association with Archaic geometric pottery. The models bear between four and nine spokes and from the centre of these rise shafts (elongated naves) supporting ducks, heads of goats, cows or rams (Walters, 1899, 12, nos. 158, 159, 162, 164) ; and in one instance a crude winged human figure is depicted mounted on a wheel (Cook, 1914, 330ff). It is of interest that, according to Cook, the principal cult of the early Rhodians was that of Helios (*ibid.*). On Delos too model wheels are frequent finds in temples ; they are presumably votive offerings rather than amulets since there is no suspension-loop on any of the examples discovered. The religious occupation of Delos began possibly as early as the 10th Century B.C. and it became a Roman settlement in the 1st Century B.C. At least one lead wheel could be Archaic, but they probably date for the most part from the Classical or Hellenistic periods (Bruneau & Ducat, 1966, 16-23 ; Deonna, 1938, 341).

The foregoing evidence indicates that at a relatively early date there is material in the Greek archaeological record showing an association between Zeus, the Hellenic Sky-God, and axe-symbolism, and between a probable solar cult and wheel-symbolism. We cannot be certain about the divinity-associations with wheels at Delos, but there is evidence both for Apollo and for Zeus at the temple-complex. It will be seen (below) that the axe and wheel both appear to be connected with a Romano-Celtic sky and solar deity.

In North-West Europe model objects occur as early as the Earlier Bronze Age in the Wessex Early Bronze Age in Britain, where there are records of miniature items, presumably of a talismanic nature. Tiny bronze halberd-pendants decorated with gold and amber were perforated at the butt-end of the haft for suspension (Piggott, 1938, 84). Also in 'Wessex Culture' graves appear miniature mace-pendants and ingot-torcs, once again probably amulets for the protection first of the living and subsequently of the dead (Piggott, 1973, 361-363 ; Green, 1975c, 56). There is a dearth of evidence for models during the later Bronze Age in Britain, but it is possible that the bronze socketed axe-models from Wiltshire, for example those in Devizes Museum, may be later Bronze Age rather than Iron Age, as has been suggested (Manning & Saunders, 1972). The Caergwrle Bowl from Flintshire (Clwyd) in North Wales may possibly be a boat-model (Green *et al.*, 1980, 26-30). It is shale and probably dates to the later Bronze Age, and has an association with solar-symbolism in its gold-foil disc-decoration. In this connection the much later gold boat-model from Broighter in County Derry (Farrell & Penny, 1975) should be borne in mind ; this particular model comes from a 1st Century B.C. hoard.

The occurrence of wheel-models in Central and North-West Europe is discussed in Chapter I.

In assessing the religious significance of Romano-Celtic models, and of wheel-miniatures in particular, the question should first be asked what exactly prehistoric models, and more specifically wheel-models, represent and the precise nature of their function. We have the situation, both in the later Bronze Age and the Iron Age in Europe, of the presence of tiny wheel-shaped objects with no intrinsic function (see Chapter I). In Gaul, at the end of the Bronze Age, there are pendants representing wheels associated with boats, of which the prow and stern terminate in the heads of aquatic birds (Gimbutas, 1965, 310, 316 ; Holste, 1951 ; Hampel, 1887). This occurrence appears to associate wheel-pendants with the great sun/sky-cult of the Urnfield and Hallstatt phases of continental Europe, represented by sun and bird-boat images on sheet-bronze vessels and other metalwork (see Chapter I). The Iron Age occurrence of wheel-models in graves appears to substantiate the idea of the possession of talismanic properties. The hundreds of wheel-models from French rivers (Courcelle-Seneuil, 1910, 73) may be Roman or pre-Roman (Flemming,

1908, 391ff. ; Déchelette, 1910, 409ff.) ; there is no way of distinguishing which, but they must have been deliberately cast into the water, and one may thus presume a ritual significance of some kind. Blanchet, among other scholars (1912) argues for the use of miniature wheels as currency and (1905, 27) cites circumstances where wheels and Gaulish coins are found in association, for example at Naix (de Villefosse, 1881, 12) and at La Tène (Zürich Museum). In the same way the numerous plain bronze rings found together with model wheels at, for instance, Bibracte, Alesia and Sainte-Geneviève (de Longpérier, 1867 ; Blanchet, 1912 ; 1905) may have been utilized in some kind of monetary system. It is the sheer numbers of model wheels occurring on Gaulish sites (Lambrechts, 1942, 64-80) which argues most strongly for their use as currency. In the later La Tène, miniature wheels and rings are recorded at, for example, Naix, where they were slung together on metal strips (Déchelette, 1914, 1296, fig. 560q ; de Mortillet, 1876). This mirrors the situation in late pre-Roman or Roman contexts at Lavoye (see below) where lead wheels were cast in strips or bands (Chenet, 1919). If Gaulish wheel-models, in the Iron Age, were used as money, it is probable that there was also a religious symbolism. Coins themselves (Allen, 1958, 43-63) certainly appear to have a ritual as well as an economic function ; it may well be significant in this respect, that there are a number of instances of sun-symbolism on the coins of Gaulish tribes (e.g. British Museum, 1925, 167 ; and information from Dr. D. Nash, Ashmolean Museum).

Iron Age model axes are recorded at various sites. They are rare in Britain and rarer on the Continent. In British contexts they occur, for example, at a Long Wittenham settlement site (Oxon) (Savory, 1937, 3) ; at an Arras grave in East Yorkshire (Manning & Saunders, 1972, 281 ; Evans, 1881, 134, fig. 161) and at the Meare Lake Village (Manning & Saunders, 1972, 282 ; Bulleid & Grey, 1953, pl. XLIX, E74). Model weapons are also not unknown in British Iron Age contexts. Iron Age-style shields are recorded at Frilford, Oxon (Bradford & Goodchild, 1939, 1ff.) and at Worth, Kent (Klein, 1928, 76ff.) ; both sites have evidence of Iron Age occupation, and both are ritual sites. Other Iron Age models include the shield-model from Breedon-on-the-Hill (Wacher, 1979, 44, pl. 22) ; and a cauldron from Ancaster (Anon, 1957-8, 99-101), which would appear to hark back to the pre-Roman custom of manufacturing globular sheet-bronze cauldrons (Hawkes, 1951 ; 1956) both for culinary and for ritual purposes (Ross, 1967, 31, 179, 183, 246, 357).

Where there is specific evidence for the function of models, they appear very frequently in prehistory to have been worn. We have evidence of their attachment as pendants, to brooches, belts and torcs, presumably as good-luck talismans ; they were buried with the dead in graves. In order to be worn as amulets or charms model objects generally would need evidence of suspension-rings or loops ; this is not the case with an openwork wheel, since a thong or wire could be threaded between the spokes. So we do not necessarily know whether wheel-models were amulets or were votive offerings to a divinity in the pre-Roman period. Certainly, in the Iron Age, not all models were talismans worn as good-luck symbols. The Frilford sword and shield and the Worth shields, for instance, were true votive offerings in temples.

The Significance of Romano-Celtic Models

Origins of British Models

Although the distribution of British model objects demonstrates a concentration in the southern and eastern regions it is necessary, in my opinion, to seek an indigenous origin for them rather than to assume them to be the result of imports from the Continent. The prehistoric material mitigates against the latter proposal. Whilst it is true, however, that model wheels occur in Britain during the Iron Age, their frequency in Romano-Celtic Gaul and the Rhineland, contrasted with their scattered occurrence in Britain, argues for a major centre of development on the Continent. Certainly the Wheel-God himself, as manifested in iconography, is concentrated in Gaul.

Chronology of British Models

Certain models occur during the Early Iron Age – for example the Stanwick and (possibly) the Hounslow wheels, the Frilford and Worth weapons (see Chapters I, II). It is possible to demonstrate, from a few sites, that models continued to be manufactured and used right through the Roman period. The Backworth hoard (AB1) was deposited around the reign of Antoninus Pius ; the Felmingham deposit (AB5) was accompanied by a coin of A.D. 260 ; the South Shields axe-brooch apparently comes from a 3rd or 4th Century context ; the Housesteads wheel-brooch (AB7) comes from a 4th Century context ; the Maiden Castle hammer and the Lydney axe-pin (see Chapter II) come from temples built or refurbished in the mid 4th Century A.D. after Christianity had become the State Religion (Wheeler, 1943 ; Wheeler, 1932). One Colchester wheel (AB25) is probably very early Claudian.

Chronology of Continental Model Wheels

As in Britain, wheel-models, whether true models, brooches or pendants, appear to have been made right through the Roman period on the Continent, and of course before. The Basel models are 1st Century B.C. date (see Chapter I), and we have already noted the Iron Age model tradition. The wheel-brooches at Augst, near Basel, date from the early Claudian period until the 2nd Century A.D. (A146). The true wheel-models from Insula 17 (A137-141) were found with pottery of 1st-3rd Century A.D. date. It is almost inconceivable that the Augst models are earlier than Roman. The inscribed example must be Roman. Dr. Martin points out (personal communication) that Augst itself has produced virtually no Iron Age finds, except five coins compared with over 10,000 Roman coins. The swastika-brooch from here (A151) appears to be late 2nd Century/early 3rd Century (agreeing with the Dura Material [Frisch & Toll, 1949] which dates between A.D. 165 and 256). The Augst wheel-on-bow brooch is 1st-2nd Century (A152) ; the wheel-bracelet may be 1st Century A.D.

Where there is dating evidence available, other wheel-brooches appear to have been most popular during the 2nd and 3rd Centuries. The Zugmantel (A25, 89, 127-128) and Saalburg (A20-24, 129-131) wheel and swastika-brooches are 2nd/early 3rd Century A.D. The Vesqueville brooch (A167) is possibly 3rd Century ; that from Bazoches (A170) was found with material including coins of 1st-4th Century but occupation was especially intense during 2nd and 3rd, concentrating in the Antonine period. Néris (A176) dates to the end of the 2nd Century ; the Villeneuve brooch (A179) comes from a 2nd Century cremation-cemetery ; the Lanslevillard cemetery (A100) dates from the 1st/2nd Century ; the Weissenthaum brooch (A119) is probably 2nd-3rd Century. At Hüfingen (A132) solid or openwork disc-brooches date from the earlier 1st Century to the time of Commodus (Rieckhoff, 1975, 5-105) ; knobbed solid disc-brooches, like that from Watercrook, Lancs., are common in the 2nd Century (Potter, 1979, 211, fig. 84). The occupation at Sarre-Union (A39) is mainly 1st-2nd Century ; the Argentomagus brooches (A193) are associated with 2nd Century material ; Blanc Pavé (A196) probably dates to the 3rd Century. Exceptions to this include the Montot brooch (A178) which was associated with mainly Claudian material, and possibly that from Guiry-Gadancourt Villa (A182) where occupation appears to have been concentrated in the 4th Century.

With regard to true models (apart from the Augst group already dealt with) the Meuse examples are the most informative chronologically. The lead wheels from Pont Verdunois (A186) could have been manufactured from the 1st Century A.D. until the time of Commodus. The earliest Lavoye lead wheels (A187-192) may date as early as late La Tène, but one of the bronze ones was found with pottery of 2nd-3rd Century date. The dating evidence for the Rhineland multi-model grave-groups (from two of which come wheel-models [A12 ; 12a]) rests on coinage of Alexander Severus, Maximinus Thrax, Elagabalus, and Gallienus, demonstrating the use of wheels as late as the mid 3rd Century on the German frontier.

The evidence of pendants bears out other chronological patterns. The bronze pendant from Aizanville (A103) was associated with coins from Antoninus Pius to Severus Alexander, and probably dates to the late 220s or 230s A.D. The gold wheel-jewellery was manufactured from about the 1st-3rd Centuries A.D. (Galliou, 1974 ; Higgins, 1961 ; Charlesworth, 1961 ; Mann, 1975). The Ardennes pendant (A172) is suggested as being as early as late La Tène ; the Augst and Backworth material (A149 ; AB1) is probably 2nd Century. The Obfelden gold wheel (A135) was found in an allegedly 3rd Century hoard of goldwork. Gold wheel-jewellery from non-Celtic sites appears mostly to be dated to the 1st and 2nd Century A.D. The Pompeii and Boscoreale goldwork must be pre A.D. 79. The Eleutheropolis wheel is perhaps 2nd Century (Higgins, 1961, 186).

Function

Like prehistoric examples, Romano-Celtic models may be functionally divided into those which were probably worn and those which were votive offerings. As stated above, there is a fundamental problem in the interpretation of wheel-models in that they may be suspended as ornaments without trace of extra attachment for a wire, chain or thong surviving. However, we have more external evidence for wheel-symbols being worn as talismans than for any other miniature object. There is a certain amount of both direct and indirect iconographic material to support the amulet-hypothesis. There is the carving of a Celtic warrior from Fox-Amphoux in southern France (B45), who wears a six-spoked wheel as a pectoral pendant (Espérandieu, no. 8613). Another such example is the Metz figure found in 1749 (B80), a stone sculpture of an individual with a wheel-shaped amulet worn slung on a chain or thread round the neck as a pendant. Both these carvings recall the gold, silver and bronze chains with wheels known in the archaeological record of the Roman Empire (Galliou, 1974). I should stress that there is no intrinsic reason, apart from occasional context (see Chapter II) to support the ritual function of these chains. A number of horseman figures from 'Jupiter-gigantensäulen' groups, for example from Luxeuil (B72), Obernburg (B102) and Meaux (B77) are portrayed with their arms thrust through the spokes of wheels, as if the symbolism of a wheel-amulet and the functionalism of a shield are being combined. Certainly the wheel-shaped brooches of the Rhineland, Gaul and Britain were worn, and one could argue that the elements of function and ritual symbolism were combined, the latter perhaps having, by the Roman period, faded into an amorphous and vague good-luck motif, rather as the Christian cross or Egyptian ankh are sometimes employed at the present day.

The gold and silver wheel-pendants from, for example, Thérouanne, Arras, Dolaucothi, Backworth and Newstead (A74 ; A75 ; AB4 ; AB1 ; AB12) were, like the brooches, parts of jewellery items − gold, silver or bronze necklaces or bracelets. It could be argued (Higgins, 1961, 186 ; Galliou, 1974) that these are purely decorative pieces, and it has been suggested that the Backworth material (Mann, 1975) was an Italian import. This it may well be but the necklaces could equally be of Gaulish make (witness the Thérouanne and Arras examples). The Dolaucothi wheel was found in a goldwork hoard in the vicinity of the Roman goldmines and goldmining activity, and the circumstances are suggestive of the wheels and chains having been made at the site by a resident craftsman.

Where a wheel-brooch (or an axe-brooch) bears a ring for suspension, it could be that the item has a double function, as decorative and functional brooch and as amulet. However (see also Chapter II) there may be a more mundane interpretation ; brooches of all kinds were chained together in pairs, for example those from Argentomagus (Albert & Fauduet, 1976, pl. IV, no. 20). The same problem of ritual versus secular interpretation manifests itself with other functional items which appear to incorporate sky-symbolism in decoration. A case in point is the class of stone 'spindle-whorls', decorated with radial lines emanating from a central perforation (Savory, 1976, 104, e.g. fig. 34), which were perhaps either worn as talismans or were used as spindle-whorls whose decoration, not being visible in use, was of some ritual significance.

Spindle-whorls similar to the North Welsh ones described by Savory (1976) are recorded on the Continent, for example that from the Bonn area ornamented with radial lines (Hinze, 1969, 221).

All one can do, with regard to jewellery, or any other item which has a function apart from an overtly ritual one, is to say that ritual may have a role to play. Certainly it is sometimes difficult to distinguish a true model wheel (which I would argue must be of religious significance) from a brooch or pendant.

We have evidence, from Britain and from the Continent, of models – wheels, axes and other items – bearing suspension-rings (apart from brooches already discussed). Wheels we know were sometimes worn as pendants but evidence for others is usually lacking, although model bells, for instance, could have been attached to ceremonial rattles or *sistra* in order to make a tinkling sound when shaken in a ritual procession. However, there is no direct evidence for this but there does exist an association of bell-models with chain necklaces, for instance that from Pfünz (*O.R.L.*, 1901, pl. LXIII, no. 8), and at Daubeuf-la-Campagne (Indre) where a 'charm'-bracelet with a ring, discs and a bell-model are recorded (de Boüard, 1968, 347-372). This wearing of models as jewellery may be a secular or a religious custom and there is no means of being certain. Bertrand (1897, 167) would see the wearers of brooches which incorporate sun or sky-symbolism as possible priests of a sky-cult, but this is pure speculation and, in any case, need not apply to all models. However, one does not require a great deal of imagination to see the Backworth, Dolaucothi and Newstead necklaces as badges of office – perhaps somewhat akin to mayoral chains, even if originally these were merely items of jewellery, as Higgins (1961) and Galliou (1974) would suggest. Drioux (1934, 42) believes that model wheels did retain their cult-significance and are definitely to be considered as amulets, although their original specific importance in religious terms may have been forgotten. As regards true models as opposed to jewellery, the amulet theory is still valid since, as stated above, one can attach a wheel by a thread through the space between the spokes. The Mainz silver pin (A28) is of interest in this respect, since from a wire attached to the cone-shaped terminal of the pin was suspended a wheel-model. In this connection, Cook's view (1914, 254) is relevant in that he suggests that a bronze wheel-model slung on a double thread and spun would look quite like the sun; the miniature wheel from Engelhalbinsel (A136 ; Pl. LIX) should be recalled here, with its nave indented as though for a thread. Presumably a brass example –

like that from Colchester (AB17) — would be even more sunlike than bronze because of its yellower colour (one should remember how difficult brass was to produce [Craddock, 1978, 4]) ; and gold would have been the most authentic of all. Tinned brooches like that from Icklingham (AB27 ; Pl. LX, Fig. 21) could incorporate similar ideas of brightness. Lambrechts (1942, 64-80) is firmly convinced, like Drioux, that the wheel-models, for instance in the collections of St.-Germain Museum, are charms. De Villefosse (1881, 12) makes a similar contention, and poses the question whether the little bronze wheels so common particularly on eastern Gaulish sites, are merely for keeping away evil or whether they embody a stronger, more direct sun-symbolism as Gaidoz (1884) would seem to think. An interesting point concerns the pipe-clay model wheels in Cologne Museum (A10). We know that identical wheels were attached as part of four-wheeled carts of pipe-clay. Nevertheless it is possible that isolated ones were also talismans, and would of course have been cheaper to buy than bronze models. The whole question of clientèle should always be borne in mind. After all it is assumed that it would be the higher classes of Romano-Celtic society that would have bought bronze figurines of deities and the poorer folk those of pipe-clay, so it is equally feasible that pipe-clay models were also in demand as votive offerings. Certainly the Cologne clay wheels could have been worn as amulets by means of a cord threaded through the central perforation in the nave ; and we do have bronze true wheel-models from the city.

The function of other models (see Chapter II for summary of evidence) has to be looked at in terms of ritual significance. In the first place axes and axe-brooches or pins frequently occur at the same sites, for instance at Straubing in South Germany, and Richborough in southern Britain. This probably means that there is no sharp division to be made between the religious purpose of jewellery or true models. The question has to be asked why models of particular tool-types were manufactured, often accurately and painstakingly. One answer is that perhaps the implements copied were in some respect relevant to the devotee or to the divinity or both. One could argue that the model spears from the temple-sites of Woodeaton and Harlow (see Chapter II) were offered up by people about to go on or just returned from a hunting expedition, to propitiate Silvanus, Diana or the local equivalent. In the same way the smiths' equipment depicted as models, for example from Chesters, Brough or Chester (Green, 1978), may have been offerings to appease a smith-deity, by a blacksmith. It is interesting, in this context, that there is a great deal of evidence for a smith-god in the archaeological record, especially of northern Britain (Leach, 1962 ; Green, 1978). It is thus perfectly possible that the owner of a model offered up miniature replicas of the tools of his trade either to a local multi-functional godling or to a 'saint-patron' of smiths, hunters, soldiers or potters. Where one has tiny copies of what one might call temple-furniture, it may be that a miniature shrine is being depicted, perhaps for a domestic sacred place or a grave.

One fundamental question concerning function is whether miniaturization itself was entirely governed by secular motives, like economy of cost or material, convenience, aesthetics, or by ritual factors (as if somehow the very size of the object were important). In my opinion there are elements of both. The concept of models as economical and convenient representations of life-size offerings is a reasonable one. A small model could be made in bronze, at little cost compared to, for instance, a full-size axe of wood and iron. Bronze would be aesthetically more pleasing than iron, and it would probably have been too expensive for most people to commission a craftsman to manufacture a full-scale bronze implement as a votive offering. Convenience is probably just as important as the cost-factor. If one considers that, where evidence for functional context exists, models were either worn as jewellery, amulets or were offered as votive items in graves or shrines, then the small size of such offerings was essential. The miniature sheet bronze mirrors known in Greece (Oberländer, 1967) could well have been miniature offerings to Aphrodite, whose emblem was the mirror ; likewise the model pots at a temple dedicated to Demeter at Sparta (personal information from Prof. John Ferguson) could easily have been made so small for convenience. Nevertheless I believe that miniaturization has an intrinsic ritual significance. It is possible to donate a full-size implement to a divinity in a shrine. Large altars, carvings and full-size pots are frequent discoveries in the small Romano-Celtic shrines both of Gaul (de Vesly, 1909) and Britain (Lewis, 1966). Graves too can normally accommodate at least a few largish objects. Thus mere convenience of size, although probably a major factor, is not necessarily the only criterion for the existence of models. It may be that, just as some miniatures – like the Woodeaton spears (Kirk, 1949, 32ff.) – were deliberately damaged, presumably to defunctionalize them and render them more suitable as divine offerings, so the act of modelling of life-size items may itself have sanctified them. No one can use an axe 2 cm long and that in itself was perhaps considered to place these copies beyond the human scope and render them divine.

If a model object has a votive inscription, then that makes it unequivocally religious in function. This is true of the Augst wheel-model fragment (A140 ; Pl. LVIII, Fig. 16) and of certain Swiss axe-models (Forrer, 1948 ; see AX1) which are actually dedicated to known divinities (see below).

Two final points about function are concerned with context. The first is that, in Britain, wheel-symbols, unlike axes and other models, are not found directly associated with shrines. This may mean that they were talismans rather than votive offerings. The second point is a fundamental one about models in general. It has been suggested that models are simply toys, as is put forward in the case of wooden Viking models (Herteig, 1975, Pl. XVIb, 82), but I think this is untenable on grounds of context alone. So many models are from temples or graves that to regard them all as the playthings of children is to misunderstand concepts which are fundamental to the ancient world. It is my belief that if some models are religious then the chances are that most are. To reinforce the 'contra-toy' theory (if that expression may be excused) one has only to look at the beautifully-enamelled bronze stands from a number of British sites (Green, 1978, pls. 126-129).

Intrinsic Symbolism

One phenomenon of certain model objects is that they do incorporate within their physical form some features which may themselves point to a ritual significance. If we look first at wheels, we see that the number of spokes appears to be entirely random, both on British and on continental examples (Toutain, 1920, 192ff.). The evidence suggests that there is no 'sacred number' as one might have expected, though there are clusters of numbers (see Chapter IX). This presumably means that it is the wheel itself which is symbolic, and it was evidently not considered necessary to demonstrate or enhance its power with a constant and symbolic number of 'sun-rays'.

The materials with which wheel-models were made may or may not be important. Generally they were made of bronze, but (see Chapter II) they may be of lead, gold, silver or brass. The brightness of bronze, gold and brass has been considered above; Lead wheel-models, like those from Naix (A78) and Lavoye (A187-192) are more enigmatic. Other lead models are recorded, for example the spears and anvil from Chester (Green, 1978, 54), and the lead mirror-models from, for example Carnuntum grave-contexts (Lloyd-Morgan, 1977). A lead axe is recorded from Springhead (Kent) (see Chapter II). Specifically associated with the

Romano-Celtic Sky-God is the lead wheel from Plessis-Barbuise (A73) inside which, in a break in the spokes, is depicted a figure of the divinity. It may be that lead was sometimes chosen to manufacture votive offerings simply because it was cheaper and technically easier (Manning, 1979, personal communication). The statement by Tudor (1976, 61) that bronze is cheaper and that therefore lead would be purposely and ritually chosen, is nonsense. Lead may, in certain religious circumstances, have had magical properties. In the Roman world gold tended to be used for benevolent spells (Sieburg, 1898, 123-153) and lead, a dark, heavy metal, was almost invariably employed for curses or *defixiones* (Ferguson, 1977, 52). It is possible that lead was regarded as an earthward-looking, dull, heavy, element whilst gold was light, pure and of bright sun-colour. The lead female figurine from Caerleon (Green, 1978, 49) has a curiously 'closed', malevolent look about her features, and could well have underworld connections. It will be seen below (Chapter VI) that there is evidence of a chthonic aspect to the Celtic sky-cult, which may account for the occasional use of lead for wheel-models.

Before we leave the subject of lead wheel-models, we should recall the long 'bands' of lead wheels, very small in size, found at, for instance, Lavoye (A187ff.). Chenet (1919) has put forward the suggestion that these joined wheels could almost have been a form of Celtic 'rosary', but my own opinion is slightly less romantic. If they do have a purely ritual rather than an economic function, then the idea may well have simply been enhancement of power by means of multiplication.

The most important intrinsic symbolism on models is that of decoration. If it is assumed, from their frequent association with shrines and graves, that models do have a ritual importance, then, in my opinion, it is valid to assume that decorative features too may have had religious motivation, though it is important not to read too much into the evidence; Looking first at wheel and swastika-models, various decorative features should be noted. The denticulate ornament on certain Gaulish wheels (A82) could be interpreted as symbolizing sun-ray terminals ; perhaps if the wheels were spun on a thread the jagged outline would blur to a realistic sun-image (cf. Cook, 1914, 254). The Engehalbinsel model (A136) has already been mentioned in connection with spinning (above). The pointillé decoration on the felloe of a Lavoye bronze model (A191) may also have been to catch the light when turned. This particular model had a very highly polished surface and Chenet suggests (1919) that this wheel appears to combine the functions of jewellery, money and amulet.

Two further phenomena commented upon in the descriptive analysis (Chapter II) are the features of spoke (and occasional felloe) ribbing, and of knobs or lugs attached to the circumference and sometimes also to the nave of a wheel-brooch. The ribbing is enigmatic; it may be purely decorative; a model sickle from one of the Rhineland grave-groups (Cologne Museum) has a ribbed haft. However, it could be that the horizontal lines or grooves on wheel-spokes are either representative of wood-grains on a real wheel or they could have been added to give an impression of rotary motion. In this connection the Hallstatt full-size bronze wheel from Byčiskala Höhle (see Chapter I) with ribbed spokes should be remembered. It was sheathed in bronze and when new, if the wheel were turned, the ribs would catch and reflect the light. The semi-circular excrescences or lugs on the felloe and sometimes the nave of some wheel-brooches are also not easy to explain. It is possible that, like the toothed felloe on French wheels already considered, the idea was to break up the smooth wheel-surface to give a notion of sun-like rays. Sometimes the knobs coincide with the outer spoke-terminals; in these instances it is possible that the knobs represent spoke-ends sticking through the felloe (as sometimes occurs in real wheels [see Chapter IX]); the Iron Age model from Fully bears protruding spoke-ends. It is just possible that there is a deeper significance attached to the presence of knobs. Deonna (1917, 124ff.) would see the knobs terminating the horns of bull-images as sun-symbols, similar to that of wheel-circles. Knob-horned bulls occur both in stone, for example at Langres (Drioux, 1934, 73) and in bronze (Reinach, 1896, 553). Langres is of interest since there is evidence from here both of wheel-symbolism (A80), three-horned bulls (Drioux, 1934, 73) and knob-horned bulls (*ibid.*). The bull did have a definite association with the Gallo-Roman Jupiter in Britain (see Chapter VI). For instance, the bull-mounts with eagle-heads from Thealby (Green, 1977b, pl. 12, VIII, a, b) have knobbed horns. If knobs on bull-horns were connected with sky or sun-symbolism, then it would be feasible to think in terms of potency-enhancement for a wheel-shaped object by the addition of knobs or lugs. The only other possible reason for knobbing, if it has a ritual significance at all, is that of defunctionalizing a wheel-model.

Certain other decorative features of wheel-models or brooches may have religious symbolism. The Silchester (AB30) and Villeneuve (A179) wheel-brooches bear concentric circle (or ring-and-dot) ornament, as does the true model from Champagne (A210); this feature could, in this context, have solar significance; The Bavay wheel-brooch (A59 ; Pl. LIII, Fig. 9) has a dolphin at the nave. This may have significance if one bears in mind the association of dolphin and Wheel-God on the Willingham sceptre-terminal (C6). Perhaps the most important decoration occurs on brooches like that in the British Museum, from a French or German context (A104) and those from Trègnes (A155), Bavay (A166) and Nijmegen (A160). All of these bear solar or floreate decoration in the enamel of the felloe. It may be mere decoration, but to my mind the coincidence of wheel-symbol and solar-ornament on the one object is too great for dismissal.

Swastika-shaped brooches, axe-models and occasional other models bear ornamental features which are possibly significant. Common to all these model-types is decoration in the form either of ring-and-dot (or concentric-circle) or incised 'binding marks' the most frequent of which is a straightforward X. On swastika-brooches this occurs at the junction of the four arms ; on axes it may occur either where the haft and blade join or on the blade itself, as at Bern (AX2) and at Kirmington (AX15). Either the cross represents cord or rope binding copied in bronze as a skeuomorph of a full-size axe-model or it has some deeper significance, or it is purely decorative. W. H. Manning (personal communication 1979) has suggested that thongs around a life-size axe would be totally useless on a Roman shaft-hole axe and he very much doubts whether such representation on model axes and other implements could be given a functional interpretation. Nevertheless, there are one or two axe-models from Britain where the argument for the presence of binding-marks is extremely strong. The axes from Woodeaton (Green, 1975c, fig. 5, 30c), Hockwold (*ibid.*, fig. 4, 17), and Richborough (Bushe-Fox, 1949, pl. 52, 189, 190) bear lines which do not seem to be merely crosses. The Woodeaton one has double lines as if a thong has been passed twice around the blade and haft-junction. The Hockwold and one Richborough axe have marks which irresistably suggest a cord being passed repeatedly around the blade.

Binding-marks occur on a number of the Cologne multi-model grave-group miniatures. The rake-model from one of them has incised lines crossing over one another on the back of the blade ; the keys from these burials (Rottländer, 1973-1974, 143-152) and from the barrow in Sussex (Green, 1975c, fig. 5, nos. 65a, b) bear ornament in the shape of crosses, vertical lines and alternate parallel lines (one diagonal, one vertical etc.). Sometimes there is evidence for, at any rate, the diagonal 'St. Andrew's Cross' being other than a binding representation. For instance, where it occurs on a swastika-brooch it would surely be folly to suggest that a wooden prototype is being copied, the arms bound together with thongs. Likewise, the diagonal cross-marking on the recently-discovered model axe from Kirmington (AX15) is definitely on the blade itself rather than where the haft and blade meet. It is worth noting that the diagonal sign appears on a Romano-British shovel-model from Oxfordshire (Green, 1977a, 256-260), at a position halfway up the haft. This is of particular interest because it can hardly be seen, which argues against it being purely decorative, and because in this position it is not convincing as a cord-mark. It should here be noted that it is not only on models that the sign occurs (see Chapter VI).

In my opinion, shared by at least one continental scholar (Rottländer, 1971, 94-109) the ritual interpretation of the 'X' sign should be followed up. If, as I attempt to demonstrate below, there is some common symbolism behind, for instance, wheel and some axe-models, then one may perhaps look for a sky-sign in these markings. In the first place, we do have the mark on some swastika-brooches; second, a ligatured cross appears on a Woodeaton axe-model (AX20; Pl. LXIV, Fig. 27), and from the same site comes an axe-miniature bearing a swastika-motif. Third, the very sign itself could easily be a stylized sun or wheel-symbol. What may be represented is a simplified motif of four spokes without the surrounding circle; the idea could even be a combination of wheel and swastika, or an attempt to include elements both of sun and stars (day and night symbols). In this connection it is interesting to note particular figurines of Gallo-Roman divinities which bear celestial signs including crosses. Elsewhere in this study (Chapter VI) I attempt to show a necessary association between the Sky-God and the god with long-handled hammer (who often bears 'X' signs).

The ring-and-dot motif occurs on swastika-brooches, axe-models and a model shovel from a Cologne grave-group (Rottländer, 1973-4, Abb. 14). One has to be careful with ring-and-dot decoration in terms of ritual since it is a ubiquitous method of ornamenting objects from the Bronze Age right through and after the Roman period. Powell (1968, 155) comments upon its use in later prehistory. It is also a common means of decoration on Iron Age bonework (it occurs at Danebury; information in Society of Antiquaries Lecture, 16.10.80, by B. W. Cunliffe), and on late Roman jewellery, for example on bracelets (Wheeler, 1932, 82, fig. 17E; Keller, 1971). It may be, however, that on models there is a more than purely secular significance. It occurs (see Chapter I) on later Bronze Age wheel-pendants in Europe, and on Hallstatt axe-models. The 'barillet' on the Vienne Sucellus figure (C15) bears concentric circle decoration ; the sign occurs on Sucellus-statuettes themselves, for example on a Cologne bronze (C34) ; it occurs on Vosges tombstones along with wheels and crosses (Linckenheld, 1927). The appearance of this motif *and* the 'X' symbol on swastikas and axes may link the two model-types together. From one and the same site — Richborough — came axe-models both with cross and with circle motifs (Green, 1978, 67-70 ; AX16-18). Of even greater significance is the bronze axe with 'X' motif from the Romano-Celtic site at Woodeaton, a second with a ring-and-dot mark, and a third with a swastika-sign (AX20). One of the shovels from a Cologne grave-group bears such ring-and-dot marks and another, from Oxfordshire, has an 'X'. It should not be forgotten (Manning, 1966, 50-59) that Sabazius is probably represented by the Cologne burial-finds, and that this divinity is known to have occasionally been equated with Jupiter (Oxford Classical Dictionary, 1970, 941).

One rather curious item remains to be examined for intrinsic significance connected with physical characteristics. This is the swastika-shaped brooch from Cologne with horse-head terminals to the four arms (A7). The brooch has a direct parallel with an example from Romania, at Buciumi (Miclea & Florescu, 1980, no. 235). This may be of extreme importance since there is evidence (see Chapter VI) that the Celtic Jupiter has associations with horses and a horseman cult. Horses pulling solar-chariots are common features of a prehistoric sun-cult (see Chapter I) and, on Jupiter-columns, the Sky-God is depicted on horseback. There is an association of a horseman portrayal and wheel-symbols at, for instance, Willingham Fen (horsemen and wheel-bearing deity found together in a hoard [see Chapter VII]. Hallstatt graves have yielded axe-models with ring-and-dot motifs and bearing a miniature horseman-image (Kromer, 1959, 138, pls. 137, 222). Thevenot (1951, 130ff.) has produced a substantial amount of data relating to sun, sky and horse symbolism. Pipe-clay horses from Assche-Kalkoven in Belgium (C52) are sometimes decorated with celestial symbols (see Chapter V).

Finally in this sub-section the Swiss model axes with inscriptions should be considered. Apart from association and context this group, and the wheel-model from Augst (A140), are the only models with concrete evidence for a religious function. Inscriptions occur on a number of Swiss axes, with dedications to Minerva (2), Mercury, Neptune, the Mothers (2) and Jupiter (2) (Forrer, 1948, catalogue). It is tempting to link the occurrence of the 'classical' divinities with those frequently associated with Jupiter-columns (Bauchhenss, 1976). In any event we do have a positive link in the two Jupiter-dedications (AX1, 8 ; *C.I.L.*, XIII, 5172, 5158) between the sky-cult and axe-models. Of the two axes dedicated to the Mothers, there is, as can be seen below (Chapter VI), other evidence for an association between the Sky-God and Earth-Goddesses, as represented by models.

Context and its Significance

Much has already been said concerning the context of these models (Chapter II). However, in order to draw together the threads, it is useful to consider it with regard to specifically ritual significance. British models in general are twice as common on rural as on urban sites ; this could suggest a bias towards native rather than romanized cults. They do infrequently appear on villa-sites, and are far more common in rural shrines than in any other type of site. It is of interest that British wheel-models do not occur in shrines and only occasionally in graves. This may suggest, as we have seen, that they are here to be regarded as amulets, personal talismans or good-luck tokens rather than as votive objects. The Felmingham Hall wheel (AB5) on the other hand, may be an ex-voto since it and the other items in the hoard probably came from a sacked or looted shrine ; the same may be true of the Backworth cache (AB1). Continental wheel-models, like those from Gusenburg (A50) ; Dhronecken (A51) ; Lardiers (A180-181) ; Bolards (A173-175) ; Bourbonne (A206) and Argentomagus (A193) come from temple-contexts. This and the occurrence, both in Britain and in Europe, of wheel-miniatures in graves, appears to be an unequivocal pointer to their ritual importance ; the grave-association (already noted in Iron Age contexts, see Chapter I) may mean a specifically funerary cult (cf. wheel-symbols on Vosges steles) or they may just be personal amulets buried with the dead as treasured possessions.

In Britain, but not on the Continent, axe-models are very frequently found in or near shrines, generally of Romano-Celtic type. The appearance of a number of these models at the site of Richborough (Green, 1978, 67-70) is interesting since, alone of military sites, it possesses Romano-Celtic temples. Axe-models are common also as finds in graves, especially in the Rhineland (Rottländer, 1973-4, 143-152). Lead model mirrors are recorded in sepulchral contexts at Carnuntum, perhaps for the use of beauty-conscious women in the afterlife (and/or as dedications to the goddess Venus) (Lloyd-Morgan, 1977, personal communication). Miniature pots from Luxembourg graves are generally thought to have accompanied the burials of children (Luxembourg, Musée des États). One interesting point about model findspots is their occurrence on the Continent in riverine or lacustrine deposits. There is a substantial amount of evidence for miniature wheels having been cast into rivers in Gaul (Courcelle-Seneuil, 1910, 73 ; Reinach, 1894, 34ff.). Two Swiss axe-models, from Solothurn and Allmendingen (Toutain, 1907, 287) are also from aquatic deposits. The former comes from the bed of the river Aar ; the latter from in or near the Lake of Thoune. We have abundant evidence for water-deposits both in pre-Roman (Torbrügge, 1972) and Romano-Celtic contexts. One has only to recall the British well-finds, some of which are undoubtedly of a ritual nature (Ross, 1968) ; the Llyn Fawr (Savory, 1976, 46-47) and Llyn Cerrig Bach (Fox, 1946) lacustrine hoards, the Lake Neuchâtel deposit (Vouga, 1923) and the finds from the Source of the Seine (Corot, 1927-32, 9-10) and from Bath (Cunliffe, 1969).

The occurrence of wheel-symbols, and of axe-models bearing dedications to Jupiter, as water-offerings (AX1, 8), may seem curious. If wheel-models, by the Roman period, were simply vague good-luck talismans (a theory perhaps belied by the Augst example which is inscribed), without an association with a particular divinity, then the miniatures may have been cast into water in order to appease a local water-spirit. However, this cannot explain the specifically-dedicated axe-models. In my opinion, there is a chthonic aspect to the cult of the Celtic Sky-God (Chapter VI). This is evidenced by the wheel-symbols on the Alsace tombstones, by the occurrence of wheel-symbols in graves, and by the association of wheels with chthonic beasts such as the ram-headed snake on the Lypiatt Park altar (BB13), and on the Gundestrup Cauldron (Olmsted, 1976 ; 1979, Pl. C). In addition, as will be seen below (Chapter VI), there is a link between the Mothers and the Celto-Roman Jupiter, and there is an association between Mother-Goddesses, water and chthonicism. Finally, if one does regard water-cults as chthonic (presumably the idea is that springs emanate from underground and that rain soaks into the earth) then there is plenty of evidence for chthonicism associated with Romano-Celtic sky-symbolism (Chapter VI).

Association of Models with Divinities (other than the Sky-God)

The direct association of models, notably wheels, with sky-symbolism and therefore with the Gallo-Roman Jupiter himself; is discussed below.

For the present, I wish to consider the evidence of various other divinities in relation to models. First, it should be said that caution should be employed in using the term 'association'. Models may occur in shrines or other contexts where there are representations of certain deities. However, there need be no special significance since Celtic and Roman shrines, whether dedicated to particular beings or not, frequently housed images of more than one cult. A hoard, on the other hand, may be more enlightening. Even so, in the case of the Felmingham Hall deposit, already noted (AB5), we may have a cache of items originally from a temple-context and so the same criteria of judgement may apply. It is important to bear this in mind when assessing the religious importance of cult-associations.

Model objects (including wheels) may have direct or indirect links with oriental, classical or Romano-Celtic divinities. Taking eastern connections first, the most important evidence must be that pertaining to the Rhineland multi-model grave-groups containing agricultural, symbolic and other models (Rottländer, 1973-4, 143-152). These groups are anomalous in the wide range of consistently recurring models — pitchforks, axes, adzes, ladders, sickles and many others — and of the presence, in the majority of the graves, of reptile and amphibian figurines — lizards, snakes and batrachians. For some time the presence both of agricultural implements and of the figurines of these beasts has led to their interpretation as emblems of an eastern mystery-cult. In the past they have been termed by German scholars 'Mithrassymbole' (Behrens, 1939, 56-59), but this is now seen to be almost certainly incorrect and, in any case, would be too simplistic an interpretation (Manning, 1966, 50-59). It is probably sensible to be looking, in this Rhineland context, for a soldier's god, and the Thraco-Phrygian divinity Sabazius appears to be a likely candidate for the worshippers offering symbols in Rhine-frontier graves. The presence, among German military installations, of votive bronze hands dedicated to Sabazius (for example Ristow, 1975, pl. 56) which also bear these particular symbols, does suggest cult-associations between this deity and the German sepulchral models. A further point is the occasional presence in the grave-groups, of wheel-models; these are exclusive of wheels belonging to model carts, for instance those from Rodenkirchen (Rottländer, 1973-4, 143-152). The inclusion of such models introduces a sky or sun element into the cult. Sabazius is generally interpreted as being a Lord of Heaven, commonly identified with Dionysus. His cult, like the other mysteries, offered, to those who had successfully undergone the initiation-process (Diodorus Siculus, IV, 4, 1), a happy sojourn in the afterlife and a personal communion with the god. He was considered by his devotees to have a special regard for agriculture (Manning, 1966, 52). Sabazius was the son of Persephone (Diodorus, *ibid*.) and thus the symbolic items in the grave-groups, like keys and balance-beams, fit in with this cult — the keys, perhaps, being those of the Kingdom of Heaven, and the scales representing the weighing of the soul in judgement. Sabazius, however, was sometimes identified with a Sky/Light deity. Not only do the wheel-models on some of the votive bronze hands, like that from Aquileia (Blinkenberg, 1904, 71), bear this out, but a model hand from Vado-Sabatia bears a Greek dedication to Zeus Sabazius, offered by a soldier (*ibid*., 69). A lost dedication from the Trieste area of North Italy (Pascal, 1964, 59 ; Unione Accademica Nazionale, 1935) bore evidence of an equation between Sabazius and Jupiter.

Other evidence of a possible (?) association between models and oriental cults is connected with the double-axe (see Catalogue AX). Apart from this symbol's very early association with Minoan Culture and with Zeus as a Sky-God, it is linked, in the Roman period, with a number of oriental mystery-cults incorporating celestial symbolism, including that of the Danubian Riders (Tudor, 1976) and, more importantly, Dolichenus, equated in the Roman era with the Roman Sky-God (Merlat, 1960 ; Speidel, 1978). The miniature double-axe representations from, for instance, Trier (AX10, 11), Richborough (AX18) and elsewhere, may be connected with this cult. However, we may go further and draw an inference about single-edged axes. At Trier (AX10) and at other German sites were found brooches incorporating both single and double-axes. More significant is the occurrence at Mainz of a Jupiter Dolichenus figure wearing a conical helmet or hat and carrying in his hand a model of a single-edged rather than a double-axe (Mainz Mittelrheinisches Landesmuseum). It is possible that some axe-models, whether single or double-edged, may have some relevance to a Jupiter Dolichenus cult. Finally, in looking at oriental cult-symbolism one should recall the occurrence, in the Felmingham Hall hoard (AB5 ; Pl. LXII, Fig. 24), of a wheel accompanied by the radiate head of a possible Jupiter Helioserapis.

We may now look at the evidence for an association between classical and Romano-Celtic cults and models. I shall not divide the evidence into classical and Romano-Celtic components since, as will be seen below (Chapters VII, VIII), *interpretatio romana* and *interpretatio celtica* frequently make it impossible to dissociate Roman from Celtic deities and representations. As regards a connection between models and divinities with Roman names, the most unequivocal evidence is that of the Swiss models (see above). There is other evidence to link model axes with a Jupiter-cult (see below). The other deities named on the Swiss axes (AX1) could, likewise, be concerned with Jupiter since Jupiter-Giant columns frequently portray these divinities. There is evidence linking wheel and club-motifs, the club normally being associated with the demi-god Hercules. The Thérouanne gold chain with its wheel-pendant is associated with a miniature club-pendant hanging from the same chain (A74); the Willingham Fen (C6) and Corbridge (C10) wheel-bearing deities are associated with clubs (although the former example could perhaps be interpreted as a stylized thunderbolt). If the seeming association between the Wheel-God and Hercules is meaningful, then we either have a syncretism and confusion between the elements of two deities or else a conflation of concepts, since Hercules was the natural son of the Roman Sky-Father. If that is so it is interesting that Celtic (wheel) and classical (club) motifs are compatible enough to appear together, and in the case of the Willingham club-thunderbolt the ambiguity may be deliberate.

The Celtic Mother-Goddesses or *Deae Matres* have a connection with certain models. Of the group of axe-models found in the vicinity of Allmendingen (AX1) two are dedicated to the Mothers. This establishes at least a general link between the *Matres* and axe-models. The Romano-Celtic temple-precinct of Springhead in Kent produced a lead axe-model, and also fragments of pipe-clay 'Venus' figurines. If, as I think likely (Green, 1976), these clay figures and those of *Deae Nutrices* incorporate elements of the Great Mother-cult of the Celts, then this latter may be an instance of axe and *Matres* association. It is of interest that here the axe was of lead; this suggests that the possible identification of lead with chthonicism and of chthonicism with water, healing and Mother-Goddesses, already alluded to, finds expression at this therapeutic cult-site. The Mothers appear in association with wheel-models in the Durham ritual cache from Backworth (AB1). Two dedications are present here – one to the *Deae Matres*, inscribed on the handle of the *patera* containing the hoard, and another on a gold ring inscribed to the *Matres Coccae*. The term *Coccae* may mean 'red'. If there is a genuine association between the Wheel-God cult as evidenced by this hoard, *Coccae* may refer to the red-gold of the sun and the wheel-pendants in the deposit; alternatively, one could interpret the term as meaning the red of blood and slaughter. We know that on Rhineland Jupiter-columns the Sky-God is depicted as a warrior representing light and good. We also know (see Chapter VI) that there was a Celtic association between Jupiter and Mars. There is plenty of other evidence too for the association of Mothers and wheel-signs. At Langres a wheel-symbol occurs at the same site as a dedication to the goddesses (A80). The two elements occur in association on two Mother-Goddess carvings from the Cotswolds (Green, 1976, 18). The Gundestrup Bowl from Jutland (C1), probably a 1st Century B.C. cult-vessel depicting Celtic mythological scenes (Hatt, 1965, 80-125 ; Olmsted, 1976, 95ff.), portrays a deity associated with a wheel, and on another plate a female (who may be a Mother-Goddess) flanked by two stylized wheels. The pipe-clay 'Venus' figures from Gaul bearing sun-symbols (see Chapter V and Catalogue C) may also be relevant, as may be the possibly meaningful association between pipe-clay figures of 'Venus' and 'Dea Nutrix' with a wheel-brooch at Nor'nour on Scilly (AB19). One final point is that both the pipe-clay figures (for example at Springhead [Green, 1976, 228]) and the *Deae Matres* (for example at Bath [Green, 1976, 186]) were connected with water and thermal springs. The wheels tossed into Gaulish streams could have relevance in this context. The chthonic aspect of wheel-models, evidenced by grave-finds and water-finds, linked perhaps with the representations on the Alsace tombstones, could mean that a nameless divinity is involved. One should remember, in this respect, that axes too are associated with burials and with water.

We have already noted other deity-associations in connection with intrinsic significance of models, and have alluded to Sucellus, horses and horsemen. Further identifications may be noted, for example, with the Hounslow material (AB6 ; Pl. LXIII, Fig. 25) comprising a wheel-model and three boar-figurines. It is interesting that the boar occurs with wheel-symbolism on one of the Netherby sculptures (BB18), depicting a local *Genius* holding a wheel over an altar, in company with a tree and a boar. The boar and wheel again appear together on the Farley Heath sceptre-binding (C7 ; Pl. LXXXII). Finally, in looking at deity-association, we should recall the Felmingham Hall material (AB5 ; Pl. LXII, Fig. 24), a cosmopolitan group incorporating Celtic, classical and oriental elements. The association of a dancing *Lar* with a wheel-model and other possible representations of Jupiter in some form is not easy to interpret, but one thing of interest in this deposit is the connection between the wheel and two bronze raven-figurines. These birds may be portrayed on the Farley Heath binding ; they are also common associates of Sucellus on the Continent (Krappe, 1936, 236-246), and we know (Chapters V, VI) that the Celtic Jupiter and Sucellus have a close connection ; ravens also appear in later Bronze Age prehistoric Urnfield contexts possibly associated with solar symbolism (Ross, 1967, 242).

Models and Sky-Symbolism

Although both in the descriptive analysis (Chapter II) and elsewhere in the present section allusions have been made to the sky-symbolism of various models, it is, in my opinion, necessary to consider in conclusion what definite and unequivocal evidence exists for an association between certain miniature objects and a celestial cult. The most obvious group of models to which such an attribution must apply is wheel-models. The wheel is the only category of model apparently with a specific connection with a known and identifiable deity, a Romano-Celtic Sky-God, a provincial version of the classical Jupiter (Green, 1979a, 345-368). There is definite evidence for a divine representation accompanied by a wheel in Romano-Celtic iconography (Gaidoz, 1884, 7-37 ; Green, 1979a). Thus it is reasonable to suppose that wheel-pendants, brooches and true wheel-models could have a link with the cult of the Wheel-God. In this respect, both British and continental distribution-patterns of wheel-models must be taken into account (Pls. XIX-XXIII). One of the two British areas of concentration − Hadrian's Wall − coincides with other iconography pertaining to the cult. On the Continent, it is eastern and central Gaul and the Rhineland which have produced the largest number both of wheel-models and of stone representations, though there are distinct differences in concentration (Pls. XIX-XXVII). The use of a wheel as an attribute for a sky-divinity need not be discussed in detail here. It is a natural and long-standing symbol of the sun embodying, at one and the same time, elements of revolution through the sky, rotation, the sun's rays, and the nimbus surrounding them. The sun, in the ancient world (Bailey, 1932, 260), was envisaged as ever-revolving ; in the day, it was thought to traverse and fertilize earth and, at night, to visit the lower regions. In this connection one should recall the evocative association at the Lardiers Romano-Celtic shrine (A180, 181) where wheel-model, swastika-brooch and 'sun-discs' are recorded. De Villefosse's view (1881, 10) is that wheels represented apotropaic devices in Gaulish symbolism precisely because of the image of light/sun versus darkness/evil. Of interest here is that the association of the wheel with the Gallo-Roman Jupiter means that, in Celtic terms, he was the god of both sky and sun (Toutain, 1920, 192ff.). This point has to be emphasized since sun and sky were regarded as different elements and certainly were distinct from each other in the Graeco-Roman world where Zeus (Jupiter) was the celestial divinity and Helios (and later Apollo) was the solar god. One or two wheel-models themselves show a direct connection with Jupiter of which the most important is the lead wheel from Plessis Barbuise (A73) containing a figure of a being with sceptre and thunderbolt.

Certain associations between the Celtic sky-god and wheel-motifs must also be examined. The Wheel-God from Le Châtelet (C2 ; Pl. LXXIX, Fig. 57) is one of the very few bronze figurines to portray the Gallo-Roman deity. Nearby to the findspot of this statuette, at Grignon (A76) a number of wheel-models are recorded. In Britain, at Icklingham in Suffolk (Green, 1975b) the wing of a bronze eagle (the emblem of Jupiter) was found at the same site as a bronze wheel-model fragment (AB8) and a wheel-shaped brooch (AB27). At Felmingham Hall (AB5) a wheel was associated (Pl. LXII, Fig. 24) with a hollow bearded bronze mask which may well represent Jupiter. The Le Châtelet bronze figure (C2) is further connected with wheel-model symbolism in the presence of 'S'-symbols, which also recur on the Grand-Jailly wheel-model (A101) along with rosette-decoration on the nave (it is interesting that certain wheels themselves are roseate in appearance. The meaning of the wheel and 'S' motifs, which occur also on the small pot painted with alternating wheel and 'S' symbols from Silchester (C54) is obscure. Thevenot (1968, 22) would like to see the nine 'S' shapes attached to the ring on the Le Châtelet figure as 'spare' lightning-flashes ; elsewhere I have suggested that the symbol could possess links with swastika-motifs or that it could even have more enigmatic and obscure associations with the stylized aquatic bird-shapes of Urnfield/Hallstatt sky-sun imagery.

There are other, but perhaps less direct, connections between wheel-models and celestial iconography. The fact that swastika and wheel-symbols occur in close distributional proximity on the Continent – the Rhineland – is of interest. At Saalburg and at Zugmantel, swastika-brooches appear to be favoured, rather than the more conventional wheel-shape itself; The solar shape of a swastika-sign is not in question (see Chapter VI) and, in a Gallo-Roman context, one has only to look at the south-west group of French sites yielding altars, presumably dedicated to Jupiter, and decorated with wheels and with swastikas (see Chapters IV, VI), to believe in an intrinsic association. The star-sign in the Cologne grave-group (A13) is interesting in that it may have a solar significance similar to that of wheels and swastikas, but it could instead embody the night-heavens. In this connection the association between wheel-models and crescents should be noted. At Dolaucothi (AB4), Newstead (AB12) and on one Backworth example (AB1), we find chains of precious metal attached to which are wheel-pendants and minute *lunulae*. At Starigrad (A204) bronze bracelets bear wheel and crescent respectively. At Rembrechts, Kr. Ravensburg (Baden-Württemberg) a silver chain bears a crescent alone in place of the more usual wheel-symbol (Böhme, 1974). It seems reasonable to interpret these ornaments as representative of the sun and the moon (or light-symbols of night and day). The Balèsmes wheel-pendant (A102) from Gaul is of particular interest in that it bears not only a crescent soldered onto the spokes but has, in addition, a double-axe motif. If the double-axe may be correctly interpreted as a thunderbolt-sign, then it could be that three different aspects of sky-symbolism — sun, moon and storm-energy — are here portrayed.

Apart from wheel-models themselves, other miniatures have direct links with the Gallo-Roman Sky-God. The two Swiss axe-models, from Allmendingen (AX1) and Solothurn (AX8) bear inscribed dedications to Jupiter. The miniature thunderbolts found near a spring (note the apparent water-connection again) at St. Tau (Drioux, 1934, 40) are probably connected also with a Jupiter-cult. The miniature bronze altar to Jupiter from an unprovenanced French locality (Babelon & Blanchet, 1895, 14, no. 31) has specific Celtic symbolism in the association of a thunderbolt with two snake-limbed creatures. Another miniature altar, this time in stone, from Périgueux (St-Germain-en-Laye, Acc. no. 77126) is also dedicated to Jupiter.

One particular class of models, apart from wheels, may have a consistent and possibly necessary connection with a sky-cult; namely the very large group of axes. There are one or two intrinsic associations which deserve special notice; One is the Woodeaton axe-model (AB20) with its incised swastika-symbol (Green, 1979a, fig. 20), which is all the more interesting when seen in the context of other finds from the temple-site, particularly the six bronze eagles (see Chapter VII). The eagle was a constant companion of the classical Sky-God, and its presence here together with at least four axe-models (one with a swastika and another with a ligatured 'X' sign and yet a third with a ring-and-dot symbols) may be significant. I have argued above that both these signs may possess solar symbolism and certainly ring-and-dot and 'X' decoration appear on continental swastika-brooches, and occur also on model axes in Britain, Gaul and the Rhineland (see AX catalogue). Another point concerning axe-models is the association between that symbol and oriental sky-cults (alluded to above). The eastern cult of the god Sabazius is of relevance here ; Jupiter was sometimes equated with him. If the German grave-finds do refer to this cult then the association of wheels, a star-symbol and numerous axes and other models (sometimes bearing ring-and-dot or 'X' patterns [A12-13]) could be significant in terms of sky-motifs.

In discussing a possible link between axe-models and a sky-cult, the prehistoric material must not be forgotten. Of particular note is the Dürnnberg association, of Iron Age date, between wheel and axe-models in a young woman's grave (Hallen Keltenmuseum). Greek sky-cults may well have been represented by axe-miniatures. They certainly occur on Hellenic sites and are known as pendants from at least the 5th Century B.C. (Minns, 1913, 236-239). The model bronze axes from the early oracular sites at Olympia and Dodona – as early as the 13th and 12th Centuries B.C. – were probably offered by devotees of Zeus (see above). The tomb at Narce in Faliscan Italy, with its miniature diorite axe-pendant attached to a blue vitreous paste bead necklace (Blinkenberg, 1911, 29, fig. 6) could be that of a sky-god worshipper. The double-axe is perhaps of even greater significance for double-axes were of extreme antiquity in the pre-classical Greek world of southern Europe (Cook, 1925, 543-559 ; Hawkes, 1937, 145, 149, fig. 3 ; Higgins, 1974, 142) and may well have been connected very early with a sky-cult. The original interpretation of the double-edged weapon (Cook, *op. cit*.) would seem to involve either or both of two ideas – the image of an implement cutting both ways and perhaps symbolizing Sky and Earth/Underworld, or the image of a thunderbolt. The double-axe appears as a model and in iconography in the Roman world. The latter representations are generally concerned, in western Europe, with Dolichenus (Merlat, 1960 ; Speidel, 1978) but less esoteric and mysterious cults seem also to have been identified with this symbol. The model clay double-axe from Trier (AX11) comes from a Romano-Celtic temple-precinct ; the double-axe-headed pin from Richborough (AX18) comes from a fort-site which has produced no oriental material. Most interesting, for an alleged association between Romano-Celtic sky-symbolism and double-axe, is the Balèsmes wheel-pendant (A102) with its applied double-axe. Brooches from, for example Trier (AX10) and Stockstadt (AX9), with double and single-edged axe-motifs demonstrate direct associations between the two types of implement. An indirect, but nonetheless potentially relevant piece of evidence, comes from Cirencester, Glos. (Phillips, 1976a) ; this is a possible Jupiter-column fragment of which we possess part of the quadrangular base and a magnificent Corinthian capital (which might come from the same monument). The capital bears images of four humanoid divinities emerging from a foliate surround. One of these figures holds a large double-axe (see Chapter VI).

Conclusion

This chapter has necessarily dealt with extremely tenuous evidence and ambiguous data ; interpretation must be equally tentative. Models are not as evocative as iconography ; iconography is itself enigmatic without literature or, at any rate, epigraphy (Piggott, 1968b, 22-26). What I have attempted to do is, first, to establish model objects definitively as a class of ritual material in the Romano-Celtic world ; second, to endeavour to isolate a general interpretation and function based, where necessary, on parallels sometimes far removed from the Roman era in space and time ; third, to assess the importance of wheel-models and related miniature items to a Celtic sky-religion ; fourth, to look at associations and intrinsic symbolism to see if any common ground may be established between models of different types ; fifth, to examine the seemingly consistent connections between wheel and axe-symbolism. I must once again stress the insubstantial and ephemeral nature of any interpretative investigation using this evidence. Model axes and wheels may simply be good-luck emblems or amulets. Even if this is so, it appears possible, to some extent, to catch a glimpse into the origins of their talismanic significance and to gain some insight from them as to the rôle of a sky-deity in the Romano-Celtic world.

Appendix to Chapter Three

Since this work was completed, the excavation-report of a highly significant site in France has been published, and brief mention should be made of certain features relevant to the present study. The site is the shrine at Villeneuve-au-Châtelot (Aube) (Piette, 1981, 367-375). Here a coin-hoard found in 1973, dating to the beginning of the Roman Empire, contained Roman and Gaulish coins and, in addition, thirty-two silver wheel-models. The presence of structures is also attested (*ibid.*, 369-370). A number of other miniature wheels is recorded from the site, including bronze examples and very large quantities of lead models, some strung together in the manner of, for example, the Lavoie (Meuse) lead wheels (*ibid.*, 372).

CHAPTER IV

Descriptive Analysis of Stone Monuments relating to Wheel-Symbolism in Roman Gaul, the Rhineland and Britain

INTRODUCTION (¹)

There are almost two hundred stone monuments in Gaul, the Rhineland and Britain which are associated with Romano-Celtic wheel-symbolism (Catalogue B ; Pls. I-XVIII ; LXV-LXXVI). The majority of such carvings are overtly linked with the cult of a Celtic divinity who appears, during the Roman period, to have been equated with the classical Sky-Father, Zeus-Jupiter. The sixth chapter is concerned with the interpretative significance of this composite divinity represented both in stone sculpture and in miscellaneous (non-miniature) items. The present purpose is to present the evidence for stone representations, to suggest a workable classification-scheme, and to examine descriptive elements, distribution and chronology.

Stone sculpture, whether in the form of altars, representations in the round, or reliefs, has a purpose distinct from that of the model items investigated in Chapters II and III. For the most part stonework would appear to have been the result of corporate activity and worship. Although some of the southern Gaulish altars (for example B21) are extremely small, even these need not have been personal possessions. At any rate the majority of stone items were not portable in the accepted sense. They were not jewellery objects, amulets, or talismans, but were probably intended to be positioned in particular localities as focal points of devotion. Unlike the models there is no question as to their distinctively

---

(1) Nos. in text prefixed by 'B' refer to Continental Stone catalogue ; nos. prefixed by 'BB' refer to British Stone Catalogue. Main bibliographical references to sites and finds are in the catalogues.

and unequivocally ritual character. It is possible to argue that the religious significance, in the case of miniatures, of the wheel-sign, could have been all but forgotten and replaced by a simple and general good-luck symbolism by the time of the Roman period. When present on altars, for instance, wheels and swastikas may be said to have a positive, active and meaningful function. The particular interest in stone sculpture associated with wheels or swastikas is precisely that it is repeatedly connected with the worship of one known and identifiable Romano-Celtic divinity. The swastika or wheel-sign does occur elsewhere, on funerary monuments, with no indication as to deity, and is occasionally linked with other gods or divine personifications – such as Genii, or goddesses, such as Minerva. However, a great many monuments associate the symbol of the wheel with an anthropomorphic image or with an epigraphic dedication which relates the motif to a version of Jupiter.

Typological Classification [2]

Any form of necessarily unnatural classification-scheme is fraught with problems, both in terms of complication versus over-simplification, and because monuments cannot always be tidily grouped into any one category. The following attempt has no pretensions to genuine significance in any kind of ritual sense. All it seeks to do is to isolate and distinguish various types of representation associated with wheel and/or swastika symbols. The division has been done on the basis of content rather than physical shape or type. It has been the intention of the writer to divide the monuments very broadly into two groups each with a number of sub-divisions. Thus the classification or typology may be used in as little or as much detail as required.

My two main typological divisions comprise : (I) Monuments associated with an anthropomorphic image and (II) Monuments without such imagery and with or without epigraphic dedications.

I.   Monuments bearing anthropomorphic representations
Ia.   Wheel-God
        Nos. : B3 ; B4 ; B6 ; B15a ; B17 ; B35 ; B54 ; B67 ; B81 ; B86 ; B88 ; B90 ; B107 ; B120 ; B130 ; B144 ; B145 ; B149 ; B150 ; B153 ; B158 ; B164 ; BB3 ; BB8 ; BB16 ; BB17 ; BB18.

[2] Numbers refer to Stonework Catalogue.

Ib.		Jupiter-Giant manifestations
Ibi.		Wheel-God with giant

Nos.: B11 ; B18 ; B19 ; B24 ; B34 ; B36 ; B39 ; B41 ; B71 ; B72 ; B75 ; B77 ; B87 ; B89 ; B102 ; B114 ; B143 ; B151 ; B160 ; B165.

Ibii.   Wheel-God with small humanoid figure

Nos.: B5 ; B52 ; B74 ; B79 ; B91 ; B116 ; B118 ; B123 ; B124 ; B128.

Ic.   Wheel associated with other representations

Nos.: B1 ; B7 ; B9 ; B10 ; B45 ; B61 ; B78 ; B80 ; B103 ; B121 ; B125 ; B146 ; B150 ; B157 ; B158 ; B169 ; BB6 ; BB7 ; BB9 ; BB10.

II.   Non-anthropomorphic representations

IIa.   Funerary monuments

Nos.: B8 ; B15 ; B16 ; B23 ; B31 ; B42 ; B43 ; B44 ; B47 ; B50 ; B51 ; B56 ; B57 ; B63 ; B64 ; B69 ; B104 ; B115 ; B119 ; B126 ; B131 ; B132 ; B134 ; B135 ; B136 ; B137 ; B138 ; B139 ; B140 ; B141 ; B142 ; B156 ; B167 ; BB19 ; BB21.

IIb.   Altars, etc.

IIbi.   Epigraphic

Nos.: B2 ; B21 ; B25 ; B26 ; B29 ; B30 ; B39a ; B62 ; B66 ; B70 ; B76 ; B83 ; B85 ; B92 ; B95 ; B101 ; B106 ; B113 ; B129 ; B152 ; B166 ; BB2 ; BB4 ; BB5 ; BB11 ; BB12 ; BB15 ; BB19 ; BB20 ; BB22.

IIbii.   Anepigraphic

Nos.: B12 ; B13 ; B14 ; B28 ; B33 ; B40 ; B46 ; B49 ; B53 ; B55 ; B60 ; B70 ; B73 ; B82 ; B93 ; B99 ; B100 ; B105 ; B108 ; B109 ; B110 ; B111 ; B112 ; B117 ; B122 ; B127 ; B147 ; B148 ; B154 ; B155 ; B159 ; B161 ; B163 ; BB1 ; BB13 ; BB14.

DESCRIPTIVE ANALYSIS

I. *Monuments bearing Anthropomorphic Representations*

Ia. *Wheel-God*

This group comprises representations of the Wheel-God alone either seated or standing upright, occasionally with a goddess (who may be a form of Juno), but without any other imagery such as monsters. The group falls into two types. The first comprises portrayals of Jupiter seated on a throne, alone or with his consort, Juno. I have recorded four of these, from Alise-Sainte-Reine (B3) ; Alzey (B4 ; Pl. LXV, Fig. 30) ; Naix (B88) ; and Tongres (B150). Of these the first three consist of the god seated alone ; on the Tongres example (B150) he is accompanied by Juno. On B3 Jupiter is seated on a throne with high sides or arms, decorated each side with four-spoked wheels. The god holds a globe in his right hand ; he is draped ; an overlarge eagle accompanies him. The content of the piece is classical, the style native and fairly unsophisticated. The Alzey carving (B4 ; Pl. LXV, Fig. 30) is similar ; the deity is shown half-draped and is more classical in style than the Alesia carving (B3). Decorating the left side of the throne is a clearly-defined eight-spoked wheel. To the god's right is an eagle. B88 differs from the first two in the addition of two *cornuacopiae* below a six-spoked wheel which is situated exactly at the height of the left hand. B150, from Tongres, depicts the divine couple seated side by side on a throne or dais. Jupiter is semi-draped, Juno is clad in a long robe and a cloak. The god bears a thunderbolt in his right hand and a possible sceptre in his left. The goddess bears a wheel in her left hand clasped against her chest. An eagle on a globe and a peacock are carved on the rear surface of the throne.

There are similarities in all four pieces. In each of the first three the wheel-symbol decorates the sides of the chair. The Alesia example stands out as having both sides so ornamented. The Naix stone (B88) bears *cornuacopiae* in addition. What is interesting is that the wheels have differing numbers of spokes in each of these three instances – four, six and eight. Both the Alesia and Alzey pieces have Jupiter's eagle accompanying the god. Apart from the presence of the wheel the elements on these carvings would appear to represent entirely classical themes. One discordant note which should be stressed is the presence of the *cornuacopiae* at Naix (B88). This is of interest since, though this attribute is common both with certain classical and with many Celtic divinities, it is not a symbol generally associated either with Jupiter or his Celtic counterpart. However, it is not unique. As shall be seen below, the two Wheel-Gods/Genii from Netherby (BB17 ; BB18 ; Pl. LXXV, Fig. 51) also bear this emblem of prosperity (though this is more reasonable within the context of the Genius or Bonus Eventus type). The Tongres carving (B150), now lost and known only from a drawing, is of exceptional interest in that it is Juno rather than Jupiter who carries the wheel ; the god himself is occupied with thunderbolt and sceptre. Eagle and peacock are both present. The only Celtic feature is the wheel. Juno with this emblem is extremely rare ; she nearly always herself appears in classical guise even if she accompanies the Wheel-God. There is, however, other evidence for this goddess associated with the Celtic symbol, as is discussed below. It is noteworthy that on this particular carving it appears as if as many emblems or attributes as possible are portrayed. The Roman Sky-God accessories of thunderbolt, sceptre, eagle and peacock are all present here.

The second type comprises 'Viergöttersteine' (stone blocks carved on all four sides with figures of divinities). A number of these represent the Wheel-God. It is almost certain that these quadrangular steles are to be interpreted as forming an integral part of 'Jupitergigantensäulen'. However, for the purposes of Wheel-God representation, it is perfectly valid to classify them in a group apart from, for instance, the horseman-group surmounting the Corinthian capitals of such pillars. 'Viergöttersteine' showing a Wheel-God are recorded from Auberive (B6 ; Pl. II, Fig. 3) ; Dunzweiler (B35 ; Pl. XVII, Fig. 38) ; Glanmünchweiler (B54) ; Niederwürzbach (B90 ; Pl. XVII, Fig. 40) ; Speyer (B145) and Theley, Trier (B149 ; Pl. XVII, Fig. 39). At Dunsweiler a nude figure with a sceptre in his right hand carries a wheel in his left. The Glanmünchweiler stone shows a similar, beardless, figure, again with a wheel in his left hand. The Speyer sculpture portrays another young, beardless, god resting his left hand on a probable sceptre-shaft, and holding aloft a four-spoked wheel in his right hand. At Trier a youthful Jupiter wears a chlamys and an oak-leaved crown, and probably carried a sceptre in his right hand. He bears a six-spoked wheel in his left hand ; there is a small bird, perhaps an eagle, at his feet. The Auberive piece (B6 ; Pl. II, Fig. 3) is curious ; it is debatable whether one should include it at all, although Drioux (1929, 357) seems to think it valid to accept it as a probable rendering of the Wheel-God. It is of interest in that the divinity portrayed wears a long beard and a Gaulish, sleeved, belted tunic. He clasps an unspoked, solid circular object in both hands against his torso. The Gallic garb gives the deity a decidedly Celtic aspect. The circular item is too small to be a shield, and, in any case, is not held correctly for such an object. Likewise it is too large for a *patera* and, once again, is incorrectly positioned. The position and the way it is clasped against the body immediately calls to mind the Tongres relief (B150), where an unequivocal wheel is carried in just such an attitude by Juno. On the Niederwürzbach stone (B90 ; Pl. XVII,

Fig. 40) Jupiter carries a thunderbolt in the right hand and a four-spoked wheel in his left, the hand being threaded through the spokes (in just the same way as some Jupiter-horseman carvings, for example that from Butterstadt [B19 ; Pl. LXV, Fig. 29]). The interest of this particular carving lies in the wheel itself ; two of the spokes are distinctly 'S'-shaped. It should be recalled that there is direct evidence for a specific significance attached to the 'S' shape in connection with wheel-symbolism. The Le Châtelet Wheel-God (Pl. LXXIX, Fig. 57) bears nine 'S'-shaped symbols. The Grand-Jailly wheel-model (see Catalogue A) has applied 'S's ; the wheel-motifs on the Silchester pot are interspersed with 'S'-symbols.

The third type within this group comprises standing statues of the Wheel-God. They occur at Bordeaux (B15a) ; the Meuse area (B81) ; Rully (B120) and at Séguret near Vaison (B144 ; Pls. X, LXVI). The Meuse and Rully examples are only very small fragments, in each case comprising a hand clasping a wheel. The Meuse one has four spokes, the other an indistinguishable number. These two fragments may be part of a Wheel-God representation of this type, but they may equally form part of a Jupiter-horseman column-group ; it is impossible to be certain one way or the other. The Bordeaux (B15a) and Séguret (B144) stones each represent a standing figure of Jupiter. The first comprises a god, turning towards the left, wearing a chlamys. His right arm encircles a thunderbolt ; in his left hand is a seven or eight-spoked wheel (it is interesting that the way in which the attribute is carved makes it impossible to tell the number of spokes ; this could either suggest that it may not have had much importance, or, alternatively, that secrecy was the objective). The deity wears his hair and beard long. This piece portrays the divinity in civilian guise. The Séguret example, however, shows the Wheel-God in the garb of a Roman general or even the emperor. He is entirely Roman in style, with a thunderbolt in his left hand and an eagle, naturalistically feathered, at his feet. The accompanying oak-tree is an emblem of the classical Jupiter, but the snake twined round it is a curious feature which we shall meet again below. The most unroman characteristic is a large, well-carved, ten-spoked wheel standing vertically against the god's right leg, steadied by his hand (Pl. LXVI).

Nearly all other depictions of the Wheel-God in this main group take the form of reliefs. They may very roughly be divided into classically or Celtically-styled iconography. Several of the sculptures are carved on altars. In this category are included the stones from Laudun (B67 ; Pl. IV, Fig. 5), the Pyrenees (B107), Trier (B153) and Vaison (B158). On the

Laudun altar (Pl. IV, Fig. 5) a draped god with sceptre in his left hand occupies the main surface ; on the lateral faces are an eagle (on the right) and a five-spoked wheel (on the left). The Pyrenees carving (rare in the large group of Pyrenean altars with wheel-symbolism, in having a humanoid portrayal as well) consists of the bust of a divinity associated with a swastika underneath. The Vaison altar is a large and magnificent specimen with a relief of Jupiter and Juno standing side by side on a dais. Jupiter (as in the Séguret statue from nearby) wears Roman military costume. He bears a thunderbolt in his right hand and a wheel by his left side supported by his hand (again very similar to the Séguret example). He has an eagle by his feet ; Juno is accompanied by her peacock and carries a *patera*. As in the case of the Séguret statue, a snake is also present, this time situated beneath the wheel. This positioning could be extremely significant if one relates it to the 'Jupitergigantensäulen' horseman groups (see below). Another image of a god associated with wheel-sign and snake comes from Bremevaque (B17 ; Pl. VII, Fig. 14). The god is crudely portrayed as a virtually two-dimensional figure, nude apart from a possible helmet, with a spear in his right hand and a sinuous serpent-like object pouring vertically from his crooked left elbow. Above the figure is a pot ; on the altar-base is a large swastika. Essentially similar is a relief of a naked and ithyphallic divinity from Vienne, Isère (B164) who is accompanied by a wheel with ten spokes and a possible bird (impossible to distinguish which species). The other reliefs in this section form a somewhat heterogeneous group. The small stone (?) bronze-mould from Caerleon (BB3) with crudely-represented male figure is of interest in that the associated wheel-sign is multiple − one is shown at the end of each arm, another is by the left foot. An indeterminate rectangular object is positioned by the right foot. Another multi-wheeled and enigmatic item takes the form of an oblong plaque from Churcham (BB8), portraying the image of a male deity wearing a long tunic. The unequivocally Celtic nature of this being manifests itself in the enormous head and traces of possible horns. In each hand the figure grasps a tri-lobed object. At each of the lower angles of the plaque is a four-spoked wheel. The trilobate objects are curious ; it is possible that they too are stylized wheel-symbols. On some model wheels and on stonework, the wheel-shape is blurred into a floreate, petalled motif ; this is what we may have here. It is strange, if that is the case, however, that on one and the same representation one should find two totally different methods of wheel-depiction (but a similar phenomenon may be seen on the Gundestrup Bowl [C1]). Horns and over-emphasis of the head are both well-known Celtic artistic phenomena, particularly in parts of Britain, and will be discussed in the context of religious interpretation (Chapter VI). The Maryport relief (BB16) is a doubtful inclusion. It comprises an oblong stone set into the base of an octagonal column, with a dedication to Jupiter Optimus Maximus. On the stone a horseman is portrayed, associated with a rosette or wheel-shape. The horseman-image and the octagonal column-base both recall features on Jupiter-Giant pillars, but there is no evidence of a snake-limbed or other monster. Jupiter as a horseman, without the corresponding 'anguipède' is, as far as I know, unique. The two British reliefs from Netherby (BB17 ; BB18 ; Pl. LXXV, Fig. 51) are virtually identical. They are very curious in that the wheel-sign is not associated with a Jupiter-like Wheel-God at all, but instead with a Genius or Bonus Eventus art-form. In both cases the being holds a *cornucopiae* in the left hand, and in the right hand of each is a wheel over an altar. BB18 has additional iconographical features in the presence of a boar standing in front of a tree (this combination occurs also on certain Celtic coinage [Nash, personal communication]). Although it is impossible to tell what kind of tree is represented, the boar makes it at least likely that an oak could be intended. Boars are particularly partial to beech and oak since they feed on beech-mast and acorns. If the Netherby tree is an oak then it is appropriate since the oak was sacred to the classical Jupiter. However, the association between boar, tree and divinity would appear to give the complex Netherby representation a rustic, hunting aspect appropriate to a deity worshipped in the wilderness of Cumbria, which would have been quite heavily forested at the time of the Roman occupation (Pennington, 1970, 73). Elsewhere similar connections are distinguished. The Farley Heath bronze sceptre-binding, for instance (Pl. LXXXII), depicts boar-figures associated with a possible Wheel-God represented by a human head and a rosette-like wheel. The Hounslow model wheel (Pl. LXIII, Fig. 25) was found in a field with boar-figurines. The hunting link is reinforced on some southern Gaulish altars where the wheel of the Sky-God is connected with attributes of a Gaulish Silvanus (for example B2).

The final Wheel-God portrayal in this section is of extreme significance if it has been correctly interpreted. It comprises a mosaic from St-Romain-en-Gal, Vienne (B130). Strictly-speaking it does not belong in our stonework list at all. However, it comes into the category of monumental material, and it presents a phenomenon which is normally rendered in a lithic medium. The mosaic depicts two individuals possibly sacrificing in front of a tall pillar on which stands a divinity bearing a probable thunderbolt in his right hand, and with his left hand resting on a possible wheel which is positioned upright against his left leg. A tree may be distinguished behind the column. The pillar itself suggests the 'Jupitergigantensäulen' of North-East Gaul and the Rhineland. The standing figure with the wheel resting by his side immediately recalls, for instance, the Séguret monument (B144 ; Pls. X, LXVI). What is of further interest is the presence, yet again, of the tree. It is impossible to tell the *genus* ; but a tree was present, as already commented upon, on the Netherby relief (BB18) and on the Séguret monument (B144). It is particularly significant that a tree should be present on this mosaic since it is generally considered in recent scholarship (Bauchhenss, 1976) that the column of the 'Jupitergigantensäulen' is itself a tree-portrayal ; this is why there is frequently foliate decoration on the pillars themselves. The Roman stylistic nature of some of the representations we have been looking at, like those from Séguret (B144) and Vaison (B158), is manifested yet once more in this mosaic, since only a reasonably Romanized individual would possess such house-furnishing. The Celtic content of the floor-decoration recalls British mosaics, such as the possible Cernunnos example from Verulamium (Green, 1976, 207).

Ib. *Jupiter-with-Giant Representations*

Ibi. *Wheel-God with true Giant*

These manifestations may simply be divided into horsemen and non-equestrian portrayals.

The horseman-image is the most frequent method of representing the Celtic Jupiter associated with a snake-limbed or chthonic monster. It should be stressed at the outset that most Jupiter-giant depictions are not associated with the Celtic attribute of the Wheel. Thus one is, in a sense, taking those which do possess such a feature out of the general context of the monument-group as a whole. Nevertheless, I feel it is valid so to do and, in any event, at a later stage in the enquiry, I will be discussing the general significance of this class of iconography (Chapter VI).

I have recorded thirteen certain and two possible examples of an equestrian Jupiter associated with an 'anguipède' monster and accompanied by a wheel. The two uncertain ones are from Malmaison (B75) and Varenne-Reuillon (B160). Both comprise small fragments of the complete group. The Varenne-Reuillon stone consists of a hand clasping a wheel, and could perhaps have been part of a standing Wheel-God with or without a chthonic giant. The Malmaison example is more definite ; it comprises a hand holding a four-spoked wheel, thrust through the spokes like a shield, precisely in the manner of most equestrian Wheel-God images. Nos. B11, 39 and 165 should also be treated with certain reservations. All three are definitely horsemen, from Beaune (B11), Fallberg (B39 ; Pl. LXVII, Fig. 34) and Vienne-en-Val (B165) respectively. The first-mentioned stones are merely presumed, by the attitude of the deity, to have once held wheels, now lost. The Fallberg example bears a circular attribute which could be interpreted as a wheel, but the stone is fragmentary, and it is impossible to be sure.

Where there is information available (this may be lacking either owing to wear, fragmentation or incomplete archaeological recording) the number of spokes on the wheel-carvings varies between three, four, five and six. The wheel is generally held as if taking the place of a shield, in the rider's left hand, with the wrist threaded through the spokes to hold the reins of his mount. This is the case with the groups from Butterstadt (B19 ; Pl. LXV, Fig. 29) ; Les Ronchers (B71) ; Luxeuil (B72 ; Pl. XI, Fig. 24) ; Meaux (B77 ; Pl. XI, Fig. 23) ; and Obernburg (B102 ; Pl. I, Fig. 1). In the case of Eckelsheim (B36) and Quémigny-sur-Seine (B114 ; Pl. II, Fig. 2) the object is half-way between a wheel and a shield. The Eckelsheim horseman grips the item against his body as if to protect himself ; the Quémigny rider holds an oval shield, impossible to imagine as a true wheel because of its shape alone. But the shield-boss acts as a wheel-hub in sprouting six radiating 'spokes'. What one appears to have here is a composite shield/wheel, or a shield with radiate sun-symbol decoration. The physical characteristics of the wheels themselves are sometimes worthy of mention. Often, as at Butterstadt, the object is fairly simple. However, the Meaux rider bears a very roseate wheel ; and the Obernburg wheel has exaggeratedly concave-sided spokes, the spaces between them forming (Pl. I, Fig. 1) quasi-circles. This has been remarked upon in the case of some wheel-models examined in Chapter II. Where the deity himself is sufficiently preserved to examine in detail, he is generally dressed in *tunica* and *paludamentum*. This is so, for instance, at Butterstadt (B19 ; Pl. LXV, Fig. 29) ; Luxeuil (B72 ; Pl. XI, Fig. 24), and at Meaux (Pl. XI, Fig. 23) where the cloak flutters out behind the deity to simulate fast-riding (B77). The rider is often bearded, as at Luxeuil and probably at Butterstadt. The monster supporting or being ridden under the horse's hooves is usually male (though female monsters are recorded, for instance at St-Martin-du-Mont [Corot, 1927-32, 247]). The Butterstadt giant is beardless and lies on his back, turning his face towards the left side of the rider, right hand pressed palm downwards against the ground, the forelimbs of the horse resting on the monster's shoulders. The drawing of the lost Luxeuil group furnishes us with a great deal of detail. The giant, in this instance, is merely represented by a beardless head emerging from the earth, supporting the left forefoot of the horse. The Meaux giant (B77 ; Pl. XI, Fig. 23) is also beardless. The Neschers group (B89) is very broken up. The head of the monster, with horse-hooves resting on it, survives. There are separate fragments of a six-spoked wheel which is sculpted free ; the object would appear to have rested against the palm of the rider's hand and up against his head. There is certainly no evidence to suggest the wheel being held like a shield, as in the case of other, more complete, examples. Two equestrian groups possess further features of interest. The Luxeuil rider (B72 ; Pl. XI, Fig. 24) is not only accompanied by a chthonic monster, but also by a small partially-draped female torso, missing below mid-thigh, suspended in space by his side, the rider's left hand resting on her head. In the next major group of material (Ibii) the diagnostic characteristic is the presence of a small humanoid figure by the side of the Wheel-God ; this being is not a representation of the monster itself, but the sometime presence of a scroll-like tail for nether limbs is suggestive of a similar iconographic function. The Luxeuil group, with both conventional chthonic monster *and* the small anthropomorphic figure, would seem to represent particularly powerful symbolism (rather as if two giants were portrayed, as occurs at Tongres for instance, on a non-wheel-bearing rider-group). The final comment is concerned with the horseman from Scarpone (B143). He is portrayed alone and, as survives, was not even certainly associated with the essential giant. However, if he is part of such a group, then he is of special interest, not in his possession of a wheel, but in the presence of a well-marked diagonal cross on his chest. In a previous chapter (Chapter III), I have attempted to demonstrate the possible connection between this symbol and that of the wheel and swastika. I shall go into further detail when dealing with ritual significance of stonework (Chapter VI).

The next type in this section comprises representations of a non-equestrian Wheel-God, but once again associated with a chthonic, monstrous being. B24, 34 and possibly also B41 consist of representations of upright divinities associated with giants. B87 and B151 comprise giants with wheels, the (presumably originally present) god himself now missing. The Champagnat carving (B24) depicts a striding deity, with an awesome, closed physiognomy and jutting beard. He appears to be naked. His right hand holds a five-spoked wheel against the side of his head, rather in the manner of the Neschers horseman-fragment (B89). Kneeling by his left leg is a beardless figure of indeterminate sex. Dompierre-les-Églises (B34) has produced a rather similar figure ; an upright statue of the Wheel-God is portrayed with a four-spoked wheel (the spokes being wedge-shaped) held in his left hand above a humanoid, bearded head, presumably that of a giant. The whole group is very damaged and incomplete, so it is not possible to be absolutely certain of what precisely was represented. The divinity from the Forêt de Châtillon-sur-Seine (B41) is standing and clothed in Roman armour, like, for instance, the Séguret (B144) and Vaison (B158) giant-free examples considered earlier. No head nor arms survive on this particular sculpture ; there is a giant by his left side, and it is reasonable to suggest that the dominant figure once held a wheel. The Mouhet (B87) and Tours (B151) carvings are curious in that only the chthonic element is represented in anthropomorphic form, but is associated, in each case, with the celestial wheel-sign. The example from Mouhet comprises a (possibly) kneeling figure with his hands behind his back in the manner of a captive. His back balances or supports an eight-spoked wheel. Also surviving on this monument are the legs of a seated figure the left foot of whom crushes the snake-tail of the giant. The Tours sculpture is similar ; the wheel balanced on the giant's back also probably had eight spokes. There is no trace of an accompanying divinity in this instance. These two representations are of extreme interest. The horse and rider have been replaced by the wheel-motif itself as a symbol of celestial force ; there is direct contact between wheel and giant. It is unfortunate that, with the incomplete and damaged data at our disposal, it is not possible to work out whether the two types are contemporary or whether the one developed from the other.

Ibii. *Wheel-God Representations accompanied by Small Human Figure*

Most of the ten figures in this group are incomplete, and in the majority of cases the wheel itself is absent. However, from pipe-clay figurines which are essentially similar, it is possible to infer that some complete carvings in this category comprise a dominant male divinity, with a diminutive anthropomorphic figure by his side, and holding a wheel in one hand up against his ear, as on the complete example from St-Georges-de-Montagne (B124). The pipe-clay figurines themselves are discussed in

Chapter V. Sometimes the small figure is not portrayed below mid-thigh, as if kneeling ; other depictions show the little being with scroll or snake-like nether limbs, recalling the full-size giants of the main Jupiter-giant groups. This is the case, for instance, at Giaud (B52) and at Rezé (B116). The Giaud figure is of especial note in that there is a theriomorphic emblem present, surprisingly not Jupiter's eagle but the peacock of his Roman consort. The St.-Pourçain figure (B128) is noteworthy simply because it comes from the same locality as a number of pipe-clay figurines of the Wheel-God. The Luxeuil group (B72), though discussed in the preceding section, should be recalled at this time since, as well as the giant and horseman elements, a small humanoid being is also present.

One of the most informative examples in the group is that from St-Christophe-le-Chaudry (B123). A nude, bearded god with a majestic expression on his face, bears traces of ornamentation or a circular attribute on his head. Both arms are missing, but the shoulder-position indicates that the right hand was raised, perhaps supporting a wheel-symbol. To his right, resting against his leg, is a small kneeling male figure, dressed in a cloak. His head is sunk between his shoulders, and his face wears a particularly dolorous expression. Although he is bowed under the weight of neither horse-hooves nor wheel, the whole attitude is one of labouring under a great burden. In my opinion the only difference between the diminutive figures of this group and the full-size giants is one of art-form. I suggest that there is little or no difference in cult significance. The idea of making the small being so disproportionately tiny may be to enhance the power of the divinity and to demonstrate his dominion over things terrestrial and subterranean.

Ic. *The Wheel Associated with Other Anthropomorphic Images*

A substantial number of iconographic representations exist in which the symbol of the wheel or swastika occurs without the Wheel-God himself. Occasionally it is Juno who appears accompanied by such a symbol, without her consort ; this is logical and need not surprise us. The motif is found also on portrayals which one has no cause to think of as divine in themselves, and where the presence of such a symbol implies talismanic significance. Where problems may arise is where other divinities adopt these celestial signs, especially where there is no obvious sky-significance to their cult. Fortuna is an exception. This classical goddess has, as a frequent attribute, the Wheel of Chance. I have included stone representations of the deity where she is accompanied by this emblem simply because Fortuna depicted with her wheel is not particularly common on Gaulish stone carvings, and it may be that some equation between her and a Gaulish sky-consort may have taken place because of the attribute common to them both.

We have already considered portrayals of Jupiter and Juno together, accompanied by a wheel, and it has been noted that on one such occasion it is Juno and not Jupiter who carries the sky-sign. Attribute-sharing between these two deities is carried to further extremes on carvings where the goddess occurs alone with the wheel. It should be remembered that there was very close identity between pairs of Celtic divinities – witness Mercury and Rosmerta ; Sucellus and Nantosuelta – and that in the classical world Juno's emblem, the peacock, symbolizes in its spread tail the orb of the sky. In some respects, moreover, this theriomorphic symbol is closer to the Celtic wheel-element than any of Jupiter's classical attributes.

Juno occurs accompanied by Jupiter-with-a-wheel, as noted earlier, at Vaison (B158), and at Tongres (B150) where Juno holds the celestial motif. The goddess appears on her own on a stele probably from the Autun area (B7), where she is represented with a thunderbolt in one hand and a possible wheel in the other. She is also portrayed alone at Vaison (B157) where the deity appears in tunic and cuirass, holding a wheel in her right hand. On the base of the altar, to the left of the divinity, appear a bird and snake. A goddess who is probably Fortuna, but who may also be present as a feminine counterpart to the Sky-God in a Celtic context, occurs at Agey (B1), possibly at Jagsthausen (B61), Rülzheim (B121) and Wolfstein (B169). Castlesteads in Britain (BB6) has produced a relief on which Fortuna is represented with a rudder resting on top of a wheel. The Rülzheim sculpture is, interestingly, part of a 'Viergötterstein' and shows Fortuna in relief, with *cornucopiae* in the left hand, rudder on globe in the right, and with an eight-spoked wheel by her left leg. The Agey carving shows a goddess with naked torso, rudder in the right hand, *cornucopiae* in the left ; a wheel-like object is at her feet ; a naked child turns its head to gaze at her. She has been variously identified: Espérandieu (7526) thinks she may be Fortuna or some Celtic divinity ; Toutain (1925, 2ff.) regards her as Venus Victrix ; Linckenheld (1929c, 41ff.) believes her to be some kind of Mother-Goddess. The Wolfstein stele-fragment shows part of a female figure with a wheel by her left foot. The sculpture from Jagsthausen has similar characteristics ; here the foot of a draped female figure is associated with a wheel with five spokes resting against a pilaster. What is of interest is that of depictions of non-Jupiter divinities with wheels, the majority portray females. Apart from those already looked at, there are other carvings which are not certainly identifiable with one Roman deity. Interpreted by Espérandieu as Fortuna (*Germ.*, 670) is the relief from Oehringen (B103). The depiction is of a draped female seated in an armchair or armed throne with a seven-spoked wheel-carving on one side; Far from being Fortuna, and judging by items like the Alzey sculpture portraying an enthroned Sky-Father (B4 ; Pl. 37d), this particular carving is more likely to be of a Celtic Juno than anyone else. Other female figures are also recorded. An indeterminate goddess, possibly with a wheel appears on a relief from Melun (B78). A fragmentary altar from St-Just (B125) portrays a female head. On one lateral surface is an eleven-spoked wheel. An unusual but surely unequivocally celestial goddess is shown on a relief from Susa in the Cottian Alps (B146). The divinity is armed and winged, and she is accompanied by an eagle and a five-spoked wheel.

Of specifically Celtic goddesses, Epona and the Mother-Goddesses are recorded with wheel-associations. At Baudoncourt (B10) an Epona-representation on a 'stèle-maison' is recorded as bearing a circular wheel or sun-like motif at the apex of the 'roof'. Two British Mother-Goddess reliefs, one unprovenanced within the Cotswolds (BB9) and the other from Easton Grey in Wiltshire (BB10) are each associated with a wheel-symbol. Both comprise fragmentary reliefs. The Cotswold example bears a wheel-symbol at the apex of the triangular-roofed niche in which the figure was portrayed. The Easton Grey fragment consists of a detached head from a Deae Matres group, with a small Latin Cross or wheel-derivative on the edge of her cap, above the centre of her forehead.

Male divinities associated with the wheel-sign but not certainly depictions of the Wheel-God himself, include a miniature stone altar from the Chedworth Roman Villa (BB7 ; Pl. LXXVI, Fig. 52-53). On the main face is a very crudely depicted, two-dimensional and stylized 'matchstick' figure carrying a spear and possibly also Sucellus' attribute of a long-shafted hammer. On each lateral surface appear curious wheel-symbols on long stems, with the physical appearance more of Bronze Age wheel-headed pins than anything else. A very similar portrayal, in terms of content, comes from Bad Dürkheim in the Rhineland (B9). This site was a Roman military stone-quarry. On the quarry-face appear a series of graffiti and child-like sketches implemented with chisels. The carvings include theriomorphic images — bird and dog, for instance, phalli (quite common on military scrawlings), and anthropomorphic representations depicted as heads on stick-legs. Those of special interest include swastikas and stemmed four-spoked wheel-symbols similar to the Chedworth altar wheels. Of particular note is a group comprising swastikas with three horses, a man bearing two spears and a stemmed eight-spoked wheel with four rays emanating from the top. The spear-carrier bears a strong resemblance to the Chedworth being. The carvings are associated with inscriptions bearing the name of Legion XXII. It is interesting that such apparently similar depictions should come from such totally different sites. A military-run quarry and a relatively sophisticated villa do not have a great deal overtly in common. However, it should be pointed out that much of the Chedworth ritual material is extremely crude in art-style and is probably to be regarded as the property of menial workers attached to the farming establishment rather than of the villa-owners themselves. As regards the Bad Dürkheim doodlings, there is no way of telling by whom the carvings were perpetrated, but one presumes them to be the work of the ordinary soldiery, either bringing ideas from other Celtic lands or obtaining ritual expression from local devotees. I am quite certain that the scrawlings are too complex merely to be seen as secular art. It should finally be noted that tile-fragments, for example from Walldürn (see Chapter V) of this same legion, bear swastikas.

The two final pieces to be looked at in this section comprise depictions which may or may not represent divinities, but where the wheel-symbol is portrayed as a talisman or amulet in the form of jewellery. The relevant sculptures are from Fox-Amphoux (B45) and from Metz (B80). The first sculpture depicts the torso of a Celtic warrior, bearing a large oval shield. He wears a pectoral pendant in the form of a six-spoked wheel fixed by two fastenings at chin-level. Potentially significant is the decoration on the warrior's shield, taking the form of ring-and-dot motifs. In the Models section (chapters II, III) I have attempted to demonstrate an association between this symbol and the wheel or sun-sign, on models such as swastikas and miniature axes. The positioning of the decoration on the shield has parallels with the rectangular shield carried by the Corbridge Wheel-God depicted on a clay mould (see Chapter V).

The Metz stele is a funerary monument. It comprises a male human figure wearing a torc from which is suspended a six-spoked wheel. Even if all other wheel-associated carvings bearing anthropomorphic images are of divinities, this one is certainly a representation of a deceased human being ; this is of especial interest in demonstrating the function of model wheels, to be worn as talismanic pendants or other jewellery.

II. Non-Anthropomorphic Representations

I have divided this group into two basic categories — funerary monuments (with or without epigraphic dedications), and specifically religious steles and altars. Because of the identity of the divinities involved in the second sub-group, I have sub-divided this material into epigraphic and anepigraphic stones.

IIa. Funerary Monuments

It is impossible to do other than speculate upon the likelihood that wheel and swastika-symbol on tombstones have some meaning in terms of a specific Wheel-God cult. Like model objects incorporating such symbolism, the presence of wheel-motifs may have no significance other than that of a general good-luck sign. However, as will be pointed out in Chapter VI, astral symbols on burial stones, whether in a classical or Romano-Celtic context, do represent certain beliefs on the part of deceased and dedicant (Richmond, 1950).

The most important Romano-Celtic burial-monuments for present purposes are the homogeneous group of 'stèles-maisons' which are for the most part from the Alsace region, the area roughly corresponding to the tribe of the Mediomatrices. These comprise single or double house-shaped stones, or rectangular multi-epitaph blocks (often with diagonal lines to indicate the symbolic triangular shape). They come from cemeteries which were entirely given over to the rite of cremation (Linckenheld, 1927, 100). Very frequently such steles bear distinctive motifs — concentric circles, rosettes, crescents and, most significant of all, genuine wheel-symbols generally with four spokes. In the present catalogue 'stèles-maisons' with wheel (or derivative) decoration are represented by nos. B15, B42, B43, B44, B56, B64, B115, B132, B134, B135, B136, B137, B138, B139, B140, B141, B142, B167. Generally there is little symbolism on these stones apart from celestial motifs, but one or two have additional features. The stele from Bois-de-la-Neuve-Grange (B15 ; Pl. XIII, Fig. 28) bears ornamentation in the form of a conifer and a fragmentary wheel, probably originally with eight spokes but with four remaining. The stone from the Forêt de Saint-Quirin (B43 ; Pls. XIII, Fig. 29 ; LXXII, Fig. 45) bears a seven-spoked wheel and, beneath, three hammers. Apart from the aforementioned stones, the Alsace funerary monuments depict wheels and concentric circles, sometimes together, sometimes on separate stones. Of those portraying true wheel-shapes, examples may be noted at Saverne (B134) associated with a circle. The

Saverne area itself is the most prolific location for such carvings. B135 bears a wheel-shape associated with a funerary inscription ; B136 has two circles and a four-spoked wheel at the apex of the roof ; B137 is a stele with four four-spoked wheels alone ; B138 (Pls. XIV, Fig. 30 ; LXXIII, Fig. 46) is a rectangular stone bearing an inscription and six four-spoked wheels ; B140 (Pl. XV, Fig. 34), again a multiple-epitaph monument, bears four-spoked wheel-shaped symbols. A stele from the same region (B141 ; Pls. XIV, Fig. 32 ; LXXIII, Fig. 47), with an inscription in which the names are Celtic (Caratodius Carathouni), bears three wheel-shapes. From the area immediately around Saverne comes a stone of triangular shape with an eight-spoked wheel at the base (B139 ; Pls. XV, Fig. 33 ; LXXIV). Of the monuments from Alsace bearing truly identifiable wheel-shapes, the majority are four-spoked examples, but the Bois de la Neuve-Grange stone (B15 ; Pl. XIII, Fig. 28) was probably eight-spoked, as was that on the Saverne stone (B139). The St-Quirin stele (B43) portrays a complex seven-spoked wheel. By far the most overt wheel-symbolism may be seen on a 'stèle-maison' from Wasserwald (B167 ; Pl. XV), still *in situ* in the forest. It has no inscription and is bare of ornament apart from three extremely well-defined and unmistakable wheel-signs of the more usual four-spoked type.

The Alsace stones so far discussed are, it seems to me, unequivocally connected with solar wheel-symbolism. The general simple cross-type is very common on pre-Roman and Romano-Celtic sites as a bronze miniature (Chapter II), and it is difficult to dismiss the Vosges symbols as mere decoration. We have more of a problem with other motifs which occur on the stones – circles, concentric circles and rosettes, as well as moon-crescents, for example that at Walscheid (B44). Rosettes may be seen, in some cases, as wheel-derivatives. Frequently bronze model wheels are of rosette-form, but this particular symbol, as shall be seen (Chapter VI), is a common element on funerary monuments all over the Roman world (large, ornate acanthus rosettes occur, for instance on tombstones around Narbonne [Narbonne, Musée Archéologique]), and it is not easy to assess just how significant, in terms of a Romano-Celtic sky-cult, these rosettes in the Vosges may be. In southern Gaulish Celtic coinage (Allen, 1980) rosettes, wheels and concentric circles all appear to be solar. The fact that these motifs occur on similar monuments to those bearing true wheels may mean that in the present context the rosette has a Celtic significance. Rosettes occur on the house-stele at Kirchnaumen (B64) – situated at the apex of the triangular 'roof' ; and again, similarly positioned, at Reubberg (B115). The Sarrebourg monument (B132) bears at the apex of the stone roof-triangle a symbol which looks like a cross between a wheel and a rosette. The presence of simple and concentric circles on 'stèles-maisons' may or may not have relevance to a Sky-cult. In the Saverne region certain house-steles (B134, B136) have wheels and circles associated. The Forêt de Greiffenstein stele (B42) bears concentric circles ; it is worth recalling that a model wheel-brooch comes from the same area. The Forêt de Walscheid (B44) has produced a house-shaped tombstone decorated with crescent, circle and concentric circle. A double, or twin-peaked stele from Griffon, dated to the early 3rd Century A.D., bears concentric circles alone. What is of interest and could be significant, is that in several instances, the wheel and concentric circle-motifs are repeated on one and the same monument. A Saverne stone (B137) bears four wheels ; another (B138 ; Pl. LXXIII, Fig. 46) has six. B141 (Saverne) and B167 (Wasserwald) each bear three. A further point of interest lies in the absence of the swastika-motif. Whereas in some parts of Gaul (notably in the south-west of the country) swastikas and wheels appear as alternating or associated signs, in the Vosges region swastikas are not recorded on 'stèle-maisons'.

A number of other funerary steles in Gaul and the Rhineland, though not of Alsace 'stèles-maison' type, bear similar motifs. From Courbessac (B31) comes a rectangular tombstone with triangular top. It bears a funerary inscription referring to individuals with Celtic names. Represented are a hammer, axe and the remains of a wheel. A stele with three wheels comes from Hagenbach (B57), and a triangular-topped stone from Rully (B119) is recorded as bearing a 'sun-symbol' at its apex. A stele with 'astral' signs is noted at Sammuran (B131). A tombstone with wheel-shaped ornament comes from Vaison (B156). A British epitaph comes from Risingham in Northumberland with a funerary inscription and an eight-spoked wheel between two crescents (BB21). A Garin stele (B47) is ornamented with a toothed wheel-shaped carving. This is paralleled at Cazarilh, where a stone is decorated with two denticulated wheels (B23).

A heterogeneous group of funerary monuments should next be examined. From Bachos Binos comes a cinerary 'container' (B8) with, in an enclosed square, an engraved wheel within a spiralled border. It is dated to the 3rd Century. Also from the Haute-Garonne, from Le Comminges (B69), come a series of funerary 'troughs' bearing incised 'crossed-circles' (or four-spoked wheels), and in one case a six-spoked example. Again from the Comminges region of southern France come certain steles bearing busts of the deceased together with what may be interpreted as solar symbols (here is an instance of the inflexibility of any classification system since, strictly speaking, such stones should be excluded from this group on account of the presence of images of the deceased in human form). An example of such a stone is from Prieuré d'Arnes (B104) where the decoration takes the form of wheels/rosettes. Several burial plaques bearing busts of the dead, spirals and wheel/rosettes come from St-Pé-de-la-Moraine (B126). Swiss funerary steles are recorded as sometimes bearing possible solar symbols. One example, from Geneva (B51) is triangular-topped and has a concentric circle at the apex. Another, also from Geneva (B50), bears decoration in the form of 'S'-symbols.

Interestingly enough, there are few swastika-decorated gravestones, compared to those bearing other solar-signs. Examples are recorded at Bourges (B16); Juslenville in Belgium (B63) and in Britain at Peel Crags near a turret on Hadrian's Wall (BB19). This stone was re-used in antiquity and may have been brought some distance from its original provenance. It should be noted that the cemetery at Juslenville which produced the gravestone mentioned above, also produced two wheel-brooches (Catalogue A, Chapter II).

One final point may be made concerning the position of the wheel (or derivative) symbols on the monuments in the foregoing analysis. The most usual situation of wheel or rosette is at the apex of a 'stèle-maison' or triangular-summitted stone. Sometimes they are grouped, one and then two, as at Wasserwald. Occasionally, as at Saverne (B139; Pl. LXXIV) the wheel is at the base of the stone. Whereas, as will be discussed below, the top of a stele is an appropriate place for a solar-sign, it is noteworthy that such a siting is not an inevitable rule. It is of interest that on swastika-carved altars (see below) the symbol is frequently at the base of the stone.

IIb. *Altars and Dedication Slabs*

IIbi. *Epigraphic Altars*

The majority of epigraphic dedications to divinities associated with wheel or swastika-symbols mention the Roman Sky-God Jupiter, either alone or associated with another divine power. However, in some instances, it is not Jupiter but another deity with whom the signs are linked.

The first group which may be distinguished comprises stones dedicated to Jupiter alone. These occur at Collias (B27 ; Pls. VIII, Fig. 18 ; LXX, Fig. 39); Cologne (B29 ; Pl. XVIII, Fig. 42); the Reims area (B30); Lansargues (B66); Nîmes (B95, B101); Pyrénées (B113); Tresques (B152); Birdoswald (BB2); Castlesteads (BB4); Maryport (BB15). The dedications may be to Jupiter Optimus Maximus, as at Cologne (B29) and Lansargues (B66 ; Pl. IV, Fig. 6), or merely to Jupiter, as at Nîmes (B95 ; Pl. VIII, Fig. 17). Where the evidence survives completely enough it is useful to look at the precise nature of the accompanying emblems. In each instance there is a wheel, swastika or both.

Tabular representation of attributes on Type 1 Jupiter-dedications

Site	Wheel	Swastika	Other
Collias	8-spoked	—	thunderbolt or trident
Cologne	8-spoked	—	—
Reims (area)	8-spoked	—	hand holding thunderbolt
Fallberg	two 4-spoked	—	—
Lansargues	6-spoked	—	2 thunderbolts, wheel between
Nîmes	no detail	—	—
Nîmes	6-spoked	—	—
Pyrenees	no detail	present	—
Tresques	7-spoked	—	7-petalled rosette
Birdoswald	two 4-spoked	present	—
Castlesteads	six 4-spoked + 1 ?-spoked	—	thunderbolt
Maryport	?-spoked	—	—

One final thing to look at in this first group is any information obtainable from the form of dedication or the art-style of the altars. B27 is dedicated by two local Gaulish peoples or sub-tribes, called Coriossedenses and Budicenses (Pls. VIII, Fig. 18 ; LXX, Fig. 39). The Birdoswald altar (BB2) was erected by a Dacian cohort ; that from Castlesteads by the 2nd Tungrian Cohort (it is worth remembering the Wheel-God carving from Tongres itself [B150]) ; the examples from Maryport by Spaniards. The only other feature worth commenting upon in passing is the extremely classical style of some altars ; the Cologne carving, for instance (B29), apart from its wheel, has no local or Celtic characteristic either in lettering, altar-shape or workmanship. Finally, still on the subject of content, it is of interest that the Lansargues stele (B66) has evidence of an attempt, in antiquity, at erasure of wheel and thunderbolts.

Type 2 stones comprise altars or dedication-slabs combining a dedication to Jupiter with that of another divinity. B2, from Aigues-Mortes (Pl. LXXI, Fig. 42), is dedicated to Jupiter and Silvanus ; an altar-fragment from Clarensac (B25) bears an inscription to (Jupiter) and Mother Earth ; the Jublains stone links the emperor's *numen* with Jupiter Optimus Maximus (B62), as do those from Marsillargues (B76 ; Pls. V, Fig. 7 ; LXIX, Fig. 38) ; from the Nîmes area (B92) ; Saint-Privat (B129) ; Castlesteads (BB5) ; and Housesteads (BB22). A Pyrenean altar (B106) bears a joint dedication to Jupiter and Minerva.

Tabular representation of attributes on Type 2 stones

Site	Wheel	Swastika	Dedication	Other
Aigues-Mortes	6-spoked + 7-spoked	—	Jupiter & Silvanus	2 hammers, billhook, pot, thunderbolts
Clarensac	fragment	—	Jupiter – Terra Mater	—
Jublains	4-spoked + 6 or 8-spoked, four	—	Jupiter (&) Augustus	—
Marsillargues	large, open-work-naved, 8 or 10-spoked	—	Jupiter & Augustus	—
Nîmes area	fragment	—	Jupiter & Augustus	—
Saint-Privat	7-spoked	—	Jupiter & Augustus	—
Castlesteads	10-spoked	—	Jupiter & Num. Aug.	thunderbolt
Housesteads	two 4-spoked	—	Jupiter & Num. Aug.	—
Pyrenees	—	present	Jupiter & Minerva	—

If we examine the details of the dedications where information exists, it is suggested that the form of the lettering of the Aigues-Mortes inscription (B2 ; Pl. LXXI, Fig. 42) may date it to the earlier 1st Century A.D. The Castlesteads altar (BB5 ; Pl. LXXV, Fig. 50) bears the detail that the stone was erected when Gordian was emperor, in A.D. 241. The form of the dedication to the emperor's *numen* on the Housesteads altar (BB22) is similar, and a mid 3rd Century date may be given for that also (Fishwick, 1969). The British examples give us some idea as to the country of origin of the worshippers. The Castlesteads stone was set up by Tungrians (as was that inscribed with Jupiter's name alone) ; the Housesteads block was also dedicated by auxiliaries originally from Belgium.

Type 3 comprises the association of wheel-sign with deities other than Jupiter, and is a relatively small group. An altar from Montsérie (B85) was inscribed to *Erge*, a local divinity equated with Mars, and was decorated with a swastika. From Piercebridge came a lost altar dedicated to a local Mars, Mars Condatis, associated with a swastika-motif (B20). An altar from Vivarais, carved with a swastika-sign, was set up to a Gaulish version of Apollo, Belenus (B166). High Rochester (BB11) has produced an altar to Minerva and a Genius set up by a guild, bearing on the capital a wheel with four diagonally-placed spokes flanked by reverse swastikas. In this connection we should recall the altar to Jupiter and Minerva already examined (B106). Cohors I Vardullorum erected an altar to a Genius and the Standards, once more at High Rochester (BB12). This particular stone has the added information that the dedicants were Roman citizens. On the capital of the altar are two swastikas, one on each side of an incised crescent. On the question of wheel-swastika symbolism, the Netherby reliefs of a Genius or Bonus-Eventus with *paterae*/wheels should be recalled. One interesting point here is that it is generally swastikas rather than true wheel-symbols which are associated with deities not overtly connected with sky-symbolism. It is suggested (Ferguson, personal communication) that this may be something to do with the swastika being less symbolic with regard to a Romano-Celtic solar/sky cult than the true wheel.

Type 4 consists of other dedications which do not fall into any of the above groups. No divinity is specifically mentioned, but this is sometimes due to the fragmentary nature of the stones concerned. The minute Castelnau-Valence altar (B21 ; Pl. LXXI, Fig. 41) bears a remnant of an inscription mentioning a dedicant (?) named Severus, and bears a five-spoked wheel. B83 (Pl. IX, Fig. 19) comprises a fragment of an altar bearing two nine-spoked wheels and two lines of an inscription (*fulgur*) *conditum*, from Montmirat. Finally the ritual site of Le Mont-Saçon, in the Pyrenees, should be alluded to (B70). Here we have an interesting phenomenon in the presence of a number of anepigraphic altars bearing wheels and swastikas, and one fragmentary dedication, on a small altar, to Jupiter but without any such symbolism. It looks as though, in this instance, the name of the god could be readily substituted for his essential Celtic emblems and *uice uersa*.

CHAPTER IV

Positioning and Multiplication of Attributes on all Four Types

It is possible that in some instances the physical relationship between the inscription and wheel and other symbols may be of significance, as may the duplication of certain motifs. Émile Thevenot (1968, 37) suggests that on some monuments the thunderbolt is replaced by the wheel. We will be examining this hypothesis in detail in Chapter VI. It is certainly by no means the rule here. The British altars with both wheel and thunderbolt attest this. The complex altar from Aigues-Mortes (B2 ; Pl. LXXI, Fig. 42) bears a seven-spoked wheel and a thunderbolt beneath the dedicatory inscription. On another surface is a second thunderbolt and a six-spoked wheel. On a third face are a billhook, pot and hammer. Another multi-symbol altar is B62, from Jublains. Here again the wheel-sign is duplicated. There are five wheels in all, a four-spoked motif on the front accompanying the dedication, one six-spoked wheel on the left lateral face, and three six-spoked symbols grouped two and one on the right. The Clarensac (B25) and Montmirat (B83 ; Pl. IX, Fig. 19) altars bear the wheel-sign in between the lines of the inscription, as if to form as close a link as possible between name and symbol. On the Cologne (B29 ; Pl. XVIII, Fig. 42) and Marsillargues (B76 ; Pls. V, Fig. 7 ; LXIX, Fig. 39) stones, on the other hand, the wheel is beneath the dedication. At Lansargues (B66 ; Pl. IV, Fig. 6) the symbol is beneath the inscription and between two thunderbolts. The Tresques stone (B152) bears a seven-spoked wheel associated with the dedication, and the symbol is duplicated in stylized form in the two seven-petalled rosettes flanking the name of the divinity. At Birdoswald (BB2) a swastika is flanked by two wheels. On both Castlesteads altars (BB4 ; BB5 ; Pl. LXXV, Fig. 50), a thunderbolt is on the left lateral face, the wheel on the right. BB4 has the added symbolism of six 'enclosed crosses' along the top of the capital. BB11 bears a four-spoked wheel flanked by reverse swastikas ; two swastikas are also present on BB12. Both these are from High Rochester. BB12 is of especial interest in that the presence of the crescent implies both sun and moon imagery on one and the same stone (recalling the gold and silver chains from the province bearing wheel and lunar crescent) [3]. The Maryport altar (BB15) is curious in that the wheel is at the rear of the stone. If Picard is correct (1977, 97) in his interpretation of the Mouhet Jupiter-giant group as consisting of a seated god with giant and wheel at the back of the throne then the position of the Maryport wheel has a

[3] See Chapters II, III.

Gaulish parallel. The Housesteads dedication bears duplicated symbolism in the two juxtaposed four-spoked wheels in the middle of the altar-capital.

IIbii. *Anepigraphic Altars*

The last major group to be analysed is that comprising altars bearing symbolism only, with neither anthropomorphic representation nor inscription. It could be argued that this group thus represents the most primitive of the monuments since anepigraphic and non-humanoid imagery is something pertaining specifically to pre-Roman and unromanized Celtic peoples. I think that this is a somewhat dangerous hypothesis since, at one and the same site, for instance at Montmaurin, and at Le Mont-Saçon, one may find inscribed and uninscribed altars of very similar types and arguably of similar date.

Tabular representation of attributes on anepigraphic altars

Site	Wheel	Swastika	Other
Begnères	—	present	—
Begnères	—	present	—
Belbèze-en-Comminges	6-petalled, rosette-like	—	—
Collias	half 8-spoked; fragment	—	—
Dôle	4-spoked	—	bird + 8-rayed barrel and smaller barrels
Foeschen	lobed-spoked	—	—
Gard, area	no detail	—	—
Garonne/Adour (between)	no detail	present	—
Gilly, Nîmes	6-spoked	—	—
Goudex	—	present	tree
Ilheu	—	present	tree, + 3 leaves
Le Mont-Saçon	—	1, in lozenge	—
Le Mont-Saçon	—	1, in circle	—
Le Mont-Saçon	—	present	stylized tree
Le Mont-Saçon	—	present	—
Le Mont-Saçon	—	present	—
Le Mont-Saçon	4-spoked	—	—
Le Mont-Saçon	4-spoked	—	—
Mainz	8-spoked	—	—
Montmaurin	4-spoked	present	—
Nîmes	'flashing'	—	—
Nîmes	5-spoked	—	—

Site	Wheel	Swastika	Other
Nîmes	8-spoked	—	thunderbolt
Pyrenees	—	—	concentric circles + tree
Pyrenees	4-spoked	—	palm
Pyrenees	3 double spokes	present	—
Pyrenees	1 frag. + 1 4-spoked	two	—
Pyrenees	—	present	palm
Pyrenees	—	present	palm
Robernier	—	present	concentric circles, beasts (e.g. foal + mare)
St-Bertrand	—	present	conifer
St-Plancard	—	present	—
Tarbes, area	—	present	conifer
Tarbes, area	simple cross	—	several conifers
Vaison	10-spoked	—	—
Vaison	6-spoked	—	—
Valentine	no detail	present	tree + palm leaf
Vauvert	8-spoked	—	2 thunderbolts
Vernègues	6-spoked	—	2 trees, long-shafted hammer + 2 pots
Birdoswald	frag.	—	—
Lypiatt Park	4-spoked (?)	—	ram-horned snake
Maryport	frag.	—	—

The number of spokes on the wheels themselves varies between three, four, five, six, seven, eight and ten ; the commonest numbers are four and eight. Five and seven are rare and this may be because such numbers would have been difficult to lay out. Where they do occur they could possess significance in terms of the planets or the planets plus sun and moon. At Belbèze the wheel bears a strong resemblance to a petalled rosette. The Foeschen wheel is lobe-spoked, and an example from the Pyrenees has three double spokes, recalling a bronze wheel-model from Mainz (Chapter II). One Tarbes stone has a wheel not enclosed by a circle but which forms a simple, four-armed cross. A Nîmes altar is described as bearing a 'flashing' wheel. This must mean that each spoke terminates at the circumference-end in a kind of tail to one side, as if the item were on fire and rotating. Altars within this group may bear wheels alone, as at Collias (B28) and at Gilly (B53 ; Pls. IX, Fig. 21 ; LXVIII, Fig. 36) ; swastikas alone, as at Begnères (B12 ; 13 ; Pl. VI, Fig. 10) and Ilheu (B60) ; or combinations of the two, as at Montmaurin (B82).

Other attributes may take the form of familiar items, such as thunderbolts, as at Castelas-de-Vauvert (B20 ; Pl. LXVIII, Fig. 35). Repeated emblems are dendromorphic shapes — palm-branches and stylized trees (generally conifers), and occasionally isolated leaves. The foliate decoration recalls the funerary monument (B15) from Bois de la Neuve-Grange, bearing a wheel with branch-like terminals to the spokes. Two further types of attribute fall into the categories of zoomorphic and implemental items. One very curious carving comes from Dôle (Pl. XVIII, Fig. 41), bearing a four-spoked wheel above the head of an unclassifiable bird ; above this creature is a barrel-like object with eight radiating spokes, each terminating in a similar barrel or cylinder. This strange item immediately brings to mind the spoked barrels associated with figurines of Sucellus, like the bronze from Vienne, Isère (Boucher, 1976, no. 301). The bird itself is of great potential interest ; it is just possible that the sculptor meant to represent a peacock ; its crested head is surmounted by a four-spoked wheel which actually touches it, thus depicting a strong and essential link between the living being and the symbol. Other zoomorphic images occur on the (probably) La Tène Robernier stele (B117) with its quadrupeds including a probable mare and foal, and the Lypiatt Park altar (BB13 ; Pl. III, Fig. 4) which bears a worn wheel on the top horizontal surface of the stone and a ram-horned serpent twined round the outside. Implements, apart from thunderbolts, are exampled by the pots and hammer on the Vernègues sculpture (Pl. VII, Fig. 15). The significance of all these associations and their relationship to the other iconographic stone groups in this section will be fully considered in Chapter VI.

Positioning of Emblems

One feature of these altars which strikes one immediately is that the swastika-sign, where present, is frequently on the base of the altar. At Montmaurin (B82) the wheel occupies the main frontal area, the swastika the base. At Ilheu (B60) a tree is present on the front, the swastika on the base. The enclosure of swastikas on two altar-bases at Le Mont-Saçon (B70), may or may not be worthy of attention. It may be that the act of enclosure had a ritual meaning, the contained space perhaps being especially sacred, rather in the manner of a temple-temenos. Or it may be that here wheel and swastika-symbol are being conflated. At Valentine (B159), where there is composite symbolism, it is the wheel that is on the base and the swastika, tree and palm occupy the main stone surfaces. At Vauvert (B20 ; Pl. LXVIII, Fig. 35) the eight-spoked wheel decorates the front of the altar and a simple thunderbolt is present on each lateral face. This is interesting ; the position of the wheel would appear to give it dominance, but it is outnumbered by the flanking thunderbolts. This could be an equalizing gesture ; alternatively the lateral symbols could be 'attendant' on the wheel. A more mundane explanation may simply be that of symmetry and a desire to decorate all visible surfaces. On the Vernègues altar-fragment (B163 ; Pl. VII, Fig. 15) all four faces were utilized by the sculptor. On one long side is a rather compressed wheel ; on the opposite surface are a hammer and two pots ; the other two sides are occupied by stylized trees.

I myself have doubts as to whether the position of the attributes on these stones has much, if any, religious significance. The possible exception is the basal swastika which occurs so repeatedly on the south-west Gaulish altars.

A final feature to which attention should be drawn is the fact that the southern French stones, especially those from Pyrenean contexts, are of a distinct type – small and sometimes quite crudely-made.

Chronology

There is some evidence for pre-Roman wheel-symbolism on stone monuments in Gaul. The paucity of such material need not surprise us since there is little Bronze and Iron Age figured stonework of any description. The two areas which have produced relatively substantial amounts of data in the pre-conquest era are the Rhineland and the extreme south of Gaul (Liguria). In connection with pre-Roman wheel-carvings, the rock-engravings of Scandinavia (Gelling, *et.al.*, 1969) and, more immediately relevant, those of Camonica Valley in northern Italy (dating between the Neolithic and the Iron Age (Anati, 1960b) should not be forgotten. These phenomena were considered in Chapter I.

One of the earliest, possibly relevant, stone sculptures is from Substantion (Hérault) in southern France (Soutou, 1962, 521 ; Briard, 1974, 153, fig. 12 ; Coles & Harding, 1979, 439, fig. 158). It is probably a funerary stele dating to the later Bronze Age. On it is carved a notched, concentric-ringed shield of conventional later Bronze Age type (Coles, 1962), above which is a design possibly intended to represent a spearhead. At the top of the stone are three four-spoked wheels each with a series of sloping strokes leading upwards from the top quadrant of the rim. At each side of the stele is an aquatic bird. Briard (1974, 153, fig. 12) would see this sculpture as the image of a warrior's accoutrements – spear, shield and chariot. This may be so but it seems curious to represent a vehicle by three wheels, and it is possible that the three motifs may have some sun-symbolism. It is tempting to see the wheels as representative of a solar wagon carrying the sun-wheel (Gelling *et.al.*, 1969), but speculation should not be carried too far in this case.

The material from Entremont in the extreme south of Gaul (the precursor of Aquae Sextiae) is pre-Roman. At least four statues of warriors from this *oppidum* bear breastplate-decoration in the form of spiral/toothed wheel-motifs. The statues are cross-legged and wear pectoral, possibly apotropaic, pendants in the form of spirals and circles. One well-preserved torso bears a double 'sun-symbol' comprising two concentric circles with a denticulated chain weaving round them in a spiral shape (Musée Granet, Aix-en-Provence ; Espérandieu, 8653-8655 ; Benoît, 1956, 221, fig. 7). Also from Entremont is a fragmentary female stone head from whose ears are suspended pendants in the form of wheels (Espérandieu, 8671 ; Salviat, 1976, 94, fig. 4). These sculptures must predate the sack of Entremont by the Romans in 123 B.C. They may be seen as the result of Greek influence, and could be much earlier (Brogan, 1974, 205). It is more likely that the southern French sanctuaries, to which Entremont belongs, date to the 4th-3rd Century B.C. – *oppidum*-complex which flourished until the Roman Conquest in 123 (Hodson & Rowlett, 1974, 157-191). Also from southern Gaul comes the Robernier stele which has been dated within the La Tène period (Grapinat, 1970 ; Déchelette, 1910, 409ff.). The Fox-Amphoux stele, from the same region, depicting a Celtic warrior, is also perhaps pre-Roman.

Within the Roman period detailed chronological evidence is not generally forthcoming, although it is possible to distinguish some landmarks. It has been suggested that the lettering of the Aigues-Mortes altar to Jupiter and Silvanus (B2) could date it to the earlier 1st Century A.D.. The Vosges cemeteries in the Saverne area of Alsace, all contain cremation-burials right through to the 4th Century A.D. The Wasserwald cemetery apparently dates from the later 2nd-3rd Century (Linckenheld, 1927, 100). The double house-stele at Griffon is suggested as being of early 3rd Century date. In Britain, the Lower Slaughter settlement, in which the well containing the Genii Cucullati carving was found, was occupied from mid 2nd-late 4th Century. The Peel Crags tombstone-fragment found near a turret on Hadrian's Wall could be Hadrianic, but since it was re-used in antiquity, it is impossible closely to date it. The Risingham tombstone has been assigned to the 3rd Century, as has the Bachos-Binos cinerary container. Collingwood and Richmond (1969, 204) make the point that tombstones tended to be ousted during the 3rd

Century (among the well-do-do) by the more fashionable stone *sarcophagi*. One of the Castlesteads altars gives us the information that it was erected when Gordian was emperor, in A.D. 241 (*R.I.B.*, 1983). The Vivarais altar to Apollo Belenus, bearing an incised swastika-sign, is possibly 3rd Century (Grapinat, 1970, 54-56). Of especial interest is the Montmaurin villa-complex in the Pyrenees, where the shrine containing an altar of general south-west Gaulish type (small with wheel and swastika) among other altars, was probably built in the first half of the 4th Century A.D. (Fouet, 1969, 163).

Jupiter-giant columns, with or without wheel-symbols, appear to span a period between the 1st and 4th Centuries (see Chapter VI). Where a Jupiter-column was first produced is beyond our knowledge; there is evidence, however, to suggest that it could have been in the Flavian period in or near Mainz (Bauchhenss, 1976, 22). Haug (1891, 9ff.) discusses the columns set up in Raetia, Upper Germany and Gallia Belgica, and cites 218 which, where datable, are between A.D. 170 and 246. We know that the Cirencester 'Jupiter-column' (not included in the present catalogue since there is no evidence of the original group having borne a wheel) was re-erected after Britannia Prima became a separate British province in the Diocletianic reorganization of A.D. 296 (*R.I.B.*, 103). Haverfield (1893, 312) suggests that the most likely time for restoring such a monument was under Julian the Apostate (A.D. 360-363), but this can be no more than speculation.

The chronology of certain sites, notably in the German *limes* area, can sometimes bracket the date of stones, although no detailed pointer may be forthcoming. Jagsthausen and Oehringen were founded probably in about A.D. 100-120 (Schönberger, 1969, 144-197). Alzey dates from 1st-later 3rd Century, and was re-occupied as a fortress in c. 357-370. Bad Dürkheim was being quarried between 1st and 3rd Centuries A.D.; Cologne and Mainz from the last years B.C. until the 5th Century A.D.; Obernburg was occupied from A.D. 100 until the mid 3rd Century; Speyer from A.D. 45 until the 5th Century; Trier from late 1st Century B.C. until the 5th Century A.D. (von Elbe, 1975).

Distribution (See Pls. XXIV-XXVIII)

In the words of Gerhard Bauchhenss (1976, 19-20) a Celtic divinity bearing a wheel as an attribute may be found in almost the whole of Celt-occupied Europe, from Britain to the Balkans. Epigraphic dedications to the specifically Celtic (and non-local) Jupiter, Jupiter Taranis, are of little help, since they are so few and, in any case (see Chapter VIII), may not be necessarily connected with the Wheel-God cult. Wheel-God or wheel alone is present in all Romano-Celtic regions (Lambrechts, 1942, 64-80 ; Map 4). Lambrechts excludes Aquitaine, but since his survey was completed, the Bordeaux Wheel-God, for example (B15a) has been recorded. The god was especially popular in the Lower Rhône Valley (Picard, 1974 ; de Vries, 1963, note 6, 45).

The most striking clusters of monuments bearing wheel-symbolism, although rarely accompanied by representations of the god himself, are in Provence and in the mountainous valleys of the Pyrenees between the Garonne and Adour. The altars here are generally small and frequently bear wheels (generally four-spoked), swastikas or both, and often stylized trees. Bearing in mind this south-westerly distribution it is of interest that a Portuguese stele from Monté Cildad shows a horseman accompanied by two swastikas (Grapinat, 1970, 54-56). A second significantly-positioned group of monuments is the wheel-bearing Jupiter-columns. Here we cannot dissociate those where the deity bears a wheel from groups without. In any case the wheel may, in several instances, have been lost. The distribution of Jupiter-columns indicates concentrations in Upper and Lower Germany, Raetia and Belgic Gaul, being especially common in the Middle Rhineland, both east and west of the river (Haug, 1891, 9ff. ; Powell, 1958, 136). Powell (*ibid.*) would see a dispersal from the Middle Rhine (perhaps the starting-point) down into the Vosges and into North-East and Central Gaul. In Lower Germany the horseman-groups are rare and tend to be replaced by the pillars surmounted by an enthroned or standing Jupiter (Bauchhenss, 1976, 16 ; Lambrechts, 1942, 108). The centre of the main scatter of columns is in the territory of the Gaulish tribe of the Lingones (de Vries, 1963, 38-48, Map 5). A third distinct group of wheel-bearing stones is the Alsace funerary group. Finally it is worth mentioning that, in most instances, apart from the Pyrenees, wheel and swastika are mutually exclusive (at least wheel and swastika occur together in south-west Gaul, but in other regions where there are wheels, swastikas are absent, notably in Alsace, and in the Lower Rhône Valley).

In Britain the distribution is mainly in the area of Hadrian's Wall. Where traceable the dedicants are Tungrians, Dacians and Spaniards, according to the names of the cohorts mentioned. Wilkes (personal communication) has suggested that, even in the 3rd Century (when one Castlesteads altar was dedicated) there may have been Tungrians on Hadrian's Wall, since the recruiting-ground for such auxiliaries continued, throughout the Roman occupation, to be North-East Gaul. It would be unlikely that there were actual Dacians at Birdoswald, however, and the troops there were probably also from Belgica. This is interesting since this region does, itself, have evidence for wheel-symbolism (e.g. Tongres [B150]). Within Britain wheel-representations are found in South Wales and the Cotswolds. From the numbers and distribution in Britain it is plain that the Wheel-God neither originated here, nor was at his most popular. The Hadrian's Wall group may all be seen as the result of immigrant activity, since the repertoire of native religious sculptors in the North of Britain does not include the Wheel-God type. However, the Gloucestershire group may have been set up by Britons with less direct influence from outside. The Churcham, Lypiatt Park and Lower Slaughter carvings are Celtic in style; they have no necessary link with military activity, and were certainly carved locally on local stone. What is interesting is that two other distinct groups of Celtic divinities have just this dual distribution-pattern − in Gloucestershire and Hadrian's Wall − namely the Deae Matres and Genii Cucullati. We do know that the Central Roman government had Gauls in Cirencester in the late 3rd or 4th Centuries. The governor of Britannia Prima who was responsible for the restoration of the Corinium Jupiter-column was a citizen of Reims.

CHAPTER V

Descriptive Analysis of Miscellaneous Material

The Romano-Celtic (and very late pre-Roman) material which may be classified neither as models nor as stonework, may be divided simply into three major categories. These comprise : I) representations of a male divinity, probably or possibly the Wheel-God himself ; II) other anthropomorphic and theriomorphic representations associated with the wheel or related symbol ; III) objects bearing wheel (or derivative) motifs but without any specific link with a divinity.

It may be seen from Catalogue C that the material presented here is somewhat heterogeneous. Both in terms of quantity, and to an extent in quality of information, the group is, as a whole, inferior both to models and certainly to stonework. It is, therefore, perhaps justifiable to confine the non-interpretative discussion to a fairly brief analysis of types. Group I is of greatest interest since it comprises, for the most part, small cult-objects representing the Celtic Jupiter himself. Some of the items are probably to be regarded as personal possessions of devotees – such as the pipe-clay depictions. Others, like the sceptre-fittings (C6, C7), are to be interpreted as ritual furniture. Group II consists of depictions of divinities other than the Celtic Jupiter who, nonetheless, are associated with celestial symbolism and who may therefore have had some specific connection with the Wheel-God cult. Group III is of the least intrinsic significance, comprising, in the main, essentially non-liturgical objects decorated with ritual solar motifs.

Group I :
Male Anthropomorphic Representations of a Wheel-Bearing Deity
(C1-14 ; 80 ; 82)

For convenience this group may be subdivided in terms of material into objects of metal and of clay. Metal (in most cases bronze) items are likely to have belonged to members of a higher social class than ceramic items. Bronze and silver especially would have been far more costly both to produce and to purchase. As a corollary one would expect to find metal representations more rigidly stereotyped within the classical tradition than, say, stone or clay, particularly in view of the presence of centralized workshops. Within the latter media one may not be altogether surprised at Celtic individuality. These guide-lines, however, are by no means universally valid in these instances. Pipe-clay manufactories, at any rate, were centralized in Central Gaul and in the Rhineland around Cologne.

I.A *Metal Representations*

The two most important portrayals of a Celtic Wheel-God are the bronze figurines from Le Châtelet (C2 ; Pl. LXXIX, Fig. 57 + Frontispiece) and Landouzy-la-Ville (C3 ; Pl. LXXX). The two have certain stylistic similarities — the sketchy treatment of anatomical features, the facial expression, and the stocky unclassical build. The Landouzy figure is of especial interest in that, in mien, he recalls depictions of the Gallo-Roman Hercules, whereas the basal inscription indubitably points to the identification of the depiction as that of the Roman Sky-God. The association of wheel-motif with the Imperial Cult is mirrored, for instance, by the Castlesteads altar (*R.I.B.*, 1983). The presence of the wheel at Landouzy and the style of the piece betray Celtic influences, but the content of the dedication is entirely Roman. A final feature to which attention should be drawn is the curious pedestal supporting the wheel resting in the god's left hand. This support terminates in a capital-crown. Whether one interprets it as an altar on which the wheel is being offered (analogies exist, for instance, on the Netherby carvings [BB17, BB18]) or simply as a pedestal, there is an immediate physical analogy with the Corinthian capitals surmounting stone Jupiter-columns. Since these pillars frequently support representations of Jupiter accompanied by a wheel the comparison may be a valid one, and we may have a conscious attempt, by a Gallo-Roman bronze-smith, to form a link between one medium of expression and another. When we come to consider pipe-clay portrayals (below) we will see that such a phenomenon certainly seems to occur.

Like the Landouzy (C3) figurine, the god from Le Châtelet (C2) bears a six-spoked wheel. This statuette is of a less "wooden" appearance (Frontispiece) and differs both in having long hair and a long beard, and in carrying a thunderbolt rather than a sceptre. The god has an additional feature of a shoulder-ring supporting nine free-cast spiral-shaped items.

The interpretation of these is problematical. They may, as Thevenot suggests (1968, 22) be a supply of lightning-flashes carried by the divinity for his immediate requirements. It should be recalled here that the pot from Silchester (C54) bears alternating 'S' and wheel-shaped motifs ; and 'S's are associated with the wheel-model from Grand-Jailly (Catalogue A). The fact that the spirals attached to the Le Châtelet figure are free-cast and free-moving does suggest that Thevenot's hypothesis may possess some validity, although there may be other explanations (see below, Chapter VI). What should be pointed out is a functional aspect to this particular bronze, for although frequently taken as a figurine in its own right, first-hand examination reveals the presence of two rings at the rear of the figure, suggesting that its original purpose was to fit onto a wand or ritual staff. Thus the figure would have performed a function essentially similar to the Willingham Fen piece (C6).

Before we look at the sceptre-evidence, we should consider briefly the statuette from the Harzburg military installation (C4). Here the Celtic 'Jupiter' is represented with a basket, a wheel and a fish. It is tempting to see these three symbols as representative of sky, earth and underworld. The basket has analogies with those borne by the 'Deae Matres' on some reliefs ; the fish might (like the snake) have a chthonic function, being an underwater dweller, or there may be fertility symbolism here.

The two sceptre-fittings are both from Britain — from Willingham Fen (C6 ; Pl. LXXXI) and Farley Heath (C7 ; Pl. LXXXII) — but could not be more different in artistic treatment, although both comprise representations of a Wheel-God as integral parts of ritual staves. Each depiction is accompanied by composite symbolism which presumably has profound significance. Whilst the grim-faced Landouzy god (C3) looked at earlier resembles Hercules, the joyously-posed figure on the Willingham Fen bronze (Pl. LXXXI) looks like a youthful Cupid, yet is associated with the celestial emblems of eagle and wheel (the one classical and the other Celtic) and a chthonic monster. The other two beings — a dolphin and a triple-horned bull's head — are more enigmatic in this context. The latter is a well-known iconographic form in the Romano-Celtic world, especially in eastern Gaul, but it is not the normal associate of the Celtic Sky-God. The deity bears in one hand what may either be a club or a thunderbolt. The former attribute is interesting since it has been noted above that the Landouzy statuette resembles Hercules (the usual classical club-bearer). In addition the Corbridge clay mould depicting the Wheel-God (C10 ; Pl. LXXIX, Fig. 58) (discussed below) shows the deity clasping an unequivocal club ; and the gold wheel-pendant from Thérouanne in northern France (see Catalogue A) was associated with a club-model on the same suspension-chain. Both the Willingham Fen (C6) and the Farley Heath (C7) sceptre-fittings come from ritual sites. Willingham Fen was a cult-hoard, possibly a priest's cache originally from a temple-site. The deposit included other ritual material – bird-figurines, anthropomorphic busts of Mars and Minerva and two bronze horsemen.

Farley Heath in Surrey was a Romano-Celtic temple-site containing, amongst other ritual material, model enamelled stands, a plaque in bronze depicting Cupid, a bronze hawk and an eagle. The sceptre-binding (C7 ; Pl. LXXXII) is of interest both because of the mythological figures it portrays and the artistic style of representation. The human and animal figures are depicted roughly, as 'matchstick figures' and their treatment has parallels in Britain in some ritual metal plaques, such as those from Bewcastle dedicated to the Celtic god Cocidius (Richmond, 1938, 208, fig. 14 ; Green, 1978, 46, pls. 60, 61), and in some crudely-fashioned little stone altars both from North Britain (Ross, 1967, *passim*) and from the Gloucestershire area, for example at Chedworth (Goodburn, 1972, pl. 10.1, 3). There is virtually nothing Roman about the Farley Heath strip and if the style is Celtic then so is the religious content. Apart from the theriomorphic figures, the Hammer-God Sucellus is depicted, seemingly equated with a Smith-God to judge by his conical hat and the two associated pairs of tongs. Near him is an anthropomorphic head associated with a rosette-like wheel. The identification of this head as representative of the Celtic Jupiter is suggested not only by this wheel but by a thunderbolt beneath it. Thus, once again, both classical and Celtic celestial emblems are present. Whether there is any significance to be drawn from the depiction of the head alone in this case, contrasted with the completeness of Sucellus' form, is open to question. The whole scene is seemingly so lacking in attention to art, as we know it, that the artist may have miscalculated his spacing. On the other hand all the figures are simply 'sketched' and thus attention to anatomical detail was purely nominal. One is reminded of the two-dimensional, triangular bodies of some British stone carvings, for example the Mothers from Bath (Green, 1976, pl. XV,C) or the Genii Cucullati from Lower Slaughter, Gloucestershire (Ross, 1967, pl. 62b). The most interesting aspect of this bronze binding is the juxtaposition of the Hammer-God and the Wheel-God. We shall see later that there is strong evidence for a close iconographic association between them.

The item to be considered next is the lead medallion from Plessis-Barbuise (C5). This has already been included in the Models discussions (Catalogue A, Chapters II, III) but, since the object incorporates significance not only as a wheel-model but also as a small representation of the Sky-God, it seems appropriate to treat it here also. The medallion has particular significance since the discovery (see below) of identical pieces depicting Epona. There is some evidence for a connection between these two types of representation. All three lead roundels depict divinities, recognizable by their attributes, surrounded by and contained within a wheel.

The final item in this group is the representation on the Gundestrup Cauldron (C1). Strictly-speaking this is beyond the present scope, both chronologically and geographically. It has been the subject of a number of modern publications, and opinions differ as to its precise date. Piggott sees it as Middle La Tène, dating to the 2nd or 1st Century B.C. (Piggott, 1965, pl. opp. 219). Bémont (1979, 69-99) remarks that some of the vegetation-patterns on the bowl have close similarities with Danubian metalwork of the 1st Century B.C., and it has, in a recent study, been convincingly dated (Olmsted, 1979) to the mid 1st Century B.C., from an examination of, among other features, the Celtic arms depicted. It was discovered in Jutland, beyond the boundaries of the Roman Empire. However Olmsted (1979) has put forward strong evidence for the manufacture of the bowl in North-West Gaul. There are Oriental influences present; Klindt-Jensen, for instance (1976, 233-245) sees strong stylistic links with other silver, silver-gilt and gold works of art in tombs and hoards in Dacia and Thrace. There are also close reflections on the figured scenes with Gallo-Roman iconographic trends, and it appears appropriate to group it here rather than with truly prehistoric material. The cauldron (C1) consists of five inner and seven outer silver plates, once gilded (Megaw, 1970, no. 209a), depicting what appear to be Celtic mythological scenes. On one of the inner panels is portrayed a bearded god (represented by head and shoulders) associated with a wheel held by a small but complete figure of an ? attendant wearing a helmet with knobbed bull-horns. Only half the wheel is depicted, but the complete item would have had no less than sixteen spokes. Whilst the wheel could merely represent a broken chariot-wheel, as suggested by Olmsted (1979), bearing no solar significance whatsoever, its presence on a cult-vessel, associated with a deity and held by a bull-horned figure, may suggest a link with a celestial cult. Certainly Megaw (1970, no. 209a) believes that the wheel is a ritual item. The bull and wheel-association may be important. The bull does have a role to play in Celtic sky-symbolism. This is indicated by the Willingham Fen piece (C6) and by the Maiden Castle bull with its 'S'-shaped tail, recalling 'S' symbols on various cult-items of the Celtic Jupiter (Green, 1977b, pl. X,a). The Thealby and Ribble bucket-mounts (Green, 1977b, pl. VIII, a, b) associate both eagle and bull-motifs, the latter bearing, in addition, a humanoid head. As we shall see below, a bronze bull from a Gaulish site is decorated with solar symbols, and the knobs on the Gundestrup wheel-holder's helmet could be significant if, as is sometimes considered, these also represent sun-motifs. Knob-horns are common on Romano-Celtic depictions of bulls. One may cite as instances the head from Jasseines, Aube (Musée de Troyes, 1898, no. 293, pl. XXVIII) and the Ribble and Thealby items already noted. The true wheel-symbol is not the only example on the Gundestrup Cauldron. One should note also the bust of a goddess on one of the other plates, flanked by two stylized wheel-motifs with lobate spokes (Fox, 1958, pl. 37a).

I.B *Clay Representations*

These include objects of white pipe-clay manufactured in factories in Central Gaul and in the Rhineland, and terracotta items discovered (and presumably made) in Britain. The British group consists of the baked clay mould from Corbridge (C10 ; Pl. LXXIX, Fig. 58) and two antefixes from the legionary fortress at Caerleon (C11; Pl. LXXVII). The Corbridge Wheel-God (C10) is accompanied by an eight-spoked wheel. Noteworthy features include the presence of a knotted club, alluded to above in connection with Willingham Fen (C6), and the decoration on the shield. The fact that the shield itself is rectangular presumably implies its identification as a legionary rather than an auxiliary piece of armour. The ring-and-dot ornament may very well be significant in this context. In chapters II and III an attempt has been made to demonstrate that this symbol may sometimes have solar connections. The motif appears on the double-axe model from Richborough, and on more than one swastika-brooch from Continental contexts. As the mould was manufactured in order to impress the representation of the Wheel-God onto a large ceramic jar, it is a fair assumption that such a vessel may have itself had some ritual purpose. The Caerleon antefixes (C11; Pl. LXXVII) are, by contrast architectural fittings, designed for attachment to the terminals of 'imbrices' on roofs. The British examples may be compared with a similar item from Vindonissa (C79). Both Caerleon examples depict eight-spoked wheels at their apexes, rather in the manner of some of the 'stèles-maisons' of the Saverne region of Alsace (see Catalogue B). In both cases night and day are represented and in one, sun, moon-crescent and stars are all indicated. The humanoid head would appear to be that of a sky or solar deity. The whole idea of such a building-feature must have been to bring good-luck to a structure by means of having the all-powerful Sky/Sun God of the Celts as a permanent watchman over a military installation. The Vindonissa item (C79) is also from a legionary fortress. It is of interest in that here the human head is flanked by a rayed circle and a stylized conifer, recalling Pyrenean altars bearing arboreal and solar motifs.

The Gaulish and Rhineland pipe-clay figurines of the Wheel-God have fairly well-defined geographical parameters. Those made in the German centres — the Trier examples (C14) — comprise enthroned statuettes with the suggestion of a shield-wheel on one side of the throne. Analogues to this composite motif occur on some Jupiter-columns in the Rhineland, where the equestrian Sky-God carries a wheel as if it were a shield (see Catalogue B). The Allier factories produced a series of figurines of which some unequivocally represent a Gaulish Wheel-God (C8, 9, 9a, 12, 13 ; Pl. LXXXIII, Fig. 65). There are, in fact, several hundred pipe-clay figurines in the Musée des Antiquités Nationales, St. Germain-en-Laye collections, including two main Jupiter-types, one with eagle and thunderbolt and the other with wheel and thunderbolt or small individual. The fact that a Celtic Jupiter is intended seems implied by the presence of statuettes otherwise identical but where the wheel is replaced by an eagle (Rouvier-Jeanlin, 1972, Type 1). Eagle and wheel appear interchangeable, and it is perhaps worthy of mention here that, in the Willingham Fen bronze considered above (C6 ; Pl. LXXXI), the eagle and wheel are situated one on top of the other as if in deliberate association. The wheel, in all examples examined by the writer, has five or more usually six spokes, and is either held in the god's upraised hand against his right ear or down by his right side. Frequently, as at St. Pourçain, Moulins and Néris (Pl. 59), a second, much smaller, humanoid individual kneels or stands by the left side of the god, with the deity's hand resting on its head ; sometimes the smaller being's arms are upraised as if to support the weight of the hand. The small being, whether depicted as male or female, appears to echo the function of the chthonic monster of the Jupiter-columns. It was observed in chapter IV that, on these pillars, Jupiter is frequently associated with a smaller figure often portrayed with serpentiform or scroll-like lower limbs. One Néris figure (C9a i) omits the second being; instead the god bears both wheel and thunderbolt. Another Gaulish example (C9 iii) portrays the Sky-God with a wheel and a strange oblong item in his left hand. Unlike anything so far discussed, these pipe-clay statuettes represent cheap mass production for a relatively poor element in society. They are of interest in that they form a link between corporate public and individual private worship. This connection is epitomized by one small clay figure not included in our catalogue since it bears no wheel. This is a terracotta from Voirans (Musée des Antiquités Nationales, St.-Germain-en-Laye) showing a god astride a horse whose forelimbs bear down upon a monster whose body disappears into the earth (Green, 1979a, pl. XXX, figs. 43, 44). The similarity in theme between this and the stone groups upon Jupiter-columns is very striking. Bronzes of the Wheel-God are, and probably always were, relatively few. Pipe-clay is easily smashed, but yet enough fragments and whole specimens survive to indicate that they were, at the least, more popular than metal representations. Here we have an instance of an object which mirrored in miniature the activity of public groups in the worship of the Romano-Celtic Sky-Father.

Another small group of pipe-clay figures should finally be mentioned. There are three in the catalogue, from Van Oudenburg (C78), Thiel-sur-Acolin (12) and Lyon (C82). All bear marked physical similarities to the pipe-clay Wheel-God proper but instead of the conventional wheel, each bears a wheel-like *patera* in the right hand, a curious chain-like object in the left. These figures may or may not have significance in terms of a Wheel-God cult. The flat object in the right hand may simply be a decorated dish, but it is worthwhile to recall stone images of the god from Netherby (Catalogue B, BB17, 18) where a *genius*-like figure holds a wheel, *patera*-fashion, over an altar.

Group II :
Other Anthropomorphic and Zoomorphic Representations
(C15-52 ; 83 ; 84).

II.A *The Hammer-God/Sucellus*

The Gaulish Hammer-God, named on a Sarrebourg monument as Sucellus (Reinach, 1905, 218) has been noted as bearing a marked physical resemblance to Gaulish portrayals of Jupiter. The depiction from Champforgeuil, for example (Armand-Calliat, 1937, pl. XVI), is very like Jupiter in appearance, and Boucher points out (1976, 55) the similarity of

Sucellus' pose to that of bronze representations of Jupiter the Thunderer. In addition, an inscription mentioning Jupiter Optimus Maximus Sucaelus (*C.I.L.*, XIII, 6730) is recorded at Mainz (Toutain, 1907, 197ff.). Apart from this, some bronze figurines of the divinity bear what may be interpreted as solar or astral symbols, sometimes specifically of wheel-shape, suggesting a close connection between this divinity-form and Celtic versions of Jupiter. Boucher makes the interesting statement that it is the least classical bronzes which bear celestial signs, and that such figures appear typologically late (Boucher, 1976, 169 ; Lambrechts, 1951b, 205ff.). This evidence is somewhat at variance with that concerned with pipe-clay material bearing these symbols (see below), which are generally thought of as being manufactured during the 1st two centuries A.D. especially (Rouvier-Jeanlin, 1972, 27).

The most striking symbol-bearing figurine of Sucellus is that from Vienne, Isère (C15), where the pelt-clad deity bears a wheel-like object comprising a larger central and five peripheral 'barrels' joined to the main one by means of five 'spokes' or shanks. The symbolism of the figure is complex ; the lion or wolfskin implies equation or partial identification with Hercules or Silvanus. The pot (a very common attribute of the Hammer-God) may signify prosperity, as does the Celtic name *Sucellus* (the 'Good Striker'). Parts of separately-cast items, which appear to be fragmentary spoked-barrels, exist in the collections of the St.-Germain Museum.

Other statuettes of the Hammer-God indicate possible solar symbolism by means of markings on their bodies or their clothing. Drioux (1921, 67) remarks that several figurines of the god are ornamented by rosettes and diagonal crosses. The Sucellus from Saint-Vulbas (C19) wears a belt decorated with ring-and-dot motifs. The Cologne statuette (C34 ; Pl. LXXXIII, Fig. 66) bears circles and semi-circles on his tunic and legs. The Viège god (C49) holds an object which could be interpreted either as a hammer or a thunderbolt, and bears on his tunic the symbols of crosses and swastikas. The association of a known solar sign, the swastika (presumed to have been a variant wheel-symbol [Thevenot, 1968, 22]) with the cross suggests that a similar significance may be implied for this latter motif. A number of depictions of Sucellus are associated with the diagonal or 'St. Andrew's' cross, which I have elsewhere attempted to show may have solar symbolism. These include the bronze in the Musée de Châlon-sur-Sâone (C22) showing a seated male figure, the side-front panels of whose chair or throne bear such crosses. The Nolay (C29) and

Roger (C30) statuettes also bear diagonal crosses, as do those from an unprovenanced Gaulish site (50) and from Beaune (35) where the deity, in addition, carries a barrel on the end of a long staff instead of the normal long-handled hammer (recalling the Vienne figure described above). The Lyon Sucellus (C37) is of interest in that it bears not only diagonal crosses but also 'L' shapes, which are enigmatic but, according to Toutain (1916), could represent keys (presumably the keys to the afterlife [see below, and personal information from J. M. C. Toynbee]). A Sucellus figure (without celestial motifs) from Stuttgart (Toutain, 1916, fig. 4) carries in his hand an 'L'-shaped item. The Maranville figurine (C23) stands out in its corporeal decoration of celestial signs which take the form of lobed shapes, crosses, rosettes and true wheels. This association of lobe and wheel may be paralleled on the Churcham stone figure (BB8) (see Chapter IV). The Pully Sucellus (C83) bears both Latin and diagonal crosses on his body.

II.B *The Celtic 'Pseudo-Venus'*

The second major type of representation in this group is the version of the Celtic Mother-Goddess, represented by pipe-clay figurines resembling the classical Venus in art-form, which were mass-produced in Gaulish and Rhineland workshops. Blanchet (1890, 146ff.) was one of the first scholars to suggest that the pipe-clay 'Venus' was a local Celtic deity rather than the classical Love-Goddess, partly because of distribution and partly because of her frequent occurrence in cemeteries. Whilst most of the several hundred figures produced are plain, devoid of any external decoration, a significant number do bear wheel (or related) motifs. C26, in the collections of Rouen Museum, has wheels and astral signs. The example from Tronëon in Brittany (C32) bears wheel-symbols on the clay outlining the body on each side. Rings, concentric-circles, stars, rosettes and true wheels occur alone or in various combinations on C40, ii ; 41 ; 43-46 ; 84. On a few figures the celestial motifs are numerous, as if to intensify their potency. For instance, C31, from Bro-en-Fegréac, is decorated with astral symbols and wheels beside the body and the rear of the statuette bears rosettes and crosses. Another multi-motif figurine is that from Caudebec-lès Elbeuf (C42) with wheels, concentric-circles and sun-signs taking the place of the breasts, on the trunk and thighs, and by the sides of the legs. The thighs also bear lunar crescents. Perhaps the most interesting pipe-clay portrayal of this type is one from the Moulins, Allier, district of Central Gaul (C40, i), one of the main centres of production. It consists of a group-representation comprising a 'Venus', accompanied by a male adult and a child. The goddess wears a sun-symbol suspended on a necklet. Large stylized sun-wheels are depicted at the rear of the group. Most interesting of all is the presence of aquatic birds associated with solar signs on the lower half of the front. It is conceivable that the water-birds (ducks or swans) could possibly have archaic connections with those frequently found associated with wheel-symbols during the later half of the Bronze Age and beginning of the Iron Age (see Chapter I). Finally one further feature of the Bro-en-Fegréac figure (C31) should be noted ; that is the presence, in the goddess' right hand, of a scroll-like object. This item may be explained in a number of ways; the scroll-motif could demonstrate a link between the 'Venus' and the 'Genii Cucullati', who sometimes bear scrolls and who are godlings of prosperity and the Underworld (Heichelheim, 1935, 187-195). Ultimately, these little hooded figures, occurring widely in Romano-Celtic iconography, are derived from the classical art-form of Telesphorus who represents wisdom as acquired through the art of writing, but in a Gaulish context the art-form does not necessarily appear to be ritually significant, and the scroll accompanying these 'Genii' may be meaningless. However, the functions of 'Cucullatus' and 'Venus' are essentially similar, and it is easy to see how a Gaulish craftsman could borrow attributes from one god for another of similar function. Alternatively the scroll in the hand of the Bro-en-Fegréac 'Venus' (C31) could be more meaningful and have connections with the spirals or 'S'-symbols carried, for instance, by the Le Châtelet Wheel-God (C2 ; Pl. LXXIX, Fig. 57). Again, there is scroll-symbolism associated with some of the small humanoid figures accompanying stone representations of the Wheel-God. Whether or not this particular emblem, occurring in one instance only, may be justified in terms of present knowledge, the most abiding interest of these 'Venus' figures is their unequivocal association with solar symbolism in its different forms ; it is especially noteworthy that on the example from Caudebec (C42) the nocturnal motif of the moon is also present.

II.C *Other Female Representations*

Fortuna, Epona, a Mother-Goddess and two indeterminate female figures are included here. Fortuna need have no significance in a Gaulish context since she is associated with a wheel in classical tradition. However, it might be argued that this very fact may have suggested a Romano-Celtic association between herself and an indigenous Wheel-God. The Echzell Roman fort, which produced a wall-painting of the goddess accompanied by a wheel (C28) was close to Saalburg, whence comes a number of wheel and swastika brooches (see Catalogue A). Both the bronze figures in the index (C16, 17) have well-defined wheel-symbols and, on the Autun example (C16), the motif is large and out of proportion to the rest of the figurine.

The Epona representations (C25) are noteworthy in that they lend weight to the idea of a connection between the Romano-Celtic Horse-Goddess and the Celtic Sky-God, already evidenced by the stone Epona-carving from Agassac (Haute-Garonne) (Magnen & Thevenot, 1953, no. 223). Other factors which strengthen this association include the equestrian attitude of the goddess, which recalls that of the god surmounting the Jupiter-Giant columns, and the almost identical distribution of the two art-forms. The present portrayals take the form of lead 'medallions' in the form of openwork wheels in the midst of which are profile-depictions of Epona. This method of representation is virtually identical to that of the Celtic Jupiter within a wheel, also in lead, from Plessis (C5); there is strong suggestion of a close ritual association between the two divinities (see Chapter VI).

Epona may well be a kind of fertility or Mother-Goddess as well as patroness of horses. This is suggested by her frequent burdens of corn-ears, loaves, fruit and other emblems of earthly prosperity. One other representation in this group consists of a standing Mother-Goddess in bronze, from Buxières-d'Aillac, Indre (C21). In her left hand is a *patera*, in the right a circular object which has been identified as a cake, but which bears six well-defined lines radiating from the centre. If the object is a ritual cake the incised markings could be interpreted as divisions into six portions. In my opinion this is an unsatisfactory explanation ; it is difficult to see why such a division should be significant. It is, I believe, more likely that the cake has superimposed and combined solar-symbolism, or that the object has been mis-identified and is in fact a true wheel. It is of interest that wheel-shaped 'cakes' are known in Italian religion, in connection with the cult of Jupiter Summanus (Pattazoni, 1954, 95).

The two final female representations in this section comprise a bronze statuette and a pottery flagon. The bronze, from Dompierre-sur-Besbre (C24) could perhaps be a priestess or a worshipper. She is fully draped, and wears a necklet suspended from which is a concentric-circle pendant, which could be significant in terms of wheel-symbolism. The Rheinzabern pot (C27) has two handles and a narrow neck on which is depicted a ? female human face. The neck is ornamented by a necklace upon which is hung a six-spoked wheel as a pendant. This depiction immediately brings to mind the genuine metal chains with wheel-shaped pendants known, for example, from northern Gaul and from the North and West of Britain (see Catalogue A). The similarity between the wheel-types is very close. The Rheinzabern pot, which is, incidentally, from the vicinity of a great tile and pottery-making establishment, bears a wheel with knobs at the hub and where the rim meets the chain or necklet. The gold wheel-pendants, like those from Dolaucothi and from Backworth, for instance, are ornamented with knobs at the centre and where the spokes meet the rim or felloe.

II.D *Other Male Representations*

The bronze figurine of Hercules (C18) from a Swiss site is a dubious inclusion here. The Latin-Cross marking on his chest is considered by the scholar who originally published the figure, as of significance. If the motif is anything other than pectoral muscle-depiction, then this particular portrayal of Hercules could be a Romano-Celtic version, perhaps allied to the Celtic Sky-God. The repeated presence of the wheel and club together has already been commented upon. In addition, the Vienne Sucellus (C15), carrying a variant wheel-symbol, considered above, wears a pelt of what may be a lion, thus connecting this deity with the Gaulish Hercules.

Three pipe-clay male figurines should next be looked at. C47, from Brittany, is only a fragment, but portrays an individual wearing Gaulish clothes and decorated with wheels and concentric circles, in much the same way as the Celtic 'Venus' figures described above. The Quilly representation (C48) is of more interest since he is in a cross-legged attitude. The figure is beardless ; sun-symbols and stars are depicted beneath his right elbow. On the back of the statuette appear semi-circles (as on the Sucellus bronze from Cologne), circles and stars. In addition the god wears a necklet decorated with small circles. At the tips of the fingers is a small aquatic bird, recalling the ducks or swans on the Caudebec 'Venus' (C42). Whilst it would be a mistake positively to identify the god represented at Quilly as the stag-horned, squatting deity Cernunnos (the antlers are not present and may never have existed, and a cross-legged position would be a natural one for Celtic peoples who habitually sat on the floor), it is worthwhile to remember that true portrayals of Cernunnos are associated with prosperity and well-being (as one presumes is the case with the Mother-Goddesses). The stag-horned god depicted on the Reims stele (Thevenot, 1968, 148) is associated with the divinity Apollo, who had a solar aspect to his cult. It looks as though the Quilly figure may have associations both with prosperity/fertility (like the similar pipe-clay 'Venus')and with solar-symbolism.

The only divinity within this group who is specifically named is a local and otherwise unknown deity 'Brixantius'. A bronze key dedicated to the god comes from Moulins-Engelberf (C36). The presence of the diagonal cross may connect both god and key with a sky-cult. It should be recalled that the Sucellus figurine from Lyon (C37) bears both 'St. Andrew's' crosses and 'L'-shaped objects which may be interpreted as keys (Toutain, 1916). At this point it may be observed that an uninscribed bronze key bearing a similar cross occurs at Maubeuge (Ozeel, 1973, 17-22), and that a number of miniature items from the Rhineland multi-model grave-groups (Rottländer, 1973-74) bear incised diagonal markings. Other sacred items, from Britain, also bear this mark, and it behoves us to be cautious in assigning celestial significance to all occurrences. It appears, for instance, on a pipe-clay 'Dea Nutrix' base at Richborough (Green, 1978, 70), and on the base of a bronze 'Bonus Eventus' from the same site (*ibid.*, 68); it appears on the knife from the Muntham Court temple-site (Green, 1976, 220); on a model shovel from Oxfordshire (Green, 1977a, 256-260); and on a ceremonial pole-tip from Milton, near Peterborough (Green, 1975a). Whilst I would assert that the diagonal cross sometimes has significance in terms of a sky-cult (see chapters III, IV) it would be dangerous to assume it is always so.

The final male representations in this section comprise oriental depictions, which probably have nothing but a superficial and physical connection with Celtic Sky-God symbolism. One is the triangular bronze plaque from Central Europe (C51) dedicated to Jupiter Dolichenus and Juno Regina. Near the apex of the triangle is an eight-spoked wheel-rosette. Whether this symbol is a straightforward Syrian representation of the sun or whether there is syncretism between Celtic, Roman and Eastern Sky-cults is problematical. The Cologne Mithras-jug falls into a similar category (C33). The pot bears depictions of Sol and the *cannophori* ; there are definite wheel-motifs painted around the vessel in pale-brown. It is impossible to tell whether or not Celtic symbolism has crept in or if it is merely Sol or his chariot which is represented. The unprovenanced Roman bronze figurine of Mithras in the Ashmolean Museum (Ashmolean Museum, 1902, no. 55), only the left arm of which survives, bears two solar asterisks and a swastika. The hand and symbols bear traces of silvering. The sun-signs occur in a similar position on a bas-relief of Mithras on the site of Antium (*ibid.*). The swastika-sign may represent Celtic symbolism, but we have no means of knowing where the figure was originally found, and both wheel-less sun-motif and swastika are acceptable in an oriental solar context.

II.E *Animals*

We have evidence that certain beasts from Romano-Celtic sites have connections with celestial symbolism. Apart from aquatic birds, already considered, bulls and horses are relevant here. The bronze bull from St.-Rémy-de-Provence (C20) wears a ritual girdle ornamented with solar circles, very similar to those on the belt of the Saint Vulbas Sucellus (C19). The bull-lamp from an unprovenanced site in the Marne area (C39) bears an incised diagonal cross at the back of the left front leg. Symbol this must surely be, since the mark would not normally be visible when the lamp was being used. Possibly the sign was scratched on in order to improve the light-output of the lamp by dedicating it to a celestial power. Of greatest interest, perhaps, is the Avrigney triple-horned bronze bull (C38) which bears a rosette-shaped growth of hair on its forehead. The association of the bull with a sky-cult is positively evidenced, for instance by the Willingham Fen sceptre (C6 ; Pl. LXXXI) with its triple-horned bull-head and Wheel-God, or by the Ribble and Thealby bucket-mounts (Green, 1977b, 297-327). The other beast with overt celestial associations is the horse, interestingly enough portrayed in pipe-clay and possibly from the same centres as produced the other pipe-clay figures already considered. The cache of horse-statuettes from Assche-Kalkoven in Belgium (C52) contains beasts wearing harness which is sometimes ornamented both with *lunulae* and with other celestial motifs. There may well have been a sanctuary here, although all traces of such a structure have vanished. The horse was associated with solar cults in Europe long before the Roman period ; in addition there is Romano-Celtic evidence for a link with the Sky-God, in the form of the equestran figures at the summit of the Jupiter-columns.

Group III : Miscellaneous Items Bearing Sky-Symbols

III.A *Pottery*

Ceramic vessels and tiles are the two categories of object under discussion. C54, 55, 56, 59, 60, 62, 65, 68, 71, 73, 75, all consist of pots or sherds with wheels or swastikas incised, stamped, applied or painted on them, unaccompanied by anthropomorphic or theriomorphic representations. The three virtually complete vessels from British sites, from Silchester (C54), Littlehampton (C55) and Caistor (C56), which are colour-coated vessels with slip or painted decoration, may be ornamented in a purely secular fashion, but it is possible that they are cult-vessels. The same may be true of the Manchester bowl (C62) with its white-painted wheel-decoration. The greyware potsherds from Malton (C59 ; Pl. LXXVIII, Fig. 56) and from Housesteads (C60 ; Pl. LXXVIII, Fig. 55) are unquestionably from ritual vessels of some kind. All three sherds come from jars, and in all instances the wheel-shapes have been made separately and applied to the smooth body of a coarseware vessel. Other ceramic material from Malton is extremely informative since it includes identical greyware sherds bearing applied tongs, hammers, anvils and human faces. Similar sherds from Corbridge bear smithing equipment, faces and actual representations of a Smith-God himself (Green, 1978, 56). In addition the Corbridge Wheel-God mould (C10 ; Pl. LXXIX, Fig. 58) was for application of its design to a pottery jar, probably of the same type. It is most unlikely that such applied motifs — wheels, human figures and faces, smithing material — have no ritual significance.

Some Gaulish pots likewise bear sky-symbols. The Pyrenean (C65) and Rouen (C68) vessels are ornamented with swastikas. Those from Lons-le-Saunier (C71) and La Graufesenque (C73) have wheel-motifs. The two last-mentioned examples are not strictly Gallo-Roman ; they probably date from the last period of the Gaulish Iron Age. Both pots only bear one wheel, and I think this fact is significant if one is weighing up the chances of symbolism versus decoration. If a potter is merely seeking to decorate a vessel, then he is more likely to repeat the pattern (as happens in the swastika-ornament on the sherd from Finistère [Clermont, 1979, fig. 1]) than to mark a single wheel or swastika. In fact the Lons-le-Saunier vessel, with its incised wheel, may have been marked by a subsequent owner or priest rather than by the manufacturer. The Pyrenean pots (C65) are of interest in that they are swastika-marked, and the swastika is an especially prominent motif on small Gallo-Roman stone altars in that region, some of them actually dedicated to a version of Jupiter (see chapters IV, VI). The Rouen vessel is noteworthy in that it was used in burial. Finally in considering ceramic material one should mention the Nene Valley Ware wheel from Stibbington in Cambridgeshire (C75), although it is not a vessel. It is a buff-pink clay wheel — too large to be classified as a true model yet not full-size. It has a central hole, as if fastened to a wagon or chariot-axle, and brown-painted spokes. It could have been part of a small cart, but, as it is hollow, it would not have stood much strain

Tiles bearing swastika-motifs are recorded on the Continent. Like some of the pot-marks described above, the motifs may merely have been goodluck symbols, if that, the original solar significance perhaps forgotten. In the Hainaut region of Belgium (C61) a *tegula* has been incised with a swastika. The Roman Villa at Anthée (C69), also in Belgium, produced two fragments of tile with incised swastikas. A rectangular piece of brick or tile from Toulouse bears the same sign. Like the Pyrenean pots already considered, this site is in the centre of a distribution-area of swastika-marked altars ; and Toulouse has itself produced two wheel-models (see Catalogue A). Finally both Walldürn and Bad Dürkheim (C64, 74) in the German *limes* area have produced tile-stamps of Legion XXII (based at Mainz) with swastika-motifs. The Bad Dürkheim example is of especial interest since it comes from the vicinity of the Roman quarry which produced curious graffiti and scrawled rock-carvings including men, horses, wheels and swastikas (see Catalogue B). Strasbourg (C67) and Augst (C70 ; Pl. LVII, Fig. 14) have produced tiles or tile-fragments with wheel-symbols. Those from the Alsace town were found in 4th Century A.D. deposits. The Augst item stands out as being, in all probability, a mould for a four-spoked metal wheel-model.

III.B *Glass*

The glass-sherds from Little Houghton (C63) and from Springhead (C57) should be considered in a similar light to the pottery vessels looked at earlier. One example (C63) bears a damaged and worn wheel-motif on the base of a flat-bottomed vessel. The other (C57) is a small sherd with a definite swastika-sign. Both may well have come from cult-vessels. It is worth recalling that Springhead was a 'Tempelbezirk' with evidence for a Jupiter-column (Harker, 1980, 285-288), healing cults, the Celtic Mother-Goddess (as represented by pipe-clay figurines of 'Venus'), a model axe-head, and a pipe-clay horse (Green, 1976, 228).

III.C *Miscellaneous Metal Objects*

A Gaulish (but unprovenanced) votive hand (C58) bears a patera ornamented with wheel-like spokes. This recalls the Mother-Goddess from Buxières (C21) ; the pipe-clay figures from Van Oudenburg (C78),

Lyon (C82) and Thiel (C12) ; and the stone Netherby carvings (BB17, 18). From Strasbourg come two copper or bronze plaques found in a Roman cemetery. Both bear punched decoration (like the Farley Heath binding) in the form of swastikas, and one also bears a Latin Cross. Finally Caerwent (C81) has produced a bronze plate ornamented with a wheel within a rectilinear frame.

III.D *Bone Items*

These comprise only the two (?) bone discs with incised spokes from Casterley Camp, Wiltshire (C76).

Chronology

Little of a significant nature may be said concerning dating. Wheel-symbolism, in this miscellaneous group of objects, occurs from the 1st Century B.C. through to the 4th Century. Gundestrup, La Graufesenque, and Lons-le-Saunier are all probably 1st Century B.C. The pipe-clay factories were in production from the 1st-3rd Centuries A.D., though the Van Oudenburg figure appears to come from a late Roman grave area. The Manchester pot, from its shape, could be of 1st Century A.D. date. The Rheinzabern and Casterley camp contexts appear to be 2nd Century. The Malton and Housesteads sherds may be 2nd-3rd Century. Bad Dürkheim was in operation from the 1st to the 3rd Century A.D. The Cologne jug is suggested as being of 2nd-3rd Century A.D. date. The Landouzy bronze figure could be mid 3rd Century, judging by the formula of the inscription (Fishwick, 1969). The Strasbourg tile-mark is reputedly from 4th Century deposits.

Context and Associations

A consideration of context or association may sometimes be informative. Some items, like the Gundestrup Cauldron, need no ritual findspot to identify them as of considerable cult-importance. Many, less definitive, objects come from military sites or villas, where no indication of a religious context exists. The items from Willingham Fen (C6) ; Farley Heath (C7) ; Trier (?) (C14) ; Assche-Kalkoven (?) (C52) and Springhead (C57) were from, or in close proximity to ritual sites. C66 and C68 come from funerary contexts. Many objects, like the pipe-clay figures, were probably for domestic use and the absence of associated shrines need not trouble nor surprise us. As regards association, it is worthwhile to recall that the Le Châtelet bronze (C2) was discovered in the same area as model wheels (see Catalogue A). The Willingham Fen hoard (C6) produced ravens, Mars and Minerva depictions, two horsemen and a bull's head. The Farley Heath binding was found in a shrine also containing an eagle-figurine. The Néris area (C9a) and Strasbourg (C66, 67) produced wheel-brooches as well as material in the present group. Corbridge (C10) and Cologne (C34) have yielded wheel-brooches ; Toulouse (C72) has produced wheel-models ; Housesteads (C60) has a wheel-brooch ; Augst (C70) has revealed a mass of evidence for wheel-symbolism (see Catalogue A).

Conclusion

Certain categories of find in this section, notably representations of the Wheel-God himself, are unequivocally relevant to this enquiry. It is at least within the bounds of probability that a number of other humanoid portrayals are also associated with the Sky-God cult. We are on less certain ground with what are essentially secular and utilitarian items which happen to be decorated with wheel or swastika-motifs. Swastikas are a common decorative pattern and occur, for instance, quite innocently on mosaics (e.g. Waywell, 1979). Whilst in my opinion there is some kind of symbolism on all the objects here indexed, it is worthwhile to introduce a note of caution in assigning direct and positive solar or celestial significance since, even if the motifs are other than purely ornamental, they may merely represent an unprofound, good-luck, 'touch-wood' symbolism, especially in the case of tile-marks and pottery incisions.

CHAPTER VI

Significance of Monuments and Cult-Objects relating to Wheel-Symbolism

The two previous chapters attempted a stylistic classification of the stone monuments and other non-model items relating to Romano-Celtic wheel-symbolism. This chapter endeavours to interpret them, as far as is possible, in terms of religious expression. I shall not necessarily keep strictly to the groups as classified, since different physical types may share elements of significance. The problem of interpretation is a complex one ; it can be seen from looking at the evidence that there is diverse symbolism. It is necessary first to isolate and examine the main items of potential significance and then to link these, where possible, with a main divinity or cult. It should be remembered that some of the following discussion will also have a bearing on the interpretation of models, in as far as it examines fundamental significance of wheels and swastikas themselves.

I. THE SOLAR MOTIFS

Wheel and Swastika as Solar Symbols

The main feature which is common to all the stone monuments catalogued, and to the miscellaneous small objects, is the presence of a true wheel-sign or its derivative. The usual alternative to the wheel itself appears to be the swastika. As already seen the true wheel may occur with a number of variations. The numbers of spokes vary ; the most common numbers are four, six and eight. But this may be for ease of carving rather than for any true significance. I shall return to the possible meaning of spoke-numbers later. The fact that has to be established at the outset is what the wheel itself stands for in the Gallo-Roman context. There are two main schools of thought — that it is a solar symbol, and that it represents thunder. I shall examine the second hypothesis first. The most prominent exponents of this view include Benoit and Espérandieu. According to the latter (1917, 82) the wheel in Gaul is a symbol of Jupiter, probably because of an allusion to the noise of rolling thunder being comparable to a chariot rumbling across the sky. As his argument Espérandieu uses the name of Taranis, occasionally linked with the name of a Celtic Jupiter (see Chapter VIII) and meaning 'Thunderer'. Benoit (1950, 13) endorses this view, that the wheel represents thunder rather than the sun. Both Thevenot (1968, 37) and Hatt (1951a, 82-87) put forward the argument that the wheel alternates with the thunderbolt on a number of Jupiter-monuments in Gaul, including those depicting the equestrian Jupiter of the columns (Lefort des Ylouses, 1949, 152). The idea of the chariot is a complicated one. First there is the probable association of the Celtic Jupiter with Apollo and with horses, to both of which we shall return. Second, Jupiter on the columns occasionally appears not as a rider but as the driver of a *biga*, as at Besigheim, Stuttgart (Reinach, 1917, 107). On a stele from Bourges it is suggested that Jupiter's wheel has been replaced by a solar *quadriga* (Espérandieu, 1510 ; Hatt, 1951a, 82-87). The alleged replacement of wheel by thunderbolt is, in my view, invalid. It can immediately be seen from the previous sections (Chapters IV, V) that on many Wheel-God monuments both wheel and thunderbolt are present. Hatt (1951a) puts forward the interesting and possibly relevant theory that there is an intimate and necessary connection in Gaulish belief between the sun and the thunderbolt. He states that the thunderbolt may have been considered as an emanation of the sun, thought of as an instrument by which the Sky-God fertilized the earth and caused the occurrence of rain. There is certainly plausibility in the thesis, although no direct evidence. Several high gods in the East, during this period and before, combined the complexities of a rain, fertility, sun and sky function. The Hadad-Zeus-Jupiter of Khirbet Tannur in Nabataea, furnished in the iconography with thunderbolt and double-axe, was concerned with the weather and the sky (Glück, 1965, 203-205). Hatt (1951a) correctly points out that the wheel itself cannot always represent thunder. Its presence, for instance, on the Gallo-Roman funerary steles of the Vosges can bear no logical interpretation as thunder-symbol.

The interpretation of the wheel as a solar sign has gained far wider credence especially among recent scholars and is, in my view, the most satisfactory explanation. The wheel's solar symbolism has been assumed, for example, by Brogan (1953, 182ff.) and by Bauchhenss (1976). According to Gaidoz (1884, 14) the symbolism is obvious since the sun, like the wheel, is circular and moves in space. For Cook (1925, 57-93) the wheel is an unequivocal sun-motif, thought of in these terms in Greek as well as Celtic expression (*ibid.*, 288ff.). He makes the point that in Greece the evidence for Zeus' association with the wheel is literary rather than archaeological. The wheel as the sun appears in classical Greek literature not necessarily associated with a deity :

> 'The eye to menace the wheel of the sun'
>
> Aristophanes, *Thesm.* 17.

and

> 'Stage-carpenter, when you want to send the wheel spinning aloft, say Hail, thou light of the Sun'
>
> Aristophanes, *Daedalos* Frag. 234.

According to Bailey (1932, 260) the sun in Graeco-Roman religion was thought of as an essentially moving object, traversing the earth by day and the lower regions by night ; this movement could, quite logically, be expressed by a wheel-sign. Gaidoz also makes the suggestion (1885, 191-193) that Fortuna's wheel could originally have had some solar symbolism. The Wheel of Fortune is, he attests, a symbol of movement and the mutability of human affairs ; the globe is a substitute. But the ancient Italian goddess Fors Fortuna apparently had a festival at the time of the summer solstice. Other Italian wheel-symbolism may be of interest. Coin-types of Etruria and Umbria bear a wheel on one side and a crescent and star on the other (Bücheler, 1883 ; Pettazoni, 1954, 105). Umbrian religion, at the time of the Roman Republic, had a ritual connecting Jupiter with wheel-symbolism (Pettazoni, 1954, 96-97 ; Devoto, 1940, 366). The Italian god Summanus, a thunder-deity, had offered to him flourcakes in the form of spoked wheels (Pettazoni, 1954, 95).

Looking now outside the classical world, Linckenheld (1927, 100ff. ; also Forrer, 1935, 139) avers that the wheel was already invoked as a sun-sign in Gaul before the appearance of Roman influence and persisted especially on the funerary monuments of Alsace. Hatt points out that the Acts of St. Vincent, a martyr remarking on pagan Aquitanian cults at the beginning of the 4th Century, talk of a custom involving a flaming wheel, presumably representative of the sun (Zwicker, 1936, 302-303 ; Hatt, 1951a, 82-87). According to Tudor the Dacians in the Roman period had a symbolic image of the sun represented on plaques of the Danube region sometimes by simple discs, but on one engraved gem belonging to the cult the sun and moon deities are represented by an eight-spoked wheel and a crescent respectively (Tudor, 1976, 184). It is of interest that in Dacia there are occasional stone monuments representing wheels. The museum of Tropaeum Traiani in Romania has such a monument.

Of the several wheel-derivatives occurring on Gaulish and British cult-items the swastika is perhaps the most important. It is necessary to be cautious in ascribing ritual significance to swastikas in general since the shape can be and was used entirely as a decorative motif and was, as such, diffused throughout the Mediterranean world (Duval, 1957, 13). Grapinat (1970, 54-56) makes the point that the beauty of the swastika means that its use may frequently be ornamental and entirely secular. However, he himself states that the swastika-shape, in a religious sense, represents rotary movement, as does Courcelle-Seneuil (1910, 70). Another idea (Ferguson, 1979, personal communication) is that the swastika represents a maze guarding against evil. Again one has to exercise care in ascribing purely Celtic cult-significance for the motif. It is common in Greek art. It appears, for instance, on a red-figure krater on the breast of a chariot-driver whose vehicle is surrounded by a rayed disc next to which is a thunderbolt (Cook, 1914, 233ff. ; fig. 269). In Roman symbolism the swastika occurs, albeit very occasionally, on North African funerary monuments (*C.I.L.* VIII, 1908, 5192 ; Linckenheld, 1927, 78). Its occurrence, for instance, within a circle at the entrance to a room, on a mosaic at Herculaneum, presumably means that it was a good-luck symbol. In Roman iconography, however, there is no doubt that the swastika was adopted 'par excellence' by the Celts, and it is of interest that Galatian shields of Celtic design, carved on the great Pergamene frieze of Attalus I, bear both swastika and 'S' symbols (Linckenheld, 1927). In the Romano-Celtic world of Gaul and Germany the swastika's associations show it to be of cult-importance. The Bad Dürkheim petroglyphs (B9), suggested as being of 1st Century A.D. date (Thevenot, 1951, 130ff.) are associated with wheel-signs, wheels on stems, stylized human figures and horses. The bronze hammer-deity from Viège (C49) has thunderbolt, key, hammer or barrel on long handle and a tunic decorated with crosses and swastikas (Deonna, 1915b, 145-147 ; 1916, 193-202). Most significant of all is the group of south-western Gaulish altars, some of which appear merely with a swastika but some with the motif associated with other symbolism including the wheel itself, for example at Montmaurin (B82) (Fouet, 1969, pl. XLVIII). The association of several of these altars is with a version of Jupiter, as at Montmaurin, and possibly also with a solar

Mars-cult at St.-Plancard (Haute-Garonne) where Mars Sutagius was worshipped (see below 'Mars'), and near which swastika-altars are recorded (Laffargue & Fouet, 1948 ; Thevenot, 1955). Certain features of these swastika-decorated monuments should be noted here. First, the altars are mainly found, as is the case with the wheel-incised examples, in the mountainous districts of the Pyrenees (Courcelle-Seneuil, 1910, 70). Second, if one bears in mind the geographical proximity of these altars, which are unequivocally religious, the swastikas on coarse pottery of the Pyrenees take on possible significance (Bertrand, 1897, 145ff.). Third, I would argue that whilst wheel and swastika may both have solar associations, they are not representative of exactly the same thing ; if that were the case there would be little point in depicting both symbols on the same monument. Finally the Robernier stele should be mentioned (B117). Probably of immediately pre-Roman date, from the Argens Valley of southern Gaul, it bears equine depictions and a swastika-symbol. Duval (1957, 13) asks the question as to whether the Sky-God was represented here before the Romano-Celtic symbolism was fully introduced. The question is difficult to resolve. There is immediate similarity in content between this stele and the Bad Dürkheim (B9) petroglyphs ; both monuments associate swastikas and horses. But there is probably at least a century and several hundred miles between them. In any case, the later popularity of the swastika-motif as a ritual sign in the area of south-western France, coupled with the undoubted significance of the horse in Romano-Celtic sky-symbolism, make it at least a strong possibility that a sky-cult of some kind is represented. Two final distributional points should be made about the swastika-motif. Whilst wheels and swastikas occur frequently either together or at least in close geographical association in the Pyrenean regions, in the Lower Rhone Valley wheel-bearing monuments are common, but not swastikas. Likewise the swastika does not occur among the wheel-decorated tombstones of Alsace.

In my opinion wheel and swastika are close in ritual symbolism, though one is not an absolute substitute for the other. The wheel appears to represent the sun itself (the wheel-nave), its rays (the spokes) and either an outer nimbus or a sacred boundary (felloe). The swastika has no nave, it has 'spokes' and it has a semi-rim in the crooked angle of the arms. With the swastika, if the maze idea is not valid in this context, the movement of the object is more important than the idea of a wheel itself.

Rosettes and Circles

Other wheel-derivative signs occurring on Romano-Celtic ritual monuments appear to include rosettes and circles, either plain or concentric. The rosette, perhaps more than the swastika, derives from Mediterranean symbolism and by itself need have no Celtic significance whatever. Greek steles bear rosettes (Linckenheld, 1927, 78ff.). In Roman contexts roses are frequently mentioned as gifts to the dead, pledges of eternal Spring in the life beyond the grave. Roses are mentioned in funerary inscriptions and painted on the walls and vaults of tombs (Toynbee, 1971, 63). Rosettes occur both on Spanish and on German monuments of Roman date. Roman influence in the Rhineland was particularly strong because of the military occupation, and the rosettes occur with other flowers, stars and circles (Hatt, 1951b, 146). The Mediomatrician carvers of the Gallo-Roman tombstones of Alsace adopted and adapted the rosette as a funerary motif. Rosettes do occur on these stelai, and Linckenheld's view (1927) is that sometimes they are merely added to fill spaces or as the centre of a floreate arrangement. But the frequency and popularity of the rosette on the Alsace tombstones of 'stèles-maisons' type, coupled with the possibility that the wheel was frequently a Celtic substitute for this symbol on these stones, could mean that in, North-East Gaul, the essentially Roman rosette did have a solar significance, in terms of Celtic beliefs, and represents the survival of a Gaulish sun-cult. It should be recalled that many other Gallo-Roman funerary monuments, for example in the Comminges area (Hatt, 1970, 9-97 ; 1945, e.g. no. 24) bear rosettes, circles and other, probably astral, symbols like wheels and swastikas. Hatt's series E monuments (1945), including a stone from Garin ; series G (e.g. no. 48) from Trébons, with rosettes and semi-circles ; and series J (e.g. no. 74) from Loures Barousse, with rosette and semi-circles, demonstrate the insistent use of the motif on southern Gaulish tombstones. In the Comminges region we also have the great group of altars decorated with wheels and/or swastikas.

Certain other features of rosettes should be mentioned in connection with their possible celestial significance. One is their association with the unequivocally Celtic goddess Epona. At Meursault (Magnen & Thevenot, 1953, no 181) a carving of an Epona-figure is accompanied by a rosette. The St.-Lieu (Algiers) stele is similar (*ibid.*, no. 216). Epona is one Celtic goddess who is mentioned in some detail in Roman literature ; and she is commented upon as having roses offered to her (Juvenal, *Satires*, 8, 157 ;

Apuleius, 3, 27). It will be seen below that Epona would appear to have an important and close connection with the Gaulish Sky-God whose emblem was the wheel ; it is at least possible that the rosette as her symbol could have solar connotations.

Other Romano-Celtic divinities have associations with the rosette-symbol. Pipe-clay 'Venuses' decorated with celestial signs bear the motif (C41). A fragment of such a figure comes from a tumulus at Toulvern in Baden (Linckenheld, 1929a, 72). The fact that a number of these statuettes also bear wheel-signs argues for a link between the two motifs. The same is true of bronzes depicting Sucellus or the Celtic Hammer-God, who frequently appears with wheels, crosses, swastikas, circles and rosettes (Drioux, 1934, 100 ; Linckenheld, 1929a, 69, 74). Boucher makes the interesting observation that it is the least classical, and typologically late, figurines which bear astral signs such as circles and rosettes (Boucher, 1976, 169 ; Lambrechts, 1951, 205ff.). The lateness of manufacture postulated by Boucher is curious when it is recalled that the pipe-clay figures were probably manufactured quite early on in Central Gaul, during the 1st Century A.D. Perhaps the most important link between the rosette and the wheel is demonstrated by the Jupiter-giant horseman from Meaux (B77 ; Pl. XI, Fig. 23) whose left arm is threaded through the spokes of a rosette-like wheel. Another point is that a number of model wheels or wheel-brooches are of roseate form. Third, it is possible that the lobed object in the hands of the Churcham (BB8) stone figure, who appears also with wheels, could represent the petals of a rosette. The wheel on the Foeschen monument (B40) is lobed ; a bronze Sucellus from Maranville (C23) bears wheels, crosses, lobed shapes and rosettes (Drioux, 1934, 100 ; 1929, 67-68).

Two other rosette-contexts in Gaul should be noted. One is the presence on pre-Roman-Gaulish coinage of horses surrounded by rosettes, presumably as solar symbols (Lambrechts, 1942, 73). Allied to this is the point made by Allen (1980, 54-55) that Celtic copies of Greek rose-decorated coins misunderstood the rose and converted it to a wheel or sun. The other context is the presence of rosettes on terracotta andirons from Gaulish settlements also ornamented with diagonal crosses (see below) (Lambrechts, 1942, 49 ; Déchelette, 1898, 245ff.).

Taking all the foregoing evidence into account, the rosette appears, in some cases at least, to have a definite association with the Sky-God. Ritual stone monuments endorse this view. Apart from the Meaux horseman, the Maryport relief (BB16) associates column, horseman and rosette. The stone from Tresques (B152) bears a seven-spoked wheel, a dedication to Jupiter and seven-petalled rosettes on the same monument. The Belbèze stele (B14) bears a symbol which looks like a cross between wheel and rosette.

Circles, concentric circles and semi-circles are commonly also associated with conventional wheel-signs on monuments, and may well have a similar significance. Allen (1980) believes that circles and wheels on Celtic coins are both solar symbols. It could be argued that the semi-circle represents a crescent and therefore a lunar sign ; we shall look at crescents below. However it is my contention that the physical association of semi-circles with other solar motifs may mean that they are stylistic representations of true circles. Looking first at concentric circles and the, in my opinion, related ring-and-dot motifs, a note of caution should first be sounded. 'Boss and ring is a dull repetitive motif turned out in great quantity in central and northern Europe from about the twelfth Century B.C. ...' (Powell, 1968, 155). The concentric circle is ubiquitous in European art, and it behoves us to beware of ascribing too much significance to it on its own. Ring-and-dot patterns can, as we have seen in chapters II and III, be purely secular decoration, but the symbol does occur on miniature axes and other models, and on swastika-brooches. Both the Corbridge Wheel-God (C10) and the, probably, immediately pre-Roman sculpture from Fox-Amphoux (B45) are relevant here. On the shields of both warriors is depicted ring-and-dot ornamentation. Both items are associated with wheels. The British god (Pl. LXXIX, Fig. 58) bears a wheel by his left ankle ; the Fox-Amphoux warrior wears a wheel-shaped pectoral pendant. The true concentric circle appears on Gaulish monuments predominantly on the house-shaped tombstones of the Alsace region (Pl. XIII) and on some south Gaulish funerary stelai. Certain of the north-eastern examples (for example B135, 136) bear true wheels and circles associated. Non-funerary stones, like that from Castelnau-Valence (B21), also carry this association. Hatt (1945, e.g. nos. 48, 74, 92) has produced a number of southern French tombstones bearing circles, rosettes and wheels together. Hatt's no. 63, from St.-Bertrand, is the roof of a cinerary trough decorated with semi-circles, two humanoid busts, an axe, hammer and bird. The association of circles and other celestial symbols occurs both on pipe-clay 'Venus' figures and on bronzes of Sucellus (see Chapter V, Catalogue C) (Lambrechts, 1942, 110). The Sucellus from Santenay bears concentric circles together with diagonal crosses on his body and legs (Reinach, 1894, 171).

Before proceeding to the discussion of other possibly relevant symbols, a point which needs to be raised is that of the multiplication of symbols, either of the same or of different forms on one and the same item. On certain altars, tombstones and figurines, several wheels may occur together or may be associated with one or more rosettes, circles and other 'solar' signs. This occurs, for example, on the (?) mould from Caerleon (BB3), the Churcham plaque (BB8) and on a number of Gaulish stones. Sometimes in the Pyrenees, as already said, wheels and swastikas occur together. Where one has on one object a number of symbols of the same type − multiple wheels, circles or rosettes − then one may assume that the purpose is intensification of the force of that particular motif (if one disregards artistic eclecticism). But when two different but overtly celestial or solar symbols occur together the significance is more obscure. Why should a craftsman represent the same idea with different symbols at the same time ? One explanation − particularly with wheels and rosettes − is the possible marriage between Roman and Celtic forms. This does not work so well with swastikas and wheels occurring together. There is no entirely satisfactory solution. Pure intensification could be the answer if wheel and swastika are interchangeable and the actual form of portrayal is unimportant ; it is more likely that there are subtle differences in meaning which must escape us. A swastika-substitute for a wheel is reasonable since it is simpler to carve straight than curved lines, but sometimes both signs occur together, as already pointed out. The answer may be intensification of the solar motif where wheel and swastika represent different solar properties, hinted at above (physical appearance + movement).

The Significance of 'St. Andrew's' and Other Crosses

In certain circumstances crosses, especially the diagonal cross, would appear to have relevance to wheel and solar symbolism. We have seen that the sign occurs on a number of model objects, notably axes, and on certain swastika-brooches (see Chapters II, III). Whilst I would not wish to aver that in all cases the 'X'-sign bears a celestial meaning, in some instances it may be so. The association of the sign on swastika-brooches is important. Second, the equestrian Jupiter from Scarpone (B143) appears with such a symbol across his chest. We shall be discussing the solar significance of such horsemen below. On Gaulish monuments the 'X' may appear alone or with other markings ; it may occur on ceremonial implements or with deities. Examples of the former include the bronze 'pole-tip' from Milton near Peterborough (Green, 1975a); and, of the latter, the bronze key from Moulins-Engelberf dedicated to a god Brixantius (C36). The name of this god could be important in a celestial context, as will be seen below. A miniature clay altar from La Celle, Aix-en-Provence, bears lozenge, chevron and diagonal-cross decoration (Benoit, 1964, 592, fig. 35). A sacrificial bronze knife with an 'X' mark at the handle-terminal comes from a shrine in Sussex (Green, 1976, 220); a similarly decorated knife is known at Neuss (Novaesium) (von Petrikovits, 1957, pl. 35, no. 73). A stone altar from Chedworth bears nothing but this symbol. Four votive stone hammers from Côte-d'Or, found in a Roman context, bear these marks. One came from a temple dedicated to Apollo at Beire-le-Châtel (Thevenot, 1952, 99-103). The presence of the sign on hammers is of interest because these may have been offered by devotees of the Hammer-God Sucellus. A number of bronze statuettes of this deity bear cross-markings of this nature; an example from Prémeaux near Beaune, has 'X's all over his body (Reinach, 1894, 137). The Santenay example (*ibid.*, 171) bears ring-and-dot and associated diagonal-cross motifs. It is of note that the clay firedogs from Gaulish sites cited by Lambrechts (1942, 49) bear both rosettes and 'X'-symbols. These andirons are ram-headed; in a domestic context such as this one might reasonably interpret the decoration in terms of general wellbeing and prosperity. However, a pre-Roman bronze bracelet from the Oppidum-de-la-Cloche (Bouches-du-Rhône) bears ornament in the form of a ram-horned serpent and a diagonal cross. Certainly the ram-horned serpent is a well-known cult-beast both in pre-Roman and Romano-Celtic contexts. One such animal appears to have a direct association with sky-motifs, occurring on a Gloucestershire altar together with a wheel (BB13). Snakes, as discussed below, have a strong significance in the Romano-Celtic Jupiter-cult, and it is therefore just conceivable that a tenuous link between celestial symbolism and the cross may be maintained with this theriomorphic association. If we look for a moment at the Danubian Rider-plaques of Dacia, it is noteworthy that on stone figured monuments stars appear to be represented by simple 'X's, whereas on lead plaques, which were easier to work in detail, stars are portrayed more realistically (Tudor, 1976, 190). So in one provincial Roman cult at least the astral (if not solar) symbolism of such a sign is fairly sure, though in Dacia night rather than day is represented. Returning to Gaul the presence of a 'St. Andrew's Cross' on an Epona-monument is of potential significance. The stone in question, from Gourzon, is a funerary stele of 'stèles-maisons' type, bearing a depiction of the horse-goddess, with a diagonal cross at the apex of the triangle (Magnen & Thevenot, 1953, no. 228). If, as I shall attempt to show, Epona has a close link in symbolism with certain aspects of the Celtic Sky-God, then her association with such a cross-pattern may endorse the connection. Finally, an idea of Hatt's may have some relevance to the problem. He draws attention (1950, 427-436) to Gaulish coins (Hucher, 1874, pl. I, 2 ; pl. VI, 1) representing a deity in a *biga* drawn by a monstrous winged figure. The god carries a banner on which is a diagonal cross. Hatt suggests (1950, 1951a) that this symbol, like the double-axe or hammer, could represent a thunderbolt. In fact, if we look closely at some of the Alsace funerary monuments, like that at Wasserwald (B167, Fig. 35), it is immediately apparent that the three four-spoked wheels are carved so that the spokes are diagonal to the observer. If we forget the outer rim, then what we have are 'St. Andrew's Crosses'. On this monument the set of the wheels appears to imply movement. I suggest that in some instances, the 'X' may be a 'short-hand' version of a solar wheel-motif.

The Spiral

The most important item here is the Le Châtelet bronze figure of a Wheel-God (C2 ; Pl. LXXIX, Fig. 57) with six-spoked wheel, thunderbolt, and with free-cast 'S'-shaped objects slung from a ring on the god's shoulder. Thevenot suggests (1968, 22) that they may be stores of lightning-bolts carried by the god in reserve. However the 'S'-shapes do not look like lightning, and on depictions of Jupiter's lightning the shape is either jagged to represent forked flashes or the bolt itself looks rather like a loaf of French bread – as on the Le Châtelet statuette itself. The association of wheel and spiral or 'S'-shape is not confined to this figurine. A pot from Silchester (C54) bears ornamentation in the form of wheels and alternating 'S's. On certain stone monuments spirals occur, for example at Bachos-Binos (Haute-Garonne) (B8) where a cinerary container is recorded, with decoration in the form of a swastika with a spiral border. Spirals and wheels or rosettes occur on the St.-Pé burial plaques (B126) ; Geneva (B50) produced a funerary stele with 'S'-shaped symbols ; the same place yielded an example with a concentric circle at the apex (B51). The association of spirals or 'S' shapes and wheels occurs frequently enough for us to assume some connection between them. A further link is provided by the occurrence of two three-horned bulls from Britain. The Willingham Fen 'sceptre-terminal' (C6 ; Pl. LXXXI) bears depictions of a

Wheel-God and a triple-horned bull. The Maiden Castle three-horned bull (E79) bears no wheel-symbolism but its tail forms an unnatural 'S'-shape ; the remains of humanoid busts on its back may indicate that the Celtic Sky-God plus his associates is represented (Frend, 1955, 13). If one is postulating a link between solar symbolism and 'S's then the Pergamene frieze showing La Tène Celtic weapons may be relevant (see Chapter I). Here 'S' signs are represented on Galatian shields together with swastikas. In this connection, much later 'Galatian' evidence from Phrygia takes the form of tombstones, reputedly of 3rd Century A.D. date, bearing astral signs including spirals (Mendel, 1909, 283ff). Returning to Romano-Celtic material, certain other items should be mentioned. The Niederwürzbach 'Viergötterstein' (B90 ; Pl. XVII, Fig. 40) depicts a god holding a wheel the spokes of which are curvilinear and 'S'-shaped. Two pipe-clay figurines of Mother-Goddesses (Blanchet, 1890) are depicted with spiral symbols on their diadems, which might conceivably have a solar association (see below 'Mother Goddesses'). The Bro-en-Fegréac pipe-clay 'Venus' with scroll may embody the same idea. The Grand-Jailly wheel-model (see Chapters II, III) is decorated with 'S'-motifs which were soldered on. An early Gaulish monument bearing a spiral-sign is one of the stones from Mavilly, probably the site of a thermal spring-sanctuary. The Mars figured on the stone bears a La Tène III shield ornamented with spirals. This is of particular note for a number of reasons. First there is evidence, examined later, that the Romano-Celtic Mars had a solar aspect. Second, even considering earlier comments on the possible explanation of 'S's as lightning-flashes, there is apparently a very great similarity between the spirals on the Mavilly item and those depicted on a silver-leaf plaque to Jupiter Sabazius at Vichy, where the god bears a spiral-shaped thunderbolt (*C.I.L.*, XIII, 1496). Vichy was also a thermal cult-establishment, at which another Mars, surnamed *Vorocius* was worshipped (Thevenot, 1955). The Mavilly evidence leads me to consider a further possible interpretation of the spiral, that is as a snake-symbol. As I shall discuss below, there is substantial evidence for the close association between the Romano-Celtic Jupiter and serpents. For the moment the material from Mavilly is sufficient to establish possible connections between spiral and serpent. The Mavilly Mars is associated with a ram-horned serpent (Espérandieu, 2067, 4 ; Ross, 1967, 141, fig. 99). On a second Mavilly stone a ram-horned snake is entwined round an altar on one face, whilst on another a goddess holds two normal snakes (Espérandieu, 2072). Vichy once again is relevant since from here comes a potsherd portraying a helmeted figure of Mars with an oval shield and horned serpent (Thevenot, 1955). Two other possible, though perhaps too speculative and far-fetched, interpretations for the 'S' or spiral, come to mind. One is that (though, by the Roman period, it could have lost all true significance save for a vague solar connection) in origin the 'S' could derive from the profiles of aquatic birds depicted with solar signs especially on sheet metalwork of the Urnfield and Hallstatt periods in Central European contexts (see Chapter I). The other is that the 'S' is a derivative of the swastika-motif – a 'half-swastika', perhaps a 'short-hand' version, just as the 'X' could be interpreted as a sun-wheel without the tedium of portraying the outer rim. Whatever the precise explanation, it seems indubitable that spiral and celestial cult are in some sense intermingled.

Solar, Sidereal and Lunar Motifs

Crescents as well as solar or astral symbols appear on the Alsace funerary stones ; the Forêt de Walscheid stele (B44) bears circles and crescents. The British epitaph from Risingham bears an eight-spoked wheel between two crescents (BB21). The High Rochester altar (BB12) bears swastikas and a crescent. The lunar motif is of interest in association with solar symbols. We have already noted (Chapters II, III) that certain gold and silver chains bear wheel and crescent-signs together. Although Linckenheld (1927) avers that the crescent is Gaulish and a relatively unromanized concept, this is not entirely tenable. For instance, North African stelai of Roman date frequently bear crescents and stars though no actual wheels (Toutain, 1911, 165-175). Linckenheld does make the interesting observation that crescents are not particularly common in very romanized areas. He cites the military stones of the Rhineland, which are generally crescent-less, as being too romanized to bear such barbaric symbolism (1927, 78). The appearance of essentially nocturnal motifs such as the crescent is of note especially where they occur together on the same monument with solar motifs. Study of the Jupiter-giant groups (see below) demonstrates probable dualism and interaction between light and dark or sky and underworld elements. If a gravestone in provincial Gaul bears both solar and lunar signs it may be that both aspects of one and the same divine entity are being acknowledged, or that the deities of both upper and lower worlds are being propitiated. The whole question of solar symbols on funerary monuments will be assessed later in this chapter.

II. ASPECTS OF JUPITER AS A WHEEL-GOD

The Wheel-Symbol Itself

The constant association on the stone and on some bronze and clay items of the wheel or derivative with a deity who may be physically identified with Jupiter (either by depiction or epigraphy) makes it certain that the wheel was a symbol of a Romano-Celtic version of this god. Even where wheel or swastika occurs alone we may be fairly sure of its cult-associations. For instance, at Montsérie, Le Mont-Saçon and Montmaurin, the wheel-sign appears on altars without overt Jupiter-connections, but at the same sites occur Jupiter-inscribed altars of exactly the same type. In these instances and elsewhere in the Pyrenees, the sign alone was obviously sufficient and was sometimes interchangeable with an actual dedication. In the case of funerary monuments such direct evidence for deity is not forthcoming but there is every reason to suppose a celestial connection.

Certain features of wheels themselves may aid in interpretation or they may be entirely incidental. Most physical characteristics have been fully discussed in chapters IV, V and IX. Here I wish merely to recall points which may be significant. One or two comments about the shape of the symbol may be made here. One is that the association between shield and wheel is very powerful and occurs on a number of stones. The Auberive (B6) object is solid like a shield but is held close to the body like the Tongres wheel (B150). The Eckelsheim monument (B36) bears a rider with a very shield-like wheel ; at Quémigny (B114 ; Pl. II, Fig. 2) the item is oval but with a central boss radiating sun-like rays or spokes. On a number of horse-and-rider stones the wheel is gripped by the left hand being thrust through wheel-spokes (see Chapter IV). The warrior-element as shown by other features (discussed below) on many monuments, is very prominent. If, as shall be seen later, there is a close link between the Romano-Celtic Mars and Jupiter, this shield-element endorses the thesis.

A further point regarding a composite function for the wheel-symbol concerns the Netherby stones (BB17, 18 ; Pl. LXXV) where a god, looking like a Genius, holds a wheel-shaped object over an altar. Here the wheel replaces the usual *patera*. One of the Netherby reliefs portrays a true wheel, the other shows a concentric circle-like object with four spokes, but is otherwise identical. Either the *patera*-element is more important on the latter relief or the concentric-circle is simply acting as a wheel-derivative, as suggested above (see 'Symbols'). The pipe-clays from, for example, Van Oudenburg (C78) and Lyon (C82) may suggest similar symbolism.

Other curious features concerning wheel-shape include the Nîmes altar (B93) where the wheel appears to be on fire and at the same time moving very fast (it recalls the Acts of St. Vincent with its tale of a flaming wheel [Hatt, 1951a, 82-87]). The idea may be similar to that on a Garin stone (B47) where the wheel is denticulated, like some models recorded from Gaulish contexts (see Chapter II). We have already mentioned the roseate wheel from the Meaux Jupiter-horseman group, and the 'S'-shaped spokes on the Niederwürzbach 'Viergötterstein'. Finally the Dôle monument should be considered. Here a possible peacock has a tiny four-spoked wheel resting on its head; the bird faces a large spoked barrel whose spokes terminate in smaller barrels, precisely in the same fashion as the 'barillet' carried by the bronze Sucellus from Vienne. This particular phenomenon is difficult to explain. On the bronze the items may be barrels or hammers; the same may be true of the Dôle stele (B33; Pl. XVIII, Fig. 41) – in which case the connection with the Hammer-God is self-evident (see below).

The positioning of wheel and swastika-symbol on stone monuments has been commented upon in Chapter IV. The actual placing of the wheel when associated with the god himself is probably of little significance; but there is an interesting difference between two types of wheel-bearing monument where the god himself is not represented in anthropomorphic form. Whilst the wheel-motifs on Alsace house-shaped stelai are generally at the apex of these stones, the swastikas carved on the south-western Gaulish altars are usually on the base. The latter incidences may be entirely motivated by convenience, but the position could imply a lesser importance for swastikas than for wheels – which are generally (on these altars) in the middle of the front altar-face. The solar symbolism on the Alsace tombstones could embody the idea of the soul rising to heaven.

It is difficult to establish whether or not the number of wheel-spokes depicted on the various monuments is significant in religious terms. On the one hand, the number varies to such a degree that it is hard to see a regular, thought-out pattern. On the other, symbolism was rarely at random in the ancient world and one may be simplistic if one does not recognize that a hidden significance may have been present. One or two monuments may give us a clue in that they bear seven-spoked wheels. The number 7 may have special symbolism as representative of the sun, moon and five planets then known (suggestion from Prof. John Ferguson). Seven-spoked wheels occur, for instance, at Saint-Privat (B129) ; Tresques (B152) and Aigues-Mortes (B2 ; Pl. LXXI, Fig. 42). All are from Gard in the area around Nîmes. It is interesting that the occurrence of seven spokes is so comparatively rare. On the Aigues-Mortes stone a six-spoked wheel is also present and one wonders whether there is any significance in having two wheels with differing numbers of spokes — other than carelessness on the part of the mason.

Size of Attributes

Three points may be made here. Certain attributes on Wheel-God monuments are disproportionately large or small, as if particular features need to be stressed or diminished. The large eagle on the Alise-Sainte-Reine carving (B3) may indicate that the Roman sky-element is of especial importance. The enormous head of the Churcham figure (BB8), with its traces of horns, may indicate the desire to emphasize the head as the most important feature of the carving (Ross, 1967, 61-127). The horns may well be a fertility element (Ross, 1961, 63ff.), and may thus tie in both with Mother-Goddess associations (see below) and with the presence of *cornuacopiae* on some monuments (for example at Netherby [BB17, 18] and at Naix [B88]). The most important comment to be made regarding size is the small proportions of the snake-limbed humanoid creatures accompanying the Wheel-God on some stone and pipe-clay items. As will be seen below, this small being probably represents the chthonic element in the Celtic Jupiter-cult and the difference in size may indicate Jupiter's dominance over the terrestrial and subterranean worlds.

Jupiter's Military Garb

The Wheel-God as Jupiter appears either naked, half-or fully-draped, in tunic and cloak or in full Roman armour. In classical iconography Jupiter is not normally a warrior, and the presence of the soldier-image on some Gaulish monuments has given rise to the figure's identification with the Emperor. Certainly Jupiter Optimus Maximus was a symbol of loyalty and allegiance, rather than simply a divinity, from the 1st Century B.C. Soldiers renewed their pledges to Rome each year by dedicating new altars in Roman forts. We also have the evidence of a number of epigraphic dedications to Jupiter and Augustus on wheel-bearing stone monuments (see Chapter IV) and on the bronze statuette from Landouzy-la-Ville (C3 ; Pl. LXXX). Certainly the presence of armour on the Wheel-

God has led to his equation with the *praeses bellorum* of the Bern scholiast on Lucan (Usener, 1869, 30-31 ; Zwicker, 1934, 50). Cook suggests (1925, 57-93) in talking of Jupiter-horseman groups, that because the sculptors of the columns took their inspiration from the Graeco-Roman gigantomachy − the Battle of Olympian gods and Titans (Charbonneaux *et al.*, 1970) − Jupiter is naturally shown on these monuments as a warrior. But this does not explain the Séguret Jupiter who is not linked with a chthonic being, and who is, on the surface, entirely romanized as a Roman general apart from his large wheel (B144 ; Pls. X, Fig. 22 ; Pl. LXVI) (Courcelle-Seneuil, 1910, 68). I myself wonder whether the military dress is as significant as sometimes thought. Speidel (1978, 39-40) has an interesting point to make about the armour of Jupiter Dolichenus. Whilst the cuirass is normally taken as a sign of the god's military character, the Greek anatomical cuirass was in fact adopted in the Near East in Hellenistic times as the state costume of gods and rulers, simply a standard feature employed in Greek art to represent Oriental deities (Will, 1955, 255-271). This may not be the case in Roman Gaul, but it is worth remembering that armour could be a standardized phenomenon, and that it is in southern, and Greek-influenced, Gaul that the non-Jupiter-giant-type with armour sometimes occurs. However, a war-element may be of significance. The Corbridge god (C10) bears weapons (albeit curious ones) ; the attendant holding the wheel on the Gundestrup Cauldron (C1) is also armed ; if the wheel here is solar, then this may be significant.

The Different Types of Wheel-God Representation

Certain features of some Wheel-God depictions require further discussion in order to try and understand the true significance of the cult. If the god appears as Jupiter, with Roman and Celtic symbols, as at Séguret (B144) and at Landouzy (C3), then as far as physical characteristics are concerned, the symbolism is reasonably straightforward, and rests on the equation of solar and sky-god − Gaulish and Roman (the conflation of solar and sky-deity is a non-Roman association). We have already looked at some individual peculiarities, such as 'S' symbols at Le Châtelet (C2) ; and we will discuss the presence of *cornuacopiae* when looking at Mother-Goddesses and fertility symbolism. Three features remain to be examined. One is the occurrence of the wheel at Gundestrup ; the second is the appearance of a second smaller being in company with the Wheel-God ; the third, which is allied, is the occurrence of Jupiter, generally on horseback, accompanied by a snake-limbed monster — the so-called 'Jupiter-Giant' column groups.

Gundestrup

The wheel occurs twice on this great cult-bowl, held once by a bull-horn-helmeted individual, associated with the bust of a (?)god, the other in company with the bust of a (?)goddess. The first wheel is depicted as a half of a true cart-wheel; the second appears twice as a stylized, lobe-spoked, example flanking the goddess. Olmsted (1979) does not consider the wheel here to be solar, but regards it as half a chariot-wheel, relating it to one of the Dagda myths of the Early Irish sagas. It is impossible to be sure what the wheel represents here, but its occurrence in company with a bull-horned creature who is apparently offering it to a divinity, would seem to suggest that it is a ritual wheel of some kind. If the Cauldron does date to the immediate pre-Roman period and if, as seems likely (see Chapter I), the Wheel-God in some form was known in the Iron Age, then it is not inconceivable that the wheel on this bowl does represent an attribute of the Celtic Sky-God. Likewise the lobed wheels are not inappropriate here. If the goddess is a Mother-Goddess, the association of solar wheels is not unknown (see below). The wheels themselves appear to possess solar qualities in the short 'rays' emanating from the felloes (see Chapter IX).

The Small Individual

The diminutive size of these humanoid individuals has already been noted. What is of interest is a) that the stone monuments and the pipe-clay figurines are virtually identical and b) that in my opinion there is absolutely no difference in symbolism between these small human figures and the chthonic monsters of the true Jupiter-giant groups. This view is enhanced by the Luxeuil group (B72 ; Pl. XI, Fig. 24) where an equestrian wheel-bearing Sky-God has the forefoot of his horse on the head of a chthonic being and also has a small figure by his side (Espérandieu, 1917, 76). The scroll or snake-tail links this figure inextricably with the 'anguipède' of the true giant-groups. The hand of the god on the shoulder or head of the little being is probably indicative of the god's domination, in the same way as the horse-hoof on the giant's shoulders. The miserable expression of the little figure on some pipe-clay statuettes and, for instance, on the St.-Christophe-le-Chaudry stone figure (B123), indicates that the domination is perhaps not always welcome. The 'scroll-tail' on some monuments is of interest. It presumably reflects a serpentine element, but its stylization as a spiral or 'S'-shape may indicate a connection between snakes and spirals already hinted at (above). If, as I believe, both giant and diminutive figure represent a chthonic element in the Sky-God cult, there is still no need to invoke Benoit's thesis of the classical allegory of dead hero offering heads of humans to underworld gods in order to conquer death (Benoit, 1950). Benoit would link the sculptures and pipe-clay figures with the carvings at, for instance, Entremont, where hands rest on heads with closed eyes. As Lambrechts remarks, I think rightly, (Lambrechts, 1951a) Benoit is too much influenced by Mediterranean themes ; he would like to see all Jupiter-giant and 'small individual' groups as essentially funerary, but the evidence does not justify this. One powerful argument against Benoit's thesis is that the small pipe-clay figures are never found in tombs. Whilst, in my opinion, Benoit goes too far in interpreting Celtic in terms of classical thought, he may well have a point as regards art-form borrowing. Just as one can see the Graeco-Roman gigantomachy in the iconography of the Jupiter-giant groups, so there may be classical art-forms which influenced the 'Jupiter-with-a-small-person' depictions. For instance, a sculpture identified as Nemesis from Dionysias in Egypt, dated to the Trajanic or Hadrianic period (Schwarz, 1969, pls.XV-XVII), portrays a fragmentary standing figure with a wheel by its side and with its left foot resting on a small fallen creature.

III. THE EVIDENCE OF JUPITER-GIANT COLUMNS

I discuss these as a group, because, though it is generally the figured sculpture at the summit of the columns which is the most important, the other elements in these composite monuments are also of extreme significance. I should emphasize that only a very small proportion of the 150 or so columns recorded have wheel-bearing depictions, but it is necessary to survey the whole phenomenon of the columns since they do form such a homogeneous and striking iconographical feature. Another point is that it is not only the topmost in-the-round carving that is directly relevant to our study ; the descriptive analysis demonstrates that it is sometimes the 'Viergötterstein' or base stone which incorporates wheel-symbolism.

Construction of the Monuments

A preliminary point which should be made is that frequently, as at Heidelberg, Jupiter-giant columns are associated with altars whose inscriptions bear witness to the existence of a column dedicated to Jupiter (Bauchhenss, 1976, 1ff.). If we look at examples of complete columns (such as that from Merten [Espérandieu, 4425] which is fifteen metres high) we can see all the possible elements, not all of which always occur. There is generally a quadrangular base or 'Viergötterstein' bearing carvings of deities ; above this is an octagonal stele decorated with figures of gods, usually connected with the sun, moon and planets, and with a dedication to Jupiter or Juno. This stele supports a column topped by a Corinthian capital and a horseman-group at the top. The octagonal and quadrangular stone bases are usually outwardly romanized but occasionally, as seen above (Chapter IV), Jupiter is depicted on a 'Viergötterstein' carrying a wheel. A large number of the columns are actually dedicated to Juno (Bauchhenss, 1976, 22-25), suggesting a very close association between Jupiter and his consort, closer than in conventional Roman religion. This may be because of the Celtic trait of worshipping pairs of deities identical in form and function to each other (for example, Mercury and Rosmerta).

The columns themselves may be plain, or with a scale-pattern, or more specifically tree-like, as at Hausen-an-der-Zaber (Bauchhenss, 1976, 1) where it was decorated with oak-leaves and acorns. The species of tree chosen here is of especial relevance to a Jupiter cult since the oak was sacred to the classical god. The tree-element in the columns has been noted (see below 'trees'), but Wightman (1970, 224-225) has the idea that the column could represent a 'cosmic pillar' to keep up the sky. Duval's thesis is that the column was simply to raise the Sky-God as high as possible (Duval, 1957, 264-275). I myself think that both column and tree represent the idea of a link between upper and lower worlds, just as deep pits may mirror a connection between the earth's surface and the nether regions. After all the interpretation of the column's function must be judged in relation to the other elements in the whole monument (see below). Benoit (1970, 87ff.) believes that the column itself could be funerary, and cites columns in Italy (Quagliati, 1932, 69), but Bauchhenss (1976, 14-16) sees as the column-prototype a Jupiter-column set up in the Capitol in Rome in 63 B.C., mentioned by Cicero (*In Catilinam* 3, 19ff. ; *de Diuinatione* 1, 19ff.). A Jupiter-column appears in relief on Constantine's Arch in Rome erected in A.D. 303. Picard sums up the general principle which appears to be present, where he says that the Jupiter-giant columns represent a Celtic iconographical theme fused with a Roman monumental form (Picard, 1977, 89-113).

The Jupiter-Giant Group

Some Celtic Jupiter-columns bear a standing or enthroned Jupiter at the top. Apart from the wheel-element at, for example, Alzey, these sculptures are extremely romanized. The Mainz column, the earliest example in the western provinces and, according to Bauchhenss, the formal prototype, was erected by the *canabae* of the city, on the occasion of Nero's salvation from the 'conspiracy' of Agrippina. The column had a bronze statue of Jupiter at the summit (Körber, 1906, 54ff. ; Strong, 1913, 321-332 ; Reinach, 1917, 23ff.). The Hausen-an-der-Zaber group comprises an armoured warrior, leaping on horseback over a cowering giant. Bauchhenss (1976, 1) insists that the sculptor of the column and group had a very precise knowledge of Greek mythology and that the group represents the Olympian god fighting with the earthbound Titan, the earth-element being portrayed by the snake-limbs of the giant ; thus the old classical gigantomachy art-form was being utilized in a Celtic context to depict a Celtic theme. This idea gains credence if one looks at other media such as coins. Phrygian money minted during the reign of Alexander Severus and Gordian show Zeus on a throne with sceptre and thunderbolt and with two giants with snake-limbs looking up at him (Lelong, 1970, 123-126). Lambrechts (1942, 92) agrees with the thesis of classical iconographic forms being present but stresses that the symbolism is entirely different ; for instance the classical Jupiter is never portrayed on horseback, so the gigantomachy was not completely right for a certain Celtic religious theme. Bauchhenss uses as his argument for the gigantomachy the fact that Jupiter sometimes wears armour, that very occasionally the giant bears arms (for example Bauchhenss, 1976, pl. 25, 27), and that the column-drum at Hausen (*ibid.*, pl. 33) shows evidence of a definite struggle (*ibid.*, 17-19). Bauchhenss would argue further that the peaceful attitude of the giant and horseman, seen for instance at Limbach-Kohlhof, Kr. Homburg (Kolling, 1958, 160-162), shows an allegory of Caesar conquering the province. Bauchhenss would say that the horse and wheel elements are Celtic idiosyncrasies in an essentially classical art-form.

In my opinion certain features in the equestrian Jupiter-group indicate more Celticism than, for instance, Bauchhenss gives credit for. In the first place the snake-element is common both to the giants on these groups and to other portrayals of the Celtic Jupiter accompanied by a wheel (see below, 'snakes'). In the second place constant depiction of the god on horseback is too significant to be explained away without detailed examination. As stated earlier, this equestrian element is never present with the god as a classical being (Lambrechts, 1942, 92). There certainly is a Celtic religious element in this type of monument — already manifested in the wheel, horse and other factors. The distribution of the columns indicates that the religious concepts must be Celtic. A few literary allusions may also be relevant. Maximus of Tyre in the 2nd Century A.D. states (*Logoi*, 8, 8) that the Celts worshipped Zeus, but their portrayals of him were high in oak-trees. A Pannonian Christian, Martin of Tours, apparently saw (according to Sulpicius Severus in A.D. 372) huge columns with idols at the summit (Brogan, 1953, 208). Valerius Flaccus' remark (*Argonautica* 6, 89) on the (probably) Celtic Coralli, worshipping gods associated with wheels and columns (Lambrechts, 1942, 54 ; Green, 1979a, 347), may likewise be relevant :

> ... the serried Corallians left their banners ; barbaric wheels are their emblems, and the shapes of swine with iron-coated backs, and broken columns, effigies of Jove.

A final Celtic feature is the parallel between the column-groups and certain pre-Roman Gaulish coins showing a man emerging from the earth (Lambrechts, 1942, 93).

If the wheel, where it appears on the columns, is solar and native, then it seems to follow that the giant is essentially a native chthonic element, represented as subservient to a sky and sun-deity. Whilst it is true that the motif usually represented is one of support for the horse and rider rather than resistance, this does not mean that the idea of superiority on the part of the rider is absent. I would not go so far as to say that Jupiter represents good and the giant evil ; I do not think that Celtic religion worked in such 'black-and-white' terms. My belief is that there is a dualistic element in the cult and that, just as the wheel itself depicts movement (perhaps from upper to lower regions), so this group may represent day and night, light and darkness, and the higher and lower elements in a Celtic mythology. According to Lambrechts (1951a) the god was the supreme ruler of life and death ; Wightman's related view (1970) is that the antithesis of life and death is portrayed. There is a marriage here of Graeco-Roman and Celtic iconography and belief. The Celtic theme of dualism, light and dark, found a ready formalized outlet in various classical mythological themes. Thus we should not be surprised if we cannot entirely disentangle what is classical from what is Celtic. The two elements came together precisely because there was a certain similarity in thought. The only danger is in interpreting religious expression in terms of foreign art-forms simply because those art-forms were borrowed. Once again Picard expresses what has probably taken place fairly clearly, where he says that, in the case of the Jupiter-giant groups, there has been a replacement of indigenous concepts with a Graeco-Roman divinity of corresponding function (Picard, 1977, 89-113).

The idea of the rider himself representing the Emperor (Bauchhenss, 1976, 22) is a problem ; Picard (1977, 89ff.) is of the opinion that the column-groups express loyalty to Rome and thus are a form of imperial cult-expression. I myself think that the rider is definitely Jupiter himself, as does Espérandieu (1917, 77). The dedications prove this. But it is not impossible that the conqueror-idea was not totally absent from some sculptors' minds. Credence is lent to this by some of the epigraphic evidence on some Gaulish altars which combine the worship of the Emperor with that of Jupiter, and bear wheel-symbolism (see Chapter IV). In this context we should not forget the Landouzy bronze statuette (C3 ; Pl. LXXX) of a Wheel-God dedicated to Jupiter Optimus Maximus and the Numen of the Emperor.

The upper and lower world-element embodied in the groups gains validity when we look at some further features of the columns. For instance, we shall see that Epona and the male equestrian of the columns have similarities both in distribution and in the presence of the horse (Magnen & Thevenot, 1953). Epona has fertility, earth and underworld symbolism. Jupiter-columns and Epona are sometimes found associated with water (Hatt, 1951a, 82-87) and associated with tombs (Lambrechts, 1949, 145ff. ; Picard, 1977, 89ff.). Richmond (1950, 22-23) would see parallels between 1st Century Rhineland tombs showing horsemen riding down enemies and Jupiter-giant groups. The solar element, shown sometimes by the wheel, is further suggested, for example, by the Besigheim, Stuttgart, Jupiter-group where the god drives a chariot and where there is an 'anguipède' on the ground (Reinach, 1917, 157). The interpretation of the horse as a solar beast is shown at its most powerful (see also below 'Horses') by, for example, the giants from Mouhet (B87) and Tours (B151) where the wheel itself is on the back of the giant as if replacing the horseman. A further indication of sun and light-symbolism is offered by the close proximity, in the Bourgogne and Nièvre area, between Jupiter-giant groups and a number of god-epithets recalling the sun — for instance 'Candidus' at Entrains (Nièvre), associated with the spring-deity Borvo ; 'Vindonnus' (clear) at Essarois, associated with a spring ; 'Lussovius' (bright) at Luxeuil (Haute-Saône), associated with a water-spirit Brixia (Lebel, 1940-46, 61-64). The Luxeuil evidence is of extreme interest since we have a Light-deity, a Jupiter-group with a wheel, and Brixia, in close proximity. This last name recalls the deity Brixantius (C36) to whom a bronze key decorated with a diagonal cross was dedicated (see above 'St. Andrew's Crosses).

The final physical element in Jupiter-giant columns to be looked at is the Corinthian capital. According to Benoit (1970, 51ff.) the capital with stylized acanthus leaves and four humanoid heads or busts has Graeco-Italian origins and appears in southern Italy in the 4th Century B.C., being adopted in Gaul for Jupiter-columns. Benoit suggests that the combination of foliage and human heads has a nature-cycle/saviour-god symbolism, which would fit in well with ideas of dualism postulated for the Jupiter-groups. This may be the reason for the Bacchic symbolism on the possible Jupiter-column capital from Cirencester (Phillips, 1976a, 35-41). Other Jupiter-groups do have wine/saviour symbolism. For instance, the Walheim column (Bauchhenss, 1976, 22-25) bears vine and grape-motifs. There may, however, be other causes for the, somewhat curious, Dionysiac symbolism. It occurs on an altar to Jupiter from Irgeitscheim (Phillips, 1976a, 40) ; and Rose (1948, 78) mentions that 'Liber,' the name of a Roman wine-god, was a title also used of Jupiter. The precise connection between the two is unknown.

The Presence of the Wheel on Jupiter-Giant Groups

One more interpretative point has to be considered, and that is the precise role of the wheel in this context. It occurs very infrequently and is therefore by no means an essential element like those represented by the snake-limbed giant and the (frequently) equestrian Sky-God. It is my opinion that the solar symbolism of the wheel-motif doubles that already evinced by the horse-element. The horse itself very probably has a solar element (see below) in Gaul, and the wheel-presence may intensify or reinforce the solar force of the iconography. Thus, for instance, if the Alzey (B4) and Séguret (B144) Wheel-God monuments are portions of Jupiter-columns as Bauchhenss believes (1976), the Celtic solar element is indicated just by the wheel, the horse being absent. On Jupiter-column groups with no wheel or horse, one can only assume that the romanization of those individual sculptures is of particular strength. In these cases either the solar element is entirely absent or it is known and 'silently' acknowledged. The absence of the wheel-symbol on some monuments need not surprise us. At Montmaurin, for instance (B82) there is an altar decorated with wheel and swastika, and another dedicated to Jupiter but without such symbolism. In this instance the solar motif must be tacitly present but not, of necessity, depicted.

The Siting of the Columns

Destruction, possibly Christian destruction (Bauchhenss 1976) has reduced the potential evidence of these columns. The Wasserwald Jupiter-group was found in fragments which were dispersed over 100 metres; the fragmentation could have been deliberate (Colin, 1927, 173ff.); the phenomenon could tie up with the deliberate attempt at erasure of the wheel and thunderbolts on the Lansargues stone (B66; Pl. IV, Fig. 6). Still, the physical composition of the monuments would mean that they were vulnerable, especially the sculptured groups which were perched at the top and would be the first things to smash if the columns toppled, even accidentally. Thus it is frequently difficult to pinpoint the exact provenance of a column or group. Many appear to be from the vicinity of villas, which is interesting considering how extremely costly they must have been to set up. But many were erected publicly in cities – as at Mainz and Paris. Others again were put up in remote sanctuaries, as, for example, at the shrine of Le Donon, on a Vosges peak 1000 metres above sea-level. At Heidelberg-Neuenheim a column was found on the site of a Mithraeum (of possible significance if one looks at Mithraism, its dualism and light-symbolism). One point of interest is that the columns were not often set up actually within the forts of the *limes* (Bauchhenss, 1976, 7ff.). We assess the evidence for dedicants, patrons and craftsmen at the end of this chapter.

IV. INANIMATE ATTRIBUTES ASSOCIATED WITH WHEEL- AND RELATED SYMBOLS

Trees

Oak-trees (the classical dendromorphic attribute of Jupiter) and other species, are frequently represented on wheel-bearing monuments. On the Trier 'Viergötterstein' (B149), the youthful Jupiter wears an oak-leaved crown. The Séguret figure (B144) is accompanied by an oak tree. On one of the Netherby reliefs (BB18) a boar stands in front of a tree (which may well have been an oak). This iconographic theme is of extreme potential significance. There are certain pre-Roman Celtic coins which bear the associated symbols of boar, tree and solar-motifs (personal information, Dr. D. Nash ; Allen, 1980, nos. 376-377). What we may have at Netherby is a theme remembered and handed down to a Romano-Celtic craftsman who depicted a 'Genius' with a wheel instead of a *patera* and with the ancient symbols of boar and tree (we should remember the Coralli with their wheels and boar-likenesses, and the Hounslow association (see Chapters II, III) between boars and wheel-model). The association of boar with tree may serve to symbolize that the tree was an oak (boars being especially fond of acorns), and thus there is a neat association with the Roman Jupiter. An indeterminate tree is represented on the St.-Romain-en-Gal mosaic (B130). Although by no means the majority of Jupiter-giant column-groups bear wheels (see above) some do, and thus it is of interest that a number of the columns represent trees. We have already seen that the Hausen column actually had depictions of oak-leaves and acorns. Many other columns bear scales which it is suggested (Bauchhenss, 1976, 1ff.) are stylistic representations of bark. On Trajan's Column, for instance, trees are thus portrayed. Early scholars studying the phenomenon of Jupiter-columns, such as Hertlein (1910) and Cook (1925, 57-93), suggest that the column itself is representative of a tree-trunk, especially where scales or vine-leaves are present, as at Heddernheim. Powell goes further (1958, 136) to postulate that Jupiter-giant columns had native forerunners in wood with, as their ultimate model, a growing sacred tree. There appears to be true equation here between Roman and native Gaulish beliefs. The classical Jupiter had an oak-tree association ; the Gaulish Celts may well have had a cult involving a sacred tree. One of the Bern scholiasts on Lucan (Usener, 1869, 30-31 ; Zwicker, 1934, 50) mentions the Celtic Taranis (see below, Chapter VIII, for his connection with Jupiter) being invoked with human sacrifices by burning them in a tree-trunk. Caesar (*de Bello Gallico* VI, 16) states that some sacrifices to Gaulish deities were made by burning living beings in huge wicker images. On some wheel-bearing Romano-Gaulish items the tree depicted bears no resemblance to an oak, but is, instead, a conifer. On others again the dendromorphic image appears to represent a palm-branch. It should be noted that, if one is making a rough carving on a stone, conifer and palm-branch may look rather alike, consisting in each case of a vertical stem and upward-slanting lines on either side. A clay antefix from Vindonissa (C79), similar to those from Caerleon (C11), portrays a human head with on one side a rayed circle and on the other a stylized conifer or palm (Leibundgut, 1966-76, 84, Abb. 28). A house-stele from the Metz area (B15) bears wheel and branch decoration conflated, the wheel's spokes terminating in twig-likes extensions from the felloe. Otherwise the conifer/palm-bearing stone monuments are clustered in the Garonne region of south-western Gaul, associated either with wheels or swastikas. A stone from Valentine (B159) has a wheel, swastika, tree *and* palm-leaf. A stele from Ilheu (B60) bears a wheel and an isolated leaf. An altar to Jupiter and Minerva from Géry near Béat, in Toulouse Museum, is decorated with a tree or palm-branch (Espérandieu, 842 ; Reinach, 1917, fig. 131); interestingly, a swastika-carved altar, also from the Pyrenees (B106) is also dedicated to Jupiter and Minerva. So there appears to be a connection between conifers and/or palms, wheels/swastikas and the worship of Jupiter. The presence of conifers and palm-branches (if they can be separated) is enigmatic. If conifers grew in abundance in the Pyrenees region and oak-trees did not, then we may have a Gaulish substitution by local craftsmen, of their most familiar trees for the oak. Alternatively, it was perhaps the idea of any tree or vegetation in some form that was important, and the trees represented are merely basic stylistic representations with no particular thought as to specific type. If so, their presence may either be concerned with the symbolism of a tree stretching up into the sky and acting as a link between celestial and chthonic regions, or it is life, greenery and vegetation itself which is significant. Allied to this is the possibility that the stylized 'trees' are neither conifers nor palms but ears of corn. If that is the case then such depictions form a link with fertility symbolism, Mother-Goddess association and other signs of well-being, such as *cornuacopiae*, which, as we shall see, all have important connections with the Gaulish Sky-God cult.

Hammers, Axes and Thunderbolts

The association of hammers, either long-shafted or normal, is significant. When we come to discuss Sucellus, the Gaulish Hammer-God, and his connection with Celtic versions of Jupiter (below) it will be realized that it is the hammer itself which forms the vital link between both kinds of art-form or entity. The association between hammers and wheels is of two basic types. One concerns representations in bronze of Sucellus, where the god bears his long-hafted implement and has solar symbols marked on his body. The other is where a wheel-decorated altar also bears a depiction of a hammer. Perhaps the most important bronze figure of the Hammer-God in the present context is that from Vienne (C15) where, instead of the hammer proper, the deity bears a long staff on top of which is a central 'barrel' or cylinder, with five radiating spokes each terminating in a smaller barrel. Bearing in mind other Sucelli with solar symbols on body or clothing, it seems inescapable that what we have here is a hammer/wheel. According to Chassaing, the 'barillet' is bound up with sun-symbolism (Chassaing, 1956, 156ff.); indeed, it seems difficult to interpret the object and other small isolated spoked-barrels occurring in the French archaeological record any other way. In this context, the stone monument from Dôle in the Jura should be recalled (B33 ; Pl. XVIII, Fig. 41). The carving comprises a four-spoked wheel touching the head of a crested bird, and an eight-spoked barrel with the spokes terminating in smaller barrels. Here wheel-symbolism and 'barillet' are directly associated. The species of bird is equivocal but it is possibly a peacock, Juno's classical attribute. There is one further point here. Stone representations of Sucellus frequently bear barrels by the god's feet (Lambrechts, 1942, 100ff.). These may be interpreted as signs of the god's prosperity-symbolism. It is just possible that the curious 'barillet' may incorporate wheel, hammer and barrel.

Returning to true hammers, on a number of monuments wheel and hammer are juxtaposed. This is the case with a stone from St.-Quirin (B43 ; Pl. XIII, Fig. 29), a funerary stele from Alsace bearing a radiate sun-shape and hammers. Another funerary monument, from the Gard region of southern France (B31), bears a wheel and a hammer. A Vernègues stone bears a six-spoked wheel, two trees and a long-shafted hammer (B163 ; Pl. VII, Fig. 15), together with two pots (Chaillan, 1907, 357-358, pl. on 357). The most informative carving is that from Aigues-Mortes (B2 ; Pl. LXXI, Fig. 42), where wheels of six and seven spokes respectively, two hammers, a billhook and two thunderbolts are associated with a dedication to Jupiter and Silvanus (Jullian, 1918a, 244).

The problem is the interpretation of the hammer in connection with the wheel. Hatt (1951a, 82-87) suggests that both the axe (especially the double-axe) and the hammer could represent thunderbolts, in which case the link with a Celtic, wheel-bearing Sky-God is an obvious one. Credence is lent to this theory by an altar from around Carpentras (*C.I.L.*, XII, 1179) with a hammer on one side and a double-axe on the other. A bronze Sucellus from Viège (C49) bears a 'barillet' without spokes, swastikas and crosses on his tunic, and a thunderbolt. The connection between the Hammer-God (see below) and a Celtic Jupiter seems firmly established. On one Jupiter-giant group, Jupiter bears Sucellus' hammer (Benoit, 1950, 15 ; Lambrechts, 1942, 97). Boucher's recent and comprehensive work on Romano-Gaulish figured bronzes (1976) has demonstrated that there are strong similarities between some representations of different god-types. For instance, take away Jupiter's sceptre and give him a long-shafted hammer and he becomes Sucellus — facial features and stance are very alike. Attempts are made below to show further links between Sucellus and Jupiter in Gaul (see also Chapter VIII).

The resemblance between axes, double-axes and hammers is apparent, and there may be a similarity in meaning to some craftsmen and devotees. That the axe is not a hammer-substitute on monuments is suggested by the Courbessac stele (B31) which bears wheel, axe and hammer. The same is true of the Carpentras altar mentioned above. Hatt's idea of the axe or double-axe representing a thunderbolt may not be all that far-fetched. Certainly eastern Baals like Dolichenus (Merlat, 1960 ; Speidel, 1978) and Hadad-Zeus the storm, weather and thunder-god of Nabataea (Glück, 1965, 203), all carry double-edged axes. Both Dolichenus and Hadad, however, bear thunderbolts as well, so there is some distinction in function even though both may be sideral symbols. Linckenheld (1929a, 84) draws attention to a possible axe-hammer associated with a 2nd Century inscription with a depiction of Leto or Artemis/Diana and Apollo. In Britain the double-axe occurs in possible association with the Celtic Jupiter at Cirencester ; on a Corinthian capital with four humanoid busts, possibly once attached to a Jupiter-column (Pl. LXXXV) a possibly Bacchic figure of a bearded individual with a vine-branch and double-axe is depicted. As the other three busts appear to have Dionysiac associations (Phillips, 1976a, 35-41) the author has interpreted the axe-bearer as Lycurgus, the king of the Edones who attacked the Maenad Ambrosia with an axe. Whatever the interpretation of the double-axe in this context, it may have sidereal connotations in Romano-Gaulish iconography ; there may be a weather/thunderbolt connection, and there could be some conflation between axes, axe-hammers, double-axes and conventional hammers. In Chapters II and III the significance of miniature double and single axes has been discussed at length, and a probable celestial link established.

The thunderbolt itself appears to be extremely important in connection with a wheel-bearing divinity. It has already been established that it cannot be seen as a wheel-substitute or *uice uersa*. On a great many Romano-Gaulish monuments wheel and thunderbolt appear together and seem very closely linked. I have counted some seventeen stones where both occur. In addition the Le Châtelet bronze Wheel-God (C2) bears a thunderbolt as well as a wheel, as does the pipe-clay figurine from Néris (C9ai). The Montmirat stele (B83) bears two wheels and part of an inscription referring to the burial of a thunderbolt (Espérandieu, 1924, 28, no. 106). It is worth remembering that to the Romans the ground hit by a thunderbolt was thereafter held sacred, presumably to Jupiter. The question has to be asked as to why there was a frequent association of wheel and thunderbolt on altars and stelai, whilst on Jupiter-giant groups the thunderbolt is an infrequent accompaniment to the wheel. The case of the latter is unproven since most of the wheel-bearing equestrian Jupiter-figures are fragmentary, and it is not possible to ascertain whether both wheel and thunderbolt were ever present. Where wheel and thunderbolt do occur together on monuments, the most reasonable explanation must be that both Roman and native elements are portrayed. The classical Jupiter is represented by his thunderbolt, demonstrating his role as commander of sky, weather and rainfall. The solar and Gaulish element is indicated by the wheel. Hatt (1951, 82-87) would see a Gaulish as well as a classical meaning to the thunderbolt on Celtic monuments. He suggests that the item was regarded by the Gauls as an emanation of the sun striking the earth to fertilize it and induce rain (see above 'wheels and thunderbolts'). He further postulates that the association of the thunderbolt with these connotations of storms and rain explains the frequent siting of Jupiter-columns near water, or connected with springs and thermal sanctuaries.

Pots

Small vessels of 'olla' type are occasionally associated on the monuments with wheel or swastika-symbols. A deity appears with swastika and pot at Bremevaque (B17 ; Pl. VII, Fig. 14). The Aigues-Mortes stone (B2 ; Pl. LXXI, Fig. 42) bears wheels, hammers, billhook, thunderbolts and a pot. The Vernègues stele (B163 ; Pl. VII, Fig. 15) depicts a wheel, trees, a hammer with long shaft and two pots. The presence of such vessels may merely imply an offering of wine or oil to the deity invoked, but the occurrence also of hammers on two stones may give the item a deeper significance. Sucellus, the Hammer-God, frequently bears a pot, both on bronzes, for example on the figurine from Lyon which has a pot and also bears crosses and diagonal crosses on his tunic (C37), and in stone iconography, for instance on an altar-fragment from

Nîmes bearing the figure of Sucellus and a dog (Espérandieu, 1924, 42, no. 157). Once again there appears to be a direct link between some aspects of the Gaulish Hammer-God and the Celtic god of the Wheel.

The Billhook

This is an instrument used essentially for clearing woodland. It would not be a normal implement to find associated with the repertoire of a sky and solar deity, yet it does appear on one southern Gaulish stone, at Aigues-Mortes (B2). This stone, as already commented upon, has a complex and varied group of attributes (pot, thunderbolts, wheels and hammers). Most interesting is its dedication to Jupiter (hence the wheels and thunderbolts) and to Silvanus, a woodland god, hence the billhook. The conflation between these two divinities is unthinkable in the classical sense of their two cults. Indeed the dedication is to the two gods, not one equated with the other, and therefore there may be simply altar-sharing, with the attributes of both occurring. Yet, as shall be seen later, there is evidence that in this part of Gaul Jupiter was associated with prosperity and fertility. The situation is even more complicated in that Sucellus and Silvanus are sometimes confused in Gaul (see below), and here at Aigues-Mortes both hammer and pot are present in addition to the billhook.

Keys

Whilst the Wheel-God himself has no direct association with keys, two bronze items representing the Gaulish Hammer-God are worth noting. One is the figure from Viège (C49), with Sucellus' 'barillet', thunderbolt (linking him with Jupiter), swastikas and crosses on his clothing (thus having solar connections) and appearing with what is described as a key or a nail. The other bronze figurine is from Lyon (C37) with diagonal crosses and 'L'-shapes on his body. If keys are what are represented on these depictions, then the two bronze keys, from Moulins-Engelberf (C36) and Maubeuge (Ozeel, 1973, 17-22), both decorated with 'St. Andrew's Crosses', may be relevant. It is difficult to see what exact interpretation may be put on these implements. They do occur in the German multi-model grave-groups (see Chapter III). As we have seen, these groups occasionally include wheels. Keys are also sometimes linked with the cult of Epona (see below), where the most likely interpretation would seem to be their representation as keys to the afterlife (personal communication, Prof. J. M. C. Toynbee). This, too, is how Manning (1966, 50-59) would explain the keys in the Sabazian cult probably represented by some of the

Rhineland model grave-groups. If this interpretation is correct, we have an aspect of the Celtic Sky-God which has concern with death and the afterlife. Death is certainly relevant to this cult (see below). One final connection with keys is between the Brixantius whose name is inscribed on the Moulins key, and the Brixia who occurs as a water-spirit at Luxeuil, in company with a light-deity called 'Lussovius' and a wheel-bearing equestrian Jupiter in close proximity.

Spears

Spears occur, for instance at Bad Dürkheim (B9) associated with stylized human figures, horses and swastikas ; and on the stele from Bremevaque (B17 ; Pl. VII, Fig. 14) where a naked and snake-bearing deity holds a probable spear. The warrior-element implied by this evidence is of interest if one considers the bellicose nature of some depictions of the Wheel-God (for example at Séguret) and of some Jupiter-giant equestrian groups (see above). Finally, as shall be seen below, there is substantial evidence for a connection between the Gaulish Jupiter and an aspect of the Celtic Mars.

V. ZOOMORPHIC ASSOCIATIONS

Snakes

It has already been suggested that snake, spiral and 'S'-shape may have some shape-association. In any case the serpent has a very positive link with the Wheel-God. On the Séguret monument (B144 ; Pls. X, Fig. 22 ; Pl. LXVI) a snake is twined round an oak-tree ; at Vaison (B158) a serpent lies beneath the wheel. The nude Bremevaque god (B17 ; Pl. VII, Fig. 14) depicted as a warrior, is associated with a pot, swastika and a sinuous (?)snake rippling vertically downwards from his arm. The bronze from La Bouëxière (Lantier, 1936, 218-220) depicts a god, interpreted as Jupiter, with a human-headed snake. The Vaison altar to Juno (B157) shows the snake associated with a bird. The snake, in the Greek and Roman world, from very early, had a chthonic or earth-and-death bound association. In the Graeco-Roman world, according to Toynbee (1973, 223-236), serpents were regarded as representative of the beneficent spirits of the dead, associated with deities of healing and fertility. This would account for the snakes, both ram-headed and normal, at the (probably) therapeutic site of Mavilly, associated with Mars (Duval, 1957, 39ff. ; Thevenot, 1955). However, in association with the Romano-Celtic Jupiter, snakes do not always appear to represent benign and helpful entities. Although a benign connection between Jupiter, the Mother-Goddesses (*Vacallinehae Leudinae*) and a serpent seems to exist at the Romano-Celtic shrine of Pesch (Lehner, 1918-21, 74ff., pl. XXI, 4, 5), yet, at Trier, an altar to Jupiter Optimus Maximus depicts on one side an eagle fighting two snakes (*C.I.L.*, XIII, 3648). Toynbee points out (1973, 262) that this theme of eagle and snakes is a common Roman art-motif. There is too the whole problematical question of the role of the snake-limbed monsters on the Jupiter-columns (see above). Sometimes, as at Hommert (Espérandieu, 4557), the snake-legs have heads of their own ; so here the reptiles are entities in their own right. In view of the possible association between the Gaulish Hammer-God and the Celtic Jupiter, a Nîmes stele (Espérandieu, 1924, 42, no. 158) is of interest in that on it a snake curls round a hammer-handle. Apart from the Trier altar and possibly the Jupiter-giant groups, the snake as linked with the Romano-Celtic Jupiter does seem to be a beneficent element, either as a chthonic/death symbol, or as a fertility attribute. In this context we should remember Jupiter, Silvanus and wheel at Aigues-Mortes (B2) ; and the association of the Celtic Sky-God with the Mother-Goddesses (see below). The ram-horned snake is of relevance here. Both ram and serpent have fertility connotations in the classical world (Toynbee, 1962, 132). There is a possible association between solar symbolism and the horned snake, as depicted on the Iron Age bronze bracelet bearing 'X's and a ram-horned snake, from the Oppidum-de-la-Cloche (Chabot, 1975, 261, fig. 1). More important is the direct association between ram-horned snake and wheel at Lypiatt Park (BB13 ; Pl. III, Fig. 4).

The Bull

The three-horned bull will first be considered. There is little direct association between the triple-horned bull and a Gaulish or Celtic Wheel-Cult. However, such a connection does occur on the Willingham Fen sceptre-terminal. The craftsman and/or patron involved has shown a certain eclecticism here inasmuch as both bull and dolphin are associated with wheel, humanoid divinity, monster and eagle. The temple of the Celtic Apollo at Beire-le-Châtel (Côte-d'Or) has produced rare stone depictions of this fabulous beast (de Vries, 1963) ; some of them bear lunar crescents between their horns (Colombet & Lebel, 1953, 111, fig. 22, 121). Deonna would also suggest (1954, 409-410) that there must be a link between the three-horned bull and 'Tarvostrigaranos' on the

Tiberian Paris pillar dedicated to, and bearing a depiction of, Jupiter (Duval, 1961). If, as seems likely, the triplication is connected with the enhancement of the fertility aspect of the horns (Green, 1976, 13), then the three-horned creature of the Willingham Fen bronze may well represent the fertility facet of the cult of the Celtic Jupiter. In this connection, two other bulls may be relevant. One is the silvered bronze triple-horned bull from Maiden Castle, with 'S'-shaped tail (E79). The other is a bronze three-horned bull from Avrigney (C38), which has a rosette-shaped growth of hair on its forehead.

The normal, two-horned, bull is a natural accompaniment to any version of Zeus-Jupiter. If one glances at Greek mythology, there is a great deal of evidence of bull-sacrifice to the Hellenic Sky-God (Harrison, 1912, 148ff.). Harrison suggests (*ibid.*, 145) that the bull may have been an intrinsically holy beast not necessarily originally or always connected with Zeus. However, the association between beast and god is very early. The temple to the Cretan Zeus on Mount Ida, as early as the Middle-Late Minoan Period, produced ox-skulls with the horns intact ; the shrine dates to the time when Zeus was still the male vegetation-god of the Cretans, before he became the high Sky-God of the Greeks (Dietrich, 1973, 81). In a dedication to Zeus Olbios (Prosperous) on a votive relief in the Musée Impérial Ottoman, Zeus wears bull-horns ; above in a gable is represented a bull's head ; below is an ox-sacrifice (Bey, 1908, pl. V). The classical association of bulls with the Graeco-Roman Sky-God need not be laboured. It is interesting that Oriental Sky and Weather-deities later associated with Zeus or Jupiter, also have close links with the bull. Zeus/Hadad/Jupiter of Nabataea has a bull, thunderbolt and double-axe (Glück, 1965, 203). The bull is present as a fertilizing power. Dolichenus too (Merlat, 1960) is necessarily linked with the bull.

As early as the pre-Roman Iron Age (and probably before) the bull appears in the iconography of the Celtic world (see Chapter VII). Thus, when we find the bull associated with the Romano-Celtic, wheel-bearing Jupiter, it is difficult to know whence comes the association. The thing to remember is that in many respects Celtic and Mediterranean religion is closely linked, and it is probable that in both the bull represented power, fertility, strength and ferocity. Two points concerning Romano-Celtic representations of bulls are of particular note. One is the possible solar association of beasts with knob-tipped horns, which Deonna (1917, 124ff. ; Drioux, 1934, 73) suggests may be sun-symbols. This is of especial interest if we look at the wheel-bearer on the Gundestrup

Cauldron (C1). Whilst it is not certain that the wheel has any solar significance (Olmsted, 1979), it is worth recalling that the being actually in contact with the wheel (possibly as an offering to the associated god) is dressed as a warrior wearing a helmet with knobbed bull-horns. Related to this is the second point, namely that three bull-mounts from Britain, all with knob-horns (E95 ; E108), of late Iron Age or early Roman date (a pre-Roman date is suggested by other, similar mounts, like the knob-horned one from the Celtic *oppidum* of Heidetränk [Müller-Karpe, 1977, 33-63]), are directly linked with the Romano-Celtic Jupiter. The Thealby examples (E108) (Green, 1977, 311, pl. 12, VIII, a, b) show a bull-head topped by that of an eagle with very prominent eyes. The River Ribble item (E95) (*ibid.*, 311) is similar except that a humanoid (and very Celtic) head is also represented. The juxtaposition of the various heads is not a classical but a native phenomenon. It is impossible to prove the alleged solar symbolism of the knobs but, at least in Celtic Britain, the celestial association is apparent.

Eagles and Peacocks

Little need be said regarding the interpretation of these birds. Both appear on a number of wheel-depicting monuments, and the eagle is also present, for instance, on the Willingham Fen bronze (Pl. LXXXI). The peacock, classical emblem of Juno, its tail symbolizing the orb of the sky, is of interest since it is not as common in classical iconography as Jupiter's eagle ; its presence implies a reasonable amount of knowledge on the part of the craftsmen carving the stones. Both the peacock and, to greater extent the eagle, were used by Gaulish and British craftsmen to symbolize the sky-element in the celestial cult of the Wheel-God. At Dôle (Pl. XVIII, Fig. 41) there is physical contact between a four-spoked wheel and a possible peacock with crested head. In Dacia, plaques of the Danubian Rider-God sometimes bear eagles, presumably a sky-motif (Tudor, 1976, 285). It is interesting, in view of hints that the Celtic Sky-God has a chthonic side to his cult, that eagles have a death-aspect in the classical world. It was a widely-held belief (Cumont, 1922, 158-159 ; Toynbee, 1971, 242) in the Roman world that one's soul at death was carried away by a bird, frequently a bird of prey and sometimes an eagle. It may be that the eagle, on Romano-Celtic monuments to the Sky-God, embodies this concept in addition to the pure sky-element. In this context the small eagle made of lead, from a cemetery at Shefford (E99) should be recalled. Apart from the cemetery-association, lead itself may represent a chthonic metal (Green, 1978, 11).

Other Birds

Ravens, indeterminate birds and aquatic birds are occasionally connected with wheel-symbolism. It is sometimes a problem, when studying iconographical evidence, to identify particular bird-types. For instance it is easy, on a crude or worn carving, to mistake a raven for an eagle and *uice uersa*. It is impossible to distinguish the species of bird scrawled on the Bad Dürkheim petroglyph (B9). One cannot be certain that the Dôle bird (B33 ; Fig. 41) is a peacock, though it is crested. Birds which are probably ravens are associated with other beasts and with the Wheel and Hammer-deities on the Farley Heath bronze sceptre-binding (C7 ; Pl. LXXXII). This probability ties in with the Felmingham Hall hoard with its model wheel and two (?)raven-figurines (Pl. LXII) (see Chapters II, III). The raven is a bird in constant attendance with Sucellus and his consort Nantosuelta (Linckenheld, 1929a, 40-92 ; Krappe, 1936, 236-246). The bird also appears to have had early and pre-Roman links with solar cults in Central Europe in Urnfield and Hallstatt contexts (Ross, 1967, 242). The association of wheel and other symbols with aquatic birds is of interest since, once again, one can see such a connection in later Bronze Age prehistory in Europe (see Chapter I). A pipe-clay 'Venus' figure with a child, from a Central Gaulish factory around Moulins (C40i), bears sun-symbols including wheels and two water-birds. At Quilly a pipe-clay cross-legged divinity (C48) is recorded, with a small water-bird at the tips of the fingers of one hand. Circles, stars and solar-motifs decorate the figure. If one can really link later prehistoric solar-cults with those occurring in Romano-Celtic Gaul, what we may see is a reminiscence of an association between sun and water-bird depictions so common in Central and Eastern European contexts from a thousand years before the Roman conquest of Gaul.

Dolphins

This sea-mammal appears associated with wheel-symbolism on the Willingham Fen terminal (C6 ; Pl. LXXXI) as an attribute of the Wheel-God, and on a wheel-brooch from Bavay (see Chapter III). The dolphin appears constantly in Graeco-Roman art ridden by a boy, often identified as Cupid (Toynbee, 1973, 207). The connection here may be Venus, Cupid's mother, who as Anadyomene also possessed this sea-symbol

(Stebbins, 1929, 119). The Greek Poseidon (Zeus' brother) had the dolphin as an emblem in Greek art (*ibid.*, 117). Connection between Zeus or Jupiter himself and a dolphin are uncommon, but the dolphin-rider does appear on a metope-fragment from the east side of the temple of Zeus in Olympia (*ibid.*, 120). The motif of the dolphin, symbolizing marine connections appears in funerary contexts in Roman art as a symbol of the journey of the soul across the ocean to the Isles of the Blessed. Toynbee cites as an instance of this (1973, 207) a 4th Century A.D. Christian sarcophagus found in Rome. Linked to this thought is the Greek custom (Glück, 1965, 315ff.) of placing dolphin-tokens in the hands of the dead to ensure a safe voyage for those traversing the uncharted regions of the afterlife.

The Willingham Fen dolphin may be present with the Wheel-God for any one of a number of reasons. First, the youthful, almost dancing attitude of the god here (Pl. LXXXI) is very Cupid-like and there may have been confusion on the part of the bronzesmith, artist or patron. Second, the relationship between Poseidon/Neptune and Zeus/Jupiter may be referred to. Third, and possibly most likely, the dolphin has been selected out of a number of classical art-motifs to symbolize the underworld element in the Celtic Sky-God cult. If this is the case, the attributes are ethnically well-balanced. The wheel and eagle may be seen as representing the Roman and Celtic celestial elements; the chthonic monster beneath the Wheel-God's foot and the dolphin the Celtic and classical attributes of the Underworld.

Dogs, Stags and Boars

These three beasts are all represented on the Farley Heath sceptre-binding (C7; Pl. LXXXII), associated with the Wheel-God and the Hammer-God. The dog appears elsewhere with wheel-symbolism on the Bad Dürkheim quarry-face. The interpretation of stag and dog is problematical. Their only apparent relevance is through reference to Silvanus and Sucellus, both of whom, as we have seen and will see, have some association in Gaul, with the Celtic Sky-God. Sucellus is frequently accompanied by a dog (Linckenheld, 1929a, 40ff.; Lambrechts, 1942, 100ff.). Silvanus' stag-connection is well-known. The dog in Gaulish, as in Roman religion, may have links with cults of healing and with death (Jenkins, 1957a, 60-76).

The boar occurs on two items connected with the Wheel-God. One is the Farley Heath binding (C7; Pl. LXXXII); the other is the relief of a wheel-bearing deity from Netherby (BB18 ; Pl. LXXV). Like the bull, in the Celtic world the boar was a symbol, from pre-Roman Iron Age times, of strength, ferocity and indomitability. Thus it is an appropriate emblem for any high divinity. The craftsman who fashioned the Farley Heath sceptre seems to have wanted to crowd in as many theriomorphic motifs as possible, presumably to augment the power of a ceremonial and, very probably, priestly item. However, like the stag, the boar may represent hunting and woodland and, therefore, once again Silvanus may be symbolized. In this respect the Netherby god is also relevant since the boar is associated with a tree.

Horses

It is difficult to dissociate horses themselves from divinities connected with them. I shall make certain observations here but I should stress now that any interpretative exercise concerned with equine depictions will have to take into account humanoid deities still to be assessed, such as Epona, Mars, Apollo and the Dioscuri, in addition to the equestrian Jupiter himself, already examined above. At this stage I will be confining myself to consideration of horses without riders, directly associated with wheel-symbolism on Romano-Celtic monuments. This occurs at Bad Dürkheim (B9) where swastikas are associated with three horses and other animals, stylized human figures, including a spear-carrier, and stemmed and unstemmed wheels on a carving possibly of 1st Century A.D. date. On the Robernier stele (B177), probably immediately pre-Roman, a mare and foal appear on a stone carved also with a swastika. In prehistoric Europe (see Chapter I), from the middle part of the Bronze Age, the horse appears to possess a solar significance. Pre-Roman Gaulish coinage bears horses and solar symbols (Lambrechts, 1942, 73 ; Nash, 1978 ; Allen, 1980), apart from chariot-wheels. Iron Age Treveran coins of Allen's 'Star-Wave-Lyre' type (Allen, 1971, 95-110) depict a horse and sun or star replacing the charioteer. The solar symbolism attached to this beast seems to remain throughout the Roman period. The classical connection would appear to stem from the sun-chariot of Helios or Apollo (confused with Helios from the 5th Century B.C. and re-associated with the Sun from the time of Augustus [Rose, 1933, 33, 134 ; Fairbanks, 1908, 126 ; Altheim, 1938, 394ff., 398, 400 ; Oxford Classical Dictionary, 1978, 999 ; Gage, 1955, 639ff.]). Certainly in the Gallo-Roman context there appear to be connections between horses and Apollo, who was first and foremost a god of healing both in the Roman and in the Gaulish world. The link between sun and healing (as indeed between water and healing) is a natural one (Ferguson, 1970, 218). The Gaulish association between Apollo and horses may be a solar one (see below, Apollo). Horse-figurines occur at healing water-shrines to Apollo, for instance that of Apollo Belenus (Brilliant One) at Sainte-Sabine (Côte-d'Or) (Thevenot, 1951, 131). There are certain other hints at solar-horse symbolism in Gaul. At Neuvy-en-Sullias a bronze horse dedicated to Rudiobos is known. The name implies the meaning 'Red Striker or Cutter' and could have links with a Mars Rudianos who occurs more than once in Gaul (Loth, 1925, 210-227) (see also Mars). Mars has a solar aspect in Gaul and the term 'red' may possibly have a sun-connection. It should be recalled, for instance, that the 'Matres Coccae' (? red) appear associated with gold wheel-symbols in northern Britain (see Chapter II, III). There is a substantial amount of evidence for horses associated with a Mars-cult in Gaul and in Britain. A connection with a sky-cult seems to occur where Jupiter on Jupiter-giant columns appears on horseback, sometimes as a warrior. What is interesting here is that occasionally Jupiter appears not on horseback but in a chariot, as at Weissenhof (Benoit, 1950, 15). On a funerary stele from Bourges (Espérandieu, 1510), it is possible that the chariot at the apex of the gable is a solar one and replaces a wheel-symbol (Hatt, 1951a, 82-87). Monuments like the Mouhet stone (B87) depict a giant with a wheel directly on its back instead of the usual horse. Cook makes the point that the symbol of the wheeled chariot may overlie the belief in the sun as a horse. Wheel and horse, he suggests, may easily and naturally become a chariot. He cites, as an example of the solar connection, the Attic red-figure krater (1914, 233ff. ; fig. 269) with a chariot surrounded by a rayed disc, a thunderbolt on its left and a driver with swastika on his breast. Horse, Mars and sky-symbolism appear to exist together in Carinthia where there is a shrine of Roman date with a mosaic depicting a horse carried in a boat, a large bronze horse (now lost) and a portrayal of a young warrior. Nearby is a sanctuary to a Celtic Mars, Latobius, with inscriptions both to Mars and to Jupiter (*C.I.L.*, III, 5097-5098 ; Thevenot, 1955 ; Alföldy, 1974, 46). Sidereal connection with horses appear to exist at Assche-Kalkoven in Belgium (De Laet, 1942) (C52) where a cache of pipe-clay horses has been discovered, some of them decorated with lunar symbols. Finally, glancing at a possible chthonic element to the Sky-God's cult, it is suggested (Malten, 1914, 179ff. ; Benoit, 1950, 7) that horses themselves may have chthonic and underworld aspects.

Horsemen

An immediate sky or solar symbolism is apparent in the equestrian groups on Jupiter-giant columns. There are, in addition, other indications of solar connections with horsemen. The Willingham Fen Wheel-God representation (C6) was found in a hoard in association with bronze figurines of horsemen. Two rider-god brooches from Spanish contexts, from Luzaga and Gormaz, probably of pre-Roman Iron Age date, bear ring-and-dot decoration (Krüger, 1940, Abb. 10, 11). A human head and stylized body can be seen under the front hooves of the horse. Whilst I am reluctant to see a direct association between these occurrences and Jupiter-columns (which are at least geographically far removed from each other), it is nevertheless of interest that a solar element is hinted at by the concentric-circle ornamentation on the Spanish horses' bodies. We have already seen that Apollo in Gaul has some horse-connection. He is known also as a horseman himself, as 'Atepomarus' (Great Horseman) at Mauvières (Indre) (*C.I.L.*, XIII, 1318 ; Picard, 1977, 89-113). La Tène III Gauls already knew a horseman-god ; on certain coins of, for example, the Andecavi, charioteers guide human-headed horses accompanied by wheels. At pre-Roman Entremont, the *oppidum* of the Salii or Saluvii, a sculpture of a galloping, armed horseman is recorded (probably of 3rd and 2nd Century B.C. date) (Lambrechts, 1954, Chapter II). Sky-symbolism connected with horsemen occurs on the Danube in the Roman period among the Dacians, who possessed an equestrian Sky-God armed with a double-axe (Tudor, 1976, 283). There is a parallel between this god and Jupiter-giant groups, both of whom ride down an enemy (*ibid.*, 118).

Gods who may have some connection with horses, horsemen and Sky or Sun may be the Dioscuri, generally portrayed with horses and with evidence of a cult both in Gaul and in Germany (Krüger, 1940, 8-27 ; 1941, 1-66). Their cult is particularly prevalent in south-east and in eastern Gaul. They appear, for example, at Annecy (Haute-Savoie) (*C.I.L.*, XII, 2561, 2526), once linked with a god named Vintius, identified elsewhere with Mars (Krüger, 1940, 8-27). Diodorus Siculus (IV, 56, 3ff.) mentions that the Celts of the 'sea-shore' worshipped the Dioscuri above all. Classical mythology makes Castor and Pollux sons of Zeus (Oxford Classical Dictionary, 1978, 354) ; they fairly early have an astral connection and represent interaction between light and dark, heaven and underworld. Thevenot suggests that, in Gaul, Dioscuri and horsemen in general were considered as helpers of the dead (1951, 130ff.) and believes that both the heavenly Twins and Mars (*ibid.*, 133) are concerned in Gaul with light and darkness.

Epona

This Gaulish goddess is necessarily connected with horses, it being the very meaning of her name (Magnen & Thevenot, 1953). On stelai dedicated to her she is frequently depicted with mares and/or foals ; in this context she may possibly have an association with the Robernier stone (B117). At Baudoncourt (B10), Epona occurs on a 'stèle-maison' at the apex of which is a (?)solar symbol. At Agessac, Comminges, a marble funerary Epona-plaque bears sea-monsters and solar symbols. Hatt (1945, no. 23) would date this plaque to the mid 2nd Century A.D. A funerary stele from Gourzon, of 'stèle-maison' type bears a diagonal cross at its apex (Magnen & Thevenot, 1953, no. 228). The Meursault carving (*ibid.*, no. 181) depicts Epona with a rosette, as do other sculptures (see above 'rosettes'). Another possible solar association occurs on the Epona-carving from Fontaine-les-Châlon, where the goddess has a nimbus around her head (Benoit, 1950, 32). We have already seen that the rosette or rose was sacred to the goddess, and that these could have been regarded by Gaulish Celts as solar. There is further evidence that the Horse-Goddess may be connected with the cult of the Celtic Sky-God. Lead medallions in the shape of wheel-models from La-Villeneuve-au-Châtelet (C25) bear depictions of Epona and may be paralleled almost exactly by the lead model from Plessis Barbuise (C5), except that the latter portrays a standing figure of Jupiter instead. At Cilli in Yugoslavia (Magnen & Thevenot, 1953, no. 26) was found a dedication to Epona, Jupiter and a presumably local goddess Cdeia. At Entrains-sur-Nohain (Nièvre) is recorded a dedication mentioning a shrine to Epona, and, in the same spot, inscriptions to Jupiter are known (*ibid.*, 28). Lambrechts (1951) makes the observation that Epona and the Jupiter-horseman of the columns are distinguishable from the rest of the Gaulish pantheon by virtue of the horse-element, and by the almost identical distribution. The Epona-carving from Saulon-la-Chapelle (Côte d'Or) is of interest here (Thevenot, 1950, 22-25, pl. 1, fig. a). The site is by the bank of the stream 'de la Varaude'. Epona (unusually) is portrayed nude (like a water-nymph) and sits astride the horse (she is generally depicted side-saddle or seated between two horses). Here she takes on the stance of a male equestrian deity, like the Jupiter of the columns. The bronze plaque from Mont Auxois (Alise-Sainte-Reine) in St-Germain is of particular note since here

Epona herself is missing, but present instead are a *biga*, mare and supplicant ; the dedication is to Epona (Benoit, 1950, 65). The introduction of the chariot may be interpreted in terms of solar symbolism ; the Weissenhof Jupiter-chariot immediately comes to mind. A further common ground between Epona and Jupiter-columns is their frequent association with water. Epona is connected with sacred waters, for instance at Allerey (Magnen & Thevenot, 1953, 16-18), at Saulon-la-Chapelle (Thevenot, 1950, 22-25), ad at Néris (Espérandieu, 1568). There is substantial evidence that Jupiter-giant groups too are associated with water (Lambrechts, 1949, 145-158).

The depiction of Epona and solar-symbols on funerary monuments is interesting, and indicates an aspect of her cult which is concerned with death. The paradoxical link between sky and death-elements is one with which we repeatedly come into contact. The constant portrayal of wheels on funerary monuments ; the dualistic motif of the Jupiter-giant groups ; the casting of wheel-models into water, or their burial with the dead (see Chapters II, III), all demonstrate this. If Epona, as is likely, has a strong association with the Mother-Goddesses (her fertility attributes are virtually identical to those of the Mothers), then the life-death element may be understood. Death, water-healing and rebirth are all connected in their cult (see below). At any rate Epona herself has a firm link with death. At La Horgue-au-Sablon (Magnen & Thevenot, 1953, no. 190), she appears on the site of a huge cemetery. Another vast burial-ground near to the Gallo-Roman town of Metz has produced several stelai representing Epona (Lambrechts, 1949, 158 ; Toussaint, 1948). Luxeuil (incidentally also the site of a wheel-bearing equestrian Jupiter-group) has produced a 'stèle-maison' with an Epona-relief (Linckenheld, 1927, 17). A further funerary or afterlife aspect to Epona's cult is her association with keys, for example at Gannat (Espérandieu, 1618) and at Grand (Espérandieu, 4894), which may be the key to the stable-door and, allegorically, to the afterlife.

Finally some mention should be made of the association of Epona with the Mother-Goddess cult. Her attributes of *patera, cornucopiae*, ears of corn, etc., are shared by the Deae Matres (Magnen & Thevenot, 1953). Epona and the Matres seem to have in common the double function of guardians both of life and death. A form of Mother-Goddess, portrayed by pipe-clay 'Venuses' in Gaul, frequently bear sun-symbols. In Britain too there is evidence of an association between the Mothers and a sky-cult. We should recall the Backworth hoard dedicated to the Mothers containing gold wheel-models (see Chapters II, III). We also have the evidence of the two Cotswold stelai (BB9, BB10), where Mothers are directly associated with wheel-symbols.

A final point should be considered. It may not be of any true significance, but the Epona fashioned out of clay from Rheinzabern (Colin, 1927, 185) sits on a beast which resembles a bull rather than a horse. This is perhaps worth remarking on in view of the association between bull and Sky-God. Related to this is the stone Epona from Gannat (Musée des Antiquités Nationales, St-Germain-en-Laye) which depicts the goddess on a horse, but with her cloak billowing out in a nimbus around her head in exactly the same manner as conventional depictions of Europa and the Bull (for example a mirror-back in the Ashmolean [Acc. no. 1971.822]).

VI. FEMALE DEITIES WITHOUT A ZOOMORPHIC ELEMENT

Fortuna

This goddess is, in classical contexts, associated either with a wheel or a globe. The symbol is that of movement and mutability of human affairs, conditions and activities. Isis also (Cook, 1914, 254ff.) sometimes carries a wheel ; she is often equated with Fortuna in post-classical syncretism. Nemesis in Greek art (*ibid.*) and Dike too bear this symbol, presumably representing inexorable rotation and the inescapable results of one's actions. We have already looked at the Nemesis-sculpture from Dionysias in Egypt (see above 'Jupiter with small individual').

The classical association of a goddess with a wheel, especially Fortuna, may have attracted Gallo-Roman craftsmen simply because it was easy to associate this deity with the Celtic Wheel-God of their own. We have seen in Chapter IV that stone images of Fortuna are recorded at, for instance, Agey (B1), and bronzes, for example at Autun (C16), where the wheel is exaggerated in size, possibly deliberately. The Autun bronze is of especial interest since the same place has produced a stone image (B7) of a goddess with Jupiter's thunderbolt and a wheel. Coupled with this, in the same area, around Dijon, inscriptions to Jupiter Optimus Maximus and Fortuna Redux together are recorded, as if Fortuna is purposely being chosen as a consort for a Gallo-Roman Jupiter (Gaidoz, 1885, 194 ; *C.I.L.*, XIII, 5474-6), a kind of Celtic Juno. Gaidoz (1885, 191-3) has an interesting theory regarding this possible solar aspect of Fortuna, pointing out that the ancient Italian Fors Fortuna could have had a solar association (her festival being at the time of the summer solstice). However, (Oxford Classical Dictionary, 1978, 445) there is evidence that this goddess was originally a divinity of fertility (hence her frequent association with *cornuacopiae*).

Juno

A goddess who may be Juno accompanies the Wheel-God on some stone monuments. Sometimes there is direct evidence for her identification ; more often her attributes make it uncertain. The Tongres monument (B150) is interesting since it is the goddess herself who bears a wheel ; her classification as Juno is here assured by the presence of a peacock. The fact that it is Juno rather than Jupiter who carries the wheel is of exceptional importance since it indicates far-reaching conflation between classical and Celtic couples. Juno, normally a non-celticized divinity, is here an integral part of the Wheel-God cult ; without her, Jupiter himself on the carving appears entirely Roman ; it is Juno who is needed for the identification. This transference of symbols from Wheel-God to goddess attains further lengths where a female divinity occurs alone with the wheel-symbol, as at Vaison (B157) and at Autun (B7). At Autun she bears a thunderbolt. At Vaison equation between herself and Jupiter goes to the incredible length of her portrayal in military costume; The Oehringen goddess (B103) may also be Juno. The Agey (B1) and Autun (B7) portrayals are noteworthy in the context of another relief from Dijon, depicting a goddess with a thunderbolt (Espérandieu, 3452 ; Drioux, 1934, 52).

Juno and Fortuna seem to be very closely associated in Gallo-Roman thought as expressed by some stone sculpture and by one or two bronzes. Both appear to have been selected as likely and appropriate consorts for a Celtic wheel-bearing Sky-God. Fortuna, as already emphasized, was an obvious choice since she already possessed associations with wheels ; Juno was the classical Jupiter's companion, and as such, was also a natural choice. She appears, on the few reliefs just recalled, to have taken over the Wheel-God's role in a manner uncommon in classical iconography. This can perhaps be better explained in looking (below) at the fertility aspect to the Sky-God cult, and at his associations with Gaulish Mother-Goddesses.

Minerva

In classical iconography Minerva, though the daughter of Jupiter, has no connection with his role as Sky-Father. Nevertheless in Gaul and in Britain there are occasional hints at such an association. An altar from Géry in south-western Gaul bears a dedication to Jupiter and Minerva and is carved with a stylized conifer (Espérandieu, 842 ; Reinach, 1917, fig. 131). Another Pyrenean altar (B106) bears a similar tree, a swastika and a dedication to Jupiter and Minerva. A High Rochester altar bears an inscription to Minerva and a Genius loci, with four-spoked wheel and swastika-carvings (BB11). This last immediately recalls the Genii from Netherby bearing wheels in place of *paterae*. At Willingham Fen the same hoard which produced the Wheel-God depiction, also yielded a bronze owl (Minerva's theriomorphic emblem) (Green, 1976, 210). Two Celtic epithets for Minerva should be looked at in this context. One is the surname *Belisima* meaning 'Lightning' given to the goddess, in Gaul, at St-Lizier (Ariège) (*C.I.L.*, XIII, 8). Belisima alone appears near Vaison (*C.I.L.*, XII, 162 ; de Vries, 1963, 86). The other name is *Sul* or *Sulis* in Britain, at Bath, a name having solar connotations. The identification of Minerva with Sul is curious since *Sul* is a masculine name ; yet certainly at Bath the temple was dedicated to a goddess (Cunliffe, 1971, 10-11, pl. XXXVIIIa). There is further interest here in that Bath was a curative establishment connected with sacred springs ; we have seen that the Celtic Jupiter in Gaul would appear to have had therapeutic associations. Finally, on occasions the Celtic Mother-Goddesses are called *Suleuiae*, for example at Cirencester in Britain (Green, 1976, 174), and in Gaul (de Vries, 1963, 131), as well as in Bath itself (Cunliffe, 1971, pl. XXXVIIId). This epithet would appear to form a direct link between solar (Sul was probably a solar deity in origin), healing and fertility symbolism.

One further comment concerning Minerva should be made, and that is the possible connection with Medusa. Minerva is frequently depicted in iconography with the gorgoneion-aegis on her breast. A male Medusa-mask with moustache is portrayed on the pediment of the great shrine to Sul-Minerva at Bath, where the shape of the hairstyle resembles a solar-symbol. The possible sun-symbolism of the Medusa-head is further indicated by some southern Gaulish funerary monuments (Hatt, 1945, Series I) from the Comminges region. Hatt's no. 69 from Czarin consists of a triangular roof of a cinerary trough with the head of a stylized, heliolatric Medusa. No. 70 from Benqué is similar and the Medusa is accompanied by two small wheels. Once again an essentially classical element may have been picked out by Gaulish craftsmen and adapted to fit in with their own native motifs.

The Mother-Goddesses

Two British fragmentary Mother-Goddess reliefs are relevant here (BB9, BB10) both from the West Country and each bearing wheel or derivative symbols. This is not the only British connection between the Deae Matres and a Sky-cult. The Backworth gold models associated in a hoard with the Mothers (see Chapter II, III) should be recalled. There is a considerable amount of evidence in Gaul for solar and fertility symbolism having an association. At Clarensac in southern Gaul (B25), a stone bears a fragmentary wheel and a dedication to Jupiter to Terra Mater, which may mean that here in Narbonensis Jupiter is linked with crop-growth and prosperity (Duval, 1957, 76). The most important association between the two concepts is shown by pipe-clay representations of Mother-Goddesses, either in the guise of a 'Venus' figure (the classical cult of Venus is rare in Gaul) or as a 'Dea Nutrix' based on the art-form of Juno Lucina (see Chapter V). Two pipe-clay Deae Nutrices bear 'S' symbols on their diadems (Linckenheld, 1929a, 57 ; Bertrand, 1897, 243, fig. 55). We have seen (above) that 'S' shapes appear to have a solar significance closely linked with that of the wheel. More importantly, the number of pipe-clay 'Venus' figures with sun-symbols on their bodies, both at front and back, are unequivocal evidence for this sky-association. Linckenheld (1929a) would link these 'Venus' statuettes with bronzes of Sucellus bearing similar symbols. But in my opinion it is not necessary to do this. For one thing the media are totally different. For another only the sun-symbols link these two entities and this is not sufficient to postulate anything as close as a 'marriage' between them. The connection would seem to be *through* the association of both with a Celtic sky-cult.

There is further evidence in Gaul of a link between Jupiter and the Mothers. First a figure of Jupiter from Harzburg (C4) bears a wheel, a fish and a basket, the two last-mentioned items being frequent attributes of the Mothers. Whilst this may be a somewhat dangerous speculation, the three emblems present here could be seen as symbolic of sky, earth and chthonic elements. The wheel is self-explanatory ; the water-aspect of the fish could mean an underworld association ; the basket may symbolize plenty, prosperity and fertility (like the fish). A bronze Mother-Goddess from Buxières bears a *patera* and also a flat wheel-shaped object with radiating spokes ; it has been interpreted as a cake (this brings to mind the wheel-shaped flour-cakes offered to the Thunder-God Summanus, equated with Jupiter, in Italy [Pettazoni, 1954, 95]). There is also the material pertaining to the cult of Epona, who has features in common with Celtic aspects of Jupiter, as we have seen, and who also bears attributes identifying her with fertility and the Mothers. Second there is the solar epithet *Suleviae* attached to some Mothers. Third, at Pesch, the temple of the Matronae Vacallinehae has produced part of a standing statue of Jupiter (Lehner, 1918-21, pl. XXI, 4) and a snake twisted around an altar (like the Gloucestershire example [BB13 ; Pl. III] associated with a wheel-symbol). Fourth, there is evidence that the Matres have links with healing springs and water in general, as shown, for instance, by the Matrones Comedovae at Aix-les-Bains (de Vries, 1963, 130) or by Coventina in North Britain (Ross, 1967, 29ff.). There is much material reflecting the Celtic Jupiter's connection with water (Lambrechts, 1949, 149). Fifth, a possible death-connection manifests itself. We have seen that several funerary monuments, especially in Alsace and in southern Gaul, bear wheel-symbolism. The pipe-clay Venus with sun-signs from Toulvern in Baden (C43) was buried in a barrow. Pipe-clay Mother-Goddesses are frequently found in graves, as at Ballestein (Moselle) where one was buried under a 'stèle-maison' (Linckenheld, 1929a, 67) (in the same general area as so many wheel-bearing house-stelai), and in Britain at Hassocks, Sussex (Green, 1976, 221). The association between Mothers and death, though seemingly strange, is a natural one. As Richmond states (1950, 25) in a Roman context Mother Earth enfolds the dead in her bosom and there is a life-after-death symbolism here too. The whole business of the relationship between life and death shows great complexity in Gaul. Healing springs are associated with Mothers. Therapeutic waters are associated with the sun as a healing power, and thus possibly with Celtic aspects of Jupiter. The little wheels thrown into Gaulish rivers are probably evidence of the close link between life-giving water/fertility and solar cults. Finally the association between stylized wheels and a (?) Mother-Goddess depiction on the Gundestrup Cauldron (C1) should not be forgotten.

Finally in this fertility connection the role of *cornuacopiae* should be assessed. The stone from Naix (B88), bearing a depiction of the Wheel-God, is unusual in that it also bears two *cornuacopiae* below a six-spoked wheel. It is not a normal symbol either for the classical or the Celtic Jupiter or his counterpart Juno. However, in this context the two

Netherby reliefs (BB17, 18 ; Pl. LXXV) are relevant. Here the Wheel-God is portrayed as a Genius of prosperity holding a wheel over an altar in one hand and a *cornuacopiae* in the other. Taking all into account, the association in Celtic belief between the Sky-God and fertility in its various forms is inescapable. The Agey goddess (B1) with wheel and *cornuacopiae*, interpreted as a possible Fortuna, may even be a feminine version of the entity represented at Netherby.

VII. MALE DIVINITIES

Apollo

Although mainly a prophetic and healing deity in classical contexts, there is evidence of a solar connection and a certain conflation with Helios as early as the 5th Century B.C., although as Rose states (1933, 134) the identification has nothing to recommend it save that both deities were archers. Helios, although universally acknowledged as a god, was little worshipped in Greece except on Rhodes. According to Guthrie (1954, 211) the Greeks could see that the Sun remained in its heaven and did not interfere with the lives of men, so there was no point in worshipping him as a humanoid divinity. In art and literature Helios was depicted as a charioteer with *quadriga* or occasionally on horseback (Rose, 1933, 33). Apollo came to be regarded as a similar image. 'Phoebus' or 'Bright' Apollo is referred to in classical literature (e.g. Homer, *Iliad*, 1, 43) ; the *Bassarai* of Aeschylus and the *Phaethon* of Euripides both acknowledge the identification (Altheim, 1938, 394ff.). From the time of Augustus a new equation or link between Helios or Sol and Apollo was established (*ibid.*, 394ff.). According to Altheim (*ibid.*, 398) the reason for confusion between the two was because Apollo was spiritual and Helios was bound up with a close link to the physical sun. Only as a giver of light, the most sublime and godlike element, not as a mere cosmic force, could Helios be found in unity with Apollo. The Sun and Apollo were never considered as one and the same being, but Apollo was seen as master of the Sun (Altheim, 1938, 401).

It is important to sort out the role of Apollo in connection with Solar force in order to understand the Gaulish interpretation of the god. In Gaul Apollo's main function appears to have been that of a healer (thus not deviating from his classical role). But there are certain solar associations (see also 'Horses' above). Presumably (Ferguson, 1970, 218), as already suggested, any Roman or Celtic assimilation between Helios/Sol and

Apollo would naturally come in recognition of the sun's healing properties. Thus the little horses sometimes found in sanctuaries of the Healer Apollo in Gaul may owe their presence to the horse-element in Helios' classical portrayal. Apart from the link between Apollo and horses in Gaul, there is evidence of a direct association between Apollo and solar-symbolism on a stone monument from Vivarais (B166) which bears a dedication to Apollo Belenus (Brilliant One) and a swastika-motif. The surname of Apollo here is indeed a direct acknowledgement of a light-element in the god's Gaulish cult ; this particular aspect is localized in the Alps of southern Gaul and North Italy (de Vries, 1963, 83ff. ; Duval, 1957, 77). Tertullian (*Apologeticus* 27, 4) mentions Belenus as a local cult among the Noricans. The same god is recorded at a healing-spring shrine at Sainte-Sabine (Thevenot, 1951, 131), associated with horses. It is interesting that at the shrine of Apollo Grannus (Healer), at Grand, horses are present and the same place also produced a number of Jupiter-giant groups, one of which was found close to the sacred baths (Lambrechts, 1949, 146-7). Mars who, as we shall see, had a solar aspect in Gaul, has connections with the Celtic Apollo. For instance the two gods occur together at Bains d'Yverdon in the Jura, near Lake Neuchâtel (*C.I.L.*, XIII, 11472, 11473). Mars is here called 'Caturix' (King of Combat).

Apollo in Celtic guise appears to have some connection with the Romano-Celtic Jupiter. Lambrechts (1942, 76 ; 1949, 154) goes so far as to say that Taranis links the attributes of Jupiter and Apollo. Hatt (1951a, 87) has much the same view. In this connection we should mention the Jupiter-giant group where a chariot takes the place of the horse (Lambrechts, 1949, 154). At Monthelon near Autun, an epithet belonging to Apollo Grannus is 'Amarcolitanus', possibly meaning a 'mounted horse' (Thevenot, 1951, 131). Jupiter and Apollo in Gaul are definitely sometimes linked. From Phalsbourg, Nancy (*C.I.L.*, XIII, 5991), comes a dedication to Jupiter, Apollo and a native deity Visucius. Some Pyrenean altars decorated with wheels and swastikas were found in close proximity to others dedicated to Apollo or a local god Abelio who, Bertrand (1897, 145ff.) suggests, may have been a solar deity. There was a temple to Apollo Moritasgus at Mont Auxois, Alesia, where the god physically resembles Jupiter (Lambrechts, 1949, 154) ; there are miniature wheels from here (Anon, 1912c, 270) and we do have a stone wheel-god also from Alesia (B3).

Two other possible pieces of evidence should be mentioned. One comprises Treveran coins — gold staters and quarter-staters — bearing a human-headed horse, a charioteer and a 'winged-mannikin' beneath the horse-hooves which rest on the humanoid being's body. Allen (1971, 91-110) sees a connection between the positioning of horse and winged being and later Jupiter-columns (which are abundant among the Treveri). On the obverse of these coins is a regular radiate Apollo-head. The other point concerns a votive stone hammer with diagonal cross-marking from the temple of Apollo at Beire-le-Châtel (Côte d'Or). If (see above) this 'St. Andrew's Cross' is connected with celestial symbolism, then there is a possible further link between Apollo and sky-motifs.

Mars

The Roman War-God appears to have had a variety of functions both in Gaul and in Britain, far removed from his normal classical role. A few monuments connect either Mars himself, or at any rate a warrior-deity, with sky-symbolism. The miniature altar from the Chedworth Roman Villa (BB7) portrays a spear-carrying warrior on the front, and curious stemmed four-spoked wheels at each side (Pl. LXXVI). This is very similar to the depictions on the Bad Dürkheim petroglyphs (B9). From Piercebridge comes a (lost) altar, dedicated to a local Mars — Condatis — and bearing a swastika (BB20). Bremevaque (B17 ; Pl. VII, Fig. 14) produced an altar depicting a nude male with helmet and spear, snake and pot, and with a swastika on the base. The humanoid figure is ithyphallic (thus perhaps linking wheel-symbolism with fertility). At Monsérie (Languedoc) fifteen altars to 'Erge' (one of which bears a swastika-motif), five to Mars and three to Jupiter are recorded (Thevenot, 1955).

There is plenty of evidence in Gaul and Britain that deities given the name of Mars were not necessarily anything to do with war. They may be healers (like Mars Lenus at Trier and Caerwent) ; local domestic protectors, as is the case in Gloucestershire (Green, 1976, 29-30) ; and have many other identities (Benoit, 1953 ; Thevenot, 1955). The sky-association is of particular potential significance in that it may be that Mars' original Italian functions of (?) storm/weather-god and agriculture (fertility) are being invoked. Certainly in Gaul the celestial and/or solar aspect of Mars is amply demonstrated not only when he is found directly in association with wheel-symbolism. One should also remember that if the Lucan scholiast is to be believed at all (Zwicker, 1934, 50), then the Celtic Jupiter had a 'Mars' function as *praeses bellorum*. In addition, if the armed Jupiter of southern Gaul (for example at Séguret) is meant to represent a warrior, we have another Mars-connection.

Several epithets of Mars hint at a celestial and Jupiter-shared facet. Mars Rudianos (Loth, 1925, 22-25) may refer to the colour 'red'. Mars Mullo may also be linked to this colour. Whilst 'Mullo' is generally thought of as having reference to a mule-cult, it is possible that 'Mullo' refers instead to *mulleus*, the red shoe worn by senators (Terouanne, 1965, 209ff.). Interestingly enough it is possible that Mullo pre-dates the Roman conquest of Gaul since he occurs in four widely separated tribal areas and the name is not the kind of geographical or descriptive epithet normally invented for classical gods in Romano-Gallic contexts. The name Rudianos could possibly have a solar function (de Vries, 1963, 68) and certainly the colour red could have connections with gold and the sun. The epithet of Mars Loucetius (Brilliant, Bright) invoked, for instance at Bath with a consort Nemetona (Cunliffe, 1971, 69), at Angers in Britanny (*C.I.L.*, XIII, 3087) and at Mainz is, as Wightman says (1970, 208), more suitable for Apollo or Jupiter than Mars. Indeed Jupiter Leucetius (recorded as Lucetius in the classical world [Ogilvie, 1969, 12]) is known in the Rhine Valley (Thevenot, 1955). The Mavilly Mars from a probably therapeutic spring-sanctuary bears an 'S'-decorated shield, and is associated with a ram-horned serpent. Mars is frequently linked both with healing establishments, in the same way as Apollo, and with horses. At Bolards (Nuits-St-Georges) a bronze mule bears a dedication to Mars Segomo (Victorious) (Thevenot, 1951, 130ff. ; *C.I.L.*, XIII, 2846). Wheel-symbols also come from this site (see Chapters II, III), although the association may not be archaeologically significant. Mars Segomo is known also among the Sequani nearby and in the Jura, for example at Arinthod (*C.I.L.*, XIII, 5340). A Mars sanctuary at Sougères-en-Puisaye (Yonne) produced Mars and horse figures. The horse association is of interest in that an equestrian aspect of Mars is known in the classical world (Oxford Classical Dictionary, 1978, 651). Whether or not the horse-connection with Mars in Gaul is solar, it is impossible to judge but there is a possibility that the localized horseman-warrior, as evidenced by Catuvellaunian bronzes in Britain (Green, 1976, 1977b), may have some link with the equestrian (and warrior-like) Jupiter of the columns. Finally in this connection we should recall the hoard-association of the Willingham Fen Wheel-God with bronze horsemen (C6).

Other connections between Mars and Jupiter in Gaul may briefly be summarized. At Dhronecken in the Moselle region, a Romano-Celtic sanctuary near Trier, which dates from 1st-5th Century A.D., the finds comprise large and elaborate wheel-brooches (see Chapters II, III), statuettes of Mars, a bronze Jupiter with thunderbolt and sceptre, and a number of pipe-clay figurines including those of Jupiter (Grenier, 1958, Chapter IX). The association between the Celtic Jupiter and trees (see above) may be reflected in dedications to Mars Olludius (Tree) in Gloucestershire (Green, 1976, 170) and in the area around Aquae Sextiae (Clerc, 1916, 284). Several instances occur in Gaul of the worship of a Mars linked with high places and mountain-tops, which may indicate a sky-connection. This is the case in Mars shrines around Lake Antre in the Jura (Thevenot, 1955). In the southern Gaulish Alps many local Celtic epithets for Mars are concerned with the summits of mountains ; for example Rudianos dwelled in the high mountain-sanctuary of St-Michel de Valbonne. The pre-Roman horseman from here should not be forgotten (Thevenot, 1955). On the mountain of the Magdalensberg, Carinthia (*ibid.*) a warrior-god depiction could be connected with the nearby shrine of Mars Latobius (*C.I.L.*, III, 5097-9) in the Vale of Lavant, where Latobius-Mars and Jupiter are represented (Obermayr, 1971, 76). Other hints at a solar or sky-association include two dedications to Vintius Pollux in the Savoie area near Seyssel (*C.I.L.*, XII, 2561-2) which have links with a Mars Vincius in the Maritime Alps (de Vries, 1963, 115) at Vence (*ibid.*, 64). Some Comminges tombstones bearing wheels are in close geographical proximity to a sanctuary to Mars Sutagius at St-Plancard (Haute-Garonne) (Thevenot, 1955).

The association of a Romano-Celtic Mars with a Romano-Celtic Sky-God is tenuous and scattered but it is there and there is enough of it to be reasonably definite. Such a link need not surprise us ; in the words of Grant (1971, 100) Mars was in origin much more than a War-God ; he was also an agricultural deity ; he was a high god of the Italians with a similar kind of function to that of Jupiter.

Sucellus, Silvanus and Dispater

I discuss these three entities together since there is a great deal of confusion between them in representation. For instance, there is interaction between the Hammer-God and Silvanus. They are assimilated in a limited geographical region of Narbonensis (Duval, 1957, 39ff. ; Musée de St-Rémy). The Vienne bronze Sucellus with his wheel-shaped 'barillet' (C15) taking the place of his long-shafted hammer, may have a connection with Silvanus in his possession of a wolf-skin (*ibid.*, 81). The most significant piece of evidence, as far as we are concerned, is the Aigues-Mortes altar (B2 ; Pl. LXXI, Fig. 42) bearing a dedication to Jupiter and

Silvanus, along with carvings of hammers, a pot (both belonging to Sucellus), billhook (Silvanus), thunderbolts and wheels (the Celtic Jupiter). It is hard to see a logical association between the Sky-God and Silvanus (to whom the stone is dedicated) unless the fertility aspect of the sky-cult is represented, or unless such an association occurs through the medium of the Hammer-God, who appears to have links with both. It may just be that the association between the deities on this altar should be taken as coincidental and does not necessarily imply a religious connection. Linckenheld (1929a, 75) suggests that the link between Silvanus and Sucellus may be to do with their respective functions of primitive nature and domestic entities. De Vries (1963, 99ff.) is of the opinion that the common factor is the hammer itself which, because of its long shaft, could be interpreted as a wood-cutter's axe.

Certainly Sucellus himself has powerful associations with the Sky-God in Gaul (the Hammer-God is named Sucellus, for instance, on inscriptions from Sarrebourg [Toussaint, 1928, 169]). Babelon (1916, Chapter VII) goes so far as to equate Taranis with Sucellus (see Chapter VIII for discussion of equation of Taranis with the Wheel-God). At Mainz a dedication to Jupiter Optimus Maximus Sucaelus (*C.I.L.*, XIII, 6730) is recorded (Toutain, 1907, 197ff.). Various scholars have assumed links between hammers and stylized thunderbolts, as may be the case with double-axes (see above 'Hammers' etc.). Lambrechts (1942, 100ff.) thinks that the hammer could represent a sceptre. Certainly some bronzes of Sucellus resemble Jupiter closely, like that from Lillebonne (Seine-Maritime) (Espérandieu & Rolland, 1959, nos. 9, 24), and the figure from Champforgeuil (Châlon-sur-Saône) (Armand-Calliat, 1937, Pl. XVI). One Jupiter with thunderbolt type of statuette very much resembles the Maligny and Autun Sucellus-figures (Lebel & Boucher, 1975, no. 46, 39 ; nos. 99, 98) and Lebel and Boucher suggest (1975 ; Boucher, 1976) that Sucellus' *olla* is a substitute for Jupiter's thunderbolt. Both Sucellus and Jupiter have one arm outstretched (with thunderbolt or pot) and one holding a long-hafted item (sceptre, hammer). This common stance occasionally also occurs in pipe-clay. A pipe-clay bearded Sucellus wearing a belted Gaulish tunic and conical hat, bears a hammer against his shoulder in very similar position to that adopted by the Gaulish Wheel-God in pipe-clay (Habert, 1901, no. 4816). Other possible connections between the Celtic Jupiter and Sucellus include distribution and siting. The divine couple Sucellus and Nantosuelta in stone are limited to north-eastern Gaul, precisely where depictions of the Celtic Sky-God are particularly popular (Lambrechts, 1942, 115). Sucellus, like the Celtic Jupiter, is found on the site of thermal waters, for example at Antigny-la-Ville (Canton Arnay-le-Duc) (Thomasset, 1956, 7-9). Linckenheld (1929a, 79-80) endorses the spring-siting of the god.

In the present context the connection between Sucellus and Celtic wheel-symbolism is demonstrated both in Britain and in Gaul. The Chedworth stone altar bearing the incised figure of a nude god with a spear possibly attests the link. The human figure also possibly holds a long-shafted hammer and there are wheel-symbols on the sides of the stone (Pl. LXXVI). On the Farley Heath sceptre-binding (C7 ; Pl. LXXXII), a human head next to a wheel-shape shares the bronze strip with a stylized Sucellus with his hammer. In Gaul there is a large group of bronzes depicting the Hammer-God bearing swastikas, wheels, circles, crosses and other celestial signs. Linckenheld lists such occurrences (1929a, 54, Table V). This apparent conflation between the Gaulish Hammer-God and the Celtic Sky-God is generally explained by reference to Dis Pater (Linckenheld, 1929a, 40-92 ; Deonna, 1915b, 1916). This is partly because one of the Bern scholiasts on Lucan equates Taranis with Dis Pater and partly because Caesar (*De Bello Gallico* VI, 18, 1) states that the Gauls thought they were descended from him and so time was counted by night rather than by day. It is by no means proven that Sucellus has any connection with Dis whatever. Sucellus' name means 'Good Striker'. Even the fact that he occurs with a three-headed dog (Linckenheld, 1929a, 84) need not mean a funerary significance. Cerberus is not necessarily being invoked ; triplication is well-known in Gaulish iconography as is the dog. The domestic nature of Sucellus, as shown, for instance, by his companion's long-shafted house (Toussaint, 1928), may simply mean that he occurs as a mediator between the Sky-God and ordinary people. There is no evidence that he is chthonic or funerary. His sky-symbolism, need not be tied in with wheel-symbols on Mediomatrician house-steles, as is often considered to be the case (for example Drioux, 1934, 100) ; and the fact that, for instance, the Viège god (C49) looks like Sucellus and bears thunderbolt and swastikas, must surely mean that an aspect of the Celtic Jupiter is represented.

Vulcan and Hercules

In Britain two types of item demonstrate possible associations between a Smith-God and a Celtic Wheel-Cult. One is the Farley Heath sceptre-binding (C7 ; Pl. LXXXII) ; the other is the coarse grey-ware sherds from

North Britain, notably from Malton (C59 ; Pl. LXXVIII, Fig. 56). On the Farley Heath sheet-bronze strip smithing equipment is depicted in close proximity to a conical-hatted figure with long-shafted hammer, and the head of a wheel-deity. Sherds from Malton bear applied wheels and also applied hammers, tongs and anvils (Leach, 1962). It is only these items of equipment that are depicted here, together with human faces ; it is difficult not to see an association. At Corbridge too actual depictions of a Smith-God are recorded, on moulds for application to large pottery jars ; it is from here that the mould portraying the Celtic Wheel-God (C10 ; Pl. LXXIX, Fig. 58) comes. If there is in Britain some conflation between the two deities the problem is why. The immediate answer may be in the common factor of attributes, the fire of the smithing-furnace in the case of one and of the sun in the other. It is not only in Celtic iconography that there is an association between the two motifs of wheel and smith. On some Graeco-Italian vases, for example one from Capua, the Smith-God is linked with Ixion and his wheel (Cook, 1914, 198ff. ; Brommer, 1978, 23). Some Graeco-Roman bronzes of a Smith-God look very like Jupiter (Brommer, 1978, 53, Abb. 26). Jupiter was the father of Vulcan, and Zeus Areios was sometimes identified with Hephaistos (*ibid.*, 135 ; Robertson, 1975).

The association of smithing-equipment on the Farley Heath sheet-bronze strip (C7 ; Pl. LXXXII) is interesting if one recalls the Sucellus in pipe-clay with long-handled hammer against his shoulder and conical smith's hat (Habert, 1901, no. 4816). One thing about Celtic equation or association between Vulcan and the Sky-God should be remembered. Smiths were extremely important in Celtic society. Henig (1972, 212) draws attention to their depiction on some Celtic coins in Britain, for example on a bronze of Cunobelinus, and a silver of Dubnovellaunus. Finally we should recall that on the Paris Pillar dedicated to Jupiter (Duval, 1961) there are images and inscriptions pertaining to, among others, Jupiter himself, Castor and Pollux and Vulcan (Duval, 1961, 264-275).

Hercules has associations with both Sucellus and with solar cults. Sucellus once has a club (Linckenheld, 1929a, 79-80). The wolfskin worn by the Vienne bronze Hammer-God (C15) may represent some half-remembered allusion to Hercules' lion-pelt. Hercules Saxanus represented on a rock at Brohl in the Rhineland (*ibid.*) is accompanied by sun and moon symbols. The bronze Hercules from (?) Neuchâtel has a cross on his chest which could be a solar motif, though in my opinion it could equally represent pectoral muscle (C18). The gold chain from Thérouanne (see Chapters II, III) bears a wheel and club-pendant associated. Two pieces of British evidence are important in connection with Hercules/Celtic Jupiter-identification. One is the Willingham Fen sceptre-terminal, where the youthful Wheel-God brandishes what may either be a club or a club-like thunderbolt (C6 ; Pl. LXXXI). The other is the Corbridge Wheel-God (C10 ; Pl. LXXIX, Fig. 58) armed, like Mars, but with a large, knotted club which he leans on. Some continental material may endorse this association. Wightman (1970, 210) suggests that a statue of a seated Jupiter from behind the Petrisberg in Trier, from a small shrine near a suburban villa, may not be entirely Roman because of the presence of a relief of Hercules carved on the back. The Celtic-looking Jupiter in Rouen Museum, portrayed with stylized curls, barbarian dress and an eagle perched on his outstretched left arm, looks very like some Romano-Gaulish bronzes of Hercules (Espérandieu & Rolland, 1959, 22, no. 1). If the apparent association between these two entities is valid, then it may occur partly on account of Jupiter's classical kinship with the demi-god and partly because Hercules symbolized force and strength.

VIII. Aquatic and Chthonic Aspects to the Wheel-God Cult

Both of these have already been touched upon in a number of preceding sub-sections. However, it is necessary generally to assess these two somewhat obscure aspects to what is essentially a celestial and solar cult. We have seen that Romano-Celtic divinities such as Apollo, Mother-Goddesses and Epona — who do have a solar or sky facet to their cult — are found frequently associated with healing water-sanctuaries. The connection may well have something to do with the sun's healing power. Water, in the classical world, was considered absolutely essential to the curative process. There was, for instance, an actual spring at the Asklepieion in Corinth (American School of Classical Studies at Athens, 1977, 12). The solar association is best seen perhaps at Bath, where a solar deity (in existence before the Roman period since 'Sul' is a proper name, not a descriptive epithet) had a large shrine and hot baths dedicated to him/her. We have noted that miniature wheels were flung into Gaulish rivers, and that Jupiter-giant columns (Lambrechts, 1949) were associated frequently with water (Hatt, 1951a, 82-87 ; Lambrechts, 1949, 149 ; Reinach, 1913, 126). Riverine associations for Jupiter-columns include Montgeraud near the Loire, and Beaune near the Bouzaise (Lambrechts, 1949, 145).

Column-fragments have been found in river-beds, for example at Auberive (*ibid.*, 146-147) in the vicinity of which (B6) a (?)wheel-bearing sculpture is recorded (Pl. II, Fig. 3). Luxeuil was a thermal establishment which produced a Jupiter-group with a wheel (B72 ; Pl. XI, Fig. 24) (Espérandieu, 1917). Springs and wheel-symbols are associated in Côte-d'Or, for example with the Agey Wheel-Goddess (B1) ; and at Néris, where a wheel-brooch and pipe-clay Wheel-God (C9a) are recorded. At Bourbonne-les-Bains miniature wheels are known (see Chapter II). On one occasion fragments of a Jupiter-column were discovered in a Roman pit 16 metres deep at Montiers-sur-Saulx (Meuse) (Lambrechts, 1949, 78). This pit-association is of potential significance since it could have a connection with chthonicism and the underworld. According to Benoit water aided communication with the lower world (1970, 65). Tacitus (*Annals* 2, 54) mentions a sanctuary of Apollo Claros near Colophon on the Ionian coast in the Roman period, where the priest drank the water of a sacred pit beneath the temple before revealing the oracle. Water in Romano-Gaulish beliefs may well have had a chthonic as well as a healing element. Epona is associated with horses, with water, with fertility and with death ; so are the Deae Matres. There is substantial evidence that the Sky-God also had such an association. The occurrence at Nîmes both of water-cults and solar emblems may have a death as well as a healing significance.

In the previous chapter it was put forward that there can be no unequivocal evidence for beliefs in a Gaulish Sky-God being reflected on wheel-bearing funerary monuments, but that nevertheless there may be such an association. Strong chthonic evidence has been seen in connection with the iconography of Jupiter-giant groups but, for the present, we confine ourselves to items of a specifically funerary nature. One thing that can be stated here about Jupiter-columns is that they themselves are sometimes found in sepulchral contexts (Picard, 1977, 89-113), and Picard further maintains that some early monuments bear a strong resemblance to military funerary stelai of the Rhineland where an equestrian, armed, figure rides down a fallen enemy. Benoit goes so far as to suggest that the columns themselves may be funerary (1970, 87), though this is not necessary to explain the monumental structure of these items (see above). The two major groups of funerary stones in Gaul bearing solar symbolism are from the Comminges and neighbouring area of south-western Gaul (Hatt, 1945) and, above all, from Alsace (Linckenheld, 1927) (though others are recorded, like the tombstone of Quintus Fortesius from

Petronell in Austria [B170]). The two aforementioned groups are associated with cremations. Hatt (1945) would date relevant stones from SW Gaul mainly to the mid 2nd - end of 3rd Century A.D. The Alsace cemeteries lasted from the 1st to at least the 4th Century. Linckenheld himself (1927, 76) admits the problems implicit in distinguishing between ornament and symbolism. The rosettes on some Rhineland funerary stones (Hatt, 1951b, 106) may be decorative or they could be romanized symbols of eternal life and spring beyond the grave (Toynbee, 1971, 63). Linckenheld is of the opinion that the Mediomatrici of the Vosges adapted the Roman rosette and formed it into a true wheel, a solar symbol which was already in mental if not physical existence before Roman influence. This same phenomenon certainly seems to have taken place during the Iron Age on Celtic coins of southern Gaul (Allen, 1980). At any rate it is easy to see how rosette can be transformed into wheel, especially in a province where this motif may have been familiar as a cult-symbol from the pre-Roman era (see Chapter I). It is of interest that Vaison, which has produced powerful Wheel-God evidence for the Lower Rhône Valley, has yielded a tombstone to the four-year-old Julius Severianus, bearing wheel-ornament (Sautel, 1926, 90, no. 152). Rosettes and wheel-symbols are associated with cremation rather than inhumation. Toynbee (1971, 33-34) postulates a change in the method of disposal of the dead in Rome and Italy about the turn of the 1st Century A.D., gradually spreading to the rest of the Empire. But, as we have seen, in the Vosges cremation lasted a very long time. Toynbee suggests that people in the Roman world did generally believe in an afterlife, and, to some extent, in theories of an astral apotheosis, where in death the soul rejoined the pure, fiery element whence it came (*ibid.*, 35). The astral glorification, as stated by Cicero in his *Somnium Scipionis* is, according to Richmond (1950, 13-14), a very naïve and unspiritual conception of the afterlife ; it means that a sentient deity rewards a good and successful creation by transforming it into a star, *per ardua ad astra*. Cremation does fit well into Cicero's ideas, whereas inhumation accords better with later anthropomorphic views of the otherworld (*ibid.*, 19). There is both literary and iconographic evidence that in the Roman Empire a belief existed that the sun was a god of the dead. Emperors were borne to heaven in the chariot of Helios. A funerary altar from Rome bears the inscription *Sol me rapuit* (*C.I.L.*, VI, 29954 ; Cumont, 1922, 102).

With the abundance of wheel-symbolism occurring in all areas of Gaul, both in small models, other items and stone monuments (sometimes, in the case of models, buried with the dead), coupled with the rosette, solar and sidereal symbolism attached to death in the Roman world, it would seem a fairly natural phenomenon for wheel and derivative motifs to occur, even if in some instances reduced to good-luck signs, on Romano-Celtic tombstones.

IX. Function, Craftsmen and Dedicants

Of the stone monuments and small objects bearing wheel-symbolism, the majority either bear dedications to Jupiter or, if the wheel accompanies a humanoid figure, it is generally this divinity who is represented, identifiable by his stance, physiognomy and by classical attributes — thunderbolt, eagle or sceptre. The portrayals range from large stone monuments — such as Jupiter-column sculptures, which must have normally been the result of corporate organization — to small pipe-clay figures, which were cheap and mass-produced for an amorphous market, and presumably originally the property of individuals. In between come the few bronze items — like the Landouzy (C3) and Le Châtelet (C2) figures, and the Willingham Fen sceptre (C6). The former, though expensive, could belong to an individual ; the latter in all probability belonged to priest or temple. At the very base of a hypothetical 'triangle of sacredness' come the utilitarian items — pieces of pottery and tile — which were marked with wheel or swastika.

Small bronzes and pipe-clay figures were made by artisan-craftsmen in centralized workshops and disseminated throughout the provinces of Gaul and, to a lesser extent, Britain (Boucher, 1976 ; Jenkins, 1957b ; 1958). According to Boucher classical art-forms were adopted for bronzes as soon as the Romans arrived and the indigenous ideas crept back later (1976, 173). What of stone sculptures and their makers ? Who made the large stone monuments and how did they work ? Even the stonework may be sub-divided. The small swastika-altars of, for instance, the Pyrenees may have been made by local craftsmen without a great deal of organization or expertise. But the large and ornate Jupiter-columns are another matter entirely. Bauchhenss states (1976, 1) that the sculptor of the Hausen column had precise and detailed knowledge of Greek mythological themes and art-forms ; yet the patron of this monument bears a Celtic name, and the mason himself was probably a Celt. Bauchhenss maintains that the erection of the columns was above all at the instigation of the native population. Both Bauchhenss (1976) and Phillips (1976a, 35-

41) believe that knowledge of classical art-forms was disseminated to craftsmen either through apprenticeships or via pattern-books. Liversidge has an interesting observation to make about the latter thesis, with regard to wall-paintings :

> 'The artists seem to have used pattern-books full of favourite scenes and motifs ; and the client must have ... chosen whatever appealed to him... Occasionally ... he did not understand the significance of the designs he chose.' (Liversidge, 1968, 84).

If this state of affairs may be assumed for sculptures, it goes some way towards explaining the use in Jupiter-column groups of the gigantomachy to symbolize an essentially Celtic dualistic theme. Phillips (1976b, 50-57 ; 1976c, 101-109) has some useful comments on stonemasons in north-western Britain. In his examination of unfinished stone monuments he has concluded that all his pieces were made in local sandstone and therefore carved locally, though not necessarily always by British masons. He recognizes a broad correlation between style and technique (the more classical the theme the more Roman the tools used). In looking at Carlisle sculptures Phillips has identified a local workshop ; he comments (1976c, 101) that popular sculptures of the Roman Empire were usually produced by local artists working for local patrons. This is clear both from distinctive regional characteristics and from geographical distribution. Any community of sufficient size to provide sculptors with a living would have had at least one workshop with its favoured motifs, types of monument and stylistic idiosyncrasies. There would not have been a great trade in non-high quality and non-classical carvings.

If we accept that large stone monuments would have been too expensive for most individuals to afford, there is a problem with regard to the siting of some of the more remote Jupiter-columns — on the sites of private estates or secluded temple-sites. One can only assume that some farmers were wealthy enough to commission such an item and that a community united in religious beliefs would have been able to pool their resources. The dedicants of Jupiter-giant columns, where the evidence survives, were not normally soldiers but, above all, members of the local population (Bauchhenss, 1976, 7ff.).

Picard maintains (1977, 89-113) that although some dedicants were Gaulish and Celtic, in Germany some were soldiers or decurions. He is of the opinion that the cult was brought to the Rhineland by Gauls in the army or attracted by frontier prosperity. Certainly, where there are indications on other types of wheel-bearing monument, there is evidence of Celtic dedications, for instance at Saverne (for example B141) and at Collias (B27) where a group, clan or sub-tribe of people is involved. Where military altars are concerned the northern British evidence points to dedications by Tungrians. Spaniards and Dacians are also mentioned but Wilkes (personal communication) is of the opinion that the cohorts so named would in fact contain recruits from the north-western provinces rather than from the original homeland of the battalion.

Conclusion

Any interpretation of Celtic religion is made the more difficult because of the lack of indigenous literary sources for the La Tène and even the Roman period (Harmand, 1970, 113ff. ; Piggott, 1968b, 22-26). This has been amply demonstrated in this chapter. Brogan (1953, 178) states that the function of native deities may be deduced by the symbols or attributes carried by their images. As the foregoing discussion has attempted to indicate, one such divinity can be identified by the bearing of a wheel-symbol. There are immediate problems. Whereas in Roman religion the chief feature is that all important world processes were divinely activated and thus all deities had charge of particular functions and spheres of activity (Ogilvie, 1969, 10), Celtic religion appears to have been based far more on locality for deity-identification, and one god may have had a number of different functions. Nevertheless, Jupiter, or a Celtic Sky-God, seems to have differed from the general rule. The Roman Sky-Lord did have a locality – the sky – as well as a set of limited functions and a Celtic divinity, later equated with him, seems to have had a solar role above all. However, this uneasy marriage between different methods of identification led, in Gaul and Britain, to a great diversity in wheel-bearing monuments so that, as we have seen, there is a substantial amount of assimilation of other divinities besides Jupiter himself. It is true that the vast majority of such monuments can, where the necessary data exist, be identified with Jupiter but the formal, physical religious expression stimulated by such a cult is by no means clear-cut.

CHAPTER VII

Classical Jupiter and Celtic Sky-God in Britain (¹)

INTRODUCTION

The purpose of this chapter is to present and analyse the totality of archaeological evidence for a sky-divinity within the Roman province of Britain, both overtly classical and Romano-Celtic. The main problem is that of interpretation of the very varied art-forms by which this entity is represented as a classical or Celtic deity. In other words what we are attempting to assess is the relative roles of *interpretatio romana* and *interpretatio celtica* (Green, 1976, 2).

The Roman Sky-God Jupiter was of the utmost import to Rome, not merely, or even first and foremost, as a god to be worshipped in the purely religious, individual sense, but as an epitome of the Roman state itself (Altheim, 1938). By the time of the early Empire, and indeed before (Ogilvie, 1969), Jupiter had become a political rather than a religious symbol. However, we have evidence (see for example chapters IV, V, VI, VIII) that the Celtic peoples of Gaul and Britain had a Sky-God of their own, probably originating long before the Roman era in those two areas (Green, 1974, 2-6 ; 1979a, 345-368). After the Roman Conquest this god appears to have attained close associations with the classical Jupiter. Overt Celticism is expressed by the presence of a wheel in the iconography, generally a Celtic rather than a Graeco-Roman symbol (see Chapter VI). In Gaul, as we have seen, a god accompanied by a wheel is a reasonably common occurrence, and this has long been recognized as a specific art-

---

(1) See Catalogue E for material referred to in this chapter : in order to avoid too much repetition in the case of wheel-bearing items, the reader is referred, in Cat. E, to the main catalogues — A, B, C.

form (Courcelle-Seneuil, 1910 ; Lambrechts, 1942 ; Duval, 1957 ; de Vries, 1963 ; Thevenot, 1968). In Britain, as in Gaul, there are a number of instances where well-defined emblems or attributes are depicted, which argue for a Celtic as opposed to a purely classical interpretation. However, this clarity of definition is in some cases lacking. It is necessary to examine content, style, context and association of the material in order to evaluate its role in Sky-worship in Britain.

I. THE NATURE OF THE EVIDENCE

The archaeological evidence for a Roman or a Romano-Celtic Jupiter in Britain falls into a number of classifiable groups. These categories may be defined as follows :

    A. Epigraphy
    B. Representations of the deity in Roman or Celtic guise
    C. Classical or Celtic emblems of the god

A. *Epigraphic Dedications*

Of more than a hundred dedications to *Iupiter Optimus Maximus* in Britain (recorded in *R.I.B.*) ([2]) and carved on stone altars, a minute fraction only bear witness to any form of celticism. This is no surprise since, in the first instance, Jupiter is only infrequently equated with a named Celtic divinity anywhere in the Celtic provinces (see Chapter VIII). Second, epigraphy is a specifically Roman method of expression, so the bias will naturally be towards the mention of classical divinities. One or two British dedications to Jupiter Optimus Maximus do bear possible signs of 'contamination' of the Roman State-Deity. The inscription on the upper half of a fragmentary limestone altar at Aldborough in Yorkshire links Jupiter Optimus Maximus with the Mother-Goddesses (*R.I.B.*, 708). At Binchester (*R.I.B.*, 1030) an altar was dedicated to Jupiter Optimus Maximus and the Mother-Goddesses Ollototae (overseas). We have seen (Chapter VI) that there is substantial evidence for a connection between the Celtic Jupiter and the Deae Matres, but one must also bear in mind that the presence, in army ritual, of the Matres of the Parade-Ground, reminds us just how far originally Gaulish deities eventually infiltrated the

---

([2]) *R.I.B.* = COLLINGWOOD, R. G. & WRIGHT, R. P., 1965, *The Roman Inscriptions of Britain*, Vol. I, *Inscriptions on Stone*.

State ritual (Howell, 1969). Jupiter, Cocidius and a Genius were linked on an altar from the Housesteads Mithraeum (Lewis, 1966, 104).

About a dozen dedications to Jupiter are worthy of detailed scrutiny in the present context. Only one of these, however, has an overt association between Jupiter and a Celtic Sky-deity. The Chester altar to *I.O.M. Tanarus* (E21) refers to a Sky- and Thunder-deity — with classical and Celtic conflation (see Chapter VIII). It is conceivable that the 6-petalled rosette on the right lateral surface of the stone is a stylized wheel-symbol (see Chapter VI). It is worth noting that a similar, 8-petalled example decorates the apex of a bronze plaque to the Syrian Baal Jupiter Dolichenus at Mauer-an-der-Url (C51).

Four altars, three from Hadrian's Wall forts (E5, E18, E19) and one from the Cumberland coast defence post at Maryport (E84), bear dedications to the conventional *I.O.M.* but, in each case, associated with wheel-motifs. At Birdoswald and Maryport respectively, twenty-two altars to the god were discovered. At each site one of these was decorated with the symbolism of the Celtic divinity — the Wheel. The Birdoswald altar was set up by a Dacian cohort (*R.I.B.*, 1877); the Maryport stone was dedicated by a battalion of Spaniards (*R.I.B.*, 827). It is probable, however, that the content of these cohorts, by the time they came to the Wall area, would have come from the North-East provinces of Gaul rather than from the named homeland of the battalion. Both of these forts also produced carved reliefs of wheels (Wright & Phillips, 1975, 69; Bailey, 1915, 135ff.). The other two altars in question come from Castlesteads (*R.I.B.*, 1981, 1983) (Pl. LXXV, Fig. 50). Both were commissioned by the 2nd (part-mounted) Cohort of Tungrians (from the Tongres area of modern Belgium, a region which has itself produced wheel-symbolism, e.g. B150). One of the altars (*R.I.B.*, 1983) was dedicated to Jupiter Optimus Maximus and to the 'Numen' of the Emperor. It is not easy to evaluate the significance of the wheel-motifs in such an otherwise normal Roman context. They were dedicated by auxiliary army-groups, and obviously the first importance was to pledge renewed allegiance to the reigning emperor (Richmond, 1943). From alternative evidence, discussed below, it would appear that soldiers stationed in Britain were well aware of the cult-expressions evoked by the presence of a Celtic sky-power, although his popularity was of prime importance only across the Channel. It says much for the tenacity of the cult that the Celtic wheel-emblem was able to penetrate that most Roman of customs — the annual pledge of loyalty to the Roman State and the Imperial House.

One or two other dedications to Jupiter from Britain may have possible Celtic influence. Chichester (E25) and Cirencester (E27) have produced dedications to the god which could just possibly be part of 'Jupitergigantensäulen', though in neither case does enough of the monument survive for this to be more than speculation. The Cirencester example is by far the most interesting and informative. The monument comprises a rectangular base with small attached columns at the two surviving angles (*R.I.B.*, 103 ; Green, 1976, 174). An elaborate Corinthian capital from the site (Phillips, 1976a ; Pl. 69) may belong to the same monument. The dedication on the inscribed block is somewhat ambiguous. The inscription refers to the erection of a statue and a column to Jupiter Optimus Maximus, by a governor of Britannia Prima, which was apparently erected under the 'Old Religion'. The governor's name is given as Lucius Septimius, a citizen of Reims. The mention of Prima dates the inscription post A.D. 296 when Britain was divided into four provinces in the Diocletianic reorganization. The dedication here implies the renovation of an old monument after years of neglect. Haverfield (1893) suggested that the dedication may date from the time of Julian's Apostasy in the mid 4th Century, when Christianity lapsed for a brief period. The fact remains, however, that whereas the inscription implies the presence of a column and statue, it is impossible to say whether the classical pagan State Cult, or a Celtic Jupiter is referred to in the statement 'erected under the Old Religion'. On the one hand one might expect an official Roman governor to adhere to the strictly classical deities, even though Lucius Septimius was, in origin, a citizen of Reims (the more especially if, as Wacher [1978, 55] has suggested, Corinium was the capital city of Britannia Prima). On the other hand, Reims was an area within Gaul abounding in Celtic cult-expression. One should also bear in mind the essentially Celtic nature of a great deal of cult-evidence from Corinium — Cernunnos with ram-horned serpent, Mother-Goddesses and others (Green, 1976, 172-174).

There is no indication, among other dedications to Jupiter in Britain, of anything other than straightforward classical allusion. The numerous military altars to Jupiter Optimus Maximus are too standardized to be worthy of detailed attention. A new dedication from excavations of the City of London (E76) Hobley & Shofield, 1977, 63) refers to a (?)temple to Jupiter Optimus Maximus which had collapsed on account of age, and had been restored by a freedman and three others. It is perfectly feasible that whatever collapsed was not a temple but a column or pillar. A wooden oath from Lothbury in London (E75) reads 'By almighty Jupiter and the Genius of the Imperial Majesty Domitian...' (Green, 1976, 224). There is Celtic as well as classical religious evidence from London, but only one item relating to Celtic Jupiter-worship − a miniature six-spoked wheel (E76a) − hints at a Gaulish rather than a Roman cult of the Sky-God. The classical State deity appears to be virtually untarnished here. The lead curse from Ratcliffe-on-Soar (E94) − presumably once nailed up on the door or wall of a shrine − likewise need have nothing to do with a Gaulish or Celtic cult. Lead curses are common finds both in the classical and Celtic worlds, originating in the former. The dedication and carved stone figure from York (E123) appears classical.

Judged on its own merits the silver votive plaque found with others in an urn at Windmill Hill, Stony Stratford (E107), appears as an unequivocal dedication to Jupiter and Vulcan. The leaf-pattern of the plaque's edges, however, is Celtic in style (Ross, 1967), and there are other indications that the hoard may have been deposited in a Celtic context. First, the plaque was found associated with parts of native-style ceremonial headdresses of chains and plaques of a type known at the rural Romano-Celtic shrine at Hockwold, Norfolk, and at Cavenham, Suffolk (Layard, 1925). Second, at Barkway in Hertfordshire, similar plaques are recorded of which two were dedicated to Celtic deities − Mars Alator (known also at South Shields [Green, 1978]), and Mars Toutatis − and a third, to Vulcan, as at Stony Stratford. In Gaul, Mars and Mercury have perhaps the largest number of Celtic epithets applied to them of all Roman deities (Benoit, 1953), whereas Jupiter has very few indeed (see Chapter VIII), as has Vulcan. It may be that the Mars dedications from Barkway have implications for the Jupiter/Vulcan plaque, and that Celtic influence is present. Hoards and caches of ritual material in Britain do tend to represent native cult-activity. Those at, for example Willingham Fen, Cambridgeshire, and Felmingham Hall, Norfolk, were not deposits in response to classical methods of worship.

B. *Representations of the Sky-God*

As is the case with epigraphic dedications, there is a certain ambiguity in the interpretation of this group of artifacts. I shall discuss the overtly classical images first. It should be emphasized, however, that visual 'classicism' does not necessarily or automatically imply religious classicism, although in many instances that is the most likely interpretation.

One of the great altar corner-stones at Bath (E3), which come from the temple of Sulis-Minerva, depicts a draped figure of Jupiter with his emblems and thunderbolt, sceptre and eagle. Another stone represents an equally classical Hercules. The images are of Graeco-Roman deities — of that there is no doubt — but the temple was dedicated to Sul-Minerva, a Celtic deity existing probably long before the advent of the Roman pantheon to south-west Britain (Cunliffe, 1966 ; 1969, 1). Moreover, the bronze head of the goddess (Toynbee, 1962, 135-6, pl. 20, no. 25), hacked at some time from the body, could not be more classical in concept. 'There can be little doubt that this is the head of a once helmeted Minerva — of Sulis-Minerva in purely Graeco-Roman guise' (*ibid.*, 136). The two cultures are inextricably intertwined here. The point I would make is that however Roman an effigy of a divinity appears to be, knowledge of its context may cause one to reconsider a classical attribution. From York comes a not dissimilar figure to the Bath image (E123). On the right side is a weathered upright deity holding a staff ; on the left a figure wearing a tunic and bearing a large animal faces right — a scene, perhaps, of a suppliant offering a sacrifice. The accompanying dedication reads 'To Jupiter Optimus Maximus, to the gods and goddesses of Hospitality and to the Penates' (*R.I.B.*, 649). There is no evidence of a Romano-Celtic version of Jupiter.

Other 'classical' images of the Sky-God are mainly of bronze, taking the form of small figurines, presumably personal property or ex-votos from shrines. Bronze figurines of the god come from a number of Romano-British sites including Brampton (E7) ; Colchester (E30) ; Ilkley (E58) ; Kirkby Thore (E64) ; Langham (E65) ; Leicester (E68) ; London (two statuettes) (E72, E73) ; Manchester (E81) ; Southbroom (E103) ; Sea Mills (E97) ; South Shields (E104) ; West Stoke (E112) ; and York (E121). Of these only the West Stoke figure is seated. The Langham, London and Manchester examples are particularly classical in style ; the Southbroom statuette, on the other hand, is one of a number of highly stylized Celtic bronzes found in a ritual hoard in a pot (British Museum, 1964) ; other figures include Mars with ram-horned snakes. Other sites have produced bronze busts or masks of the god (sometimes intended for attachment to other objects, as at Caerleon [E11 ; Green, 1978, 48]). Grays (E47) has yielded a small bust of the deity, while from the Roman town of Ilchester (E57) comes a medallion depicting a head of Jupiter. The hollow bronze mask from the hoard at Felmingham Hall (E43) is interesting, since it was discovered in a ritual context — a cache of religious material — including a

Celtic wheel-symbol, a ceremonial pole-tip and a small mask depicting Jupiter Helioserapis ; the whole group being dated by a coin of the 260s A.D. (British Museum, 1964 ; Gilbert, 1978). London (E74) has produced an oddity in the bronze thunderbolt decorated with planetary deities, presumably a Jupiter-symbol, but unconnected with any effigy of the god himself. The object could, with its planetary associations, be connected with Celtic 'Jupitergigantensäulen' (Bauchhenss, 1976), or with an oriental cult — such as that of Sabazios (personal communication, Professor J. Ferguson).

Several representations from Britain are very definitely depictions of a Romano-Celtic or Celtic Sky-God rather than the classical Jupiter. We will examine first the evidence of stone carvings. At Churcham (E26) an oblong stone plaque bears a depiction of a huge-headed god, possibly horned, a trilobate object in each hand and accompanied by two four-spoked wheels. This representation very obviously bears no resemblance whatever to the Graeco-Roman celestial divinity depicted, for instance, at Langham (E65). The fact that the head is overlarge reflects the Celtic emphasis of the head noted, for example, on the bronze statuette of the cross-legged deity from Bouray in France (Pobé & Roubier, 1961, pls. 12-13). The presence of the wheel-motif suggests that we have here a thoroughly native depiction of the Romano-Celtic Sky/Wheel-God. Another stone carving of relevance from Britain, that from Great Chesterford, should also perhaps be mentioned (E48). It comprises a half-octagonal 'trough' decorated with busts of deities round its edge. It is conceivable that one of the divinities is Jupiter and that the monument is part of a 'Jupitergigantensäule' (Richmond, 1963, 1ff.). Other possible monuments of this type have been mentioned in the epigraphic section above. However, one or two possible such columns, but without inscriptions, exist, including a fragment from Irchester (E60) (Haverfield, 1902, 157ff.) and from Springhead (E106) (Harker, 1980). These have been included here because if they are fragments of Jupiter-columns, when complete they could have carried an effigy of the god.

Netherby ([3]) has produced two curious stone carvings (E86, E87) of Wheel-bearing deities in the guise of Genii sacrificing with a wheel instead of the more usual *patera* over an altar (for type of classical Genius

---

[3] Wheel-bearing items are dealt with cursorily here since they are considered in detail elsewhere (Catalogues A, B, C ; Chapters II-VI).

or Bonus Eventus see Toynbee, 1962, 139, Cat. no. 32, pl. 25). This confused Romano-Celtic image could be interpreted as a depiction of the Wheel-God being invoked by a suppliant Genius on behalf of or as representative of the owner of the sculpture. The figures both bear *cornuacopiae*, as well as wheels, thus apparently marrying the two overtly alien concepts of sky-power and prosperity (see chapters IV, VI) (Pl. 49).

Three clay objects may next be considered. Two are triangular clay antefixes from Caerleon (E9, E10 ; Pl. LXXVII), and the third, from Corbridge, a clay mould for application to pottery vessels (E33 ; Pl. LXXIX, Fig. 58). The Caerleon examples (see Chapter V and Catalogue C) take the form of depictions of human heads each associated with wheels at the apex of the triangle. It may be that the humanoid heads here represent the Celtic Sky-God. It is noteworthy that of the other antefixes from the site one has a human head associated with stars and crescents, and another consists again of a head, this time surrounded by what appears to be a stylized conifer. This association brings to mind the Netherby carving (E87) with boar and tree and, more immediately, an antefix from Vindonissa in Switzerland (C79), with head, celestial symbol and tree. Such antefixes would have been fixed in the end-tiles of the roofs of barrack-blocks or other buildings within the legionary fortress. It is possible that the image of the Celtic divinity served both as good-luck symbolism and as protection against evil forces. Perhaps the soldiery, ever superstitious with regard to alien powers (Wacher, 1977), thought it prudent to propitiate a potent foreign deity — so like their own omnipresent Jupiter — on whose land they were trespassing. The representation from Corbridge is in the form of a mould bearing an impression of a deity with shield, club, helmet and wheel. It may be that here also Roman soldiers were seeking to appease a Celtic deity in whose territory they had set up their fort and supply-depôt. On the other hand, if we are correct in surmising that the wheel-bearing Sky-God was introduced from Gaul to Britain, it may be that the cult was brought to Corbridge by a soldier.

Three bronze cult-representations of a presumed Romano-Celtic Sky-deity remain to be discussed. The first comprises the iconography on the sheet-bronze sceptre-binding from the Farley Heath Romano-Celtic temple near Albury in Surrey (E41 ; Pl. LXXXII). The binding, when discovered, was curved into a spiral as though it had been wrapped around a cylindrical rod ; traces of iron suggest that this shaft may have been of iron. The decoration punched on the sheet-bronze is unequivocally ritual in character (see Chapter V). Among other iconography, including birds, boars, stags and indeterminate creatures, a figure of a deity in 'matchstick' style bearing a long-shafted hammer, and associated with two pairs of tongs, is represented. Nearby is the head of another deity associated with a stylized wheel and a thunderbolt. It is reasonable to assume that this may represent the Celtic Sky-God — the wheel and thunderbolt respectively identifying Celtic and Roman aspects of his cult-imagery. As regards stylization of this and many other items of Celtic iconography, one should remember comparisons with other pre-industrial societies. 'The Negro artist ... accentuates whatever has spiritual significance, without regard for natural proportions. Whatever is unessential is excluded' (Leuzinger, 1960, 13).

The composite bronze bucket-mount found in the River Ribble (E95) very possibly represents the Romano-Celtic Sky-God, even though no wheel-imagery is present. The mount comprises three flat-backed heads, of which two are linked by a rivet from which hangs a loop. The head of a bird of prey (probably an eagle) surmounts the head of a knob-horned bull. From the bird's head a rivet connects with that of a human being. If the bird depicted is an eagle, then its association with the portrayal of an anthropomorphic divinity perhaps means that a version of Jupiter is the cult-figure. Animal bucket-mounts, especially with bull-depictions, are common occurrences in the pre-Roman and early Roman archaeological record in Britain (Hawkes, 1951). The bull is a ubiquitous Celtic cult-animal from the Iron Age to the end of the Roman period both in Britain and in Gaul. Moreover, as will be demonstrated below, the bull appears to have definite and consistent associations with the Romano-Celtic Sky-God (the animal also has close associations with the classical Jupiter but, I would argue, not in such an essential or equalized manner as in the Celtic world). The bull on the Ribble bucket-mount has horns terminating in knobs which would appear to be a Celtic rather than a classical method of stylization (Ross, 1967). Drioux (1934) has an interesting point to make about this phenomenon, although it is of course no more than speculation. His view is that the knobs could represent sun-symbols, and other continental scholars (Reinach, 1896 ; Deonna, 1917) have thought on similar lines. It is of interest that the attendant holding the wheel on the Gundestrup Bowl has a knob-horned helmet (C1). Two other bucket-mounts, from Thealby (E108) bear eagle and bull iconography similar to the Ribble item, but without the anthropomorphic element.

The Willingham Fen (E114) evidence is perhaps more enigmatic and at the same time potentially illuminating than any other item so far considered. A ritual hoard of bronzework found in Cambridgeshire includes a composite bronze-casting, perhaps to be interpreted as a sceptre-terminal. The imagery depicted comprises a youthful, naked and beardless, curly-haired divinity whose foot rests on the head of a humanoid monster. This human form is associated with the head of a triple-horned bull, a dolphin, an eagle and a wheel. The god wields either club or thunderbolt (see Chapter V). Once again we have the association of an eagle with a bull – this time of the Celtic three-horned variety common in eastern Gaul. Although the appearance of the god has little in common with the normal representations of Jupiter, the presence of the wheel would seem to indicate that the Celtic Sky-God is to be identified here. The eagle's presence is presumably representative of the classical Jupiter element. The (?)club brings to mind the implement on the Corbridge depiction. The 'monster' underneath the deity's foot may have associations with the chthonic being on the Jupiter-columns (see Chapters IV, VI). What remains puzzling is the choice of physical type for the god himself. It is difficult to see why the craftsman has deviated from the usual image, since the idea must have been to be able to identify the god. The rather Cupid-like image could have a connection (in art-form at least) with the presence of the dolphin (Stebbins, 1929). What is interesting is the balance on this piece of iconography, between classical emblems (such as eagle and dolphin) and Celtic ones (monster, wheel and three-horned bull-head) (Pl. LXXXI).

It is appropriate here to analyse the significance of one further piece of bronze figure-work, even though the Sky-God is by no means certainly represented. The item in question is the Maiden Castle bull (E79). The figurine consists of a silvered bronze three-horned bull bearing the remains of three figures on its back. As described, there appears to be no reason to connect it with the cult of Jupiter. However the treatment of the bull's tail gives cause for comment since it has been cast into a very pronounced 'S' shape. While this might possibly be a purely decorative feature, it suggests a tentative connection with another item. This is a small pot from Silchester (E101) decorated on the body with wheels alternating with 'S' symbols. A figurine from Gaul (C2) provides confirmation that 'S' symbolism is associated with the cult of the Celtic Wheel-God (see Chapter VI). If the 'S' shape of the bull's tail from a 4th-century shrine at Maiden Castle has religious meaning, then the question remains as to the significance of the three figures on its back. Triads of deities are common to both Graeco-Roman and Celtic mythology, religion and iconography. One of the figures on the bull may be female ; it may be that the classical Capitoline triad of Jupiter, Juno and Minerva are depicted. However, the Celtic symbolism of the tail and the three horns must make it more likely that a Celtic interpretation of the figures is to be sought. One could speculate that the three divinities could be Lucan's three gods – Taranis, Esus and Teutates (*Pharsalia* I, 445) – though I have argued elsewhere (Chapter VIII) that these deities may not have been of much importance. Still in this context it is worth recalling the Paris 'nautes Parisiacae' monument (Duval, 1961) which bears carvings of the god named Esus and of 'Tarvostrigaranos' – the bull with three cranes. It is quite feasible to think in terms of deliberate ambiguity on the part of the maker or patron of the Maiden Castle bronze, and that the three figures perched on the back of the creature have flexible, personal explanations and symbolism. Finally, the context of the find should be noted. The statuette comes from a late Romano-Celtic temple built in the mid 4th Century A.D. (Lewis, 1966, 53), not so very far removed in time from the restoration of the Corinium column. Both items appear to flout the State Christianity of the period, although both may have come into being at the time of Julian the Apostate's rule (the actual building of the temple, however, being earlier than this).

Two important points emerge from consideration of the smaller representations of the Celtic Sky-God : one is the frequent balance of iconographical detail between Graeco-Roman and Celtic. The other is the frequent association between bull and Sky-God.

C. *Emblems of the Sky-God*

The categories of Romano-British object which remain for discussion in this study are portrayals of eagles alone and of wheels when not directly associated with epigraphy or composite iconography linked specifically with the Sky-God himself. Both types of item have associations with the Roman or Celtic Sky-Father, the eagle appearing to represent the classical and the wheel the Celtic element in the cult's symbolism.

Depictions of eagles occur at some forty sites in Britain. In the majority of instances there is no reason not to interpret their presence as an entirely Roman phenomenon – the eagle being the symbol of Jupiter and thus also of the army and its standards. In some cases, however, there may be slightly more to it than that. Eagles occur both at military and at civilian sites and, naturally, those from army-contexts are likely to have a normal

Roman significance. Eagles certainly or probably from inside or close to military installations occur in bronze at Ambleside (E1); Burgh Castle (E8); Carvoran (E16); Chesterholm (E23); Chesters (E24); Corbridge (E33); Ilkley (E59); Keighley (E62). Several of these are in the form of attachments to fit onto a helmet or staff — such as examples from Corbridge and Keighley. A rather crude terracotta 'eagle' with stylized feathers in the form of stamped circles comes from the legionary fortress of Chester (E22). The item looks as though it was made in an idle moment by a potter with a spare piece of clay and has much the same look about it as a terracotta 'Bacchus'-head from the same site (Green, 1978, 53). A point of possible significance is the occurrence of Celtic Sky-God symbolism at the same site as the presence of eagles. This happens, for instance at Chester and at Corbridge.

It is of interest that eagles occur more frequently in civilian contexts, although in some instances this could be due to the presence of veterans. Bronze examples have been found at Bath (E3a); Caistor-by-Norwich (E14); Corby (E36); Currie (E37); Farley Heath (E42); Fenny Stratford (E44); Icklingham (E54); Leicester (E68a); Little Heath (E70); Newport (E89); Oxford (E93); Silchester (E100); Verulamium (E111); Wickham-Brook (E113); Winterton (E115); Woodeaton (E116) and York (E122) (in the form of a bronze enamelled brooch and therefore perhaps not a cult-object). A number of eagles occur in material other than bronze. Caerwent has produced the head of a bird in bone (E13). One of the Lydney eagle-representations is in the form of a bone plaque with the incised figure of an eagle (E77). The Langton eagle (E66) is also carved on a bone plaque. A Roman cemetery at Shefford (E99) has produced a lead eagle designed to fit onto a staff. The use of lead is of interest. A lead female figurine was found at Caerleon (Green, 1978, 49) and a lead Mercury-plaque was recovered from Chesters (*ibid*., 55). Elsewhere (1978) the writer has suggested that the use of lead might be deliberate rather than fortuitous (or cheap) and that an underworld interpretation is perhaps to be sought in the case of lead cult-figures, just as curses are made of lead — a heavy, dull base-metal being especially appropriate for destructive purposes. Whether one can stretch the evidence to explain a lead eagle is a moot point, but the burial-context at least would fit (and there is evidence, see Chapter VI, that the Celtic Jupiter did have a chthonic aspect).

Stone eagles occur at Cirencester (E28); Cole's Hill (E32) and Exeter (E40) — the last in Purbeck Marble. The Exeter eagle was found in a rubbish-pit with late 1st-century pottery, and was, possibly deliberately, decapitated. It is roughly life-size and could have been part of a Jupiter statue or have represented the emperor Nero. Toynbee (1979, 131-133, pl. XX, fig. 44) suggests that the latter may have been the case − hence the mutilation of head, back, wings and claws and the deposition in a rubbish-pit. A pipe-clay eagle comes from Wroxeter (E119) − in the form of a miniature column with an eagle depicted on one side. The Oundle figure (E92) comprises a bust of a helmeted Minerva, the lower half of the object being in the form of a spatula (Webster, 1968, 303). The Leicester example occurs carrying a food-pellet or (?)sacrificial cake in its mouth. This probably has a certain significance. The two bronze ravens in the Felmingham Hall hoard bear these pellets (Pl. LXII). The ritual figure of the water-bird carrying Sequana, goddess of the Seine (Boucher, 1976, 293), also bears such a pellet, as does the bronze duck from the Iron Age hillfort of Milber Down (Ross, 1967, 236, fig. 149).

One or two other eagle-depictions are worthy of mention. An un-inscribed altar from Sea Mills (E96) bears on one side the carving of an eagle perched on a globe, and a *cornucopiae* ; on another side is a *patera* and a (?)bull's head ; on the third, a knife and dagger ; and, on the fourth, columns and either a trident or thunderbolt. Here we have an association between a classical sky-emblem and a prosperity symbol (as at Netherby there is a link between prosperity and a Celtic sky-sign). From Sea Mills also comes a small bronze Jupiter (E97) ; the site was probably a military supply-base (Frere, 1978). The Silchester bronze eagle (E100) is really in a class by itself being thoroughly classical and 'superbly naturalistic' (Boon, 1974, 119). Boon suggests that it was a permanent ornament of the basilica, probably part of a large group accompanying a figure of Jupiter or perhaps the emperor (*ibid*., 120). By contrast there is little that is classical about the Thealby and Ribble bucket-mounts. The latter has already been discussed in connection with representations of the Sky-God himself. The two Thealby mounts have no humanoid head but each comprises conjoined heads of bull and eagle (E108). The iconography here is extremely unclassical in style. The fact that the heads only are portrayed and the janiform positioning of the two heads, quite apart from the styling itself, suggest Celticism.

The site in Britain which has yielded most eagles is the Romano-Celtic temple at Woodeaton (E116). The context of the finds is native rather than Roman, although the architecture of shrines of Romano-Celtic type owes something to classical style (Lewis, 1966 ; Rodwell, 1980). There are few, if any, overtly classical bronzes from the temple but a number of items — the model tools (including two with overt sky-symbolism of ligatured diagonal cross and swastika); the 'kilted' Mother-Goddess; the votive chain-mail — suggest that the worshippers were simple rural Britons with few pretensions to Roman-ness. If the bronze eagles (six in number) do represent Jupiter, I would suggest that it could be a Celtic Sky-God rather than the Roman State deity who is being invoked. An interesting aside is that from the site (Kirk, 1949, 32ff.) comes a sheet-bronze plaque with the figure of a god in 'matchstick-man' style, with large head, very similar in treatment to the Farley Heath sceptre-binding, and, indeed, to other Celtic representations — like the silver plaques to Mars Cocidius at Bewcastle (Green, 1978, pls. 60, 61).

The occurrence, on one and the same site, of Graeco-Roman and Celtic elements relating to Jupiter-worship, is much more frequent on civilian than on military sites. Caistor-by-Norwich produced a bronze eagle (E14) and a pot bearing wheel-symbols (E15); Cirencester has a stone eagle (E28) and part of a possible Jupiter-column (E27); Caerwent has wheel-symbol (E12) and bone eagle (E13); Chester's altar mentions Tanarus (E21) and a terracotta eagle (E22) comes from the same fortress; at Colchester was found an eagle (E31), a Jupiter-figure and model wheels (E29; E31a); Corbridge has yielded a Wheel-God representation (E33), a wheel-brooch (E35) and an eagle (E34); Farley Heath produced the sceptre-binding (E41) and an eagle (E42); Icklingham has an eagle's wing, a fragmentary bronze wheel-model, and a wheel-brooch (E54-56); from Silchester came a bronze eagle, a wheel-ornamented pot and two wheel-brooches (E100-102); and from Verulamium (E109-111) come a possible *Capitolium*, a bronze eagle and a wheel. The site at Woodeaton, already looked at (E116-117), produced half-a-dozen figurines of eagles and, in addition, bronze axe-models bearing sky-symbols. Wroxeter has yielded a miniature pipe-clay column and a bronze wheel-brooch (E118-119). It is quite out of the question to ascribe positive significance to this kind of 'association'. Occurrences of both types of evidence may be meaningful in the context of a shrine, such as Woodeaton or Farley Heath (and even that is questionable given the long life of some temples), but, in a town-situation, the appearance of an eagle and a wheel, perhaps of widely differing dates on the same site, may well mean nothing at all. Even with shrines there is no certainty; one has only to glance at the evidence from the Walbrook Mithraeum — with its cosmopolitan set of deities — to see that (Grimes, 1968).

Wheels occurring alone (without representations of the Wheel-God) fall into a number of sub-groups : jewellery − brooches, necklaces or bracelets ; metal objects decorated with wheel or swastika-motifs ; bronze wheels as models ; stone wheel-carvings ; ceramic items ; miscellaneous.

Jewellery

Wheel-brooches (see Chapters II, III, main Catalogue A), enamelled or plain, and always in bronze, come from a number of sites including Colchester (E31a) ; Corbridge (E35) ; Hadrian's Wall (E49) ; Housesteads (E51) ; Icklingham (E56) ; Islip (E61) ; Kettering (E63) ; Lakenheath (E64a) ; (?)Liverpool area (E71a) ; Margam Beach (E83) ; Nor'nour (E91) ; Sewingshields (E98) ; Silchester (E102) ; Wroxeter (E118). Swastika-brooches come from Benwell (E4) and Denholme Hill Farm (E37a) (see Pls. LIV, LV, LVI for examples of wheel-brooches).

Other wheel-jewellery, rarer than brooches, takes the form of bracelets or necklaces of gold and silver chain, incorporating gold or silver wheel-ornaments. These all occur in the North and West of Britain (the largely unromanized and mainly military regions of the province). They occur at Backworth (E2) where three were found associated and two at Dolaucothi, in the vicinity of the Roman gold-mines (E38). A silver necklace probably associated with a silver eight-spoked wheel, comes from Newstead (E90). Of the group only the Backworth finds have any sort of ritual context. The function of the precious metal has been looked at in detail in Chapter III. Here all one need say is that they may have Romano-Celtic sky-symbolism and could have been worn as priests' regalia, rather in the manner of mayoral chains. The Backworth context (in a hoard associated with cult-items connected with the Mother-Goddesses) reinforces a generally ritual interpretation of some kind.

The question of the brooches is more difficult (again see Chapters II, III). At, for example, Icklingham and Colchester wheel-models and brooches were found at the same site − in the case of Icklingham there was also an eagle's wing, lending credence to the idea of the presence of a Jupiter-cult. Nor'nour, on Scilly, is the only possible ritual site in itself, where a cache of pipe-clay Mother-Goddess figurines was also unearthed (Dudley, 1967, 1ff.). It is of interest that both gold-necklace wheels (at Backworth) and wheel-brooches (at Nor'nour) have such fertility associations (see Chapter VI for fuller discussion). Wheel-brooches, like gold wheel-necklaces, do have Italian parallels (Higgins, 1961, 186), but they are much more common in the Romano-Celtic provinces than elsewhere within the empire.

True wheel-models, usually of bronze (not jewellery items) are recorded in various parts of Britain. They occur at Chester (E22a); Colchester (E29) (of brass); Felmingham Hall (E43; Pl. LXII); Hounslow (E50); Icklingham (E55; Pls. LX, Fig. 21); Leatherhead (E67); London (E76a); and Verulamium (E110). Of these Colchester and Leatherhead are potentially most interesting since their wheels apparently come from sepulchral contexts; the Hounslow one may have been associated with boars found in the same field, all possibly of Iron Age date (it is worth recalling the association of boar and wheel on the Netherby relief [E86]). The Felmingham wheel comes from a ritual hoard including a Jupiter-mask, a bust of Helioserapis and a pole-tip. The hoard is dated to the mid 3rd Century A.D. The Icklingham brooch and eagle-fragment are very possibly in direct association (Green, 1975b). Icklingham has produced a number of cult-items, and there was perhaps a domestic shrine associated with a villa — which has long been suspected.

Stone Wheel-Carvings

Isolated stone wheels, unassociated with Sky-God depictions, occur at Birdoswald (E6) and Maryport (E85). It may be significant that both have also yielded altars dedicated to Jupiter Optimus Maximus, bearing wheel-carvings. In both instances, the wheels are carved in relief and must come from larger monuments depicting the Wheel-God himself (see Chapter IV).

Two Cotswold carvings (E39) consist of Mother-Goddess portrayals with stylized wheel-signs (Green, 1976, 190). Once again, as at Backworth (AB1), there is apparent association between Mothers and a Sky-cult (see Chapter VI). This is reinforced by a pipe-clay 'Pseudo-Venus' from London (probably a Celtic Mother-Goddess type; see Chapter VI) bearing astral signs on her body. Finally the Nettleton Shrub (E88) and Lypiatt Park (E78a) carvings should be noted. The former stone depicts a cross; the latter a wheel-symbol associated with a ram-horned serpent. The Lypiatt find has no religious context but the Nettleton site is of great interest; it comprises Romano-Celtic, simple circular and rectangular shrines and we know that Mercury and Rosmerta, and Apollo Cunomaglus were worshipped there (Green, 1976, 189-190).

Ceramic Wheel-Depictions

The ceramic group is heterogeneous in that several sub-groups may be distinguished. The first is represented by one item only, the large (c. 18 cm diameter) pottery wheel in colour-coated ware from Stibbington near Castor (E20), the centre of the Romano-British Castorware industry. The wheel is virtually complete and consists of a buff fabric with brown-painted spokes. It is presumably a votive piece, and it is an interesting item of evidence for a potter manufacturing a ritual object out of his own materials, perhaps for his personal religious use. A comparable situation pertains at Islands Thorn in Hampshire, where, in a potter's hut in the New Forest, two minute pots were fashioned to the exact design of life-size models — one was in fact a 1.5 cm high 'tulip-beaker' (Green, 1975c, 54-70).

Housesteads (E52; Pl. LXXVIII, Fig. 55) and Malton (E80; Pl. LXXVIII, Fig. 56) have produced rather different ceramic wheel-evidence from the Stibbington example. From both sites come fragments of grey ware (one at Housesteads, two at Malton), applied to which are fired clay wheel-symbols. Originally the surviving sherds must have formed part of quite substantial 'cooking-jars'. The Housesteads fragment stands alone (except for the occurrence at the same site of a large sheet-bronze, undecorated, wheel-brooch with convex spokes [Pl. LXI]). However the two Malton sherds are only part of a larger group of ceramic pieces in the same fabric which bear appliqué symbols in the form of hammers, tongs and anvils. In this context, we may note the occurrence at Corbridge not only of the Wheel-God himself but also of sherds of pottery bearing figures of smith-deities in relief. It is particularly interesting to see this apparent association between the cult of a Smith and that of a Wheel-God (see Chapter VI). The question remains as to how one should assess the complete vessels from which these appliqué symbols come — whether the motifs are purely decorative, having lost all original cult-significance, or whether they were part of vessels employed in religious ceremonies, presumably conducted in shrines.

The last suggestion leads directly to a final category of ceramic Sky-God evidence, namely the three complete ritual vessels respectively from Caistor-by-Norwich (E15); Littlehampton (E69); and Silchester (E101). The Silchester example is the most elaborate, being a vase decorated with wheel-motifs, interspersed with 'S'-symbols. We noted earlier connections between this 'S' shape, that formed by the tail of the Maiden Castle bull, and the Le Châtelet figure (C2) (see Chapter V). It is assumed that these little vessels were part of the ceremonial and ritual regalia of priests engaged in the worship of the Romano-Celtic Wheel-God. It seems to the writer unlikely that the three pots were ornamented with these signs merely as a decorative feature, although this is of course a possibility incapable of disproof. A bowl from Manchester (E82) is an imitation of Samian form 30, and may also belong to this group. It is made of a pink clay fabric and bears white-painted wheel-decoration. Interestingly Manchester had earlier yielded a classical bronze figure of Jupiter (Bruton, 1909, 182) (E81).

Miscellaneous Items

Finally, various miscellaneous objects complete this survey of items relating to the Wheel-God in Britain. Two glass fragments should first be mentioned, since there are probable functional similarities between these and the ceramic vessels considered above. One glass item, from Little Houghton (E71) consists of a piece, from the base of a flat-bottomed vessel, bearing a raised wheel-symbol. The second piece is from a fragment of glass with a swastika-symbol (E105) from Springhead. Both sherds may have belonged to cult-vessels of some kind ; Springhead was a large and elaborate temple-complex, which revealed a possible Jupiter-column (Harker, 1980), further evidence of a Celtic Sky-God cult. Another object bearing a swastika-motif is the model axe from the Romano-Celtic temple-site of Woodeaton (E117). Woodeaton was occupied from the 1st-4th Century A.D. (Kirk, 1949). It is an extremely rich site (compared to many Romano-Celtic shrines in Britain), and one of the most abundant types of ritual object is that of model tools (Green, 1975c, 54-70). About a dozen of these have been discovered, including axes, spears (sometimes deliberately bent double to 'kill' them [see Grinsell, 1953, 36-37 for antiquity of ritual breakeage]), and a model anchor (one of two found in Britain, the other being from a villa at Barton Hill Farm [Green, 1979b]). On the blade of one of the Woodeaton axes is an incised swastika-motif. On another is a ligatured diagonal cross, which may be a stylized wheel-symbol (E117). It is noteworthy that whilst Woodeaton did not produce model wheels – although other model types are well-represented – the site has produced six eagle-figurines. The significance of axe-miniatures is fully discussed in Chapter III.

A find unique in Britain, from Gateshead (E46), is a stone mould for the manufacture of miniature bronze wheels or wheel-brooches – more probably the latter. The mould may be paralleled, on the Continent, with a stone mould for a four-spoked wheel, found in the late Celtic *oppidum* of Bibracte (Mont-Beuvray) (Musée des Antiquités Nationales, St-Germain-en-Laye).

Two final items come from Caerwent (E12) and Casterley Camp (E17) respectively. The South Wales find comprises a bronze plate ornamented with a wheel in a square frame. It came from a well (Ross, 1968, 262). The plate may have been a cult-object similar in function to the (?)cult-vessels discussed above. One is put in mind also of the wheel-*patera* representation borne by the Netherby depictions (E86-87). The only other evidence of a Sky-God cult in Caerwent is the bone head of an eagle (E13) (Ashby, 1910, 1-20). The Casterley Camp item (E17) comprises a bone disc inscribed on one face with a wheel or 'representation of the Sun' (Cunnington, 1896, 111). The disc was found in a T-shaped hearth, presumably a corn-drying oven, together with 2nd Century pottery, and the author of the report mentions another similar disc apparently discovered there by General Pitt-Rivers.

II. Distribution and Association:
A Survey of the British Evidence

Site-Context (see Tables I-II)

In Table I evidence for the Sky-God, which includes the use of the wheel-motif, is differentiated from other evidence; This is not a division between classical and Celtic iconography; it is an arbitrary distinction based on the unequivocally non-classical nature of the wheel-symbolism compared to the ambiguous material comprising eagles, thunderbolts and Celtically 'styled' representations.

Fourteen forts have yielded non-wheel evidence for a Sky-God and ten have produced items incorporating wheel-symbolism. Of legionary fortresses Caerleon and Chester have produced both types of material, whereas the fortress and *colonia* at York only yielded 'classical' symbolism for the god. Four hoards include wheels; Felmingham Hall has a wheel and probable mask of Jupiter; Southbroom revealed a Jupiter figurine in very non-classical style; Stony Stratford has an inscribed Jupiter and Vulcan-plaque. Only Backworth and Willingham Fen revealed unequivocal Gaulish contextual influence – one in terms of association, the other within the complexities of the wheel-bearing item itself. Graves are poorly represented with regard to both types of evidence. Probably only burials from Colchester and Leatherhead included wheel-symbols; a cemetery at Shefford produced an eagle. Temple-material should be of the most interest of all, but relevant finds are disappointingly sparse, although British temples in general (Lewis,

TABLE I

Site-Context of Classical and Romano-Celtic Sky-God Symbolism
(+ = wheel ; × = other)

Site name	Fort	Fortress	Hoard	Grave	Temple	Town	Villa	Stray	Other site
Ambleside	×								
Backworth			+						
Bath					×	×			
Benwell	+								
Birdoswald	× +								
Brampton								×	
Burgh Castle	×								
Caerleon		× +							
Caerwent					× +	× +			
Caistor					× +	× +			
Carvoran	×								
Casterley Camp									+
Castlesteads	× +								
Castor/Stibbington									+
Chester		× +							
Chesterholm	×								
Chesters	×								
Chichester						×			
Churcham								+	
Cirencester						×			
Colchester			+			× +			
Cole's Hill							×		
Corbridge	× +					× +			
Corby								×	
Currie								×	
Denholme Hill								+	
Dolaucothi									+
Easton Grey								+	
Exeter						×			
Farley Heath					× +				
Felmingham Hall			× +						
Fenny Stratford								×	
Frilsham								×	
Gateshead								+	
Grays								×	
Great Chesterford						×			
Hadrian's Wall									+
Hounslow				+					
Housesteads	× +								
Icklingham									× +
Ilchester						×			
Ilkley	×								
Irchester						×			

CLASSICAL JUPITER AND CELTIC SKY-GOD IN BRITAIN 237

Site name	Fort	Fortress	Hoard	Grave	Temple	Town	Villa	Stray	Other site
lip								+	
eighley								×	
ettering								+	
irkby Thore	×								
angham								×	
angton							×		
eatherhead				+					
eicester						×			
ittlehampton								+	
ittle Heath								×	
ittle Houghton								+	
)Liverpool									+
ondon						× +			
ydney					×				
aiden Castle					×				
alton	+								
anchester	× +								
argam Beach								+	
aryport	× +								
etherby	+								
ettleton Shrub					+				
ewport								×	
ewstead	+								
or'nour									+
undle								×	
xford								×	
atcliffe-on-Soar					×				
ibble								×	
ea Mills									×
ewingshields									+
hefford				×					
ilchester						× +			
outhbroom			×						
outh Shields	×								
pringhead						× +			
tony Stratford			×						
healby								×	
erulamium					×	× +			
est Stoke								×	
ickham-Brook								×	
illingham Fen			+						
interton							×		
oodeaton					× +				
roxeter						× +			
ork		×				×			
ypiatt								+	

1966) are not renowned for their proliferation of cult-objects of any description (some, like Brean Down in Avon, have produced virtually nothing). It is uncertain whether the finds from Caistor and Caerwent were originally from temple-sites, but it is probable. Excavation at both civilian tribal capitals revealed a number of shrines. The Caerwent plate (found in a well but possibly originally used in a shrine) and the Caistor pot are both items which would fit well into the category of 'temple-furniture', as sacrificial or cult-vessels. Springhead, Farley Heath, Nettleton Shrub and Woodeaton are all temples that have produced evidence for a Romano-Celtic rather than a classical Sky-cult. If we may assume that the triple-horned bull with 'S'-shaped tail has a link with the Sky-God, then Maiden Castle too should be grouped here. It is strange that the overtly Celtic shrine at Lydney dedicated to a native deity – Nodons – should have produced eagles but no Celtic evidence for the Sky-deity.

Towns are reasonably well-represented in both varieties of material. Wheel-motifs occur at Caerwent ; Caistor ; Corbridge (a town as well as a military establishment) ; London ; Silchester ; Verulamium ; and Wroxeter. Bath, although Celtic in origin and in resident divinity, was extremely romanized and it is not surprising that there is no celticism about the Jupiter present here. Cirencester, as is discussed above, is an unknown quantity. There is a great deal of religious celticism here, but we have no means of knowing how to interpret the curious inscription set up by Britannia Prima's Reims-born governor. Villas are poorly represented (as they are in all kinds of cult-material [Green, 1976]). The Cole's Hill find of a sculptured eagle is included here since it was found only half a mile away from the rich and prosperous villa of Spoonley Wood and could possibly have come from such a romanized establishment. Icklingham was also very probably a villa but there is no concrete evidence to justify its being put into this group in the present context. Among other types of site we may note the Hadrian's Wall turrets, and the gold-mining site of Dolaucothi in Dyfed. The Nor'nour site too is noteworthy. It appears to have contained a bronzesmith's workshop (Dudley, 1967), although whether this context should be applied to all of the finds is unclear.

Site Associations : Jupiter/Sky-God Representations (Table II)

It is important to be extremely careful with the use of the term 'association', as emphasized already above. With this note of caution it is of interest, and perhaps informative, to plot the number of instances where more than one type of cult-object relating to the Sky-God appears.

This happens on no less than twenty-six sites out of over eighty. The proportion may not at first glance seem remarkable, but when one considers the overall paucity of religious evidence from Roman sites, even in the larger towns (Green, 1976, 1978), more than coincidence may be involved in some of these twenty-six instances. Even if a site is large, like a town, and frequently multi-period in date, that is not to say that valid conclusions may not be drawn. Traditions in temples may well continue from generation to generation, and even in the towns, which were, after all, minute by modern standards (Frere, 1978), a single family may have had a specific patron-deity, handed down within that kinship group.

TABLE II

Site "Associations"

Site name	Class. rep.	Rom.-Cel. rep.	eagle	wheel	Class. name	Cel. name	misc. Class.	misc. Rom.-Cel.
Bath	×			×				
Birdoswald					×	×		
Caerleon	×	×		×				
Caerwent			×	×				
Caistor					×	×		
Castlesteads					×	×		
Chester			×	×			×	
Cirencester				×	×			×
Colchester	×		×	×				
Corbridge		×	×	×				
Farley Heath		×	×	×				
Felmingham Hall	×			×				
Housesteads	×			×				
Icklingham			×	×				
Ilkley	×	×						
Leicester	×	×						
London	×			×	×		×	
Manchester	×			×				
Maryport					×	×		
Sea Mills	×		×					
Silchester			×	×				
Springhead				×				×
Verulamium				×	×			×
Woodeaton			×	×				
Wroxeter			×	×				
York	×		×		×			

Table II tabulates eight sub-groups of Roman or Romano-Celtic representation. A word of explanation of these sub-divisions may be appropriate at this point. The term 'classical representations' means depictions of the god Jupiter himself, in more or less purely classical guise, however excellent or poor the standard of workmanship may have been – whether the craftsman came from Italy, Gaul or Britain. The point here is that the artist was aiming at a certain clientèle (Boucher, 1976), a sophisticated market with at least a deep veneer of romanization. Whether, of course, the god worshipped in classical art-form was really Jupiter or merely a native deity of similar appearance, is a point difficult to resolve. One may enquire whether the bronze figures of the god were genuinely cult-objects in all instances, or whether they were sometimes put on show in town or country houses as marks of romanization and therefore civilization. The Langham Jupiter was never a personal votive item, and one could argue that, for instance, the broken London statuette, from the Thames, was also meant for public display rather than private worship. Only at Caerleon legionary fortress do you find classical and Celtic portrayals of the Sky-God from one and the same site. Here it is interesting that the clay antefixes, which must have been inspired by army officials, indicate celticism. The bronze Jupiter-attachment from here is purely Roman in idea, but Boucher reminds us (1976) that bronze much more rarely shows overt native or Gaulish influence than objects made from other media such as stone or clay.

Looking at Table II the most striking point is the frequency of occurrence of wheels and eagles at the same sites. This happens eleven times (not counting instances of the two symbols appearing on the same item, as at Willingham Fen). The Silchester eagle must stand by itself as a purely classical emblem, and in any case apparent associations within towns can have no necessary credibility in terms of true archaeological association. However, the temples of Farley Heath and Woodeaton have both produced examples of eagles and wheel-symbolism, as did the probable villa-site of Icklingham, Suffolk. As suggested above, it is possible that we do have two sides of a coin represented here – the Roman and the Celtic expressions of sky-cults.

The Romano-Celtic Sky-God and other Divinities (Table III & Appendix)

On a number of sites in Britain there is evidence not only of the Sky-God but also of other deities. Again, certain and true association occurs only infrequently but, when it does arise, it is of considerable interest.

Only Romano-Celtic Sky-symbolism has been included here. Purely classical-seeming depictions of Jupiter or his eagle have been omitted. When looking at the appearance of more than one type of religious symbolism on a given site, it should be remembered that even in a shrine there may not be any profound significance. Roman religion was extremely accommodating and one should, as said before, recall, for example, the Walbrook Mithraeum, where classical and oriental deities were very obviously worshipped together.

It may be that hoards of religious material, perhaps buried at a time of political or religious unrest, offer the most informative source for cult-association. In a number of cases it may be assumed that a buried hoard represents the action of a priest or a group of priests burying the entire contents of a shrine, since items of priests' regalia are frequently included. Contexts which may be classified as hoards, comprise the following: Backworth; Felmingham Hall; Hounslow; Southbroom; Stony Stratford; Willingham Fen. Stony Stratford, strictly speaking, has no overt celticism, but the presence of the plaques in a situation directly comparable to those of Barkway, which do possess Celtic influence (*R.I.B.*, 218, 219), and the presence in the Stony Stratford hoard of ritual crowns and headdresses (British Museum, 1921) suggests its essential ties with native worship. Of the hoards listed Backworth, Felmingham Hall, Hounslow, Southbroom and Willingham Fen involve other Gaulish or native divinities. 'Classical' deities are represented at Felmingham, Southbroom, Stony Stratford and Willingham. Oriental gods appear at Felmingham, Southbroom and Willingham.

The Backworth hoard is of especial interest because of the association of the Deae Matres, referred to on the handle of the *patera* containing the hoard, and on a gold ring inside the vessel. Elsewhere in Britain only at Easton Grey and at an unlocated Cotswold site is there a similar association – in the form of stylized wheels incised upon the Mother-Goddess depictions themselves. At Felmingham Hall and Willingham Fen figurines of ravens are present. This may be significant since ravens also apparently occur with the wheel-deity on the Farley Heath sceptre-binding. The Willingham Fen material included a bull-figure. The Southbroom hoard contained a number of bronze statuettes of divinities all of whom except one are classical or oriental in concept although thoroughly non-roman in style and treatment. The exception is a little figure of Mars clutching in his hands two ram-horned snakes. Thevenot (1955) cites several instances of this association with Mars but ram-horned snakes are rare in Britain. The Hounslow association comprised a wheel and three Iron Age bronze boars of native style. Horsemen are present at Willingham Fen. It is probable (Green, 1976, 30) that horsemen are a Celtic version of Mars, and this type of portrayal and its associations with the Celtic Jupiter are fully discussed in Chapter VI. All that should be said here is that the Horseman and the Sky-God are both clustered in eastern Britain.

Among the Roman-inspired divinities represented in the Sky-God hoards Minerva is depicted at Felmingham Hall. She also occurs at Southbroom. In addition the Wiltshire hoard has produced figures of Mercury, Venus and Mars. A *lar* is present at Felmingham.

Oriental divinities appear occasionally in these hoards — surprisingly, because they are all in remote rural areas where one would expect native cults to be rife and eastern gods non-existent. Even if deities in classical guise were accepted in these regions (since it appears to have been easy to invoke *interpretatio celtica*), it is going one step further in the romanization-process to absorb the mystery-cults of the east. The radiate mask from Felmingham Hall is perhaps best interpreted as Jupiter Helioserapis (Harris & Harris, 1965). The whole hoard seems to have been centred on Jupiter-worship in some form; we would appear to have classical, Celtic and Oriental versions or aspects of the Sky-God at the same site. A Phrygian-capped figure, who may be Atys, occurs at Southbroom — but with the same Celtic styling as the other statuettes in the hoard. A bust, possibly representing Cybele, was found with the Willingham Fen material. Cybele was the Great Mother-Goddess of Anatolia, absorbed into the Roman pantheon as early as 204 B.C. (Ferguson, 1970, 26ff.); it is possible that her presence in this context may simply be another expression of the Deae Matres Celtic cult in Gaul and Britain.

Associations between the Romano-Celtic Sky-God and other divinities occur at certain shrines, including composite symbolism on one item. Celtic associations at shrines include Mercury and Rosmerta (at Nettleton); Genius Cucullatus and pipe-clay 'Venus' (at Springhead), and a very Celtic god with the emblems of Hercules (at Woodeaton). Classical deities associated in temples include eagles (representing the classical Jupiter) at Farley Heath and Woodeaton; Minerva at Maiden Castle and Woodeaton; Cupid at Farley Heath and Woodeaton; Diana at Nettleton Shrub; Venus and Mars at Woodeaton. Oriental divinities occur only at Farley Heath — in the form of a hawk possibly connected with the cult of Horus. The cockerel at Nettleton is probably to be connected with the cult of

Mercury known there (but the idea of a cockerel heralding the new dawn and thus, indirectly, the sun, suggests a possible connection with a sky-cult, hinted at in the stylized (?)sky-symbol inscribed on a stone from the site). Although at least three different temples have been identified at Nettleton, all the above-mentioned finds came from Temple I (Lewis, 1966, 75-77).

Ritual items from temples, unconnected with a specific divinity of any ethnic origin, occur in a number of shrines associated with the Sky-God. A model hammer comes from Maiden Castle ; a miniature axe from Nettleton ; another (lead) from Springhead, and a number of axes, spears and a model anchor from Woodeaton (see Chapter III for significance of models, especially axes). Items of priests' regalia include the sceptre-bindings from Farley Heath and Woodeaton ; plaques from Maiden Castle and Woodeaton ; and finally crown-fragments from Woodeaton.

Ritual items associated with shrine furniture are also known from most of the hoards discussed above, thus increasing the possibility that the hoards were buried by priests taking religious material from temples into a place of safety. The Backworth group was contained in a *patera*, and the inscribed gold ring may itself have been the property of an officiating priest, as may the wheel-ornamented chains. Pole-tips, perhaps part of ceremonial staves (Green, 1975a), occur at Felmingham Hall and were found in the sacred precinct at Brigstock in Northamptonshire (Greenfield, 1963). Willingham Fen also produced pole-tips and fragments of sceptres as well as the well-known Wheel-God sceptre-terminal.

Composite associations of deities on single objects may finally be examined. Such occur at Easton Grey and on another site in the Cotswold region ; Farley Heath ; Malton ; Netherby ; the River Ribble ; Lypiatt ; Stony Stratford ; Thealby and Willingham Fen. Although the aforementioned 'associations' could be and, in some instances doubtless are, merely instances of physical contiguity and therefore of no religious significance, the occurrence of different types of cult-symbolism on one and the same item is worthy of careful consideration to see whether any patterning, of potential significance, is detectable.

The Easton Grey wheel/Mother-Goddess association has already been noted in connection with Backworth. The sceptre-binding at the Surrey shrine of Farley Heath, with its association with a Wheel-God, a Smith-God, Sucellus and various cult-beasts is obviously an extremely important religious find and probably embodies a native or Gaulish mythology. Associations between the Sky-God and other deities in Gaul and Britain are fully considered elsewhere (Chapter VI). One can say that all the motifs and entities identified in the Farley Heath item may be connected with other ritual phenomena concerned with Gaulish Sky-cults ; and the same may be said of the Willingham Fen piece. Vulcan and Jupiter (possibly the Romano-Celtic version) occur on the same object at Stony Stratford. The Malton finds cannot, strictly speaking, be termed association on one item, but the objects in question — sherds of grey ware — are all of the same kind and could have come from one or two cult-vessels, ornamented 'en appliqué' with wheels and smithing equipment. The finds from Thealby (Lincs) and the River Ribble (Lancs) should be considered together. All three are bronze bucket-mounts, the two Lincolnshire examples comprising a composite bull and eagle-head and the Lancashire mount consisting of a similar group but with the addition of a human head. The Netherby sculptures fall into a category very much by themselves as associations between *Genii loci* or *Bonus Euentus*, both with wheel-symbolism and, in one case, with a boar-emblem. It should be remembered here that Felmingham Hall produced a *lar* and that an altar from High Rochester dedicated to a Genius, was decorated with swastika-symbols (Bruce, 1875, no. 553). The Lypiatt Park altar associates on one and the same cult-item a wheel and a ram-headed serpent ; such an association occurs also on the Danish immediately pre-Roman cult-bowl from Gundestrup (see Chapter VI).

The final item which should be mentioned in this survey of associations is the model axe from Woodeaton, ornamented with a swastika-motif. The link here is not between deities, but it may, nevertheless, be significant. An altar from High Rochester, dedicated to Minerva (Bruce, 1875, no. 546), was decorated with the sign of the crooked cross. Model axes from Switzerland were dedicated to Minerva (Forrer, 1948). Finally, if one looks at associations of divinities in Britain (Table II), Minerva figures a number of times. In any case, however, axes and the Sky-God have a probable association (see Chapter III).

It is extremely difficult to assess the true significance of the associations and connections considered above. Table III shows that the numbers are in all cases pitifully small and no statistical conclusions may be drawn. All one can say is that religious finds on Roman sites are always scarce bearing in mind the length of occupation of many and considering too that some sites are temples. Numbers in Britain cannot be a concern. The continental evidence for Sky-God worship is therefore of the greatest importance for the light it throws on apparent links between divinities (see Chapter VI).

TABLE III

Frequencies of Associations between Romano-Celtic Sky-Symbolism and other deities, ritual items, emblems, etc. (*)

Subject	Number of instances (sites)
Apollo	1
Atys	1
Axe, model	3
Boar	3
Bull	4
Bull, triple-horned	2
Cockerel	1
Crown/plaque	1
Cupid	2
Cybele	1
Dea Nutrix	1
Diana	1
Dog	1
Dolphin	1
Eagle	2
Genius	1
Genius Cucullatus	1
Goddess, indeterminate	1
Goddess, Celtic	1
Hammer, model	1
Hawk	1
Helioserapis	1
Hercules	3
Horseman	2
Lar	1
Mars	4
Matres, Deae	3
Mercury	2
Minerva	5
Owl	1
Pole-tips	1
Ram-horned snake	2
Raven	2
Rosmerta	1
Smith-God	2
Snake	2
Spear, model	1
Stag	1
Sucellus	1
Venus	2
'Venus', pipe-clay	2
Victory	1
Vulcan	3

(*) See also Appendix.

Table IV

Tribal Frequencies for Sky-God Symbolism in South-East Britain
(more than one item for each site counts as single entry)

Overtly classical		Overtly Romano-Celtic	
Atrebates	2	Atrebates	2
Belgae	1	Belgae	1
Catuvellauni	7	Catuvellauni	9
Catuvellauni/Dobunni	2	Catuvellauni/Dobunni	1
Catuvellauni/Cantiaci	2	Coritani	2
Coritani	6	Cornovii	1
Dobunni	4	Dobunni	4
Dumnonii	1	Dobunni/Belgae	1
Durotriges	1	Dumnonii	1
Iceni	4	Durotriges	2
Regnenses	3	Iceni	3
Silures	1	Regnenses	3
Trinovantes	2	Silures	1
		Trinovantes	0

NB. Where e.g. Catuvellauni/Cantiaci etc. occurs this denotes location on a probable tribal boundary.

Sites in the North and West of the country have not been divided tribally since for the most part distribution of Jupiter cult-material reflects the presence of the army, and the majority of items come from military installations or their *uici*.

Tribal Frequencies in South-East Britain (Table IV)

Once more the numbers are minute in all tribal regions. However, one or two tentative conclusions may be drawn from the evidence we have. One is that overtly classical references to a Sky-God tend to be more frequent in tribal areas where the Romano-Celtic sky-symbolism also prevailed. A striking example of this is the tribe of the Catuvellauni, whose huge territory included a large part of south-eastern Britain – from Essex and Hertfordshire to Northamptonshire and part of Oxfordshire. Ritual finds in general (Green, 1976, 65ff.) are relatively common in Catuvellaunian lands. This must be the result of early and fast romanization – whether the items are of classical or native influence. Celtic as well as classical art and expression received an enormous stimulus in the Roman era. If, as I have sought to show above, there is a valid link between the Romano-Celtic cult of the Horseman and the Celtic

Sky-God (Chapter VI), then again the Catuvellauni seem to have been particularly devoted to this cult (Green, 1976, 65ff.). If Woodeaton may be assigned to the Catuvellauni rather than the Dobunni (it is right on the inferred boundary between the two tribes) the emphasis is even stronger. Evidence for a Sky-God in Dobunnic lands is scarce compared to their powerful neighbours, even though general cult-expression is just as prolific. Apart from the Catuvellauni and Dobunni, other tribes have a comparative dearth of general cult-material. The Iceni and Regnenses are best-represented by classical and Romano-Celtic sky-symbolism. Nowhere is there evidence that a tribe plumped for Celtic rather than classical forms or *uice uersa*; this suggests that, in many cases, classical and Gaulish art-forms portrayed the same god in different form. The Trinovantes, although adjacent to the Catuvellauni, do not seem actively to have adopted devotion to a Jupiter-cult of any description, but this apparent *lacuna* may result merely from the sparsity of the surviving evidence.

Summary

It cannot be overstressed that any interpretation drawn from such very small numbers is bound to have some element of doubt. Nevertheless what we do have in Britain is of intrinsic interest and of possible significance when assessed together with the material from the Sky-God's Gaulish homeland. There are hints in Britain, of associations between divinities, which may be clarified, to some extent, in a study of the continental evidence (Chapter VI).

I have attempted to show that celticism and classicism cannot and should not be categorically separated, notwithstanding the existence of entirely classical or entirely native representations; for example the Langham Jupiter and the stick-like figures on the Farley Heath binding; the Silchester eagle and the Icklingham wheel. But in between these extremes, there is a great deal of material which it is impossible confidently to place in an ethnic group. The romanization process was a two-way affair. *Interpretatio romana* and *interpretatio celtica* appear to have become inextricably intertwined.

Appendix

Index of Associations between Romano-Celtic Sky-Symbolism and other Divinities

The association may not be archaeologically sound or significant. Even within a shrine there may be vast differences in chronology between one object and another. The occurrence of two types of cult-material in a given town is not counted unless there is proven association within it. Naturally the most significant connections will be those in sealed hoards or where two types of symbolism occur on one and the same item.

Backworth (Durham) : Hoard
    Deae Matres, Matres Coccae
Easton Grey (Wiltshire) : One object
    Mother-Goddess
Farley Heath, Albury (Surrey) : Shrine
    1. On sceptre-binding : ravens, bull, boar, stag, dog, Sucellus, Vulcan
    2. Other items : hawk, eagle, Cupid.
Felmingham Hall (Norfolk) : Hoard
    Minerva, ravens, Helioserapis, Lar.
Hounslow (Middlesex) : (?)Hoard
    Three 'Iron Age' boars
Lypiatt Park (Gloucestershire) : One object
    Ram-horned snake.
Maiden Castle (Dorset) : Shrine
    Model hammer, draped nude female figure, Minerva.
Malton (North Yorkshire) : Fort and town. (Association comprises similar objects with different cult-symbols.)
    Sherds bearing applied smiths' tools.
Netherby (Cumbria) : Fort : One object
    Boar, Genius.
Nettleton Shrub (Wiltshire) : Shrine
    Diana, cockerel, Mercury and Rosmerta, votive miniature axe.
Nor'nour (Scillies) : Small island
    Pipe-clay 'Venus', pipe-clay 'Dea Nutrix'.

Ribble (Lancashire): One object
Knob-horned bull.
Southbroom (Wiltshire): Hoard
Mercury, Mars, Atys, Venus, Minerva, Hercules, Mars with two ram-horned snakes.
Springhead (Kent): Temple-complex
Pipe-clay 'Venus', model axe, Genius Cucullatus, possible Jupiter-column.
Stony Stratford (Buckinghamshire): Hoard
Vulcan (on same object).
Mars, Victory, Apollo.
Thealby (Lincolnshire): One object
Bull.
Willingham Fen (Cambridgeshire): Hoard
1. On same object: Sky-God, three-horned bull, dolphin, Hercules' club.
2. In wooden box with hoard: pole-tips, horsemen, Minerva or Mars, owl, raven, bull, (?)Cybele.
Woodeaton
Model axes, model spears, crowns, etc., Venus, Celtic goddess, Mars, sceptre-binding, (?)childbirth amulet, Minerva, Cupid, Celtic Hercules, snakes, eagles.

CHAPTER VIII

Taranis and the Celtic Jupiter

In this chapter I shall attempt to analyse two main issues. The first is the role that 'Taranis' plays, both in connection with the Romano-Celtic Jupiter and with the Wheel-God. The second involves examination of non-wheel-bearing, but nevertheless not wholly Roman, representations of, or epigraphic allusions to, Jupiter.

TARANIS

Lucan in his *Pharsalia* (*de Bello Ciuili* I, 444-446 ; Getty (ed.), 1940, 15) mentions three Celtic divinities :

> *Et quibus inmitis placator sanguine diro*
> *Teutates horrensque feris altaribus Esus*
> *et Taranis Scythicae non mitior ara Dianae.*

Two Bern scholiasts, probably dating to the ninth Century A.D. (Usener, 1869, 30 ; Zwicker, 1934, 50), each equate Taranis with different Roman deities. One links him with Dispater ; the other equates him with Jupiter, and furthermore describes him as *praeses bellorum*. The Jupiter-equation has frequently (for example Lambrechts, 1942, 64ff.) led scholars to identify Taranis with the Romano-Celtic Wheel-God who, as we have seen in previous chapters, frequently appears in the guise of the Roman Sky-God. There are a number of points at issue here. One is whether the equation of Taranis with Jupiter is valid ; another is whether the equation of Taranis with a Wheel-God is valid. A third is whether Taranis is of the importance apparent in Lucan's poem, since epigraphic allusions to him are so scarce. A fourth is the difference in name-form between the *Taranis* of the literature and the *Taranus*-derivations occurring in the epigraphy.

I shall discuss name-form first. Lucan calls the god in question *Taranis*. But the half-dozen mentions of a *Taran*-derivative on stone inscriptions

(Catalogue D) all stem from a *Taranus*-root with a *u* not an *i*, for example *Taranucnus* (D1 [Pl. LXXXIV], D2) ; *Taranucus* (D4) ; *Taranus* (D6). *Taran* is a Celtic word and should behave in the same way as *Garan* which in Gaulish Latin becomes *Garanus*. Taranus means 'Thunder' but in the forms on epigraphy the word 'Thunderer' is generally expressed, with notable exceptions as at Chester (D7). It is quite possible, according to Cerquand (1883, 382) that *Taranis* could exist as a god-name 'Thunderer' or 'Thunder-God' side by side with *Taranus* (the element itself) and its derivatives.

A problem arises with the inscriptions from Chester, which occurs on an altar dedicated to *I.O.M. Tanarus*, and from Orgon (D3). There are two points here ; one is that the term 'Thunder' itself is used (as is the case with the Tours inscription) as if Jupiter is being equated with the elemental force itself. The other is that for example at Chester (D7), we have the apparent metathesis *Tanarus* instead of *Taranus*. To take the latter point first, we need to establish whether *Tanarus* is a faulty rendering of *Taranus* or if it means something different. There is no known meaning of *Tanarus*, but on the other hand one would have thought it unlikely that a mistake would have been made over the name of a god although, according to Susini (1973, 39ff.), it is important not to disregard plain inattentiveness as a possible cause. After all literacy is widespread today but glaring errors occur. There are many stages at which such a fault could have occurred. The mistake could have been made by the *scriptor* (text-drafter), or by the *ordinator* (who combined the functions of guide and stonecutter [Susini, 1973, 41]). It is possible also that the *scriptor* was dictated to and therefore never saw the god's name in writing (Susini, 1973, 42). Another possibility, suggested by Cerquand (1883, 382ff.) is that one of either craftsman or patron was illiterate, although it is doubtful that the *princeps* of a legion (the Chester dedicant) would be unable to read. An alternative solution is that the metathesis or transposition of *r* and *n* is a legitimate one, a possibility borne out by both Latin and Teutonic words for 'thunder' (*Tonans, Tonare, Tonitrus, Tonitralis*, and 'Donar', 'Thonar'). The craftsman could have had both Celtic and Latin forms in his mind as he worked.

The next point to be considered also concerns the Chester (D7), Orgon (D3) and Tours (D6) inscriptions. If we accept that *Tanarus* means 'Thunder' then, as at Tours (Taranus) we have three dedications to 'Thunder' and, in the case of Chester, to 'Jupiter Best and Greatest Thunder' (not Thunderer as in Jupiter Tonans or Taranucnus). An essentially similar inscription occurs in Vienne (Isère), to *I.O.M. Fulguri Fulmini* (*C.I.L.*, XII, 1807). We have to analyse the significance, if any, of such dedications. Do they mean that the personality of the god is confused with the thunderbolt itself, and therefore that Jupiter could be thought of as an elemental force, undetached from it and without human form ? Does such a formula mean that the elemental concept is of particular importance here ? It is dangerous to speculate too far. The patron of the Chester altar was a legionary officer worshipping in A.D. 154, in a remote corner of Britain, far away from Gaulish religious centres (and the dedicant himself came from Spain). All we can say is that on this occasion the devotee ventured to conflate the official god *Iupiter Optimus Maximus* with what may have been an instrument of the Gaulish Thunder-God. The other inscriptions are ordinary adjectival derivatives of *Taranus* and thus fall into the large category of Celtic epithets — like Andescocioucus (Green, 1976, 216), or Corotiacus (*ibid.*, 218).

The next major point for discussion is whether Taranis was a great Celtic divinity, implied as such in Lucan's poem and in the Bern scholiasts' comments on Lucan. The straightforward answer is that there is little archaeological evidence to back this up. The epigraphic material is extremely scanty, scattered and, in any case, for the most part appears outside Gaul itself (see Pl. XXXIII). It is the opinion both of Reinach (1897a, 139) and Powell (1958, 128) that one should not necessarily take much notice of Lucan's statement. In the eyes of modern scholars the three divinities Esus, Teutates and Taranis, are generally considered as important and major universal beings, and there is thus surprise at there being so little in the way of epigraphic information. Powell asserts (1958, 128) that the obscurity and sparseness of the inscriptions deny the importance of any of these deities. It is possible, according to Reinach (1897a, 144) that Lucan may have obtained his information from lists of peoples, rivers and mountains in Gaul, and could have condensed and twisted his impressions. Lucan did not travel in Gaul himself. If, as is generally suggested (Getty, 1940, xxix ; Pichon, 1912), Lucan found his historical source in the lost books of Livy, then this geographical and ethnic information may have come from these. Alternatively Lucan could have obtained references from Caesar (Pichon, 1912). As Reinach points out (1897a, 144) a great many tribal areas were traversed by Caesar's army in its evacuation of Gaul. Lucan does not specify *who* it was that offered human sacrifices to the Triad ; he does not even state whether the three deities belonged to the same tribe or group. There is an interesting point to be made about the other two gods in Lucan's triad. Reinach remarks that *Esus* occurring in the *Pharsalia* and in the Parisian inscription (*C.I.L.*, XIII, 3026) could be derived from the common noun *esus* meaning 'lord' or 'ruler' (Reinach, 1897a, 149). Likewise *Teutates* refers to a word meaning 'tribe' or 'people' (Ross, 1967, 171). So again this is a general term rather than a specific god-name. One should always remember that Lucan was writing an epic poem, so antiquarian 'learning' could be a factor (personal suggestion from Dr. C. Emlyn-Jones). Several points may be made with regard to *Taranis*. If he is a major Celtic god it could be argued that he should appear in Rome and Roman literature (like Epona). Against this it could be said that very few Celtic deities are thus recognized. Second, although inscriptions mentioning him are very sparse, they are also extremely scattered, with the inevitable conclusion that the god was known in many different parts of the Romano-Celtic world. One thing which should be said about *Taranis* is that he is a deity in his own right rather than a mere adjectival epithet to a Roman god. He is equated with Jupiter on a few inscriptions, as we shall see below, but he appears on his own on others.

Two final points regarding *Taranis* need to be examined – whether he should be identified with a Wheel-God and whether with Jupiter. We should remember that equation or identification implies complete oneness of identity. One Bern scholiast (Zwicker, 1934, 50) equates Taranis with Jupiter, and some inscriptions (D4, D5, D7) also carry this equation. Alone the scholiasts need not carry much weight; they need not have been all that familiar with the details of Celtic mythology. It has been established that in Romano-Celtic Gaul and Britain Jupiter was very frequently equated with a Wheel-God. We have no specific evidence whatever that Taranis was equated with a Wheel-God. None of the inscriptions bear a wheel-symbol (with the possible and doubtful exception of the Chester altar [D7] with its rosette). Since there is no concrete evidence we should look next at circumstantial data. On the one hand it may be argued that because the Romano-Celtic Jupiter was frequently represented with a wheel, and because three times epigraphically and once literally Jupiter is equated with Taranis, then therefore Taranis = the Wheel-God. In my opinion the conclusion does not follow logically from the premises. Jullian (1909, 140-1) suggests that the Sky-God Taranis had a sun-wheel as an emblem of his 'investiture'. He thinks (1920, 35) that Jupiter is the Roman successor of the Gaulish Taranis. Duval's opinion (1957, 7) is that the reason that the Celtic Jupiter is only infrequently named as Taranis is because of true Gallo-Roman equation or assimilation of Celtic by Roman forms. There may be some sense in this. There is evidence with other gods that Roman and native divinities are equated on inscriptions and at other times the native name appears alone – for example Mars Cocidius or Cocidius alone in North Britain (Ross, 1967, 169-171), and Nodens in Gloucestershire (Wheeler, 1932). Conversely it may be that the appearance of a Roman god-name alone may sometimes hide a Celtic connection. So one cannot say just because only three inscriptions mention Taranis and Jupiter, that on those where Taranis alone is mentioned Taranis has nothing to do with Jupiter and *uice uersa*.

An argument put forward for Taranis' equation with the solar Wheel-God – and I think a weak one – is that, according to one of Lucan's commentators (Duval, 1957, 33-34 ; Powell, 1958, 154), Taranis was appeased by burning sacrifices in tree-trunks, and thus fire might have an association with the heat of the sun. There is an interesting aside here in that Caesar (*de Bello Gallico* VI, 16) mentions the burning of human sacrifices in huge wicker man-shaped frames. The evidence is too tenuous to be paid too much attention. Lambrechts (1942, 76) states that Taranis unites the attributes of Jupiter and Apollo ; Hatt (1951a, 87) says more or less the same thing. They appear to be saying that the Wheel-God occurring in the Roman period has elements both of Jupiter and a solar deity and is called Taranis. The Jupiter-equation with Taranis is enhanced (de Vries, 1963, 70) by the Bern scholiast who mentions Jupiter-Taranis as *praeses bellorum*, and an armed, armoured Jupiter with or without a wheel is a frequent occurrence in Romano-Celtic iconography (see Chapter VI). Lambrechts (1942, 77) also points out that the figure holding the wheel on the Gundestrup Cauldron is armed, at least helmeted. This may or may not be significant since it is at least possible (see Chapter V) that the wheel here is nothing to do with solar-symbolism or a cult-wheel in any strict sense, but could represent a chariot-wheel.

One thing should be emphasized here ; the word *Taranus* or *Taranis* implies nothing more than a 'Thunder' deity. There is nothing intrinsic to the name which hints at a solar symbolism. The three inscriptions which do equate Jupiter and Taranus are examples of a particular and personal devotion, and need not imply a general faith. Just as in purely Latin dedications (like Jupiter Tonitrator, at Sarajevo, Dalmatia [*C.I.L.*, III, 2766]) Taranus in Jupiter Taranus could be thought of as an epithet demonstrating one aspect of Jupiter's function. However, in the present instances, we have both a Roman and a Celtic title. Secondly, we do have Taranus on his own without the Jupiter-element. Still, all we have is the equation between Jupiter and a Celtic entity who may be identified with one aspect of the Roman god. *Taranus* embodies only the concept of a noisy lord of thunder, weather and storms ; a power-struggle perhaps in the sky, with undertones of battle and of fertility. But thunder is only one of Jupiter's attributes and instruments, and his role of wielder of the thunderbolt only one of his functions. Jupiter has a much wider role as all-powerful over the immensity of the luminous atmosphere. Jupiter does bear a thunderbolt, but the lightning, flashing element is more important on representations, which frequently portray it as a jagged lightning-fork (for example on the Hausen Jupiter-column ; Bauchhenss, 1976, 1, pl. opp. p. 1) than the noise-factor which is all-important to a god called a thunderer. By definition Taranus cannot escape from his noise-role to attain greater significance. Jupiter's first role is as a god of the ethereal infinite ; and his light-giving force establishes him above all as High-God and Father. One can see why Jupiter among the Gauls was conceived of as a solar, wheel-bearing divinity. One can also perceive an occasional equation between a Thunder-God of the Celts and part of Jupiter's function as a celestial lord of rain, sun, light and storms. But it is probably simplistic to assume that Taranis and Jupiter/Wheel-God were considered as equals or that one was exactly the same as the other. If, as Cerquand suggests (1883, 381ff.) one could equate the functions of *Taranis* with those of the Teutonic 'Thor', then the hammer could be significant. If one may accept that, because of the noise-element, Taranus had a hammer where Jupiter had a sceptre, then confusion between the two could have led to the evolution of the long-shafted hammer (sceptre and hammer combined). If one accepts this possibility then Sucellus (see Chapters V and VI) may come into his own. We have already seen that the Hammer-God of the Gauls with longshafted hammer, when occurring in bronze, frequently bears solar symbols. If there is in the Roman period total (and therefore confused) conflation between Thunder-God and Solar-God, this might account for the presence of the entity known as Sucellus.

It is my opinion that there may well have been a Celtic solar deity or entity, thought of in terms of wheel-symbolism before the Roman period. At the time of the Roman conquests of Gaul and Britain, there could have been a natural conflation between this solar divinity and the Roman Sky-Father Jupiter. The Thunder-God Taranis, also pre-existing Roman influence in some form, was not a solar deity but simply a thunder/storm-god, and was also occasionally equated with Jupiter since Jupiter was also a wielder of a thunderbolt. Where one finds solar symbols on bronzes of the Romano-Gaulish Hammer-God, it may be that because Taranis was sometimes linked with Jupiter and, because a Celtic solar-god was also thus linked, to a Romano-Celtic mind it may have followed that Taranis, a Thunder-God, was sometimes identified with solar symbolism, but mistakenly, since in essence Taranis or Taranus can be no more than a Thunderer. With this in mind one does well to remember Jupiter-Sucaelus at Mainz (*C.I.L.*, XIII, 6730).

A further point concerns the equation of Taranis with Dispater made by one Bern scholiast (Zwicker, 1934, 50). As the Roman Dispater was an underworld deity, in order for this equation to have any validity we have to seek an underworld facet to the cult of the Thunder-God. If the god has connections with Sucellus, then there is little of any direct relevance here (although much is made, among continental scholars, of the fact that the wheel occurs both on Vosges tombstones and on bronzes of Sucellus [see Chapter VI]). But if we consider the role of the Celtic Jupiter in Gaul, we do possess evidence of a chthonic association. We have already seen that both water and graves have a bearing on the cult (see Chapter VI). The water-link is especially striking. In this connection Albenique's remark (1948, 19) could be of significance. He comments that the river Tarn or Tarnis, located in the territory of the Ruteni, could have associations with *Taranis*.

Finally the Bern scholiast's identification of Taranis with Jupiter should be looked at once again in terms of his sacrifices. Apparently human heads were once offered for his appeasement. Only one doubtful piece of evidence exists in the iconography. This is a stone from a temple-site at Wall, Staffordshire, carved on which is a naked figure holding a circular object (thought by the excavator to be a wheel) over an altar. Beneath this figure is a human severed head (Birmingham City Museum & Art Gallery). The relief is extremely worn, and in my opinion the round object could as easily be a *patera* as a wheel.

Celtic Influence on the Roman Jupiter in Gaul and other Western Provinces

Epigraphic Evidence

Jupiter in Gaul has nowhere near as many Celtic epithets recorded on inscriptions as, say, Mercury or Mars, but those which do occur, for the most part, have topographical or local implications, thus indicating Jupiter's identification with local spirits or entities presumably existing before the Roman period. The notable exception is of course *Taranis* or its derivatives, discussed above. Allied to the thunder-epithet is the dedication to Jupiter Fulminans at Este in northern Italy, attesting the firmamental or celestial role of the god (*C.I.L.*, V, 2474 ; Pascal, 1964, 76-83). Pascal's opinion is that, alongside official Jupiter Optimus Maximus cults there was perhaps in Cisalpine Gaul a worship of Jupiter which was more narrowly restricted to Jupiter's primitive celestial role ; Jupiter here is perhaps the name given to a local pre-Roman god whose own indigenous name survives either as an epithet or has been lost altogether. Another surname occurring in Narbonensis, which is not a local name as such, but appears only once in this area, is *Frugifer* or 'fruitful' (Clerc, 1916; 289) ; the find-spot is Rougiers (*C.I.L.*, XII, 336). This association of Jupiter with agricultural prosperity and crop-protection is of great interest since in the same region we have a dedication (see Chapter IV) to Jupiter and Terra Mater, associated with a wheel-symbol ; there are other indications (see Chapter VI) of a link between Jupiter and fertility, in particular with the Celtic Mother-Goddesses and with Epona. Jupiter Optimus Maximus and the Mothers were worshipped together at Mainz (*C.I.L.*, XIII, 6729). In ancient Roman religion too (Warde Fowler, 1922, 121) *Tellus* or Earth is combined with Jupiter in a Roman formula of *deuotio*, where the speaker touches the ground as he mentions her name, and then stretches his hands up towards the sky when he names Jupiter (Macrobius, *Saturnalia* III, 9, 11). According to Warde Fowler however (1922, 156), there is nothing in the Roman religion to suggest that the Sky-Father and Earth-Mother personally unite in marriage or in the sexual act. It is difficult not to believe in a somewhat closer relationship of the two concepts of sky and fertility in Romano-Celtic cult, as evidenced by the archaeological record. In the Mainz region (*C.I.L.*, XIII, 6730) Jupiter is equated with Sucaelus (Sucellus) the 'Good Striker', the Gaulish Hammer-God who has connections both with prosperity (fertility) and solar symbolism. Jupiter Olbius (again a prosperity-title) is recorded at Heddernheim (*C.I.L.*, XIII, 7346) ; he is linked with Nemausus, a water-deity, at Nîmes (*C.I.L.*, XII, 3070).

Jupiter appears thus to have had multiple aspects in the Roman provinces of Gaul. On the one hand he is the great imperial guardian, and on the other he is identified with ancient pre-Roman gods or localities (Toutain, 1907, 197ff.). Toutain comments (*ibid.*) that the cult of the official Jupiter Optimus Maximus within the provinces was really only popular where city-life was active and where military and administrative personnel were in evidence. Jupiter Brixianus at Brescia in Cisalpine Gaul (northern Italy) is a local god equated with Jupiter (*C.I.L.*, 4233 ; Pascal, 1964, 76-83). The Celtiberian divinities of the North-West mountains of Spain are sometimes assimilated with the Roman Sky-God, for example Jupiter Ladicus − the god of Mount Ladicus (*C.I.L.*, II, 2525 ; Toutain, 1920, 143ff.). At Morestel (Isère), in the territory of the Allobroges (*C.I.L.*, XII, 2383) Jupiter is called *Baginas* (Toutain, 1920, 143ff. ; Vallentin, 1879-1880, 21). Among the Bigerriones, Jupiter Optimus Maximus was called Beisirissa, at Cadéac (Hautes-Pyrénées) (*C.I.L.*, XIII, 370 ; Toutain, 1920, 143ff.). Both the last-mentioned names are entirely local. *Saranicus* and *Poeninus* are also recorded (de Vries, 1963, 39).

Among the Noricans, some of whom were Celts, some mountain-deities were identified with or conflated with the Roman Jupiter (Alföldy, 1974, 23). On the loftiest peak of Koralpe, on the Steinschneider, between the Lavant and Mur valleys, 2000 metres above sea-level, a votive inscription was set up to a native god identified with Jupiter (Alföldy, 1974, 9 ; Leber, 1965, 25f. ; Leber, 1967, 517-520). Jupiter Arubianus was entirely local to this region of Austria (*C.I.L.*, III, 5443, 5532, 5575, 5185, 5580 ; Alföldy, 1974, 22), as was another mountain-god Uxellinus, also assimilated with Jupiter (Alföldy, 1974, 135 ; *C.I.L.*, III, 5145).

In Pannonia and Moesia Superior, until Severan times, little attention was paid by natives to Roman gods and they did not erect altars to their own gods. Thus the native population showed little interest in the religion of their conquerors, which is the reason why native gods were not identified with those of the classical pantheon (Mócsy, 1974, 182). However, later one does find an equation in Pannonia between Jupiter Optimus Maximus and Teutanus (Mócsy, 1974, 253 ; Mócsy, 1962, 740, 745). This is interesting because the epithet or surname might refer to a tribal aspect of the god's cult. Mars Toutatis is recorded at Barkway, Herts (Green, 1976, 209 ; Toynbee, 1964, 328-330) and possibly also at Castor, Cambs (Green, 1976, 208 ; *R.I.B.*, 232). At Aquincum Jupiter was surnamed Accionis (de Vries, 1963, 38 ; *C.I.L.*, III, 3428). According to Alföldy (1964, 54-59) the high god of Pannonia Inferior was identified with the Celtic Jupiter. In a temple-precinct at Carnuntum in eastern Austria a dedication was found to *I.O.M. K*....., which, it is suggested (Jobst, 1977, 155-165) could either mean Jupiter Kapitolinus or Karnuntinus (though neither need be so).

On the borders of North-East Dalmatia and Upper Moesia (*C.I.L.*, III, 8353, 14613) Jupiter was known as Parthinus or Partinus. The first-mentioned inscription was dedicated to *I.O.M. Partinus*. There were Celtic peoples living in the North-East of Dalmatia (Čremošnik, 1959, 207ff.), and Wilkes suggests (1969, 165) that *Partinus* could be connected with a local native group called the Partheni.

So in widely differing areas outside Gaul, and also in the south of Gaul, one finds native epithets to Jupiter, generally, with certain exceptions, referring to topographical *Genius loci*-type allusions, and frequently associated with high places, as befitted the supreme god of the sky. These local names are of great interest. One presumes that spirits of places were recognized and identifiable to the indigenous population before the period of Roman influence and therefore there must have been deities of mountain-summits who were probably also storm, weather and celestial entities, easily and naturally conflated with the classical 'Olympian' Sky-God after the conquest. The equation of mountain-deities with Jupiter all over the Roman empire is well-established. As far away as Nabateia the Zeus-Jupiter-Hadad of Jebel (Mount) Tannus was worshipped on a sacred mountain, commanding springs and the Wadi of La'aban. Hadad was a Thunderer existing long before the Greek and Roman periods (Glück, 1965, 203, 205). He was both a celestial and a fertility-god, with dominance over weather and rain — exactly as is the case with the Romano-Celtic Jupiter of southern Gaul.

Other Celtic Influence on the Roman Jupiter (outside Britain)

Apart from wheel-symbolism and indigenous names, there are other indications that Jupiter in Gaul sometimes has Celtic influence. It should be remembered that Caesar mentions Jupiter in fourth place among the Gauls (*de Bello Gallico* VI, 17). He takes religious romanization as if it were total, but this, as we have already seen, is questionable, to say the least. Apart from Jupiter's association with, for example, the Celtic Mothers at Pesch (Lehner, 1918-21, 74ff.), and with Epona at Entrains-sur-Nohain (Nièvre) (Magnen & Thevenot, 1953, 28), other Celtic associations include the dedication at Phalsbourg, Nancy (*C.I.L.*, XIII, 5991) to Jupiter, Apollo and a native deity Visucius (Reinach, 1917, 97). Two early monuments attest at least a close connection between Jupiter and other 'Roman' gods on the one hand, and Celtic divinities on the other. The most significant of these is the Parisian Pillar dedicated by the *Nautes Parisiacae*, elevated to the glory of Jupiter Optimus Maximus by the sailors of Paris, and erected in the reign of Tiberius (*C.I.L.*, XIII, 3026). The monument was found in 1711 in five blocks (a sixth stone has been lost) at Notre-Dame. Probably the whole column was originally six metres high (Duval, 1961, 264-275). The juxtaposition of gods in native and classical form (Espérandieu, nos. 3132, 3133, 3134, 3135) indicates close association between them, and one can at least say that Jupiter here is not entirely divorced from Celtic influence, though he bears no such Celtic attribute as a wheel and is overtly Roman. The gods portrayed here include Jupiter himself, Vulcan, the Dioscuri, Mars, Mercury, Venus, Fortuna, Esus, Tarvostrigaranus, Cernunnos and Smertrios. On one face six men, possibly Severi Augustales, are depicted ; the emperor is being offered a torc (a Celtic symbol) of honour. Duval suggests (1961) that the face bearing the Jupiter-representation was probably in the highest position, the intention being, as is the case with the later Jupiter-columns and with mountain-worship, to raise Jupiter as high as possible.

The other important Gaulish monument depicting Jupiter in association with Celtic deities is the pillar from Mavilly (Côte-d'Or) (Espérandieu, nos. 2067, 2072). Jupiter is portrayed seated (Mackendrick, 1971, 155-156) with other deities including Roman gods such as Vulcan, Neptune, Apollo and Fortuna, but also Mars in company with a ram-horned serpent (Duval, 1957, 39ff.).

There are plenty of further indications of overtly classical depictions of Jupiter being somewhat 'contaminated'. Wightman suggests (1970, 210) that although an inscription in Trier dedicates an ornamental gateway to *I.O.M.* (*C.I.L.*, XIII, 3647) the temple within the precinct could have been associated with a not entirely Roman divinity. A Celtic Sky-God is presumably being worshipped at the sanctuary associated with the large southern Gaulish villa of Montmaurin, a possibly late establishment (coins dating mostly to Constantine − A.D. 312-337), where several altars to Jupiter are recorded (Mackendrick, 1971, 135) associated with similar altars engraved with wheels and swastikas. At Dhronecken near Trier, in the Hunsrück, a Romano-Celtic shrine dating from 1st-5th Century A.D. has produced a classical-looking bronze statuette of Jupiter, but also pipe-clay figurines of the god (Grenier, 1958, Chapter 9, 2) (it should be remembered that some of these from the Allier factories bear wheels, and all seem to have catered for a Romano-Celtic clientèle), and two magnificent wheel-shaped brooches.

Some representations of Jupiter indicate Celticism by virtue of their style alone rather than by attribute or association. From Escornebœuf

(Midi-Pyrénées) comes a very Celtic-looking stone figure of a standing Jupiter, with an over-large head and lentoid eyes (Labrousse, 1974, 478, fig. 25). A bronze from Strasbourg depicts a Gaulish-garbed divinity bearing a thunderbolt (Forrer, 1922-26, 334, fig. 197 ; Strasbourg, Musée Archéologique, 1973, pl. 15). A stylized bronze head of Jupiter, in Périgueux Museum, comes from Eymet, Dordogne (Eydoux, 1962, 277, ill. 322), and two extremely unroman-looking bronze figurines of Jupiter are from the Speyer area of the Rhineland (Menzel, 1960, Taf. 1, nos. 1-2). In my opinion it is fair to assume that the further away one gets from naturalistic, and therefore essentially classical, styles of representation, the less romanization is present. A really romanized worshipper, one would have thought, would not have appreciated a grotesque portrayal of his god, or even have understood the meaning of an over-large head, shuttered features, and other Celtic stylistic traits.

To the Celtic peoples Jupiter seems to have been identifiable with their own divinities. As we have seen, the thunder-element and the higher celestial concepts of the classical cult led Jupiter to be conflated sometimes with thunder, and more importantly, with solar deities belonging to Gaulish peoples. Among the Celts (Duval, 1957, 6) Jupiter became multi-functional and had associations with sky, combat, fields, fertility, and perhaps even smithing. The Celtic peoples do not appear to have grasped the concept of fixed function for a particular god. However, these Gaulish roles for Jupiter may have little to do with the official state-cult role for the god. Granted that the cult, as exported to Gaul at the time of the conquest, was the official state-religion, embodying loyalty and allegiance to Rome (the cult of Jupiter Optimus Maximus was firmly established in Rome by the 1st Century B.C. [Ogilvie, 1969, 15-16]), Jupiter as worshipped as a true god in Gaul has much more in common with older Mediterranean conceptions of a sky-cult. In Gaul, Britain and the Rhineland, there is abundant evidence for the official state-religion in areas where army or central administration was active. It is interesting that although *capitolia* were present in the large towns of Gaul, where the capitoline Triad was worshipped (Mackendrick, 1971, 174ff.), Jupiter had few other sanctuaries in the province. In Gaul the state-cult of Jupiter was present but his worship was by no means confined to this.

When conflation between Roman and native deity occurs there is an immediate problem since rigid functionalization existed in Rome but not among the Celtic peoples. In Rome generally locality is superseded by function (Bailey, 1932, 110-111). Jupiter-Zeus is different from the general run of Olympian deities, however, in that he has a locality (the sky) as well as his role as controller of celestial phenomena. It is locality which appears, from our evidence in the period of Roman influence, to have defined Celtic divine entities. This may have made it easy for Celts to identify a Roman with their own sky-deity. If we go back to the origins of Jupiter in Italy we see that, apart from his celestial function, the god was a tribal god, pre-eminently the deity of Latium. When Rome took over headship of the Latin League and removed the religious centre to Rome, the temple of Jupiter Latiaris – the original god of the League – was rebuilt on its Alban Hill and a new temple was also built in Rome itself probably in the late 6th Century B.C. (Warde Fowler, 1922, 237). Whilst as a wielder of thunder and raiser of storms Jupiter had limited *auctoritas* it was his new role as city-guardian of Rome – a magnified tribal god – from which his real importance emanated (Bailey, 1932, 167-168). If we take away Jupiter's role as god of the City of Rome (in which context he was almost, like Roma, the personification of Rome) we are left with a deity who is in essence very similar to our Romano-Celtic entity, except that in Gaul and Britain the solar element is of particular significance. In a solar context however, Bailey has an interesting point with regard not to the Roman Jupiter but to the Greek Zeus. There was, he states, dualism in Greece with Zeus/Pluto. This could possibly adapt itself to solar functions, in that the sun was thought to traverse earth by day and visit the lower regions at night (Bailey, 1932, 260). If we have, as suggested above, a division in Gaulish concepts of sky-divinity, into 'thunder' and 'sun' powers, then this may be reflected also in Greek antiquity where the powers of the sun appear to have been split up into 'weather' and the celestial bodies (Harrison, 1912, 523ff.). The fertility-aspect of the Celtic Jupiter also has parallels in the classical and pre-classical world. According to James (1957, 198) the youthful Cretan Zeus became, with the development of agricultural society, a Sky-Father or Weather-God pouring down rain to fertilize earth and water the crops. The solar element in sky-religion manifests itself, again presumably at least partly as a fertility-concept, in Egypt with Horus – a god with the theriomorphic form of a falcon. Horus appears to have been a sky- and sun-deity represented as a source both of life and death, rain and celestial fire (James, 1957, 210). There is great similarity between the functions of this god and the Sky-God of the Gaulish Celts. To return for a moment to Greece, the Indo-European Sky-God Zeus, before the end of the Bronze Age and before the Dorian invasions (according to information from

Linear B) (Dietrich, 1973, 240-241), superimposed his name on the prehistoric sky and weather-deity of the Cretans (James, 1957, 259 ; Dietrich, 1973, 59). Zeus became the head of a mountain-pantheon in Thessaly, thus accentuating his celestial role and raising him above the essentially storm and vegetation-functions of his predecessors. The mountain-element is interesting. A high peak is a natural locality for a sky-lord. He is as close to the sky as he can be, and at the same time, can survey his territory from a lofty position, thus commanding, and, as a corollary, being superior to earth. Height is something which preoccupied worshippers of the Celtic Jupiter — we can see it in the local mountain-gods' assimilation to Jupiter ; we see it in the Jupiter-giant columns. We also possibly see it in the wheel-symbols at the apex of triangular 'stèles-maisons' of the Bas-Rhin area.

What we appear to have among Celtic peoples, is the worship of a Sky-God, as it were frozen in time, before becoming developed as a city and later a universal imperial deity. Weather, Sky, Fertility, Death, Healing were all important. The solar element, worshipped as a deity in human form, is perhaps the most alien to Mediterranean civilizations.

CHAPTER IX

Realism and Non-Realism in Cult-Wheel Representation

INTRODUCTION

A study has been made of the physical characteristics of Romano-Celtic cult wheels as represented by stone sculpture and small votive objects. This has been undertaken for a number of reasons. One is in order to attempt to discover the degree of realism or stylization, with a view to possible significance in terms of cult. This problem has necessitated a brief examination of the evidence for surviving Romano-Celtic non-cult wheels, both real examples and the utilitarian specimens represented on secular sculpture. A further reason for such a study has been to ascertain differences in physical form between cult-wheels on monumental stonework and those depicted in other media. A third is to analyse differences and similarities of construction within the categories of monumental and other religious representations.

I emphasize at the outset that the present exercise may have no bearing whatever on Romano-Celtic wheels as cult-symbols. However, I feel it obligatory to gain as much information as possible from the raw data at my disposal ; in my opinion, even negative evidence for a correlation between physical form and cult-relevance is of interest. A sample ([1]) of 274 wheels, drawn both from the literature and from my own museum research, was analysed and a number of variables were defined (see Attribute-list, p. 289, and analysis, pp. 283-288). It is important to note that, for purposes of immediate comparability, the illustrated wheels (Pls. XXV-XLIX) have been standardized both in respect of size and circularity.

---

(1) Numbers in this chapter, preceded by 'S' refer to sample-number in illustrations (Pls. XXV-XLIX). S1-S95 are stone ; S96-118 are miscellaneous depictions (not stone or models) ; S119-274 are models, all of metal. For sample site-list see pp. 290-293.

Ancient Wheel-Construction

Piggott (1979) has recently surveyed the evidence for wheeled vehicles and their construction in earlier prehistory, and there is no need to discuss this here. During the Roman period both spoked and solid-wheeled vehicles were in use. According to Piggott (1979) the invention of the spoked wheel was triggered by the introduction of the light, horse-drawn cart or chariot as a fast motive force. Spoked wheels (Piggott, 1979, 10-11) were made for a light, swift and manoeuvrable vehicle (Jenkins, 1961, 22-24). One should maintain the distinction (Piggott, 1979, 4 ; Harding, 1978, 15) between four-wheeled domestic wagons (not necessarily requiring spoked wheels) and two-wheeled carts (with spoked wheels) which could be driven with ease and comparative speed over uneven and hilly terrain.

Later prehistoric representations of spoked wheels (as opposed to true utilitarian examples) cause problems of interpretation similar to those encountered during the Roman period. The question has to be asked as to how close miniature wheels and other depictions are to real wheels. To what extent are wheel-portrayals faithful reflections of the real thing ? Piggott makes the valid point (1979, 12) that the representation of a simple, four-spoked, wheel (occurring, for instance, in European, especially Scandinavian, rock-art [Filip, 1969, 1612]) may either be interpreted as a realistic depiction or as a short-hand, stylized method of representing any wheel, with no attempt at reproducing the correct number of spokes.

Later Bronze Age miniature wheels with only four spokes could be faithful copies, since there were in existence cast bronze wheels, found, for instance, in the later Urnfield hoards. Such wheels include that from Abos, Hungary (Kossack, 1971, 147, fig. 30, 1, 2). The Cortaillod bronze wheel from Lake Neuchâtel is a four-spoked specimen 47.5 cm in diameter (of metal felloe), cast in one piece. An oak tyre, probably in separate segments, was fixed to the U-channelled felloe by means of eight nails (Sauter, 1976, 106, fig. 39).

Where Mediterranean vase-painting (Jope, 1956, 540, fig. 483 ; 541, fig.485) shows four-spoked wheeled chariots, either the wheels represented must be of this type of cast bronze or they are probably not true copies (though Jenkins [personal information] is of the opinion that a four-spoked wooden wheel is feasible if only used for very light loads). Jope cites a model classical Greek chariot for the Olympian games, with four spokes (1956, 542, fig. 487), but also an Etruscan relief of 6th Century B.C. date depicting a chariot with eight-spoked wheels. Kossack would suggest (1971, 147-148) that Greek vase-paintings are dubious evidence but that in his opinion it is permissible to say that they present contemporary bronze wheels in Europe at the time. The Tiryns Fresco, with oblique bands on spoke-terminals could, Kossack suggests, reflect faithful reproduction of binding a separately-segmented rim. In the context of true copying it is of interest that certain later Bronze Age wheel-shaped amulets, occurring in Italian graves, are extremely realistic, as if from wagon-models ; the hub or nave in particular is sometimes very naturalistically constructed (Woytowitsch, 1978, Taf. 50-51). Some of these, like that from Fontanella di Casalromano (*ibid.*, Taf. 51) actually have suspension-rings, demonstrating their definite use as talismans. Other, Central European, wheel-amulets (for example in the Schweizerisches Landesmuseum, Zürich [Wyss, 1967, Taf. 10]), however, are stylized, with no effort at realism in respect of hub or felloe.

It is worthwhile to look in some detail both at Hallstatt and La Tène wheel-construction since we have good evidence, in both periods, for wooden construction which, in many essentials, has strong affinities with later Romano-Celtic technological methods. In both periods too we have evidence of cult-wheel representation, for instance in the form of amulets. In Hallstatt C chamber-graves, for example that from Hradénin (Czechoslovakia), evidence is provided for wagon-wheels with fourteen parallel-sided spokes (a curious and difficult number) and a very thick felloe (Kossack, 1971, 150, fig. 31). A second grave, at Grossabstadt, Bavaria, has produced a similar wheel but with sixteen converging-sided spokes. This evidence is of interest since it demonstrates non-uniformity in construction both in numbers of spokes and in spoke-shape. A grave of similar date (c. 7th Century B.C.) but from a Cypriot context at Salamis, has produced a vehicle with two eight-spoked wheels one metre in diameter (*ibid.*, 155), with board felloes and no iron tyre (*ibid.*, fig. 34). Kossack also cites an Assyrian relief from Nineveh (fig. 35, 4) showing a wheel of constructional interest, with a very thick felloe and sixteen very narrow, convex-sided spokes. It is the felloe-construction which is interesting here. There is an important technological distinction between Hallstatt and La Tène wheels (Kossack, 1971 ; Piggott, 1979). The Hallstatt group comprises composite, massive board or plank felloes (like the Assyrian and Cypriot examples), whereas the La Tène ones (like the much earlier specimens in vehicle-burials of the Armenian Caucasus [Piggott, 1979, 11]) are of single-piece, bentwood construction. This fact is of relevance to Romano-Celtic wheel-production since, in this period (see below), both felloe-types may be seen, on one and the same site.

Iron Age Italy has produced similar evidence to that in Hallstatt and Urnfield Central Europe. A large cast bronze wagon buried with the dead at Montelione di Spoleto, Perugia, has eight cast-bronze spokes (Woytowitsch, 1978, Taf. 15, no. 85). Variety, especially in number of spokes, is borne out by the Italian models of this period, for instance that from Ca'Morta, Corno (*ibid.*, no. 129, Taf. 26) with ten-spoked wheels ; the unprovenanced example from Italy with 6 cm diameter wheels and four thick spokes (*ibid.*, no. 126, Taf. 22) ; and the clay wagon-model with two horses and two four-spoked wheels each with wedge-shaped spokes (*ibid.*, no. 166, Taf. 35). All these date from c. 7th-6th Century B.C.

Two Hallstatt vehicles, both models, demonstrate interesting evidence for wheel-construction. The question has to be asked whether the wheels are as they are because they reflect reality or simply because they are models. We have seen that functional wooden wheels of this period have certain characteristics. How far do the models copy these ? One model is the bird-decorated cult-wagon from Orastie (Szasvarosszek, Czechoslovakia). It dates from the 7th-6th Century B.C. and is 10 cm high. Realism is present in the elongated nave and in the metal plates at the junction of felloe and spokes. The felloe is thick, which fits in well with functional construction ; but the spokes are but four in number and very thin (Anon, 1980a, no. 3.30). The other model is that from Strettweg in Austria. It is probably of 7th Century B.C. date. It is much bigger than the first model, being 48 cm in length. It is a cult-wagon, from a chief's grave, but the wheels are very naturalistic with long naves, thick felloes and eight narrow spokes.

Hallstatt-period wheel-amulets are not necessarily realistic. Examples from Hallstatt itself, for instance those in the Vienna Naturhistorisches Museum, exhibit stylization, and realism has been forsaken to a certain extent in favour of ritual function. One such wheel (Grave 507) is part of a ceremonial 'rattle' with chains and other amulets hanging from it.

Iron Age functional wooden wheels have survived well enough to allow for fairly accurate reconstruction. As is the case in earlier prehistory, there is evidence for solid as well as spoked types. In the Netherlands, in the Terp of Ezinge (Province of Groningen) fragments of at least six tripartite disc-wheels with lunate openings are recorded (Van der Wals, 1964, 121-124). The lunate openings are interesting ; the author suggests their purpose to have been to facilitate carrying or lifting of the carts they supported. However, there may be a weight-factor here, with its implications for the need for speed and manoeuvrability, as is the case in the adoption of spokes. It is of interest here that the disc-wheels appear to have lasted at least until the early Imperial Roman period, with no evidence for spoked wheels until (probably) after A.D. 400 at Ezinge.

At Llyn Cerrig Bach (Anglesey) the remains of a number of chariots or carts are recorded, represented by broken iron tyres (Lynch, 1970, 258). Between ten and twenty vehicles were deposited in the lake, very probably coming originally from different regions and of varying dates. The number of spokes appears to have varied from six to twelve ; the tyre-diameter could be as small as 40 cm but most commonly measured about 90 cm (*ibid.*, 259).

Celtic wheel-wrights were apparently famous for the lightness and strength of their vehicles (Lynch, 1970, 259, fig. 86). By early La Tène, Celtic craftsmen were skilful in shaping the felloe from a single piece of ash steamed or heated into shape (Jope, 1956, 549), as was the case at the site of La Tène itself (Vouga, 1923, 92f., fig. 9). The felloe was held and strengthened by an iron tyre heated and shrunk onto the rim (Jenkins, 1961, 24-25). The tyre was placed red-hot over the wooden wheel and shrunk on, the quenching of the hot metal hardening it (Jope, 1956, 551) (see Jenkins [1961, 72-73] for views of 'modern' tyre-making). At Llyn Cerrig the tyres were of high-quality carbon-steel skilfully welded into a full circle out of several pieces of metal (Jope, 1956, 551). It is the absence of nail- or rivet-holes which proves the method of attaching tyre to felloe during this period.

Other evidence for wheel-type during the Iron Age includes material from Britain and the Continent. The wheels found at the Glastonbury Lake Village had turned ash hubs and evidence of twelve circular spoke-mortices (Jenkins, 1961, 25). Remains survive from 'Marnian' graves in eastern Yorkshire (Stead, 1965). At Kärlich in the Rhineland, the wood and iron wheel had eight spokes ; a wagon-wheel of La Tène date from Bell in the Hunsrück had a felloe eight cm thick (unusually thick) and ten spokes. Both had spokes with diverging sides (Kossack, 1971, 145, fig. 28, 2 ; 146, fig. 28).

General characteristics both of Hallstatt and La Tène wooden wheels include the relatively large number of spokes, with short spoke-tongues, and long, small-diametered hubs (Jenkins, 1961, 25). The Djejberg cult-wagon from central Jutland has four wheels with twelve or fourteen spokes, a single-piece felloe 5 cm thick and with a running surface 3.3 cm wide. The diameter of each wheel is 95 cm. The felloes were shod with iron tyres (Jenkins, 1961, 25 ; Kossack, 1971, 144-145, fig. 28, 5). Like the Bell and Kärlich wheels the spokes of this cult-wagon are of diverging type.

Jenkins (1961, 25) makes the point that Iron Age wheel-wrights, in Britain for instance, developed techniques which remained virtually unchanged for the next 2000 years — lathe-turned hubs of elm or oak, bound each end with cast bronze collars ; spokes with square tenons and round tongues to pass through hub and felloe, lathe-turned and of oak, willow or hornbeam (in recent personal communication Jenkins has in fact denied the probability of lathe-turning for spokes, as cleaving with the grain using a spoke-shave would make better sense in terms of strength) ; bentwood ash felloes and iron tyres. Iron Age wheel-models, certainly sometimes amulets (as at Mannersdorf, Austria, c. 350-300 B.C. [Anon., 1980b, no. 50]), are sometimes extremely realistic, with tyre, nave and spokes faithfully represented. Others, like that from a Dürnnberg girl's grave (c. 430-400 B.C.), are stylized, with no hub and tyreless felloe (Anon., 1980b, no. 98).

One final point of interest with regard to Iron Age vehicle-function is the possibility that two-wheeled vehicles may not have been chariots as is generally supposed, but were carts (Harding, 1978, 16-17). However in Britain at any rate in the 1st Century B.C. chariots were being used against Julius Caesar (*de Bello Gallico* IV, 33). In this connection, it is of interest to reflect that where Greek light chariots, as portrayed on vase-paintings, were designed to carry one individual, Celtic 'chariots' were built for two.

Romano-Celtic Wheel-Construction

We do not know a great deal in detail about Roman wheel-making. Jope suggests (1956, 550) that Celtic workmanship is discernible in some cases. Certainly the Glastonbury (Iron Age) and Bar Hill (Roman) wheels are very similar (Curle, 1911, 293). However, there are a number of survivals of Roman functional wheels and enough secular representations (as well as cult ones) to show that radially-spoked specimens were common in the Roman world.

Jenkins suggests that the Newstead Roman wheels may well have been made by native Celtic craftsmen. In Pit XXIII at Newstead two almost entire wheels were found, and a third in Pit LXX, as well as other fragments (tyres and isolated spokes) (Curle, 1911, 292-294, fig. 2). The two lighter wheels have elm hubs, willow spokes and a single-piece, bentwood felloe of ash, bent by artificial softening. The ends were bolted together by means of a metal plate, the whole being bound by a tyre. The diameter is about 90 cm ; there were ten spokes convex in shape and a long hub or nave c. 38 cm long with a diameter of 20.5 cm at the centre and with fitted iron rings at both ends (Curle, 1911, 292-294 ; Jope, 1956, fig. 504A ; Jenkins, 1961, 25). The third complete wheel from this South Scottish site is of different construction, with a larger diameter of c. 105 cm, and was heavier altogether. It has a multi-piece felloe comprising six wooden segments dowelled together, with two almost square spokes mortised into each felloe-segment (Jenkins, 1961, 25 ; Curle, 1911, 294). According to Jenkins (*ibid.*) this larger wheel is very reminiscent of a 19th Century English farm-wagon wheel ; and Curle sees in this specimen an example of a wagon or freight vehicle rather than a 'Caledonian chariot' (Curle, 1911, 294).

At Bar Hill there is similar evidence for Roman wheels both of single and multi-piece felloe construction. In Refuse Pit no. 6, close to the bottom, was a complete wooden wheel (Robertson, Scott and Keppie, 1975, 22, 48, and opp. fig. 14). The external diameter was 88 cm, with a one-piece ash felloe and eleven lathe-turned ash spokes c. 27.5 cm long, with square tenons at each end. The elm nave had a total length of 32 cm, each side protected by an outer rim and inner lining of iron. The felloe was enclosed by a one-piece iron tyre 4.5 cm wide. As is the case at Newstead there is also evidence for multi-piece-felloed wheels on the site (*ibid.*, 50, fig. 15, 2). One segment of a (probably) six-segmented felloe survives, probably originally with twelve spokes and with a diameter of c. 90 cm. What is of particular interest about this specimen is that the wear suffered by the spoke-ends protruding from the rim demonstrates their non-enclosure by a metal tyre. Extra wooden knobs set into the outer face of the rim between the spokes would have helped protect it from excessive wear. There is a parallel here with the Iron Age wheel-model from Fully in Switzerland, where the spokes are represented as protruding from the felloe-surface. Although this Bar Hill example is published as never having had a tyre, Jenkins (personal communication) sees this as an unfinished wheel, suggesting that the spoke-ends would, in construction, be made too long, but when the tyre was shrunk on the spoke-ends would be driven back and the whole would be extremely taut as a result. The presence of the bronze Fully model appears to strengthen the original (Bar Hill authors') hypothesis.

Elsewhere in the Romano-Celtic world functional wheel-remains also exist. At Augst (Römermuseum Augst) is the narrow iron tyre of a wooden cart-wheel. At Zugmantel (Anon, 1912b, 68ff.; Abb. 27, 28) wooden cart-wheels survive, with ten parallel-sided spokes, heavy-duty one-piece felloe, long well-turned nave and metal tyre (White, 1967, 167; White, 1975, 82).

The extant wooden wheels from the Celtic provinces demonstrate that Geraint Jenkins' view (1961, 22-23), that even up to the Medieval period spoked wheels were limited to vehicles of war and ceremony, and that disc-wheels were invariably used for freight, is untenable. In any event the large number of Gallo-Roman and other stone monuments showing freight-vehicles, frequently depict spoked wheels. The Buzenol relief of a Gaulish reaping-machine has ten-spoked wheels, like the Newstead and Zugmantel wooden specimens (White, 1967, 164, 168, pl. 15). The Buzenol wheel has a broad nave, thick felloe and convex-sided spokes. Other animal-drawn wagons with spoked wheels are depicted, for example, at Dijon (Espérandieu, 3522), Arlon (with eight narrow spokes and thick felloe) (Espérandieu, 4031, 4092) and Neumagen (Espérandieu, 5759). The Trier *uallus* (White, 1975, pl. 16) has a thin felloe and diverging spokes. The hub is broad in diameter. Trajan's Column has plentiful evidence of Dacian wagons with spoked wheels (presumably depicted as if they were Roman examples). 'Metope no. XLIII' shows a battle among the wagons. A Roman soldier stands on a wagon on which sits a Dacian woman as a suppliant. The wagon is four-wheeled and has eight parallel-sided spokes (Rossi, 1971, 63, pl. 25). Several other Dacian wagons depicted have eight spokes (*ibid.*, 151, pl. 33). An ox-cart is portrayed, however (*ibid.*, 163, pl. 52) with twelve parallel-edged spokes. On one panel a Roman *carroballista* on a mule-drawn cart is depicted with eight-spoked wheel, spokes tapering towards the felloe, and a clearly-visible tyre (Rossi, 1971, 153, pl. 36; Webster, 1969, pl. XXIXa, 235). A relief of Roman Imperial date from Klagenfurt (Austria) depicts a four-wheeled travelling-wagon with eight-spoked wheels (Jope, 1956, 546, fig. 494). A similar relief, depicting either a travelling-vehicle or a funerary car, also with eight-spoked wheels, comes from Vaison (Vaucluse) (*ibid.*, 553, fig. 506). A Rhineland relief of a wagon for transporting wine-barrels, has eight parallel-sided spokes, small nave and thick felloe (Günther & Köpstein (eds.), 1975, Abb. 88). The Roman (Imperial date) bronze model of a chariot or two-wheeled cart found in the Tiber has very similar wheel-construction — thick felloe and eight parallel-edged spokes

(Jope, 1956, 541, fig. 484), but the relief of a boy's 'chariot' on a Trier sarcophagus of 3rd Century A.D. date has six spokes (*ibid.*, fig. 489). A Bordeaux sarcophagus of 3rd Century A.D. date shows a wheeled vehicle intended to be naturalistic, but with very floreate spokes with exaggeratedly convex edges (Bordeaux, Musée d'Aquitaine, 1973, 107, no. 95).

There is substantial evidence, from secular representation, of solid wheels in the Roman period. This is of interest since we appear to have an example of a solid cult-wheel, on a relief from Auberive (B6). Cato's *plaustrum maius* (Cato, 10, 2) – a four-wheeled cart, was clumsy, with solid wheels (White, 1975, 81). A number of bas-reliefs and wall-paintings (*ibid.*) show wagons with solid wheels formed from a single drum (*tympanum*) of timber. A funerary monument from Sulmona, Abruzzi, depicts a primitive two-wheeled vehicle with solid wheels (*ibid.*, 82). A vintage scene from Rome (Palazzo Mattei) represents a two-wheeled cart with wicker body and solid wheels (*ibid.*, pl.7). The evidence seems to suggest that solid-wheeled vehicles were used on farms, especially outside the Gallic provinces ; it may be that Roman carriage-builders to some degree lacked the skill of Celtic craftsmen (Jope, 1956, 545). Certainly many Latin terms for wheeled vehicles are of Celtic derivation (*ibid.*, 537).

The foregoing survey of Roman secular wheel-representation raises a number of questions also of relevance to cult-depictions. First, there are differences between true wheels and portrayals. For instance, the nave on stone sculptures is frequently wider and flatter than the functional specimens would suggest. Second, the tyre is rarely shown on secular sculpture. Third, there is sometimes stylization of the spokes (cf. the Bordeaux sarcophagus mentioned above). Another point of interest is that, for instance on the Trier *uallus*, no attempt has been made faithfully to represent the spokes – some are parallel-sided, some diverge. Thickness of the felloe in some cases argues for a multi-piece, segmented felloe, whereas a bentwood type of construction is clearly depicted on some examples. Fourth, though spoke-numbers do vary, eight is the favoured number on representations, whereas more – frequently ten or twelve – often occur on functional wooden survivals. On Trajan's Column eight is almost universal but the exceptions, like the ox-cart with twelve spokes, demonstrate that eight was not simply a schematized method of representing wheels on the column. A final point concerns odd and even numbers of spokes. Oddness is uncommon on functional examples, but eleven spokes are recorded at Bar Hill. This rarity is in fact reflected on Romano-Celtic cult-wheel representations. Odd numbers of spokes are known, for example at Aigues-Mortes (S24), but where it does occur the total is generally five or seven, and it could be argued (see previous chapters) that ritual significance should be assumed.

Romano-Celtic Cult Wheels

We may turn now to examine the cult-representations in detail to see how they compare with true wheels of the period and to assess the degree of realism, arguing from my analysis-sample of 274. The S-numbers quoted in the text refer to individual wheels in the sample (see Tables I-III [pp. 283-288] and figures [Pls. XXV-XLIX ; and pp. 290-293 for key to figures]). I turn first to the stone depictions. Immediately certain portrayals may be distinguished as having little or no attempt at realism. These include the barrel-wheel from Dôle (S21), the lobate-spoked examples from Belbèze (S22), Foeschen (S96) and Churcham (S43), the voluted wheel from Agey (S50), the exaggeratedly concave-edged spokes of the Obernburg (S75) and Meaux (S30) wheels (both carried as shields as part of Jupiter-groups), and the very stylized Saint-Pé example (S87). Perhaps also in this group should come the Quémigny carving (S76) where spokes and nave are reasonably realistic but the enclosing shape is oval, not round and the 'wheel' is again held as a shield (like the stylized Jupiter-wheels mentioned above [S75, 30]). Another schematized group comprises wheel-carvings which are mere incisions rather than attempts at in-the-round sculpture. These include the Risingham (S44) wheel, and a number of others, for example from Saverne, and some of the Pyrenean examples (S52-73), in addition to Petronell (S81-83), Chedworth (S84) and Bad Dürkheim (S93-95). Allied to this group are those where the nave or hub is entirely missing, as at Lypiatt Park (S6), Speyer (S92) and many others. Even more significant is that fact that a number of these stone representations have only four spokes, an unlikely number for a real wheel (unless of cast metal, like some later Bronze Age specimens alluded to above). At the very least, I should have thought, six spokes would be necessary, and eight is a much more realistic number. Other points of non-realism include the uneven distribution of spokes, as on the Garonne and Adour monument (S75) and at Petronell (S83) ; the grotesquely wedge-shaped spokes at Dompierre-les-Églises (S26) ; the curious placement of spokes at Valentine (S79), the missing spokes at Laudun (S14) ; the 'stalks' at Chedworth (S84) and at Bad Dürkheim (S94, 95), and the 'rays' at the latter site (S93 ; 94) ; and the curious branch-like spoke-extensions at Bois-de-la-Neuve-Grange (S40). Some of these stylistic anomalies may have cult-significance. The tree-feature just mentioned may have a connection with the association on many south-western Gaulish monuments of wheels with trees. The 'rays' at Bad Dürkheim may well represent solar symbols ; the stalks at this site and at Chedworth imply depiction of a carried standard. Whilst not suggesting any cultural link, this phenomenon does recall prehistoric Scandinavian rock-carvings (Gelling, 1969). The 'hanging' wheel at Saverne (S17) could (if one may be allowed to stretch speculation to its limits) represent an amulet worn around the neck. Once again the suspension-motif may be paralleled on the Late Bronze Age wheel-carved stone from Hérault (Briard, 1973, 153, fig. 12). The Dôle 'wheel' (S21) has possible associations with the Gaulish Hammer-God (see Chapter VI). The small number of spokes on many stone examples may or may not be of significance. As Piggott suggests (1979) four spokes may simply be a short-hand way of depicting a wheel on a monument or small object ; the same may be true of simple incision. If one looks at many Celtic cult-representations, for example the Genii Cucullati from Cirencester (Corinium Museum) and a large number of northern British examples (Ross, 1967, *passim*), it appears that naturalism is not necessary for ritual purposes as long as the idea of the god comes across to the spectator. The fact remains, however, that realism has been attempted by a number of craftsmen in carving cult-wheels.

In a few cases, as at Aigues-Mortes (S23, 24) ; Agey (S50) ; Obernburg (S75) ; Alzey (S4) ; Oehringen (S86) and Vaison (S9, 10), the iron tyre has been faithfully copied, demonstrating great attention to realism and to detail. This is curious at Agey and at Obernburg since otherwise these wheels are very stylized. In some instances, as at Mainz (S18), Aigues-Mortes, Vaison, Alzey, Castlesteads (S2, 3) and Oehringen, the wheel closely resembles a contemporary cart-wheel, and there are a number of other representations, as at Tongres (S91), Luxeuil (S34), Netherby (S1), where realism is aimed at if not actually achieved. Great care is sometimes taken, as at Vaison (S9, 10), to reproduce a three-dimensional nave ; in most cases the nave or hub appears in relief as a largish circle (unrealistic, as we have seen from looking at functional examples, but present on most of the secular depictions we have studied). In some instances, as at Saverne (S15, 16), the nave is shown as an open circle. One further point concerning spokes should be examined. Even with fairly naturalistically-portrayed wheels on cult-monuments, the spokes are sometimes impossibly wide, as at Dompierre (S26), at Malmaison (S39) and Jagsthausen (S85), or very narrow, as at Tongres (S91) and Vauvert (S49). Finally the Tongres (S91) wheel should be singled out since it has the appearance of being 'dished' or saucer-shaped. As will be seen below, this also occurs on one figurine and on a bronze model. If this 'dishing' is not simply a stone-working quirk, then it may be of significance for wheel-construction as a whole, since it is generally considered that purposeful 'dishing' did not come into being before the 16th Century (Jenkins, 1961, 27-28). The innovation appears to have occurred because such wheels were supposedly better able to take sideways thrusts as the vehicle jolted, and, in addition, gave more room for the body of a wagon (Thompson, 1976, 23).

Comparison between wooden, functional wheels, secular depictions and stone cult-representations demonstrates features of interest. Certain types of very stylized physical form appear on cult but not on real examples. The four-spoked type does not occur on the secular representations that I have been able to examine. Both categories possess a number of spoke-shapes (parallel, diverging, converging or convex-sided). But the very wedge-shaped or grotesquely concave-sided examples only appear on cult-portrayals. Likewise, odd disposition of spokes and uneven distribution of spokes occur on cult-representations only. Any conclusion drawn from such a comparison must be equivocal. We have seen that there are certain similarities in the realism of secular and cult-depictions. Nevertheless there are quite distinct differences. The lack of realism in some examples may be due to the desire for the *idea only* of a wheel to be represented. We have already seen that for a cult-object realism is not necessarily important and this may be true especially where a sun-symbol is being depicted. However, the very accurate cart-wheels sometimes represented argue for a very close association in ideas between wheels both as wheels and as solar symbols. If we may count the solid circular object clasped by the Auberive 'Wheel-God' (B6) as a solid, spokeless wheel then this lends credence to this association. One must therefore assume that the wheel as a cult-symbol, though in all probability representing the sun, had an entity of its own and did not lose it in order to become particularly sun-like. In other words the wheel frequently remains as a wheel rather than as a collection of radiating lines enclosed by a circle.

Finally, when talking of realism in stonework, one must remember the constraints of stoneworking. If you really want to represent a faithful copy of a functional wheel there is a limit to the three-dimensionalness that you can readily achieve.

I turn now to other cult-depictions, namely small cult-objects and models. These fall into two sub-groups, models and miscellaneous cult-items. Of the latter group the items from Le Châtelet (S100) ; Landouzy (S101) ; Willingham Fen (S102) ; the Allier factories (S104-106) ; Autun (S117) and Stobi (S118) are all figurines (the Allier examples being of pipe-clay, the others of bronze). Other clay items are in the form of reliefs. The wheel from Corbridge (S107) belongs to a mould and is associated with a deity and allied to this are the antefixes from Caerleon (S112, 113). The Housesteads (S108) and Malton (S109) items were once applied to pots and the Littlehampton (S115) and Manchester (S116) examples were painted on pots. The remaining specimens in the 'Miscellaneous' category are heterogeneous. Two Casterley Camp wheels (S197, 198) are scratched on bone discs ; the Farley Heath 'wheel-shape' (S103) was punched on a bronze sheet ; the Little Houghton (S114) depiction was moulded on a glass vessel. Finally we have two totally different types of wheel-depiction on the Gundestrup Bowl (S96, 111).

I intend to examine the physical forms grouped by raw material, since it may well have significance for wheel-type. Looking first at metal objects, the Gundestrup Cauldron silver wheel-symbols (S96, 111) were produced in the same way − by chasing on the upper surface of the metal after the rough shape had been hammered up from beneath (Olmsted, 1979, 15). The two accompanying the goddess are totally unrealistic, having delicate lobed spokes ; in contrast the wheel associated with a god and held by a being with horned helmet, is a naturalistic cart or chariot-wheel with narrow, tyred felloe, small-diametered hub and sixteen (if reconstructed whole) spokes. The two lobate wheels (S96) must be taken as purely symbolic, stylized portrayals ; the multi-spoked example (S111) has significance as a wheel (of Iron Age type) in its own right.

Of the bronzes the Farley Heath strip has a stylized sun-wheel produced by punch-technique. All the motifs on this complex mythological item are schematized, and include 'matchstick men' and sketchy depictions of beasts. The figurines divide quite sharply. The wheels accompanying Fortuna are four-spoked and the Autun example is nave-less. By contrast, the wheels accompanying the Wheel-God Jupiter himself are more realistic, with six spokes, and, in the case of the wheels at Landouzy and Willingham Fen (S101, 102), care has been taken with naturalistic nave-depiction showing characteristically Celtic long, small-diametered hubs.

Of possible significance is the 'dishing' of the Le Châtelet wheel (S100). It should be remembered that the bronze figures would have been cast and it is relatively easy to cast a complicated shape – so realism is more possible here than on, for example, stonework ; but at the same time decoration, if required, is also easier to achieve. The non-ornamentation here could be important.

The clay figurines and other clay items are distinctive in being a particularly realistic group. The Allier examples, and those from Corbridge and Housesteads (S104-108) all have felloe-tyres. The naves are usually naturalistic. Spoke-numbers vary between five (Allier) (an unusual number) and twelve (Housesteads). The latter number reflects the construction of functional Roman examples looked at above. The Caerleon wheels (S112, 113) are curious in this group in being naveless. The clay wheel-portrayals were produced in one of two ways. The figurines and the antifixes were either moulded (the Corbridge item was itself a mould) or, as at Malton and Housesteads, wheels were applied from strips of clay. The incised spindle-whorl from Casterley is very stylized ; it is difficult to judge whether it is a ritual or entirely secular item. The two pots decorated with painted wheels are semi-naturalistic ; neither possess hub or tyre but each has eight spokes. The Littlehampton example (S115) is curious in that one spoke continues beyond the felloe, presumably a mistake. This recalls the error made by the stonemason of the Bachos-Binos wheel (S51) where a spoke was originally placed in the wrong spot.

The remaining wheels in this miscellaneous category are of glass and bone. The Casterley Camp bone discs bear incised rays similar to many stone examples cited above. The Little Houghton glass wheel (S114) was moulded and has eight narrow spokes and a thick felloe. Apart from the lack of nave (the glass is damaged anyway) this wheel is fairly realistic.

There are a number of similarities between stone and miscellaneous votive objects. Incision, four spokes, navelessness, lobate spokes all occur as stylistic characteristics on both types. Realism is demonstrated in the two groups by multi-spoked wheels, tyres and three-dimensional hubs (some larger – as on secular and cult stonework – than functional examples). Parallel, convex, and diverging spokes appear in both groups.

As a generalisation it is fair to state that there are less eccentric decorative elements among the small cult-objects than in the stonework. As far as one can say with such a small sample, realism is more predominant within the miscellaneous category. As regards cult-significance and stylization the most important item is the sheet-bronze strip from Farley Heath, which is only *just* a wheel, and looks much more like a heliolatric symbol than a copy of an utilitarian object.

The final, and largest category in our sample comprises the models. For the purpose of the present survey I have excluded the gold and silver filigree specimens since they are first and foremost pieces of Roman jewellery and may only have a secondary significance within the Celtic provinces as cult-symbols (see Chapters II, III). With models we have to make it clear that many are brooches, not true models, although wheel-brooches have a significantly Romano-Celtic distribution. It is among this group that one, naturally, finds the most unrealistic and stylized items. This is because decorative and ritual elements are, in my opinion, being combined. However, in some instances, in looking at the wheel-element alone, it is impossible to tell wheel-models from brooches and it therefore seems valid to group the two object-types (model and brooch) in terms of ritual. I do not examine wheel-brooches and wheel-models separately ; in a number of museums in France it has been impossible to study the reverse of the items since only closed display-cases were made available to me. In any case, if the catch-plate is completely broken and/or worn or corroded, the evidence is ambiguous. It is of interest that although proven true models are generally the more realistic, in some instances known brooches are equally faithful copies of functional wheels.

It is among the models (used hereafter as a blanket-term for all miniatures) that the most variation and stylization occurs. Realism is muted and it is quite rare that all the major naturalistic features − felloe, tyre, long nave, large number of spokes − are present on one item. One of the most realistic models in the illustrated sample is not Roman but an Iron Age example from Stradonice Hradiste (S126). Other, Roman, wheels of realistic type include those from Icklingham (S145) (found close to a wheel-brooch) ; Verulamium (S147) ; Felmingham Hall (S148) ; some Gaulish wheels in St.-Germain (S166, 167) ; Hautepin (206) (a definite brooch) ; Böhming (236, 237) ; Cologne (S247) ; Lavoye (256, 257) ; Bazoches-les-Hautes (S264) ; Mainz (S274) and the Dinant area (S273). The Kettering wheel (S146) is also realistic. A group of wheel-models of great interest came to my notice too late to be included in the sample. These are from Augst in Switzerland. They are naturalistic, in all probability come from shrines, one bears a votive inscription and is a particularly faithful copy of a cart-wheel, with long nave and careful moulding (Pls. 23-25). The large number of spokes on many examples cited above, like that from Felmingham Hall with twelve spokes, also betokens realism.

Other miniatures, like those from Trier (S121, 124); Gusenburg (S122-123) and Zugmantel (S127) are semi-realistic, with flat or perforated naves and six or eight spokes. The brooches with rim-knobs (and these are all brooches) have obvious decorative elements. In many instances, however, as at Corbridge (S138),the knobs coincide with the felloe-ends of the spokes. It may be purely fanciful, but it could be that the knobs represent an exaggerated form of spoke-endings. The wooden wheel from Bar Hill and the model from Fully (see above) should be recalled in this connection. Another decorative element which may reflect accurate copying of true wheel-features is that of spoke-ribbing (already discussed in a ritual context, see Chapter III). This could possibly mirror the marks left in lathe-turning on wooden spokes. But there is possible cult-symbolism also. At an exhibition held at the Schloss Lamberg in Steyr (Austria, 1980) entitled 'Die Hallstattkultur', I was struck by the reconstruction of a Hallstatt funerary wagon [2] of 7th Century B.C. date, from Býčískála-Höhle, Mähren (Czechoslovakia). The wheels had horizontal groups of ribbing and were sheathed in new bronze. Another such wheel was mounted on a vertical turn-table and rotated at speed. The result was extremely heliolatric, and the facets of the ribs particularly caught the light (an original wheel from the site, with ribbing on the spokes, is in the Naturhistorisches Museum, Vienna). The Romano-Celtic ribbed models may have the same function, as may the decoration on the felloes of some examples – as at Lavoye (S257); Kettering (S146); Amiens (S140); Pfünz (S233) and Villeneuve (S242). Even the knobs (including nave-knobs at, for example, Cologne [S174]) and the denticulations on French examples (175-177) could have a solar effect, especially if rotated. Other decorative features which may be solar include the thick, grooved, felloe at Langenhain (S235) and on a French specimen (S165); the swastika-spokes at Slavonin (S248); the rim-circles at Sarre-Union (S268) and the scallopped rim-edges at Cologne (S136).

The reason why there is much more stylization, decoration and variety among models than in either of the other two categories may be partly, as I have said, due to the combined function of ritual talisman or votive object and jewellery. Also the raw material may be relevant. It is easier to

---

[2] Dr. Kromer (personal info. 1/12/80) interprets this vehicle as part of a two-wheeled cart/chariot.

cast metal into complicated shapes than it is to carve stone and there may also have been more individuality amongst bronzesmiths than stonemasons, even though there were centralized workshops among the former. There are nonetheless certain, sometimes unnaturalistic, similarities between this third group and the other two. Four-spoked, naveless examples occur among models, for instance at Wederath (S227-231); Toulouse (S265); and Cologne (S240). The Augst (S238) and Magdalensberg (S134) moulds imply very thin, almost two-dimensional, spokes. The Hounslow model (S149) has four very narrow spokes but a thick felloe. Lobate wheels occur at Dieburg (S244). A Cologne model (S247) with six spokes and flat nave closely resembles several stone cult and secular wheel-representations. The Iron Age model from Fully (S249) recalls the Bad Dürkheim quarry-carvings (S93-95). One French model (S171) reflects the cult-wheels from Tongres and Le Châtelet in its apparent dishing. I cannot be certain of this particular instance since I was unable to examine the wheel except through glass.

As regards spoke-shape, all three categories possess realistic, parallel-sided, diverging/converging and convex-sided spokes. In addition models like that from Kapersburg, with very concave spokes (S234), bear close resemblances to the Obernburg and Meaux stone wheels. Models such as two from France (S172) and a Saalburg brooch (S128) are similar in spoke-shape to, for instance, the Butterstadt stone wheel (S5). A Trier brooch (S119) reflects the stone wheel from Dompierre (S26). One general statement is that convexity and concavity in spoke-shape are particularly over-emphasized on some models. The Lakenheath brooch (S132), for example, has convex spokes like some realistic wheel-carvings on secular and ritual monuments, but the shape is exaggerated so that the spokes terminate almost in a point. Likewise the very concave examples – as at Icklingham (S162); Andernach (S143); Trier (S144); Augst (S210-218) and Pfünz (S232) recall stone Jupiter-column wheels like Butterstadt and Meaux.

Models of unrealistic form (mainly brooches) arrange themselves into types more readily than do any other group of wheels but, for present purposes, it would be inappropriate to concoct a rigid typological scheme. There seems to be little, if any, distributional significance apart from the clustering of certain shapes at individual sites, as at Augst. The same is true of stone and other cult-representations.

A final note should be taken of raw material. The majority of the sample is bronze but, whilst one Lavoye lead example is of eight-spoked type, over 200 lead examples of simple, four-spoked, type are recorded (from one and the same site) ; I have come across no elaborately-decorated lead specimens. Although strictly excluded from the sample, I should state that the gold and silver jewellery-pendants from, for instance, Dolaucothi and Newstead are all virtually identical to each other, with grooved filigree spokes and felloes, and circular three-dimensional (though schematized) naves.

Note on Absolute Frequency of Attributes (see Tables I-III)

Certain points of interest emerge on examination of absolute frequencies of the attributes applied to the sample (see pp. 283-288 and 289). The three groups are I - Stone ; II - Miscellaneous ; III - Models.

The figures for attribute 1 show the predominance of single, regularly-spaced, spokes in all three groups. The numbers in attribute 2 demonstrate that in group I three spoke-numbers stand out — 4, 6 and 8, with 4 being twice as common as either of the others. In group II, 6 and 8 are the most frequent spoke-numbers. In the case of group III the same thing occurs but with 6 being more common than 8. With attribute 3, thin spokes are the most frequent type, but in the case of group I, linear incision is of importance. As regards spoke-shape (attribute 4), there is overwhelming evidence for shape 'a' (parallel-sided). Spoke-ribbing (attribute 5) only occurs on models (group III) ; spoke-decoration (attribute 6) is uncommon in all three groups. The presence of a tyre (attribute 7) does occur on a significant number of examples, but it is absent in most cases in the three groups. Linear representations of felloe-thickness (attribute 8) occurs almost exclusively on stonework and, in this group, thin and thick felloes are equally common ; the latter is true of group II, but in group III thick felloes predominate. Like ribbing, knobbing (attribute 9) only occurs in group III, and felloe-decoration apart from knobs (attribute 10) is infrequent in all groups. In group I the nave or hub (attribute 11) is present and absent on an equal numbers of examples ; in groups II and III, however, the hub is more often present than absent, strikingly so in the case of group III. With regard to attribute 12, nave-shape, in group I realism and non-realism are close in frequency ; by contrast stylization is much more common in groups II and III. Hub or nave-decoration (attribute 13) is absent in group I and II and uncommon, though sometimes present, in group III. Raw material (attribute 14) speaks for itself. In overall design (attribute 15), stylization is more frequent than realism in groups I and III ; realism and schematization are evenly balanced in group II.

Many of the above frequencies seem to reflect not only the constraints of the different media employed but also the ambivalent role of models as decorative pieces and as items of religious symbolism.

TABLE I : Group I

Frequencies of Attributes : *Stone*. Sample = 95
(See Attribute-List, p. 289)

1. *Spoke-disposition*			
single, regularly-spaced	(I)	82	
paired, regularly-spaced	(II)	1	
irregularly-spaced	(III)	12	
2. *Spoke-numbers*			
three		1	
four		43	
five		2	
six		18	
seven		2	
eight		23	
nine		1	
ten		4	
eleven		0	
twelve		0	
thirteen		0	
fourteen		0	
fifteen		0	
sixteen		0	
?		1	
3. *Spoke-thickness*			
linear	(i)	29	
thin	(ii)	40	
thick	(iii)	26	
4. *Spoke-shape*			
a		64	
a/b		1	
b		4	
c		7	
d		6	
e		5	
f		4	
g		1	
h		3	
a = 64			
other = 31			

Table I (cont'd)

5. *Ribbing*	0
6. *Other spoke-decoration*	5
7. *Tyre on felloe*	
present	8
absent	87
8. *Felloe-thickness*	
linear (i)	34
thin (ii)	31
thick (iii)	30
9. *Knobbing*	none
10. *Other felloe-decoration*	
present	7
absent	88
11. *Hub/Nave*	
present	45
absent	48
uncertain	2
12. *Hub-shape*	
realistic (a)	20
stylized (b)	25
13. *Decoration on hub*	none
14. *Raw Material* (E)	stone, all examples
15. *Overall design of wheel*	
realistic (a)	19
stylized (b)	76

TABLE II : Group II

Frequencies of Attributes : Miscellaneous. Sample = 23
(See Attribute-List)

1. *Disposition of spokes*		
single, regularly-spaced	(I)	19
paired, regularly-spaced	(II)	0
irregularly-spaced	(III)	3
uncertain		1

Table II (cont'd)

2. *Spoke-number*		
	three	0
	four	3
	five	1
	six	7
	seven	0
	eight	9
	nine	0
	ten	0
	eleven	0
	twelve	1
	thirteen	0
	fourteen	0
	fifteen	0
	sixteen	1
	?	1
3. *Spoke-thickness*		
	linear (i)	3
	thin (ii)	14
	thick (iii)	5
	?	1
4. *Spoke-shape*		
	a	12
	a/b	1
	a/c	2
	b	0
	c	4
	d	0
	e	2
	f	1
	g	0
	h	0
5. *Ribbing*		
	present	none
6. *Other spoke-decoration*		1
7. *Tyre*		
	present	6
	absent	17
8. *Felloe-thickness*		
	linear (i)	2
	thin (ii)	9
	thick (iii)	12

Table II (cont'd)

9. *Knobbing*	
present	none
10. *Other felloe-decoration*	
present	2
absent	21
11. *Hub/Nave*	
present	14
absent	9
12. *Hub-shape*	
realistic (a)	9
stylized (b)	5
13. *Hub-decoration*	
present	none
absent	all
14. *Raw Material*	
Bronze (A)	6
Silver (B)	2
Gold (C)	0
Lead (D)	0
Stone (E)	0
Bone (F)	2
Pipe-clay (G)	3
Terracotta (H)	9
Glass (I)	1
15. *Overall design of wheel*	
realistic (a)	11
stylized (b)	12

TABLE III : Group III

Frequencies of Attributes : Models. Sample = 156
(See Attribute-List)

1. *Disposition of spokes*		
single, regularly-spaced	(I)	110
paired, regularly-spaced	(II)	3
irregularly-spaced	(III)	7

Table III (cont'd)

2. *Spoke-numbers*
three	1
four	51
five	2
six	53
seven	1
eight	40
nine	1
ten	2
eleven	0
twelve	5
thirteen	0
fourteen	0
fifteen	0
sixteen	0

3. *Spoke-thickness*
linear	(i)	0
thin	(ii)	104
thick	(iii)	45
thin/thick	(ii/iii)	7

4. *Spoke-shape*
a	100
a/b	1
b	7
b/d	3
c	1
c/d	14
d	9
e	12
f	1
g	1
h	6
a/h	3

5. *Ribbing*
present	17
absent	139

6. *Other spoke-decoration*
present	6
absent	150

7. *Tyre*
present	33
absent	123

Table III (cont'd)

8. *Felloe-thickness*			
	linear	(i)	0
	thin	(ii)	40
	thick	(iii)	116
9. *Knobbing*			
	present		32
	absent		124
10. *Other felloe-decoration*			
	present		30
	absent		126
11. *Hub/Nave*			
	present		136
	absent		20
12. *Hub-shape*			
	realistic	(a)	49
	stylized	(b)	87
13. *Hub-decoration*			
	present		22
	absent		114
14. *Raw Material*			
	Bronze	(A)	150
	Lead	(D)	6
			(only in sample. Over 200 lead examples come from one site)
15. *Overall design of wheel*			
	realistic	(a)	58
	stylized	(b)	98

ATTRIBUTE-LIST

Spokes

1. Position — single, regularly-spaced   I
     — paired, regularly-spaced   II
     — irregularly-spaced   III
2. Number — 3-16
3. Thickness — linear (i)
     — 2-dimensional :   < 3% thin   (ii)   (3% = 2.83 mm my drawings : percentage is of circumference)
             > 3% thick   (iii)
4. Shape — || \| /\ )(( ) () ((other
      a   b   c   d   e   f   g   h
5. Ribs — present − +
   — absent − −

Felloe

7. Presence of tyre − +
 absence of tyre − −
8. Thickness — linear (i)
     — 2-dimensional :   (ii) < 3% of circumf. thin (3% = 2.83 mm)
            (iii) > 3% of circumf. thick
9. Knobs − + or −
10. Other decoration − + or −

Hub

11. Presence of − +
 absence of − −
12. Shape — realistic   (a)
    — stylized   (b)
13. Decoration − + or −

14. *Raw Material*
 Bronze   A
 Silver   B
 Gold   C
 Lead   D
 Stone   E
 Bone   F
 Pipe-clay   G
 Terracotta   H
 Glass   I

15. *Overall Design of wheel*
 realistic   (a)
 stylized   (b)

Sample Site-List

Group I (Stone)

1. Netherby
2. Castlesteads
3. Castlesteads
4. Alzey
5. Butterstadt
6. Lypiatt Park
7. Nimes area (Esp. 428)
8. Gilly, Nimes (Esp. 430)
9. Vaison
10. Séguret
11. Nimes, Notre-Dame-de-Laval (Esp. 2681)
12. Marsillargues (Esp. 524)
13. Lansargues (Esp. 517)
14. Laudun, near (Esp. 513)
15. Saverne (Esp. 5691)
16. Near Saverne (Esp. 5687)
17. Saverne (Esp. 5688)
18. Mainz (Esp. 5771)
19. Theley (Esp. 5116)
20. Niederwürzbach
21. Dôle
22. Belbèze
23. Aigues-Mortes
24. Aigues-Mortes
25. Garonne & Adour
26. Dompierre-les-Églises
27. Between Salon and Aurons (Esp. 1691)
28. Pyrenees (Esp. 863)
29. Wasserwald
30. Meaux (Esp. 3207)
31. Jublains (Esp. 3058)
32. Jublains (Esp. 3058)
33. Jublains (Esp. 3058)
34. Luxeuil
35. Saverne area (Esp. 5969)
36. Saverne area (Esp. 5969)
37. Saverne area (Esp. 5705)
38. Saverne (Esp. 5688)
39. Malmaison, near (Esp. 4666)
40. Bois-de-la-Neuve-Grange (Esp. 4526)
41. Forêt de Saint-Quirin (Esp. 4528)
42. Saverne
43. Churcham, Gloucestershire
44. Risingham
45. Courbessac
46. Cologne
47. Commetreuil
48. Saverne
49. Vauvert
50. Agey
51. Bachos Binos
52. Prieuré d'Arnes
53. Birdoswald
54. Saverne
55. Saverne
56. Saverne
57. Saverne
58. Saverne
59. Housesteads
60. Le Mont-Saçon
61. Le Mont-Saçon
62. Hagenbach
63. High Rochester
64. Pyrenees
65. Pyrenees
66. Pyrenees
67. Pyrenees
68. Pyrenees
69. Montmaurin

70. Nîmes
71. Pyrenees
72. Pyrenees
73. Castlesteads
74. Mouhet
75. Obernburg
76. Quémigny
77. Susa
78. Tours
79. Valentine
80. Vienne (Isère)
81. Petronell
82. Petronell
83. Petronell
84. Chedworth
85. Jagsthausen
86. Oehringen
87. Saint-Pé
88. Sammuran
89. Foeschen
90. Wolfstein
91. Tongres
92. Speyer
93. Bad Dürkheim
94. Bad Dürkheim
95. Bad Dürkheim

Group II (Miscellaneous)

96. Gundestrup
97. Casterley Camp
98. Casterley Camp
99. Casterley Camp
100. Le Châtelet
101. Landouzy-la-Ville
102. Willingham Fen
103. Farley Heath
104. Allier area (factories)
105. Allier area (factories)
106. Allier area (factories)
107. Corbridge
108. Housesteads
109. Malton

110. Malton
111. Gundestrup
112. Caerleon
113. Caerleon
114. Little Houghton
115. Littlehampton
116. Manchester
117. Autun
118. Stobi

Group III (Models)

119. Trier (Maar, Trier Nord)
120. Trier (Saarstrasse)
121. Trier (unprovenanced)
122. Gusenburg
123. Gusenburg
124. Trier (unprovenanced)
125. Baden-Württemburg (unprovenanced)
126. Stradonice-Hradiste (Iron Age)
127. Zugmantel
128. Saalburg
129. Saalburg
130. Rheingönheim
131. Wederath-Belgium
132. Lakenheath
133. Kapersburg
134. Kapersburg
135. Cologne
136. Cologne
137. Southern France
138. Corbridge
139. France (Ashmolean Museum)
140. Amiens
141. Augst
142. Icklingham
143. Andernach
144. Trier
145. Icklingham
146. Kettering
147. Verulamium
148. Felmingham Hall

149. Hounslow
150. Lavacherie
151. France (unprovenanced)
152. Balastière de Guignicourt
153. Balastière de Guignicourt
154. France (unprovenanced)
155. Naix
156. France (unprovenanced)
157. France (unprovenanced)
158. Marne
159. Marne
160. Marne
161. Marne
162. Mont-Berny
163. France (unprovenanced)
164. France (unprovenanced)
165. Magny-Lambert (?)
166. France (unprovenanced)
167. Seine, Paris
168. Champlieu
169. France (unprovenanced)
170. France (unprovenanced)
171. France (unprovenanced)
172. Southern France
173. France (unprovenanced)
174. Cologne
175. France, possibly Paris area
176. France, possibly Paris area
177. France (unprovenanced)
178. France (unprovenanced)
179. Weissenthaum
180. Lanslevillard
181. Lanslevillard
182. Lanslevillard
183. Lanslevillard
184. Lanslevillard
185. Lanslevillard
186. Lanslevillard
187. Housesteads
188. Sewingshields
189. Sâone-et-Loire
190. France (unprovenanced)

191. Marne
192. Seine, Paris
193. France (unprovenanced)
194. Southern France
195. Southern France
196. London
197. Bavay
198. Cologne
199. Juslenville
200. Juslenville
201. Mainz
202. Elouges
203. Tongres
204. France (unprovenanced)
205. Cologne
206. Hautepin
207. Dinant area
208. France or Germany
209. Carnuntum
210. Augst
211. Augst
212. Augst
213. Augst
214. Augst
215. Augst
216. Augst
217. Augst
218. Augst
219. Saalburg
220. Sâone-et-Loire
221. France (unprovenanced)
222. France (unprovenanced)
223. Rhine
224. Strasbourg
225. Zugmantel
226. Zugmantel
227. Wederath-Belginum
228. Wederath-Belginum
229. Wederath-Belginum
230. Wederath-Belginum
231. Wederath-Belginum
232. Pfünz

233. Pfünz
234. Kapersburg
235. Langenhain
236. Böhming
237. Böhming
238. Augst
239. Staré Hradisko (Iron Age)
240. Cologne
241. Wederath (late Iron Age)
242. Villeneuve d'Asq
243. Jonvelle
244. Dieburg
245. Lille Museum
246. Pas-de-Calais
247. Cologne (model)
248. Slavonin
249. Fully (Iron Age)
250. Lavoye ⎫
251. Lavoye ⎬ lead + over
252. Lavoye ⎬ 200 joined
253. Lavoye ⎬ in bands
254. Lavoye ⎭

255. Lavoye (lead)
256. Lavoye
257. Lavoye
258. Néris-les-Bains
259. Montot. Châtelet de Nambon
260. Guiry-Gadancourt
261. Blois
262. Argentomagus
263. Alesia (Alise-Sainte-Reine)
264. Bazoches-les-Hautes
265. Toulouse
266. Vesqueville
267. Bolards
268. Sarre-Union
269. Vienne (?)
270. Vienne (?)
271. Besançon
272. Nijmegen
273. Dinant area
274. Mainz

Note on sample-illustrations. – For purposes of comparability, the wheels have all been reduced to fit within a true circle of constant diameter.

CHAPTER X

Conclusion

The task of drawing together the threads of this complex subject is a difficult and formidable one. We will first recapitulate the nature of the evidence for the Wheel as a Cult-Symbol. This thesis is based primarily upon archaeological evidence, which comprises epigraphy, stone sculptures, statuettes, models, ritual furniture, miscellaneous ritual objects and utilitarian items. Of these categories some are unequivocally religious, others primarily secular. One may in fact construct a hypothetical 'triangle of sacredness' with altars and sculptures at the apex, statuettes, temple-furniture and miniature items below ; and, finally, such objects as swastika-decorated pottery at the base.

Models

Of the categories outlined above the only one about which there is particular ambiguity is that of models. One of the conclusions of this study has been firmly to establish models as objects of ritual significance, even if this significance often took the form of their use as talismanic 'good-luck' symbols. Models in general frequently come from ritual contexts (Green, 1975c). The votive nature of wheel-models is occasionally beyond question, as in the Augst example (A140) with its votive inscription. The positive identification of wheel-models with deities is sometimes demonstrated, for example at Plessis (A73) where a wheel-model is an integral part of a Jupiter-representation. A further point concerns wheel-models as jewellery items. Both necklaces and brooches may be decorative in primary function but I have attempted to establish a ritual aspect. In the first place, both brooches and necklaces sometimes have a religious context, as at Backworth (AB1). Second, brooches and true models may be found together, as at Icklingham (AB8, 27) suggesting that there may be little difference between their respective functions. Third, on some gold necklaces (for example Thérouanne [A74] and Balèsmes

[A102]), other symbols accompany the wheel, indicative, perhaps, of other than secular significance for the wheel itself.

Symbols

It is necessary to examine the evidence for the function of the wheel as a symbol. There is good evidence for the wheel-motif representing the sun. We know from classical literature that the wheel could be a solar sign. We have also the physical form of the wheel with its undertones of sun-rays, movement across the sky, and the surrounding nimbus. In Romano-Celtic contexts certain decorative elements appear to enhance the solar image – sun-symbols themselves appear on brooches ; knobbing and ribbing appear ; finally the media for representation could be important – gold, bright bronze, and sometimes tinned or silvered metal. However, in Romano-Celtic cult contexts it appears that the wheel is not important merely as a solar motif but also in its own right. This is implied by the very realistic design of a number of wheels. Nevertheless, extreme stylization does occur, and comparisons between non-liturgical representation and cult-depiction indicate that a schematic rendering of the symbol was sometimes enough to conjure up the correct image for god and worshipper. For example, simple four-spoked wheels are more common on cult-depictions than on secular representations of functional wheeled vehicles.

Other heliolatric symbols appear to have a strong cult relationship with the wheel in Romano-Celtic contexts. These include the swastika (perhaps the most important), the rosette, the 'S' sign, the concentric circle motif and the 'St Andrew's Cross'.

The purpose of the swastika on Romano-Celtic cult items seems to be similar to, though not identical with, the wheel itself. The idea of rotary motion is again expressed by its physical form. The crooked arms may represent spoke and rim combined. The association of wheel and swastika is a recurrent one. Wheel and swastika-brooches are both concentrated on the Rhine frontier. Swastikas and wheels are associated on Pyrenean altars frequently dedicated to Jupiter. It is of interest that swastika-marks on pottery are also concentrated in this region of south-west France, and the swastika appears to have been favoured particularly by the people of this area. Finally, 'X' mark and concentric-circle decoration on swastika-brooches may attest heliolatric or celestial significance. The 'X' sign sometimes appears to have wheel-associations in Romano-Celtic cult contexts. In physical form it resembles a rimless wheel (of stylized four-spoked type), but it could equally represent a thunderbolt (see below) or may combine the symbolism of both. That it is a ritual sign is attested by its presence on other sacred items. The concentric circle or ring-and-dot is controversial. The motif occurs throughout prehistory and in the Roman world as a secular decorative mark. However, there are later European prehistoric solar associations, for instance on petroglyphs, and on Hallstatt wheel-pendants. In some instances then this symbol may be a heliolatric alternative to the wheel. The association of both X-motif and concentric circle with Sucellus (see below) and with axes (see below) may lend credence to the motifs as sky-symbols. Finally, both the Wheel-God from Corbridge (C10) and the Celtic warrior with wheel-pendant from Fox-Amphoux (B45) bear the concentric circle motif on their shields.

The rosette is of some interest. We know that the rose had celestial implications in classical funerary ritual. Its physical form is sun-like. On Celtic coinage the rosette was converted to a wheel and a sun-sign (Allen, 1980, 54-55). In Romano-Celtic iconography the solar significance of the rosette is sometimes very striking. For instance the wheel-model from Grand-Jailly (A101) bears both 'S' and rosette-symbols. Some wheel-models and sculptures are very roseate in form, as at Meaux (B77). The Tresques stone (B152) bears both wheels and rosettes, each with seven spokes or petals, suggesting a strong association between wheel and rosette.

It is difficult to see what the 'S' symbol represents. It could be a lightning-flash, a snake, or a symbol of unknown significance. That it has an association with wheel-symbolism is not in doubt. 'S' and wheel-sign occur on Celtic coinage (Allen, 1980). The 'S' appears on the Grand-Jailly model (A101); it occurs with the Le Châtelet Wheel-God (C2); it appears on the Silchester wheel-decorated pot (C54). The latter, with alternating 'S' and wheel-symbols, recalls the Urnfield and Hallstatt sun and water-bird motifs but the hypothesis of duck-symbolism for the 'S' in a Romano-Celtic context may be too tenuous to maintain.

The last symbol which has strong celestial associations with the wheel is the axe (and double-axe). Axes and wheels appear frequently as models in later prehistoric Europe and here axes occasionally appear to possess overt solar associations. The ritual significance of axes as Romano-Celtic models has been discussed (Green, 1975c). In Britain certain axe-models demonstrate solar or sky-symbolism. They are decorated with 'X's, concentric circles and once, at Woodeaton, with a swastika. At the same site there occurs an axe-model with a ligatured 'X' – possibly a degenerate wheel-sign — and six eagles (the Roman theriomorphic sky-symbol of Jupiter). The double-axe as a model is an even stronger candidate for sky-symbolism. At Balèsmes for instance (A102) wheel-sign, crescent and double-axe occur together. The double-axe, at least, may be a storm, rain or thunderbolt sign. It certainly has this significance in other sky-religions, notably that of Jupiter Dolichenus, the Syrian Baal of Commagene (Merlat, 1960). If the double-axe does represent a weather-symbol, the Balèsmes item is of interest in that sun, moon and storm-energy are all represented. This brings me to thunder-symbolism in general. The 'X' could be a thunderbolt sign in that its physical appearance is not unlike a stylized double-axe. There is also a similarity in physical form between 'X' and thunderbolt on some wheel-bearing monuments, notably that from Vauvert (B20). The Romano-Celtic Sky-God, like his Roman counterpart Jupiter, has strong associations with thunder and thunderbolts. On wheel-bearing monuments the thunderbolt is frequently present. This association culminates at Vauvert (B20) where the wheel and thunderbolt signs possess virtually identical stylization apart from the presence of the rim in the case of the wheel. If solar and thunderbolt elements are closely associated the reason may lie in the fertilization weather-aspect of thunderbolt-symbolism. Both sun and rain make crops grow (we shall see, below, the importance of fertility to the Sky-God cult). It is necessary, at this juncture, to examine the Romano-Celtic Wheel-God in general before considering thunder-symbolism further.

The Wheel-God and Sky-God

There is a deity occurring in the Romano-Celtic provinces of North-West Europe who is consistently represented bearing a wheel. He may be depicted in human form, or epigraphically, or both. In the majority of cases this deity appears, from art-form, dedication or associated emblems, to be equated with the classical sky-god Jupiter. That he is not a straightforward representation of the Roman god is indicated by the fact that in classical contexts the wheel and Jupiter are not generally associated, neither is Jupiter a solar god in classical religion. The presence of the wheel as a symbol in pre-Roman Celtic and pre-Celtic Europe, and its non-association with the classical Jupiter leads one to believe that there may have been a Celtic solar power represented by a wheel before the Roman period. At the time of the conquests of the North-West provinces there was a natural conflation between Celtic solar god and Jupiter because the realm of both was the sky. So the resulting Romano-Celtic

Sky-God was both a solar and a celestial deity with all the other functions of the classical Jupiter.

In returning to the thunder-element in the Sky-God cult, the question must be raised as to whether Taranis may be equated with the Celtic Wheel-God. Taranis is a Thunderer by definition. He is linked with Jupiter epigraphically and in one literary source. Taranis may be linked with an aspect of a Romano-Celtic Jupiter but without equation with the Celtic god with a wheel. As well as a solar entity there may have been a pre-Roman Celtic Thunder-God, who was also equated with an aspect of Jupiter because of Jupiter's thunder-element. Whilst wheel and thunder symbols are closely associated in Romano-Celtic religion, Taranis cannot by definition be identical with the Wheel-God.

Certain features of the Romano-Celtic Wheel-God, arising from this study, are of extreme interest. They include various aspects of his function, and his association with certain other divinities. First, one or two points arise from aspects of the wheel-symbols themselves. In the Pyrenees, where one finds small altars with wheels, swastikas and dedications to Jupiter, there are instances where there appears to be substitution of the heliolatric symbol for an epigraphic dedication and *uice uersa*. If this is significant in religious terms it implies that the name of the god is to an extent interchangeable with his symbols. Whilst I would not like to read too much into this, it does suggest great Celticism. A second point concerns the multiplication of the solar symbol on certain monuments. For instance on the tombstone from Wasserwald (B167), in Alsace, the wheel occurs several times on the same stone. Likewise in the Pyrenees swastika and wheel sometimes occur on the same altar. The intensification by multiplication of the sky-motif occurs and, at Tongres (B150), wheel, peacock, thunderbolt, eagle and sceptre all appear.

Some aspects of the Romano-Celtic Wheel-God are of significance in that they are not obvious and natural aspects of Roman sky-symbolism. Perhaps the most overtly alien concept associated with the cult is chthonicism. The Romano-Celtic Sky-God on the Jupiter-Giant columns (sometimes accompanied by a wheel) appears to be a dualistic divinity necessarily connected with the forces of darkness and evil as well as with light. This dualism may be reflected in wheel-symbolism. Wheel-Models occur in sepulchral contexts, for instance on funerary monuments in Alsace. Wheel-models and lunar crescents occur in association, for example at Backworth (AB1) and Balèsmes (A102). Wheel-God and snake are associated on Jupiter-columns at, for example, Séguret (B144), and once with a ram-horned snake (possibly combining fertility and chthonicism) in Gloucestershire (BB13). Wheel-models of lead — a heavy base metal used for *defixiones*, and possibly with a chthonic element — sometimes occur. This seemingly paradoxical dualism is not as curious as may at first appear. There are parallels, for example, in Mithraism. The classical world had the idea that the sun itself revolved through the sky visiting the lower regions at night. Jupiter-Giant columns themselves could have been a development from sacred trees, in this case possibly linking upper and lower worlds.

Another curious association is that between wheel-symbolism and water. It is interesting that such an association occurs first in the Bronze Age where, on metalwork, sun-wheel and water-bird are connected. In a Romano-Celtic context we occasionally have the same association between aquatic bird and wheel-sign. Wheels may be associated with springs, as at Bourbonne, and rivers, as in the Loire and the Seine. Allied to this a number of Jupiter-Giant sculptures were sited near water and there is the occurrence of axe-models dedicated to Jupiter in aquatic contexts and of miniature thunderbolts associated with a spring. The fertilizing element in the thunderbolt sign may be recalled here.

Fertility and healing may be associated with water-symbolism attached to the Celtic Sky-God. One major role for the classical Apollo was that of healer. By Imperial Roman times he was also a solar deity. In Romano-Celtic contexts the epithet 'Belenus' for Apollo implies a solar aspect and he is occasionally associated with a swastika, as at Vivarais (B166) and with horses (known to have a solar aspect in Gaul).

There is strong evidence for the fertility aspect to the cult of the Celtic Sky- (and specifically Wheel-) God. We have the association both between the Celtic Mother-Goddesses and the Wheel-God and between Epona and the Sky-God. Genius or Bonus Eventus with wheel and *cornuacopiae* occurs at Netherby (BB17, BB18) and *cornuacopiae* are associated with the Wheel-God at Naix (B88). Trees, including conifers, and possibly corn-ears associated with wheel-symbols appear, especially in the Pyrenees. Finally, a dedication to Jupiter and Terra Mater associated with a wheel-symbol is known from Provence (B25).

There is a warrior facet to the Celtic Wheel-God. First, there is good evidence for an association between the Celtic Jupiter and the Celtic Mars. Second, we have the Wheel-God himself as a warrior, both on Jupiter-Giant columns and on other monuments. There is an interesting link here between later prehistory and the Roman world. Armour, from the Bronze

Age onwards, bears the wheel-sign as an apotropaic symbol and in Romano-Celtic contexts the Wheel-God frequently bears the wheel as if it were a shield. The Jupiter-Giant sky-god is a fighter against evil. Can one say that this is the entire reason for the warrior-aspect to the Wheel-God ? It may be that, like Mars, a high god such as the Celtic Sky-God would sometimes automatically be represented as a conqueror and victor.

Allied to the warrior-element in the Sky-God cult is the role of the horse, apparently a solar animal since the Bronze Age. The Celtic Sky-God appears on horseback on Jupiter-Giant columns but the classical Jupiter never appears mounted. Gods who may be Celtic versions of Mars occur together in a hoard with the Wheel-God at Willingham Fen (C6) and both sky and horseman gods are concentrated in eastern Britain, especially among the Catuvellauni. A swastika-symbol with horse-head terminals is known from Cologne (A7). In eastern Gaul the distributions both of the horse-goddess Epona and the equestrian Jupiter coincide. Finally, and perhaps most importantly, there is the phenomenon of the wheel actually replacing the horse on the back of the giant on some Jupiter-Giant groups, as at Mouhet (B87). This latter occurrence, together with the close association of horse and sun-sign on Celtic coins implies that the Jupiter-Giant horses may always be solar, and that where wheel and horse both occur we may have intensification of solar imagery.

Certain other humanoid deities and theriomorphic emblems associated with the Wheel-God cult demonstrate its composite and complicated nature. The most complex and enigmatic of these is Sucellus. The Gaulish god of the long-hafted hammer is frequently depicted with celestial symbols on his body or clothing. The Vienne Sucellus (C15) bears a spoked 'barrel' looking very like a wheel ; there is similar symbolism on the Dôle sculpture (B33). On a Mainz inscription the Sky-God is called Jupiter Sucaelus. At, for example, Aigues-Mortes (B2) and Farley Heath (C7), wheel and long-hafted hammer-signs are associated. It is possible that Sucellus represents a thunder element in the Celtic Sky-God cult, for if, as in other European cultures, the hammer can represent thunder, then the long shaft and hammer on Sucellus' imagery could represent the combination of Jupiter's sceptre and a thunderbolt symbol. Where Sucellus possesses celestial, wheel-like symbols, the association of sun, sky and hammer-bearing god is close. If one accepts that hammer-symbolism may have a celestial role, then it may explain the occasional association between smithing equipment and the Wheel-God. This occurs, for instance, at Malton (C59) and at Farley Heath (C7). Silvanus' connection with wheel-symbolism is obscure. A billhook, hammer and wheels are present on the Aigues-Mortes stone (B2), and the boar and wheel links apparent for example at Netherby (BB18) and at Hounslow (AB6) could be associated. However, boar and Sky-God could equally be linked because of the indomitability of the boar and its long-term veneration by the Celtic people.

Of other deities associated with the Cult of the Wheel in Gaul and Britain, notable are Hercules, Fortuna and Minerva. Of other beasts the most important is the bull, an animal long held sacred to the Celts (possibly of solar significance in pre-Roman times) and one of the faunal associates of the classical Jupiter.

Two conclusions must be noted. One concerns the prehistoric antecedents of a Celtic sky-cult represented by wheel-imagery. The evidence of later prehistory indicates that the recognition of celestial and solar powers depicted by a wheel or derivative symbol was familiar to the peoples of non-Mediterranean Europe before the first historical recognition of Celtic culture. Unilinear continuity within prehistory or between prehistory and the Roman period is not necessarily argued but, rather, a common heritage of ideas for cult-expression. One specific feature of prehistoric wheel-symbolism recurring in the Romano-Celtic era is the presence of models used in ritual, particularly wheels and axes. Related to this is the evidence for a possibly solar association between wheel- and axe-symbols. A second, also related, feature is the wearing of wheel-models for talismanic or apotropaic purposes. A third is the apparent association in the prehistoric and Romano-Celtic periods between, on the one hand, sky and funerary ritual and, on the other, sky and water. Fourth, certain beasts with apparent solar associations in the later prehistoric archaeological record sometimes turn up in similar contexts in the Romano-Celtic period, notably the Bronze Age horse, bull, water-bird and the Iron Age ram-headed serpent. Finally, one may glimpse occasional humanoid representations associated with solar cult-expression, especially during the later Iron Age, which may be the antecedents of the Romano-Celtic Wheel-God image.

My final point is concerned with classicism and celticism in Romano-Celtic cult-representations. First the Wheel-God is only one aspect of a great Romano-Celtic Sky-God equated with Jupiter. Jupiter as a horseman, or as a local mountain deity, represents other aspects, not necessarily associated with wheel-symbolism. Second, it should be emphasized that wheel-symbolism is common to deities otherwise extremely Celtic or extremely classical. At Churcham (BB8) the celticism of the Wheel-God is demonstrated by the over-emphasis of the head ; at Castlesteads (BB5) a normal classical altar to Jupiter Optimus Maximus bears the wheel-sign. Third, Jupiter as a Wheel-God or as a wheel-less Sky-God in Gaul and Britain becomes much more multi-functional than his classical counterpart. As a Celtic divinity he is concerned not only with sky but with sun, fertility, combat, water and death. Fourth, one cannot necessarily use art-form distinctions between 'classical' and 'Celtic' representations in order to recognize classical or Celtic religion. The two ethnic cultural elements are very closely associated. Celtic craftsmen knew a great deal of classical mythological iconography. This is evidenced, for instance, by the imagery of Jupiter-Giant columns, even though such imagery may have been misunderstood and the religion represented may be non-classical. On one and the same object one may find classical and Celtic Sky-God attributes. This is epitomized at Willingham Fen (C6) where the classical sky-emblem of the eagle is balanced by the Celtic wheel-sign and where the classical funerary symbol of the dolphin is balanced by the chthonic monster beneath the wheel-god's foot. Finally, a case-study of Jupiter as classical and Celtic Sky-God in Britain has shown that the same sites and regions tend to produce Celtic and classical representations of the god and that where the Celtic style is not found neither is the classical. This implies that a common cult, however represented, is present.

Romanization, evidenced by religion, appears to have been a two-way process. This is shown very clearly by study of the Romano-Celtic Sky-God and of the Wheel-symbol. *Interpretatio romana* and *interpretatio celtica* are employed together to produce a composite cult born both of a pre-existing sky and solar cult and of the cult of the classical Jupiter introduced to Gaul and Britain at the time of the Roman conquests. Whilst this equation has perhaps produced an easier, less confused, form of physical representation than is the case with other Romano-Celtic cults, such a marriage has nevertheless given birth to a complex and sometimes enigmatic imagery.

When dealing with a cult for which there is virtually no literary evidence, interpretation, necessarily from iconography alone, can at best be tentative. One is in constant danger of imposing one's own present-day values and arguments upon a people at a very different developmental stage in religious thought-processes. It is all too easy totally to misunderstand the purposes behind iconographical representation.

Nevertheless, if no attempt at interpretation is made, one is simply left with a series of descriptive analyses. What has been essayed here is an examination of the physical imagery of one particular iconographic theme, its contexts and associations, in order to gain as much understanding of the physical manifestations of expression associated with one specific cult-form as the archaeological parameters will allow.

CATALOGUE A

Selected Model Items from Continental Sites

Concordance Table for Catalogue A

Aizanville, 103
Alise-Sainte-Reine, 183-185
Alpentäler, 96, 97
Amiens, 88
Andernach, 86
Ardennes, 172
Argentomagus, 193
Arras, 75
Augst, 126, 137-153
Baden-Württemburg, 116, 117
Balastière, 63
Balèsmes, 102
Bavay, 34, 59, 166
Bazoches, 170
Bern-Engehalbinsel, 136
Besançon, 171
Blanc-Pavé, 196
Blois, 195
Böhming, 123
Bolards, 173-175
Bonn, 14-18
Boos, 32
Bordeaux, 157
Bourbonne-les-Bains, 206
Buch, 120
Cannstatt, 154
Carnuntum, 98, 197
Châlon-sur-Saône, 161-164
Champagne, 210
Champlieu, 72
Charnes, 79
Cologne, 1-13, 200
Compiègne, 125
Dalheim, 49
Dhronecken, 51
Dieburg, 31

Eining, 30
Eisenstadt, 114
Élouges, 56
Feldberg, 121, 133
France, unprovenanced, 62, 82-83, 87, 104-105, 201, 202
Grand-Jailly, 101
Grignon, 76
Guignicourt, 77
Guiry-Gadancourt, 182
Gunzenhausen, 94
Gusenburg, 50
Haegen, 43
Hautepin, 55
Hüfingen, 132
Ilkirsch-Griffenstein, 38
Juslenville, 58
Kapersburg, 122
Koblenz, 19, 33
Köln, see Cologne
Langenheim, 119
Langres, 80
Lanslevillard, 100
Lardiers, 180-181
Lavacherie, 57
Lavoye, 187-192
Lille, 35
Luxembourg, 53
Lyon, 198
Mâcon, 37
Magny-Lambert, 65
Mainz, 26-28, 158
Marne, 64
Metz, 203
Miltenburg, 91
Mont-Berny, 71

Montot, 178
Naix, 70, 78
Namur, 124
Néris, 176, 177
Nijmegen, 160
Nîmes, 207-208
Obfelden, 135
Oise, 67
Orléans, 84
Pas-de-Calais, 36
Pfünz, 110-112
Plessis-Barbuise, 73
Pont-Verdunois, 186
Reims, 85, 108
Rennes, 107
Rheingönheim, 113
Rhine, 199
Rückingen, 92, 93
Saalburg, 20-24, 129-131
Saint-Léonard, 205
Salzburg, 134
Sâone-et-Loire, 66
Sarre-Union, 39
Seine, 68

Slavonin, 159
South of France, 69
Starigrad, 204
Stockstadt, 90
Strasbourg, 40-42
Straubing, 29
Thérouanne, 74
Titelbourg, 54
Tongeren, 60-61
Toulouse, 168, 169
Trègnes, 155
Trier, 44-48, 109
Überackern, 99
Vaison, 115
Vesqueville, 167
Vienne, 165
Viet, Dinant, 156
Villeneuve d'Asq, 179
Voves, 194
Wederath, 52
Weisenthaum, 118
Wetteraulinie, 95
Zugmantel, 25, 89, 127-128

Cologne, Nordrhein-Westfalen, Germany

A1. Six-spoked wheel-brooch ; spokes and circumference bear ribbed decoration ; 4 cm diameter. Köln Römisch-Germanisches Museum (hereinafter referred to as Cologne Museum ; Acc. no. 712.

A2. Four-spoked wheel-brooch decorated with knobs around the outside circumference ; 3.6 cm diameter excluding knobs. From St. Kunibert (N. part of Roman City). The location is in an area where many Roman graves have been recorded. Cologne Museum Acc. no. 8651.

A3. Four-spoked wheel-brooch with knobs ; 3 cm diameter excluding knobs. Cologne Museum.

A4. Wheel-brooch decorated with external curlicues and pronounced knobs ; 4 cm diameter. No exact provenance but local to Roman city. Cologne Museum Acc. no. 440.

A5. Large, eight-spoked wheel-brooch with knobs around outside and also on nave itself ; 5.2 cm diameter. Cologne area. Cologne Museum Acc. no. 455.

A6. Plain swastika-brooch with central arm-join decorated with St. Andrew's Cross ; 2.6 cm diameter. Cologne Museum (Pl. LX, Fig. 20).

A7. Swastika-brooch with arms terminating in horse-heads ; 3.1 cm diameter. Cologne Museum.

A8. Miniature bronze wheel (not part of brooch or attachment) ; 2.5 cm diameter. Cologne Museum Acc. no. 24.53.567.

A9. Miniature bronze wheel ; c. 2 cm diameter. Cologne Museum Acc. no. 1045.

A10. Several terracotta model cart-wheels, each with eight or nine spokes. Cologne Museum.

A11. Three pipe-clay carts with pony and humanoid rider, four-wheeled. Cologne Museum.

A12. Grave-group comprising two model adze-hammers, two yokes, a ladder, two keys, two lizards, a pair of scales and a four-spoked wheel ; c. 2 cm diameter. (?) Cologne Museum (Behrens, 1939, 56-59 ; Rottländer, 1973-74, Abb. 9).

A12a. Grave-group including model bell, mattock, axe, key, yoke, and six-spoked wheel (Rottländer, 1973-74, Abb. 15).

A13. Bronze star (?wheel derivative) from Cologne grave-group. Cologne Museum Acc. no. 337.

Bonn, Nordrhein-Westfalen, Germany

A14. Bronze swastika-brooch ; c. 3.5 cm diameter. Bonn Rheinisches Landesmuseum (Hereinafter referred to as Bonn Museum) Acc. no. 15574.

A15. Clay spindle-whorl in form of spoked wheel, Bonn area (Hinz, 1969, 221, Taf. 22, no. 13).

A16. Bronze wheel-brooch. Bonn Museum Acc. no. 1546.

A17. Bronze swastika-brooch. Bonn Museum Acc. no. u. 1376.

A18. Two fragmentary wheel-brooches with most of spokes missing ; one is not exactly provenanced, the other is from Bonn. Bonn Museum Acc. no. 5273.

Koblenz, Weisenthaum, Rheinland-Pfalz, Germany

A19. Wheel-brooch with openwork knobs. Bonn Museum Acc. no. 13071.

Saalburg, Hessen, Germany

A20. Wheel-brooch ; 2.8 cm diameter. Saalburg Museum (Jacobi, 1897, Fig. 82, no. 17).

A21. Two 'S'-shaped brooches. Saalburg Museum (Anon., 1913, 2, 63, no. 16, Taf. XXII).

A22. Triskele-brooches. Saalburg Museum.

A23. Two model wheels, possibly attachments. Saalburg Museum.

A24. Ten swastika-brooches, all c. 2.5 cm diameter. Saalburg Museum (Jacobi, 1897, e.g. fig. 82, no. 7, 508 ; Böhme, 1972, nos. 1041ff.).

Zugmantel, Hessen, Germany

A.25 About thirty swastika-brooches, all c. 2.5 cm diameter. Saalburg Museum (O.R.L., 1909, 84, e.g. no. 103, Taf. X, fig. 17, 27 ; Böhme, 1972).

Mainz, Rheinland-Pfalz, Germany

A26. Wheel-brooch with four double spokes. Mainz Mittelrheinisches Landesmuseum.

A27. Swastika-brooch, c. 2.5 cm diameter. Mainz Mittelrheinisches Landesmuseum.

A28. Silver pin decorated with cone-shaped coil terminal from which hang three wires with pendants attached. Two of the pendants are mere knobs, but the middle one comprises a miniature wheel. In private hands (Mainz Museum Photographic Record no. 588);

Straubing, Bayern, Germany

A29. Silvered bronze swastika-brooch, with St. Andrew's Cross at junction of arms. From Roman fort. Straubing Museum (Walke, 1965, pl. 95, 37).

Eining, Bayern, Germany

A30. Gold wheel-pendant; late Roman date. Landshut Museum (Mainz Museum Photographic Record, R15, 88).

Dieburg, Hessen, Germany

A31. Bronze wheel-shaped amulet with spokes alternating with foliate lobes. Early Roman date. Dieburg Kreis und Stadtmuseum (Mainz Museum Photographic Record, R72, 86).

Boos, O.A. Saulgau, Baden-Württemberg, Germany

A32. Wheel-brooch, found on Roman site. Stuttgart, Württemburgisches Landesmuseum (Mainz Museum Photographic Record, R13, 86).

Weisenthaum, Mayen-Koblenz, Rheinland-Pfalz, Germany

A33. Six-spoked, enamelled wheel-brooch with ring for suspension. The spokes are formed by oval holes in a solid circle. Koblenz Museum (Mainz Museum Photographic Record, R8, 86).

Bavay, Pas-de-Calais, France

A34. Two wheel-brooches. Lille Museum (Mainz Museum Photographic Record, R20, 86).

(?) Lille, region of, Pas-de-Calais, France

A35. Wheel-brooch; no precise provenance. Lille Museum (Mainz Museum Photographic Record, R20, 86).

Pas-de-Calais, France

A36. Wheel-brooch with one elaborate knob at top and smaller lateral knobs. Lille Museum (Mainz Museum Photographic Record, R20, 86).

Mâcon, Saône-et-Loire, France

A37. Wheel-brooch (Mainz Museum Photographic Record, R20, 86).

Illkirsch-Griffenstein (10 km. south of Strasbourg), Bas-Rhin, France

A38. Bronze double wheel-brooch; Strasbourg, Musée Archéologique, Château des Rohan Acc. no. 6914.

Sarre-Union, Moselle, France

A39. Bronze wheel-brooch, heavy-cast, with four spokes, and decorated with open circles around outside. Occupation of site concentrated in 1st-2nd Century A.D. Strasbourg, Musée Archéologique (Uhlhorn, 1927-30, 145, fig. 79).

Strasbourg, Bas-Rhin, France

A40. Five-spoked wheel-brooch with spoke-ribbing. Strasbourg, Musée Archéologique.

A41. Six-spoked, enamelled wheel-brooch, from Roman cemetery. Strasbourg, Musée Archéologique Acc. no. 1933a (Forrer, 1927, pl. 39, 324). No size given in publication.

A42. Sheet-bronze wheel-model ; c. 2 cm diameter. Strasbourg, Musée Archéologique Acc. no. 3278.

Haegen, Bas-Rhin, France

A43. Large, beautifully-made, enamelled wheel-brooch ; c. 5 cm diameter ; six convex-sided spokes. Saverne, Musée Archéologique.

Trier, Rheinland-Pfalz, Germany

A44. Wheel-brooch, Maar (Trier-Nord) ; grave-find. Trier Landesmuseum Acc. no. P.M. 143 (Pl. LIV. Fig. 10, right).

A45. Fragmentary wheel-brooch (approx. half survives) ; Trier West, Aachenstrasse, 1887. Some graves exist in this area but this is not a certain grave-find. Trier Museum Acc. no. 16607.

A46. Knobbed wheel-brooch, Saarstrasse/Gerberstrasse, 1887. Trier Museum Acc. no. 16718 (Pl. LIV, Fig. 10, left).

A47. Wheel-brooch with millefiori enamelling. Unprovenanced but probably Trier. Trier Museum Acc. no. P.M. 1113.

A48. Wheel-brooch, Paulin (Trier Nord), bought 1881 ; grave-find. Trier Museum Acc. no. 4998 (Pl. LIV, Fig. 10, centre).

Dalheim, Luxembourg

A49. Spiral/swastika-brooch. Trier Museum Acc. no. 18934.

Gusenburg, Hunsrück, Rheinland-Pfalz, Germany

A50. Two identical large wheel-brooches with suspension-loops, and each with six ribbed spokes. Enamelled. Found 30 km south of Trier in or near temple-precinct of Gusenburg. Trier Museum Acc. no. 20110 ; 20111 (Pl. LV, Fig. 11).

Dhronecken, Hunsrück, Rheinland-Pfalz, Germany

A51. Bronze wheel-brooch with four ribbed spokes ; from temple-precinct. Trier, Museum Acc. no. 653 (Hettner, 1901, Taf. V, no. 54, 51).

Wederath-Belginum, near Trier, Rheinland-Pfalz, Germany

A52. Several miniature wheels, from later pre-Roman and Roman cemetery at Belginum (Wederath). C. 1.5 cm diameter. Trier Museum (Haffner, 1971, 1974, 1978).

Bronze wheel-brooch, Roman (Schindler, 1970, pl. 60).

Luxembourg, area of, Luxembourg
A53. Five-spoked wheel-brooch. Luxembourg, Musée des États.

Titelbourg, Luxembourg
A54. Three miniature wheels ; two are brooches, but one has no such fitting. Luxembourg Museum.

Hautepin (Cabaret), Hainault, Belgium
A55. Bronze enamelled wheel-brooch. Brussels, Musées Royaux (Pl. LVI, Fig. 13).

Élouges, Hainault, Belgium
A56. Enamelled wheel-brooch, from Roman cemetery. Brussels Museum (Pl. LVI, Fig. 12).

Lavacherie, Luxembourg, Belgium
A57. Small four-spoked enamelled wheel-brooch, from Roman cemetery ; found in excavations of Abbé Baltus, 1871. Brussels Museum.

Juslenville, Liège, Belgium
A58. Two bronze wheel-brooches ; (?)Roman cemetery. Liège, Musée Curtius.

Bavay, Pas-de-Calais, France
A59. Bronze four-spoked wheel-brooch, with lugs or knobs, and dolphin at central nave. Liège, Musée Curtius (Pl. LIII, Fig. 9).

Tongeren, Belgium
A60. Four wheel-brooches, possibly from graves, but records burnt during World War II. Tongeren Museum.
A61. Two swastika-brooches, with ring-and-dot decoration at arm-joints and at central junction of arms ; c. 3.5 cm diameter. Possibly stray finds. Tongeren Museum.

France, unprovenanced
A62. Several hundred bronze wheel-models. Musée des Antiquités Nationales, St-Germain-en-Laye (hereinafter referred to as St.-Germain) (Pl. LIII, Fig. 8).

Balastière de Guignicourt, France
A63. Bronze wheel or wheel-brooch. St-Germain-en-Laye.

Marne, France
A64. Seven wheel-models or wheel-brooches. St-Germain-en-Laye.

Magny-Lambert, Côte-d'Or, France
A65. Bronze wheel-model. St-Germain-en-Laye.

Saône-et-Loire, France
A66. Wheel-model. St-Germain-en-Laye.

Oise, France
A67. Wheel-model. St-Germain-en-Laye. (Pl. LII, Fig. 6).

Seine, Paris, France

A68. Two wheel-models. St-Germain-en-Laye. (Pl. LII, Fig. 6).

South of France, unlocated within

A69. Four model wheels, possibly true isolated models, but probably from model chariots or wagons. St-Germain-en-Laye. (Pl. LII, Fig. 7).

Naix, Meuse, France

A70. Wheel-model. St-Germain-en-Laye.

Mont-Berny, Oise, France

A71. Wheel-model; probably from *oppidum*, possibly from Romano-Celtic shrine. St-Germain-en-Laye.

Champlieu, Oise, France

A72. Wheel-model, possibly from Romano-Celtic shrine. St-Germain-en-Laye.

Plessis-Barbuise, Aube, France

A73. Lead ornament composed of wheel-model inside which is figure of deity with sceptre or lance in right hand and thunderbolt in left. Musée d'Épernay (Thevenot, 1968, fig. opp. p. 25).

Thérouanne, Pas-de-Calais, France

A74. Gold chain suspended from which are model wheel and club. Found near Thérouanne (de Villefosse, 1881, 12).

Arras, Pas-de-Calais, France

A75. Gold chains with attached wheels recorded (de Villefosse, 1881, 12).

Grignon near Le Châtelet, Haute-Marne, France

A76. Several model wheels discovered, allegedly, in same area as Jupiter statuette (C2) (de Villefosse, 1881, 1-13).

Guignicourt, France

A77. More than forty wheels reported as having been found in sand or gravel-pit (*ibid.*).

Naix, Boviolles, Meuse, France

A78. Two vessels found, one filled with tiny silver and lead wheels; the other containing model wheels mixed with coins (*ibid.*)

A78a. Six-spoked gold wheel-pendant (Abel, 1865, 303).

Charnes, Vosges, France

A79. Gold wheel-model. Epinal Museum (de Villefosse, 1881, 1-13; Abel, 1865, 300).

Langres, Haute-Marne, France

A80. Gold wheel-model (de Villefosse, 1881, 1-13).

A81. Miniature wheels found associated with mosaics, wall-paintings, Gaulish and Roman coins, an altar and *Matres* carving (Espérandieu, 3226 ; Drioux, 1934, 111).

France, possibly Paris region

A82. Two bronze wheel-models, with denticulate ornament around outside circumference. No size given in publication (Babelon & Blanchet, 1895, 631).

A83. Lead wheel-model ; 3.6 cm diameter (*ibid.*, 656).

Orléans, near, Loiret, France

A84. Several hundred model wheels apparently found in bed of river Loire (Reinach, 1894, 34ff.).

Reims, Marne, France

A85. Knobbed or lugged wheel-brooch. Ashmolean Museum Acc. no. 1927, 335.

Andernach, Rheinland-Pfalz, Germany

A86. Silver-washed wheel-brooch ; 2.5 cm diameter. Ashmolean Museum Acc. no. 1927, 333.

France

A87. Enamelled, knobbed wheel-brooch, pin missing ; c. 3 cm diameter. Ashmolean Museum Acc. no. 1927, 298.

Amiens, Somme, France

A88. Wheel-brooch with wheel as part of bow of otherwise conventional *fibula*-type ; separate catch-plate ; c. 2 cm diameter of wheel. Ashmolean Museum Acc. no. 1927, 442.

Zugmantel, Hessen, Germany

A89. Six-spoked wheel-brooch, 2.8 cm diameter (*O.R.L.*, 1909, 81, Taf. X, fig. 11).

Stockstadt, Bayern, Germany

A90. Swastika-brooch, c. 2.6 cm diameter (*O.R.L.*, 1910, 50, no. 19).

Miltenburg, Hessen, Germany

A91. Tin brooch in form of swastika (*O.R.L.*, 1911, 43, no. 5).

Rückingen, Hessen, Germany

A92. Swastika-brooch (see following reference).

A93. Enamelled wheel-brooch ; c. 3 cm diameter (*O.R.L.*, 1913, 16, nos. 8, 14, Taf. II, fig. 4).

Between Gunzenhausen & Kipfenburg, Bayern, Germany

A94. Swastika-brooch (*O.R.L.*, 1928, Taf. 16, no. 22).

Wetteraulinie, Die (Stretch 4-5), Bayern, Germany

A95. Swastika-brooch (*O.R.L.*, 1936, 199, no. 6, Taf. 17, fig. 27).

Alpentäler, Switzerland

A96. Lugged, four-spoked wheel-brooch (Schültzer, 1924, 25, Abb. 10).

A97. Eight-spoked, convex-spoked wheel-brooch (*ibid.*).

Carnuntum, near Vienna, Austria

A98. Circular brooch with enamelled swastika-motif (*R.L.O.*, 1917, 58, Abb. 21, no. 11).

Überackern, Austria

A99. Bronze wheel-brooch with blue glass decoration on nave, six spokes ; found in bath-hypocaust (*R.L.O.*, 1917, 158, Abb. 73, B 1549 [1]).

Lanslevillard, Savoie, France

A100. Several wheel-brooches from 1st-2nd Century A.D. Roman cemetery. About fifteen of a hundred or so brooches from here are of wheel-type. 1 has six narrow spokes, with ring at side by hinge ; 2 have six spokes with concave edge between spokes and inner circumference edge ; 2 have convex spokes − one with eight spokes, the other fragmentary ; others very fragmentary but of wheel-type. No sizes given, but all appear to be 5.0-6.0 cm in diameter (Prieur, 1968, 153-158, pl. 27, pl. 24 ; Prieur, 1977, 130 ; Courtois, 1961, 245-248, figs. 2, 3).

Grand-Jailly, Côte-d'Or, France

A101. Eight-spoked wheel-model decorated with three small 'S'-shaped plaques, welded or soldered onto one surface. Only one such plaque survives, but the solder indicates the onetime presence of the other two. On each side the nave is ornamented with a rosette (Corot, 1911, 12ff., pl. III, fig. 6 ; Drioux, 1934).

Balèsmes, Haute-Marne, France

A102. Gold wheel-model with eight filigree spokes. On the two central spokes (making up the horizontal diameter) are soldered a double-axe symbol and a crescent (Déchelette, 1913b, 260ff.).

Aizanville, near Chaumont, Haute-Marne, France

A103. Bronze wheel-model with suspension-ring, identical to Balèsmes example (no. 102). Associated coins date from Antoninus to Severus Alexander (Valdan, 1921, 49, pl. IV).

France or Germany

A104. Large, enamelled, six-spoked wheel-brooch ; 6.2 cm diameter excluding external suspension-loop ; along felloe black rectangles of enamel or niello ; some traces of alternating red enamel. The black panels have incised into the middle of each a stylized sun or flower-symbol. The spokes are convex-sided and bear blue enamel-decoration. Very large conoid-centred nave tipped with orange/red enamel and surrounding cone ornamented in black enamel open-centred circles. Short, deep catch-plate taking up whole width of felloe and most of one spoke. Pin-spring takes up most of felloe-width. Suspension-loop springs from external surface of rim immediately adjacent to catch-spring. Ribbing around outer surface of nave. British Museum Acc. no. 52.42.1 (Walters, 1899, no. 2200).

France
A105. Six-spoked enamelled wheel-brooch ; c. 3.6 cm diameter (Babelon & Blanchet, 1895, no. 1782).

Rennes, area of, Ille-et-Vilaine, France
A107. Four four-spoked wheel-models, one from river Vilaine (Reinach, 1894, 34ff. ; Banéat, 1909, nos. 1367-1370).

Reims, Marne, France
A108. Bronze openwork wheel-model (Habert, 1901, no. 1351).

Trier, Rheinland-Pfalz, Germany
A109. Bronze six-spoked wheel, from Altbachtal temple precinct ; one spoke broken (Göse *et al.*, 1938, 51, pl. 23, 7).

Pfünz, Bayern, Germany
A110. Swastika-brooch, from *uicus* ; 2.8 cm diameter (Winkelmann, 1926, Abb. 48, no. 17 ; *O.R.L.*, 1901, 23, no. 35, Taf. XII, fig. 50).
A111. Wheel-brooch, 4 cm diameter, excluding knobs (Winkelmann, 1926, Abb. 48, no. 16 ; *O.R.L.*, 1901, no. 29, Taf. XII, fig. 49).
A112. Five-spoked wheel-brooch ; 2.4 cm diameter (*O.R.L.*, 1901, 37, no. 27, Taf. XII, fig. 45).

Rheingönheim, Rheinland-Pfalz, Germany
A113. Bronze double cone-shaped wheel-pendant in filigree-work, from early Roman fort ; 2.7 cm diameter. The ornament has parallels in an example from the Roman cemetery at Wederath (Ulbert, 1969, pl. 40, no. 5, 49 & pl. 55, nos. 20-21).

Eisenstadt, Austria
A114. *Fibula* with catchplate decorated with openwork wheel-motif (Schober, 1935, pl. 71).

Vaison, Vaucluse, France
A115. Late Iron Age or, more probably, early Roman red-enamelled wheel-pendant (Sautel, 1926, 76-77).

Baden-Württemburg, Germany
A116. Swastika-brooch with ring-and-dot decoration (Filtzinger *et al.*, 1976, Taf. 46).
A117. Six-spoked wheel-brooch, 3rd or 4th Century A.D. (*ibid.*, Taf. 46).

Weisenthaum, Rheinland-Pfalz, Germany
A118. Large wheel-brooch, enamelled ; 6.5 cm diameter (Eiden, 1976, Taf. 50, 63).

Langenheim, Hessen, Germany

A119. Six-spoked wheel, from Roman fort ; 2.4 cm diameter (*O.R.L.*, 1897, 8, no. 5, Taf. III, fig. 14).

Buch, Baden-Württemberg, Germany

A120. Swastika-brooch, found in Room 2a of *praetorium* building ; ring-and-dot decoration at joints and centre ; c. 2.5 cm diameter (*O.R.L.*, 1899, 13, no. 12, Taf. III, fig. 3).

Feldberg, Hessen, Germany

A121. Swastika-brooch, 2.8 cm diameter (*O.R.L.*, 1905, 29).

Kapersburg, Hessen, Germany

A122. Openwork three-spoked wheel-shaped object ; 3.7 cm diameter. Pendant attached to circumference (*O.R.L.*, 1906, 26, no. 12, Taf. VII, fig. 14).

A122a. Large four-spoked wheel-brooch ; 7.8 cm diameter (*ibid.*, Taf. VII, fig. 6).

Böhming, Baden-Württemberg, Germany

A123. Two wheel-models, each with eight spokes, 8.5 cm and 9 cm diameter respectively. Possibly from model cart (*O.R.L.*, 1907, 9, Taf. II, fig. 1 & 1a ; 10, Taf. II, fig. 7).

Namur, Belgium

A124. Enamelled brooches, including swastika-type found and probably made around Namur (Reinach, 1921, 152).

Compiègne, de, Oise, France

A125. Wheel-brooch (Reinach, 1921, 152).

Augst, Switzerland

A126. Mould for miniature wheel scratched onto piece of Roman tile. Wheel four-spoked, c. 1.5 cm diameter. Augst Römer Museum Acc. no. 60.1558 (Martin, 1978, 118, Abb. 16) (Pl. LVII, Fig. 14).

Zugmantel, Hessen, Germany

A127. Large enamelled wheel-brooch, with ring attached to outside of rim ; eight ribbed spoked ; 5.3 cm diameter (Anon., 1912b, 49, Taf. XI, no. 19).

A128. White-metal swastika-brooch (*ibid.*, 49).

Saalburg, Hessen, Germany

A129. Swastika-brooch of unusual form ; arm-joints are at obtuse angles ; side-loops above central junction (Anon., 1913, 1, Taf. III, no. 4).

A130. Enamelled wheel-brooch, with openwork petals and four concave spokes ; suspension-ring ; 3.8 cm diameter (Anon., 1914-24, 53, Taf. IV, Abb. 8).

A131. Bronze filigree or knobbed wheel-shaped object, possibly a pendant ; twelve spokes ; 2.9 cm diameter (*ibid.*, 56, Taf. VIII, Abb. 13).

Hüfingen, Bayern, Germany

A132. Wheel-brooch, from *uicus* ; six-spoked. Dating of disc-brooches of all kinds here (solid or openwork) earlier 1st Century A.D. - time of Commodus (Rieckhoff, 1975, 93, Taf. IX, no. 142).

Kleinen Feldberg, Hessen, Germany

A133. Swastika-brooch (Böhme, 1974, 14, Abb. 3, no. 54).

Salzburg, Austria

A134. Six-spoked wheel-brooch with millefiori enamelling, from Roman settlement. Salzburg Museum (Information Dr. Moosleitner, Keeper of Archaeology).

Obfelden, ZH Lunnern, Zürich, Switzerland

A135. Hoard of goldwork, allegedly of 3rd Century date. Gold chains with pendants, including two very stylized wheel-pendants with volutes between the spokes. Schweizerisches Landesmuseum, Zürich (Acc. nos. of whole hoard 4551-1 - 4551-9) (*Die Schweizerisches Landesmuseum*, 1969, 20, pl. opp. p. 20).

Bern-Engehalbinsel, Tiefenau, Switzerland

A136. Celtic *oppidum* and Roman *uicus*. Eight-spoked, naturalistic wheel-model ; late Iron Age or, more probably, early Roman date ; 5 cm diameter. Indented nave as if cord-bound and twirled. Felloe has dotted decoration. Bern Historisches Museum Acc. no. 12946 (Pl. LIX, Figs. 18, 19).

Augst, Basel, Switzerland

A137. Miniature wheel with six spokes and openwork nave ; 2.2 cm diameter. Augst Römermuseum Acc. no. 1937.843.

A138. Large wheel-model, broken but originally eight-spoked ; c. 10.5 cm diameter. Augst Römermuseum Acc. no. 1937.658.

A139. Fragment of large wheel-model (similar to A138). Augst Römermuseum.

A140. Fragmentary wheel-model with realistic nave c. 8 cm diameter. Inscription on felloe *PER BENEFICIARIVS V... S...*. Could be from model cart (long iron tang attached to nave). Augst Römermuseum Acc. no. 1937.865 (Laur-Belart, 1942, 20-23, Abb. 11) (Pl. LVIII, Fig. 16).

A141. Fragmentary wheel-model (size impossible to gauge). Possibly inscribed. Augst Römermuseum Acc. no. 1937.844.

The above were found together in Insular 17. Pottery 1st-3rd Century A.D. Probably fom temple-site (suggestion from Dr. Max Martin, Konservator, Augst Römermuseum).

A142. Two wheel-models (currently on exhibition at the Schweizerisches Sportmuseum, Basel). Augst Römermuseum Acc. no. 1937.842.

A143. Wheel-model (currently on exhibition at Schweizerisches Sportmuseum, Basel). Augst Römermuseum (unnumbered).

Kaiser-Augst, Augst, Switzerland

A144. Wheel-model fragment. Augst Römermuseum Acc. no. K.A. 68.1586.

A145. Wheel-brooch/model with ribbed felloe. Augst Römermuseum Acc. no. 68.2201b.

Augst, Switzerland

A146. Eight four-spoked wheel-brooches with concave spokes, broad felloes and ringed naves, some with knobs round felloe. Augst Römermuseum Acc. nos. 68.7597 ; 58.6207 ; 64.7501 ; 65.2454 ; 69.12880 ; 60.8423 ; 70.7110b ; 70.6559. Dating : early Claudian - 2nd Century ; nos. 1560, 1561 : early Claudian ; 1557 : Claudian-Neronian ; 1555,1559 : Neronian-Flavian ; 1554 : 2nd Century (Riha, 1979, nos. 1554-1561, Type 7.6) (Pl. LVIII, Fig. 17).

A147. Fragmentary wheel-brooch with ribbed spokes. Augst Römermuseum Acc. no. 10498.

A148. Wheel-model with six short spokes, broad felloe ; projecting nave ; c. 2.5 cm diameter. Augst Römermuseum Acc. no. 61.7135.

(The Augst wheel-models are likely to be Roman rather than Iron Age since there is virtually no other Iron Age material from the site).

A149. Gold wheel-pendant with volute-decoration between 'spokes'. Dated to 2nd Century A.D. c. 2.5 cm diameter. Augst Römermuseum (Tomasevic, 1968, 6-8, fig. 1).

A150. Swastika-in-circle brooch (Riha, 1979, Type 3.19, no. 312).

A151. Swastika-brooch, dated to late 2nd - beginning of 3rd Century (Riha, 1979, Type 3.19, no. 313).

A152. Wheel-on-bow brooch. 1st-2nd Century (Riha, 1979, Type 7.16, no. 1666).

A153. Bronze bracelet with six-spoked silver wheel in relief. Dated to 1st Century A.D. (Tomasevic, 1968, 8, fig. 5).

Cannstatt, Stuttgart, Baden-Württemburg, Germany

A154. Eight-spoked wheel-model ; c. 2.5 cm diameter. Württemburgisches Landes-museum, Stuttgart.

Trègnes, near Namur, Belgium

A155. Belgo-Roman cemetery ; two wheel-brooches. One is four-spoked with enamelwork and solar decoration on felloe, convex spokes and four-knobbed nave ; c. 3.5 cm diameter. The other is six-spoked, with broad felloe decorated with dots ; thin spokes ; c. 2 cm diameter. Namur Museum (permission not granted to study in detail or to photograph).

Viet, Dinant area, Belgium

A156. Large wheel-brooch with eight convex spokes and enamel ; c. 5.5 cm diameter. Namur Museum Acc. no. 287 (permission not granted to study or photograph) (Henry, 1933, fig. 34, 1).

Bordeaux, Gironde, France

A157. Six-spoked wheel-brooch ; broad felloe, narrow spokes ; c. 3 cm diameter. Exact provenance unknown. Bordeaux, Musée d'Aquitaine Acc. no. 208.

Mainz, Rheinland-Pfalz, Germany

A158. Eight-spoked wheel-brooch, enamelled, with convex spokes ; c. 5 cm diameter (no size quoted) (Henry, 1933, fig. 34, 3).

Slavonin, Mähren, Czechoslovakia

A159. Swastika-in-circle brooch. 3rd Century date suggested. Apparently a number of these come from Pannonian sites (Peškař, 1972, pl. 19, no. 6, no. 64).

Nijmegen, Netherlands

A160. Six-spoked enamelled wheel-brooch ; ribbed spokes (one of a number from Nijmegen) ; no size quoted. Solar symbols around inner rim. 2nd Century date (Van Es, 1972, 189, pl. 133 ; Brunting, 1969, 41, pl. 45). Rijksmuseum Kam, Nijmegen.

Châlon-sur-Saône, area of, Saône-et-Loire, France

A161. Six-spoked wheel-brooch (very similar to London wheel-model, not brooch) ; 2.8 cm diameter (Feugère, 1977, 154, no. 93, pl. 15).

A162. Wheel-brooch with four wedge-shaped spokes and very broad felloe ; 2.9 cm diameter (Feugère, 1977, 154, no. 97, pl. 15).

A163. Enamelled wheel-brooch with four ribbed spokes and with continuous knobs around outside ; suspension-ring ; maximum diameter 4.4 cm (Feugère, 1977, 156, no. 103, pl. 17).

A164. Wheel-brooch with four convex/lobed spokes, openwork knobs around outside of felloe ; elaborate cruciform nave with four knobs ; maximum diameter 5.8 cm (Feugère, 1977, 156, no. 102, pl. 17).

(?) Vienne, Isère, France

A165. Exact provenance uncertain. Six-spoked wheel-brooch decorated with red enamel ; 3.8 cm diameter. Vienne, Musée des Beaux-Arts (Boucher, 1977, no. 225).

A165a. Four-spoked wheel-brooch ; small trilobate ornament outside rim where terminals of spokes positioned ; no size given (Boucher, 1977, no. 226). Vienne Museum.

Bavay, Pas-de-Calais, France

A166. Bronze wheel-model or brooch ; six spokes and enamel with flower or solar decoration around rim (De Caylus, 1752-67, 405, pl. CXXV, II).

Vesqueville, Ardennes, France

A167. Roman Villa. Enamelled wheel-brooch with eight thin spokes and octagonal nave ; suspension-ring with pin through it ; 5.65 cm diameter. Possibly 3rd Century date (Matthys, 1974, 25, no. 60).

Toulouse, Haute-Garonne, France

A168. Miniature four-spoked wheel-model. Old find from site of Roman town ; 1.6 cm diameter (Fouet & Savés, 1971, 65, fig. 9, bottom right).

A169. Miniature wheel with eight holes indicating spaces between spokes ; 2.2 cm diameter (Fouet & Savés, 1971, 65).

Bazoches-les-Hautes, Sarthe, France

A170. Enamelled wheel-brooch ; eight convex-edged spokes, possible fragment of suspension-ring ; 6.1 cm diameter. Found with remains of tile and other objects including 1st-4th Century coins ; occupation especially in 2nd-3rd Century with emphasis on Antonine period (Dauvois, 1957, 359-360, pl. 10). Forms one of Lerat's Group 2 (Lerat, 1956, 1, fig. 1).

Besançon, Doubs, France

A171. Enamelled wheel-brooch with ten spokes ; 5 cm diameter (Lerat, 1956, pl. XV, no. 290).

Ardennes, France

A172. Gold wheel-pendant with suspension-ring. Eight ribbed spokes ; circumference in form of ribbed concentric circles ; 2 cm diameter. Dated by author to La Tène III (Guérin, 1965, 274-275, fig. 1).

Bolards, Nuits-Saint-Georges, Côte-d'Or, France

A173. Sanctuaries containing a number of votive objects including miniature bells and wheel-models (Thevenot, 1948, 321). Deities represented include Jupiter (clay head), and the Hammer-God (*ibid.*, 301, 304).

A174. Six-spoked enamelled wheel-brooch with eight openwork knobs around outside of felloe, every alternate one having three excrescences. Decorated with green and blue enamel. No size given (Colombet, 1950-52, 178, pl. 10).

A175. Two simple four-spoked wheel-models (*ibid.*, 179).

Néris-les-Bains, La Pechin, Allier, France

A176. Enamelled wheel-brooch with six knobs at external spoke-terminals, and with circular depressions in enamel. Probably dates to end of 2nd Century. No size given (Poursat, 1975, 425, fig. 7).

Néris-les-Bains, Allier, France

A177. Double chain gold necklace with eight-spoked wheel-pendant. Spokes turn back on themselves to form symmetrical volutes. No dating information available (Galliou, 1974, 265-266 ; Massoul, 1930, fig. 1).

Montot, Château de Nambon, Franche-Comté (unlocated Département), France

A178. Four-spoked wheel-brooch, six external knobs ; c. 4 cm diameter. Found with other objects including brooches ; mostly Claudian material (Morel, 1974, 422, fig. 35).

Villeneuve d'Asq, Nord, France

A179. Enamelled wheel-brooch with six narrow spokes ; four knobs cluster at nave. Outer circumference-ring decorated with circles. No size given. From small cremation-cemetery. 2nd Century (Pietri, 1973, 317, fig. 9).

Lardiers, Basses-Alpes, France

A180. Miniature wheel found with several 'votive' rings, 'sun-disc' fragments and three bronze snakes, in Romano-Celtic sanctuary (Rolland, 1964, 547).

A181. Swastika-brooch found in vicinity of Romano-Celtic shrine. Dating of site is Iron Age through Roman period (coinage) (Salviat, 1967, 387ff., fig. 26a, b).

Guiry-Gadancourt, Seine-et-Oise, France

A182. Roman Villa. Coins 1st-4th Century A.D. Bronze wheel-brooch with six narrow spokes ; 3.1 cm diameter. Occupation concentrated in 4th Century (according to finds) (Mitard, 1958, 275, fig. 13).

Alise-Sainte-Reine, Mont Auxois, Côte-d'Or, France

A183. A number of four-spoked wheel-models, probably Roman, or late Iron Age (Espérandieu, 1906-7, 42, no. 2).

A184. Ten bronze rings and wheel-model found in 1915 investigations (Pernet, 1914-16, 35-38).

A185. Four-spoked enamelled wheel-brooch with knobbed nave ; found 1925 ; 4.8 cm diameter. 2nd-3rd Century A.D. (Toutain, 1923-25, 124-158, 147, fig. 14-15).

Pont Verdunois, Meuse, France

A186. Between Reims and Metz, on great Roman road. Two miniature four-spoked lead wheels found together ; each 0.6 cm diameter. Gallo-Roman material includes samian Form 37, coins of Antoninus Pius, Aurelius, Faustina the Younger and Commodus (Chenet, 1919, 243-251).

Lavoye, Meuse, France

A187. 1) Roman road site : nine lead wheel-models, including two or three identical to A186 examples.

A188. 2) In Roman house-foundations at same site, signs of smithing work. In front of room more than 200 lead wheel-models, some grouped in long chain-like lines by lead bars. Mostly four-spoked but some eight-spoked (Chenet, 1919, 246, fig. 2).

A189. 3) In another area dating to the beginning of the Roman period (La Tène III brooches, pottery, etc.) band of fifteen joined lead wheels ; four-spoked ; 0.8 cm diameter (Chenet, 1919, fig. 2A).

A190. 4) In same field as above large bronze eight-spoked wheel-model ; 5.5 cm diameter (Chenet, 1919, fig. 3).

A191. 5) 400 metres West of Lavoye : bronze wheel-model (size not stated). On polished surface pointillé decoration. Found with pottery dating to 2nd-3rd Century A.D. (Chenet, 1919, fig. 4).

A192. 6) 200 metres West of Lavoye: four-spoked 'potin' wheel-model; 1.3 cm diameter. Found with La Tène III brooches, La Graufesenque samian etc. (Chenet, 1919, fig. 2d).

Argentomagus, Commune de St-Marcel, Indre, France

A193. Two six-spoked enamelled wheel-brooches; diameter of one (no. 141): 3.3 cm. Found with 2nd Century material in vicinity of two Romano-Celtic temples (Albert & Fauduet, 1976, 211, 216, nos. 141, 142).

Vovès, Eure-et-Loire, France

A194. Enamelled wheel-brooch with eight convex-edged spokes; minutely-executed panels of mosaic-enamel; 5.5 cm diameter. Found in garden (Dabat, 1972, 196-197, photos 1-3).

(?) **Blois**, area of, Loire-et-Cher, France

A195. Enamelled wheel-brooch with four ridged spokes, and eight circular knobs around felloe. No size given. Château-Musée de Blois (Piron, 1970, 118, fig. on Pl. IV, 119).

Blanc-Pavé, Pas-de-Calais, France

A196. Enamelled wheel-brooch from burial-ground; probably 2nd-3rd Century date (Couppé et al., 1977, 71, no. 998, fig. 4).

Carnuntum, near Vienna, Austria

A197. Disc-brooch; decoration in the form of eight openwork spokes, but with solid back-plate. Mosaic-glass ornament; 7.5 cm diameter. Very heavy felloe, short spokes with arched space between them (Swoboda, 1964, 100, Taf. XXIV, 2).

Lyon, La Guillotière, Rhône, France

A198. Gold wheel-pendant; eight ribbed spokes and ribbing along middle of felloe; 1.5 cm diameter. Suspension-loop. At rear of wheel are two applied gold pieces at ends of horizontal diameter – one in shape of 'W' and the other a perforated circle. Dating of 2nd Century suggested. British Museum (Marshall, 1911, no. 1975).

Rhine, Germany

A199. Wheel-brooch; 3 cm diameter. No trace of enamelling survives, and it may never have been present. Slightly dished felloe; ribbing present on very narrow band along inner and outer surfaces of rim. Six spokes two of which are thicker where catchplate fitted. Large nave with dished upper surface (perhaps once bearing enamel). Rear surface of nave hollowed out or dished. Spokes rectangular-sectioned and not cast in round (flat at back). Thin, light-weight bronze. British Museum Acc. no. 55.8 4.55 (Walters, 1899, 2201).

Cologne, Nordrhein-Westfalen, Germany

A200. Six-spoked plain bronze wheel-model. New stray find, Spiesergasse 13. Cologne Museum (information from Peter Nölke, Konservator). Acc. no. 64.194. 1-5.

France (?), uncertain provenance

A201. Gold filigree wheel-pendant ; eight spokes ; 1.5 cm diameter. Each spoke terminates in knob at felloe-end. Nantes Museum (Galliou, 1974, 260, fig. 1 ; Costa, 1964, no. 341 ; Higgins, 1961). Inventory no. 882-1445.

A202. Gold filigree wheel-pendant ; diameter 2 cm. Four filigree spokes, each quadrant ornamented with double volutes. Centre of nave ornamented with seven knobs. Attached to *fibula*-like suspension-agent at top of which is further loop. Nantes Museum Inventory no. 882-1441 (Galliou, 1974, 260-261, fig. 2 ; Costa, 1964, no. 342).

Metz, Moselle, France

A203. Eight-spoked gold wheel-pendant (Parenteau, 1878, pl. 13, 3, 32).

Starigrad, Yugoslavia

A204. Bronze bracelet with silver wheel-model in relief (or set into the bracelet). Eight spokes ; knobs on rim at terminal of each spoke. A Roman cemetery here has produced a similar ornament but with a *lunula* instead of a wheel (Abramic & Colnago, 1909, 103-104, fig. 73).

Saint-Léonard, River Mayenne, Mayenne, France

A205. Bronze wheel-model found in river (Reinach, 1894, 34ff.).

Bourbonne-les-Bains, Haute-Marne, France

A206. Bronze wheel-models from sacred spring sanctuary (Chabouillet, 1880-1881, 15ff.).

Nîmes, Gard, France

A207. Four-spoked bronze wheel-model ; 2 cm diameter. From cemetery in the Quartier de Complanier. Found with other items. 1st Century B.C. date. Nîmes, Musée Archéologique.

A208. Four-spoked bronze wheel-model ; 1 cm diameter. Stray find. Nîmes, Musée Archéologique (Pl. LVII, Fig. 15).

Dietikon, near Zürich, Switzerland

A209. Four-spoked wheel-brooch with concave spokes and four knobs (similar to Augst examples). 2nd Century pottery and Trajanic coinage. Schweizerisches Landesmuseum, Zürich.

Champagne, France

A210. Bronze six-spoked wheel-model ; realistic nave ; concentric-circle decoration on felloe at spoke-ends ; 4.3 cm diameter (de Villefosse, 1881, 11, fig. 3).

CATALOGUE AB

British Model Wheels

Backworth, Tyne & Wear (NGR NZ 2972)

AB1. Saucepan-shaped silver *patera* with handle inscribed with dedication to the Mother-Goddesses (*C.I.L.*, VII, 1285). The vessel contained two gold chains, the longer with *lunula* or crescent attached, a gold bead bracelet, and three eight-spoked wheel-models in gold, with eye-fastenings. Also in the vessel were five gold rings of which one was dedicated to the *Matres Coccae* (*C.I.L.*, VII, 1299), and over 280 coins, the latest of which date to the reign of Antoninus Pius. British Museum (Haverfield, 1892, 314ff. ; Romilly-Allen, 1901, 32 ; Charlesworth, 1961, 34).

Benwell, Tyne & Wear (NGR NZ 2164)

AB2. Bronze swastika-brooch. Newcastle University Museum of Antiquities (Petch, 1927, 135-193).

Corbridge, Northumberland (NGR NY 9964)

AB3. Bronze enamelled wheel-brooch with knobs or lugs. Corstopitum Museum, Corbridge Acc. no. 75.472 (Pl. LXIII, Fig. 26).

Dolaucothi, Dyfed (NGR SN 6640)

AB4. Gold chain necklace found with two wheel-shaped pendants (the surviving example had eight spokes, one of which is missing ; the lost wheel had six spokes), each fixed with eye-fastenings. The chain has a small crescent-shaped pendant attached. Found in goldwork hoard. The surviving wheel measures c. 2 cm diameter. Remains of rod with looped ends soldered behind the wheel, probably original attachment for chain. Carmarthen Museum (Nash-Williams, 1950-52, 78-84).

Felmingham Hall, Norfolk (NGR TG 2529)

AB5. Bronze twelve-spoked wheel-model found in hoard in assocation with bronze ravens, masks, pole-tips and other ritual items, in a pot with coin dating to A.D. 260. British Museum Acc. no. 1925.6-10, 1-23 (British Museum, 1964, 60 ; Gilbert, 1978) (Pl. LXII, Fig. 24).

Hounslow, Middlesex (NGR TQ 1276)

AB6. Bronze four-spoked wheel, possibly Iron Age, found in same field with three bronze boar-figurines and other beasts. Wheel has very broad felloe and very narrow spokes. British Museum (British Museum, 1925, 147-148) (Pl. LXIII, Fig. 25).

Housesteads, Northumberland (NGR NY 7968)
AB7. Bronze fragmentary wheel-brooch with eight spokes. Thin bronze, no trace of enamelling. 4th Century A.D. Housesteads Museum (Birley et al., 1934, 197) (Pl. LXI, Fig. 23).

Icklingham, Suffolk (NGR TL 7772)
AB8. Bronze wheel, in two fragments, found with bronze eagle-wing ; possibly from villa-site. Ashmolean Museum (Green, 1975b, 55-61) (Pl. LXI, Fig. 22).

Leatherhead, Surrey (NGR 1656)
AB9. Bronze wheel-model ; from grave (Smith, 1901, 255).

London (NGR TQ 3079)
AB10. Bronze six-spoked wheel-model, well-made ; stray find from within Roman town. Museum of London.

Margam Beach, West Glamorgan (NGR SS 7787)
AB11. Bronze, four-spoked, wheel-shaped brooch ; c. 3 cm diameter. National Museum of Wales.

Newstead, Border Region (NGR NT 5634)
AB12. Links of silver chain with miniature silver filigree eight-spoked wheel, fitted with solid bar across back, ending on either side with suspension-loop ; crescent-shaped ornament associated (Curle, 1911, pl. 87, no. 34).

Sewingshields, Turret 35A, Hadrian's Wall, Northumberland (NGR NY 8068)
AB13. Bronze wheel-shaped brooch, with six spokes (Woodfield, 1965, 155).

Turret 18B, Hadrian's Wall, Northumberland (NGR NY NZ 0168)
AB14. Bronze, enamelled, six-spoked wheel-brooch. Newcastle University Museum of Antiquities.

Verulamium, Hertfordshire (NGR TL 1307)
AB15. Bronze wheel-model ; stray find from within Roman town. Verulamium Museum.

Wroxeter, Shropshire (NGR SJ 5608)
AB16. Bronze wheel-brooch or wheel-shaped belt-fitting. Shrewsbury Museum.

Colchester, Essex (NGR TM 0025)
AB17. Miniature brass wheel ; found in urn with beads and a shale armlet. Colchester & Essex Museum.

Kettering, Northamptonshire (NGR SP 8778)
AB18. Bronze wheel-shaped brooch. Westfield Museum Kettering.

Nor'nour, St. Martin's, Isles of Scilly (NGR SV 9111)

AB19. Enamelled wheel-shaped brooch with lugs or knobs. St. Mary's Museum (Dudley, 1967, 1ff.).

Islip, Northamptonshire (NGR SP 9879)

AB21. Bronze wheel-brooch (Baker, 1881-1883, 90).

Gateshead, Tyne & Wear (NGR NZ 2562)

AB22. Stone wheel/wheel-brooch mould. Newcastle University Museum of Antiquities.

Chester, Cheshire (NGR SJ 4066)

AB23. Fragment of wheel-model or wheel-brooch (probably the former), from Abbey Green Site. Diameter c. 3 cm ; thickness 0.1 cm. Grosvenor Museum, Chester (Excavation no. AG 75 IV. 693. 2061).

Colchester, Essex (NGR TM 0025)

AB24. Wheel-shaped bronze brooch with projecting nave and 'bold marginal ribs' (Hawkes & Hull, 1948, 326, no. 176).

AB25. Wheel-shaped bronze brooch ; hinged pin, flat wheel-shaped plate, with central knob within stamped disc. From Ditch 1, Upper Filling, Region 5 (Period III). Claudian date (A.D. 43/44-48) (Hawkes & Hull, 1947, 326, no. 177).

Denholme Hill Farm, Southern Region, Scotland

AB26. Swastika-brooch, suggested as being of 2nd Century A.D. date. National Museum of Antiquities of Scotland Acc. no. FA88.

Icklingham, Suffolk (NGR TL 7772)

AB27. Four-spoked wheel-brooch ; pin broken off ; hole in centre of nave ; 2.4 cm diameter. Ashmolean Museum Acc. no. 1927.269 (Pl. LX, Fig. 21).

Lakenheath, Suffolk (NGR TL 729835)

AB28. Turkey Farm Roman Site : wheel-brooch with elaborate enamel-decoration in red, green, blue and white. Six convex-edged spokes ; large, perforated nave ; 5.7 cm diameter. Cambridge University Museum of Archaeology & Anthropology Acc. no. 76.1588.

(?) **Liverpool**, area of, Lancashire (NGR SJ 3591)

AB29. No exact prov. Wheel-brooch of Augst type with wide, knobbed felloe, ringed nave and four concave spokes. Pin missing. No traces of enamelling or gilding, tinning, etc. Maximum diameter 3.3 cm. Merseyside County Museums, Liverpool Acc. no. CS.20.

Silchester, Hampshire (NGR SU 6462)

AB30. Two wheel-shaped brooches. About one no information available ; the other has six angled, convex spokes, raised concentric circles on felloe and eight external knobs. Reading Museum (information George Boon Esq., National Museum of Wales).

CATALOGUE AX

Continental and British Axe-Models with Possible Intrinsic Solar or Sky-Symbolism

Allmendingen, Lake of Thun, Switzerland

AX1. Model axe bearing dedication to Jupiter: *IOVI* (*C.I.L.*, XIII, 5158 ; Toutain, 1907, 287). Six other model axes, dedicated to Minerva, the Matres, Matronae, Mercury, also from this area. Bern Historisches Museum (Forrer, 1948).

Bern, area of, Switzerland

AX2. Cast of axe-model with 'X' on blade, not at blade and haft-junction. Schweizerisches Landesmuseum, Zürich.

Bern, Engehalbinsel, Switzerland

AX3. Model axe, with ring-and-dot decoration on blade ; 6 cm long. Seven other, undecorated axes found in this area, in the vicinity of a shrine. Bern Historisches Museum.

AX4. Model axe decorated with ring-and-dot motifs ; 6.2 cm long ; one of five from here. Bern Historisches Museum.

Cologne, Nordrhein-Westfalen, Germany

AX5. Bronze axe-headed pin with cross-pattern on blade. Cologne area. Cologne Museum.

AX5a. Bronze axe-model with 'X' on blade. From 'Sabazian' grave-group. Cologne Museum.

Pfünz, Baden-Württemburg, Germany

AX6. Two bronze model axe-headed pins, one with ring-and-dot mark at junction of blade and haft (*O.R.L.*, 1901, Taf. XII, 14 & 15 [marked example]).

Saalburg, Hessen, Germany

AX7. Bronze brooch in form of axe/double-axe (Anon., 1930, Taf. V, no. 7).

Solothurn, Switzerland

AX8. Found in bed of River Aar : model axe with dedication to Jupiter : *DECIMIVS IOVI VOT* (*C.I.L.*, XIII, 5172 ; Toutain, 1907, 287 ; Forrer, 1948, no. 14). Solothurn Museum.

Stockstadt, Bayern, Germany

AX9. Bronze brooch in form of axe/double-axe (*O.R.L.*, 1910, Pl. VII, no. 18).

Trier, Rheinland-Pfalz, Germany

AX10. Bronze brooch in form of axe/double-axe. Trier Museum.

AX11. Terra-cotta double-axe model; c. 5 cm long. Altbachtal Temple-precinct. Trier Museum Acc. no. 14009.

Winterthur-Lindberg, Switzerland

AX12. Five axe-models, one with ring-and-dot decoration. Found with statuettes of Mercury, a dog and a horse. Roman site. Schweizerisches Landesmuseum, Zürich.

Zugmantel, Hessen, Germany

AX13. Bronze brooch in form of axe/double-axe (Anon., 1908-9, Taf. XII, Abb. 11).

Cranborne Chase, Dorset, England

AX14. Two bronze axe-models decorated with crosses; stray finds (Kirk, 1949, 32ff.).

Kirmington, Humberside, England

AX15. Bronze axe-model with 'X' on blade. Scunthorpe Museum (information from K. Leahy, Curator).

Richborough, Kent, England

AX16. Two bronze axe-models with incised skeuomorphic binding-marks. On blade of one is 'X', in addition to similar cross where blade meets haft. Found below stone fort road (189) and top soil (190) (Bushe-Fox, 1949, 145, nos. 189-190, pl. 52).

AX17. Two bone axe-headed pins, one with 'X' binding pattern (*ibid.*, 146, nos. 195-6, pl. 53).

AX18. Bronze double-axe-headed pin; ring-and-dot decoration on blade. Surface find in S.W. corner of fort (Cunliffe, ed., 1968, 100, no. 170, pl. 42).

South Shields, Tyne & Wear, England

AX19. Bronze brooch in form of axe/double-axe (Green, 1978, 71; Birley *et al.*, 1934, 197). Housesteads Museum.

Woodeaton, Oxfordshire, England

AX20. Four bronze axe-models from Romano-Celtic shrine. One is decorated with a 'X' and ligatures; one with a swastika; one with triangles and one with lines. Another example bears what may be ring-and-dot markings (Green, 1975c, fig. 3) (Pl. LXIV, Fig. 27).

Gestingthorpe, Essex, England

AX21. Bronze axe-model with 'X' at junction of haft with blade (in possession of Department of Environment) (Pl. LXIV, Fig. 28).

Addendum

Straubing, Bayern, Germany

AX22. Bronze axe-model with two ring-and-dot marks on blade ; from Roman fort (Walke, 1965, pl. 98, 27).

CATALOGUE B

Stone Monuments relating to Romano-Celtic Wheel-Symbolism in Gaul, Germany and Britain

I. CONTINENTAL MATERIAL

B1. **Agey**, in region of, Côte-d'Or (France)
Mutilated statuette of youthful female individual, seated, legs crossed ; naked torso, drapery from left shoulder. In right hand rudder, in left *cornucopiae* ; behind right leg circular, shield-like object with four spokes. Naked infant at her right side turns its head to look at her. Figure is probably to be interpreted as Fortuna. 65 cm high (Espérandieu, 7526 ; Corot, 1927-32, 243-264 ; Toutain, 1925, 2ff.).

B2. **Aigues-Mortes**, between here and St-Laurent d'Aigouze, Gard (France)
Altar dedicated to Jupiter and Silvanus ; form of lettering may date it to the earlier 1st Century A.D. Attributes sculpted on three faces as follows : a) thunderbolt and six-spoked wheel on one short side ; b) hammer, seven-spoked wheel and thunderbolt, under inscription on long side ; c) billhook, pot and hammer, on other short face. 65 cm high. Nîmes, Musée Archéologique (Jullian, 1918b, 113-115 ; Jullian, 1918a, 244 ; Espérandieu, 1924, 33, no. 121, pl. 6 ; Espérandieu, 6849) (Pl. LXXI, Fig. 42).

B3. **Alise-Sainte-Reine** (Alesia), Mont Auxois, Côte-d'Or (France)
Fragmentary stone statue of Jupiter with globe in right hand, seated on throne sides of which are decorated each with a four-spoked wheel ; trace of over-large eagle in front of Jupiter's knees ; fairly rough workmanship. Surviving fragment 25 cm high (Espérandieu, 2375 ; Lambrechts, 1942, 64-80 ; Drioux, 1934, 41 ; Espérandieu, 1906-1907, 41, pl. X, 2).

B4. **Alzey**, Rheinland-Pfalz (Germany)
Statue of Jupiter, comprising naked torso and draped nether limbs, seated on throne. To his left eight-spoked wheel, to his right eagle. 74 cm high. Alzey Museum (Espérandieu, 7749 ; Lambrechts, 1942, 64-80 ; Künzl, 1975, Taf. 29 ; Bauchhenss, 1976, Abb. 32) (Pl. LXV, Fig. 30).

B5. **Andernos**, Basin of Arcachon, Gironde (France)
Relief of Jupiter with wheel and small humanoid figure. 64 cm high (Espérandieu, 1237 ; Lambrechts, 1942, 64-80).

B6. Auberive, Haute-Marne (France)
Possible Wheel-God sculpture, now lost. Relief of deity on 'Viergötterstein' wearing beard and Gaulish tunic. He clasps an unspoked, solid circular object in both hands against his abdomen. Known only from drawing (Drioux, 1929, 357, fig. 2 ; *ibid.*, 1934, pl. II, 44), (Pl. II, Fig. 3).

B7. Autun, region of (?), Saône-et-Loire (France)
Stone statue representing goddess, probably to be interpreted as Juno, holding thunderbolt in one hand and possible wheel in the other ; stone extremely worn. 65 cm high (Espérandieu, 1824 ; Drioux, 1934, 52 ; Lambrechts, 1942, 64-80). Autun Museum.

B8. Bachos-Binos, Haute-Garonne (France)
Cinerary container ; in enclosed square area is engraved wheel ; spiral border ; dated to 3rd Century A.D. 40 cm high (Espérandieu, 8052).

B9. Bad Dürkheim, Rheinland-Pfalz (Germany)
Chiselled carvings on Roman stone-quarry face, including swastikas, stemmed four-spoked wheels, stylized heads on stick-legs, bird, dog, phalli. Of particular interest are associated swastikas, three horses, a man with two spears, and a stemmed eight-spoked wheel with four 'rays' emanating from the top of the wheel. Carvings occur between graffiti of Legion XXII, based on Mainz. Quarry in use from 1st to 3rd Century A.D. (Spräter, 1948a, 52 ; Spräter, 1935, 32-39, pl. 3 ; Röder, 1969, 110-135 ; Spräter, 1948b).

B10. Baudoncourt, Haute-Saône (France)
Two house-shaped steles, funerary, bearing representations of Epona ; one with circular, possibly wheel-shape at apex (Lerat, 1964, 378, fig. 4).

B11. Beaune, Côte-d'Or (France)
Horseman-fragment from Jupiter-column, probably once having held wheel, now missing. 67 cm high (Thevenot, 1936-39, 427-498 ; Espérandieu, 2085 ; Thevenot, 1971, 49, no. 64).

B12. Begnères, Hautes-Pyrénées (France)
Altar bearing swastika-symbol. Collection Frossard, Musée des Antiquités Nationales, St-Germain-en-Laye (Reinach, 1917, 121).

B13. Begnères, Hautes-Pyrénées (France)
Altar bearing swastika-symbol. Collection Frossard, Musée des Antiquités Nationales, St-Germain-en-Laye. 29 cm high (Reinach, 1917, fig. 127 ; Espérandieu, 854) (Pl. VI, Fig. 10).

B14. Belbèze-en-Comminges, Haute-Garonne (France)
Small altar, from sanctuary of 'Pédegas-d'En-Haut', a small rectangular shrine. On front of altar is floreate wheel/rosette with six spokes/petals. 18 cm high (Labrousse, 1966, 419, fig. 9).

B15. **Bois-de-la-Neuve-Grange**, between Niederhoff and Saint-Quirin, Bas-Rhin (France)
House-shaped stele with half of wheel surviving, with four remaining spokes. Curious branch-like spoke-extensions. 31 cm high. Metz Museum (Espérandieu, 4526) (Pl. XIII, Fig. XIII, Fig. 28).

B15a. **Bordeaux**, Gironde (France)
Statue found in 1900 amid purely Roman remains. Deity stands turning to left, left leg in front ; wears chlamys held at shoulder. Right arm held aloft holds thunderbolt ; in left hand, in relief, seven or eight-spoked wheel. Long hair and beard. 2 m 50 m high. Bordeaux, Musée Archéologique (Courcelle-Seneuil, 1910, 68 ; Lambrechts, 1942, 64-80 ; Étienne, 1962, 167 ; Espérandieu, 1064 ; Reinach, 1917, 100 ; Mensignac, 1905, 156, fig. on p. 156).

B16. **Bourges**, Cher (France)
Funerary monument decorated with swastika (Hatt, 1970, 7-97).

B17. **Bremevaque**, Haute-Garonne (France)
Relief of naked god, perhaps wearing helmet, with spear and snake ; on front of stele, above figure is pot ; on base is swastika. 48 cm high (Espérandieu, 871 ; Thevenot, 1955) (Pl. VII, Fig. 14).

B18. **Bruchstück**, Hessen (Germany)
Horseman from Jupiter-column ; arm thrust through spokes of wheel (Hertlein, 1910, 9).

B19. **Butterstadt**, near Hanau, Hessen (Germany)
Part of Jupiter-column, horseman group. Left hand of rider is thrust through four-spoked wheel and holds reins ; wears tunic and *paludamentum*. Giant is beardless but male ; lies on back and turns face towards left side of rider ; right hand pressed against ground ; left probably held right front hoof of horse on left shoulder ; left hoof of horse resting on right shoulder. 82 cm high. Museum des Geschichtsverein, Hanau (Espérandieu, *Germ.* 76 ; Bauchhenss, 1976, 44, Abb. 26 ; Reinach, 1897-1910, III, 151, 7 ; Grenier, 1945, pl. XIV ; Drioux, 1934, 43 ; *ibid.*, 1929, 355) (Pl. LXV, Fig. 29).

B20. **Castelas de Vauvert**, Nîmes, Gard (France)
Stone altar ; on front eight-spoked wheel, on each lateral face thunderbolt ; on fourth side *patera*. Mutilated and worn. 87 cm high. Nîmes, Musée Archéologique (Musée Lapidaire) (Espérandieu, 6843 ; Espérandieu, 1924, 29, no. 108) (Pl. LXVIII, Fig. 35).

B21. **Castelnau-Valence**, Nîmes area, Gard (France)
Fragment of very small altar, with remains of five-spoked wheel below inscribed dedication by 'Severus'. 7 cm wide. Nîmes, Musée Archéologique (Musée Lapidaire) (Espérandieu, 1924, 13) (Pl. LXXI, Fig. 41).

B23. **Cazarilh, Laspernes**, Haute-Garonne (France)
Funerary stele decorated with two denticulated wheels (Espérandieu, 883 ; Hatt, 1945, no. 97 ; *ibid.*, 1970, 7-97).

B24. **Champagnat**, Creuse (France)
Stone group ; principal figure is shown walking ; right arm holds five-spoked wheel which rests against his head. By left leg is kneeling, headless figure of indeterminate sex. The standing god has closed facial features, and a beard. Main figure 1 m 60 cm high (Blanchet, 1923, 156-160, pl. VII).

B25. **Clarensac**, Nîmes area, Gard (France)
Altar-fragment with remains of inscription *(Ioui) et Terrae Matri*. In between lines of inscription remains of wheel. Nîmes, Musée Archéologique (Musée Lapidaire). 1 m 4 cm high (Espérandieu, 6825 ; Lambrechts, 1942, 64-80).

B27. **Collias**, Nîmes area, Gard (France)
Altar dedicated to Jupiter, by Coriossedenses and Budicenses. Large eight-spoked wheel beneath inscription, and possibly either thunderbolt or trident. Nîmes, Musée Archéologique (Musée Lapidaire). 1 m 53 cm high (*C.I.L.*, XII, 2972 ; Espérandieu, 1924, 14, no. 38 ; Espérandieu, 2681) (Pls. VIII, Fig. 18 ; LXX, Fig. 39).

B28. **Collias**, near, at Notre-Dame-le-Laval
In chapel, fragment of altar with half of eight-spoked wheel surviving. 49 cm high (Espérandieu, 7621).

B29. **Cologne**, 'Kleinen Griechenmarkt', Nordrhein-Westfalen (Germany)
Altar dedicated to *I.O.M.* (Jupiter Optimus Maximus). Beneath inscription is eight-spoked wheel. Apart from wheel, normal, classical-looking altar. 86 cm high. Bonn Rheinisches-Landesmuseum (Acc. no. 7625) (Espérandieu, 6380 ; Lambrechts, 1942, 64-80 ; *C.I.L.*, XIII, 8194 ; Schoppa, 1959, pl. 19 ; Fremersdorff, 1963, pl. 119 ; Ristow, 1975, Taf. 37). (Pl. XVIII, Fig. 42).

B30. **Commetreuil**, near, Villen-en-Tardenois, Marne (France)
Altar, at one time situated in vestibule of Château de Commetreuil, near Bouilly ; undoubtedly local. Destroyed in World War II. On front was eight-spoked wheel and hand holding thunderbolt ; inscription to *I.O.M.* (Jupiter Optimus Maximus). c. 95 cm high (Demaison, 1926, 132-134 ; Espérandieu, 7201).

B31. **Courbessac**, Nîmes area, Gard (France)
Stele with triangular top. Inscription *Nundins patri et maternae matri ; Paternus fil(ius) posuit*. On top of front surface is hammer, axe, and remains of wheel. 77 cm high (Espérandieu, 6829 ; Lambrechts, 1942, 64-80).

B33. **Dôle** area, Jura (France)
Stele bearing depiction of bird whose head is surmounted by a small, four-spoked wheel. Above is item comprising a small barrel-shape with eight spokes radiating from it, each terminating in a smaller barrel or cylinder-shape. Musée de Dôle. 82 cm high (Espérandieu, 5303) (Pl. XVIII, Fig. 41).

B34. **Dompierre-les-Églises**, Haute-Vienne (France)
Mutilated statue of Jupiter with wheel. The god wears a tunic. Head, both arms and right leg destroyed. Left arm held wheel with four wedge-shaped spokes above humanoid, bearded head (probably that of giant). Very damaged, but Jupiter probably stood upright. 1 m 3 cm high (Eygun, 1965, 381, 382, fig. 51).

B35. **Dunzweiler**, Amt Homburg, Rheinland-Pfalz (Germany)
'Viergötterstein', bearing depiction of naked Jupiter, with sceptre and with battered wheel in left hand. 1 m 19 cm high. Speyer Museum (Cook, 1925, 57-93 ; Espérandieu, 5940 ; Drioux, 1934, 44) (Pl. XVII, Fig. 38).

B36. **Eckelsheim**, Hessen (Germany)
Jupiter-giant rider-group with horseman holding circular shield like a wheel or solar-symbol. 92 cm high (Behn, 1936, 256-258, Taf. 53, 1-4, Abb. 1 ; Künzl, 1975, Taf. 26, no. 11).

B39. **Fallberg**, near Saverne, Bas-Rhin (France)
Sanctuary containing several fragments of Jupiter-columns ; one horseman-group has probable wheel held in left hand. Saverne Museum (Pl. LXVII, Fig. 34).

B39a. **Fallberg**, near Saverne, Bas-Rhin (France)
Altar dedicated to *I.O.M.* (Jupiter Optimus Maximus), with at top stylized four-spoked wheel-symbols. Saverne Museum.

B40. **Foeschen**, Bas-Rhin (France)
Relief bearing lobed wheel. Sarrebourg Museum (Linckenheld, 1927, 78ff.).

B41. **Forêt de Châtillon-sur-Seine**, Côte-d'Or (France)
Gallo-Roman sanctuary containing figure of a standing, armoured god, with no head or arms, with giant by left side. Suggested that standing figure originally held wheel balanced on giant's head (Martin, 1964, 316-317, figs. 31-32).

B42. **Forêt de Greiffenstein**, near Saverne, Bas-Rhin (France)
House-shaped funerary stele bearing concentric circles. Strasbourg, Musée Archéologique (Acc. no. 40166). c. 60 cm high.

B43. **Forêt de Saint-Quirin**, Meurthe-et-Moselle (France)
Stele decorated with complex seven-spoked wheel, and, beneath, three hammers. Saverne Museum. 48 cm high (Espérandieu, 4528) (Pls. XIII, Fig. 29 ; LXXII, Fig. 45).

B44. **Forêt de Walscheid**, Vosges (?) (France)
House-shaped stele with decoration in form of crescent, circle and concentric circles. 92 cm high. Musée des Antiquités Nationales, St.-Germain-en-Laye (Espérandieu, 4549).

B45. **Fox-Amphoux**, Var (France)
Torso of Celtic warrior with large oval shield. Wears pectoral pendant in form of six-spoked wheel, fixed by two fastenings at level of chin. Shield decorated by

ring-and-dot ornament. 42 cm high. Musée Borély, Marseille (Espérandieu, 8613 ; Benoit, 1954, 436, fig. 20).

B46. **Gard**, Département du (France)
Altar with wheel-carving (Allmer, 1878-83, 202 ; Gaidoz, 1884, 14).

B47. **Garin**, Le Comminges, Hautes-Pyrénées (France)
Funerary stele decorated with denticulated wheel. 56 cm high. (Hatt, 1945, no. 92 ; Hatt, 1970, 7-97 ; Espérandieu, 884).

B49. **Garonne and Adour**, between (no exact provenance) (France)
Altar with swastika and wheel-decoration. c. 30 cm high (Courcelle-Seneuil, 1910, 70, fig. 23).

B50. **Geneva** (Switzerland)
Funerary stele with 'S'-symbol decoration. Musée Archéologique de Genève (Deonna, 1915a, 50, fig. 25, 2, 49).

B51. **Geneva** (Switzerland)
Funerary stele with concentric circles at apex. Musée Archéologique de Genève (Musée Épigraphique de Genève) (Deonna, 1915a, 49, fig. 25, 1).

B52. **Giaud**, Haute-Vienne (France)
Relief of Jupiter, small humanoid figure with scroll-tail, and Juno's peacock ; Jupiter very possibly originally held wheel. 1 m 50 cm high (Espérandieu, 1581 ; Lambrechts, 1942, 64-80).

B53. **Gilly**, Nîmes area, Gard (France)
Altar decorated with six-spoked wheel. 26 cm high. Nîmes, Musée Archéologique (Musée Lapidaire) (Espérandieu, 1924, pl. 3 ; Espérandieu, 430) (Pls. IX, Fig. 21 ; LXVIII, Fig. 36).

B54. **Glanmünchweiler**, Speyer area, Rheinland-Pfalz (Germany)
'Viergötterstein' ; beardless Jupiter holds wheel in left hand (number of spokes indistinguishable). 1 m 15 cm high (Espérandieu, 6077 ; Lambrechts, 1942, 64-80).

B55. **Goudex**, near Toulouse, Haute-Garonne (France)
Small votive altar with tree-carving, and with swastika on base. 20 cm high (Labrousse, 1962, 558, 559, fig. 10).

B56. **Griffon**, near Saverne, Vosges (France)
Double 'stèle-maison' with concentric circle-decoration. Dated to early 3rd Century (Hatt, 1964, pl. 135).

B57. **Hagenbach**, Speyer area, Rheinland-Pfalz (Germany)
Funerary monument decorated with three wheels. 75 cm high (Espérandieu, 7415 ; Hatt, 1970, 9-97).

B60. **Ilheu**, Hautes-Pyrénées (France)
Small altar ; swastika on base, tree above ; at top are three leaves. Built into church wall. 28 cm high (Espérandieu, 8900 ; Labrousse, 1954, 220, fig. 8).

B61. **Jagsthausen**, Baden-Württemburg (Germany)
Fragmentary sculpture comprising five-spoked wheel against pilaster, and foot of draped (?)goddess, possibly Fortuna. 21 cm high. Württemburgisches-Landesmuseum, Stuttgart (Espérandieu, *Germ.*, 667).

B62. **Jublains**, Mayenne (France)
Altar inscribed *Aug. Deo Ioui Optimo Max//ximo*. On front band is four-spoked wheel ; on left side is six-spoked wheel and on right three six-spoked wheels placed two and one ; the whole group is engraved on a hollow space. Lambrechts thinks that the six-spoked wheels have in fact eight spokes. Lost. 90 cm high (Lambrechts, 1942, 64-80 ; Espérandieu, 3058 ; de Villefosse, 1881, 1-13) (Pl. XII, Figs. 25, 26).

B63. **Juslenville**, Liège (Belgium)
Funerary stele decorated with swastika (wheel-brooches also from this cemetery, see Catalogue A). 1 m 5 cm high (Espérandieu, 4002 ; Hatt, 1970, 7-97).

B64. **Kirchnaumen**, Bas-Rhin (France)
'Stèle-maison' with rosette at apex of 'roof' ; c. 90 cm high. Saverne Museum (Linckenheld, 1931-34, 212-219).

B66. **Lansargues**, near Montpellier, Hérault (France)
Altar dedicated to Jupiter ; fragmentary stone bearing six-spoked wheel between two thunderbolts ; inscription to *I.O.M.* (Jupiter Optimus Maximus). Wheel and thunderbolts once raised in normal carved style, but deliberate attempt at erasure of symbols means that only the scar and outline of shapes remain. Musée de la Société Archéologique de Montpellier (*C.I.L.*, XII, 4179 ; Espérandieu, 517 ; Lambrechts, 1942, 64-80) (Pl. IV, Fig. 6).

B67. **Laudun**, near, Gard (France)
Altar depicting draped Jupiter with sceptre in left hand. On lateral surfaces : left − five-spoked wheel ; right − eagle. 21 cm high (Espérandieu, 513 ; Lambrechts, 1942, 64-80 ; Prieur, 1968, 177ff. ; de Vries, 1963, 39) (Pl. IV, Fig. 5).

B69. **Le Comminges**, Hautes-Pyrénées (France)
Near sanctuary of Mars Sutagius, funerary 'troughs' bearing incised crossed circles, a six-spoked wheel and other symbols (Hatt, 1945, 169-254).

B70. **Le-Mont-Saçon**, Hautes-Pyrénées (France)
i) Two altar-bases with incised swastikas, one in lozenge, other enclosed by circle ; c. 12 cm high (Fouet & Soutou, 1963, 275-295, 280, fig. 10).

ii) One altar bearing stylized tree and with swastika on base ; c. 20 cm high (Fouet & Soutou, 1963, 284, fig. 13, no. 3).

iii) Two altars bearing swastikas ; 20 cm and 18 cm high (Fouet & Soutou, 1963, fig. 14, nos. 44, 47, 285).

iv) Two altars bearing wheels. Exact sizes not given but c. 20 cm high (Fouet & Soutou, 1963, nos. 1, 47).

v) One altar bearing fragmentary inscription to Jupiter (Fouet & Soutou, 1963, no. 12).

The site would appear to be a sanctuary of the Celtic Jupiter (Fouet & Soutou, 1963, 275-295).

B71. **Les Ronchers**, Meuse (France)
Rider-god sculpture from Jupiter-column ; left arm thrust through spokes of wheel (Hertlein, 1910, 26).

B72. **Luxeuil**, Haute-Saône (France)
Drawing of lost Jupiter-Giant horseman group, damaged when illustrated. Shows rider wearing tunic, right hand thrust through five-spoked wheel, left resting on partially-draped female humanoid figure suspended in space at his side. The giant is represented by a head emerging from the earth, supporting the left forefoot of the rider's horse. The rider-god is bearded. 1 m 65 cm high (Cook, 1925, fig. 48 ; de Caylus, 1759, iii, 367f., pl. 99, 3 ; Espérandieu, 1917, 72ff. ; Espérandieu, 5357) (Pl. XI, Fig. 24).

B73. **Mainz**, Rheinland-Pfalz (Germany)
Altar bearing eight-spoked wheel. 27 cm high. Mainz Mittelrheinisches-Landesmuseum or Zentralmuseum (not specified in publication) (Espérandieu, 5771 ; Lambrechts, 1942, 64-80) (Pl. XVI, Fig. 37).

B74. **Mainz**, Rheinland-Pfalz (Germany)
Relief of Jupiter accompanied by small humanoid figure ; possibly the god once held a wheel. 49 cm high (Espérandieu, 5772 ; Lambrechts, 1942, 64-80).

B75. **Malmaison**, Ronchers (near), Meuse (France)
Two fragments of Jupiter-Giant statues, one comprising hand holding four-spoked wheel as if it were a shield. 14 cm diameter (wheel). Musée de Bar-le-Duc (Espérandieu, 4666, 4670 ; Drioux, 1934, 43) (Pl. XVI, Fig. 36).

B76. **Marsillargues**, between here and Lunel, Hérault (France)
Altar dedicated to Jupiter and Augustus. On front, under text, is large wheel (remains of), with prominent openwork hub and once with eight or ten spokes. A break has removed lower half of altar and wheel. 62 cm high. Musée de la Société Archéologique de Montpellier (de Villefosse, 1881, 1-13 ; Espérandieu, 524 ; Lambrechts, 1942, 64-80 ; *C.I.L.*, XII, 4172) (Pls. V, Fig. 7 ; LXIX, Fig. 38).

B77. **Meaux**, Seine-et-Marne (France)
Rider-god from Jupiter-column group, wearing wide tunic, fluttering cloak, hose ; arm thrust through rosette-like wheel with four spokes. Beardless giant. 50 cm high (Hertlein, 1910, 27 ; Gassies, 1902, 287-297 ; Espérandieu, 3207) (Pl. XI, Fig. 23).

B78. **Melun**, Seine-et-Marne (France)
Goddess, possibly with wheel, on relief. 84 cm high (Espérandieu, 2933 ; Drioux, 1934, 52).

B79. **Merkenich**, Nordrhein-Westfalen (Germany)
Relief of god, once possibly with wheel, and small humanoid figure. 32 cm high (Espérandieu, 6337 ; Lambrechts, 1942, 64-80).

B80. **Metz**, Moselle (France)
Funerary stele found in 1749, portraying figure with torc from which is suspended a six-spoked wheel (Courcelle-Seneuil, 1910, 73 ; Gaidoz, 1885, 199, fig. 13).

B81. **Meuse**, Département of (France)
Stone fragment of relief or statue or relief, showing hand clasping four-spoked wheel. Musée de Bar-le-Duc. (possibly same as B75) (Gaidoz, 1885, 199, fig. 15).

B82. **Montmaurin**, Haute-Garonne (France)
From temple of Villa de Montmaurin ; small altar with four-spoked wheel on face and swastika on base. Another, similar, altar bears an inscription to *I.O.M.* (Jupiter Optimus Maximus) (though without the incised decoration). 19 cm high (Fouet & Soutou, 1963, 290, fig. 19 ; Lefort des Ylouses, 1955, 8-9 ; Espérandieu, 8873 ; Fouet, 1969, pl. XLVIII).

B83. **Montmirat**, Gard (France)
Altar-fragment. On front is wheel between two lines of inscription (*fulgur*) *conditum*. On opposite face is similar wheel. Both have nine spokes. 19 cm high (Espérandieu, 832 ; Lambrechts, 1942, 64-80) (Pl. IX, Fig. 19).

B85. **Montsérie**, Haute-Garonne (France)
Altar dedicated to *Erge* (equated in this area with Mars), decorated with swastika. 57 cm high (Espérandieu, 851 ; *C.I.L.*, XIII, 205e ; Thevenot, 1955).

B86. **Moos**, near Linz (Austria)
Relief of Wheel-God, preserved on dedication by *Ti. Claudius Soni fil. Prouincialis*. No other details available (Linz Museum closed when area visited) (Alföldy, 1974, 22 ; Egger, 1956-58, 44f. ; Polaschek, 1942, 53ff.).

B87. **Mouhet**, Indre (France)
Kneeling 'anguipède' giant with hands behind back ; on back is balanced an eight-spoked wheel. On side, on right of monster are legs of seated being of which left foot crushes the serpentine tail of the monster (Lelong, 1970, 123-126, fig. 1, 2).

B88. **Naix**, Meuse (France)
Statuette of seated figure. On side of throne are two *cornuacopiae* above which is six-spoked wheel placed precisely at height of left hand. Upper half of figure destroyed (de Villefosse, 1881, 1-13 ; Lambrechts, 1942, 64-80).

B89. **Neschers**, Puy-de-Dôme (France)
Fragment of Jupiter-Giant group including head of monster with horse-hooves resting on it, and fragments of six-spoked wheel. The wheel is sculpted free and must have rested against the palm of the hand and against the head of the horseman (Fournier, 1962, 114-116, fig. 9).

B90. **Niederwürzbach**, Amt Zweibrücken, Rheinland-Pfalz (Germany)
Wheel-God portrayed on 'Viergötterstein', with probably Juno, Hercules and Minerva. On one face Jupiter holds a four-spoked wheel through the spokes, in the left hand. Two of the spokes are 'S'-shaped. The god also holds a thunderbolt. 92 cm high. Speyer Museum (Cook, 1925, 57-93 ; Espérandieu, 5939 ; Drioux, 1934, 44) (Pl. XVII, Fig. 40).

B91. **Nijmegen** (Netherlands)
Relief of god accompanied by small humanoid figure, probably once with wheel. 38 cm high (Espérandieu, 6623 ; Lambrechts, 1942, 64-80).

B92. **Nîmes** area, Gard (France)
Dedication to Jupiter and Augustus. Remains of wheel (*C.I.L.*, XII, 2981 ; Lambrechts, 1942, 64-80).

B93. **Nîmes**, Gard (France)
Small altar with 'flashing' wheel (de Villefosse, 1881, 1-13).

B95. **Nîmes**, Gard (France)
Altar with six-spoked wheel, and inscription *Ioui*. 12 cm high (Espérandieu, 2650 ; Espérandieu, 1924, 13 ; Lambrechts, 1942, 64-80) (Pl. VIII, Fig. 17).

B99. **Nîmes**, Gard (France)
Altar with five-spoked wheel. 11 cm high (Lambrechts, 1942, 64-80 ; Espérandieu, 6817).

B100. **Nîmes**, Gard (France)
Altar without inscription with, on front, eight-spoked wheel above thunderbolt. 80 cm high. Nîmes, Musée Archéologique (Musée Lapidaire) (Espérandieu, 428 ; Harrison, 1912, 523ff., fig. 147 ; Espérandieu, 1924, pl. 1) (Pls. IX, Fig. 20 ; LXX, Fig. 40).

B101. **Nîmes**, Gard (France)
Small altar dedicated to Jupiter, with wheel-decoration. 15 cm high (Allmer, 1884-89, 11 ; Gaidoz, 1884, 14).

B102. **Obernburg**, Bayern (Germany)
Jupiter-Giant column horseman-group ; left arm of rider thrust through wheel with three concave-edged spokes. 66 cm high (Kellner, 1971, pl. 85) (Pl. I, Fig. 1).

B103. **Oehringen**, Baden-Württemburg (Germany)
Draped relief of goddess seated in armchair which has wheel carved on the side, (?)seven-spoked. Espérandieu thinks the representation to be Fortuna, but in the

writer's opinion it is more likely to be a Celtic version of Juno. Cast is in Württemburgisches-Landesmuseum, Stuttgart (Espérandieu, *Germ.*, 670).

B104. **Prieuré d'Arnes**, Haute-Garonne (France)
Marble stele portraying busts of persons associated with wheel-like rosettes. 77 cm high (Espérandieu, 8069).

B105. **Pyrénées**, unprovenanced within (France)
Altar with stylized tree and with concentric circles on base. 23 cm high (Espérandieu, 862) (Pl. VI, Fig. 11).

B106. **Pyrénées**, unprovenanced within (France)
Altar with swastika and inscription to Jupiter and Minerva. No size given but probably c. 20 cm high. Musée des Antiquités Nationales, St-Germain-en-Laye (Bertrand, 1897, 145ff.).

B107. **Pyrénées**, unprovenanced within (France)
Altar with representation of bust of divinity with, beneath, a swastika (Reinach, 1917, fig. 136).

B108. **Pyrénées**, unprovenanced within (France)
Altar bearing portrayal of palm and enclosed cross (or four-spoked wheel). Toulouse, Musée St-Raymond (Reinach, 1917, fig. 129) (Pl. VI, Fig. 13).

B109. **Pyrénées**, unprovenanced within (France)
Altar with wheel on face and swastika on base. 21 cm high. Toulouse, Musée St-Raymond (Reinach, 1917, fig. 130 ; Espérandieu, 863).

B110. **Pyrénées**, unprovenanced within (France)
Altar-fragment with wheel on face and on base two swastikas flanking four-spoked wheel. 13 cm high (Espérandieu, 863) (Pl. V, Fig. 8).

B111. **Pyrénées**, unprovenanced within (France)
Altar decorated with swastika and palm. Toulouse, Musée St-Raymond. 25 cm high (Espérandieu, 865) (Pl. VI, Fig. 12).

B112. **Pyrénées**, unprovenanced within (France)
Altar decorated with swastika and palm. 25 cm high. Toulouse, Musée St-Raymond (Espérandieu, 865, 1).

B113. **Pyrénées**, unprovenanced within (France)
Altar with wheel, swastika and dedication to Jupiter. 20 cm high (Thevenot, 1968, 26ff.).

B114. **Quémigny-sur-Seine**, Côte-d'Or (France)
Fragment of Jupiter-Giant horseman-group. Rider holds in left hand an oval shield with the boss forming a wheel-like disc with six radiating spokes. 50 cm high. Châtillon-sur-Seine, Musée Archéologique (Drioux, 1929, 355, fig. on p. 356 ; Espérandieu, 7098) (Pl. II, Fig. 2).

B115. **Reubberg**, near Zinswiller, Bas-Rhin (France)
'Stèle-maison' with rosette at apex. Niederbronn Museum (Linckenheld, 1931-34, fig. 66, 212-219).

B116. **Rezé**, Loire-Inférieure (France)
Relief of Jupiter accompanied by small humanoid figure with scroll-like tail. Jupiter possibly once held wheel. 69 cm high (Espérandieu, 3016 ; Lambrechts, 1942, 64-80).

B117. **Robernier**, Montford, Var (France)
Fragments of stele. On one face is stylized squatting beast, traces of standing beast and swastika. On right side possibly a foal and mare. Both faces are decorated with concentric circles. Very late Iron Age or early Roman date. 60 cm high (Espérandieu, 10 ; Déchelette, 1910, 409ff. ; Duval, 1957, 13 ; Grapinat, 1970, 54-56, fig. 10).

B118. **Rottweil**, near Stuttgart, Baden-Württemburg (Germany)
Relief of god and small humanoid figure. Deity possibly held wheel. 64 cm high (Espérandieu, *Germ.*, 644 ; Lambrechts, 1942, 64-80).

B119. **Rully**, Châlon-sur-Saône, Saône-et-Loire (France)
Funerary stele with 'sun-symbol' at apex (Armand-Calliat, 1937, pl. XXIII).

B120. **Rully**, Châlon-sur-Saône, Saône-et-Loire (France)
Statue, possibly portraying Jupiter with wheel, or Jupiter-horseman with wheel (Armand-Calliat, 1937, 37).

B121. **Rülzheim**, Speyer area, Rheinland-Pfalz (Germany)
Relief of Fortuna with *cornuacopiae* in left hand, rudder on globe in right. By left leg is eight-spoked wheel. On other faces of 'Viergötterstein' are Hercules, Apollo, Minerva. 93 cm high (Espérandieu, 5994).

B122. **Saint-Bertrand**, Le Comminges area, Haute-Garonne (France)
Altar with relief of conifer and faint traces of swastika on base. 19 cm high (Espérandieu, 859).

B123. **Saint-Christophe-le-Chaudry**, Cher (France)
Group comprising naked, bearded god with majestic visage. On head traces of ornament or circular attribute. Two arms missing. Shoulder-position indicates right hand was raised. To his right, resting against his leg, is small kneeling male, in cloak ; head sunk between shoulders ; dolorous facial expression. The standing god possibly once bore a wheel. 1 m 85 cm high (Cravayat, 1955, 210-228 ; Louis, 1954, 502, fig. 7).

B124. **Saint-Georges-de-Montagne**, Gironde (France)
Relief of Jupiter with a wheel resting against his head, and small kneeling figure. Lost (no size available) (Espérandieu, 1249, 1250 ; Blanchet, 1890, 159 ; *ibid.*, 1923, 157-160 ; Lambrechts, 1942, 64-80).

B125. **Saint-Just**, Ardèche (France)

Fragmentary altar with indeterminate female head portrayed. On one side of altar is wheel with eleven spokes. 80 cm high (Lambrechts, 1942, 64-80 ; Espérandieu, 421).

B126. **Saint-Pé-de-la-Moraine**, Le Comminges, Haute-Garonne (France)

One of a number of marble funerary plaques of similar type. Busts of two males, two females, associated with spirals and wheel-like rosettes. 38 cm high (Espérandieu, 8053).

B127. **Saint-Plancard**, Haute-Garonne (France)

Altar decorated with swastika on base ; very mutilated stone. 1 m 20 cm high (Espérandieu, 8127 ; Thevenot, 1955 ; Laffargue & Fouet, 1948).

B128. **Saint-Pourçain-sur-Besbre**, Allier (France)

Depiction of deity with small humanoid figure, and possibly once with wheel. Musée de Moulins (Louis, 1954, 502 ; Musée de Moulins, ?, 44, no. 625, pl. XXIV).

B129. **Saint-Privat**, Gard (France)

Altar to Jupiter and Augustus, with seven-spoked wheel-decoration (de Villefosse, 1881, 1-13).

B130. **Saint-Romain-en-Gal**, Vienne, Isère (France)

Mosaic depicting two individuals, man and woman (?) sacrificing by altar ; behind this is column bearing statue of upright deity. Tree stands behind column. The god stands with right arm held high holding possible thunderbolt. Left arm by side, hand appears to rest on wheel (Picard, 1974, 127-137, pl. XVI).

B131. **Sammuran**, Haute-Garonne (France)

Funerary stele decorated with lobe-spoked wheel and concentric semi-circles. 60 cm high (Espérandieu, 8051).

B132. **Sarrebourg**, Moselle (France)

Funerary 'stèle-maison' with rosette/wheel at apex (Linckenheld, 1931-34, 212-219).

B134. **Saverne** area, Bas-Rhin (France)

'Stèle-maison' with wheel-shape and circle. Saverne, Musée Archéologique.

B135. **Saverne**, Bas-Rhin (France)

'Stèle-maison' with funerary inscription and four-spoked wheel. Saverne, Musée Archéologique.

B136. **Saverne**, Bas-Rhin (France)

'Stèle-maison' with two circles, and with four-spoked wheel at apex. Saverne, Musée Archéologique.

B137. **Saverne**, Bas-Rhin (France)
Funerary stele with four four-spoked wheel-symbols. Saverne, Musée Archéologique (Forrer, 1935, 139, pl. XXIV).

B138. **Saverne** area, Bas-Rhin (France)
Rectangular stele with funerary inscription and six four-spoked wheels. 1 m 20 cm high. Saverne, Musée Archéologique (Espérandieu, 5705 ; Lambrechts, 1942, 64-80 ; Hatt, 1951b, 161) (Pls. XIV, Fig. 30 ; LXXIII, Fig. 46).

B139. **Saverne** area, Bas-Rhin (France)
Triangular tombstone. At base eight-spoked wheel. 83 cm high. Saverne, Musée Archéologique (Espérandieu, 5687 ; Lambrechts, 1942, 64-80) (Pls. XV, Fig. 33 ; LXXIV, Fig. 48).

B140. **Saverne**, Bas-Rhin (France)
Multiple rectangular gravestone with wheel-symbols (all four-spoked). 1 m 40 cm high. Saverne, Musée Archéologique (Espérandieu, 5688).

B141. **Saverne**, Bas-Rhin (France)
Stele with inscription ; above are three wheel-shapes. Inscription reads *Caratodius Carathouni (filius)*. 1 m 24 cm high. Saverne, Musée Archéologique (Espérandieu, 5691 ; Lambrechts, 1942, 64-80 ; Hatt, 1951b, 161) (Pls. XIV, Fig. 32 ; LXXIII, Fig. 47).

B142. **Saverne**, Bas-Rhin (France)
Several tombstones decorated with wheels, rosettes, circles. Saverne, Musée Archéologique (Espérandieu, 5696 ; Lambrechts, 1942, 64-80) (Pl. XIII, Fig. 27).

B143. **Scarpone**, Moselle (France)
Lost figure of horseman, probably from Jupiter-giant group ; with diagonal cross on chest (Espérandieu, 4612).

B144. **Séguret**, near Vaison, Vaucluse (France)
Stone statue of wheel-bearing divinity wearing garb of Roman general, entirely Roman-looking, with eagle at feet. The god wears cuirass, chlamys hanging from shoulder ; ten-spoked wheel in right hand and thunderbolt in left. Snake climbs oak-tree behind the god. 2 m 5 cm high. Avignon, Musée Lapidaire (Musée Calvet) (Courcelle-Seneuil, 1910, 68 ; Espérandieu, 303 ; Lambrechts, 1942, 64-80 ; Toutain, 1920, 192ff. ; Gaidoz, 1884, 12 ; Sautel, 1926, no. 501, pl. LIII) (Pls. X, Fig. 22 ; LXVI, Figs. 31, 32).

B145. **Speyer**, Rheinland-Pfalz (Germany)
Quadrangular block found at cemetery at Gangloff. 'Viergötterstein'. Four deities are represented, one on each face − Hercules, Juno, Vulcan and naked, beardless young Jupiter holding aloft a four-spoked wheel in his right hand. Rests other hand on (?)sceptre-handle. 88 cm high. Speyer Museum (Espérandieu, 8531).

B146. **Susa**, Cottian Alps, near Turin (North Italy)
Relief possibly representing Jupiter-cult, comprising five-spoked wheel, eagle and armed, winged goddess (Prieur, 1968, 177, pl. XIb).

B147. **Tarbes** area, Hautes-Pyrénées (France)
Altar with conifer-carving, and with swastika on base. 27 cm high (Espérandieu, 861) (Pl. V, Fig. 9).

B148. **Tarbes** area, Hautes-Pyrénées (France)
Altar decorated with conifers and with simple unenclosed cross on base. 19 cm high (Espérandieu, 860).

B149. **Theley**, near Trier, Rheinland-Pfalz (Germany)
'Viergötterstein', portraying Hygieia or Ceres, Minerva and Hercules, and youthful deity with chlamys and crown, (?)sceptre in right hand, six-spoked wheel in left ; small bird perched at feet. 85 cm high. Trier Landesmuseum (Hettner, 1893, 29ff., no. 40 ; Gaidoz, 1884, 11, fig. 7, no. 7 ; Cook, 1914, 288ff. ; *ibid.*, 1925, fig. 40 ; Espérandieu, 5116 ; Lambrechts, 1942, 64-80 ; Reinach, 1917, 113) (Pl. XVII, Fig. 39).

B150. **Tongres/Tongeren** (Belgium)
Relief of Jupiter and Juno seated side by side on throne. Jupiter has naked torso, legs covered with a cloak ; Juno is draped. The god bears a thunderbolt in his right hand and a probable sceptre in his left. Juno, in long robe and cloak, holds a (probably) six-spoked wheel in her left hand clasped against her chest. Eagle on globe and peacock at back of throne. Neither deity has surviving head. Lost (at one time in possession of Joseph Brassinne, University of Liège) (Espérandieu, 7217 ; Lambrechts, 1942, 64-80 ; Vanvinckenroye, 1975, 73, Afb. 37).

B151. **Tours**, Indre-et-Loire (France)
Stone group comprising 'anguipède' giant with wheel against his back, probably eight-spoked. Possibly the wheel was originally held by a Jupiter-horseman figure (Picard, 1968, 343, fig. 24).

B152. **Tresques**, Gard (France)
Altar dedicated to Jupiter. Under text is carved a seven-spoked wheel. On band on each side of the word *Ioui* is seven-petalled rosette (*C.I.L.*, XII, 2752 ; Lambrechts, 1942, 64-80 ; de Villefosse, 1881, 1-13).

B153. **Trier**, Rheinland-Pfalz (Germany)
Relief of Jupiter with wheel, on altar (Reinach, 1894, 34ff.).

B154. **Vaison-la-Romaine**, Vaucluse (France)
From Roman town ; altar bearing ten-spoked wheel. Avignon, Musée Calvet (Musée Lapidaire) (Sautel, 1923, 102ff., 104, fig. on p. 105 ; *ibid.*, 1926, pl. LXVIII, 3 ; Espérandieu, 7446) (Pl. LXIX, Fig. 37).

B155. **Vaison-la-Romaine**, Vaucluse (France)
Badly-preserved altar with six-spoked wheel. Built into Notre-Dame Cathedral (Sautel, 1923, 105-106 ; Espérandieu, 7446 ; Lambrechts, 1942, 64-80).

B156. **Vaison-la-Romaine**, Vaucluse (France)
Tombstone of Julius Severianus, who died at four years. Ornament in form of wheel (Sautel, 1926, II, no. 152, 90).

B157. **Vaison-la-Romaine**, Vaucluse (France)
Uninscribed, worn altar depicting Juno with tunic and cuirass. Right hand has wheel, and on base to left of deity are bird and snake (Sautel, 1926, II, no. 717).

B158. **Vaison-la-Romaine**, Vaucluse (France)
Altar-relief of Jupiter and Juno on dais. Jupiter is in Roman military garb — like an emperor or general, with cuirass and helmet ; thunderbolt in right hand, wheel at left, eagle by feet on his right. Juno has *patera* and peacock. Traces of climbing snake below wheel. 1 m 52 cm high (Espérandieu, 299 ; Thevenot, 1968, 26 ; de Villefosse, 1881, 1-13 ; Lambrechts, 1942, 64-80 ; Toutain, 1920, 192ff. ; Sautel, 1926, III, no. 705, pl. LXVIII, 2).

B159. **Valentine**, Villa d'Arnesp, summit of Montlas, Hautes-Pyrénées (France)
Votive altar from temple, decorated with tree, palm and with swastika on one surface ; wheel on another side of base (Fouet & Soutou, 1963, 289, fig. 17).

B160. **Varenne-Rouillon**, Côte-d'Or (France)
Fragments of Jupiter-giant group, including separate hand grasping wheel. 40 cm wheel-diameter (Espérandieu, 2020, 2189 ; Thevenot, 1936-39, 427-498).

B163. **Vernègues**, near ; between Salon and Aurons, Bouches-du-Rhône (France)
Altar-fragment. On two sides stylized tree ; on third eight-spoked wheel ; on fourth are long-handled hammer and two pots. 52 cm high (Espérandieu, 1691 ; Lambrechts, 1942, 64-80 ; Chaillan, 1907, 357-358, pl. on p. 357) (Pl. VII, Figs. 15, 16).

B164. **Vienne**, Isère (France)
Roughly executed, naked, ithyphallic deity, with ten-spoked wheel, and (probably) a bird. 38 cm high (Espérandieu, 829).

B165. **Vienne-en-Val**, Loiret (France)
'Viergötterstein' found in association with horseman-group. The rider possibly held aloft a wheel or thunderbolt. Remains of right arm upraised ; forelimbs of horse rest on giant (Lebel, 1970, 167-177, pl. XVI, XVII).

B166. **Vivarais**, Ardèche (France)
Altar dedicated to Apollo Belenus, dated to 3rd Century A.D., with swastika-decoration (Grapinat, 1970, fig. 16, 54-56).

B167. **Wasserwald**, near Saverne, Bas-Rhin (France)
'Stèle-maison' tombstone with three well-defined four-spoked wheels. *In situ*. (photograph in Saverne, Musée Archéologique) (Espérandieu, 5684 ; Lambrechts, 1942, 64-80 ; Linckenheld, 1927, 128-137 ; Forrer, 1909-12, 28-34, fig. 1, Taf. II) (Pl. XV, Fig. 35).

B169. **Wolfstein**, near Speyer, Rheinland-Pfalz (Germany)
Fragment of stele showing (?)Fortuna with six-spoked wheel by her left foot. 29 cm high (fragment) (Espérandieu, 6007).

Addendum

B170. **Petronell**, near Carnuntum (Austria)
Gravestone of Quintus Fortesius, soldier of Legion XV Apollinaris. Three wheels : one eight-spoked, two flanking it five- and six-spoked respectively. 2 m 8 cm high (Krüger, 1972, no. 542, 47-48, Taf. 47).

II. BRITISH MATERIAL

BB1. **Birdoswald**, Cumbria (NGR NY 6166)
Relief of wheel. Tullie House Museum, Carlisle (Wright & Phillips, 1975, 69, no. 179 ; Green, 1979a, no. 8).

BB2. **Birdoswald**, Cumbria
Altar dedicated to Jupiter Optimus Maximus, by 1st Aelian Cohort of Dacians. Swastika-motif on front at top, flanked by two enclosed crosses (or four-spoked wheels) (*R.I.B.*, 1877 ; Green, 1979a, no. 4 ; Collingwood Bruce, 1875, 184, no. 366).

BB3. **Caerleon**, Gwent (NGR ST 3390)
Small stone object, possibly a mould for bronzework. It portrays a man, very crudely represented. At end of each arm is wheel. A further wheel is by left foot ; at right foot is rectangular object (Lee, 1862, pl. XXXVII, figs. 3, 71, 107).

BB4. **Castlesteads**, Cumbria (NGR NY 5264)
Altar with dedication to Jupiter Optimus Maximus, by 2nd, part-mounted, Tungrian Cohort. On left side is thunderbolt, on right is ten-spoked wheel. Along top of altar, series of six enclosed crosses or four-spoked wheels (could be decoration or of significance) (Collingwood Bruce, 1875, 215, no. 424 ; *R.I.B.*, 1981 ; Green, 1979a, no. 2).

BB5. **Castlesteads**, Cumbria (NGR NY 5264)
Altar dedicated to Jupiter, with ten-spoked wheel in relief. On left side is thunderbolt, on right wheel. Found in 1660. Dedication is to Jupiter Optimus Maximus and the Numen of the Emperor, by 2nd, part-mounted, Cohort of Tungrians. Tullie House Museum, Carlisle (*R.I.B.*, 1983 ; Green, 1979a, no. 1) (Pl. LXXV, Fig. 50).

BB6. **Castlesteads**, Cumbria (NGR NY 5264)
Carving of Fortuna with wheel on which rests rudder. Headless (Collingwood Bruce, 1875, 236, no. 471).

BB7. **Chedworth**, Gloucestershire (NGR SP 0511)
Miniature stone altar bearing crudely-incised figure of warrior with (?)spear, and possibly long-handled hammer. Peculiar stemmed wheel-symbols on sides of stone. 15.8 cm max. height. Chedworth Roman Villa Museum (Goodburn, 1972, pl. 10, 3) (Pl. LXXVI, Figs. 52, 53).

BB8. **Churcham**, Gloucestershire (NGR SO 7618)
Built into wall of church, oblong stone plaque. Figure in centre is male, with huge head, long tunic and possibly horns. Hands and elbows symmetrically half-extended from body. In each hand is firmly grasped a trilobate object. At each of lower angles of plaque is four-spoked wheel. 32 × 40 cm (Baddeley, 1923, 91ff. ; Green, 1976, 170).

BB9. **Cotswolds**, unprovenanced
Carving of Mother-Goddess bearing wheel-sign at apex of niche above head. Devizes Museum (Green, 1976, 17-19).

BB10. **Easton Grey**, Wiltshire (NGR ST 8987)
Carving of Mother-Goddess with stylized wheel-symbol. Devizes Museum (Green, 1976, 17-19).

BB11. **High Rochester**, Northumberland (NGR NY 8398)
Altar dedicated to Minerva and a Genius, set up by a guild. On face of capital is simple, four-spoked wheel-shape, the spokes diagonal to the spectator ; on each side is reverse swastika (Collingwood Bruce, 1875, 281, no. 546 ; Phillips, 1977, no. 212, pl. 54).

BB12. **High Rochester**, Northumberland
Altar to Genius and Standards, dedicated by Cohors I Vardullorum, Roman citizens. On front of capital are two swastikas ; in between is incised crescent. Newcastle University Museum of Antiquities (Collingwood Bruce, 1875, 287, no 553 ; Phillips, 1977, no. 188, pl. 47).

BB13. **Lypiatt Park**, Gloucestershire (NGR SO 9005)
Altar with ram-horned serpent entwined around the external surface ; worn but recognizable wheel on top *focus*. Stroud Museum (Clifford, 1938, 297ff. ; Green, 1976, 172 ; Green, 1979a, no. 44 ; Green, 1980) (Pl. III, Fig. 4).

BB14. **Maryport**, Cumbria (NGR NY 0336)
Wheel carved on stone. 20.2 cm diameter of wheel (Bailey, 1915, 135ff. ; Green, 1979a, no. 9).

BB15. **Maryport**, Cumbria
Altar. On either side *patera*, on rear wheel. Dedicated to Jupiter Optimus Maximus by 1st Cohort of Spaniards. Found 350 yards north-east of fort. Netherhall Museum (*R.I.B.*, 827 ; Green, 1979a, no. 3).

BB16. **Maryport**, Cumbria

Oblong stone set into base of octagonal column, with dedication to Jupiter Optimus Maximus. In lower, quadrangular portion is figure of horseman and stylized column. Rosette on capital at top (Collingwood Bruce, 1875, 431, no. 848).

BB17. **Netherby**, Cumbria (NGR NY 3971)

Relief of Genius, half-draped, with wheel held over altar in place of usual *patera*. Found in 1772. *Cornuacopiae* in left hand. Tullie House Museum, Carlisle (Collingwood Bruce, 1875, 402, no. 780 ; Wright & Phillips, 1975, 73, no. 196, pl. IVb ; Green, 1979a, no. 6) (Pl. LXXV, Fig. 51).

BB18. **Netherby**, Cumbria

Relief found some time before 1725. God represented as Genius, similar to BB17. Holds *cornuacopiae* in left hand and wheel over altar in right. On his right is boar in front of tree. Tullie House Museum, Carlisle (Wright & Phillips, 1975, 73, no. 197 ; Green, 1979a, no. 7).

BB19. **Peel Crags**, Hadrian's Wall, 40 yards east of Turret 39a, Northumberland (NGR NZ 0168)

Fragment of round-headed tombstone, re-used. Bears swastika-motif (*R.I.B.*, 1641).

BB20. **Piercebridge**, Durham (NGR NZ 2115)

Altar dedicated to Mars Condatis. 'To god Mars Condatis, Antonius Quintianus, surveyor, *euocatus*...'. Swastika-motif (*R.I.B.*, 1024).

BB21. **Risingham**, Northumberland (NGR NY 8383)

Gravestone of Satrius Honoratus. Dated to 3rd Century A.D. Above inscription is eight-spoked wheel between two crescents. Newcastle University Museum of Antiquities (Phillips, 1977, no. 266, pl. 72).

Addenda

B22. **Housesteads**, Northumberland (NGR NY 7968)

Altar to Jupiter Optimus Maximus and the Numen of the Emperor, dedicated by 1st Tungrian Cohort. Two four-spoked wheels on middle of top (*R.I.B.*, 1585 ; Collingwood Bruce, 1875, 90, no. 176).

BB23. **Lower Slaughter**, Gloucestershire (NGR SP 1622)

Triangular-niched plaque with three two-dimensional *Genii cucullati*, with Warrior-god or worshipper. In apex of niche rosette or four-spoked wheel. Found in well with other figures, for example Mother-Goddesses, Warrior-gods (Ross, 1967, 187, pl. 62a ; Toynbee & O'Neil, 1958, 49-55).

CATALOGUE C

Miscellaneous Romano-Celtic Wheel-Symbolism

Alphabetical Concordance Table

Angers, 45
Anthée, 69
Assche-Kalkoven, 52
Augst, 70
Autun, 16
Avrigney, 38
Bad Dürkheim, 74
Beaune, 35
Bernard, 44
Brittany, 47
Bro-en-Fégréac, 31
Buxières d'Aillac, 21
Caerleon, 11
Caerwent, 81
Caistor, 56
Casterley Camp, 76, 77
Caudebec-lès-Elbeuf, 42
Châlon-sur-Saône, 22
Cologne, 33, 34
Corbridge, 10
Corseuil, 46
Dompierre, 24
Echzell, 28
Farley Heath, 7
France, 13, 50, 58
Guerche, 41
Gundestrup, 1
Hainault, 61
Harzburg, 4
Housesteads, 60
Köln (see Cologne)
Landouzy, 3
Le Châtelet, 2
La Graufesenque, 73
La Villeneuve, 25
Littlehampton, 55
Little Houghton, 63
London, 84

Lons-le-Saunier, 71
Lyon, 37, 82
Malton, 59
Manchester, 62
Maranville, 23
Marne, 39
Mauer an der Url, 51
Moulins, 9, 40
Moulins-Engelberf, 36
Néris, 9
Neuchâtel, 18
Nolay, 29
Plessis-Barbuise, 5
Pully, 83
Pyrénées, 65
Quilly, 48
Rheinzabern, 27
Roger, 30
Rouen, 26, 68
Saint-Pourçain, 8
Saint-Rémy, 20
Saint-Vulbas, 19
Silchester, 54
Springhead, 57
Stibbington, 75
Strasbourg, 66, 67
Stobi, 17
Thiel-sur-Acolin, 12
Toulouse, 72
Toulvern-Baden, 43
Trier, 14
Tronëon, 32
Van Oudenburg, 78
Viège, 49
Vienne, 15
Vindonissa, 79
Walldürn, 64
Willingam Fen, 6

Note on size

Dimensions are given where possible. In general bronze or clay figurines are between 6 and 12 cm high. Sizes are not quoted where a scale is present on an illustration.

I. Depictions of Wheel-God

C1. **Gundestrup** (¹), Raevemose, East of Ars, Jutland (Denmark)
Silver cauldron with spherical base and cylindrical sides ; 69 cm diameter, 42 cm high. Five inner and seven outer plates. 8,885 grams of 97% pure silver used in construction. Remains of gold leaf. One inner plate depicts the bust of a male, bearded, individual with large head ; both arms raised and fingers clenched. Against right arm is half of wheel eight of whose spokes are portrayed. The wheel is supported by a small kneeling figure in short-sleeved belted tunic and helmet with long curling knobbed horns. The humanoid figures are flanked by leopards (or lions). Also present are three winged griffons and a ram-horned snake. Another plate bears a depiction of a goddess flanked by two lobe-spoked wheels each with six spokes. Date of cauldron put at 80-50 B.C. (Olmsted, 1979, pl. 2 and *passim*).

C2. **Le Châtelet**, near St. Dizier, Haute-Marne (France)
Bronze statuette 10.3 cm high (Courcelle-Seneuil, 1910, 66, fig. 21). Musée des Antiquités Nationales, St.-Germain-en-Laye, Acc. no. 32947. Discovered in 1774. The god stands naked, bearded with long hair. He bears a thunderbolt in his right hand and a six-spoked wheel in his left. From his right shoulder is slung a ring suspended from which another ring supports nine free-moving 'S' or spiral-shaped bronze items (Reinach, 1894, 33). Stylistically the figure is unroman, although, as Boucher suggests (1976, 137) the representation is of an essentially classical divinity to whom a local attribute has been added. Non-classical artistic features include the somewhat sketchy treatment of the anatomy, the stocky build (so reminiscent of many Gaulish divine portrayals) and the unroman physiognomy (Boucher, 1976, 162). Two rings at the back of the figure, at the shoulders and near the base, suggest that it was designed to fit onto a wand or staff (Green, 1979a, 345-368) (Frontispiece and Pl. LXXIX, Fig. 57).

C3. **Landouzy-la-Ville**, Aisne (France)
Bronze statuette 22 cm high (Courcelle-Seneuil, 1910, 67, fig. 22). Musée des Antiquités Nationales, St.-Germain-en-Laye, Acc. no. 26262. The figure stands naked, with sceptre (now lost) once having passed through the right hand. In the left hand is a six-spoked wheel resting on a curious capital-crowned pedestal. The figure stands on a base on which there is an inscription *I.O.M. ET Ñ AVG*. The barbarous attitude of the figure is very striking. The facial expression is wild, and

---

(1) Not strictly Romano-Celtic but not prehistoric either. I have catalogued this piece here for convenience.

the basal dedication crudely incised (de Villefosse, 1881, 1-13). The deity resembles Gaulish depictions of Hercules rather than Jupiter. Like the Le Châtelet figure (Boucher, 1976, 137, 162) the style of the statuette is fairly unclassical, although presumably a basically Roman divinity is intended (Pl. LXXX, Figs. 59, 60).

C4. **Harzburg**, Brunswick (Germany)

Bronze statuette from Roman fortress. The figure represents Jupiter with a basket in the right hand and a wheel in the left. Behind is a fish (Lambrechts, 1942, 64-80 ; Reinach, 1894, 35).

C5. **Plessis-Barbuise**, Aube (France)

Lead wheel-model (see also Cat. A, 73) inside which is figure of god with spear or sceptre in right hand and thunderbolt in left (Thevenot, 1968, fig. opp. 25).

C6. **Willingham Fen**, Cambridgeshire (England) NGR TL 4070

From hoard containing, for instance, busts of Mars, figurines of ravens, and horsemen, bronze sceptre-terminal, 12.1 cm high, decorated with composite motifs. A youthful, beardless naked deity (resembling Cupid rather than a Sky-God) bears a club or thunderbolt, and places his left foot on the head of a humanoid monster. The god is accompanied by a fragmentary wheel with four out of (?) six spokes surviving, on the right of the figure. Above the wheel is the head of a three-horned bull (Alföldi, 1949, 19ff. ; Green, 1976, 17-19, 210, pl. X, a-c ; Green, 1979a, no. 42). Cambridge University Museum of Archaeology and Anthropology (Pl. LXXXI, Figs. 61, 62).

C7. **Farley Heath**, Albury, Surrey (England) NGR TQ 0544

From Romano-Celtic temple-site, sheet-bronze binding, probably once twined round a ritual wooden stave. When discovered the sheet-metal was twisted into a spiral and attached to an iron head. Punched into the bronze is a variety of sketched symbols. At the top are a stag, dog and raven ; at the bottom are a (?) raven and other indeterminate creatures possibly including a boar ; the centre of the sheet is occupied by a god with a long-shafted hammer and a conical hat, accompanied by pairs of tongs above and below him. An axe-hammer is situated below the lower tongs. Between the upper tongs and the third of the upper group of beasts is a humanoid head associated with a stylized wheel or rosette beneath which is a trident-like thunderbolt. A bronze eagle also comes from the shrine. British Museum (Goodchild, 1938, 391ff. ; Goodchild, 1947, 83ff. ; Green, 1976, 219 ; Green, 1979a, no. 43) (Pl. LXXXII, Fig. 64).

C8. **St.-Pourçain-sur-Besbre**, Allier (France)

Workshop for the manufacture of pipe-clay items.

i) Complete pipe-clay figurine of god with six-spoked wheel resting against the side of his head and accompanied by a small figure kneeling by his side, the whole group resting on a plinth (Blanchet, 1923, 157-160). The tiny figure raises its arms above its head as if supporting the weight of the Wheel-God's hand resting on it (Blanchet, 1890 ; Rouvier-Jeanlin, 1972, Type 2, no. 513).

ii) Lower half of figure similar to (i) (Rouvier-Jeanlin, 1972, Type 2, no. 512).

iii) Pipe-clay hand holding wheel.

iv) Pipe-clay arm holding wheel against shoulder.

v) Lower half of pipe-clay figure showing standing god with small accompanying figure and possibly once with wheel (Gaidoz, 1884, no. 3).

(All in Musée des Antiquités Nationales, St.-Germain-en-Laye, Acc. nos. 28006-28007 [no. i lost]).

C9. **Moulins**, region of, Allier (France)

Pipe-clay manufactories.

i) Statuette in pipe-clay of Wheel-God similar to (C8), resting left hand on head of small nude (?) female figure by his side (Bertrand, 1897, 319, pl. 28 ; Blanchet, 1890, pl. II, 25, 187-188, no. 1, fig. 25 ; Gaidoz, 1884, 7-9).

ii) Upper half of pipe-clay statuette once bearing wheel by the right ear (now lost) (Gaidoz, 1884, no. 1).

iii) Pipe-clay male (?) bearded deity with wheel supported by upraised right hand against ear, and with indeterminate rock-like object in left hand (Gaidoz, 1884, no. 4).

iv) Pipe-clay male bearded deity with wheel by right ear and with diminutive accompanying figure (Gaidoz, 1884, no. 5).

(All in Musée des Antiquités Nationales, St.-Germain-en-Laye).

C9a. **Néris**, Allier (France)

i) Pipe-clay figurine of Wheel-God bearing both wheel and thunderbolt. Musée des Antiquités Nationales, St.-Germain-en-Laye (Rouvier-Jeanlin, 1972, Type 2, no. 519).

ii) Pipe-clay figurine of Wheel-God with left hand on head of small being by his side with raised arms (Cravayat, 1955, 213-214) (Pl. LXXXIII, Fig. 65).

NB. Wheel-brooch also from this location (Poursat, 1975, 425, fig. 7).

C10. **Corbridge**, Tyne & Wear (England) NGR NY 9964

Baked clay mould, made for impression of a design to be applied to the surface of a pottery jar. The mould depicts a male deity wearing a long tunic and a curious knobbed helmet. He bears a rectangular shield decorated with ring-and-dot motifs, a crooked club, and he is accompanied by an eight-spoked wheel by his lower left leg (Forster & Knowles, 1910, 224, fig. 6 ; Toutain, 1943-45, pl. 1, 31-34 ; Green, 1979a, no. 16). Corstopitum Museum (Pl. LXXIX, Fig. 58).

C11. **Caerleon**, Gwent (Wales) NGR ST 3390

i) Triangular clay antefix depicting human head and with an eight-spoked wheel in the apex of the triangle. Stars flank the lower part of the human face (Taylor *et al.*, 1929, 182 ; Boon, 1972, pl. 14, A ; Green, 1979a, no. 23). National Museum of Wales, Cardiff (Pl. LXXVII, Fig. 54).

ii) Triangular clay antefix depicting a human head and with an eight-spoked wheel in the apex of the triangle. Stars and a crescent are present beside the lower part of the face (Anon., 1969, 242, pl. XVIII, 3 ; Boon, 1972, pl. 14, E ; Green, 1979a, no. 24). National Museum of Wales, Cardiff (Pl. LXXVII, Fig. 54).

C12. **Thiel-sur-Acolin**, Allier (France)
Standing male pipe-clay figure, headless, with the general mien of Jupiter. In right hand is a *patera* which possibly has spokes or rays. A curious chain-like object dangles from the left hand (Vertet, 1960, 303-314).

C13. **France**, unprovenanced.
Pipe-clay figure of bearded Jupiter, once with wheel ; left hand rests on head of small naked male. Musée des Antiquités Nationales, St.-Germain-en-Laye, Acc. no. 2320.

C14. **Trier**, Rheinland-Pfalz (Germany)
Several pipe-clay figurines of seated Jupiter bearing wheel-like shield at left side of throne. Trier Landesmuseum.

II. Wheel-Symbolism (or Derivative) Accompanying Deities other than Wheel-God

C15. **Vienne**, Isère (France)
Bronze figurine of male standing deity (?Sucellus) wearing lion or wolfskin which forms a hood and is draped over the left arm. In the right hand the god bears a small circular pot ; in the left is a lance or sceptre. Behind the figure is a barrel-shaped item, supported on a long handle, from which sprout five 'spokes' each terminating in a smaller barrel or cylinder with ring-and-dot motifs (de Villefosse, 1881, 1-13 ; Reinach, 1894, 34ff. ; no. 151 ; Boucher, 1976, pl. 63, no. 301 ; Kent Hill, 1953, 204-224, fig. 1).

C16. **Autun**, Côte-d'Or (France)
Bronze figurine of Fortuna, 8.6 cm high, with exaggeratedly large four-spoked wheel (Lebel & Boucher, 1975, 35, no. 42).

C17. **Stobi** (Yugoslavia)
Superb bronze statuette of Fortuna, 8.5 cm high, with four-spoked wheel (Popovic, 1969, no. 111).

C18. **?Neuchâtel**, area of (Switzerland)
Bronze figurine of Hercules, bearing cross-pattern on breast. Deonna (1915, 96, fig. 37) suggests that the mark may be significant, but to the present writer it need only represent pectoral muscle-stylization. Musée de Neuchâtel.

C19. **Saint-Vulbas**, Ain (France)
Bronze statuette of Hammer-God (Sucellus) with wide belt decorated with ring-and-dot motifs (Colombet & Lebel, 1953, 112, fig. 23).

C20. **Saint-Remy-en-Provence**, Bouches-du-Rhône (France)
Bronze bull bearing belt decorated with concentric circles (Colombet & Lebel, 1953, fig. 21).

C21. **Buxières-d'Aillac**, Indre (France)

Bronze statuette of standing Mother-Goddess, fully-draped, bearing in right hand a 'cake' divided by six 'spokes'; in the left hand is a *patera*. Musée de Bourges (Cravayat, 1955, 215, fig. 80).

C22. **Châlon-sur-Saône**, Musée de (France)

Bronze seated male figure, named by author of publication as Sucellus. Side-fronts of chair decorated with diagonal crosses (Blanchet, 1946-49, 757, pl. XXIII).

C23. **Maranville**, Haute-Marne (France)

Bronze statuette of Sucellus decorated with 'lobed' astral signs, wheels, crosses and rosettes (Drioux, 1921, 67-68 ; Drioux, 1934, 100).

C24. **Dompierre-sur-Besbre**, Allier (France)

Bronze statuette of draped female wearing necklet with concentric-circle pendant (Poursat, 1975, 423-424, figs. 3, 4).

C25. **La-Villeneuve-au-Châtelot**, La Poterie, Ardennes (France)

Two lead medallions (and fragments of a possible third) depicting Epona within wheel-shapes. Bifurcated suspension-loops. Each complete example 5.5 cm diameter (Frézouls, 1971, 287, fig. 18).

C26. **Rouen**, Musée de (France)

Pipe-clay 'Venus' decorated with wheels and other astral signs (Blanchet, 1890, 65-224).

C27. **Rheinzabern**, Rheinland-Pfalz (Germany)

Two-handled pottery flagon dated to 2nd Century A.D., surmounted by a head, with six-spoked wheel on necklace hung around the neck. Wheel decorated with knobs in the centre and where rim meets necklace (Chenet, 1919, 250, fig. 5).

C28. **Echzell**, Hessen (Germany)

Roman fort. Wall-painting depicts Fortuna with large wheel. Preserved at Saalburg Museum (Baatz, 1968, Taf. 8).

C29. **Nolay**, Côte-d'Or (France)

Bronze statuette of Sucellus, bearded, decorated with astral signs. Musée des Antiquités Nationales, St.-Germain-en-Laye, Acc. no. 20687.

C30. **Roger**, Saône-et-Loire (France)

Bronze statuette of Sucellus, bearded, decorated with astral signs. Musée des Antiquités Nationales, St.-Germain-en-Laye, Acc. no. 81088.

C31. **Bro-en-Fégréac**, Loire Atlantique (France)

Headless pipe-clay 'Venus' minus feet. Astral signs and wheels next to her body. The figurine bears a scroll in her right hand ; at the rear of the statuette are marked rosettes and crosses (Blanchet, 1890, Type 10).

C32. **Tronëon**, Oppidum de, Finistère (France)
Pipe-clay 'Venus' statuette bearing wheel-symbols next to her body (Rouvier-Jeanlin, 1972, no. 208). Musée des Antiquités Nationales, St.-Germain-en-Laye, Acc. no. 75814.

C33. **Cologne**, Zeuhausstrasse, Nordrhein-Westfalen (Germany)
Mithras-jug bearing painted figures of Sol and the *cannophori* ; wheel-symbols painted round the pot in pale-brown. One snake and one lion-handle. Dated to 2nd or 3rd Century A.D. Römisch-Germanisches Museum, Köln.

C34. **Cologne**, Nordrhein-Westfalen (Germany)
Bronze figurine of Sucellus bearing circles and semi-circles on tunic ; c. 12 cm high. Römisch-Germanisch Museum, Köln (Pl. LXXXIII, Fig. 66).

C35. **Beaune**, Côte-d'Or (France)
Bronze figurine of Sucellus bearing a barrel on the end of a staff, and with diagonal crosses on his tunic (Encyclopaedia of Religion & Ethics, 1911, 325 ; Mainz Zentralmuseum photographic catalogue R20.23).

C36. **Moulins-Engleberf**, Côte-d'Or (France)
Bronze key dedicated to the god 'Brixantius', with diagonal cross cut deeply into business end (Toutain, 1916, 25-39, pl. III).

C37. **Lyon**, Rhône (France)
Bronze figurine of Sucellus bearing 'L' shapes and diagonal crosses on his body (Toutain, 1916, fig. 5). Lyon, Musée de la Civilization Gallo-Romaine.

C38. **Avrigney**, Doubs (France)
Triple-horned bronze bull with rosette-shaped growth of hair on forehead (Deonna, 1921-22, 22-26, pl. 1).

C39. **Marne**, Département de (France)
Bronze bull-shaped lamp with cross incised on left front leg. Suspension-ring made up of three rings and hook in form of swan's head. Fairly crude workmanship (Reinach, 1894, 279 ; Deonna, 1921-22, 22-26).

C40. **Moulins**, Allier (France)
Pipe-clay factories. Several 'Venus' figurines bearing celestial symbols :
i) Pipe-clay group comprising 'Venus', a male and a child. The goddess wears a necklet with a sun-symbol ; water-birds and solar signs on lower half of front ; large stylized sun-wheels on rear. Musée de Rouen (Blanchet, 1890, 65-224, fig. 3).
ii) 'Venus' figure bearing wheels, concentric circles and other solar symbols. No exact provenance (Blanchet, 1890, fig. 15).

C41. **Guerche**, neighbourhood of, Cher (France)
Rear half of mould of pipe-clay 'Venus' from Moulins factories, bearing rosettes and circles (Roubet *et al.*, 1888-89, 11, 21-23, pl. 5 ; Blanchet, 1890, Type 8, fig. 2).

C42. **Caudebec-lès-Elbeuf**, Seine Inférieure (France)

Pipe-clay 'Venus', inscribed on rear with maker's name. The figurine bears wheels, concentric circles and solar signs in place of breasts, on trunk and on thighs (together with crescents) and by sides of legs (Pottier, 1881, pl. 6, fig. 83 ; Blanchet, 1890, fig. 1, Type 9 ; Schliermacher, 1962, 336-341).

C43. **Toulvern-Baden**, Morbihan (France)

Pipe-clay 'Venus' decorated with circles and rosettes (Blanchet, 1890, Type 10).

C44. **Bernard**, Vendee (France)

Pipe-clay 'Venus' bearing wheels, rosettes and concentric circles (Blanchet, 1890, Type 10 ; Baudrey & Ballereau, 1873, 104, figs. 3, 4).

C45. **Angers**, Maine-et-Loire (France)

Pipe-clay 'Venus' figure decorated with stars and circles (Blanchet, 1890, Type 10).

C46. **Corseuil**, near, Ille-et-Vilaine (France)

Pipe-clay 'Venus' decorated with rings and concentric circles (Blanchet, 1890, Type 10 ; Robert, 1878, 105). Present location Rennes, Collection Fornier.

C47. **Brittany**, unprovenanced (France)

Fragment of pipe-clay statuette wearing Gaulish smock, ornamented with wheels and concentric circles (Blanchet, 1890, 65-224).

C48. **Quilly**, St.-Nazaire, Loire Atlantique (France)

Pipe-clay statuette of male, beardless, deity in cross-legged position. At tips of fingers small water-bird. Under right elbow are three incised solar-circles, and stars ; small circles on necklet. On rear of figure semi-circles, circles and stars (Coutil, 1899, 77-83, pl. VI, fig. 32 ; Blanchet, 1901, 189-272).

C49. **Viège**, Valois (Switzerland)

Bronze figurine of Sucellus, found in 1690, with hammer or thunderbolt, and with swastikas and crosses on tunic. Musée de Genève, Acc. no. M49.

C50. **France**, unprovenanced

Bronze figurine of Sucellus with diagonal crosses on body. Musée des Antiquités Nationales, St.-Germain-en-Laye, Acc. no. 32950 (Reinach, 1894, 34ff.).

C51. **Mauer an der Url** (Austria)

Triangular bronze plaque dedicated to Jupiter Dolichenus and Juno Regina. On rear of plaque are eagles ; near apex of triangle is eight-spoked wheel/rosette (Fleischer, 1967, Taf. 65, no. 119).

C52. **Assche-Kalkoven** (Belgium)

Pipe-clay figurines of horses, some with breast harness strap decorated with *lunulae* and other celestial symbols (Magnen & Thevenot, 1953, 16 ; De Laet, 1942, 41-53).

III. Miscellaneous Items Bearing Wheel-Symbolism

C54. **Silchester**, Hampshire (England) NGR SU 6462
Small pot. c. 9 cm max. diameter, decorated with painted wheel and 'S' symbols. Vessel covered with fine, reddish-purple gloss. Wheels set in circular depressions (St. John Hope & Fox, 1900, 104, fig. 5 ; Johnston, 1903, 233-234).

C55. **Littlehampton**, Sussex (England) NGR TQ 0202
Black, coarse-ware handled flagon, c. 13.7 cm high, bearing wheel-symbols on each side 'in a sort of enamel or glaze' (Johnston, 1903, 233, pl. on 233).

C56. **Caistor**, Norfolk (England) NGR TG 2303
Castor-ware pot decorated with wheel-symbols (Johnston, 1903, 233).

C57. **Springhead**, Kent (England) NGR TQ 6172
Swastika-motif on sherd of glass (Penn, 1968, 174ff.).

C58. **France**, unprovenanced
Bronze votive hand holding *patera* ornamented with wheel-like spokes. The hand hangs from a suspension-chain (Babelon & Blanchet, 1895, no. 1073, 463).

C59. **Malton**, North Yorkshire (England) NGR SE 7871
Roman fort : two grey-ware sherds decorated with applied wheels. Malton Roman Museum (Green, 1978, 63, pl. 50 ; Green, 1979a, no. 10 ; Leach, 1962) (Pl. LXXVIII, Fig. 56).

C60. **Housesteads**, Tyne & Wear (England) NGR NY 7968
Roman fort : grey-ware sherd with large applied wheel from large ceramic vessel. Housesteads Roman Fort Museum (Birley *et al.*, 1934, 197, pl. 29C, no. 1 ; Green, 1978, 61, pl. 51 ; Green, 1979a, no. 15) (Pl. LXXVIII, Fig. 55).

C61. **Hainault** (Belgium)
Tegula incised with swastika-motif. Musées Royaux, Brussels (de Löe, 1937, fig. 10).

C62. **Manchester**, Lancashire (England) NGR SJ 8397
Roman fort : clay bowl, c. 12 cm diameter, in pinkish fabric, with white-painted decoration in form of wheel. Shape of pot resembles samian form 30 (Jones & Grealey, 1974, 115, fig. 41, no. 243 ; Green, 1978, 64 ; Green, 1979a, no. 21).

C63. **Little Houghton**, Pylon Field, Northamptonshire (England) NGR SP 8160
Fragment of glass from base of flat-bottomed dish or bowl, with raised wheel-symbol. Found in 1957. Northampton Central Museums & Art Gallery (Green, 1974, 2-6).

C64. **Walldürn**, Odenwaldkreis, Baden-Württemburg (Germany)
Tile-stamp of Legion XXII (based at Mainz) in form of swastika-symbol (Baatz, 1978, 103, Abb. 33, no. 2).

C65. **Pyrénées**, unlocated (France)
Swastikas on Gallo-Roman coarse-ware vessels (Bertrand, 1897, 145ff.).

C66. **Strasbourg**, Bas-Rhin (France)
Gallo-Roman cemetery containing, in Tomb 88, a copper plaque with punched decoration in form of swastika surrounded by chevrons. A second plaque bears cross-hatched ornament, three swastikas and a cross (Bertrand, 1897, figs. 14, 15, 153-154).

C67. **Strasbourg**, Bas-Rhin (France)
Tile-marks including wheel-symbols, in 4th Century A.D. deposits (Hatt, 1953, 248, fig. 17, nos. 7, 8).

C68. **Rouen**, Seine-Maritime (France)
Cinerary urn found in 1837 ; decorated with swastika (Bertrand, 1897, 155, fig. 16).

C69. **Anthée** (Belgium)
Roman villa excavations revealed swastikas on two fragments of tile (Anon., 1896, 292).

C70. **Augst** (Switzerland)
Mould on fragment of tile, for four-spoked wheel-models (each 2.2 cm diameter) (Martin, 1978, 118, Abb. 16). Augst Römermuseum (Pl. LVII, Fig. 14).

C71. **Lons-le-Saunier**, Franche-Comté (no closer location) (France)
Large jar, probably dating to La Tène III, with incised eight-spoked wheel on belly above shoulder (Lerat, 1970, 356, fig. 20).

C72. **Toulouse**, Haute-Garonne (France)
Fragment of brick or tile bearing swastika-symbol. Found in Sept-Deniers area. Dimensions of tile 14 × 11 cm (Labrousse, 1959, 430, fig. 27).

C73. **La Graufesenque**, Aveyron (France)
1st Century (?late Iron Age) 'Vases de style campanien' including one marked on exterior surface with four-spoked wheel (Balson, 1952, 8, fig. 7).

C74. **Bad Dürkheim**, area of, Rheinland-Pfalz (Germany)
Tile-stamp of Legion XXII (based at Mainz) in form of swastikas ; from region of Roman quarry (information from Dr. D. Baatz, Director, Saalburg Museum, Bad Homburg).

C75. **Stibbington**, Cambridgeshire (England) NGR TL 1298
Nene Valley Ware wheel with painted spoke-decoration in pale-brown slip/paint. Peterborough City Museum.

C76. **Casterley Camp**, Wiltshire (England) NGR SU 1153
Bone disc with incised eight-spoked decoration on one face. 2.1 cm diameter.

Found in T-shaped furnace with 2nd Century pottery. Possibly another similar example (Cunnington, 1896, pl. LXII, no. 14). Devizes Museum.

C77. **Casterley Camp**, Wiltshire (England)

Clay spindle-whorl, 4.5 cm diameter. Decoration in form of four spokes intersected by median internal incised ring. Central hole (Cunnington, 1896, pl. LXIV, no. 23). Devizes Museum.

Addenda

C78. **Van Oudenburg** (Belgium)

Pipe-clay headless figure from late Roman grave area. Figure wears short tunic ; his left hand holds a dangling chain, his right a *patera* with wheel-shaped decoration (stylized spokes leaving circular holes in between) (Creus, 1975, Afb. 13, 14).

C79. **Vindonissa** (Windisch) (Switzerland)

Triangular clay antefix with human head in Celtic style, bearded. On one side of the head is a rayed circle and on the other a stylized conifer (Leibundgut, 1966-76, Abb. 28).

C81. **Caerwent**, Gwent (Wales) NGR ST 4790

Bronze plate bearing decoration in form of incised wheel with square frame (Ross, 1968, 262).

C82. **Lyon**, Rhône (France)

Pipe-clay figure (cf. nos. 12, 78) bearing chain-like object in left hand and wheel/*patera* in right. Lyon, Musée de la Civilisation Gallo-Romaine.

C83. **Pully**, Lausanne (Switzerland)

Bronze figurine of Sucellus, with pot, and marked with Latin and diagonal crosses (Stähelin, 1948, 531, Abb. 151).

C84. **London** (England) NGR TQ 3079

Pipe-clay 'Venus' figurine with rosette-decoration. Museum of London (Green, 1976, 20, 226).

CATALOGUE D

Epigraphic Dedications to Taranis (or Derivative)

D1. **Böckingen**, Baden-Württemburg (Germany)
Altar inscribed *Deo Taranucno ; Veratius Primus, ex iussu*. At top decoration in form of crescent and spirals. 99 cm high. Württemburgisches Landesmuseum, Stuttgart (Espérandieu, *Germ.*, no. 401 ; *C.I.L.*, XIII, 6478) (Pl. LXXXIV, Fig. 67).

D2. **Godramstein**, Rheinland-Pfalz (Germany)
Altar inscribed *Deo Taranucno* (*C.I.L.*, XIII, 6094).

D3. **Orgon**, Bouches-du-Rhône (France)
Dedication on stone to Tanarus in Greek characters, by a Gaul named Vebroumarus. Avignon, Musée Lapidaire (Espérandieu, 1924, 38, no. 40).

D4. **Scardona** (Yugoslavia)
Inscription *Ioui Taranuco* (*C.I.L.*, III, 2804).

D5. **Thauron**, Creuse (France)
Inscribed altar. On first two lines are words *Num. Aug. I.O.M.* Third line begins *Taran...*, remainder illegible (Perrier, 1960, 195-197).

D6. **Tours**, Indre-et-Loire (France)
Dedication *Taranu* (*C.I.L.*, XIII, 3086b).

D7. **Chester**, Cheshire (England) NGR SJ 4066
Altar ; on right side six-petalled flower, on rear wreath enclosing rosette. Found in 1653. Dedicated *I.O.M. TANARUS* by a Spaniard from Clunia in Hispania Tarraconensis. Ashmolean Museum, Oxford (*R.I.B.*, no. 452 ; Wright & Richmond, 1955, 13 ; Green, 1979a, no. 5).

CATALOGUE E

Objects Relating to Jupiter-Worship in Britain (*)
List Excludes Standardized Dedications
to Jupiter Optimus Maximus

E1. Ambleside (Cumbria) NY 3704
Bronze eagle. Keswick Museum. Possibly another in possession of the late Mr. Wheatley-Balme (Haverfield & Collingwood, 1914, 437).

E2. **Backworth** (Durham) NZ 2972
Saucepan-shaped silver *patera* dedicated to the Mothers, in which was gold ring dedicated to the *Matres Coccae*, and two gold chains with eight-spoked wheel-pendants, and gold bead-bracelet also with eight-spoked wheel. Also found were 280 *denarii* and two brasses of Antoninus Pius. British Museum (*C.I.L.*, VII, 1285 ; Haverfield, 1892, 314ff. ; Romilly-Allen, 1901, 32). (AB1).

E3. **Bath** (Avon) ST 7464
Great altar corner-stone depicting Jupiter with thunderbolt, sceptre, and with eagle at feet. Bath Roman Museum (Green, 1976, 187, pl. VIIe).

E3a. **Bath** (Avon)
Small bronze eagle. Bath Roman Museum (*ibid.*, 187).

E4. **Benwell** (Tyne & Wear) NZ 2164
Bronze swastika-brooch. Newcastle University Museum of Antiquities (Petch, 1927, 135-193) (AB2).

E5. **Birdoswald** (Cumbria) NY 6166
Altar dedicated to Jupiter Optimus Maximus by 1st Aelian Cohort of Dacians ; decorated with wheel-motif (*R.I.B.*, 1877) (BB2).

E6. **Birdoswald** (Cumbria)
Relief of wheel carved on stone. Tullie House Museum, Carlisle (Wright & Phillips, 1975, 69, no. 179) (BB1).

(*) Wheel-bearing depictions are fully described in main catalogues A-C : reference is here made to main catalogue numbers.

E7. **Brampton** (Norfolk) TG 2224
Small bronze Jupiter (Fox, 1889, 331ff. ; Green, 1976, 205).

E8. **Burgh Castle** (Norfolk) TG 4805
Bronze eagle. Norwich City Museum.

E9. **Caerleon** (Gwent) ST 3390
Triangular clay antefix depicting human head and, above, eight-spoked wheel (Taylor *et al.*, 1929, 182 ; Boon, 1972, pl. 14) (C11i) (Pl. LXXVII, Fig. 54).

E10. **Caerleon** (Gwent)
Triangular clay antefix depicting human head and stylized wheel above (Anon, 1969, pl. XVIII, 3, 242 ; Boon, pl. 14) (C11ii) (Pl. LXXVII, Fig. 54).

E11. **Caerleon** (Gwent)
Solid-cast bronze bust of Jupiter with square iron shank cast into back ; wears oak-leaf crown. Probably Gaulish workmanship. Caerleon Site Museum (Boon, 1962, pl. 10)

E12. **Caerwent** (Gwent) ST 4790
Bronze plate ornamented with wheel in square frame ; found in well (Ross, 1968, 262) (C81).

E13. **Caerwent** (Gwent)
Bone head of eagle (Ashby, 1910, 1-20 ; Green, 1976, 183).

E14. **Caistor-by-Norwich** (Norfolk) TG 2303
Small bronze eagle (Fox, 1889, 331ff. ; Green, 1976, 204).

E15. **Caistor-by-Norwich** (Norfolk)
Pot decorated with wheel-symbols (Johnston, 1903, 233 ; Green, 1976, 205) (C56).

E16. **Carvoran** (Northumberland) NY 6665
Bronze eagle made as attachment. Newcastle University Museum of Antiquities.

E17. **Casterley Camp** (Wiltshire) SU 1153
Bone disc inscribed on one face with wheel or representation of the sun. Found in T-shaped hearth with 2nd Century A.D. pottery. Apparently similar to one found by Pitt-Rivers (Cunnington, 1896, 111 ; Green, 1976, 192) (C76).

E18. **Castlesteads** (Cumbria) NY 5264
Altar dedicated to Jupiter Optimus Maximus and the Numen of the Emperor, by the 2nd, part-mounted, Cohort of Tungrians. On left side thunderbolt, on right wheel. Found in 1660. Tullie House Museum, Carlisle (*R.I.B.*, 1983) (BB5) (Pl. LXXV, Fig. 50).

E19. **Castlesteads** (Cumbria)
Altar dedicated to Jupiter Optimus Maximus by 2nd, part-mounted, Cohort of

Tungrians. On left side thunderbolt, on right wheel. Tullie House Museum, Carlisle (R.I.B., 1981) (BB4).

E20. **Castor** area of: Stibbington (Cambridgeshire) TL 1298
Pottery wheel, probably votive. Colour-coated ware, brown-painted spokes on buff fabric. Peterborough City Museum (C75).

E21. **Chester** (Cheshire) SJ 4066
Altar dedicated to Jupiter Optimus Maximus Tanarus, by a Spaniard from Clunia in Hispania Tarraconensis. On right side is six-petalled flower — possibly stylized wheel-motif; on rear wreath enclosing rosette. Found in 1653. Ashmolean Museum (R.I.B., 452; Wright & Richmond, 1955, 13) (D7).

E22. **Chester** (Cheshire)
Terracotta 'eagle'. Found in White Horse Yard, Foregate Street Excavations. Grosvenor Museum, Chester (Green, 1978, pl. 64a).

E22a. **Chester** (Cheshire)
Bronze wheel-model, fragmentary. Abbey Green Excavations. Grosvenor Museum, Chester (AB23).

E23. **Chesterholm** (Northumberland) NY 7766
Fragmentary bronze eagle with pellet in beak. Vindolanda Museum (Birley, 1977; Green, 1978, 54).

E24. **Chesters** (Northumberland) NY 9170
Bronze eagle. Chesters Museum.

E25. **Chichester** (Sussex) SU 8605
Pieces of possible Jupiter-column, bearing inscription to Jupiter Optimus Maximus (R.I.B., 89; Green, 1976, 197).

E26. **Churcham** (Gloucestershire) SO 7618
Oblong stone plaque in wall of church; male figure with huge head, long tunic and, possibly, horns. In each hand is firmly grasped a tri-lobed object. At each lower angle of plaque is four-spoked wheel (Baddeley, 1923, 91ff.; Green, 1976, 170) (BB8).

E27. **Cirencester** (Gloucestershire) SP 0201
Rectangular base with attached columns at two surviving angles. Dedicated to Jupiter Optimus Maximus by a Governor of Britannia Prima : 'This statue and column, erected under the Old Religion ...' (R.I.B., 103 ; Green, 1976, 174 ; Phillips, 1976a, 35-41).

E28. **Cirencester** (Gloucestershire)
Stone eagle (Frere, 1973, 307).

E29. **Colchester** (Essex) TM 0025

Miniature brass wheel found in urn with beads and shale armlet. Castle Museum, Colchester (AB17).

E30. **Colchester** (Essex)

Bronze figure of Jupiter, small. Castle Museum, Colchester (Newton, 1846, 443ff. ; Green, 1976, 216).

E31. **Colchester** (Essex)

Bronze eagle figurine (Green, 1976, 217).

E31a. **Colchester** (Essex)

Two wheel-shaped brooches, one Claudian (Hawkes & Hull, 1947, 326, nos. 176, 177) (AB 24, 25).

E32. **Cole's Hill** (Gloucestershire) SP 0425

Stone eagle, c. 25 cm long. Found half a mile south of Spoonley Wood Roman Villa. Gloucester City Museum (Green, 1976, 174).

E33. **Corbridge** (Northumberland) NY 9964

Baked clay mould of god with concave-sided rectangular shield ; wheel by feet ; crooked club in hand. Bearded, barefoot ; wears knobbed helmet. Shield has incised ornament of ring-and-dot decoration. Corstopitum Museum, Corbridge (Forster & Knowles, 1910, 224, fig. 6) (C10) (Pl. LXXIX, Fig. 58).

E34. **Corbridge** (Northumberland)

Small bronze eagle, possibly from top of helmet ; head and legs missing. Corstopitum Museum, Corbridge (Forster, 1908, 298).

E35. **Corbridge** (Northumberland)

Bronze enamelled wheel-brooch. Corstopitum Museum, Corbridge (AB3) (Pl. LXIII, Fig. 26).

E36. **Corby** (Northamptonshire) SP 8988

Bronze eagle on globe. Northampton Museum (Green, 1976, 180).

E37. **Currie** (Lothian Region) NT 1867

Bronze eagle. National Museum of Antiquities, Edinburgh (Robertson, 1970, 198ff.).

E37a. **Denholme Hill Farm** (Southern Region)

Bronze swastika-brooch, possibly 2nd Century A.D. National Museum of Antiquities, Edinburgh (Acc. no. FA 88) (AB26).

E38. **Dolaucothi** (Dyfed) SN 6640

Gold chain necklace with eight-spoked wheel-pendant fixed to eye-fastening ; found in hoard of gold-work. Remains of rod with looped ends soldered behind wheel. Carmarthen Museum (Nash-Williams, 1950-52, 79-84) (AB4).

E39. **Easton Grey** (Wiltshire) ST 890870

Fragment of Mother-Goddess relief, with small 'Latin' cross or stylized wheel carved on edge of cap above centre of forehead. Another similar fragment comes from an unprovenanced site in the Cotswolds. Devizes Museum (Green, 1976, 190, 17-19) (BB10, 9).

E40. **Exeter** (Devon) SX 9292

Life-size eagle, badly mutilated ; Purbeck Marble (Frere, 1974, 452 ; Green, 1976, 200 ; Toynbee, 1979).

E41. **Farley Heath, Albury** (Surrey) TQ 0544

Bronze sceptre-binding with punched ritual decoration, including head of god associated with wheel and thunderbolt. British Museum (Goodchild, 1938, 1947 ; Green, 1976, 219) (C7) (Pl. LXXXII).

E42. **Farley Heath** (Surrey)

Bronze eagle. British Museum.

E43. **Felmingham Hall** (Norfolk) TG 2529

Hollow bronze Jupiter-mask, and miniature bronze twelve-spoked wheel. The items were discovered in a ritual context comprising a hoard of figurines and other bronzes. They were contained in a pot with a coin dating to the 260s A.D. British Museum (Green, 1976, 205, pl. IXh ; Gilbert, 1978) (AB5) (Pl. LXII, Fig. 24).

E44. **Fenny Stratford** (Buckinghamshire) SP 8834

Bronze eagle rivetted to disc. Ashmolean Museum (Green, 1976, 179).

E45. **Frilsham** (Berkshire) SU 5375

Altar dedicated to Jupiter (Ditchfield *et al.*, 1906, 197ff. ; Green, 1976, 194).

E46. **Gateshead** (Tyne & Wear) NZ 2562

Stone wheel or wheel-brooch mould. Newcastle University Museum of Antiquities (AB22).

E47. **Grays**, near (Essex) TQ 6177

Small bust of Jupiter (Anon., 1849, 60 ; Green, 1976, 227).

E48. **Great Chesterford** (Essex) TL 5042

Half-octagonal trough with busts of deities round edges ; possibly part of Jupiter-column (Richmond, 1963, 1ff. ; Green, 1976, 211).

E49. **Hadrian's Wall** Turret 18B (Northumberland) NZ 0168

Bronze enamelled wheel-brooch. Newcastle University Museum of Antiquities (AB14).

E50. **Hounslow** (Middlesex) TQ 1276

Bronze wheel-model associated with three bronze Iron Age-type boars. British Museum (British Museum, 1925, 148 ; Green, 1976, 221) (AB6) (Pl. LXIII, Fig. 25).

E51. **Housesteads** (Northumberland) NY 7968
Bronze wheel-brooch fragment, originally eight-spoked. Housesteads Museum (Birley et al., 1934, 197) (AB7) (Pl. LXI, Fig. 23).

E52. **Housesteads** (Northumberland)
Wheel applied to grey ware potsherd ; part of large jar. Housesteads Museum (Birley et al., 1934, 197, pl. XXIX, C, no. 1) (C60) (Pl. LXXVIII, Fig. 55).

E53. **Housesteads** (Northumberland)
Stone statue of Jupiter. Housesteads Museum.

E54. **Icklingham** (Suffolk) TL 7772
Bronze wing of eagle-figurine. Ashmolean Museum (Green, 1975c, 55-61 ; Green, 1976, pl. IXk)(Pl. LXI, Fig. 64).

E55. **Icklingham** (Suffolk)
Bronze wheel-model in two fragments. Ashmolean Museum (Green, 1975c, 55-61 ; Green, 1976, pl. IXg) (AB8) (Pl. LXI, Fig. 64).

E56. **Icklingham** (Suffolk)
Bronze wheel-brooch. Ashmolean Museum (AB8b) (Pl. LX, Fig. 21).

E57. **Ilchester** (Somerset) ST 5222
Small bronze bearded head, probably medallion depicting Jupiter. Taunton Museum (Green, 1976, 184).

E58. **Ilkley** (West Yorkshire) SE 1147
Small bronze figurine of Jupiter. Manor House Museum, Ilkley.

E59. **Ilkley** (West Yorkshire)
Small bronze eagle. Manor House Museum, Ilkley (Fletcher, 1965, 16-17).

E60. **Irchester** (Northamptonshire) SP 9265
Possible fragment of Jupiter-column (Haverfield, 1902, 157ff. ; Green, 1976, 180).

E61. **Islip** (Northamptonshire) SP 9879
Bronze wheel-brooch (Anon : 1881-1883, 89-91 ; Green, 1976, 181) (AB21);

E62. **Keighley** (West Yorkshire) SE 0641
Bronze eagle with cylindrical peg between legs; feet truncated so that figure would fit onto staff. Keighley Museum (Butterfield, 1920-22, 385ff.).

E63. **Kettering** (Northamptonshire) SP 8778
Fragment of wheel-brooch. Westfield Museum, Kettering (Green, 1976, pl. IXf) (AB18).

E64. **Kirkby Thore** (Cumbria) NY 6325
Bronze figurine of Jupiter. Chesters Museum.

E64a **Lakenheath** (Suffolk) TL 729835
Bronze wheel-brooch, enamelled ; six spokes. Cambridge University Museum of Archaeology and Anthropology (Acc. no. 76. 1588) (AB28).

E65. **Langham** (Leicestershire & Rutland) SK 8411
Part of bronze Jupiter, in two pieces ; large. British Museum (Green, 1976, 167, pl. IXd).

E66. **Langton** (North Yorkshire) SE 7967
Part of small heart-shaped bone object carved from end of bone ; eagle-depiction, head missing (Corder & Kirk, 1952, 72, fig. 19).

E67. **Leatherhead** (Surrey) TQ 1656
Bronze wheel-model from grave (Smith, 1901, 255 ; Green, 1976, 220) (AB9).

E68. **Leicester** Leicestershire) SK 5904
Nude bronze Jupiter (McAlpin, 1867-70, 183 ; Green, 1976, 166).

E68a. **Leicester**
Bronze head of eagle with food pellet in beak ; probably a fitting. Leicester Museum (Green, 1976, 166, pl. VIIIe).

E69. **Littlehampton** (Sussex) TQ 0202
Small pot decorated with wheel, found c. 46 cm below ground. Black clay ; c. 16 cm high ; smooth and well-turned, with handle and elegantly moulded rim and foot. Small wheel imprinted on each side in 'enamel or glaze' (Johnston, 1903, 233 ; Green, 1976, 219) (C55).

E70. **Little Heath** (Bedfordshire) SP 9220
Bronze eagle-figurine. British Museum (Green, 1976, 180).

E71. **Little Houghton, Pylon Field** (Northamptonshire) SP 813602
Piece of glass from base of flat-bottomed vessel, with raised wheel-symbol. Northampton Museum (Green, 1974, 2-6 ; 1976, 180, pl. IXj) (C63).

E72. **London** TQ 3079
Fragment of bronze figurine of Jupiter, found in River Thames in 1837. British Museum (Roach Smith, 1839, 38-46 ; Green, 1976, 224).

E73. **London**
Bronze statuette of Jupiter with eagle, allegedly found in Bishopsgate Street (Hughson, 1805, 34ff. ; Green, 1976, 224).

E74. **London**
Bronze thunderbolt decorated with planetary deities. Museum of London (Green, 1976, 224).

E75. **London**
Wooden oath found in Lothbury : 'By Almighty Jupiter and the Genius of his Imperial Majesty Domitian ...'. Museum of London (Green, 1976, 224).

E76. **London**

Fragment of altar in oolitic limestone (Lincolnshire source): *I(OVI) O(PTIMO) M(AXIMO)* .... Inscription announces restoration of a collapsed (?)temple (Hobley et al., 1977, 31-67).

E76a. **London**

Bronze six-spoked wheel. Museum of London (Green, 1976, 226) (AB10).

E77. **Lydney** (Gloucestershire) SO 6203

Bone plaque with incised figure of eagle with outspread wings. British Museum (Green, 1976, 170, pl. VIIIi).

E78. **Lydney**

Bronze head of eagle (*ibid.*, 170).

E78a. **Lypiatt Park** (Gloucestershire) SO 9005

Stone altar bearing wheel and ram-horned snake. Stroud Museum (Green, 1980) (BB13) (Pl. III, Fig. 4).

E79. **Maiden Castle** (Dorset) SY 6688

Silvered bronze three-horned bull bearing three figures on its back; 'S'-shaped tail. Dorset County Museum, Dorchester (Green, 1976, 200).

E80. **Malton** (North Yorkshire) SE 7871

Two sherds of coarse grey ware with appliqué wheels. Malton Roman Museum (C59) (Pl. LXXVIII, Fig. 56).

E81. **Manchester** (Lancashire) SJ 8397

Bronze statuette of Jupiter found in 1839 in Tonman Street. When found one hand held sceptre and the other thunderbolt. City Art Gallery, Manchester (Bruton, 1909, frontispiece and 187).

E82. **Manchester** (Lancashire)

Pink fabric bowl with white-painted decoration in the form of wheels; shape of pot paralleled by samian form 30 (Jones & Grealey, 1974, 115, fig. 41, no. 243) (C62).

E83. **Margam Beach** (West Glamorgan) SS 7787

Bronze wheel-brooch with four spokes. National Museum of Wales (AB11).

E84. **Maryport** (Cumbria) NY 0336

Altar dedicated to Jupiter Optimus Maximus by 1st Cohort of Spaniards. On either side *patera*; on rear wheel. Found 350 yards N.E. of fort. Netherhall Museum (*R.I.B.*, 827) (BB15).

E85. **Maryport**

Wheel in relief carved on stone; 20.2 cm diameter (Bailey, 1915, 135ff.) (BB14).

E86. **Netherby** (Cumbria) NY 3971
Relief depicting deity with *cornucopiae* in left hand and in right wheel held over altar. On right is boar in front of tree. The human figure is half-draped in the manner of a Genius or Bonus Eventus. Tullie House Museum, Carlisle (Wright & Phillips, 1975, 73, no. 197) (BB18).

E87. **Netherby**
Relief similar to above (E86) but without boar and tree. Tullie House Museum, Carlisle (*ibid.*, 73, no. 196) (BB17) (Pl. LXXV, Fig. 51).

E88. **Nettleton Shrub** (Wiltshire) ST 82257696
Stone relief of cross, possibly connected with wheel-symbolism. In possession of excavator Mr. Wedlake (Green, 1976, 190).

E89. **Newport** (Lincolnshire) SE 9218
Bronze eagle. Lincoln Museum (Green, 1976, 162).

E90. **Newstead** (Border Region) NT 5634
Links of silver chain with miniature silver filigree eight-spoked wheel-pendant, with solid bar across back, each end fitted with loop (Curle, 1911, pl. LXXXVII, no. 34) (AB12).

E91. **Nor'nour** (Isles of Scilly) SV 944148
Wheel-brooch with eight knobs and four spokes. St. Mary's Museum, Scilly (Dudley, 1967, 1ff. ; Green, 1976, 198) (AB19).

E92. **Oundle** (Cambridgeshire) TL 0488
Bronze bust of Minerva, part of spatula with grip in form of eagle's head (Webster, 1968, 303 ; Green, 1976, 206).

E93. **Oxford** (Oxfordshire) SP 5305
Bronze eagle-figurine. British Museum (Green, 1976, 177).

E94. **Ratcliffe-on-Soar** (Nottinghamshire) SK 493304
Lead curse dedicated to Jupiter Optimus Maximus. Nottingham Castle Museum (Turner, 1963, 122ff. ; Green, 1976, 165).

E95. **Ribble** (?near Ribchester) SD 6435
Triple-headed bronze bucket-mount ; three flat-backed heads, two of them linked by rivet from which hangs loop. Eagle's head surmounts head of knob-horned bull. From bird's head rivet connects with human head. Rydale Folk Museum (Hildyard, 1954, 225-229 ; Green, 1977b, pl. 12, VIII, a, b).

E96. **Sea Mills** (Avon) ST 552759
Uninscribed stone altar depicting eagle on globe and *cornucopiae* ; *patera* and ram or bull-head ; sacrificial knife and dagger ; columns and trident or thunderbolt. Bristol City Museum (Green, 1976, 184).

E97. **Sea Mills**
Bronze statuette of Jupiter. Bristol City Museum (*ibid.*, 185).

E98. **Sewingshields** (Northumberland) NY 8068
Wheel-shaped brooch with six spokes (Woodfield, 1965, 155) (AB13).

E99. **Shefford** (Bedfordshire) TL 1439
Cemetery containing lead eagle designed to fit onto staff (Page (ed.), 1908, 5ff. ; Green, 1976, 207).

E100. **Silchester** (Hampshire) SU 6462
Bronze eagle. Reading Museum (Green, 1976, 196).

E101. **Silchester**
Pot decorated with wheels and 'S'-symbols (Johnston, 1903, 233 ; Green, 1976, 196 ; St. John Hope & Fox, 1900, 104, fig. 5) (C54).

E102. **Silchester**
Two bronze wheel-brooches. Reading Museum (AB30).

E103. **South Shields** (Tyne & Wear) NZ 3667
Bronze figurine of Jupiter with thunderbolt in right hand. Newcastle University Museum of Antiquities (Petch, 1925, 20 ; Toynbee, 1964, 74).

E105. **Springhead** (Kent) TQ 618725
Glass fragment with swastika-symbol (Penn, 1968, 174ff. ; Green, 1976, 228) (C57).

E106. **Springhead**
Part of possible Jupiter-column (Green, 1976, 228 ; Harker, 1980).

E107. **Stony Stratford** (Buckinghamshire) SP 7840
Silver plaque found with others in urn at Windmill Field. Inscription reads *Deo Ioui et Volca(no)* .... British Museum (*R.I.B.*, 215).

E108. **Thealby** (Lincolnshire) SE 8917
Two bronze bucket-mounts depicting conjoined heads of bull and eagle. Scunthorpe Museum (Dudley, 1949, 136, 156 ; Green, 1976, 162).

E109. **Verulamium** (Hertfordshire) TL 1307
Possible Capitolium (Lewis, 1966, 67-68).

E110. **Verulamium**
Bronze wheel. Verulamium Museum, St. Albans (Green, 1976, 207, pl. IXe) (AB15).

E111. **Verulamium**
Bronze eagle. Verulamium Museum (Frere, 1972, fig. 49, no. 158).

E112. **West Stoke** (Sussex) SU 8208
Bronze seated figure of Jupiter (Toynbee, 1964, 105 ; Green, 1976, 197, pl. IXb, c).

E113. **Wickham-Brook** (Suffolk) TL 7454
Bronze eagle (Fox, 1900, 89ff. ; Green, 1976, 213).

E114. **Willingham Fen** (Cambridgeshire) TL 4070
Bronze sceptre-terminal depicting youthful, naked, beardless deity ; head of triple-horned bull ; dolphin, eagle ; wheel. Deity's foot rests on head of chthonic giant. Found with e.g. bronze horsemen, in hoard. Cambridge University Museum of Archaeology & Anthropology (Green, 1976, 210, pl. X) (C6) (Pl. LXXXI, Figs. 61, 63).

E115. **Winterton** (Lincolnshire) SE 910181
Bronze eagle from Roman Villa. Lincoln Museum.

E116. **Woodeaton** (Oxfordshire) SP 533123
Five bronze eagles and fragment of sixth. Ashmolean Museum (Green, 1976, 178).

E117. **Woodeaton** (Oxfordshire)
Bronze model axe-head with incised swastika-motif on blade. Another with ligatured diagonal cross (Green, 1976, 178 ; 1975c, 54-70) (AX20) (Pl. LXIV, Fig. 42).

E118. **Wroxeter** (Shropshire) SJ 5608
Bronze wheel-brooch. Shrewsbury Museum (Green, 1976, 164) (AB16).

E119. **Wroxeter**
Pipe-clay miniature column bearing image of eagle on one side. Shrewsbury Museum (*ibid.*).

E120. **Wroxeter**
Bronze disc bearing device of eagle holding fish. Shrewsbury Museum (Green, 1976, 164).

E121. **York** (Yorkshire) SE 6052
Nude bronze figure of probable Jupiter, bearded. Left hand once possibly held a sceptre ; most of right arm missing. Yorkshire Museum.

E122. **York**
Bronze enamelled brooch in form of eagle ; fragmentary. Yorkshire Museum.

E123. **York**
Limestone altar. On right side weathered figure with staff ; on left figure in tunic facing right, holding large animal. Inscription reads 'To Jupiter Optimus Maximus, to the gods and goddesses of Hospitality and to the Penates ...'. (*R.I.B.*, 649).

BIBLIOGRAPHY

ABEL, Ch. 'Du Monnayage des Gaulois à propos de trouvailles faites dans le département de la Moselle', *Mémoires de l'Academie impériale de Metz*, 65, 1865, 1865-66.
ABRAMIC, M. & COLNAGO, A. 'Untersuchungen in Norddalmatien', *Jahrshefte des Östereiches Archäologisches Instituts in Wien, Beiblatt*, Bd. XII, 1909, 103-104, fig. 73.
AIGNER-FORESTI, L. 'Ein Halbplastisches Zierstück aus dem Gräberfeld von Frög', *Schild von Steier : Beiträge zur Steierischen vor- und Frühgeschichte und Münzkunde*, 15-16, 1978-79, 43-47.
ALBENIQUE, A. *Les Rutènes*, 1948.
ALBERT, R. & FAUDUET, I. 'Fibules d'Argentomagus ...', *Revue Archéologique du Centre*, 15, 1976, part 2, 199ff.
ALEXANDER, J. *Nin and the Jugoslav Iron Age*, 1958.
ALEXANDER, J. 'The Pins of the Jugoslav Early Iron Age', *Proceedings of the Prehistoric Society*, 30, 1964, 159-185.
ALFÖLDI, A. 'The Bronze Mace from Willingham Fen, Cambridgeshire', *Journal of Roman Studies*, 39, 1949, 19ff.
ALFÖLDY, G. 'Zur keltischen Religion in Pannonien', *Germania*, 42, 1964, 54-59.
ALFÖLDY, G. *Noricum*, 1974.
ALLEN, A. F. 'Chalk, Gravesend, Roman Remains', *Archaeologia Cantiana*, 70, 1956, 252.
ALLEN, D. F. 'Belgic Coins as illustrations of life in the late pre-Roman Iron Age of Britain', *Proceedings of the Prehistoric Society*, 24, 1958, 43-63.
ALLEN, D. F. 'The Early Coins of the Treveri', *Germania*, 49, 1971, 91-110.
ALLEN, D. F. 'Some Contrasts in Gaulish and British Coins', in DUVAL, P.-M. & HAWKES, C. F. C. (eds.), *Celtic Art in Ancient Europe*, 1976, 265-282.
ALLEN, D. F. *The Coins of the Ancient Celts*, 1980.
ALLMER, A. *Revue Épigraphique*, I, 1878-83.
ALLMER, A. *Revue Épigraphique*, II, 1884-89.
ALTHEIM, F. *A History of Roman Religion*, 1938.
ALTHIN, C. A. *Studien zu den Bronzeitlichen Felszeichnungen von Skane*, 1945.
ALVIELLA, COMTE, GOBLET D'. *La Croix Gammée ou Svastika, étude de symbolique comparée*, 1889.
American School of Classical Studies at Athens. *Cure and Cult in Ancient Corinth : A Guide to the Asklepieion*, Athens, 1977.

ANATI, E. 'Bronze Age Chariots from Europe', *Proceedings of the Prehistoric Society*, 26, 1960, 50-63.
ANATI, E. *Camonica Valley*, 1960.
ANON. *Journal of the British Archaeological Association*, 4, 1849, 60.
ANON. *Proceedings of the Society of Antiquaries*, 9, 1881-83, 89-91.
ANON. 'Svastika servant de marque de potier, trouvée à Anthée', *Annales de Namur*, 21, 1896, 292.
ANON. *Proceedings of the Society of Antiquaries*, 21, 1905-07, 221-228.
ANON. 'Die Ausgrabungen', *Saalburg Jahresbericht*, 1908-9.
ANON. 'Die Ausgrabungen', *Saalburg Jahrbuch*, 3, 1912.
ANON. 'Kastell Zugmantel', *Saalburg Jahrbuch*, 3, 1912, 27-71.
ANON. 'Le temple de Moritasgus au Mont Auxois', *Revue de l'histoire des religions*, 65, 1912, 270.
ANON. 'Ausgrabungen Kastell-Saalburg', *Saalburg Jahrbuch*, 4, 1913.
ANON. *Saalburg Jahrbuch*, 5, 1913.
ANON. *Saalburg Jahrbuch*, 6, 1914-24.
ANON. *Saalburg Jahrbuch*, 7, 1930.
ANON. *Lincolnshire Architectural & Archaeological Society Reports & Papers*, 7, 1957-8, 99-101.
ANON. 'Roman Britain in 1968', *Journal of Roman Studies*, 59, 1969.
ANON. *Die Hallstatt Kultur (Frühform Europäischer Einheit), (Internationale Ausstellung des Landes Oberösterreich, 25 April bis 26 Oktober 1980 : Schloss Lamberg, Steyr*, 1980.
ANON. *Die Kelten in Mitteleuropa : Kultur, Kunst, Wirtschaft. Salzburger Landesausstellung (1 Mai - 30 Sept. 1980 in Keltenmuseum Hallein, Österreich*, 1980.
ARMAND-CALLIAT, A. *Le Châlonnais gallo-romain (Châlon-sur-Saône)*, 1937.
ARMSTRONG, E. C. R. *Catalogue of Irish Gold Ornaments*, 1920.
ASHBY, T. *et al.* 'Excavations at Caerwent, Mon.', *Archaeologia*, 62, 1910, 1-20.
Ashmolean Museum. *Catalogue of the Greek and Roman Antiquities ... Ashmolean Museum ... E. Oldfield*, Oxford, 1902.
BAATZ, D. 'Römische Wandmalereien aus dem Limeskastell Echzell Kr. Büdingen (Hessen)', *Germania*, 46, 1968, 40-52.
BABELON, E. *Le Rhin : L'Antiquité Gauloise et Germaine*, 1916.
BABELON, E. & BLANCHET, J. A. *Catalogue des Bronzes Antiques de la Bibliothèque Nationale*, 1895.
BADDELEY, ST. CLAIR. 'A Romano-Celtic Sculpture at Churcham', *Transactions of the Bristol and Gloucestershire Archaeological Society*, 45, 1923, 91ff.
BAILEY, C. *Phases in the Religion of Ancient Rome*, 1932.
BAILEY, J. P. 'Catalogue of Roman Inscribed and Sculptured Stones ... at Maryport', *Cumberland & Westmorland Society Transactions*, 15, 1915, 135ff.

BAKER, R. S. *Proceedings of the Society of Antiquaries*, 9, 1881-83, 89-91.
BALSON, L. 'Reprise de Fouilles à La Graufesenque (Condatomagus), Campagne 1950', *Gallia*, 1952, 8, 1-15.
BANÉAT, P. *Catalogue du Musée Archéologique ... de Rennes*, 1909.
BARFIELD, L. *Northern Italy*, 1971.
BARKER, H. *Traditional Chinese Society*. (Lecture given in Reardon Smith Theatre, Cardiff, 5 May, 1978), 1978.
BARTHÉLEMY, A. DE. 'Le Dieu Taranis', *Musée Archéologique*, 2, 5ff.
BAUCHHENSS, G. *Jupitergigantensäulen*, 1976.
BAUDREY, F. & BALLEREAU, L. *Puits Funéraires gallo-romains du Bernard (Vendée)*, 104, 1873.
BEAUREGARD, COSTA DE. *Catalogue de l'exposition archéologique ... département de Savoie*, 1878.
BEHN, F. 'Neue Funde römischer Skulpturen aus Hessen', *Germania*, 20, 1936, 256-258.
BEHRENS, G. *Bronzezeit Süddeutschlands* (Kat. des Röm.-Germ. Zentral Museums, 6), 1916.
BEHRENS, G. 'Die Sogenannten Mithrassymbole', *Germania*, 1939, 23, 56-59.
BEMONT, C. 'Le Bassin de Gundestrup : Remarques sur les Décors Végétaux', *Études Celtiques*, 16, 1979, 69-99.
BENOIT, F. *Les Mythes de l'outre-tombe : le cavalier à l'anguipède et l'écuyère Épone*, Collection Latomus, III, 1950.
BENOIT, F. *Mars et Mercure*, 1953.
BENOIT, F. 'Monstres hippophores méditerranéens et cavalier à l'anguipède gallo-romain', *Ogam*, 1954, 6.
BENOIT, F. 'Informations-Archéologiques : XIXe Circonscription', *Gallia*, 14, 1956, 218-246.
BENOIT, F. 'Informations-Archéologiques : Aix (Sud)', *Gallia*, 16, 1958, 412ff.
BENOIT, F. 'Informations-Archéologiques : Aix-en-Provence (Région Sud)', *Gallia*, 22, 1964, 573-610.
BENOIT, F. *Le Symbolisme dans les Sanctuaires de la Gaule*, Collection Latomus 105, 1970.
BERGER, L. 'Die Mittlere und Späte Latènezeit im Mittelland und Jura', *Archäologie der Schweiz, Band IV : Die Eisenzeit*, 1966-76, 64ff.
BERGMAN, J. *Die Ältere Bronzezeit Nordwestdeutschlands*, 1970.
Bericht der Römisch-Germanischen Kommission. Volume 8, 1915, 60-61.
BERTRAND, A. *La Religion des Gaulois*, 1897.
BEY, E. 'Relief votif du Musée Impérial Ottoman', *Bulletin de Correspondance Hellénique*, 32, 1908.
BICKNELL, C. *The Prehistoric Rock Engravings in the Italian Maritime Alps*, 1911.
BIEL, J. 'Das Frühkeltische Fürstengrab von Eberdinge-Hochdorf, Landkreis Ludwigsburg', *The Archaeological Advertizer*, 3-10, 1978-79.

BING, J. *Der Sonnenwagen von Trundholm*, 1934.
BIRLEY, E. et al. 'Third Report on Excavations at Housesteads', *Archaeologia Aeliana* (ser. 4), 11, 1934, 185-206.
BIRLEY, R. *Vindolanda*, 1977.
BLAGG, T. F. C. 'The Decorated Stonework of Roman Temples in Britain', in RODWELL, W. (ed.) *Temples, Churches and Religion in Roman Britain (British Archaeological Reports)* Oxford, 77, 1980, 31-44.
BLANCHET, J. A. 'Étude sur les figurines en terre cuite de la Gaule Romaine', *Mémoires de la Société des Antiquaires de France* (ser. 6), 51, 1890, 65-224.
BLANCHET, J. A. 'Étude ... Gaule Romaine. Supplément', *Mémoires de la Société des Antiquaires de France* (ser. 6), 10, 1901, 189-272.
BLANCHET, J. A. *Traité des monnaies gauloises*, 1, 1905.
BLANCHET, J. A. *Manuel de numismatique française*, 1, 1912.
BLANCHET, J. A. 'Le Jupiter à la roue trouvé à Champagnat (Creuse)', *Bulletin Archéologique du Comité des travaux historiques et scientifiques*, 156-160, 1923.
BLANCHET, J. A. 'Notes sur deux représentations de Sucellus ...' *Bulletin Archéologique du Comité des travaux historiques et scientifiques*, 755-758, 1946-49.
BLINKENBERG, C. *Archäologische Studien*, 1904, 69.
BLINKENBERG, C. *The Thunderweapon in Religion and Folklore*, 1911, 29, fig. 16.
BOBER, P. P. 'Cernunnos : Origin and Transformation of a Celtic Divinity', *American Journal of Archaeology*, 55, 1951, 13-51.
BÖHME, A. 'Die Fibeln der Kastelle Saalburg und Zugmantel', *Saalburg Jahrbuch*, 1972, 29.
BÖHME, A. 'Die Fibeln des Kastells am Kleinen Feldberg (Hochtaunuskreis)', *Saalburg Jahrbuch*, 31, 1974, 5-14.
BÖHME, A. *Schmuck der römischen Frau*, 1974.
BONA, I. 'Clay Models of Bronze Age Wagons and Wheels in the Middle Danube Basin', *Acta Archaeologia Hungarica*, 12, 1960, 83-111.
BONNARD, L. *La Gaule thermale*, 1908.
BOON, G. C. *Isca*, 1962.
BOON, G. C. 'The Caerleon Curse', *Monmouthshire Antiquary*, 1, part IV, 1964, 128.
BOON, G. C. *Isca*, 1972.
BOON, G. C. *Silchester : the Roman Town of Calleva*, 1974.
Bordeaux, Musée d'Aquitaine. *Bordeaux : 2000 ans d'histoire*, 1973.
BOÜARD, M. DE. 'Informations archéologiques : Haute et Basse Normandie', *Gallia*, 26, 1968, 347-372.
BOUCHER, S. *Recherches sur les bronzes figurés de la Gaule pré-romaine et romaine*, 1976.
BOUCHER, S. *Vienne : Bronze antiques*, 1977.

BOUZEK, J. *Archéologické Rozhledy*, 29, 1977, 200.
BRADFORD, J. & GOODCHILD, R. G. 'Excavations at Frilford, Berks.', *Oxoniensia*, 4, 1939, 1ff.
BREUIL, H. *et al. Rock Paintings of Southern Andalusia*, 1929.
BRIARD, J. 'Bronze Age Cultures : 1800-600 B.C.', in PIGGOTT, S., DANIEL, G. & MCBURNEY, C. (eds.), *France before the Romans*, 1973, 131-156.
British Museum. *A Guide to the Antiquities of the Bronze Age* (1st ed.), London, 1904.
British Museum. *A Guide to the Antiquities of the Bronze Age* (2nd ed.), London, 1920.
British Museum. *Catalogue of Silver Plate*, London, 1921.
British Museum. *Guide to the Early Iron Age Antiquities*, London, 1925.
British Museum. *Guide to the Antiquities of Roman Britain*, London, 1951.
British Museum. *Guide to the Antiquities of Roman Britain*, London, 1964.
British Museum. *Introductory Guide to the Egyptian Collections*, London, 1969.
British Museum. *Introductory Guide to the Egyptian Collections*, London, 1971.
BROGAN, O. *Roman Gaul*, 1953.
BROGAN, O. 'The Coming of Rome and the Establishment of Roman Gaul', in PIGGOTT, S., DANIEL, G. & MCBURNEY, C. (eds.), *France before the Romans*, 1974, 192-219.
BROHOLM, H. C. *Danish Antiquities III : Early Bronze Age*, 1952.
BROHOLM, H. C. *Danish Antiquities IV : Late Bronze Age*, 1958.
BROMMER, F. *Hephaistos : Der Schmiedegott in der Antiken Kunst*, 1978.
BRONSTED, J. B. *Danmarks Oldtid II*, 1938-40.
BRUCE, J. COLLINGWOOD. *Lapidarium Septentrionale*, 1875.
BRUNEAU, P. & DUCAT, J. *Guide de Délos*, 1966.
BRUNTING, H. *400 Jaar Romeinse Bezetting van Nijmegen*, 1969.
BRUTON, F. A. (ed.). *The Roman Fort at Manchester*, 1909.
BÜCHELER, Fr. *Umbrica*, 1883.
BULLEID, A. & GRAY, St. G. *The Meare Lake Village*, 2, 1953.
BUREN, E. D. VAN. *Clay Figurines of Babylonia and Assyria*, 1930.
BURGESS, C. 'Appendix II : The Gwithian Mould and the forerunners of South Welsh Axes', in BURGESS, C. and MIKET, R. (eds.), *Settlement in the 3rd and 2nd Millennium B.C. (British Archaeological Reports*, Oxford, 33), Oxford, 1976, 69-81.
BURGESS, C. 'The Bronze Age in Wales', in TAYLOR, J. A. (ed.), *Culture and Environment in Prehistoric Wales (British Archaeological Reports*, 76), 1980, 243-286.
BURLEIGH, R. 'Calibration of C-14 Dates : Some Remaining Uncertainties and Limitations', in WATKINS, J. *Radiocarbon : Calibration and Prehistory*, 1975, 5-8.
BURY, J. B. & MEIGGS, R. *A History of Greece*, 1978.

BUSHE-FOX, J. P. *Fourth Report on the Excavation of the Roman Fort at Richborough, Kent*, 1949.
BUTLER, J. J. *Bronze Age Connections Across the North Sea*, 1963.
BUTTERFIELD, R. 'Roman Eagle Found at Keighley', *Yorkshire Archaeological Journal*, 26, 1920-22, 385ff.
CARAPANOS, C. *Dodone et ses ruines*, 1878.
CASTALDI, E. 'La Frammentazione rituale in etnologia e in preistoria', *Rivista di Scienze Preistoriche*, 20, 1965, 247-277.
CASTELIN, K. *Keltische Münzen*, 1980.
CAYLUS, A. C. P. de. *Recueil d'Antiquités Égyptiennes, Étrusques, Grecques et Romaines*, II, 1752-67.
CAYLUS, A. C. P. de. *Recueil d'Antiquités Égyptiennes, Étrusques, Grecques, Romaines et Gauloises*, 1759.
CERQUAND, J. F. 'Taranus ou Taranis ?', 'Mélanges', *Revue Celtique*, 5, 1881-83, 381-388.
CHABOT, L. 'Deux bijoux pré-romains en bronze de l'oppidum de la Cloche (Bouches-du-Rhône)', *Revue Archéologique de Narbonnaise*, 8, 1975, 259-264.
CHABOUILLET, A. 'Notice sur des inscriptions et des antiquités provenant de Bourbonne-les-Bains', *Revue Archéologique*, 1880-81, 15ff.
CHAILLAN, ?. 'L'autel à Symboles de Cuech', *Revue des Études Anciennes*, 9, 1907, 357-358.
CHANTRE, E. *Études Paléoethniques dans le Bassin du Rhône: Premier Âge du Fer*, 1880.
CHARBONNEAUX, J. et al. *Grèce Hellénistique*, 1970.
CHARLESWORTH, D. 'Roman Jewellery found in Northumberland and Durham', *Archaeologia Aeliana* (ser 4), 39, 1961, 1-37.
CHASSAING, M. 'Les Barillets de Dispater', *Revue Archéologique*, 47, 1956, 156ff.
CHENET, G. 'Rouelles de plomb et persistance d'emploi des rouelles gauloises', *Bulletin Archéologique du Comité des travaux historiques et scientifiques*, 1919, 243-251.
CHILDE, V. G. *The Danube in Prehistory*, 1929.
CHILDE, V. G. 'The First Wagons and Carts – from the Tigris to the Severn', *Proceedings of the Prehistoric Society*, 17, 1951, 177-195.
C.I.L. Corpus Inscriptionum Latinarum (Heubner Ed.).
CLARKE, D. L. *Beaker Pottery of Great Britain*, 1970.
CLARKE, D. V., BREEZE, D. J. & MACKAY, G. *The Romans in Scotland*, 1980.
CLAUS, M. *Archäologie in Südwestlichen Harzvorland*, 1978.
CLEMENT, M. 'Le Tesson aux svastikas de Trogouzel et la Pierre de Kermaria (Finistère)', *Études Celtiques*, 16, 1979, 53-63.
CLERC, M. *Aquae Sextiae*, 1916.
COCK, A. H. 'A Romano-British Homestead in the Hambledon Valley, Bucks.', *Archaeologia*, 71, 1921, 141-198.

COLES, J. M. 'European Bronze Age Shields', *Proceedings of the Prehistoric Society*, 28, 1962, 156-190.
COLES, J. M. & HARDING, A. F. *The Bronze Age in Europe*, 1979.
COLIN, J. *Les Antiquités Romaines de la Rhénanie*, 1927.
COLLINGWOOD, R. G. & WRIGHT, R. P. *The Roman Inscriptions of Britain : Volume I, Inscriptions on Stone*, 1965.
COLOMBET, A. 'Notes sur quelques objets découverts dans les fouilles Gallo-Romaines du Bolar (Côte-d'Or)', *Bulletin Archéologique du Comité des travaux historiques et scientifiques*, 1950-52, 177-182.
COLOMBET, A. & LEBEL P. 'Mythologie Gallo-Romaine', *Revue Archéologique de l'est et du Centre-Est*, 4, 1953, 108-130.
CONESTABILE, Comté. *Sopra due dischi in bronzo antico italici*, 1874.
COOK, A. B. *Zeus : A Study in Ancient Religion, I*, 1914.
COOK, A. B. *Zeus : A Study in Ancient Religion, IIi*, 1925, 57-93.
CORDER, P. & KIRK, J. L. *A Roman Villa at Langton near Malton, East Yorkshire. (Roman Malton and District Report, No. 4)*, 1932.
COROT, H. *Les Fouilles du Grand-Jailly*, 1911.
COROT, H. 'Les Sources Divinisées de la Côte-d'Or et la Reprise des Fouilles des Sources de la Seine', *Mémoires de la Commission des Antiquités du Département de la Côte-d'Or*, 19, 1927-32, 243-264.
COSTA, D. *Nantes : Musée Dobrée Art Mérovingien*, 1964.
COUPPE, J. *et al.* 'Découvertes gallo-romaines au Nord et à l'Est d'Étaples : premiers résultats', *Bulletin de la Commission Départementale des Monuments Historiques du Pas-de-Calais*, 10, 1977, no. 2, 65-87.
COURCELLE-SENEUIL, J. L. *Les Dieux Gaulois d'après les Monuments figurés*, 1910.
COURTOIS, J. Cl. 'Objets de l'âge du Bronze ... Hautes-Alpes', *Gallia*, 15, 1957, 63-85.
COURTOIS, J. Cl. 'Objets provenant d'un cimetière protohistorique et gallo-romain à Lanslevillard (Savoie)' *Gallia*, 19, 1961, 245-248.
COUTIL, L. *Les Figurines en Terre Cuite des Eburones, Veliocasses et Lexovii*, 1899, 77-83.
COWEN, J. D. 'The Hallstatt Sword of Bronze : on the Continent and in Britain', *Proceedings of the Prehistoric Society*, 33, 1967, 377-454.
CRADDOCK, P. T. 'Europe's Earliest Brasses', *Masca Journal*, Museum Applied Science Centre for Archaeology (University of Pennsylvania), 1, 1978, 4-5.
CRAVAYAT, 'Les Cultes Indigènes dans la Cité des Bituriges', *Revue Archéologique de l'Est et du Centre-Est*, 1955, 210-228.
ČREMOSNIK, I. 'Totenmatildarstellungen auf römischen Denkmälern in Jugoslawien', *Jahrshefte des Österreichischen Archäologischen Instituts*, 44, 1959, 207ff.
CREUS, I. 'De Gallo-Romeinse nederzetting onder het laat-Romainse grafveld van Oudenburg', *Archaeologia Belgica*, 1975, 179.

Cumont, F. *Afterlife in Roman Paganism*, 1922.
Cunliffe, B. W. 'The Temple of Sulis Minerva at Bath', *Antiquity*, 44, 1966, 199ff.
Cunliffe, B. W. *Fifth Report on the Excavations of the Roman Fort at Richborough, Kent*, 1968.
Cunliffe, B. W. *Roman Bath*, 1969.
Cunliffe, B. W. *Roman Bath Rediscovered*, 1971.
Cunliffe, B. W. 'The Roman Sacred Spring at Bath', *Popular Archaeology*, 1, 1978, 1, 2ff.
Cunliffe, B. W. & Wiseman, P. *The Battle for Gaul*, 1980.
Cunnington, W. *Catalogue of the Antiquities of the Museum, Devizes, Part 1*, 1896.
Curle, J. *A Roman Frontier Post and its People : The Fort of Newstead in the Parish of Melrose*, 1911.
Curle, J. 'An Inventory ... sites in Scotland', *Proceedings of the Society of Antiquaries of Scotland*, 66, 1931-32, 277ff.
Dabat, M. & Dabat, P. 'La Fibule de Voves', *Revue Archéologique du Centre*, 11, 1972, 195-198.
Dauvois, M. 'Une Fibule gallo-romaine trouvée à Bazoches-les-Hautes', *Revue Archéologique de l'Est et du Centre-Est*, 8, 1957, 359-360.
Debal, J. 'Le Cavalier au Géant de Vienne-en-Val (Loiret)', *Bulletin de la Société Nationale des Antiquaires de France*, 1970, 167-177.
Déchelette, J. 'Le Bélier consacré aux divinités celtiques', *Revue Archéologique* (fasc. II), 1898, 63ff ; 245ff.
Déchelette, J. 'Le Culte du Soleil aux Temps Préhistoriques', *Revue Archéologique*, I, 1909, 305-357.
Déchelette, J. *Âge du Bronze : Manuel d'archéologie II : Archéologie Celtique ou Protohistorique*, part 1, 1910.
Déchelette, J. *Premier Âge du Fer : Manuel d'archéologie III : Hallstatt*, 1913.
Déchelette, J. *La Collection Millon : Antiquités préhistoriques et gallo-romaines*, 1913, 260ff.
Déchelette, J. *La Tène: Manuel d'archéologie IV: Celtique et Gallo-Romaine, 2: Archéologie Celtique ou Protohistorique*, part 3, 1914.
Degen, R. 'Antike Religionen Frühes Christentum', *Archäologie der Schweiz*, 1966-76.
Dehn, W. 'Ein Quelheiligtum des Apollo und der Sirone bei Hochscheid Kr. Bernkastel', *Germania*, 25, 1941, 104-111.
Demaison, L. 'Autel antique à Commetreuil', *Bulletin de la Société Nationale des Antiquaires de France*, 1925, 132-134.
Deonna, W. 'Le Soleil dans les armoiries de la Ville de Genève', *Revue de l'histoire des Religions*, 1915, 72, 1-129.
Deonna, W. 'À propos du dieu de Viège', *Revue des Études Anciennes*, 17, 1915, 145-147.

DEONNA, W. 'Encore le dieu de Viège', *Revue des Études Anciennes*, 18, 1916, 193-202.
DEONNA, W. 'Les cornes bouletées des bovidés celtiques', *Revue Archéologique* (fasc. I), 1917, 124ff.
DEONNA, W. 'La Rosace sur le front du taureau sacré', *Pro Alesia*, 1921-22, 22-26.
DEONNA, W. 'Main et Rouelle', *Pro Alesia*, 1925, 108-113.
DEONNA, W. *Exploration Archéologique de Délos* ..., 1938.
DEONNA, W. 'Trois, superlatif absolu : À propos du taureau tricornu et de Mercure triphallique', *L'Antiquité Classique*, 23, 1954, 403-428.
Devizes Museum. *A Guide Catalogue of the Neolithic and Bronze Age Collections in Devizes Museum*, 1964.
DEVOTO, G. *Tabulae Iguvinae* (2nd ed.), 1940.
DEWEY, H. 'Discoveries at Howletts, Kent', *Antiquaries Journal*, 4, 1924, 276-277.
DHENIN, R. & DHENIN, M. 'Les Monnaies d'or gauloises conservées à la Bibliothèque municipale de Douai', *Septentrion : Revue Archéologique Trimestrielle*, 6, 1976, 1-4.
DIETRICH, B. C. *The Origin of Greek Religion*, 1973.
DITCHFIELD, P. H. 'Romano-British Berkshire', *Victoria County History Berkshire*, 1, 1906, 197ff.
DOTTIN, G. *Manuel pour servir à l'étude de l'antiquité celtique*, Paris, 1906.
DRESSEL, E. *La Necropoli presso Alife (Annali dell'Instituto)*, 1884.
DREXEL, F. 'Götterverehrung in römischen Germanien', *Bericht der Römisch-Germanischen Kommission*, 14, 1923, 1-67.
DRIOUX, G. 'Note sur un 'Dispater' provenant de Maranville (Haute-Marne)', *Bulletin Archéologique du Comité des travaux historiques et scientifiques*, 1921, 67-88.
DRIOUX, G. 'Le Dieu «à la roue» chez les Lingons', *Revue des Études Anciennes*, 31, 1929, 354-358.
DRIOUX, G. *Cultes Indigènes des Lingons*, 1934.
DRIOUX, G. 'Amulette de Bronze trouvée à Isômes (Haute-Marne)', *Bulletin de la Société Nationale des Antiquaires de France*, 1943-44, 289-290.
DUDLEY, D. 'Excavations on Nor'nour in the Isles of Scilly', *Archaeological Journal*, 1967, 124, 1ff.
DUDLEY, H. *Early Days in North-West Lincolnshire*, 1949.
DUVAL, P.-M. *Les Dieux de la Gaule*, 1957.
DUVAL, P.-M. *Paris Antique*, 1961.
DUVAL, P.-M. *Les Celtes*, 1977.
EGGER, R. *Jahreshefte des Österreichischen Archäologischen Institutes (Beiblatt)*, 1956-58, 44ff.
EGGER, R. *Die Ausgrabungen auf dem Magdalensberg, 1956 & 1957*, 1959.
EIDEN, H. *Zehn Jahre Ausgrabungen Mittelrhein und Mosel*, 1976, pl. 50, 63.
ELBE, J. von. *Roman Germany*, 1975.
Encyclopaedia of Religion & Ethics 'Crosses', 4, 325.

Espérandieu, E. 'Note sur des images de divinités', *Pro Alesia*, 1906-07, 39ff.
Espérandieu, E. *Recueil Général des Bas-Reliefs de la Gaule Romaine*, Paris, 1907-66.
Espérandieu, E. *Le Musée Lapidaire de Nîmes : Guide Sommaire*, 1924.
Espérandieu, E. & Rolland, H. *Bronzes Antiques de la Seine Maritime*, 1959.
Étienne, E. *Bordeaux Antique*, 1962.
Evans, Sir A. *The Palace of Knossos : Report for the Years 1900-1905*, 1902-03.
Evans, J. *Ancient Bronze Implements of Great Britain*, 1881.
Eydoux, H. P. *La France Antique*, 1962.
Eygun, F. 'Informations-Archéologiques : Poitiers', *Gallia*, 23, 1965, 349-387.
Fairbanks, A. *The Mythology of Greece and Rome*, 1908.
Farrar, R. A. H. 'A Bronze Hanging-Bowl and Model Axe-Head from the Roman Cemetery at Poundbury, Dorchester', *Dorset Natural History and Archaeological Society*, 74, 195, 97ff.
Farrell, A. W. & Penny, S. 'The Broighter Boat : A Re-assessment', *Irish Archaeological Forum*, 1975.
Ferguson, J. *The Religions of the Roman Empire*, 1970.
Ferguson, J. *Greek and Roman Religion* (Open University Arts Course AD208, Units 14-15), 1977.
Ferrier, J. *Pendeloques et Amulettes d'Europe : Anthologie et Réflexions*, 1971.
Feugère, M. 'Les Fibules Gallo-Romaines du Musée Denon à Châlon-sur-Sâone, *Mémoires de la Société d'Histoire et d'Archéologie de Châlon-sur-Sâone*, 47, 1977, 77-158.
Feugère, M. *Principes d'une Documentation sur les fibules d'époque romaine*, 1978.
Filip, J. *Celtic Civilization and its Heritage*, Prague, 1960.
Filip, J. *Manuel Encyclopédique de Préhistoire et Protohistoire Européennes*, 1969.
Fillioux, A. *Nouvel essai d'interprétation et de Classification des Monnaies de la Gaule*, 1867.
Filtzinger, P. et al., *Die Römer in Baden-Württemburg*, 1976.
Fischer, F. 'Die Kelten bei Herodot', *Madrider Mitteilungen*, 13, 1972, 109-124.
Fishwick, D. 'The Imperial 'Numen' in Roman Britain', *Journal of Roman Studies*, 59, 1969, 76-91.
Fleischer, *Die Römischen Bronzen aus Österreich*, 1967.
Flemming, H. 'Les Objets d'Alesia ...', *Pro Alesia*, 1908-09, 391-395.
Fletcher, E. M., *Roman Ilkley*, 1965.
Formige, J. 'Temple du Vernègues (Bouches-du-Rhône)', *Bulletin de la Société Nationale des Antiquaires de France*, 1924, 74-80.
Forrer, R. 'Ausgrabungen auf der keltisch-römischen siedlungstätte des Wasserwalden bei Stambach-Zabern', *Cahiers d'Archéologie et d'Histoire d'Alsace*, 1, 1909-12, 28-34.

Forrer, R. 'Nouvelles découvertes et acquisitions ... Musée de Strasbourg, 1914-1926', *Cahiers d'Archéologie et d'Histoire d'Alsace*, 4, 1922-26, 333-338.
Forrer, R. *Strasbourg-Argentorate*, 1, 1927.
Forrer, R. *L'Alsace Romaine*, 1935.
Forrer, R. *Die Helvetischen und Helveto-Römischen Votivbeilchen der Schweiz* (Schriften des Institutes für Ur- und Frühgeschichte der Schweiz, 5), 1948.
Forster, R. H. 'Corstopitum : Report on the Excavations in 1907', *Archaeologia Aeliana* (ser 3), 4, 1908, 205-304.
Forster, R. H. & Knowles, W. H. 'Corstopitum : Report on the Excavations in 1908', *Archaeologia Aeliana* (ser 3), 5; 1909,305-424.
Forster, R. H. & Knowles, W. H. 'Corstopitum : Report on the Excavations in 1909', *Archaeologia Aeliana* (ser 3), 6, 1910, 205-272.
Forster, R. H. & Knowles, W. H. 'Corstopitum : Report on the Excavations in 1910', *Archaeologia Aeliana* (ser 3), 7, 1911, 143-268.
Fouet, G. *La Villa Gallo-Romaine de Montmaurin*, 1969.
Fouet, G. & Saves, G. 'Le Bronze à Vieille-Toulouse : Trouvailles Anciennes', *Revue Archéologique de Narbonnaise*, 4, 1971, 46-92.
Fouet, G. & Soutou, A. 'Une cîme pyrénéenne consacrée à Jupiter : Le Mont-Saçon (Hautes-Pyrénées)', *Gallia*, 21, 1963, 75-295.
Fournier, P. Fr. 'Le Dieu Cavalier à l'anguipède dans la cité des Arvernes, *Revue Archéologique du Centre*, 1, 1962, 105-127.
Fox, A. 'Excavations at the South Gate, Exeter', *Proceedings of the Devon Archaeological Exploration Society*, 26, 1968, 1ff.
Fox, A *et al*. 'Report on the Excavations at Milber Down' *Proceedings of the Devon Archaeological Exploration Society*, 4, 1948-52, 27ff.
Fox, C. *A Find of the Early Iron Age from Llyn Cerrig, Anglesey*, 1945.
Fox, C. *Pattern and Purpose : A Survey of Celtic Art in Britain*, 1958.
Fox, G. E., 'Roman Norfolk', *Archaeological Journal*, 46, 1889, 331ff.
Fox, G. E. 'Roman Suffolk', *Archaeological Journal*, 57, 1900, 89ff.
Fremersdorf, F. *Die Denkmäler des Römischen Köln, II : Urkunden zur Kölner Stadtgeschichte aus Römischen Zeit*, 1963.
Frend, W. H. C. 'Religion in Roman Britain in the 4th Century A.D.', *Journal of the British Archaeological Association* (ser 3), 18, 1955, 1-16.
Frere, S. S. *Verulamium*, 1972.
Frere, S. S. 'Roman Britain in 1972', *Britannia*, 4, 1973, 307.
Frere, S. S. 'Roman Britain in 1973', *Britannia*, 5, 1974, 452.
Frere, S. S., *Britannia* (New Edition), 1978.
Frezouls, E. 'Informations-Archéologiques : Champagne-Ardennes', *Gallia*, 29, 1971, 287.
Frisch, T. G. & Toll, N. P. *The Excavations of Dura Europos : IV*, fasc. 1, 1949.
Furumark, A. 'The Chronology of Mycenaean Pottery', *Kunglig Vitterhetshistoria och antikvitets academien*, 1941.

GAGÉ, J. *Apollon Romain*, 1955.
GAIDOZ, H. 'Le Dieu Gaulois du Soleil et le Symbolisme de la roue', *Revue Archéologique*, 2, 1884, 7-37.
GAIDOZ, H. 'Le Dieu Gaulois du Soleil et le Symbolisme de la roue', *Revue Archéologique*, 3, 1885, 180-203.
GAIDOZ, H. 'Études sur la Mythologie gauloise, le dieu gaulois du Soleil et le Symbolisme de la roue, 1886.
GALLIOU, P. 'À propos de deux pendentifs gallo-romains du Musée Archéologique de Nantes', *Annales de Bretagne*, 81, 1974, 259-283.
GASSIES, G. *Bas-Reliefs gallo-romains trouvés à Meaux*, 1901.
GASSIES, G. 'Cavalier et anguipède sur un monument de Meaux', *Revue des Études Anciennes*, 4, 1902, 287-297.
GELLING, P. & DAVIDSON, H. E. *The Chariot of the Sun : and other Rites and Symbols of the Northern Bronze Age*, 1969.
GETTY, R. J. (ed.) *M. Annaei Lucani de Bello Civili, Liber I*, 1940.
GILBERT, H. 'The Felmingham Hall Hoard, Norfolk', *Bulletin of the Board of Celtic Studies*, 28, part 1, 1978, 159-187.
GIMBUTAS, M. *Bronze Age Cultures in Central and Eastern Europe*, 1965.
GIOT, P. R. 'Deux dépôts de bronze finistériens', *Bulletin de la Société Archéologique de Finistère*, 1949.
GIRARDOT, A. 'Station de la Pierre Polie et Sépultures gauloises de la Grotte de Courchapon', *Mémoires de la Société d'émulations de Doubs*, 1883, 273-303.
GLOB, P. V. *Helleristninger i Danmark*, 1969.
GLOB, P. V. *The Mound People*, 1974.
GLORY, A. 'Rouelle gravée et bossettes de bronze de la Grotte de Couillou (Ariège), *Gallia*, 12, 1954, 359-360.
GLUECK, W. *Deities and Dolphins*, 1965.
GOODBURN, R. *The Roman Villa Chedworth* (National Trust), 1972.
GOODCHILD, R. G. 'A Priest's Sceptre from the Romano-Celtic Temple at Farley Heath, Surrey', *Antiquaries Journal*, 18, 1938, 391ff.
GOODCHILD, R. G. 'The Farley Heath Sceptre Binding', *Antiquaries Journal*, 27, 1947, 83ff.
GÖSE, E. *et al. Der Tempelbezirk im Altbachtale zu Trier*, I, 1938.
GOZZADINI, G. *Di un Sepulchro Etrusco*, 1854.
GRANT, M. *Roman Myths*, 1971.
GRAPINAT, R. 'Les Avatars d'un Culte Solaire', *Forum : Revue du Groupe Archéologique Antique*, 1, 1970, 54-56.
GREEN, H. S. *et al*. 'The Caergwrle Bowl : its Composition, Geological Source and Archaeological Significance', *Report of the Institute of Geological Sciences*, N° 80/1, 1980, 26-30.

GREEN, M. J. 'A Symbol of the Celtic Jupiter from Little Houghton, Northamptonshire', *Journal of the Northampton Museums and Art Gallery*, 10, 1974, 2-6.
GREEN, M. J. *A Romano-British Ceremonial Bronze Object found near Peterborough* (Peterborough Museum Monograph, 1), 1975.
GREEN, M. J. 'A Romano-Celtic Cult Symbol from Icklingham, Suffolk', *Proceedings of the Cambridge Antiquarian Society*, 66, 1975, 55-61.
GREEN, M. J. 'Romano-British non-ceramic Model Objects in South-East Britain', *Archaeological Journal*, 132, 1975, 54-70.
GREEN, M. J. *A Corpus of Religious Material from the Civilian Areas of Roman Britain* (British Archaeological Reports, Oxford, 24), Oxford, 1976.
GREEN, M. J. 'A Roman Bronze Model Shovel from Oxfordshire', *Oxoniensia*, 42, 1977, 256-260.
GREEN, M. J. 'Theriomorphism in Romano-British Cult Art', in HENIG, M. & MUNBY, J. (eds.), *Roman Life and Art in Britain* (British Archaeological Reports, Oxford, 41, part ii, Oxford, 1977, 297-327.
GREEN, M. J. *Small Cult Objects from the Military Areas of Roman Britain* (British Archaeological Reports, Oxford, 52), Oxford, 1978.
GREEN, M. J. 'The Worship of the Romano-Celtic Wheel-God in Britain seen in relation to Gaulish Evidence', *Latomus*, 38 (fasc. 2), 1979, 345-368.
GREEN, M. J. 'The Romano-Celtic Bronze Model Anchor from Barton Court Farm Villa', *Council for British Archaeology Fascicule* (forthcoming), 1979.
GREEN, M. J. 'A Romano-British Model Sickle found in Aylesbury', *Records of Buckinghamshire* (forthcoming), 1979.
GREEN, M. J. 'Wheel-God and Ram-Headed Snake in Roman Gloucestershire', *Transactions of the Bristol and Gloucestershire Archaeological Society*, 99 (in press), 1980.
GREEN, M. J. 'The Gestingthorpe Models', *Department of Environment Publication* (forthcoming), 1981.
GREENFIELD, E. 'The Romano-British Shrines at Brigstock', *Antiquaries Journal*, 43, 1963, 228ff.
GRENIER, A. *Les Gaulois*, Paris, 1945, 2nd ed., 1970 (L. Haimond).
GRENIER, A. *Manuel d'Archéologie Gallo-Romaine*, 1958.
GRIMES, W. F. *The Excavation of Roman and Medieval London*, 1968.
GRINSELL, L. V. *The Ancient Burial-Mounds of England* (2nd ed.), 1953, 36-37.
GRINSELL, L. V. 'The Breaking of Objects as a Funerary Rite', *Folklore*, 72, 1961, 475-491.
GROSS, V. *Les protohelvètes*, 1883.
GUERIN, F. 'Trouvaille fortuite d'une rouelle de suspension en or dans le Département des Ardennes', *Revue Archéologique de l'Est et du Centre-Est*, 16, 1965, 274-275.
GUNTHER, R. & KOPSTEIN, H. (eds.). *Die Römer an Rhein und Donau*, 1975.
GUTHRIE, W. K. C., *The Greeks and their Gods*, 1954.

HABERT, T. *Ville de Reims : Catalogue du Musée Archéologique*, 1901.
HAFFNER, A. *Das Keltisch-Römische Graberfeld von Wederath-Belginum, 1*, 1971.
HAFFNER, A. *Das Keltisch-Römische Graberfeld von Wederath-Belginum, 2*, 1974.
HAFFNER, A. *Das Keltisch-Römische Graberfeld von Wederath-Belginum, 3*, 1978.
HAMPEL, J. *L'Âge du Bronze en Hongrie*, 1876.
HAMPEL, *Le Catalogue de l'exposition préhistorique des Musées de province ... en Hongrie*, 1876.
HAMPEL, J. *A Bronzkor emlekei Magyar Honban*, 1886-96.
HAMPEL, J. *Alterthümer der Bronzezeit in Ungarn*, 1887.
HANČAR, F. 'Ein «nordisches» Streitwagenbild im ostlichen Kaukasus', *Forschungen und Forstchrifte*, 19, 1943, 26f.
HANČAR, F. *Das Pferd in prähistorischer und früher historischer Zeit*, 1956.
HARDING, D. W. *Prehistoric Europe (Making of the Past)*, 1978.
HARDWICK, L. *Athenian Social History* (Open University Units 7-8, Course A292), 1979.
HARKER, S. 'Springhead – A Brief Re-appraisal', in RODWELL, W. (ed.) *Temples, Churches and Religion in Roman Britain* (British Archaeological Reports, Oxford, N° 77), Oxford, 1980, 285-288.
HARMAND, J. *Les Celtes au second âge du fer*, Paris, 1970.
HARRIS, E. & HARRIS, J. *The Oriental Cults in Roman Britain*, 1965.
HARRIS, W. E. *Transactions of the Newbury District Field Club*, 7, n° 2, 1935, 128.
HARRISON, J. E. *Themis*, 1912.
HARRISON, J. E. *Prolegomena to the Study of Greek Religion*, 1957 (1st edition 1903).
HARTLEY, B. R. & KAINE, K. F. 'Roman Dock and Buildings', *Journal of the Chester Archaeological Society*, 41, 1954, 15ff.
HATT, J. J. *Les Monuments Funéraires Gallo-Romains du Comminges et du Couserans*, 1945.
HATT, J. J. 'La Vision de Constantin au sanctuaire de Grand', *Latomus*, 9, 1950, 427-436.
HATT, J. J. '«Rota Flammis Circumsepta». À propos du symbole de la roue dans la région gauloise', *Revue Archéologique de l'Est et du Centre-Est*, 2, 1951, 82-87.
HATT, J. J. *La Tombe Gallo-Romaine*, 1951.
HATT, J. J. 'Les Fouilles de la ruelle Saint-Médard à Strasbourg', *Gallia*, 11, 1953, 248.
HATT, J. J. *Inventaire des Collections Publiques Françaises ... Strasbourg : Sculptures Antiques Régionales. Musée Archéologique*, 1964.
HATT, J. J. 'Essai sur l'évolution de la Religion Gauloise', *Revue des Études Anciennes*, 57, 1965, 80-125.
HATT, J. J. 'Les Croyances Funéraires des Gallo-Romains d'après la décoration des tombes', *Revue Archéologique de l'Est*, 21, 1970, 7-97.

HAUG, F. 'Die Viergöttersteine', *Westdeutsche Zeitschrift*, 10, 1891, 9-62.
HAVERFIELD, F. 'The Mother-Goddesses', *Archaeologia Aeliana* (ser 2), 15, 1892, 314ff.
HAVERFIELD, F. 'Three Notable Inscriptions', *Archaeological Journal*, 50, 1893, 308-321.
HAVERFIELD, F. 'Romano-British Northamptonshire', *Victoria County History Northamptonshire*, 1, 1902, 157ff.
HAVERFIELD, F. & COLLINGWOOD, R. G. 'Report on the Exploration of the Roman fort at Ambleside, 1903', *Cumberland & Westmorland Society Transactions* (O.S.), 15, 1914, 504-505.
HAWKES, C. F. C. 'The Double Axe in Prehistoric Europe', *Annals of the British School at Athens*, 37, 1937, 141-160.
HAWKES, C. F. C., 'From Bronze to Iron Age : Middle Europe, Italy and the North and West', *Proceedings of the Prehistoric Society*, 14, 1948, 196-219.
HAWKES, C. F. C. 'Bronze-workers, cauldrons and bucket-animals in Iron Age and Roman Britain', in GRIMES, W. F. (ed.), *Aspects of Archaeology in Britain and Beyond*, 1951, 172-199.
HAWKES, C. F. C. 'Celts and Culture', in DUVAL, P. M. & HAWKES, C. F. C. (eds.), *Celtic Art in Ancient Europe : Five Protohistoric Centuries*, 1-27, London, New York, San Francisco, 1976.
HAWKES, C. F. C. & HULL, M. R. *Camulodunum*, 1947.
HAWKES, C. F. C. & SMITH, M. A. 'On some Buckets and Cauldrons of the Bronze and Early Iron Ages', *Antiquaries Journal*, 37, 1957, 131-198.
HAWKINS, E. 'Notices of a remarkable collections of Ornaments of the Roman Period ... British Museum', *Archaeological Journal*, 8, 1851, 35-41.
HEICHELHEIM, F. M. 'Genii Cucullati', *Archaeologia Aeliana* (ser. 4), 12, 1935, 187-195.
HEICHELHEIM, F. M. 'Some Unpublished Roman Bronze Statuettes in the Museum ... Cambridge', *Proceedings of the Cambridge Antiquarian Society*, 37-38, 1935-37, 52-68.
HENIG, M. 'The Origin of some Ancient British Coin-Types', *Britannia*, 3, 1972, 209-223.
HENRY, F. 'Émailleurs d'Occident', *Préhistoire*, 2, 1933, 65-146.
HERTEIG, A. E. 'The Excavation of Bryggen, Bergen, Norway', in BRUCE-MITFORD, R. (ed.), *Recent Archaeological Excavations in Europe*, 63-89.
HERTLEIN, F. *Die Jupitergigantensäulen*, 1910.
HERTLEIN, F. 'Der Zusammenhang der Jupitergigantengruppen', *Germania*, 1, 1917, 136-143.
HETTNER, F. 'Jupiter mit dem Rad', *Westdeutsche Zeitschrift*, 3, 1884, 27-30.
HETTNER, F. *Die Römischer Steindenkmäler des Provincialmuseums zu Trier*, 1893.

HETTNER, F. *Festschrift zur Feier des hundertjahrigen Bestehen der Gesellschaft für Nützliche Forschungen in Trier*, 1901.
HIGGINS, R. A. *Greek and Roman Jewellery*, 1961.
HIGGINS, R. A. *Minoan and Mycenean Art*, 1974.
HINZ, H. *Archaölogische Bier Funde und Denkmäler des Rheinlande*, 1969.
HILDYARD, E. J. W. 'A Triple-Headed Bucket-Mount', *Antiquaries Journal*, 34, 1954, 225-229.
HOBLEY, B. & SCHOFIELD, J. 'Excavations in the City of London: 1st Interim Report, 1974-1975', *Antiquaries Journal*, 57, 1977, pt. 1, 31-67.
HODSON, F. R. & ROWLETT, R. M. 'From 600 B.C. to the Roman Conquest', in PIGGOTT, S., DANIEL, G. & MCBURNEY, C., *France before the Romans*, 1974, 157-191.
HOERNES, M. 'Die prähistorische Nekropole von Nesactium', *Jahrbuch für Altertumskunde*, 1905, 330.
HOLLEYMAN, G. & BURSTOW, P. 'Excavations at Muntham Court', *Archaeological Newsletter*, 6, 1957, N° 4, 101ff.
HOLSTE, F. 'Bronzezeit im nordmainischen Hessen', *Vorgeschichtliche Forschungen*, 1939, N° 12.
HOLSTE, F. *Hortfunde Süd-östereuropas*, 1951.
HOWELL, J. *The Religions of the Auxiliary Units ... on Hadrian's Wall*. (Unpublished B. A. dissertation, University College, Cardiff) 1969.
HUCHER, E. *L'Art Gaulois ou les Gaulois d'après leurs Médailles*, Paris, 1868-74.
HUGHES, M. J. 'A Technical Study of Opaque Red Glass of the Iron Age in Britain', *Proceedings of the Prehistoric Society*, 38, 1972, 98-107.
HUGHSON, D. *History of London*, I, 1805, 34ff.
JACOB-FRIESEN, K. *Goldscheibe von Moordorf bei Aurich mit ihren britischen Parallelen*, 1931, 25-44.
JACOBI, L. *Das Römerkastell Saalburg*, 1897.
JACOBSTHAL, P. *Early Celtic Art*, Oxford, 1944.
JAMES, E. O. *Prehistoric Religion*, 1957.
JENKINS, F. 'The Role of the Dog in Romano-Gaulish Religion', *Latomus*, 16, 1957, 60-76.
JENKINS, F. 'The Cult of the Dea Nutrix in Kent', *Archaeologia Cantiana*, 71, 1957, 30ff.
JENKINS, F. 'The Cult of the Pseudo-Venus in Kent', *Archaeologia Cantiana*, 72, 60ff.
JENKINS, J. G. *The English Farm Wagon*, 1961.
JENNY, W. VON. *Keltische Metallarbeiten aus heidnischer und Christlicher Zeit*, 1935.
JOBST, W. 'Jupiter Kapitolinus oder Jupiter Karnuntinus', *Limes : Akten des XI Internationalen Limeskongresses*, 1977, 155-165.

JOHNSTON, P. M. 'Roman Vase found at Littlehampton', *Sussex Archaeological Collections*, 46, 1903, 233-234.
JONES, G. D. B. & GREALEY, S. *Roman Manchester*, 1974.
JOPE, E. M. 'Vehicles and Harness', in SINGER, C. *et al.* (eds.), *A History of Technology : 2 : The Mediterranean Civilizations and the Middle Ages, c. 700 B.C. - A.D. 1500*, 1956, 537-562.
JOPE, E. M. 'Daggers of the Early Iron Age in Britain', *Proceedings of the Prehistoric Society*, 27, 1961, 307-343.
JORNS, W. 'Ein Hallstatt A Grab mit Bronzetasse von Viernheim, Kr. Bergstrasse', *Germania*, 38, 1960, Heft 1/2, 168-173.
JULLIAN, C. *Histoire de la Gaule, II*, Paris, 1909.
JULLIAN, C. 'L'Autel de Psalmodi', *Revue des Études Anciennes*, 20, 1918, 224.
JULLIAN, C. 'Notes Gallo-Romaines LXXVIII : Emblèmes conjugués roues et maillets', *Revue des Études Anciennes*, 20, 1918, 113-115.
JULLIAN, C. *Histoire de la Gaule, VI*, 1920.
KARO, G. 'Schatz von Tiryns', *Mitteilungen der Deutschen Archäologischen Instituts*, 55, 1930, 119-140.
KELLER, E. *Die Spätrömischen Grabfunde in Südbayern*, 1971.
KELLER, F. *The Lake Dwellings of Switzerland and other parts of Europe*, 1966-78.
KELLNER, H. J. *Die Römer in Bayern*, 1971.
KENT HILL, D. 'Le «Dieu au Maillet» de Vienne à la Walters Art Gallery de Baltimore', *Gallia*, 11, 1953, 204-224, fig. 1.
KERSTEN, K. *Zur Älteren Nordischen Bronzezeit*, 1936.
KIRK, J. R. 'The Bronzes from Woodeaton', *Oxoniensia*, 14, 32ff.
KLEIN, W. G. 'The Roman Temple at Worth, Kent', *Antiquaries Journal*, 8, 1928, 76ff.
KLINDT-JENSEN, O. *Gundstrupkedelen*, Köbenhagen, 1961.
KLINDT-JENSEN, O. 'L'Est, le Nord et l'Ouest dans l'art de la fin du IIème et du Ier siècles avant J.C.', in DUVAL, P. M. & HAWKES, C. F. C. (eds.), *Celtic Art in Ancient Europe : Five Protohistoric Centuries*, 1976, 233-245.
KOLLING, A. 'Neue Zeugnisse zur verehung des Gigantenreiters im Ostlichen Saarland', *Germania*, 36, 1958, 160-162.
KÖRBER, K. 'Die grosse Iuppiter-Saüle von Mainz', *Mainzer Zeitschrift*, 1, 1906, 54ff.
KOSSACK, G. 'Zur Ausdeutung, frühurnenfeldzeitlicher Kultgegenstände', *Archaeologia Geographica*, 1950, 4-8.
KOSSACK, G. *Studien zum Symbolgut der Urnenfelder und Hallstattzeit Mitteleuropas*, 1954.
KOSSACK, G. 'The Construction of the Felloe in Iron Age Spoked Wheels', in BOARDMAN, J., BROWN, M. A. & POWELL, T. G. E. (eds.), *The European Community in Later Prehistory*, 143-163.
KOVÁCS, T. *L'Âge du Bronze en Hongrie*, 1977.

KOZHIN, R. M. 'The Gobi Quadriga', *Sovetskaja Arheoloija*, 3, 1968, 35-42.
KRAPPE, A. H. 'Les Dieux au Corbeau chez les Celtes', *Revue de l'histoire des Religions*, 114, 1936, 236-246.
KROMER, K. *Das Gräberfeld von Hallstatt*, 1959.
KRÜGER, E. 'Die gallischen und die germanischen Dioskuren ...', *Trierer Zeitschrift*, 15, 1940, 8-27.
KRÜGER, E. 'Die gallischen und die germanischen Dioskuren ...', *Trierer Zeitschrift*, 16, 1941, 1-66.
KRÜGER, M.-L. *Corpus Signorum Imperii Romani : Corpus der Skulpturen der Römischen Welt, Österreich. Band 1, 4 ; Carnuntum*, 1972.
KÜNZL, E. *Corpus Signorum Imperii Romani : Corpus der Skulpturen der Römische Welt : Alzey und Umgebung*, 1975.
KUSTER, E. *Die Schlange in der griechischen Kunst und Religion*, 1913.
LABROUSSE, M. 'Informations-Archéologiques : Xe Circonscription', *Gallia*, 12, 1954, 211-231.
LABROUSSE, M. 'Informations-Archéologiques : Toulouse', *Gallia*, 20, 1962, 547-609.
LABROUSSE, M. 'Informations-Archéologiques : Midi-Pyrénées', *Gallia*, 24, 1966, 411-448.
LABROUSSE, M. 'Informations-Archéologiques : Midi-Pyrénées', *Gallia*, 32, 1974, 453-500.
LAET, S. J. de. 'Figurines en terre cuite d'époque romaine trouvés à Assche-Kalkoven', *L'Antiquité Classique*, 2, 1942, 41-54.
LAFFARGUE, J. & FOUET, G. *Peintures romanes, vestiges gallo-romains à Saint-Plancard*, 1948.
LAMBERT, E. *Essai sur la numismatique gauloise du nord-ouest de la France*, 1844.
LAMBRECHTS, P. *Contributions à l'étude des divinités celtiques*, 1942.
LAMBRECHTS, P. 'La Colonne du dieu-cavalier au géant et le culte des sources en Gaule', *Latomus*, 8, 1949, 145-158.
LAMBRECHTS, P. 'Divinités Équestres Celtiques ou défunts héroïsés ?', *L'Antiquité Classique*, 20, 1951, fasc. 1.
LAMBRECHTS, P. 'L'imagerie religieuse Celtique : le fond et la forme', *Mélanges H. Grégoire, III. Anneaux de l'Institut de Philologie et d'Histoire Orientales et Slaves*, 11, 1951, 205ff.
LAMBRECHTS, P. *L'Exaltation de la tête dans la pensée et dans l'art des Celtes*, Bruges, 1954.
LANTIER, R. 'Deux Figurines d'Art Celtique', *Bulletin de la Société Nationale des Antiquaires de France*, 1936, 218-222.
LAUR-BELART, R. 'Eine neue Kleininschrift von Augst', *Urschweiz*, 6, 1942, 20-23.
LAUX, F. *Die Bronzezeit in der Lüneburger Heide*, 1971.

LAWSON, A. J. 'A Late Middle Bronze Age Hoard from Hunstanton, Norfolk', in BURGESS, C. & COOMBS, D. (eds.), *Bronze Age Hoards : some Finds old and new* (British Archaeological Reports (Oxford), N° 67), 1979, 42-92.
LAYARD, N. F. 'Bronze Crowns and a Bronze Headdress from a Roman Site at Cavenham Heath, Suffolk', *Antiquaries Journal*, 5, 1925, 258ff.
LEACH, J. 'The Smith-God in Roman Britain', *Archaeologia Aeliana* (ser. 4), 40, 1962, 35ff.
LEACH, R. 'Religion and Burials in South Somerset and North Dorset', in RODWELL, W. (ed.), *Temples, Churches and Religion in Roman Britain* (British Archaeological Reports (Oxford), N° 77), 1980, 329-366.
LEBEL, P. 'Les Monuments dits du cavalier et de l'anguipède en Bourgogne et en Nivernais', *Mémoires de la Commission des Antiquités du Département de la Côte d'Or*, 22, 1940-46, 61-64.
LEBEL, P. & BOUCHER, S. *Bronzes Figurés Antiques, Musée Rolin*, 1975.
LEBER, P. 'Fund eines votiv-Altars auf der Koralpe', *Pro Austria Romana*, 15, 1965, 25f.
LEBER, P. 'Ein Altar des Mars Latobius auf der Koralpe', *Carinthia I*, 157, 1967, 517-520.
LEE, J. E. *Isca Silurum, or an illustrated Catalogue of the Museum of Antiquities of Caerleon*, 1862.
LEFORT DES YLOUSES, R. 'La Roue, le Svastika, la Spirale comme symbole du tonnerre', *Comptes-Rendus de l'Académie des Inscriptions et Belles Lettres*, 1949.
LEFORT DES YLOUSES, R. 'La Roue, le Svastika et la Spirale : Symboles antiques du tonnerre et de la foudre', *Gazette des Beaux Arts : Juillet-Aôut 1955*, 1955, 8-9.
LEHNER, H. 'Der Tempelbezirk der Matronae Vacallinehae bei Pesch', *Bonner Jahrbücher*, 125-126, 1918-21, 74ff.
LEHNER, H. 'Orientalisches Mysterienkulte im römischen Rheinland', *Bonner Jahrbücher*, 128-129, 1923-24, 36ff.
LEIBUNDGUT, A. 'Die Römische Epoche : Kunst und Kunstgewerbe', *Archäologische der Schweiz, Band V*, 1966-76, 84.
LELONG, C. 'Note sur une sculpture gallo-romaine de Mouhet (Indre)', *Revue Archéologique du Centre*, 9, 1970, 123-126.
LENORMANT, F. 'Notes Archéologiques sur la terre d'Otrante', *Bulletin Archéologique du Comité des travaux historiques et scientifiques*, 1881-82.
LERAT, L. 'Catalogue des Collections Archéologiques de Besançon, II : Les Fibules Gallo-Romaines', *Annales Littéraires de l'Université de Besançon*, 3, 1956, fasc. 1 (ser. 2).
LERAT, L. 'Informations-Archéologiques : Besançon', *Gallia*, 22, 1964; 375-410.
LERAT, L. 'Informations-Archéologiques : Franche-Comté', *Gallia*, 26, 1968, 435-472.

LERAT, L. 'Informations-Archéologiques : Franche-Comté', *Gallia*, 28, 1970, 345-365.
LEUZINGER, E. *Africa : The Art of the Negro Peoples*, 1960.
LEWIS, M. J. T. *Temples in Roman Britain*, 1966.
LINCKENHELD, E. *Les Stèles Funéraires en forme de Maison chez les Mediomatriques et en Gaule*, 1927.
LINCKENHELD, E. 'Sucellus et Nantosuelta', *Revue de l'histoire des religions*, 99, 1929, 40-92.
LINCKENHELD, E. 'Le Symbolisme astral des stèles funéraires gallo-romaines des Vosges et de l'Illyrie', *Revue Celtique*, 1929, 29-49.
LINCKENHELD, E. *Annales de la Société d'histoire et d'archéologie ... Lorraine*, 1929.
LINCKENHELD, E. 'Trouvailles anciennes et récentes du Reubberg près de Zinswiller', *Cahiers d'Archéologie et d'Histoire d'Alsace*, 6, 1931-34, 212-219.
LINDENSCHMIT, L. *Die Alterthümer unserer heidnischer Vorzeit*, I, III, Mayence, 1859-1911.
LINDUFF, K. 'Epona : A Celt among the Romans', *Latomus*, 38, 1979, 817-837.
LITTAUER, M. A. 'Rock Carvings of Chariots in Transcaucasia, Central Asia and Outer Mongolia', *Proceedings of the Prehistoric Society*, 43, 1977, 243-262.
LITTAUER, M. A. & CROUWEL, J. H. 'Terracotta Models as Evidence for Vehicles in the Ancient Near East', *Proceedings of the Prehistoric Society*, 40, 1974, 20-36.
LIVERSIDGE, J. *Britain in the Roman Empire*, 1968.
London Museum. *London in Roman Times* (London Museum Catalogue), 1930.
LÖE, Le Baron de. *Belgique Ancienne. Catalogue Raisonné III : La Période Romaine*, 1937.
LONGPERIER, H. de. 'Des Rouelles et Anneaux Antiques ...', *Revue Archéologique*, II, 1867, 343-362, 397-405.
LOTH, J. 'Le Dieu gaulois Rudiobos, Rudianos', *Revue Archéologique*, 86-87, 1925, 210-227.
LOUIS, R. 'Informations-Archéologiques : XIXe Circonscription', *Gallia*, 12, 1954, 499-525.
LYNCH, F. *Prehistoric Anglesey*, 1970.
MACGREGOR, M. 'The early Iron Age Metalwork from Stanwick, North Riding, Yorkshire, England', *Proceedings of the Prehistoric Society*, 28, 1962, 17-57.
MACKENDRICK, P. *Roman France*, 1971.
MAGNEN, R. & THEVENOT, E. *Epona*, 1953.
MAHIEU, A. 'Trouvailles Numismatiques ... faites dans la Province de Namur', *Annales de Namur*, 26, 1906, 205-220.
MAHR, A. *Ancient Irish Handcraft*, 1939.

MAJOR, E. *Gallische Ausiedlung mit Gräberfeld bei Basel*, 1940.
MALTEN, L. 'Das Pferd im Totenglauben', *Jahrbuch Deutsches Archäologisches Institut*, 29, 1914, 197ff.
MANN, J. C. *The Romans in the North*. (Catalogue of an Exhibition sponsored by the Universities of Lancester and Durham, May - October 1975), 1975.
MANNING, W. H. 'A Group of Bronze Models from Sussex in the British Museum', *Antiquaries Journal*, 46, 1966, 50-59.
MANNING, W. H. & SAUNDERS, C. 'A Socketed Iron Axe from Maids Moreton, Buckinghamshire, with a Note on the Type', *Antiquaries Journal*, 52, 1972, part 2, 276-292.
MARIANI, L. 'Aufidena', *Monumenti Antichi*, 10, 226ff.
MARICHARD, O. de. 'Découverte d'un Trésor de l'Âge du Bronze au Déroc', *Materiaux pour l'histoire primitive et naturelle de l'homme*, 1884.
MARIËN, M. E. *Oud-België*, 1951.
MARSHALL, F. H. *Catalogue of the Jewellery : Greek, Etruscan and Roman in the Department of Antiquities, British Museum*, 1911.
MARTIN, M. 'Römische Bronzegiesser in Augst BL', *Archäologie des Schweiz*, N° 3, 1978, 112-118.
MARTIN, R. 'Informations-Archéologiques : Dijon', *Gallia*, 22, 1964, 295-337.
MASSOUL, M. *Guide du Musée de Néris-les-Bains*, 1930.
MATTHYS, A. 'La Villa Romaine de Vesqueville', *Archaeologica Belgica*, 1974, 159.
MCALPIN, J. W. *Proceedings of the Society of Antiquaries*, 4, 1867-70, 183.
MEDUNA, J. 'Das Keltische Oppidum Staré Hradisko in Mähren', *Germania*, 48, 1970, 34-59.
MEGAW, J. V. S. *Art of the European Iron Age*, Bath, 1970.
MENDEL, M. G. 'Catalogue du Musée de Brousse', *Bulletin de Correspondance Hellénique*, 33, 1909, 283ff.
MENSIGNAC, C. de. 'Un nouveau Jupiter Gaulois', *Revue des Études Anciennes*, 7, 1905, 156-157.
MENZEL, H. *Die Römischen Bronzen aus Deutschland : I, Speyer*, 1960.
MENZEL, H. *Die Römischen Bronzen aus Deutschland : II, Trier*, 1966.
MERHART, G. von. 'Studien über einige Gattungen von Bronzegefässen', *Festschrift des Römisch-Germanisches Zentralmuseum in Mainz zur Feir Seines hundertjahrigen Bestehens*, 2, 1952, 1-71.
MERHART, G. von. *Bericht du Römisch-Germanischen Kommission*, 1956-57, 91-147.
MERLAT, P. *Jupiter Dolichenus*, 1960.
MICLEA, I. & FLORESCU, R. *Daco-romanii*, 1980.
MINNS, E. H. *Scythians and Greeks*, 1913, 236-239.
MISKE, K. V. *Die Prähistorische Ansiedlung Vilen St. Vid.*, 1908.

MITARD, P. H. 'La Villa Gallo-Romaine de Guiry-Gadancourt (Seine-et-Oise)', *Gallia*, 16, 1958, 266-281.
MÓCSY, A. 'Pannonia', in PAULY-WISSOWA, *Realencyclopädie der classischen Altertumwissenschaft*, G. *Wissowa*, 1962.
MÓCSY, A. *Pannonia and Upper Moesia*, 1974.
MONTELIUS, O. *Das Rad als religiöses Sinnbild*, 1901.
MONTELIUS, O. *La Civilisation primitive en Italie*, 1895-1910.
MOOREY, P. R. S. *Catalogue of the Ancient Persian Bronzes in the Ashmolean Museum*, 1971.
MOREL, J. P. 'Informations-Archéologiques : Franche-Comté', *Gallia*, 32, 1974, 401-426.
MORLEY HEWITT, A. T. *Roman Villa, West Park, Rockbourne*, 1969.
MORTILLET, G. de. 'Amulettes gauloises et gallo-romaines', *Revue d'anthropologie*, 9, 1876, fig. 2 : 14, fig. 11.
MOWAT, R. 'Les Autels Gallo-Romains de la Cité', *Bulletin Épigraphique de la Gaule*, 1881.
MÜLLER, L. *L'emploi et la signification dans l'antiquité du signe dit croix gammée*, 1877.
MÜLLER, S. 'Votivfund frä sten-og Bronzealderen', *Aarbeger von Nordisk Oldkyndighed og Historia*, 1886.
MÜLLER, S. *La représentation solaire de Trundholm*, 1903.
MÜLLER-KARPE, H. *Beiträge zur Chronologie der Urnenfelderzeit nördlich und südlich der Alpen* (Römisch-Germanisches Forschungen, 22, vii), 1959.
MÜLLER-KARPE, A. & M. 'Neue Latènezeitliche Funde aus dem Heidetränk-Oppidum im Taunus', *Germania*, 55, 1977, 33-63.
Musée Archéologique, Strasbourg. *Catalogue*, c. 1973.
Musée de Moulins. *Catalogue du Musée de Moulins*.
Musée de Troyes. *Catalogue Descriptif et Raisonné*, 1898.
NASH, D. *Settlement and Coinage in Central Gaul c. 150-50 B.C.* (British Archaeological Reports, Supplementary Series, N° 39, 1978.
NASH-WILLIAMS, V. E. 'The Roman Gold-Mines at Dolaucothi (Carms)', *Bulletin of the Board of Celtic Studies*, 14, 1950-52, 78-84.
NAUE, J. 'Eisernes Doclmesser aus dem Gardasée', *Bonner Jahrbücher*, 85, 1888, 1-5.
NEWSTEAD, R. 'Report ... Deanery Field, Chester', *Liverpool Annals of Archaeology and Anthropology*, 1928, 15, 22.
NEWTON, C. 'A Description of four bronzes found at Colchester', *Archaeologia*, 31, 1846, 443ff.
Obergermanisch-Raetische Limes des Römerreiches. Volume 8, 1897.
O.R.L. (*) *Volume 10*, 1899.

(*) *Obergermanisch-Raetische Limes des Römerreiches*.

O.R.L. Volume 14, 1901.
O.R.L. Volume 25, 1905.
O.R.L. Volume 27, 1906.
O.R.L. Volume 28 and Volume 29, 1907.
O.R.L. Volume 32, 1909.
O.R.L. Volume 33, 1910.
O.R.L. Volume 34, 1911.
O.R.L. Volume 38, 1913.
O.R.L. Volume 45, 1928.
O.R.L. Volume 53, 1936.
OBERMAYR, A. *Kelten und Römer am Magdalensberg*, 1971.
OBERLÄNDER, P. *Griechische Handspiegel* (Hamburg University Dissertation), 1967.
OGILVIE, R. M. *The Romans and their Gods*, 1969.
OLMSTED, G. S. 'The Gundestrup Version of Tain Bo Cuailnge', *Antiquity*, 50, 1976, 96ff.
OLMSTED, G. S. *The Gundestrup Cauldron*, Collection Latomus, 62, 1979.
Oxford Classical Dictionary. 1st Edition, 1970. 2nd Edition, 1978.
OZEEL, F. 'La Villa Gallo-Romaine du Bois-Brûlé à Maubeuge (Nord)', *Septentrion : Revue Archéologique Trimestrielle*, 3, 1973, 17-22.
PAGE, W. (ed.) 'Romano-British Bedfordshire', *Victoria County History Bedfordshire*, II, 1908, 5ff.
PARENTEAU, F. *Catalogue du Musée Départemental de Nantes et de la Loire-Inférieure* (2nd ed.), 1869.
PARENTEAU, F. *Inventaire Archéologique précédé d'une Introduction à l'étude des bijoux*, 1878.
PARIS, P. *Essai sur l'art et l'industrie de l'Espagne primitive*, II, 1904.
PĂRVAN, V. *Dacia : an outline of the Early Civilizations of the Carpatho-Danubian Countries*, 1928.
PASCAL, C. B. *The Cults of Cisalpine Gaul*, Collection Latomus, 75, 1964.
PASQUI, A. 'Delle tombe di Narce e dei ioro corredi', *Monumenta d'... Lincei*, 4, 1894, 490.
PATEK, E. *Die Urnenfeldkultur in Transdanubien*, 1968.
PAULI, L. *Keltischer Volksglaube : Amulette und Sonderbestattungen am Dürrnberg bei Hallein und im Eisenzeitlichen Mitteleuropa*, 1975.
PEET, T. E. *The Stone and Bronze Ages in Italy and Sicily*, 1909.
PENN, W. S. 'The Temple Ditch Site', *Archaeologia Cantiana*, 79, 1964, 172ff.
PENN, W. S. 'Springhead : Miscellaneous Excavations', *Archaeologia Cantiana*, 83, 1968, 174ff.
PENNINGTON, W. 'Vegetation History in the North-West of England: A Regional Synthesis', in WALKER, D. & WEST, R. G., *Studies in the Vegetational History of the British Isles*, 1970, 41-79.

PEQUART, M. & S. J. & LE ROUZIC, Z. *Corpus des Signes Gravés des Monuments Mégalithiques du Morbihan*, 1927.
PERNET, V. 'Les Richesses archéologiques du Mont Aussois', *Pro Alesia*, 1915, 35-38.
PERRIER, J. 'L'Autel de Thauron (Creuse)', *Gallia*, 18, 1960, 195-197.
PERRIN, A. *Études préhistoriques sur la Savoie*, 1869.
PEŠKAŘ, I. *Fibeln aus der römischen Kaiserzeit in Mähren*, 1972.
PETCH, D. F. 'Excavations in Eaton Road, Eccleston, Chester', *Journal of the Chester Archaeological Society*, 58, 1975, 35.
PETCH, J. A. 'Roman Durham', *Archaeologia Aeliana* (ser. 4), 1, 1925, 28.
PETCH, J. A. 'Excavations at Benwell (Condercum)', *Archaeologia Aeliana* (ser. 4), 14, 1927, 135-193.
PETRIKOVITS, H. VON. *Novaesium : Das Römische Neuss*.
PETRIKOVITS, H. VON. 'Fortifications in the North-Western Roman Empire from the Third to the Fifth Centuries A.D.', *Journal of Roman Studies*, 61, 1971, 179-218.
PETRY, F. 'Informations-Archéologiques : Alsace', *Gallia*, 36, fasc. 2, 1978, 347ff.
PETTAZONI, R. *Essays on the History of Religions*, 1954.
PEYRE, C. *La Cisalpine Gauloise du IIIe au Ier siècle avant J.-C.*, 1979.
PFEILER, B. *Römischer Goldschmuck des ersten und zweiten Jahrhunderts nach Chr. nach datierten Funden*, 1970.
PHILLIPS, E. J. 'A Roman Figured Capital at Cirencester' *Journal of the British Archaeological Association*, 129, 1976, 35-41.
PHILLIPS, E. J. 'Unfinished Roman Sculptures in North Britain', *Archaeological Journal*, 133, 1976, 50-57.
PHILLIPS, E. J. 'A Workshop of Roman Sculptors at Carlisle', *Britannia*, 7, 1976, 101-109.
PHILLIPS, E. J. *Corpus Signorum Imperii Romani : Great Britain, I, fasc. I : Corbridge, Hadrian's Wall East of the North Tyne*, 1977.
PHILIPS-GREG, R. 'On the meaning and origin of the Fylfot and Swastika', *Archaeologia*, 48 (part 2), 1885, 292-326.
PIČ, J. L. *Čechy Předhist, II*, 1902-03.
PIČ, J. L. *Mohyla na Hurce u Němějic*, 1905.
PIČ, J. L. *Le Hradischt de Stradonitz en Bohème*, Leipzig, 1906.
PICARD, G. Ch. 'Informations Archéologiques : Centre', *Gallia*, 26, 1968, 321-345.
PICARD, G. Ch. 'Un Sacrifice au Jupiter-gaulois sur la mosaïque calendrier de St.-Romain-en-Gal', *Bulletin de la Société Nationale des Antiquaires de France*, 1974, 127-137.
PICARD, G. Ch. 'Imperator Caelestium', *Gallia*, 35, 1977, 89-113.
PICHON, R. *Les Sources de Lucain*, 1912.
PIETRI, Ch. 'Informations Archéologiques: Nord', *Gallia*, 31, 1973, 312-321.
PIETTE, J. 'Le Fanum de la Villeneuve-au Châtelot (Aube): État des recherches en

1979', *Mémoires de la Société Archéologique Champenoise*, 2, 1981, 367-375.
Piggott, S. 'The Early Bronze Age in Wessex', *Proceedings of the Prehistoric Society*, 4, 1938, 52-107.
Piggott, S. *Ancient Europe (From the beginnings of Agriculture to Classical Antiquity)*, 1965.
Piggott, S. 'The Earliest Wheeled Vehicles and the Caucasian Evidence', *Proceedings of the Prehistoric Society*, 34, 1968, 266-318.
Piggott, S. *The Druids*, 1968.
Piggott, S. *Victoria County History of Wiltshire*, I, ii, 1973, 361-363.
Piggott, S. 'Summing up the Colloquy', in Duval, P.-M. & Hawkes, C. F. C. (eds.), *Celtic Art in Ancient Europe*, 1976, 283-289.
Piggott, S. '«The Earliest Wagons and Carts»: Twenty-Five Years Later', *Institute of Archaeology of London Bulletin*, 16, 1979, 3-17.
Piron, D. 'Les Fibules Gallo-Romaines du Château-Musée des Blois', *Revue Archéologique du Centre*, 9, 1970, 111-122.
Piroutet, M. 'Contribution à l'étude sur la préhistoire en Franche-Comté', *L'Anthropologie*, 1900.
Piroutet, M. 'Coup d'œil sommaire sur la préhistoire en Franche-Comté', *L'Anthropologie*, 1903, 677-701.
Piroutet, M. 'Sur la coexistence de populations différentes en la Franche-Comté ...', *Congrès Préhistorique de France*, 1913.
Pittioni, R. *Urgeschichte des österreichischen Raume*, Vienne, 1954.
Pobé, M. & Roubier, J. *The Art of Roman Gaul*, London, 1961.
Polaschek, E. *Carinthia*, 132, 1942, 53ff.
Popovic, Lj. B. *Antiča Bronza y Jugoslaviji*, 1969.
Potter, T. W. *Romans in North-West England*, 1979.
Pottier, E. 'Les Statuettes de terre-cuite', *Revue Archéologique*, fasc. 1, 1881, pl. 6, fig. 83.
Poursat, J. Cl. 'Informations Archéologiques ... Auvergne', *Gallia*, 33, 1975, 423-438.
Powell, T. G. E. *The Celts*, 1958.
Powell, T. G. E. *Prehistoric Art*, 1966.
Prieur, J. *La province Romaine des Alpes Cottiennes*, 1968.
Prieur, J. *La Savoie Antique*, 1977.
Primas, M. 'Die Latènezeit im Alpinen Raum', *Archäologie der Schweiz : Band IV : Die Eisenzeit*, 1966-76.
Quagliati, Q. *Il Museo Nazionale di Tarento*, 1932.
Randall-MacIver, D. *Villanovans and Early Etruscans (A Study of the Early Iron Age in Italy as it is seen near Bologna, in Etruria and in Latium)*, 1924.
Randall-MacIver, D. *The Iron Age in Italy (A Study of the Early Civilizations which are neither Villanovan nor Etruscan)*, 1927.

REINACH, S. 'La Sculpture en Europe', *L'Anthropologie*, 1890.
REINACH, S. *Bronzes Figurés de la Gaule Romaine (Description Raisonnée Musée de St.-Germain-en-Laye)*, 1894.
REINACH, S. 'Sur les cornes de bovidés terminées par des boules', *L'Anthropologie*, 1896, 553.
REINACH, S. 'Teutates, Esus, Taranis', *Revue Celtique*, 18, 1897, 137-149.
REINACH, S. *Répertoire de la Statuaire Grecque et Romaine, I, II*, 1897.
REINACH, S. *Répertoire de la Statuaire, III*, 1897-1910.
REINACH, S. *Cultes, Mythes et Religions, I*, 1905, 218.
REINACH, S. 'Le Klapperstein, le gorgoneion et l'anguipède', *Bulletin du Musée Historique de Mulhouse*, 1913.
REINACH, S. *Catalogue Illustré du Musée des Antiquités Nationales au Château de Saint-Germain-en-Laye, I*, Paris, 1917.
REINACH, S. *Catalogue Illustré du Musée des Antiquités Nationales au Château de Saint-Germain-en-Laye*, Paris, 1921.
REBER, M. B. 'Quelques séries de gravures préhistoriques', *Compte-Rendu du XIVe Congrès International d'Anthropologie et d'Archéologie préhistoriques*, II, 1907, 63ff.
RICHLY, H. *Du Bronzezeit in Böhmen*, 1893.
RICHMOND, I. A. *Archaeology, and the Afterlife in Pagan and Christian Imagery*, 1950.
RICHMOND, I. A. 'The Roman Army and Roman Religion', *Bulletin of the John Rylands Library*, 45, 1962, N° 1, 185ff.
RICHMOND, I. A. 'Roman Essex', *Victoria County History of Essex*, III, 1963, 1ff.
RICHMOND, I. A. *et al.* 'The Roman Fort at Bewcastle', *Cumberland & Westmorland Society Transactions*, 38, 1938, 195-257.
RICHTHOFEN, B. V. *Die ältere Bronzezeit in Schlesien* (Vorgeschichtliche Forschungen, I), 1926.
RIDDER, A. de *Catalogue sommaire des bijoux antiques du Musée du Louvre*, 1924.
RIECKHOFF, S. 'Münzen und Fibeln aus dem Vicus des Kastells Hüfingen (Schwarzwald-Baar-Kreis)', *Saalburg Jahrbücher*, 1975, 32, 5-105.
RIHA, E. *Die römische Fibeln aus Augst und Kaiseraugst*, 1979.
RIHOVSKY, J. *Die Nadeln in Mähren und im Ostalpengebiet : Prähistorische Bronzefunde, Abteilung XIII, Band 5*, 1979.
RISTOW, G. *Religionen und ihre Denkmäler in Köln*, 1975.
ROACH SMITH, C. 'On some Roman Bronzes discovered in the Bed of the Thames in January 1837', *Archaeologia*, 28, 1839, 38-46.
ROBERT, C. *Revue des Sociétés Savantes*, 1878, 105.
ROBERTSON, A. S. Roman Finds from non-Roman Sites in Scotland', *Britannia*, 1, 1970, 198ff.

ROBERTSON, A., SCOTT, M. & KEPPIE, L. *Bar Hill : A Roman Fort and its Finds* (British Archaeological Reports, N° 16), 1975.
ROBERTSON, M. *History of Greek Art*, 1975.
RÖDER, J. 'Der Kriemhildenstuhl', *Hundert Jahre Historisches Museum der Pfalz, 1869-1969*, 1969, 110-135.
ROLLAND, H. 'Informations Archéologiques : Aix-en-Provence (Région Nord)', *Gallia*, 22, 1964, 545-572.
R.I.B. COLLINGWOOD, R. G. & WRIGHT, R. P., *The Roman Inscriptions of Britain, I : Inscriptions on Stone*, 1965.
ROMILLY-ALLEN, J. 'Two Kelto-Roman Finds in Wales', *Archaeologia Cambrensis* (ser. 6), 1, 1901, 20-44.
R.L.O. (*) *Volume 17*, 1917.
ROSE, H. J. *A Handbook of Greek Mythology* (2nd ed.), 1933.
ROSE, H. J. *Ancient Roman Religion*, 1948.
ROSS, A. 'The Horned God of the Brigantes', *Archaeologia Aeliana* (ser. 4), 39, 1961, 63ff.
ROSS, A. *Pagan Celtic Britain*, 1967.
ROSS, A. 'Shafts, Pits, Wells — Sanctuaries of the Belgic Britons ?', in COLES, J. M. & SIMPSON, D. D. A. (eds.), *Studies in Ancient Europe*, 1968, 255-286.
ROSSI, L. *Trajan's Column and the Dacian Wars*, 1971.
ROTTLÄNDER, R. C. A. 'Das X-Motiv. Ornament oder Merkmal', *Kölner Jahrbuch für vor- und frühgeschichlichte*, 12, 1971, 94-109.
ROTTLÄNDER, R. C. A. 'Zur Deutung der Sogennanten Mithrassymbole', *Archäologische Informationen Mittelungen zur ur- und frügeschichlichte*, 2-3, 1973-74, 143-152.
ROUBET, L. *et al.* 'Collections de Moules Antiques de Céramique', *Mémoires de la Société des Antiquaires du Centre*, 16, 1888-89.
ROUVIER-JEANLIN, M. *Les Figurines Gallo-Romaines en terre-cuite au Musée des Antiquités Nationales* (XXIVᵉ Supplément à *Gallia*), 1972.
ROYSTON PIKE, E. *Encyclopaedia of Religion and Religions*, 1951, 332.
SACKEN, E. Baron von. *Grabfeld von Hallstatt*, 1868.
ST. JOHN HOPE, W. H. & FOX, G. E. 'Excavations on the Site of the Roman City at Silchester, Hants in 1899', *Archaeologia*, 57, 1900, 87-112.
SALVIAT, F. 'Informations Archéologiques : Provence (Région Nord)', *Gallia*, 25, 1967, 373-396.
SALVIAT, F. 'Statues Féminines à Entremont', *Revue Archéologique de Narbonaise*, 9, 1976, 89-104.
SANDARS, N. K. *Bronze Age Cultures in France*, 1957.
SANDARS, N. K. *Prehistoric Art in Europe*, Harmondsworth, 1968.
SAULCY, H. DE. *Revue Numismatique*, II, 1837.

(*) *Der Römische Limes in Österreich.*

SAUTEL, J. 'Note sur deux autels inédits avec roue solaire trouvées à Vaison', *Bulletin Archéologique du Comité des travaux historiques et scientifiques*, 1923, 102ff.
SAUTEL, J. *Vaison dans l'antiquité*, 1926.
SAUTER, M. R. *Switzerland*, 1976.
SAVORY, H. N. 'An Early Iron Age Site at Long Wittenham, Berks', *Oxoniensia*, 2, 1937, 3.
SAVORY, H. N. *Guide-Catalogue of the Early Iron Age Collections* (National Museum of Wales), 1976.
SCHAEFFER, C. F. A. *Tertres funéraires préhistoriques dans la Forêt de Haguenau*, 1926.
SCHAUER, P. *Prähistorische Bronzefunde : Die Schweiter in Süddeutschland, Österreich und der Schweiz, I*, 1971.
SCHINDLER, R. *Landesmuseum Trier, Führer durch die Vorgeschichtliche und Römische Abteilung*, 1970.
SCHLIEMANN, H. *Mycenae : A Narrative of Researches and Discoveries at Mycenae and Tyrins*, 1878.
SCHLIERMACHER, W. 'Ein römischer votivring aus Walheim', *Germania*, 40, 1962, 336-341.
SCHOBER, A. *Die Römerzeit in Österreich*, 1935.
SCHÖNBERGER,H. 'The Roman Frontier in Germany : An Archaeological Survey', *Journal of Roman Studies*, 59, 1969, 147ff.
SCHOPPA, H. *Römische Götterdenkmäler in Köln : Die Denkmäler des Römisches Köln*, E. Fremersdorf (ed.), 1959, XXII.
SCHÜLTZER, O. 'Ein Dezennium römischer Forschung der Schweiz, 1914-1923', *Bericht Römisch-Germanisches Kommission*, 1924.
SCHWARZ, J. *Fouilles Franco-Suisses : Qasr-Qarum/Dionysias*, II, 1950, 61-70.
SCHWEIZERISCHES LANDESMUSEUM. *Kataloge*, 1969.
SIEBURG, M. 'Ein gnostisches Goldamulet aus Gellup', *Bonner Jarhbücher*, 103, 123-153.
SIVIERO, R. *Gli ori e le ambre del Museo Nazionale di Napoli*, 1954.
SMITH, R. A. 'Notes on Excavations on Early Sites near Leatherhead and Shamley Green', *Proceedings of the Society of Antiquaries* (ser. 2), 18, 1901, 255.
SMITH, R. A. *Proceedings of the Society of Antiquaries*, 20, 1903, 6-13.
SOUTOU, A. 'La Stèle de Substantion ...', *Ogam*, 14, 1962, 521.
SPEIDEL, M. *The Religion of Juppiter Dolichenus in the Roman Army*, 1978.
SPRÄTER, F. 'Der Brunholdistuhl bei Bad Dürkheim', *Mainz Zeitschrift*, 30, 1935, 32-39.
SPRÄTER, F. *Limburg und Kriemhildenstuhl*, 1948.
SPRÄTER, F. *Die Pfalz in der Vor- und Frühzeit*, 1948.
SPROCKHOFF, E. *Jungbronzezeitliche Hortfunde Nörddeutschlands* (Kataloge des Römisch-Germanisches Zentralmusuems, 12), 1937.

SPROCKHOFF, E. 'Die Spindlersfelder Fibel', *Marburger Studien*, 1938, 205-233.
SPROCKHOFF, E. 'Nordisches Bronzezeit und frühes Griechentum', *Jahrbuch des Römisch-Germanisches Zentralmuseums*, 1, 1954, 28-110.
SPROCKHOFF, E. 'Central European Urnfield Culture and Celtic La Tène: an outline', *Proceedings of the Prehistoric Society*, 21, 1955, 257-282.
STÄHELIN, F. *Die Schweiz in Römischer Zeit* (1st ed.), 1931.
STÄHELIN, F. *Die Schweiz in Römischer Zeit* (2nd ed.), 1948.
STEAD, I. M. *The La Tène Cultures of Eastern Yorkshire*, York, 1965.
STEAD, I. M. *The Arras Culture*, 1979.
STEBBINS, E. B. *The Dolphin in the Literature and Art of Greece and Rome*, 1929.
STRONG, D. E. *Greek and Roman Gold and Silver Plate*, 1966, pl. 51a.
STRONG, E. 'On the storied column of Mayence', *Revue Archéologique* (fasc. 2), 1913, 321-322.
SUSINI, G. *The Roman Stonecutter*, 1973.
SWOBODA, E. *Carnuntum: seine Geschichte und seine Denkmäler*, 1964.
TAYLOR, M. V. *et al.*, 'Roman Britain in 1929', *Journal of Roman Studies*, 19 (part 2), 1929.
TEROUANNE, P. 'Sur les traces de Mullo', *Revue Archéologique* (fasc. 2), 1965, 209ff.
THEVENOT, E. 'Les Monuments et le Culte de Jupiter à l'anguipède dans la cité des Eduens', *Mémoires de la Commission des Antiquités du Département de la Côte d'Or*, 21, 1936-39, 427-498.
THEVENOT, E. 'La Station Antique des Bolards à Nuits-Saint-Georges (Côte d'Or), *Gallia*, 6, 1948, 289-349.
THEVENOT, E. 'L'Epona de Saulons-la-Chapelle', *Revue Archéologique de l'Est*, 1, 1950, 22-25.
THEVENOT, E. 'Le Cheval Sacré dans la Gaule de l'Est', *Revue Archéologique de l'Est*, 2, 1951, 130ff.
THEVENOT, E. 'Maillets votifs en pierre', *Revue Archéologique de l'Est*, 3, 1952, 99-103.
THEVENOT, E. *Sur les traces des Mars Celtique*, 1955.
THEVENOT, E. *Divinités et Sanctuaires de la Gaule*, 1968.
THEVENOT, E. *Le Beaunois Gallo-Romain*, Collection Latomus, 113, 1971.
THOMAS, N. 'Excavations at Vicarage Field, Stanton Harcourt', *Oxoniensia*, 20, 1955, 21.
THOMAS, S. 'Zur Verbreitung und Zeitstellung der funfscheiben Emailfibeln', *Germania*, 41, 1963, 344-350.
THOMASSET, J. J. 'Sur deux stèles du dieu Sucellus', *La Physiophile*, 45, 1956, 7-9.
THOMPSON, J. *Making Model Horse-Drawn Vehicles*, 1976.
TIHELKA, K. *Acta Musei Moraviae Scientiae Sociales*, 1952, 37.
TIHELKA, K. 'Význaný hrob velatické kultury na Čezaváh u Blučiny', *Památky Archeologické Ročník*, 52, 1961, 205-208.

TOMASEVIC, T. 'Goldfunde aus Augst 1967-1969', *Römerhaus und Museum Augst*, 1968, 6-8.
TORBRÜGGE, W. *Beilgnries vor- und frügeschichte einer Fundlandschaft*, 1964.
TORBRÜGGE, W. Vor- un Frügeschichtliche Flussfunde. Zur Ordnung und Bestimmung einer Denkmälergruppe', *Berichte Römisch-Germanischen Kommission*, 51-52, 1972, 1-146.
TORBRÜGGE, W. & UENZE, H. P. *Bilder zur Vorgeschichte Bayerns*, 1968.
TOUR, H. DE LA. *Atlas de Monnaies Gauloises*, 1892.
TOUSSAINT, M. *La Lorraine à l'époque Gallo-Romaine*, 1928.
TOUSSAINT, M. *Metz à l'époque Gallo-Romaine*, 1948.
TOUTAIN, J. *Les Cultes Païens dans l'empire romain*, I, 1907.
TOUTAIN, J. 'Les Symboles Astraux sur les Monuments Funéraires de l'Afrique du Nord', *Revue des Études Anciennes*, 13, 1911, 165-175.
TOUTAIN, J. 'Les clefs votives dans le culte païen ...', *Pro Alesia*, 3, 1916, 25-39.
TOUTAIN, J. *Les Cultes Païens dans l'empire romain*, III, 1920.
TOUTAIN, J. 'Chronique des Fouilles', *Pro Alesia*, 1923-25, 124-158.
TOUTAIN, J. *Sur quelques Monuments Gallo-Romains de la Côte d-Or* (Bulletin de la Société Nationale des Antiquaires de France : extrait 24), 1925.
TOUTAIN, J. 'Un document archéologique de la Bretagne romaine', *Bulletin Archéologique du Comité des travaux historiques et scientifiques*, 1943-45, 31-34.
TOYNBEE, J. M. C. *Art in Roman Britain*, 1962.
TOYNBEE, J. M. C. *Art in Britain under the Romans*, 1964.
TOYNBEE, J. M. C. *Death and Burial in the Roman World*, 1971.
TOYNBEE, J. M. C. *Animals in Roman Life and Art*, 1973.
TOYNBEE, J. M. C. 'A Note on the Sculptured Torso of a Bird', in BIDWELL, P. T., *The Legionary Bath-House and Basilica and Forum at Exeter* (Exeter Archaeological Reports, 1), 1979, 131-133, pl. XX, fig. 44.
TOYNBEE, J. M. C. & O'NEIL, H. E. 'Sculptures from a Romano-British Well in Gloucestershire', *Journal of Roman Studies*, 48, 1958, 49-55.
TRONQUART, G. 'Le «Camp Celtique» de la Bure (Vosges)', *Gallia*, 34, 1976, 201-215.
TRUMP, D. *Central and Southern Italy*, 1966.
TUDOR, D. *Corpus Monumentorum Religionis Equitum Danuviorum* (CMRED), 1976.
TURNER, E. G. 'A Curse Tablet from Nottinghamshire', *Journal of Roman Studies*, 53, 1963, 122ff.
TYLECOTE, R. F. *Metallurgy in Archaeology*, 1962.
UCKO, P. J. & ROSENFELD, A. *Palaeolithic Cave Art*, 1967.
UHLHORN, A. 'Monnaies trouvées à Sarre-Union et ses environs', *Cahiers d'Archéologie et d'Histoire d'Alsace*, 5, 1927-30, 143-145.
ULBERT, E. *Das Frührömische Kastell Rheingönheim*, 1969.

UNDSET, I. *Zeitschrift für Ethnologie* ..., 1891.
Unione Accademica Nazionale. *Inscriptiones Italiae*, 1935.
USENER, H. (ed.) *M. Annaei Lucani Commentaria Bernensia*, 1869, 30ff.
VALDAN, E. Compte-rendu des fouilles faites à Aizanville 1918-1919', *Annales de la Société d'Histoire et d'Archéologie de Chaumont*, 1921.
VALLENTIN, F. 'Les Dieux de la Cité des Allobroges', *Revue Celtique*, 4, 1879-80, 1-36.
VAN DER WAALS, J. D. 'Neolithic Disc Wheels in the Netherlands. With a Note on the Early Iron Age Disc-Wheels from Ezinge', *Palaeohistoria*, 10, 1964, 103-146.
VAN ES, W. A. *De Romeinen in Nederland*, 1972.
VANVINKENROYE, W. *Tongeren Romeinse Stad*, 1975.
VAUTHEY, M. & P. 'Le Cerf de Terre-Franche (Statuette en terre blanche de l'Allier)', *Revue Archéologique du Centre*, 4, 1965, 255-273.
VERTET, H. 'Cucullatus et autres figurations de l'officine de Thiel-sur-Acolin (Allier)', *Revue Archéologique de l'Est et du Centre-Est*, 11, 1960, 303-314.
VESLY, L. DE. *Les Fana ou petits temples gallo-romains de la région Normande*, 1909.
VIAN, F. *Répertoire des Gigantomachies dans l'art grec et romain*, 1951.
VILLEFOSSE, H. de 'Note sur un Bronze découvert à Landouzy-la-Ville (Aisne)', *Revue Archéologique*, 41 (fasc. 1), 1881, 1-13.
VILLEFOSSE, H. de. *Le Trésor de Boscoreale*, 1899.
VOUGA, A. *La Tène*. Leipzig, 1923.
VRIES, J. de. *La Religion des Celtes*, 1963.
WACHER, *Roman Britain*, 1978.
WACHER, *The Coming of Rome*, 1979.
WAGNER, K. H. *Nordtiroler Urnenfelder*, 1943.
WALKE, N. *Das Römische Donaukastell Straubing-Sorviodurum, Limesforschungen*, 1965, 3.
WALTERS, H. B. *Catalogue of Greek and Roman Bronzes in the British Museum*, 1899.
WARDE-FOWLER, W. *The Religious Experience of the Roman People*, 1922.
WAYWELL, S. E. 'Roman Mosaics in Greece', *American Journal of Archaeology*, 83, n° 3, 1979, 293-309.
WEBSTER, G. 'The Bronze Handle of a Romano-British Butteris', *Antiquaries Journal*, 48, 1968, 303.
WEBSTER, G. *The Roman Imperial Army*, 1969.
WESTALL, W. P. 'The Romano-British Cemetery at the Grange, Welwyn, Herts.', *St. Albans & Hertfordshire Architectural and Archaeological Transactions*, 1930, 37ff.
WHEELER, R. E. M. *Report on the Excavations in Lydney Park*, 1932.
WHEELER, R. E. M. *Maiden Castle, Dorset*, 1943, 75-76.

WHITE, K. D. *Agricultural Implements of the Roman World*, 1967.
WHITE, K. D. *Farm Equipment of the Roman World*, 1975.
WIGHTMAN, E. M. *Roman Trier and the Treveri*, 1970.
WILKES, J. J. *Dalmatia*, 1969.
WILL, E. *Le Relief cultuel gréco-romain : Contribution à l'histoire de l'art de l'empire romain*, 1955.
WILSON, R. D. *et al.* 'Roman Britain in 1970', *Britannia*, 2, 1971, 273.
WINKELMANN, F. *Kataloge West- und Süddeutscher Altertumssamlungen*, 1926.
WOELCKE, K. 'Beiträge zur Geschichte des Tropaions', *Bonner Jahrbücher*, 120 (fasc. 1 & 2), 1911, 183.
WOODFIELD, C. C. 'Six Turrets on Hadrian's Wall', *Archaeologia Aeliana* (ser. 4), 43, 1965, 87-201.
WOOLLEY, C. L. *Ur Excavations, II*, 1934.
WOSINSKY, M. *Das prähistorische Schanzwerk von Lengyel, II*, 1888-91.
WOYTOWITSCH, E. *Die Wagen der Bronze und Frühen Eisenzeit in Italien : Prähistorische Bronzefunde, Abteilung XVII, Band I*, 1978.
WRIGHT, R. P. & RICHMOND, I. A. *Roman Inscribed and Sculptured Stones in Carlisle Museum*, 1975.
WRIGHT, R. P. & RICHMOND, I. A. *The Roman Inscribed and Sculptured Stones in the Grosvenor Museum, Chester*, 1955.
WYSS, R. *Bronzezeitliche Gusstechnik*, 1967.
ZWICKER, J. *Fontes Historiae Religionis Celticae*, 1934-36.

CATALOGUE OF ILLUSTRATIONS*

FRONTISPIECE. – Bronze wheel-god ; Le Châtelet (C2). Musée des Antiquités Nationales, St.-Germain-en-Laye.

PLATE I
FIG. 1. – Equestrian wheel-God ; Obernburg (B102).

PLATE II
FIG. 2. – Fragmentary horseman ; Quémigny (B114).
FIG. 3. – Stele with ? wheel-God ; Auberive (B6)

PLATE III
FIG. 4. – Altar with wheel and ram-horned snake , Lypiatt Park (BB13).

PLATE IV
FIG. 5. – Altar with wheel, god and eagle ; Laudun (B67).
FIG. 6. – Altar to Jupiter ; Lansargues (B66).

PLATE V
FIG. 7. – Altar to Jupiter and Augustus ; Marsillargues (B76).
FIG. 8. – Altar fragment with wheels and swastikas ; Pyrenees (B110).
FIG. 9. – Altar ; Tarbes area (B147).

PLATE VI
FIG. 10. – Altar with swastika ; Begnères (B13).
FIG. 11. – Altar with circles and palm ; Pyrenees (B105).
FIG. 12. – Altar with swastika and palm ; Pyrenees (B111).
FIG. 13. – Altar with swastika and palm ; Pyrenees (B108).

PLATE VII
FIG. 14. – Relief of god with swastika ; Bremevaque (B17).
FIGS. 15, 16. – Altar-fragment ; Vernègues(B163).

PLATE VIII
FIG. 17. – Altar with wheel ; Nîmes (B95).
FIG. 18. – Altar to Jupiter with wheel ; Collias (B27).

PLATE IX
FIG. 19. – Altar-fragment with wheel ; Montmirat (B83).
FIG. 20. – Altar with wheel and thunderbolt ; Nîmes (B100).
FIG. 21. – Altar with wheel ; Gilly (B53).

PLATE X
FIG. 22. – Statue of wheel-God ; Séguret (B144).

PLATE XI
FIG. 23. – Equestrian wheel-God ; Meaux (B77).
FIG. 24. – Equestrian wheel-God ; Luxeuil (B72).

* Numbers in brackets refer to catalogues A-D.

PLATE XII
FIG. 25, 26. – Altar with wheels ; Jublains (B62).

PLATE XIII
FIG. 27. – Tombstones with wheels and circles ; Saverne area (B142).
FIG. 28. – Stele with wheel/branches ; Bois-de-la-Neuve-Grange (B15).
FIG. 29. – Tombstone with wheel and hammers ; St. Quirin (B43).

PLATE XIV
FIG. 30. – Funerary stele with wheels and inscription ; Saverne (B138).
FIG. 31. – Funerary stele with circles and crescent ; Walscheid (B44).
FIG. 32. – Tombstone with wheels and incription ; Saverne (B141).

PLATE XV
FIG. 33. – Tombstone with wheels ; Saverne (B139).
FIG. 34. – Multiple gravestone ; Saverne (B140).
FIG. 35. – House-shaped tombstone with wheels ; Wasserwald (B167).

PLATE XVI
FIG. 36. – Fragment of equestrian wheel-God statue ; Malmaison (B75).
FIG. 37. – Altar with wheel, Mainz (B73).

PLATE XVII
FIG. 38. – 'Viergötterstein', Dunzweiler (B35).
FIG. 39. – 'Viergötterstein', Trier (B149).
FIG. 40. – 'Viergötterstein', Niederwürzbach (B90).

PLATE XVIII
FIG. 41. – Stele with wheel, 'barillet' and peacock ; Dôle area (B33).
FIG. 42. – Altar with dedication to Jupiter and wheel ; Cologne (B29).

PLATE XIX
Sites producing wheel-models and brooches in Romano-Celtic Europe.

PLATE XX
Sites producing swastika-brooches in Romano-Celtic Europe.

PLATE XXI
Detailed map of Franch sites producing wheel- and swastika-models.

PLATE XXII
Detailed map of non-French sites in Europe producing models.

PLATE XXIII
Sites in England and Wales producing wheel- and swastika-models

PLATE XXIV
Sites producing wheel-decorated stone monuments in Romano-Celtic Europe.

PLATE XXV
Sites producing swastika-decorated stone monuments in Romano-Celtic Europe.

PLATE XXVI
Detailed map of French sites producing wheel- and swastika-monuments.

PLATE XXVII
Detailed map of non-French sites in Europe producing wheel-decorated stone monuments.

PLATE XXVIII
Sites in England and Wales producing wheel- and swastika-decorated stone monuments.

CATALOGUE OF ILLUSTRATIONS 405

PLATE XXIX
Sites producing miscellaneous wheel-representations in Romano-Celtic Europe.
PLATE XXX
Detailed map of miscellaneous wheel-representations in France.
PLATE XXXI
Detailed map of miscellaneous wheel-representations in Romano-Celtic Europe excluding France.
PLATE XXXII
Sites in England and Wales producing miscellaneous wheel-representations.
PLATE XXXIII
Distribution of 'Taranis' (or derivative) inscriptions in Europe.
PLATE XXXIV
Distribution of all types of wheel-representation in England and Wales.
PLATE XXXV-XLIX
Illustrations of wheel-types (see Chapter IX).
PLATE L
Fig. 1. – Late Bronze Age wheel-pendant ; Réallons (Hautes-Alpes), France. Musée des Antiquités Nationales, St.-Germain-en-Laye.
Fig. 2. – Sandstone mould for Late Bronze Age wheel-pendant or model ; Auvernier, Switzerland. Schweizerisches Landesmuseum, Zürich.
PLATE LI
Fig. 3. – Hallstatt wheel-pendant ; Most na Soci, Czechoslovakia Naturhistorisches Museum, Vienna.
Fig. 4, 5. – Iron Age bronze wheel-model ; probably France. Liège, Museum Curtius.
PLATE LII
Fig. 6. – Wheel-models ; Seine, Paris, Oise (A68, 67). Musée des Antiquités Nationales, St.-Germain-en-Laye.
Fig. 7. – Wheel-models ; Southern France (A69). Musée des Antiquités Nationales, St.-Germain-en-Laye.
PLATE LIII
Fig. 8. – Wheel-model ; unprovenanced (A62). Musée des Antiquités Nationales, St.-Germain-en-Laye.
Fig. 9. – Wheel-brooch with central dolphin ; Bavay (A59). Museum Curtius, Liège.
PLATE LIV
Fig. 10. – Wheel-brooches ; Trier (A46, A48, A44). Trier Landesmuseum ; copyright Trier Landesmuseum.
PLATE LV
Fig. 11. – Wheel-brooches ; Gusenburg (A50). Trier Landesmuseum ; copyright Trier Landesmuseum.
PLATE LVI
Fig. 12. – Wheel-brooch ; Elouges (A56). Musées Royaux, Brussels.
Fig. 13. – Wheel-brooch ; Hautepin (A55). Musées Royaux, Brussels.
PLATE LVII
Fig. 14. – Bronze wheel-model mould on tile-fragment ; Augst (A126). Augst Römermuseum.
Fig. 15. – Bronze wheel-model ; Nîmes (A208). Musée Archéologique Nîmes.

PLATE LVIII
Fig. 16. – Bronze wheel-model with votive inscription ; Augst (A140). Augst Römermuseum.
Fig. 17. – Wheel-brooches ; Augst (A146). Augst Römermuseum.
PLATE LIX
Fig. 18, 19. – Wheel-model ; Bern, Engehalbinsel-Tiefenau (A136). Bern Historisches Musem.
PLATE LX
Fig. 20. – Bronze swastika-brooch ; Cologne (A6). Römisch-Germanisches Museum, Cologne.
Fig. 21. – Bronze wheel-brooch ; Icklingham (AB28). Ashmolean Museum, Oxford.
PLATE LXI
Fig. 22. – Wheel-model fragment and eagle-wing ; Icklingham (AB8). Ashmolean Museum, Oxford.
Fig. 23. – Wheel-brooch fragment ; Housesteads (AB7). Housesteads Museum.
PLATE LXII
Fig. 24. – Part of ritual deposit ; Felmingham Hall (AB5). British Museum ; copyright British Museum.
PLATE LXIII
Fig. 25. – Bronze wheel-model and boar-figurines ; Hounslow (AB6). British Museum ; copyright British Museum.
Fig. 26. – Wheel-brooch ; Corbridge (AB3). Corstopitum Museum, Corbridge.
PLATE LXIV
Fig. 27. – Bronze axe-model with ligatured 'X' on blade ; Woodeaton (AX20). Ashmolean Museum, Oxford.
Fig. 28. – Bronze axe-model with 'binding-marks' on blade ; Gestingthorpe (AX21). Department of Environment.
PLATE LXV
Fig. 29. – Stone sculpture of equestrian wheel-god ; Butterstadt (B19). Musée des Antiquités Nationales, St.-Germain-en-Laye.
Fig. 30. – Stone sculpture of enthroned Jupiter with wheel on side of throne ; Alzey (B4). Alzey Musem.
PLATE LXVI
Fig. 31, 32. – Statue of wheel-god ; Séguret (B144). Musée Lapidaire, Avignon.
PLATE LXVII
Fig. 33. – Séguret wheel-god (B144).
Fig. 34. – Fragment of wheel-god on horseback ; Fallberg(B39). Musée Archéologique, Saverne.
PLATE LXVIII
Fig. 35. – Stone altar with wheel and thunderbolt ; Vauvert (B20). Musée Archéologique, Nîmes.
Fig. 36. – Altar with wheel ; Gilly (B53). Musée Archéologique, Nîmes.
PLATE LXIX
Fig. 37. – Altar with wheel ; Vaison area (Mislabelled) (B154). Musée Lapidaire, Avignon.
Fig. 38. – Altar to Jupiter and Augustus, bearing wheel ; Marsillargues (B76). Musée Lapidaire de Montpellier.

PLATE LXX
Fig. 39. – Altar to Jupiter ; Collias (B27). Musée Archéologique, Nîmes.
Fig. 40. – Altar with wheel and thunderbolt ; Nîmes (B100). Musée Archéologique, Nîmes.

PLATE LXXI
Fig. 41. – Small altar bearing wheel and inscription 'Severus' ; Castelnau-Valence (B21). Musée Archéologique, Nîmes.
Fig. 42. – Altar to Jupiter and Silvanus, bearing wheels and other items ; Aigues-Mortes (B2). Musée Archéologique, Nîmes.

PLATE LXXII
Fig. 43, 44 – Altar to Jupiter and Silvanus ; Aigues-Mortes (B2).
Fig. 45. – Funerary stone with wheel and hammers ; St. Quirin (B43). Musée Archéologique, Saverne.

PLATE LXXIII
Fig. 46. – Funerary stone with inscription and wheels ; Saverne area (B138). Musée Archéologique, Saverne.
Fig. 47. – Funerary stone with inscription and wheels ; Saverne area (B141). Musée Archéologique, Saverne.

PLATE LXXIV
Fig. 48, 49. – House-stelai decorated with wheels ; Saverne area (B139). Musée Archéologique, Saverne.

PLATE LXXV
Fig. 50. – Altar to Jupiter, with wheel on one side ; Castlesteads (BB5). Carlisle Museum ; copyright Carlisle Museum.
Fig. 51. – Stone relief of *Genius* bearing wheel over altar ; Netherby (BB17). Carlisle Museum ; copyright Carlisle Museum.

PLATE LXXVI
Fig. 52, 53. – Stone relief of ? Mars with wheel-marks at sides of slab. Chedworth (BB7). Chedworth Museum.

PLATE LXXVII
Fig. 54. – Clay antefixes ; Caerleon (C11). National Museum of Wales, Cardiff.

PLATE LXXVIII
Fig. 55. – Wheel applied to grey ware potsherd ; Housesteads (C60). Housesteads Museum.
Fig. 56. – Wheels applied to grey ware potsherd ; Malton (C59). Malton Roman Museum.

PLATE LXXIX
Fig. 57. – Rear view of bronze wheel-god ; Le Châtelet (C2) (see also frontispiece). Musée des Antiquités Nationales, St.-Germain-en-Laye.
Fig. 58. – Impression from clay mould of wheel-god, for decoration of pottery vessel ; Corbridge(C10). Corstopitum Museum, Corbridge ; copyright Museum.

PLATE LXXX
Fig. 59, 60. – Bronze wheel-god ; Landouzy-la-Ville (C3). Musée des Antiquités Nationales, St.-Germain-en-Laye.

PLATE LXXXI
Fig. 61-63. – Bronze 'mace-terminal' depicting wheel-god ; Willingham Fen (C6). Cambridge University Museum of Archaeology and Anthropology ; copyright Museum.

PLATE LXXXII
Fig. 64. – Bronze sceptre-binding ; Farley Heath (C7). British Museum ; copyright British Museum.

PLATE LXXXIII
Fig. 65. – Pipe-clay figurine of wheel-god ; Néris (C9a). Musée des Antiquités Nationales, St.-Germain-en-Laye.
Fig. 66. – Bronze Sucellus with 'cosmic' symbols ; Cologne. Römisch-Germanisches Museum, Cologne ; copyright Museum.

PLATE LXXXIV
Fig. 67. – Stone altar to Taranucnus ; Böckingen (D1). Stuttgart Museum ; copyright Stuttgart Museum.

PLATE LXXXV
Fig. 68. – Corinthian capital from ? Jupiter-column ; Cirencester. Corinium Museum ; copyright Corinium Museum.

PLATE I

FIG. 1. – Equestrian Wheel-God (B102), Obernburg. Height 66 cm.

PLATE II

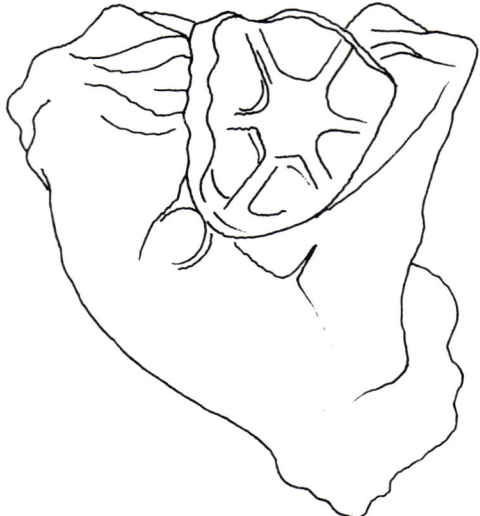

Fig. 2. – Fragmentary horseman (B114), Quémigny. Height 50 cm.

Fig. 3. – Stele with (?) Wheel-God (B6), Auberive.

PLATE III

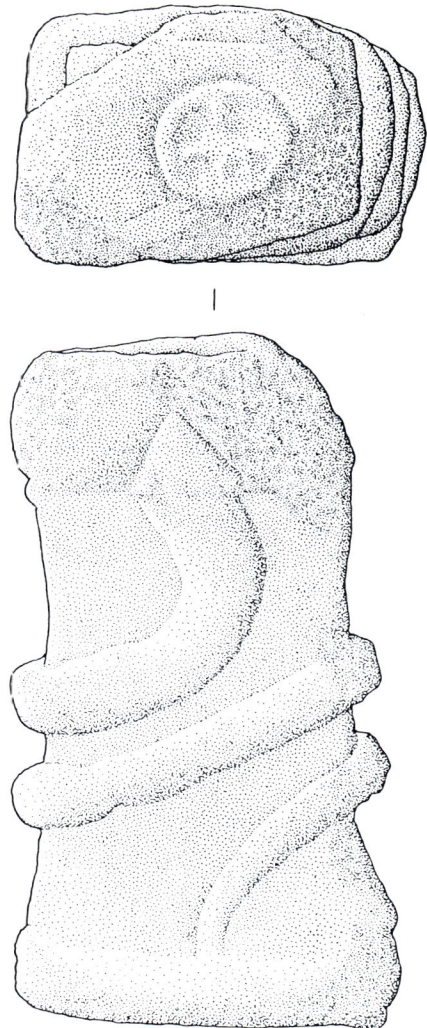

Fig. 4. — Altar with wheel and ram-horned snake (BB13), Lypiatt. Height 15 cm.

PLATE IV

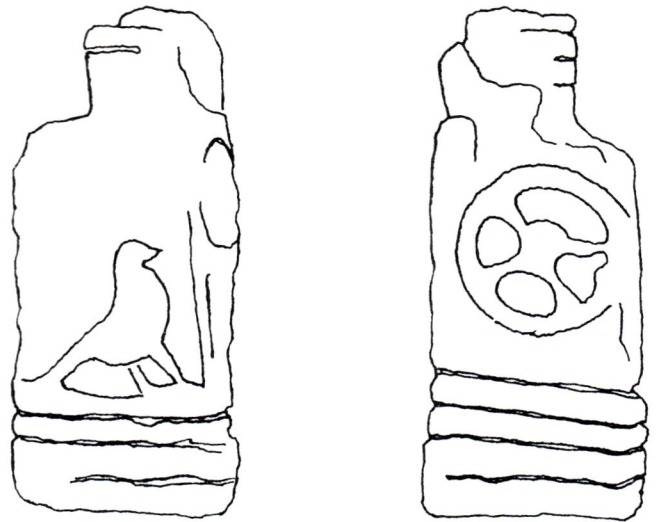

Fig. 5. – Altar with wheel, god and eagle (B67), Laudun. Height 21 cm.

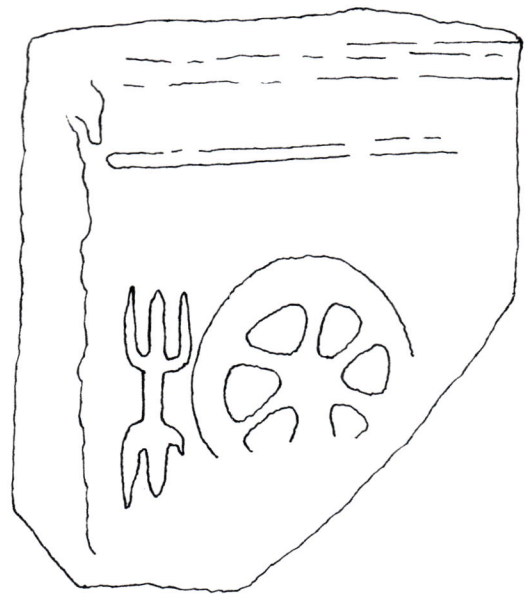

Fig. 6. – Altar to Jupiter (B66), Lansargues. Height 76 cm.

PLATE V

FIG. 7. – Altar to Jupiter and Augustus (B76), Marsillargues. Height 62 cm.

FIG. 8. – Altar fragment (B110), Pyrenees. Height 13 cm.

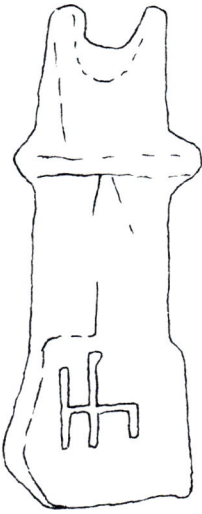

FIG. 9. – Altar (B147), Tarbes area. Height 27 cm.

PLATE VI

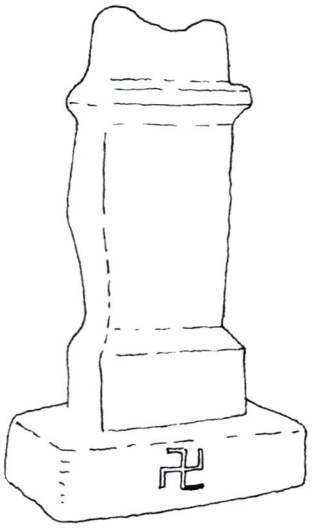

Fig. 10. – Altar (B13), Begnères. Height 29 cm.

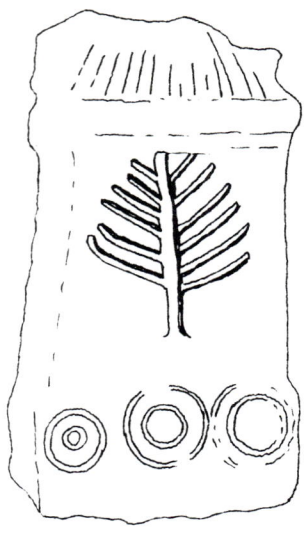

Fig. 11. – Altar (B105), Pyrenees. Height 23 cm.

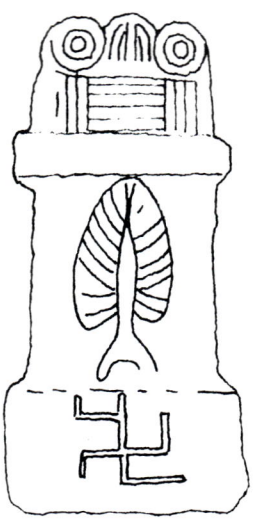

Fig. 12. – Altar (B111), Pyrenees. Height 25 cm.

Fig. 13. – Altar (B108), Pyrenees. Height c. 20 cm.

PLATE VII

FIG. 14. – Relief of god (B17), Bremevaque. Height 48 cm.

FIGS. 15, 16. – Altar-fragment (B163), Vernègues. Height 52 cm.

PLATE VIII

Fig. 17. – Altar (B95), Nimes area. Height 12 cm.

Fig. 18. – Altar to Jupiter (B27), Collias. Height 1 m 53 cm.

PLATE IX

Fig. 19. – Altar-fragment (B83), Montmirat. Height 19 cm.

Fig. 20. – Altar (B100), Nîmes. Height 80 cm.

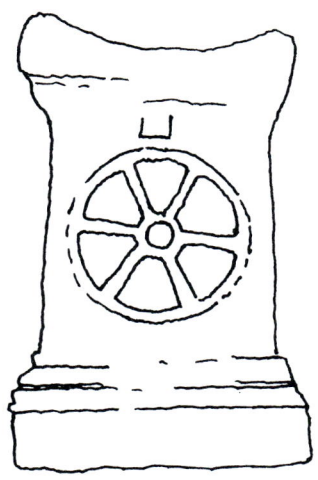

Fig. 21. – Altar (B53), Gilly. Height 26 cm.

PLATE X

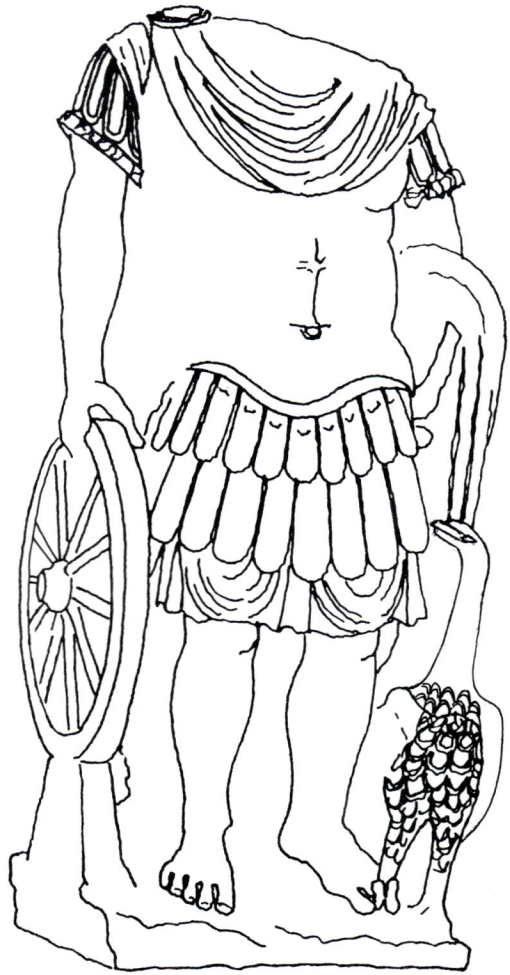

Fig. 22. – Statue of Wheel-God (B144), Séguret. Height 2 m 05 cm.

PLATE XI

Fig. 23. – Equestrian Wheel-God (B77), Meaux. Height 50 cm.

Fig. 24. – Equestrian Wheel-God (B72), Luxeuil. Height 1 m 65 cm.

PLATE XII

FIG. 25. – Altar (B62), Jublains. Height 90 cm.

FIG. 26. – Altar (B62), Jublains (alternative reconstruction).

PLATE XIII

FIG. 27. – Tombstones (B142), Saverne area. Heights between 50 cm-1 m 50 cm.

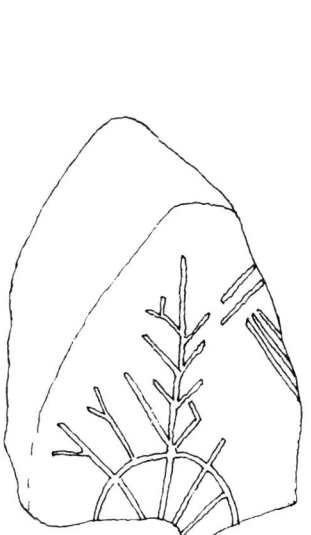

FIG. 28. – Stele (B15), Bois de la Neuve-Grange. Height 31 cm.

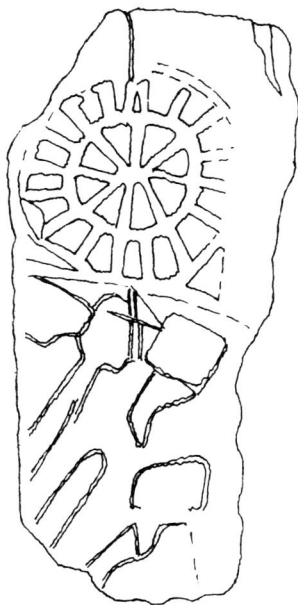

FIG. 29. – Tombstone (B43), St. Quirin. Height 48 cm.

PLATE XIV

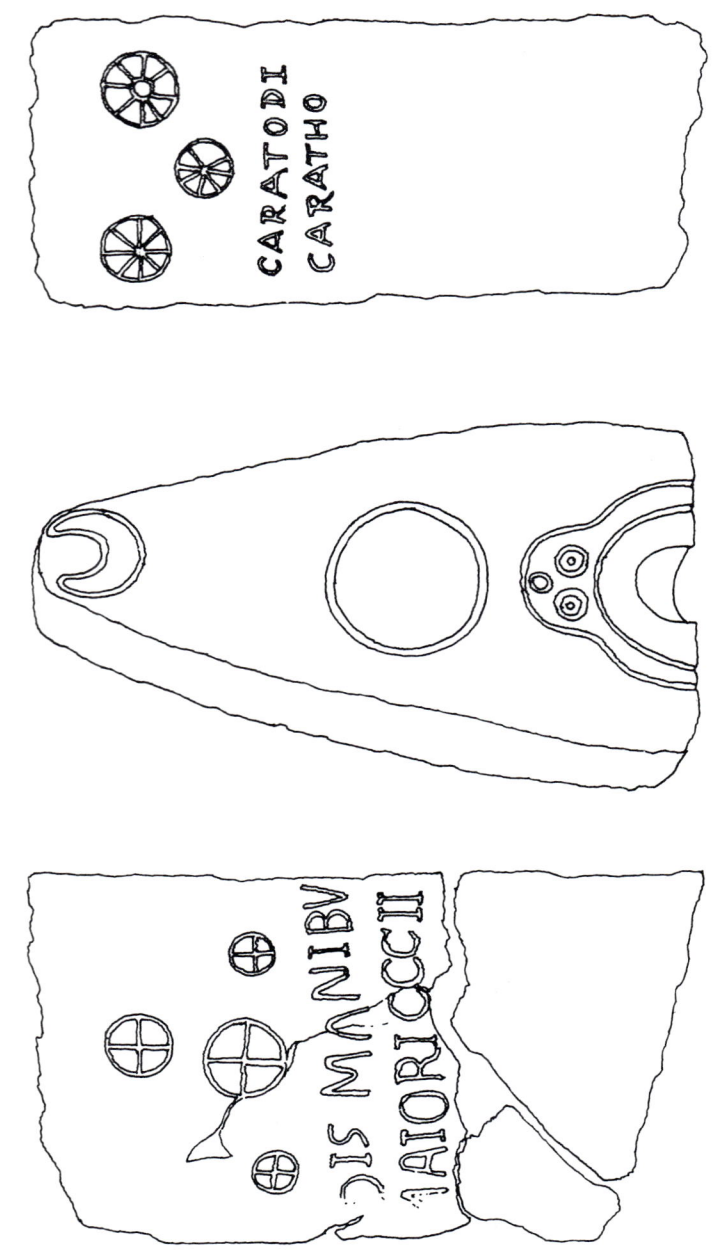

Fig. 32. – Tombstone (B141), Saverne. Height 1 m 24 cm.

Fig. 31. – House-shaped stele (B44), Walscheid. Height 92 cm.

Fig. 30. – Funerary stele (B138), Saverne area. Height 1 m 20 cm.

PLATE XV

Fig. 33. – Tombstone (B139), Saverne area. Height 83 cm.

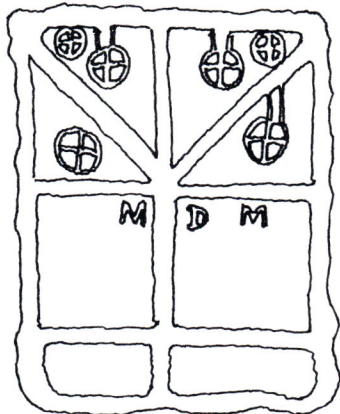

Fig. 34. – Multiple gravestone (B140), Saverne. Height 1 m 40 cm.

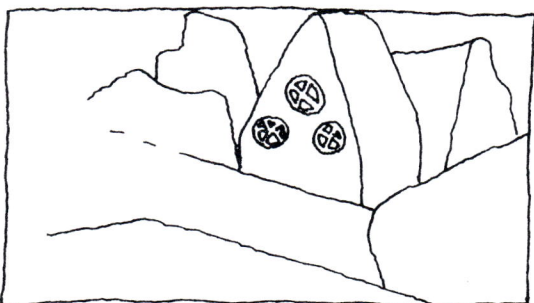

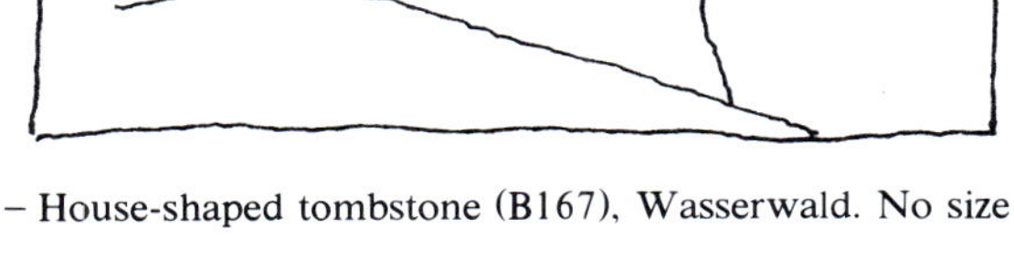

Fig. 35. – House-shaped tombstone (B167), Wasserwald. No size available.

PLATE XVI

FIG. 36. – Fragment of equestrian Wheel-God statue (B75), Malmaison. Diameter of wheel 14 cm.

FIG. 37. – Altar (B73), Mainz. Height 27 cm.

PLATE XVII

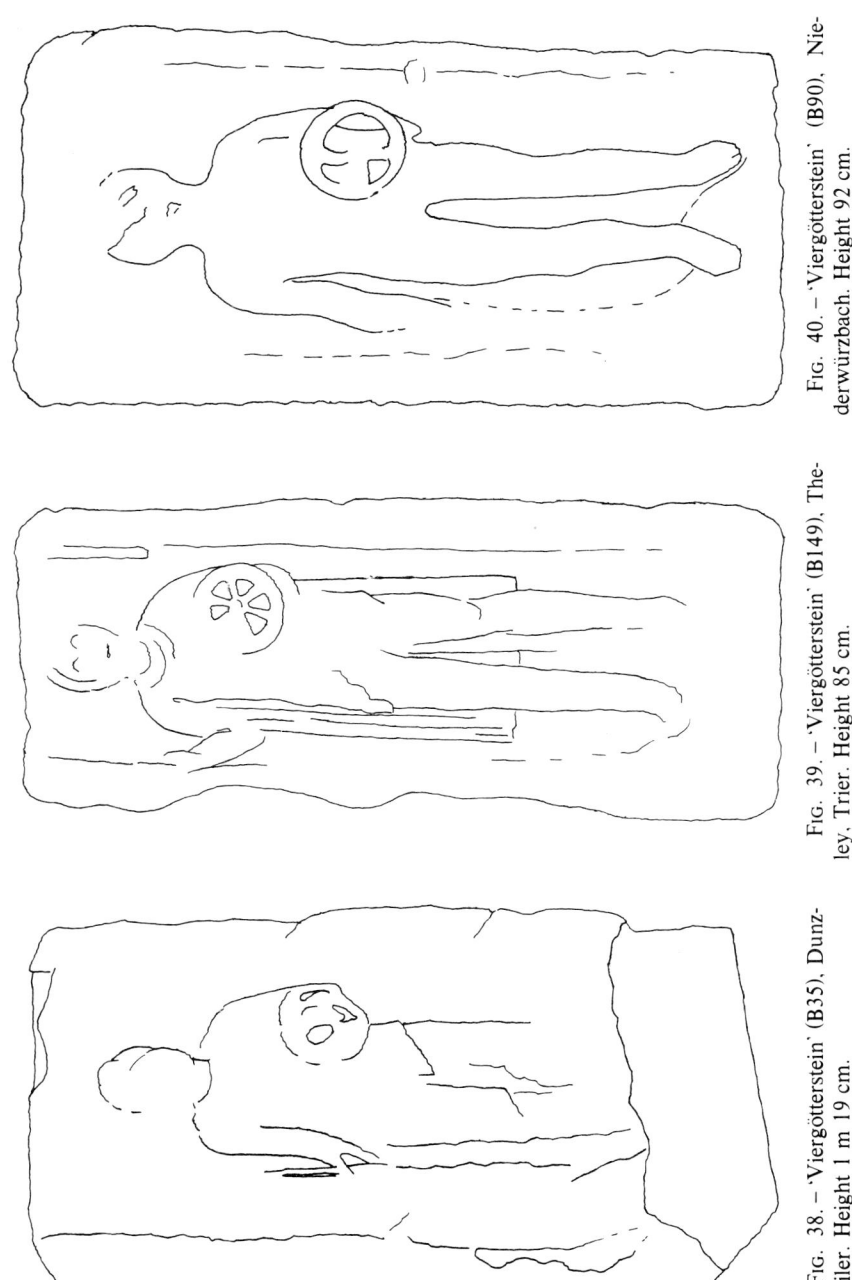

FIG. 38. – 'Viergötterstein' (B35). Dunzweiler. Height 1 m 19 cm.

FIG. 39. – 'Viergötterstein' (B149). Theley, Trier. Height 85 cm.

FIG. 40. – 'Viergötterstein' (B90). Niederwürzbach. Height 92 cm.

PLATE XVIII

Fig. 42. – Altar (B29), Cologne. Height 86 cm.

Fig. 41. – Stele (B33), Dôle area. Height 82 cm.

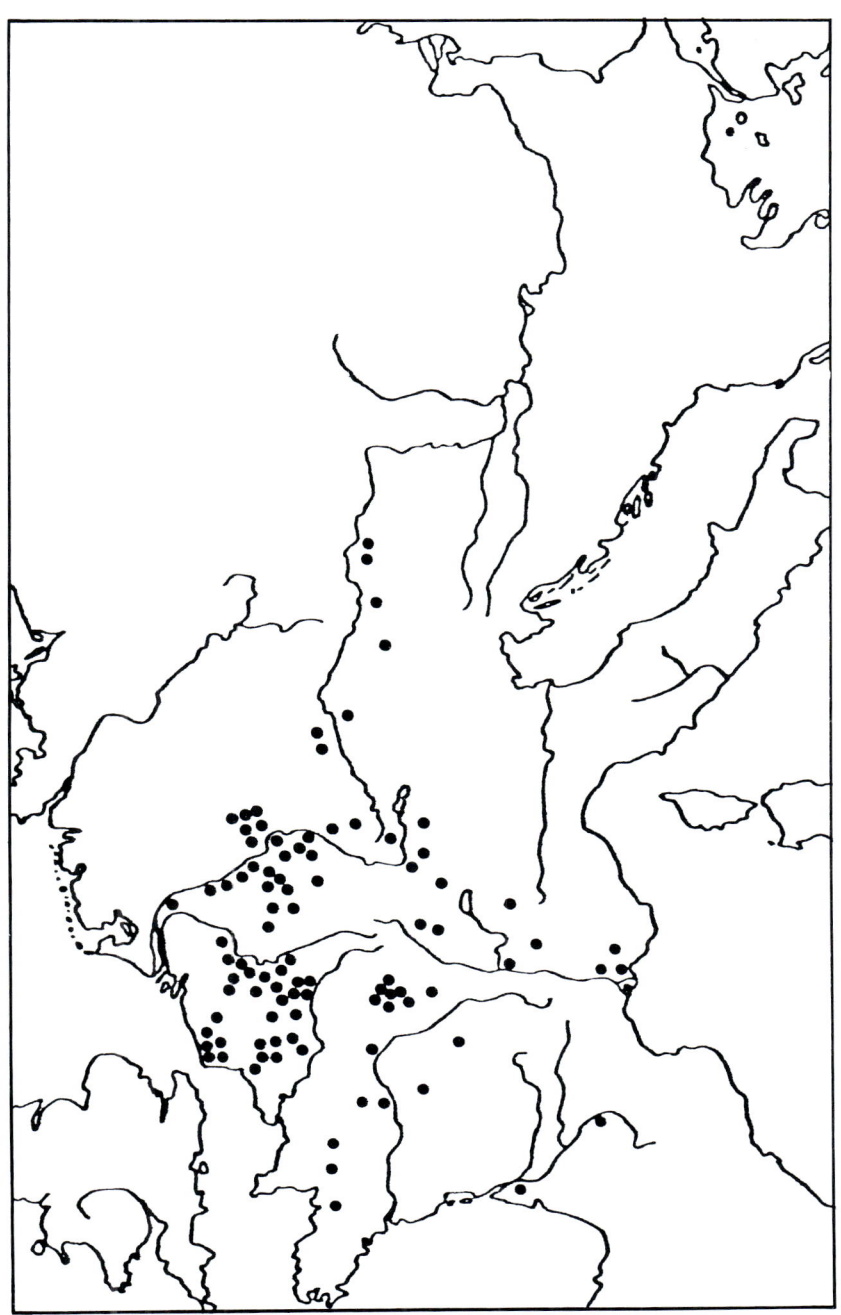

Sites producing wheel-models and brooches in Romano-Celtic Continental Europe.

PLATE XIX

PLATE XX

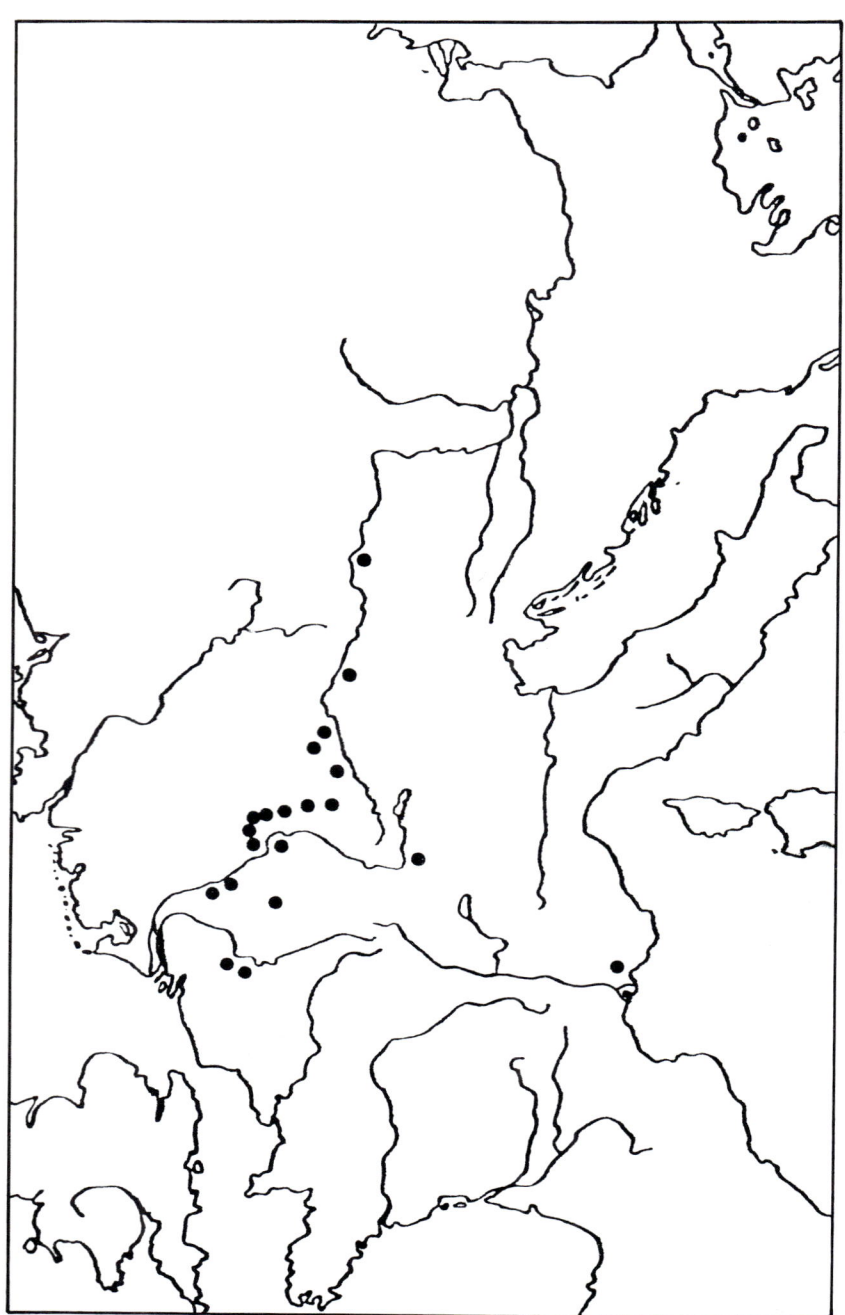

Sites producing swastika-brooches in Romano-Celtic Continental Europe.

PLATE XXI

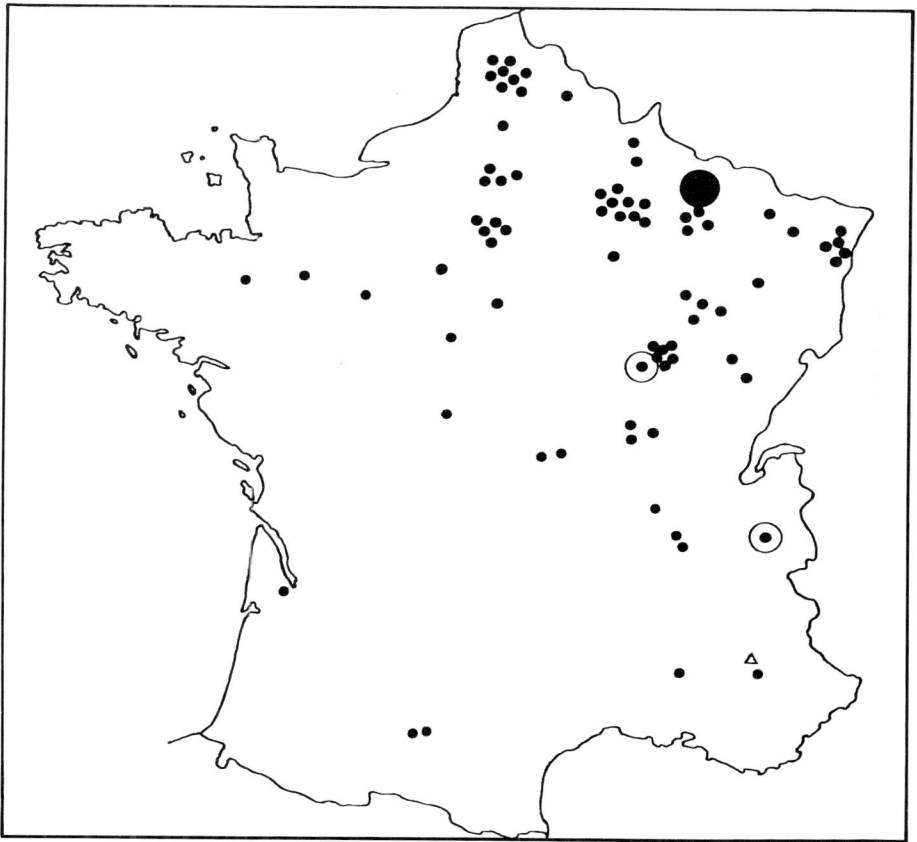

Detailed map of French sites producing wheel- and swastika-models.
- wheels
- ⊙ wheels + 10
- ● wheels + 100
- △ swastikas

PLATE XXII

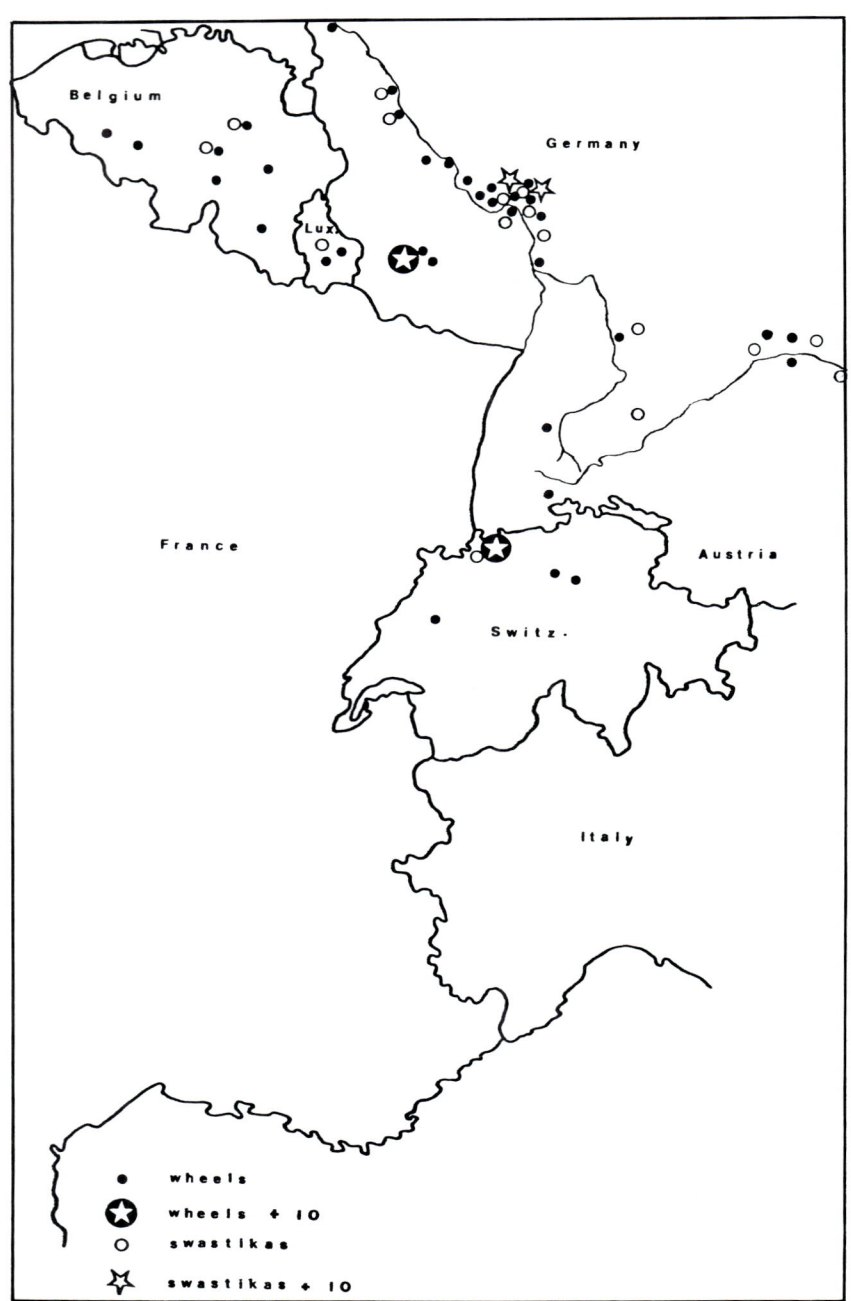

Detailed map of non-French sites in Europe producing models.

PLATE XXIII

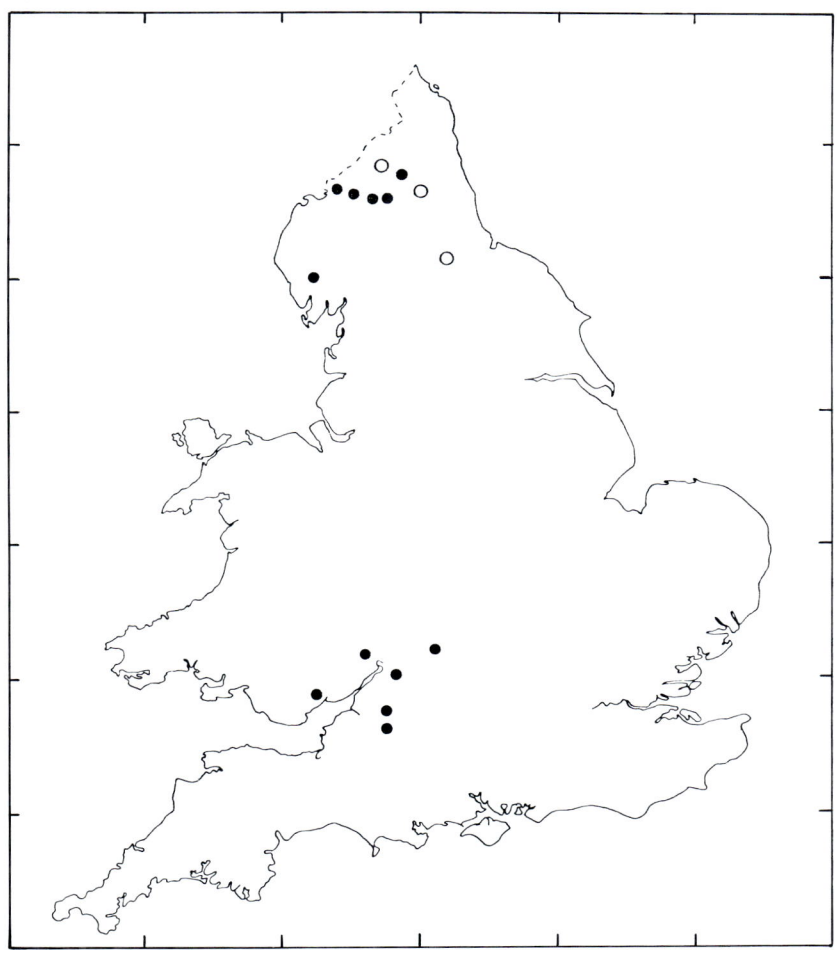

Sites producing wheel- and swastika-models in England and Wales.
- wheels
○ swastikas

PLATE XXIV

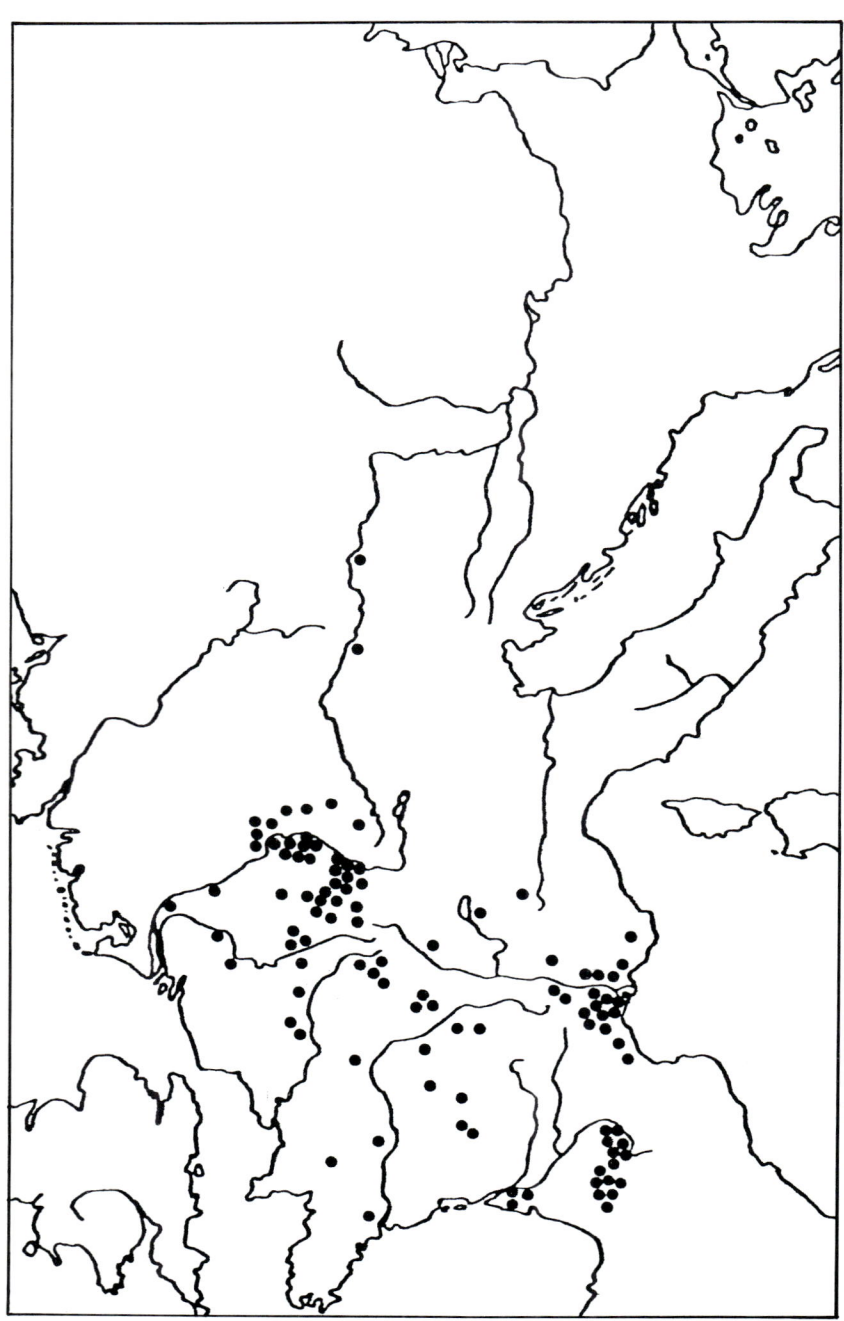

Sites producing wheel-decorated stone monuments in Romano-Celtic Europe.

PLATE XXV

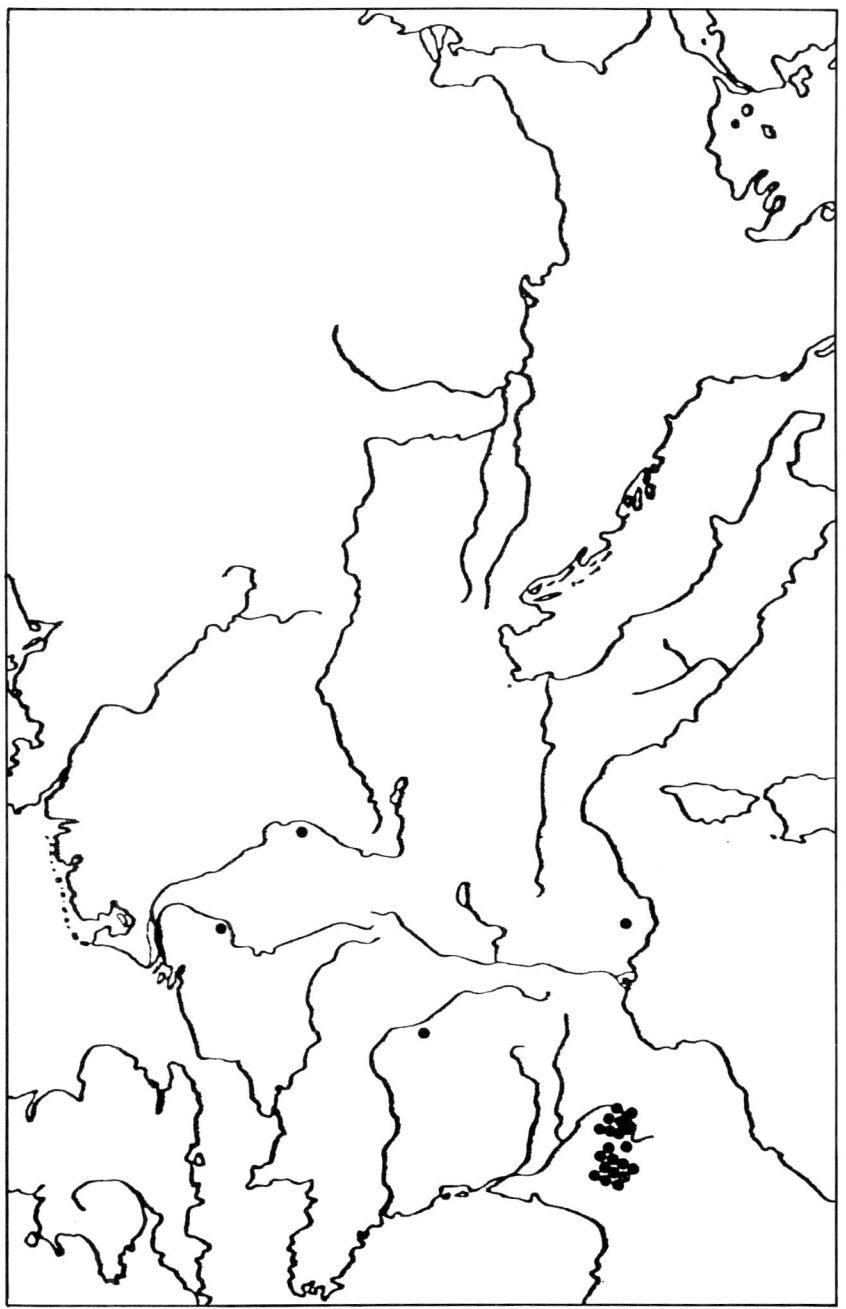

Sites producing swastika-decorated stone monuments in Romano-Celtic Europe.

PLATE XXVI

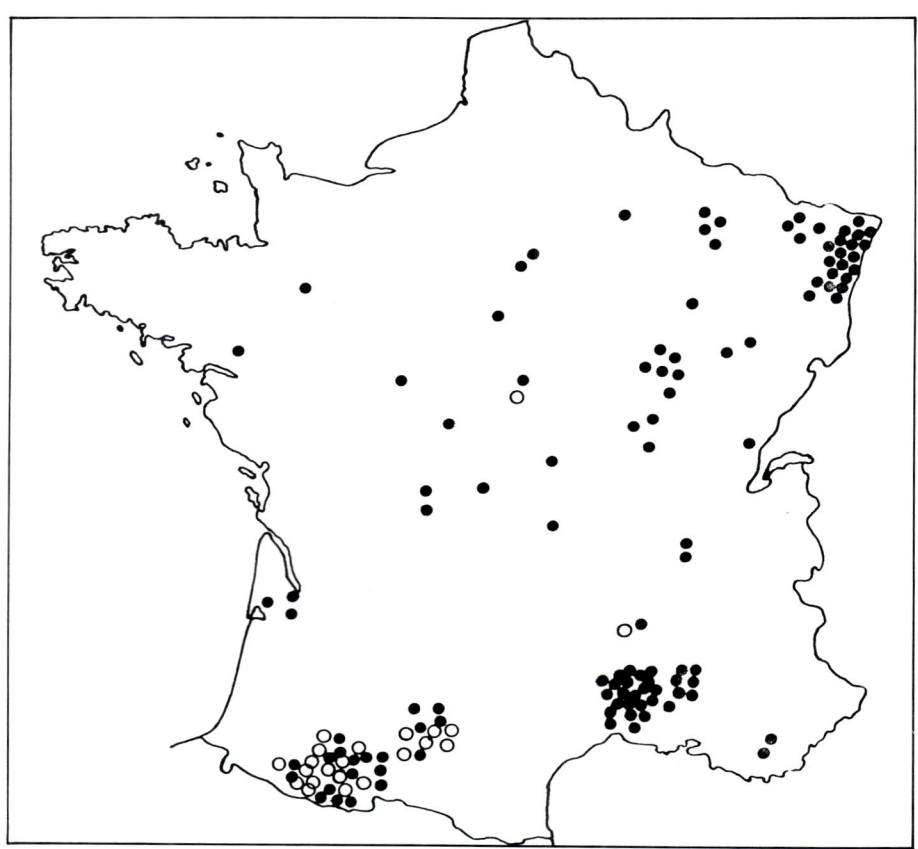

Detailed map of French sites producing wheel- and swastika-monuments.
● wheels
○ swastikas

PLATE XXVII

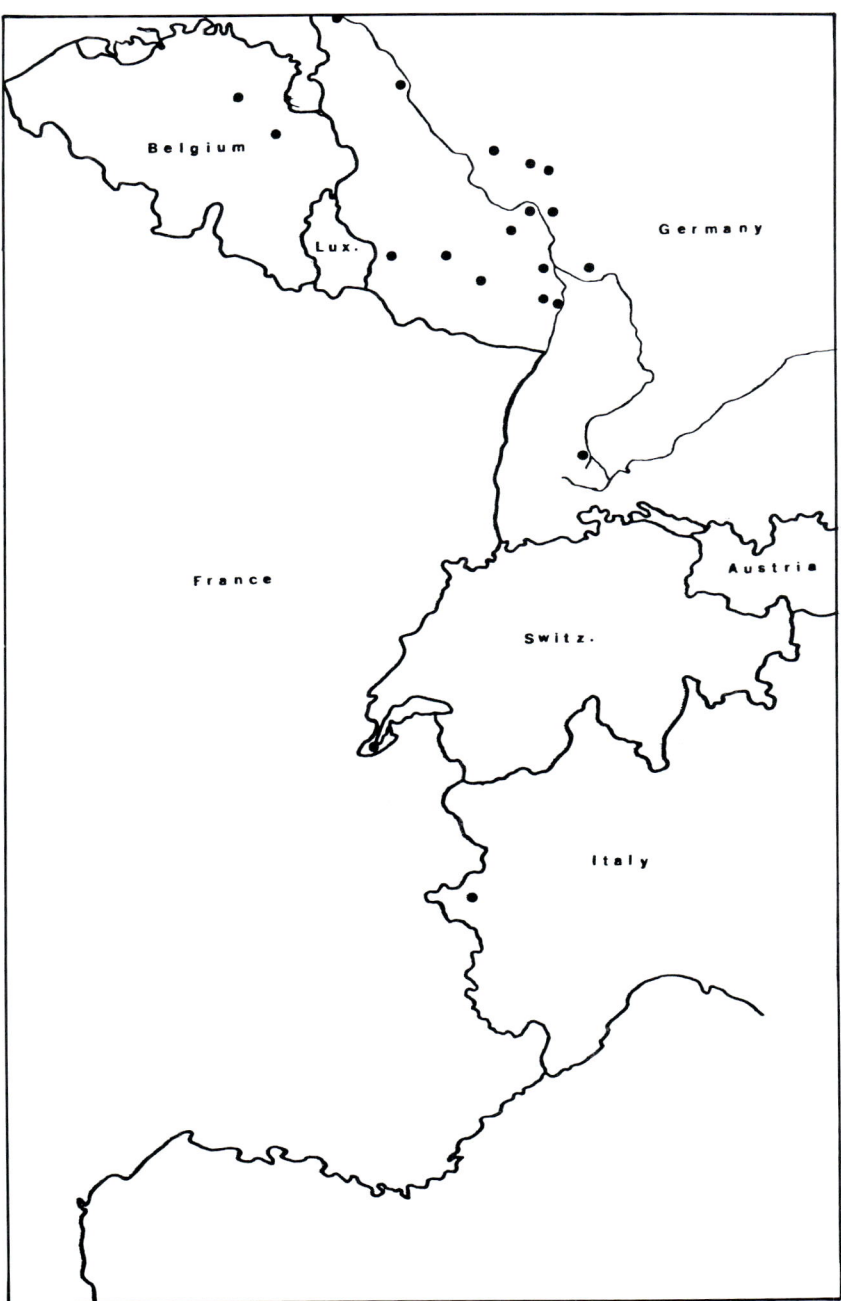

Detailed map of non-French sites in Europe producing wheel-decorated stone monuments.

PLATE XXVIII

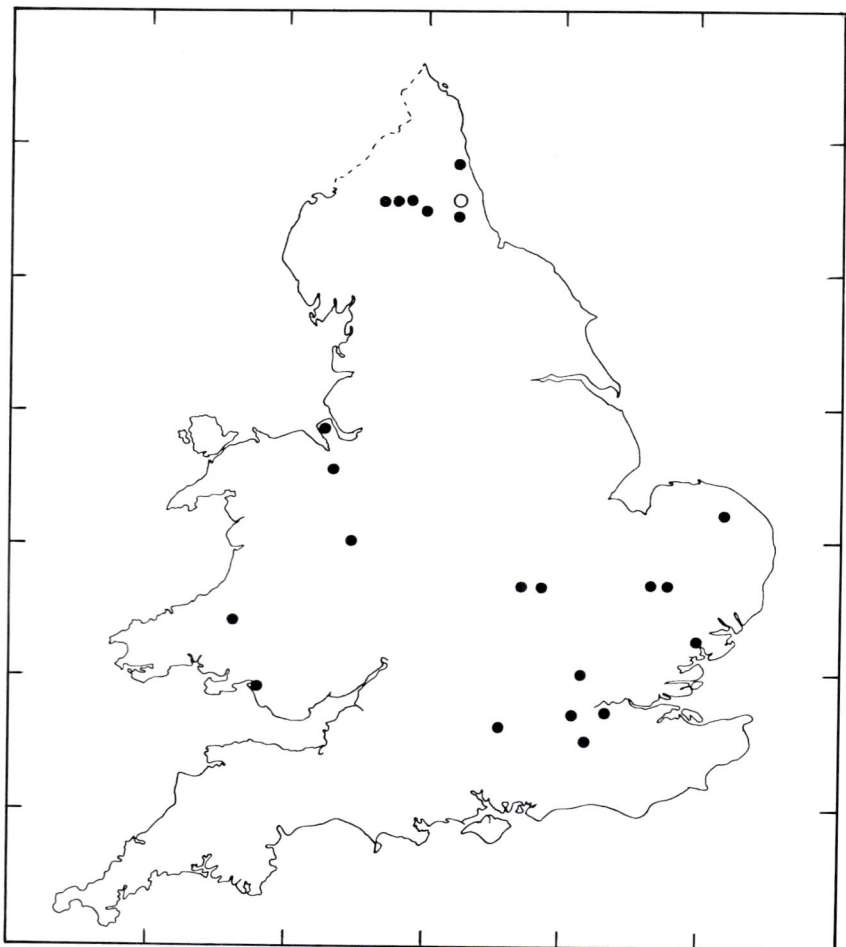

Sites producing wheel- and swastika-decorated stone monuments in England and Wales.
● wheels
○ swastikas

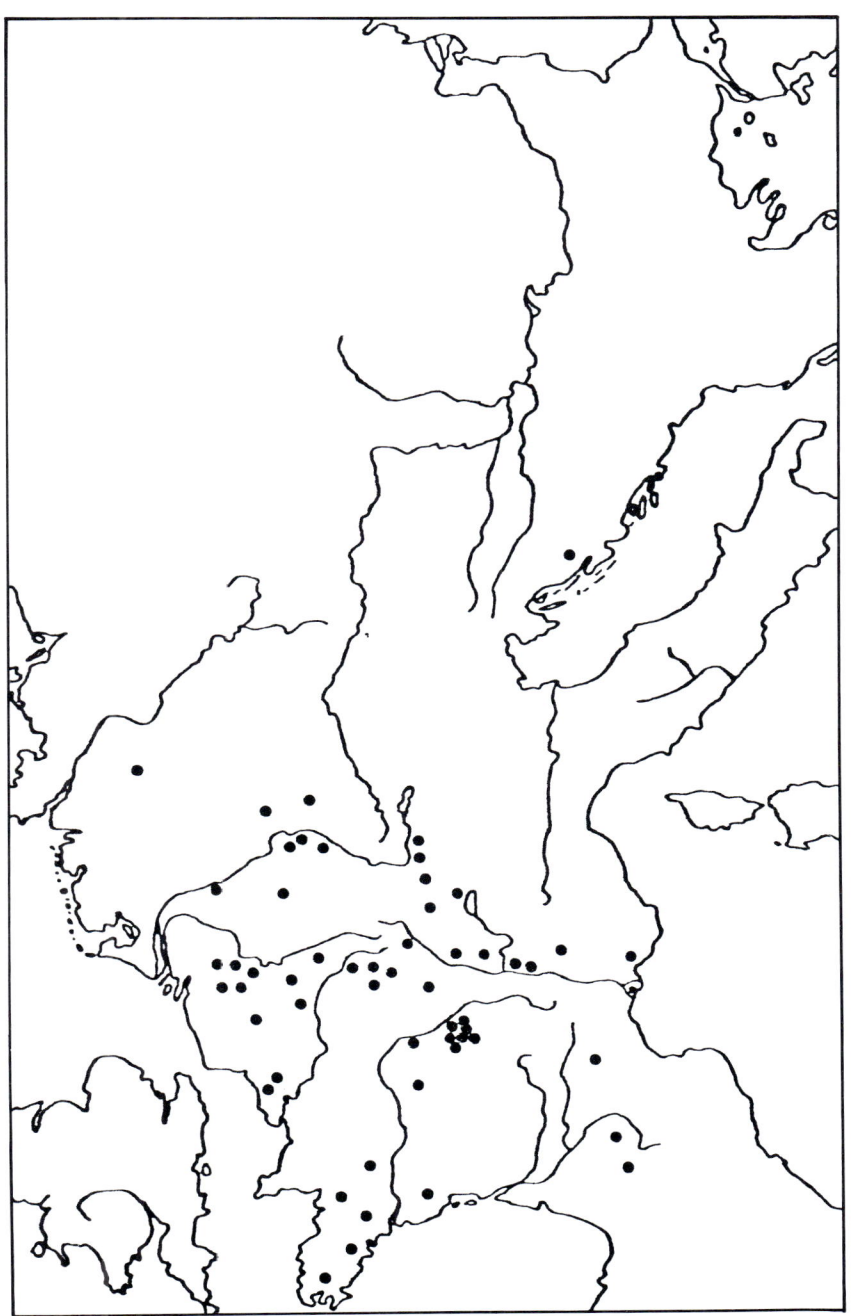

PLATE XXIX

Sites producing miscellaneous wheel-representations in Romano-Celtic Europe.

PLATE XXX

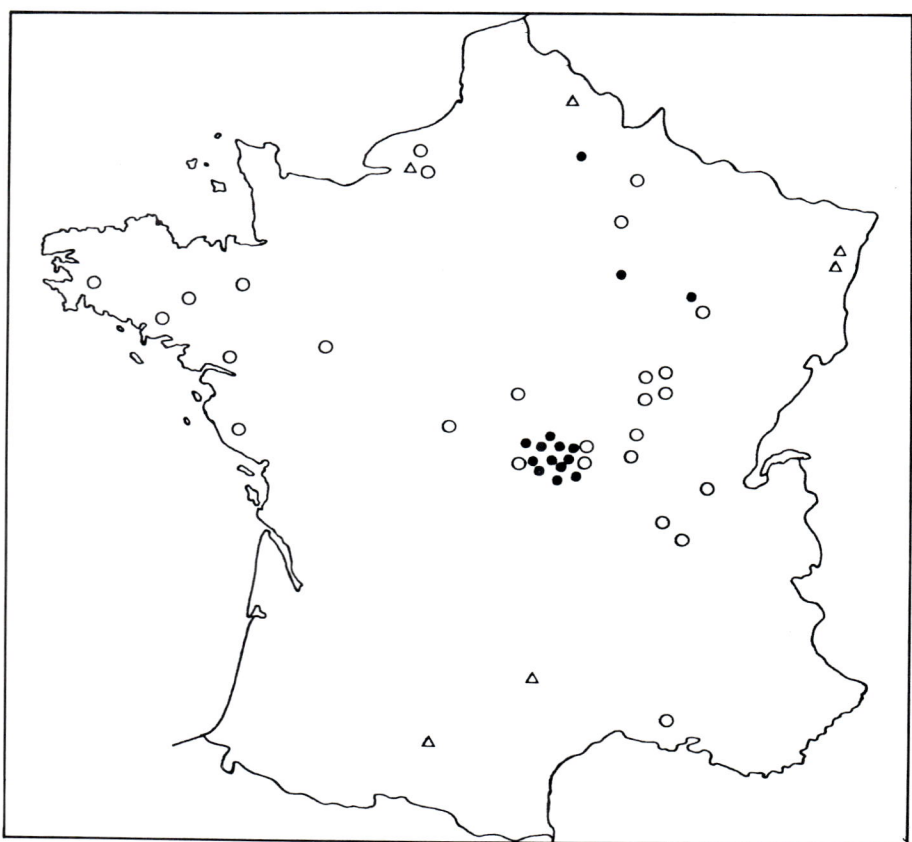

Detailed map of miscellaneous wheel-representations in France.
● Wheel-God
○ wheel accompanying other deities
△ miscellaneous symbolism

PLATE XXXI

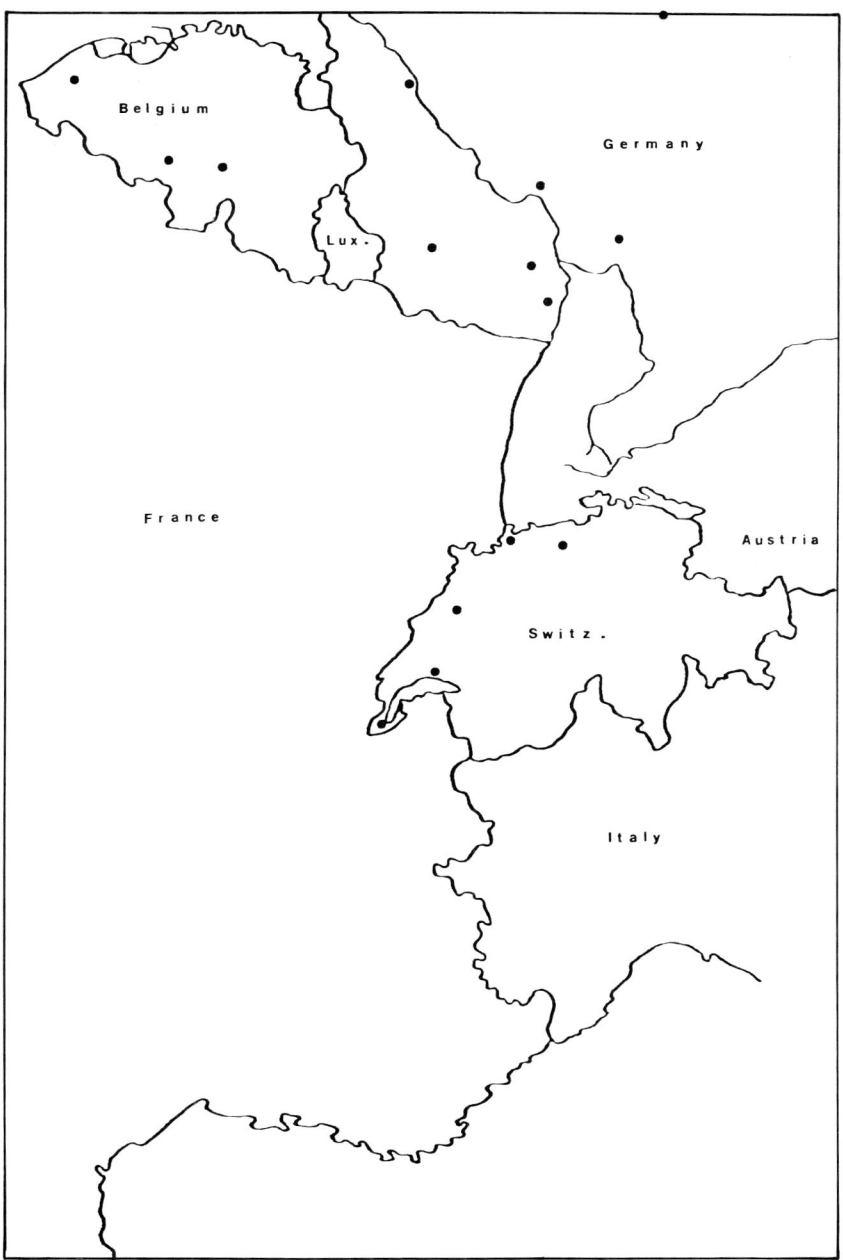

Detailed map of miscellaneous wheel-representations in Romano-Celtic Europe excluding France.

PLATE XXXII

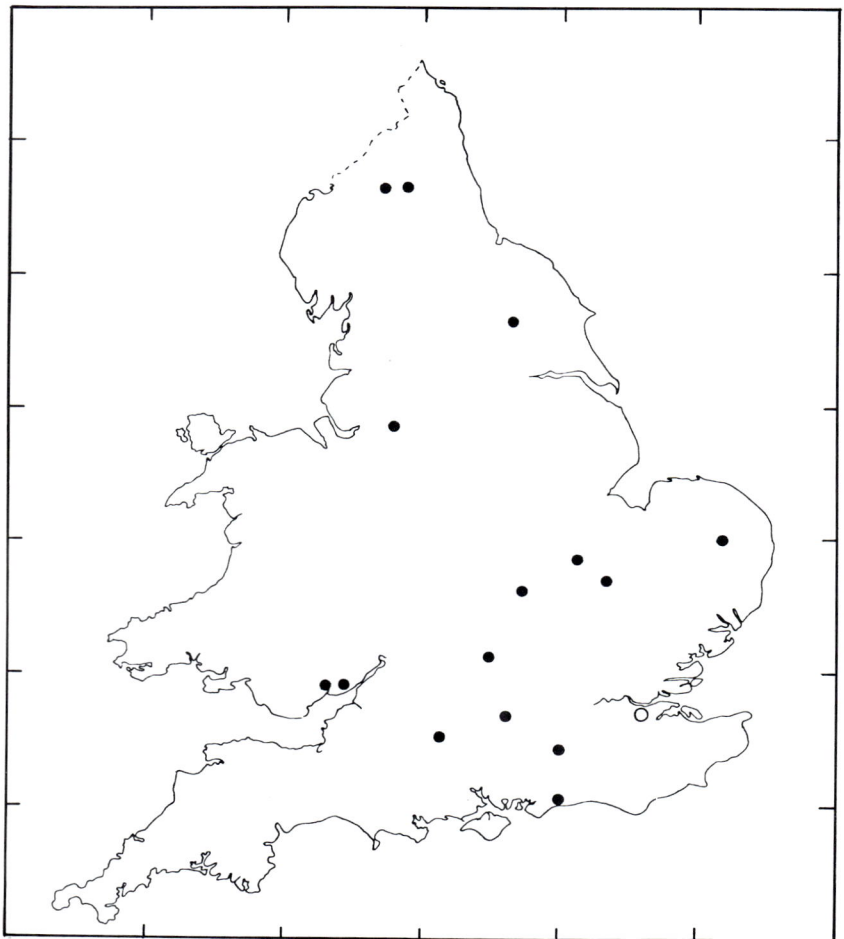

Sites producing miscellaneous wheel-representations in England and Wales.
● wheels
○ swastikas

PLATE XXXIII

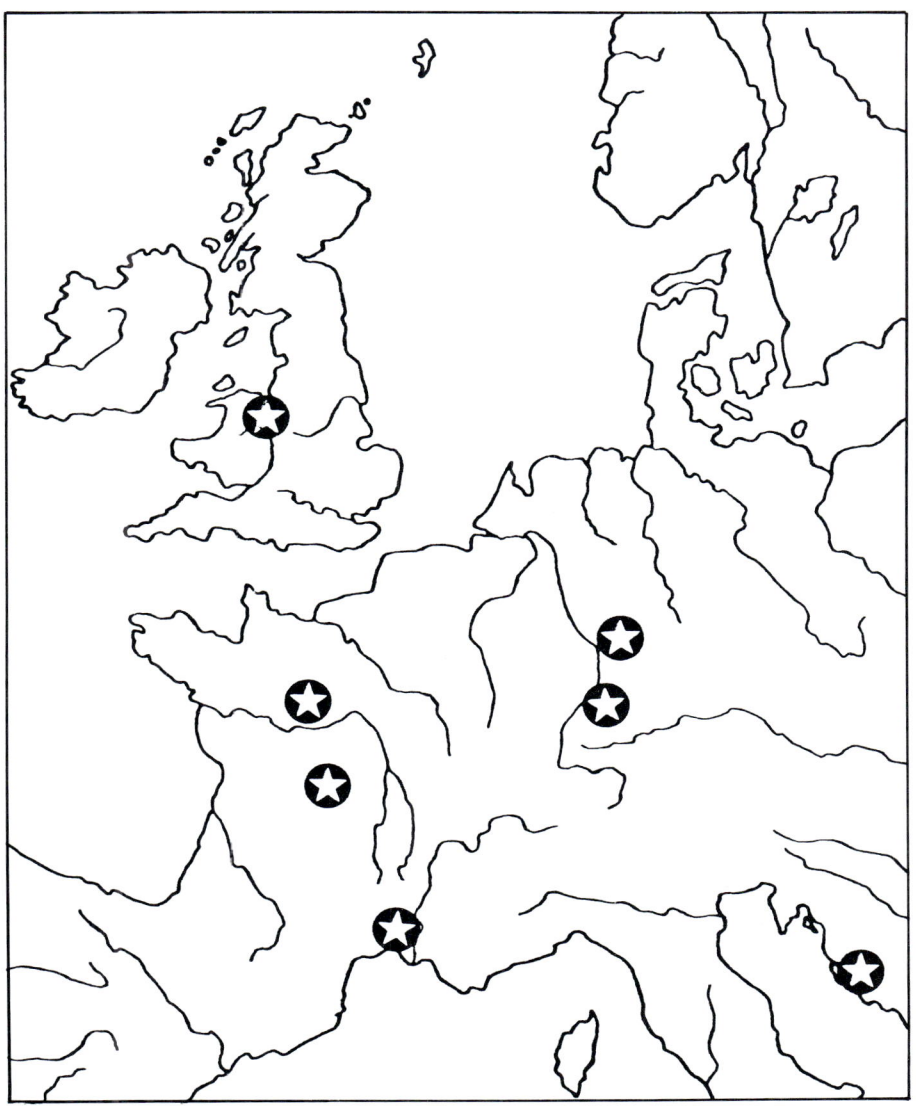

Distribution of 'Taranis' (or derivative) inscriptions in Europe.

PLATE XXXIV

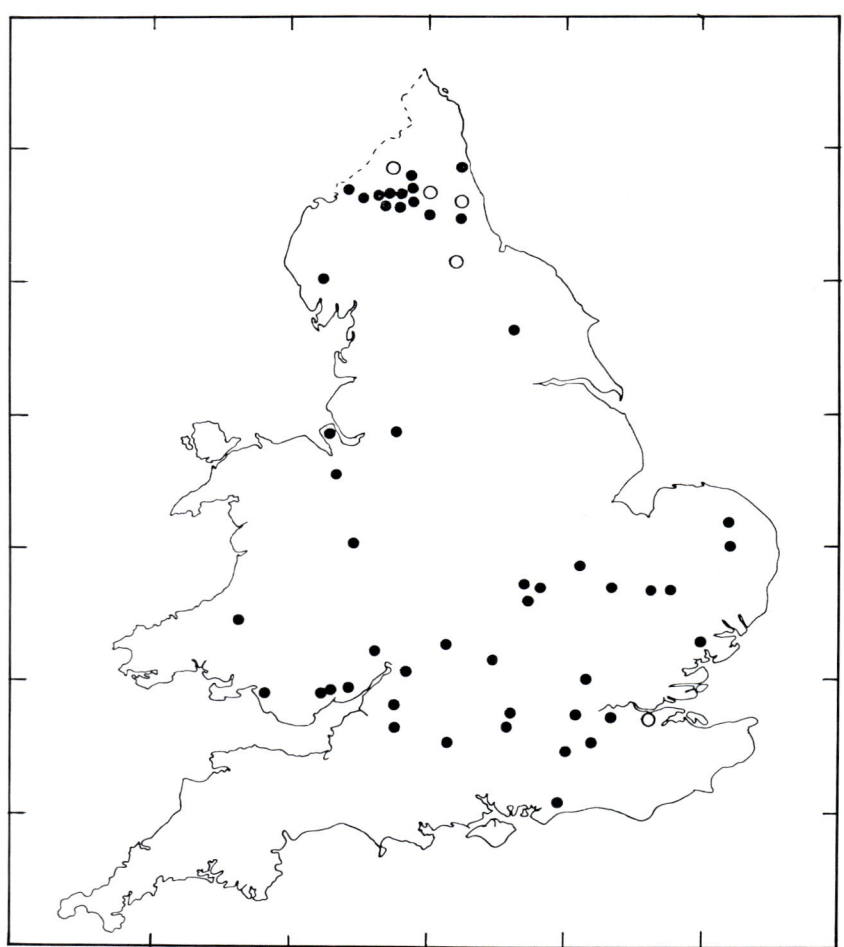

Distribution of all types of wheel-representation in England and Wales.
- wheels
○ swastikas

PLATE XXXV

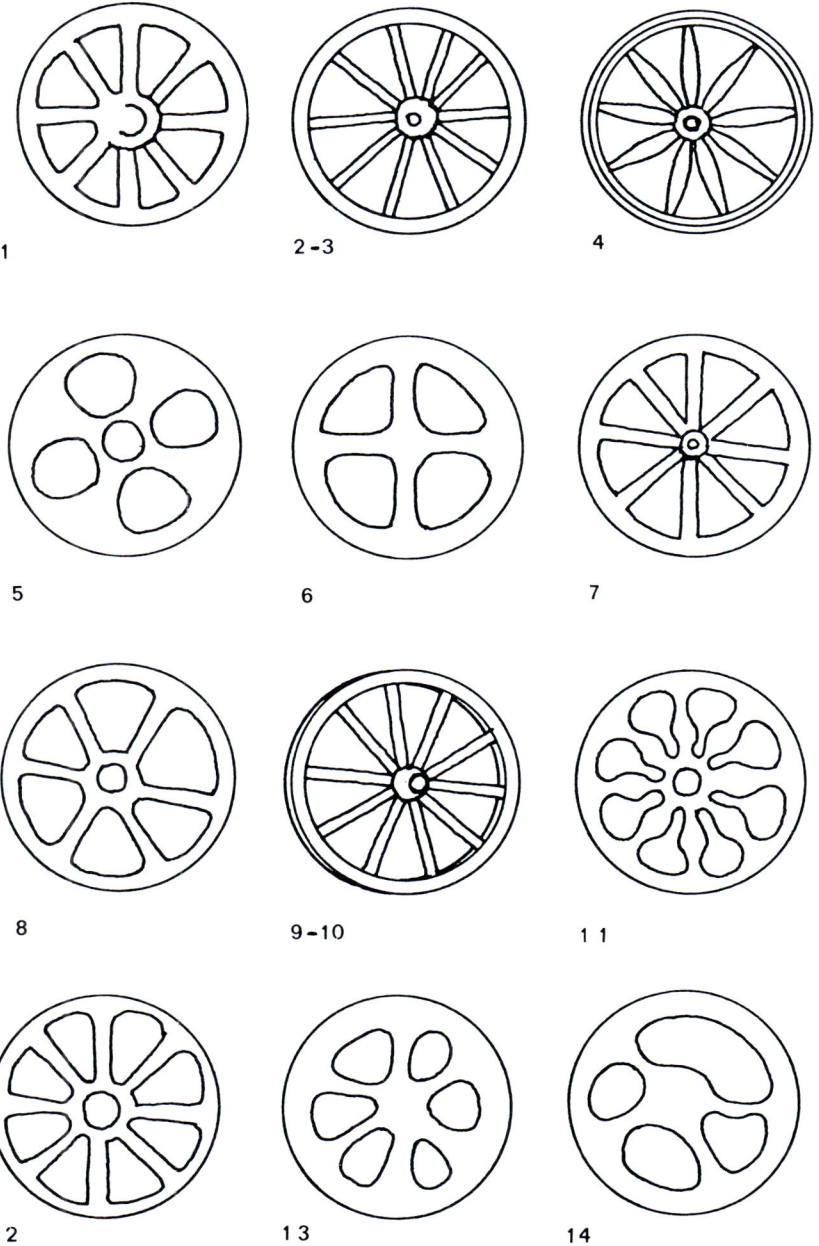

Sample of wheel-types (see Chapter IX)

PLATE XXXVI

Sample of wheel-types (see Chapter IX)

PLATE XXXVII

Sample of wheel-types (see Chapter IX)

PLATE XXXVIII

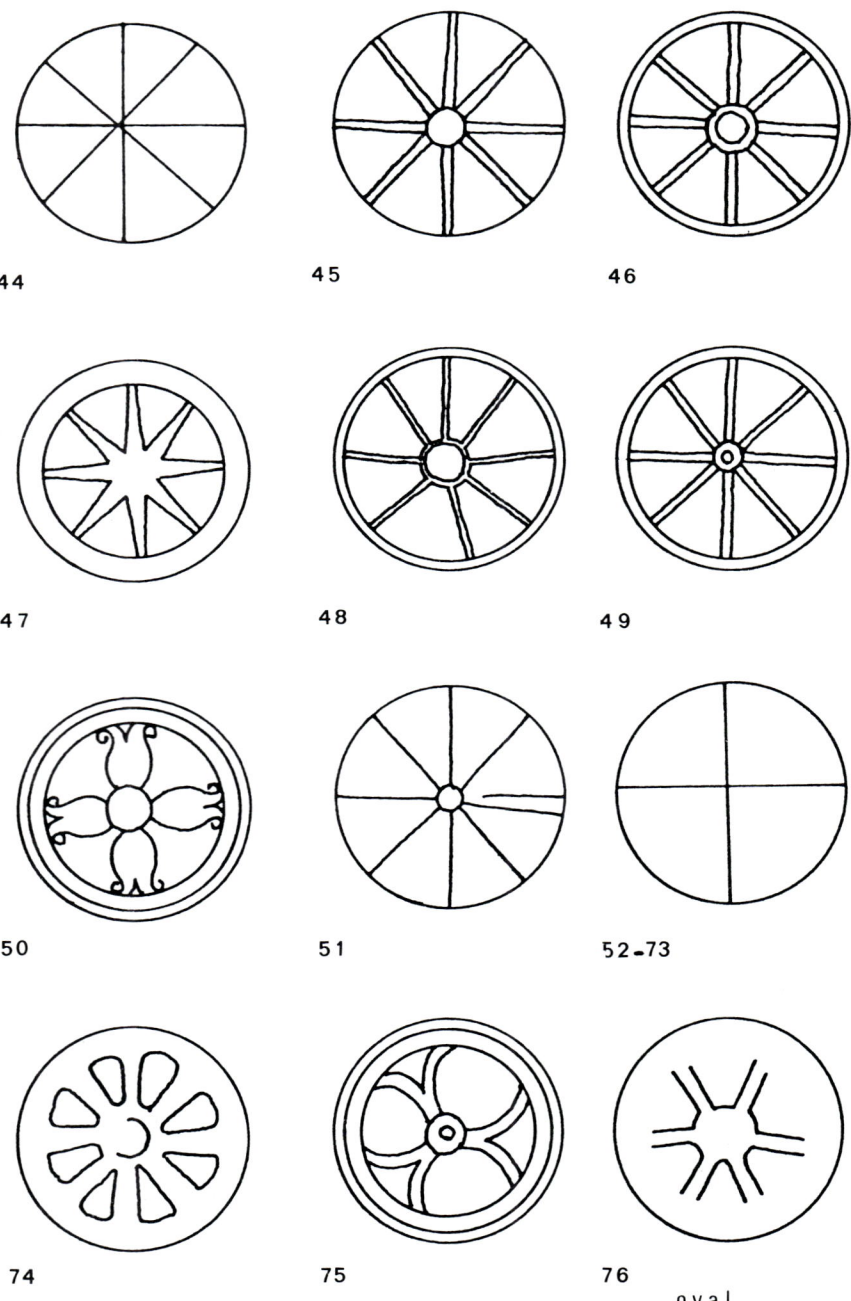

Sample of wheel-types (see Chapter IX)

PLATE XXXIX

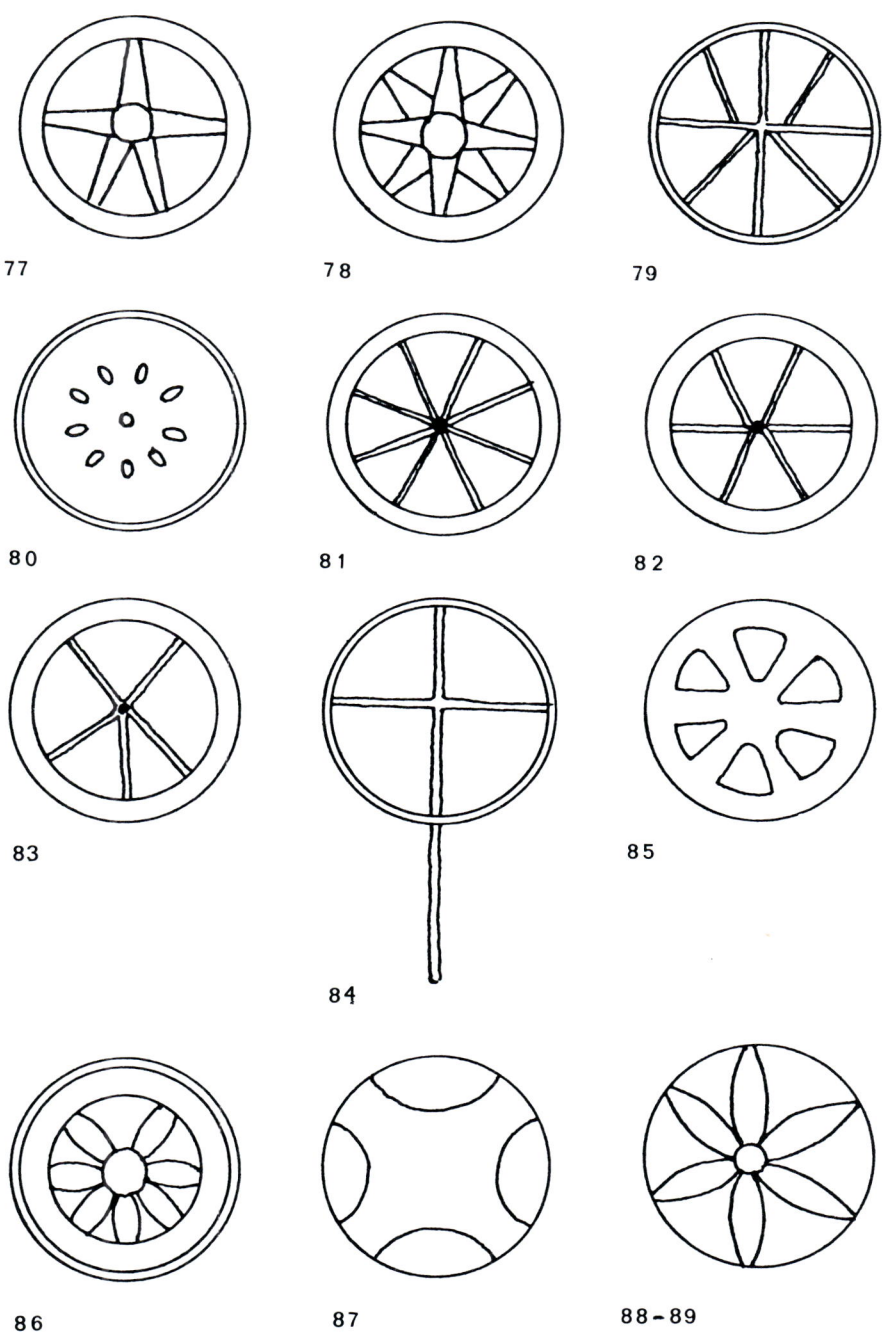

Sample of wheel-types (see Chapter IX)

PLATE XL

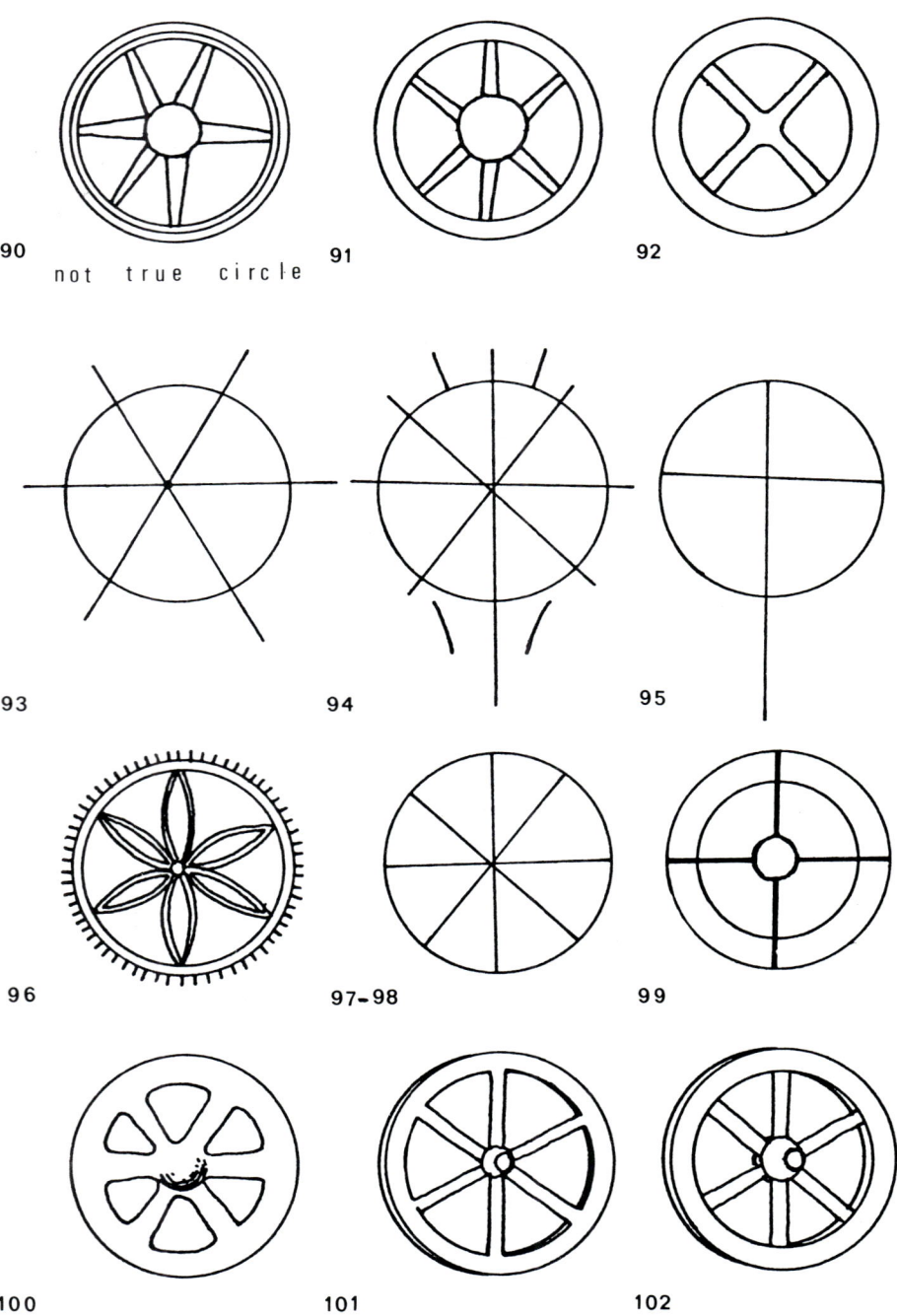

Sample of wheel-types (see Chapter IX)

PLATE XLI

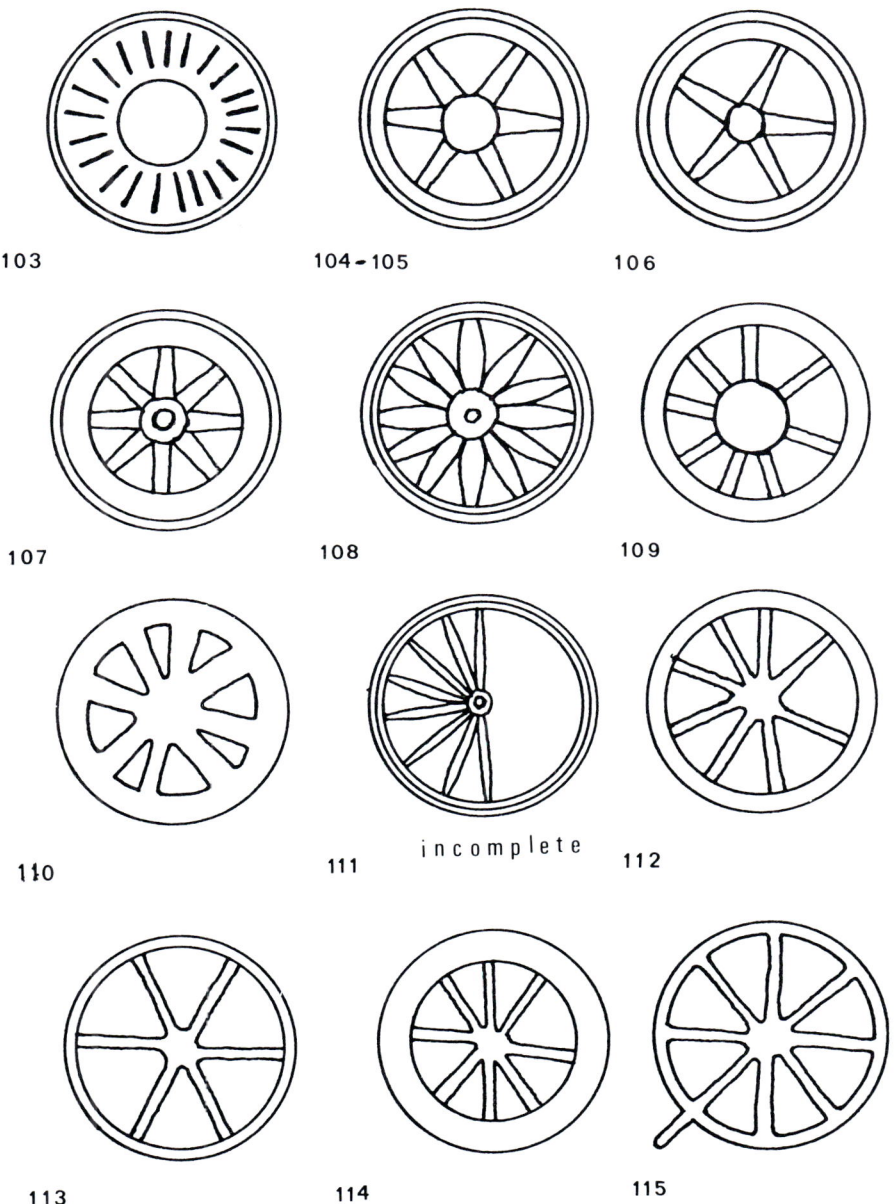

Sample of wheel-types (see Chapter IX)

PLATE XLII

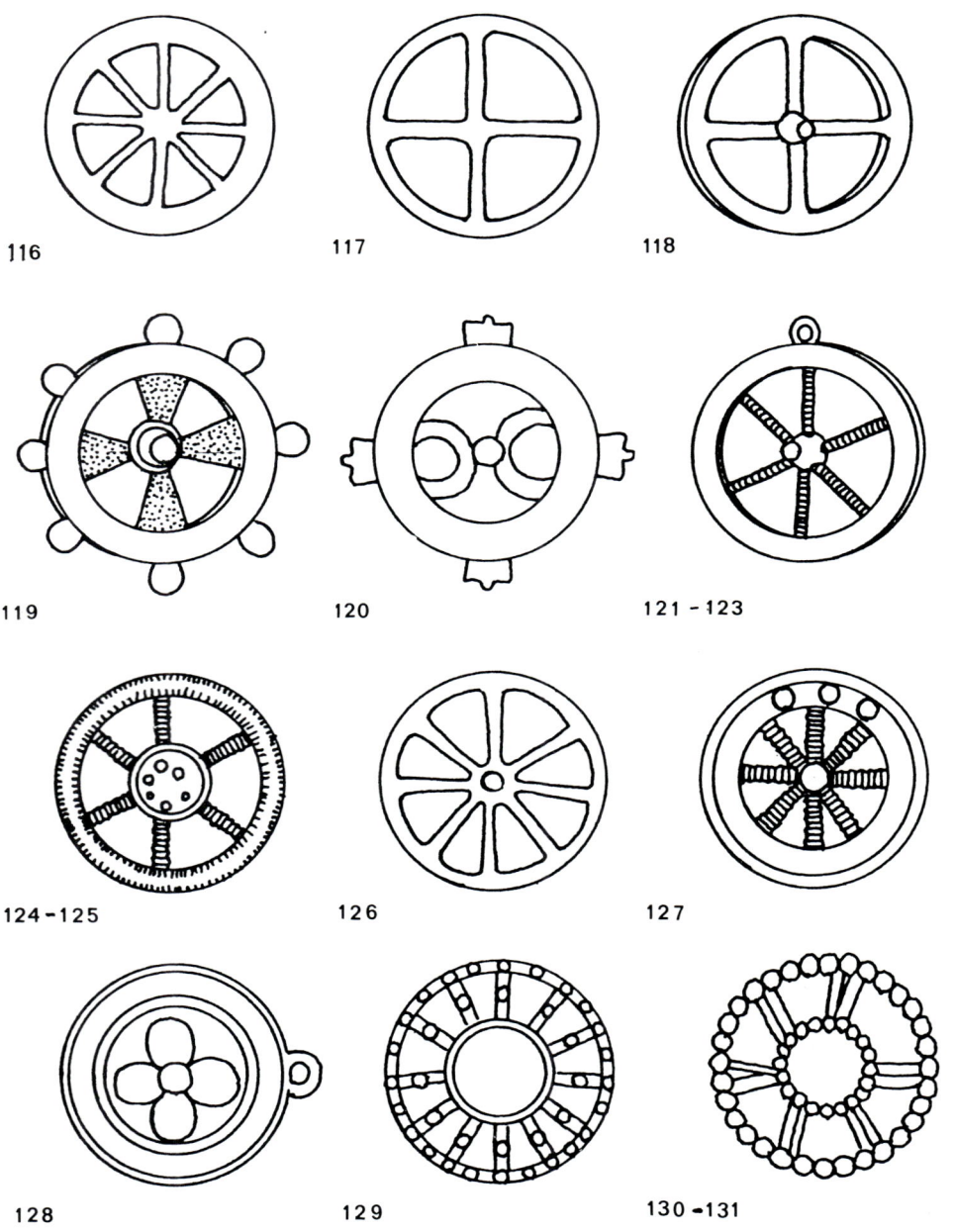

Sample of wheel-types (see Chapter IX)

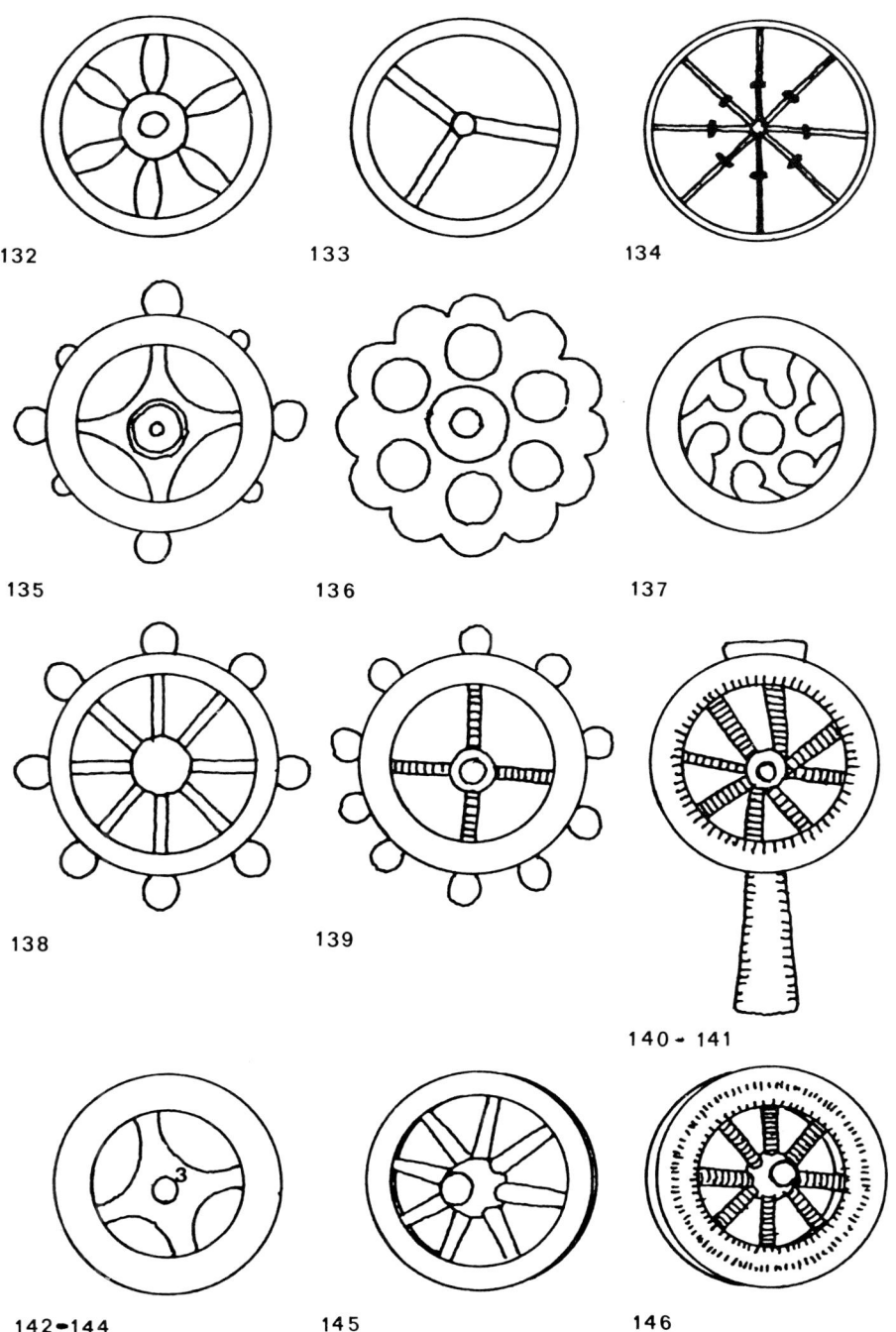

PLATE XLIII

Sample of wheel-types (see Chapter IX)

PLATE XLIV

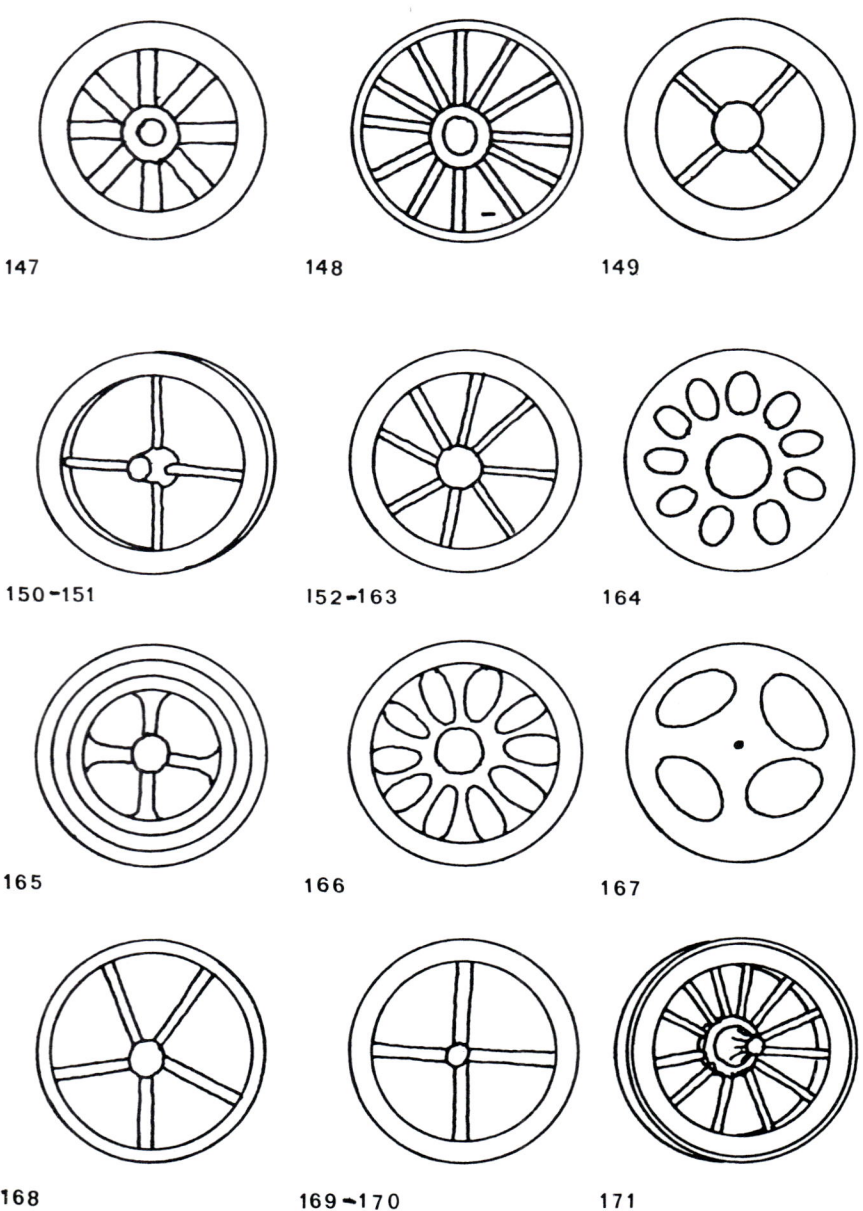

Sample of wheel-types (see Chapter IX)

PLATE XLV

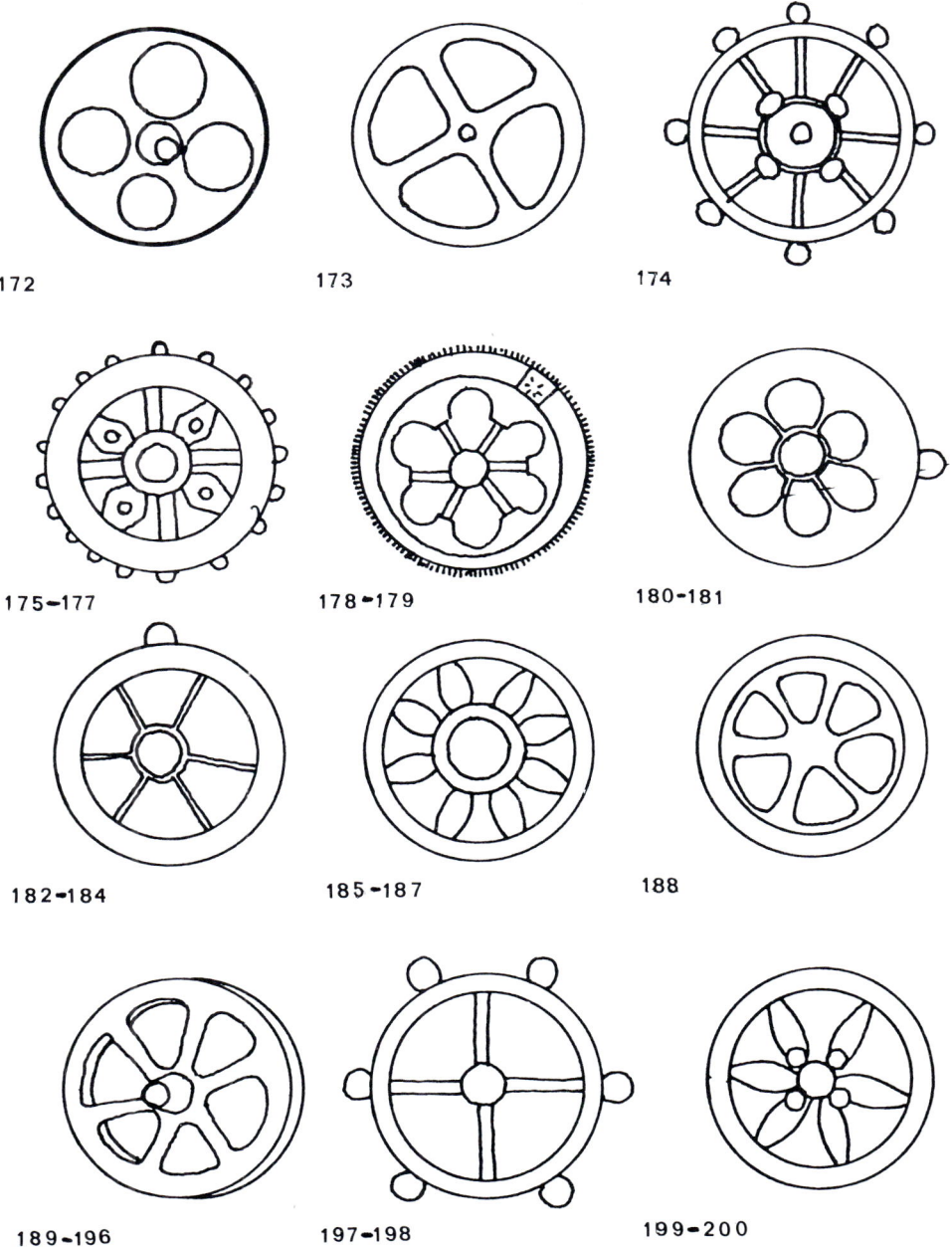

Sample of wheel-types (see Chapter IX)

PLATE XLVI

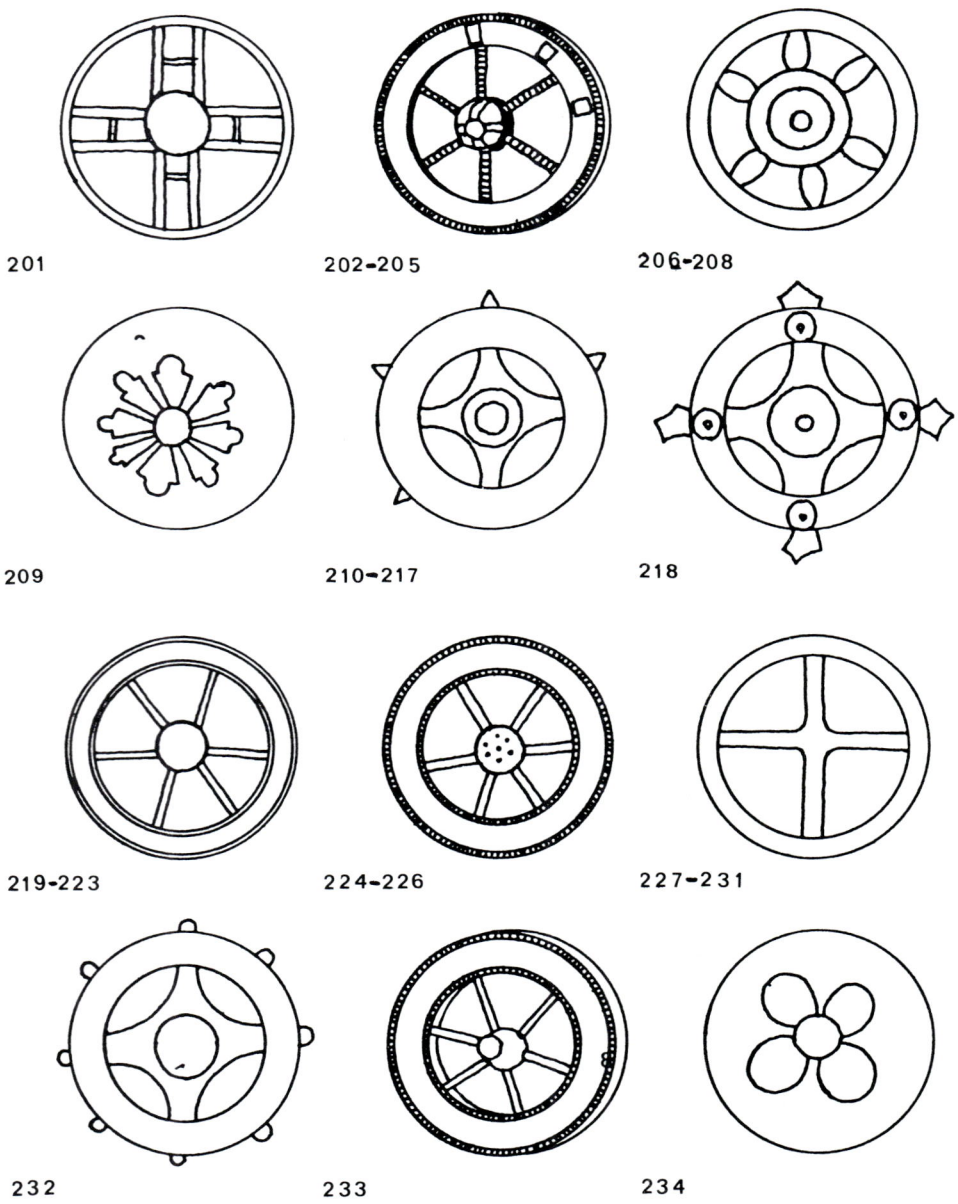

Sample of wheel-types (see Chapter IX)

PLATE XLVII

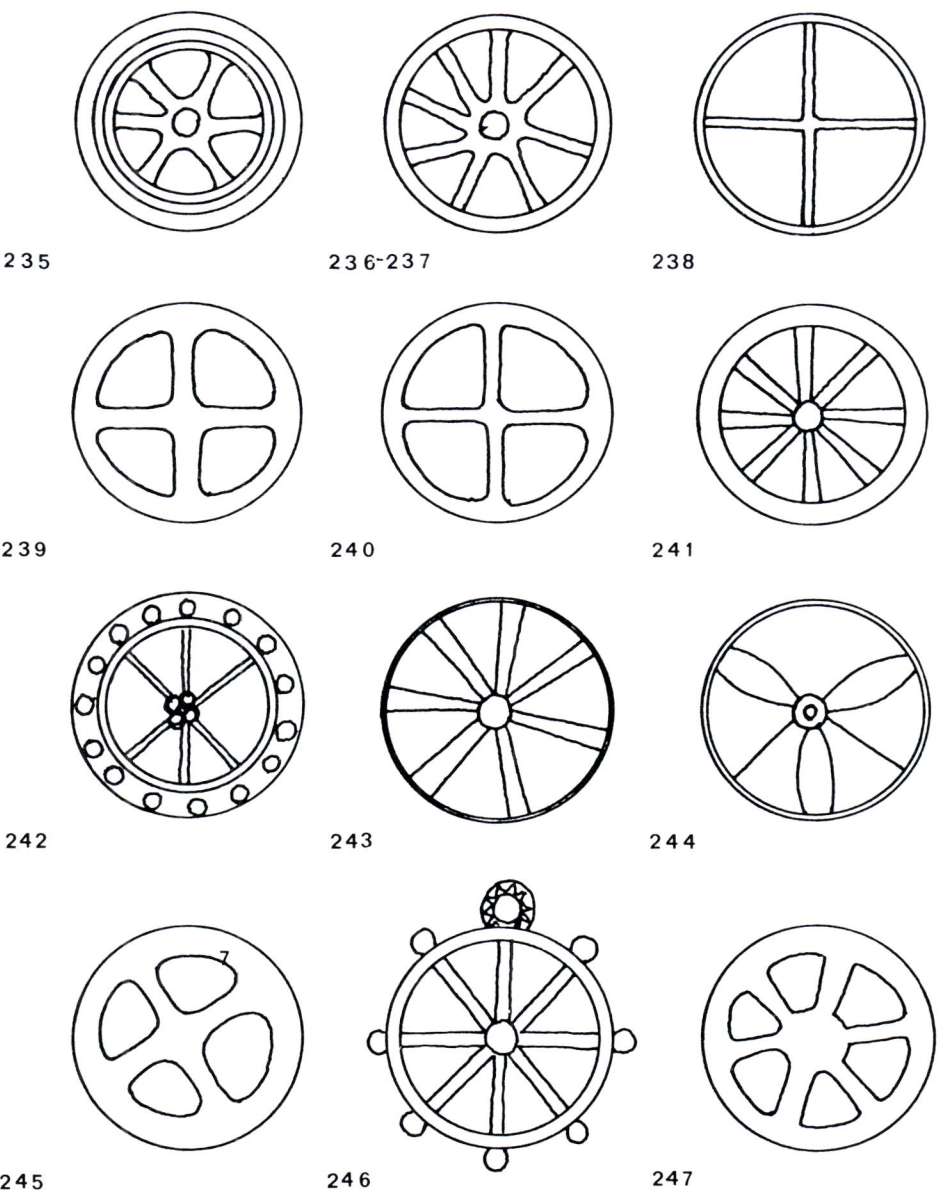

Sample of wheel-types (see Chapter IX)

PLATE XLVIII

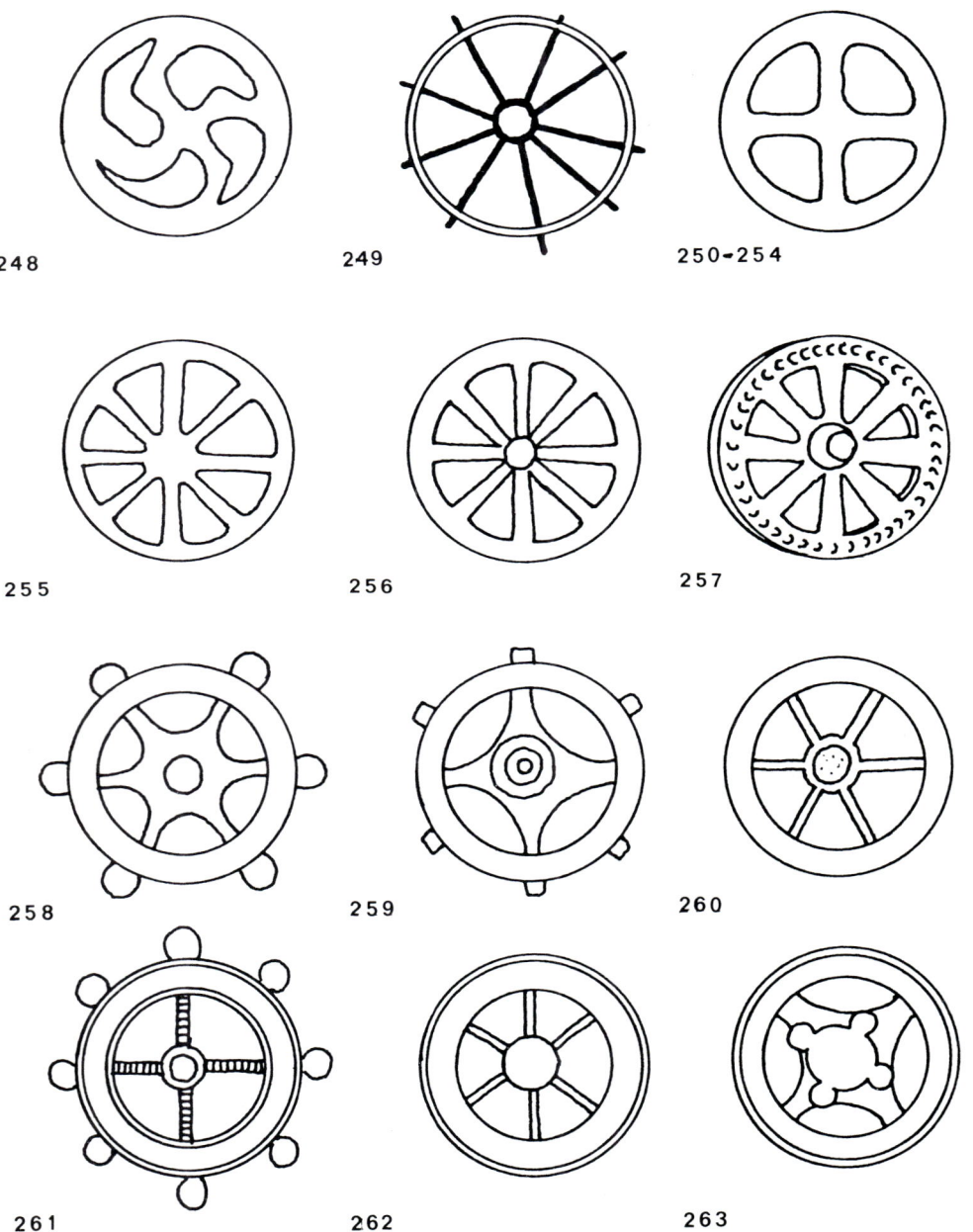

Sample of wheel-types (see Chapter IX)

PLATE XLIX

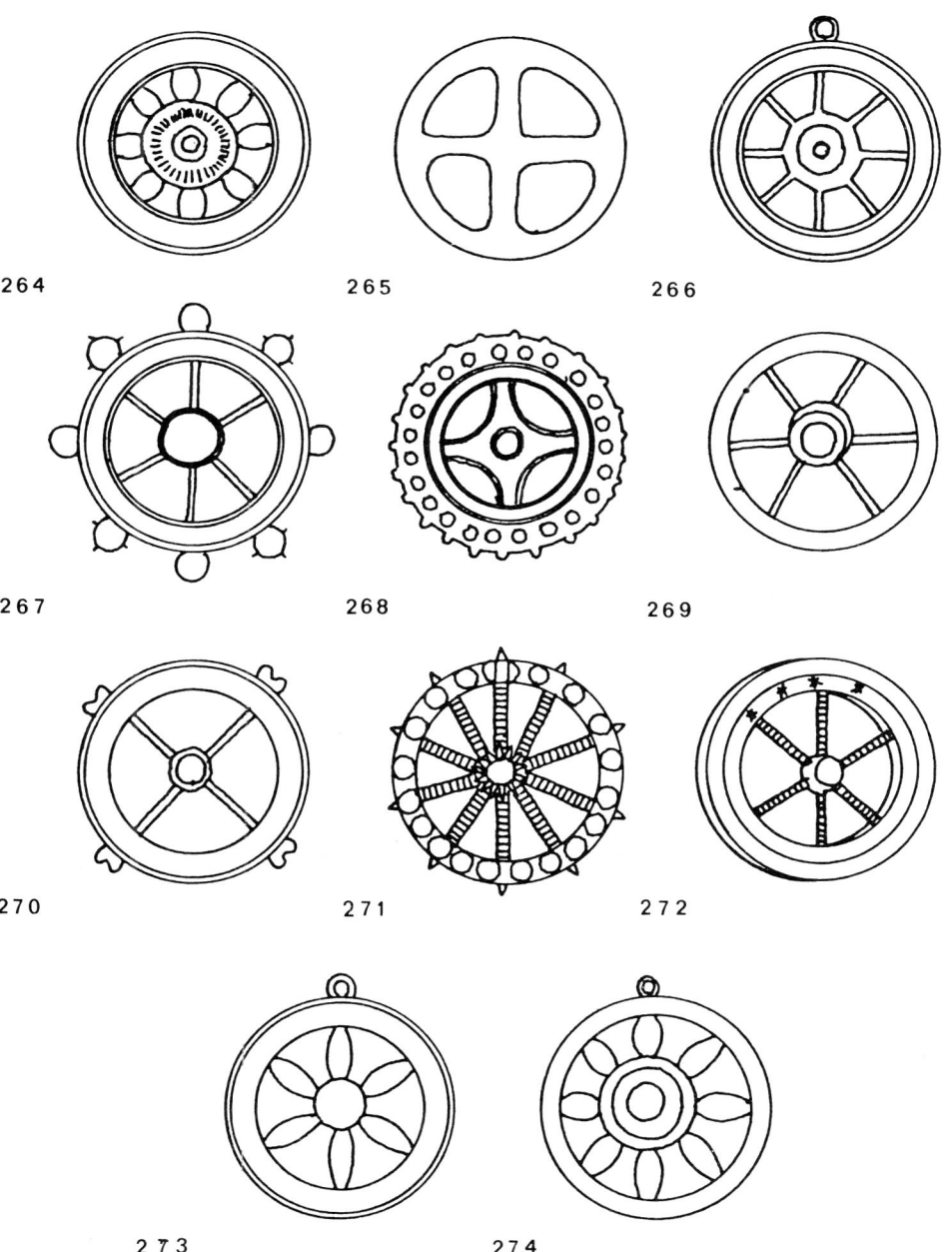

Sample of wheel-types (see Chapter IX)

PLATE L

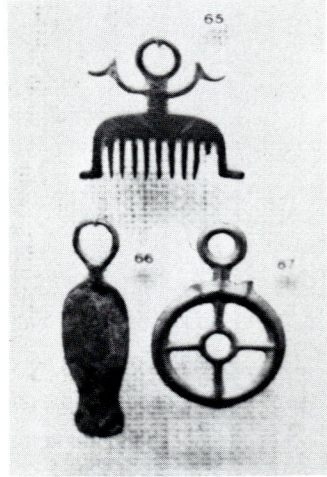

FIG. 1. – Late Bronze Age wheel-pendant ; Réallons. c. 4 cm diam.

FIG. 2. – Sandstone mould for Late Bronze Age wheel-pendant ; Auvernier. Length of mould 14.7 cm.

PLATE LI

FIG. 3. – Hallstatt wheel-pendant ; Most na Soci (Czech.). c. 5-6 cm diam.

FIG. 4, 5. – Iron Age wheel-model ; ? France.

PLATE LII

FIG. 7. — Wheel-models ; Southern France (A69).

FIG. 6. — Wheel-models ; Seine, Paris, Oise (A67, A68).

PLATE LIII

FIG. 8. — Wheel-model ; unprovenanced (A62).

FIG. 9. — Wheel-brooch ; Bavay (A59).

PLATE LIV

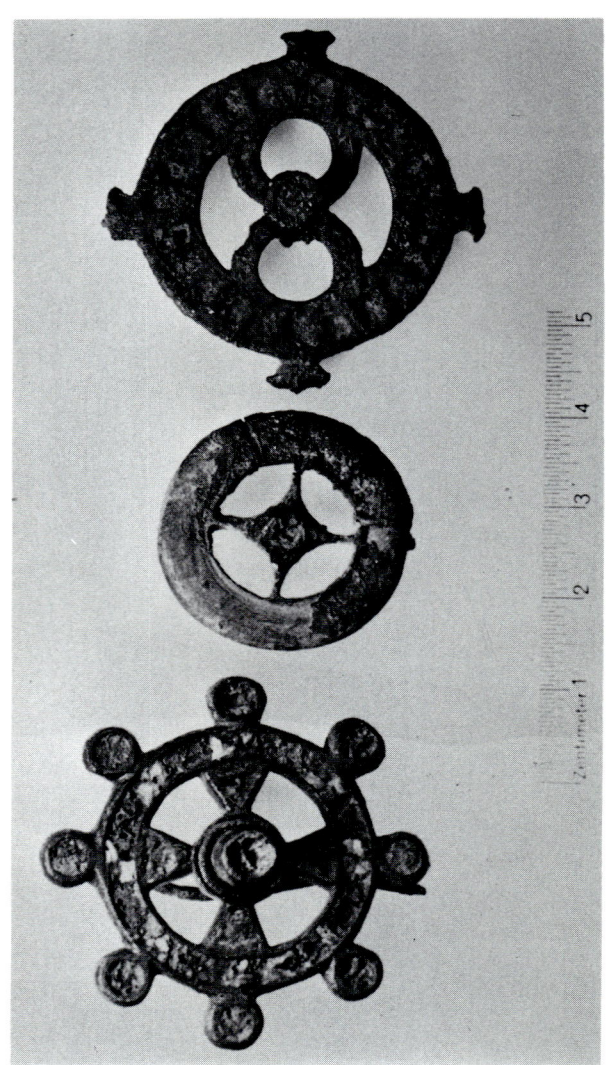

Fig. 10. – Wheel-brooches; Trier (A46, A48, A44).

PLATE LV

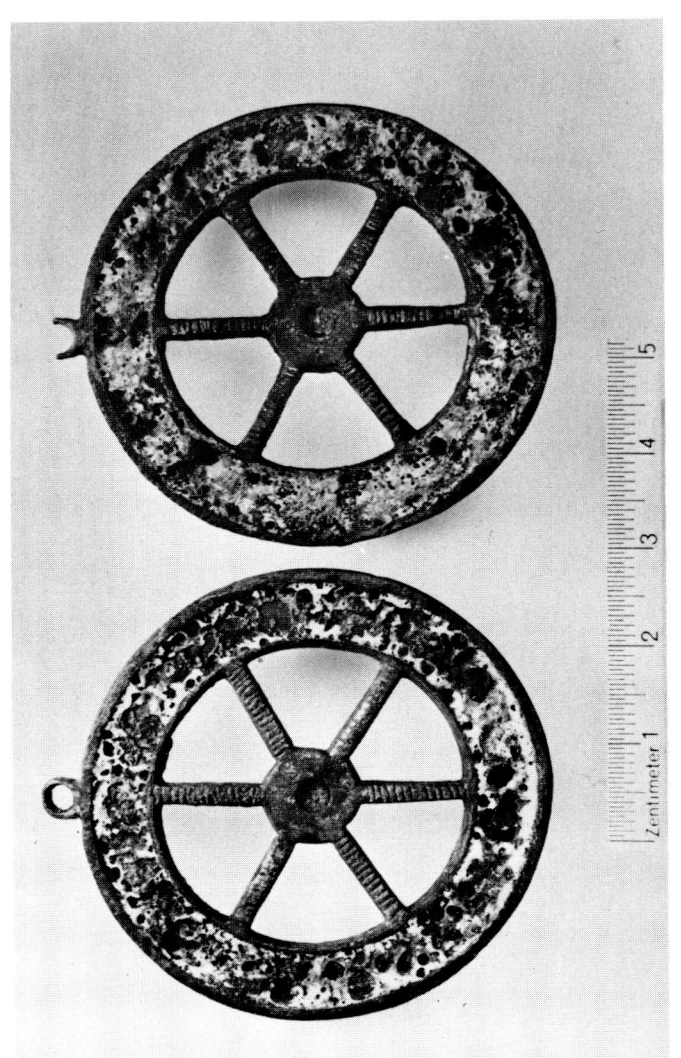

Fig. 11. — Wheel-brooches: Gusenburg (A50).

PLATE LVI

Fig. 13. — Wheel-brooch ; Hautepin (A55).

Fig. 12. — Wheel-brooch ; Elouges (A56).

PLATE LVII

Fig. 14. — Wheel-model mould on tile ; Augst (A126).

Fig. 15. — Wheel-model ; Nîmes (A208). c. 1.5 cm diam.

PLATE LVIII

FIG. 16. – Bronze wheel-model with votive inscription ; Augst (A140).

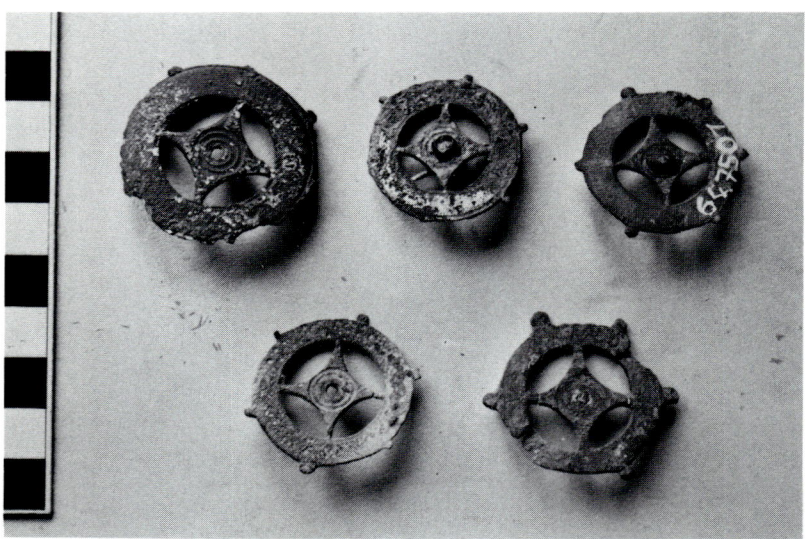

FIG. 17. – Bronze wheel-brooches ; Augst (A146).

PLATE LIX

Fig. 18. — Wheel-model ; Bern (A136).

Fig. 19. — Reverse of wheel-model ; Bern (A136).

Fig. 20. — Bronze swastika-brooch ; Cologne (A6).

Fig. 21. — Bronze wheel-brooch ; Icklingham (AB28). c. 2.5 cm diam.

PLATE LXI

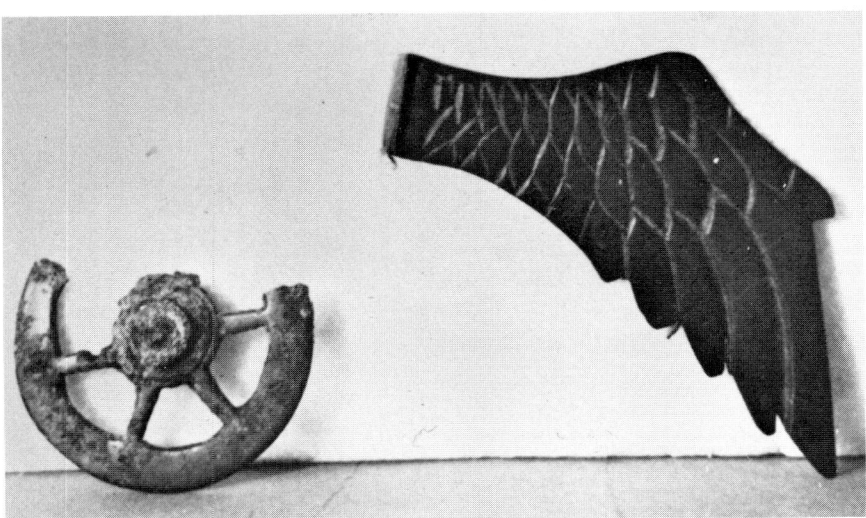

FIG. 22. — Bronze wheel-model and eaglés wing ; Icklingham (AB8). 4.1 cm diam. of wheel.

FIG. 23. — Bronze wheel-brooch fragment ; Housesteads (AB7).

PLATE LXII

Fig. 24. – Part of Felmingham board Hall (AB5).

PLATE LXIII

Fig. 25. — Bronze wheel-model and boars ; Hounslow (AB6). c. natural size.

Fig. 26. — Bronze enamelled wheel-brooch ; Corbridge (AB3). c. natural size.

PLATE LXIV

FIG. 27. – Bronze axe-model with 'X' sign ; Woodeaton (AX20). c. 5 cm long.

FIG. 28. – Bronze axe-model ; Gestingthorpe (AX21).

PLATE LXV

FIG. 30. — Seated wheel-god ; Alzey (B4). Height 74 cm.

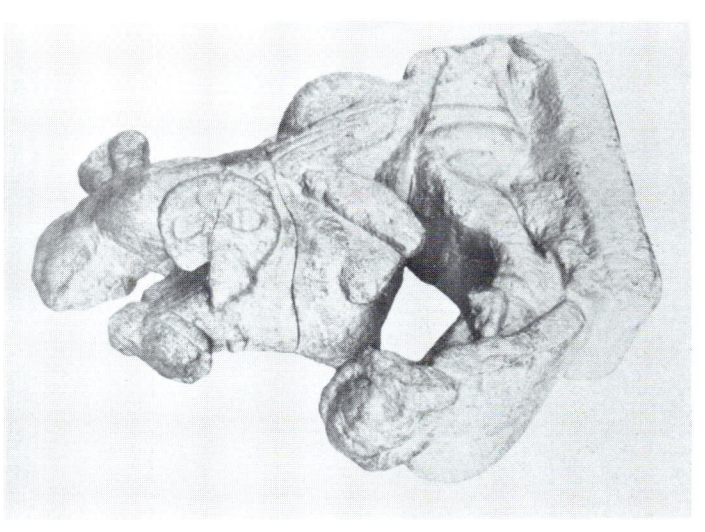

FIG. 29. — Equestrian wheel-god ; Butterstadt (B19). Height 82 cm.

PLATE LXVI

Fig. 32. — Séguret wheel-god (B144).

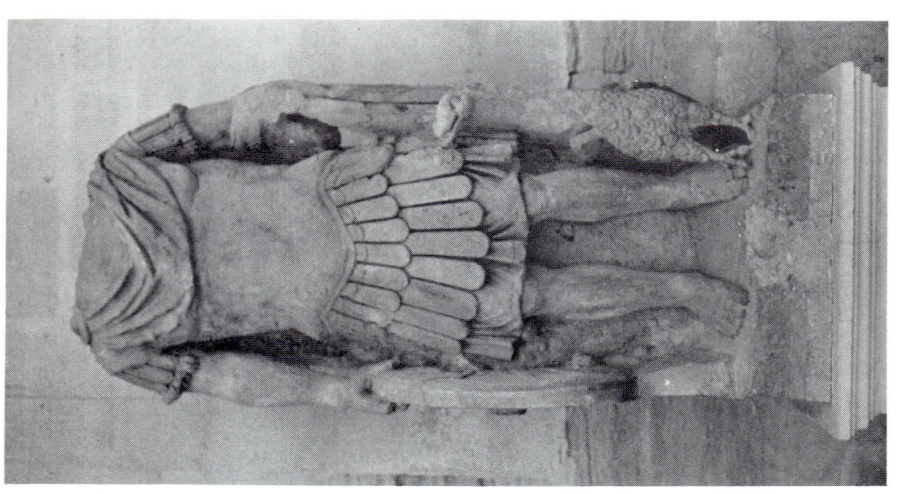

Fig. 31. — Séguret wheel-god (B144). Height 2 m 05.

PLATE LXVII

Fig. 33. – Séguret wheel-god (B144).

Fig. 34. – Fragment of wheel-god (B39).

PLATE LXVIII

Fig. 36. — Altar with wheel ; Gilly (B53).

Fig. 35. — Altar with wheel and thunderbolt ; Vauvert (B20).

PLATE LXIX

Fig. 38. – Altar to Jupiter and Augustus ; Marsillargues (B76).

Fig. 37. – Altar with wheel ; Vaison area (B154).

PLATE LXX

Fig. 40. — Altar with wheel and thunderbolt; Nimes (B100).

Fig. 39. — Altar to Jupiter; Collias (B27).

PLATE LXXI

Fig. 42. – Altar to Jupiter and Silvanus; Aigues-Mortes (B2).

Fig. 41. – Altar; Castelnau-Valence (B21).

PLATE LXXII

Fig. 45. – Funerary stone ; St. Quirin (B43).

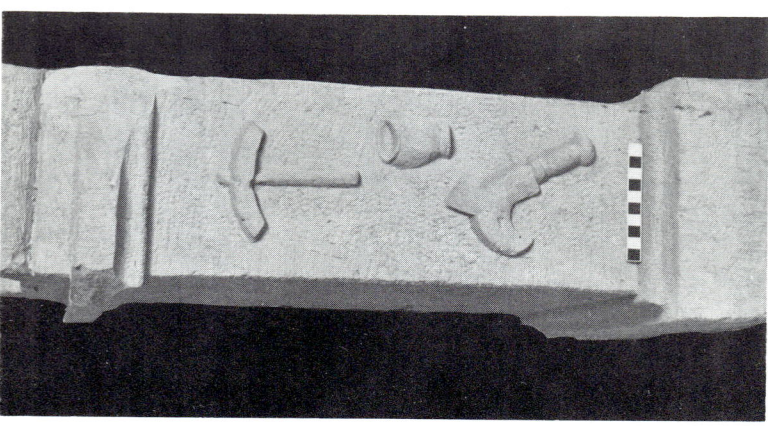

Fig. 43, 44 – Altar to Jupiter and Silvanus ; Aigues-Mortes (B2).

PLATE LXXIII

FIG. 47. – Funerary stone ; Saverne area (B141).

FIG. 46. – Funerary stone ; Saverne area (B138).

PLATE LXXIV

Fig. 49. – House-stele ; Saverne area (B139).

Fig. 48. – House-stele ; Saverne area (B139).

PLATE LXXV

Fig. 51. – Relief of *Genius* with wheel ; Netherby (BB17).

Fig. 50. – Altar to Jupiter ; Castlesteads (BB5).

PLATE LXXVI

Fig. 52, 53. – Stone ? Mars relief with wheel-marks at sides of slab. Chedworth (BB7).

PLATE LXXVII

Fig. 54. – Clay antefixes ; Caerleon (C11).

PLATE LXXVIII

Fig. 55. – Wheel on potsherd ; Housesteads (C60).

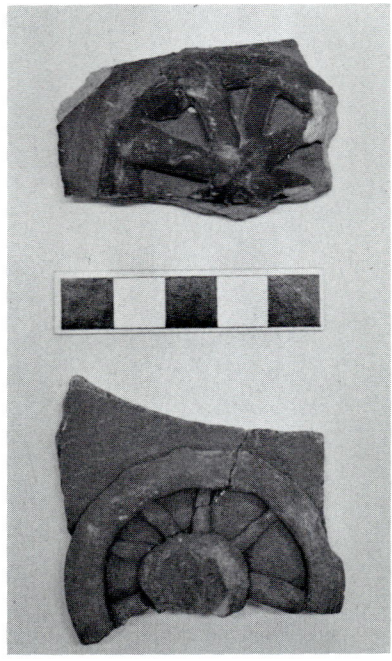

Fig. 56. – Wheels on potsherd ; Malton (C59).

PLATE LXXIX

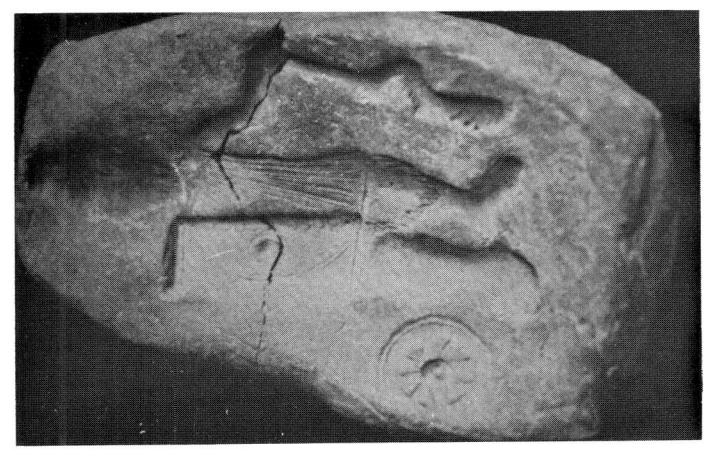

FIG. 58. — Clay mould impression of wheel-god ; Corbridge(C10). c. 10 cm long.

FIG. 57. — Bronze wheel-god ; Le Châtelet (C2). Height 10.3 cm.

PLATE LXXX

FIG. 59, 60. – Bronze wheel-god ; Landouzy-la-Ville. Basal inscription to Jupiter and the emperor's 'numen' (C3). Height 22 cm.

PLATE LXXXI

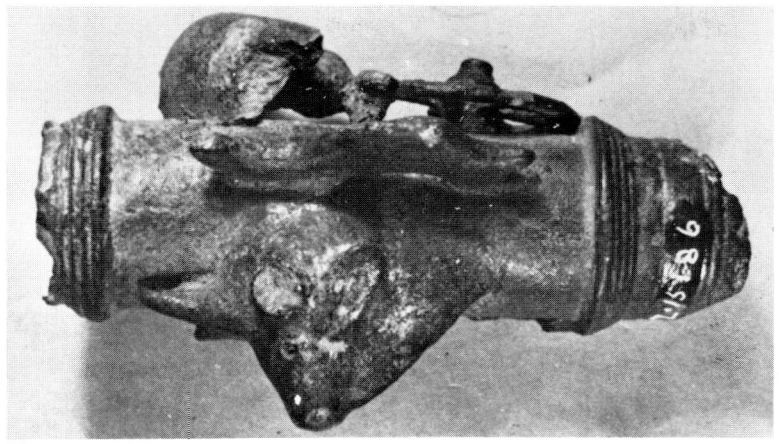

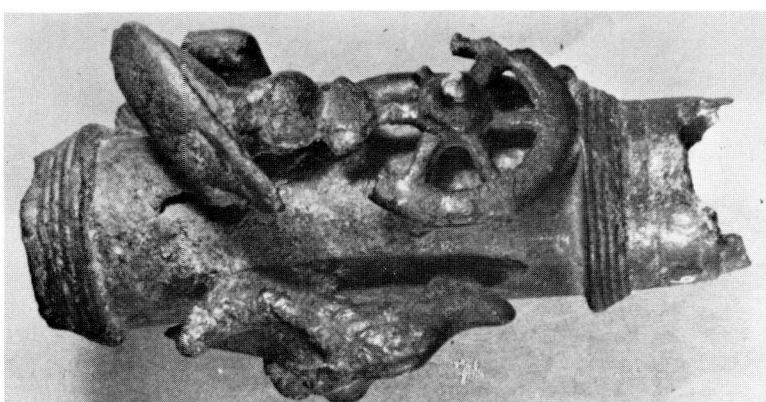

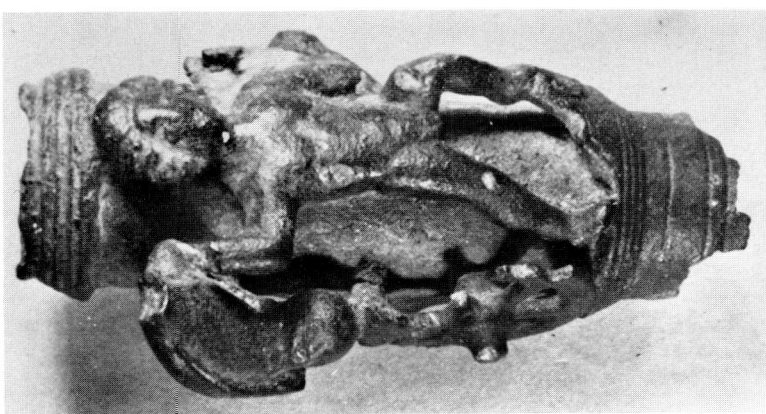

Fig. 61, 62, 63. – Bronze 'mace-terminal' depicting god, wheel, eagle, dolphin and bull's head, Willingham Fen (C6). Height 12.1 cm.

PLATE LXXXII

Fig. 64. – Bronze sceptre-binding; Farley Heath, Surrey (C7).

PLATE LXXXIII

FIG. 66. — Bronze Sucellus; Cologne (C34). c. natural size.

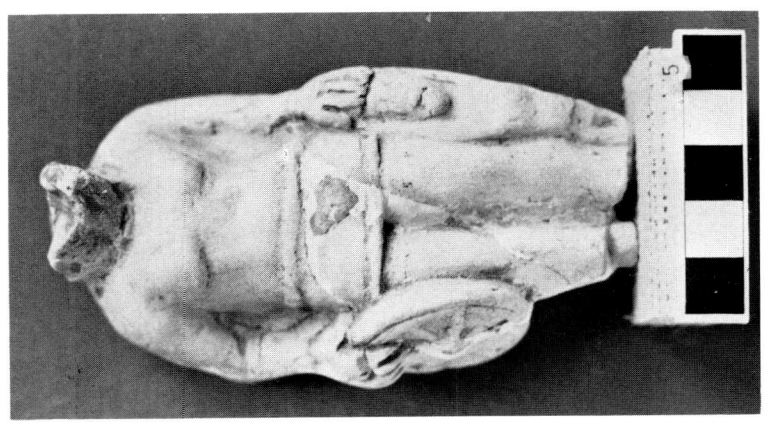

FIG. 65. — Pipe-clay wheel-god; Néris (C9a).

Fig. 67. – Altar to Taranucnus ; Böckingen (D1). Height c. 70 cm.

PLATE LXXXV

FIG. 68. – Corinthian capital from Jupiter-column ; Cirencester. Height 1 m 05.